The Presidency and the Political System

11th Edition

CQ Press, an imprint of SAGE, is the leading publisher of books, periodicals, and electronic products on American government and international affairs. CQ Press consistently ranks among the top commercial publishers in terms of quality, as evidenced by the numerous awards its products have won over the years. CQ Press owes its existence to Nelson Poynter, former publisher of the *St. Petersburg Times,* and his wife Henrietta, with whom he founded Congressional Quarterly in 1945. Poynter established CQ with the mission of promoting democracy through education and in 1975 founded the Modern Media Institute, renamed The Poynter Institute for Media Studies after his death. The Poynter Institute (www.poynter .org) is a nonprofit organization dedicated to training journalists and media leaders.

In 2008 CQ Press was acquired by SAGE, a leading international publisher of journals, books, and electronic media for academic, educational, and professional markets. Since 1965 SAGE has helped inform and educate a global community of scholars, practitioners, researchers, and students with publications spanning a wide range of subject areas, including business, humanities, social sciences, and science, technology, and medicine. A privately owned corporation, SAGE has offices in Los Angeles, London, New Delhi, and Singapore, in addition to the Washington D.C. office of CQ Press.

The Presidency and the Political System

11th Edition

Michael Nelson

Rhodes College

Editor

FOR INFORMATION:

CQ Press
An Imprint of SAGE Publications, Inc.
2455 Teller Road
Thousand Oaks, California 91320
E-mail: order@sagepub.com

SAGE Publications Ltd.
1 Oliver's Yard
55 City Road
London EC1Y 1SP
United Kingdom

SAGE Publications India Pvt. Ltd.
B 1/I 1 Mohan Cooperative Industrial Area
Mathura Road, New Delhi 110 044
India

SAGE Publications Asia-Pacific Pte. Ltd.
3 Church Street
#10-04 Samsung Hub
Singapore 049483

Printed in the United States of America

Library of Congress Cataloging-in-Publication Data

Names: Nelson, Michael, 1949- editor.

Title: The presidency and the political system / Michael Nelson, Rhodes College, editor.

Description: Eleventh Edition. | Los Angeles : SAGE/CQ Press, [2018] | Includes bibliographical references and index.

Identifiers: LCCN 2017054447 | ISBN 9781544317298 (Paperback : acid-free paper)

Subjects: LCSH: Presidents—United States.

Classification: LCC JK516 .P639 2018 | DDC 352.230973—dc23
LC record available at https://lccn.loc.gov/2017054447

This book is printed on acid-free paper.

MIX
Paper from
responsible sources
FSC® C014174

Acquisitions Editor: Monica Eckman
Editorial Assistants: Zachary Hoskins
                       and Sam Rosenberg
Production Editor: Jane Martinez
Copy Editor: Terri Lee Paulsen
Typesetter: C&M Digitals (P) Ltd.
Proofreader: Sarah J. Duffy
Indexer: Jean Casalegno
Cover Designer: Gail Buschman
Marketing Manager: Erica DeLuca

18 19 20 21 22 10 9 8 7 6 5 4 3 2 1

To my beloved wife, Linda.

She opens her mouth with wisdom,
and the teaching of kindness is on her tongue. . . .
Her children rise up and call her blessed;
her husband also, and he praises her.

Proverbs 31:26, 28

CONTENTS

PREFACE

More than three decades have passed since the first edition of this book—now in its eleventh edition—was published. The book's goal then and ever since has been to match the most important topics concerning the presidency with the best contemporary scholarship in ways that are accessible and interesting to every student of the office. Apparently this goal has been achieved: in a Hauenstein Center for Presidential Studies survey of books used in courses on the American presidency, *The Presidency and the Political System* ranked first.

The passage of time affects this book in another way. Every syllabus for a college course notes the term and year the course is offered, usually at the top of the first page. In many academic disciplines, this is simply a clerical entry: it really doesn't matter all that much whether you take Spanish or calculus in fall 2018 or spring 2019. Time matters immensely, however, in a course on the American presidency. Indeed, what makes political science so interesting is that its subject (succinctly described by political scientist Harold D. Lasswell as "who gets what, when, and how") refuses to stand still. This observation applies especially to the presidency, in which the nature of the institution is so closely intertwined with that of the person who, at any given moment, occupies it.

Consider the most important developments in the presidency since this book's tenth edition was published, including the final years of President Barack Obama's second term and, especially, the 2016 election and the early presidency of Donald Trump. These political developments, along with the new contributions to the flourishing scholarly literature on the presidency and the political system they have inspired, are treated fully in this edition. The book's twenty chapters are organized into six parts: Approaches to the Presidency, Elements of Presidential Power, Presidential Selection, Presidents and Politics, Presidents and Government, and Presidents and Public Policy. An entirely new chapter on presidential removal, a subject both timeless and timely, has been added.

To note that the authors have taken recent developments into account is not to say that this is merely a "current events" book—far from it. The presidency is an office with deep roots in history, shaped by decisions that were made at the Constitutional Convention of 1787 and by more than two centuries of change in the American political system since its founding. The presidency also is shaped by the history and current functioning of the myriad parts of the political system, such as Congress, the courts, the bureaucracy, interest groups, the media, public opinion, the electoral process, and the party system. This broader understanding of the presidency underlies all of the analyses of more recent events that the writers present.

I do not agree with everything that every author has to say in this book, nor will any reader. But together the contributors constitute an all-star team of presidential scholars, and the intellectual substance of the chapters is fully matched by their readability. Through ten previous editions, this book has been widely assigned in courses and extensively cited and reviewed in scholarly books and articles. Students may be assured of receiving the most comprehensive understanding of the presidency, and scholars will continue to find the essays valuable in conducting their research.

I am deeply grateful to those who helped in the preparation of the eleventh edition, the authors first and foremost. Thanks, too, to the editorial staff at CQ Press, including the early guiding hands of Brenda Carter and Charisse Kiino. For their fine work on this edition, I thank Executive Publisher Monica Eckman, Editorial Assistants Zachary Hoskins and Sam Rosenberg, Production Editor Jane Martinez, Cover Designer Gail Buschman, Marketing Manager Erica DeLuca, Copy Editor Terri Lee Paulsen, Proofreader Sarah J. Duffy, and Indexer Jean Casalegno. I also appreciate the helpful insights of the reviewers whose judgments we sought in preparing this eleventh edition.

Lawrence Becker, *California State University, Northridge*

Amber Boydstun, *University of California, Davis*

Daniel Franklin, *Georgia State University*

Maryann E. Gallagher, *DePauw University*

Christian Grose, *University of Southern California*

Donna Hoffman, *University of Northern Iowa*

Jennifer Jerit, *Stony Brook University*

Beth A. Rosenson, *University of Florida*

Adam Sheingate, *Johns Hopkins University*

Darren Wheeler, *Ball State University*

Donald Zinman, *Grand Valley State University*

—Michael Nelson

CONTRIBUTORS

ABOUT THE EDITOR

Michael Nelson is Fulmer Professor of Political Science at Rhodes College and a senior fellow at the University of Virginia's Miller Center. A former editor of the *Washington Monthly*, his most recent books include *Trump's First Year* (2018); *The Elections of 2016* (2018); *The Evolving Presidency: Landmark Documents* (2019); *The American Presidency: Origins and Development* (with Sidney M. Milkis, 2011); and *Governing at Home: The White House and Domestic Policymaking* (with Russell B. Riley, 2011). Nelson has contributed to numerous journals, including the *Journal of Policy History, Journal of Politics,* and *Political Science Quarterly.* He also has written multiple articles on subjects as varied as baseball, Frank Sinatra, and C. S. Lewis. More than fifty of his articles have been anthologized in works of political science, history, and English composition. His 2014 book, *Resilient America: Electing Nixon, Channeling Dissent, and Dividing Government*, won the American Political Science Association's Richard E. Neustadt Award for best book on the presidency published that year; and his 2006 book with John Lyman Mason, *How the South Joined the Gambling Nation*, won the Southern Political Science Association's V.O. Key Award.

ABOUT THE CONTRIBUTORS

Lara M. Brown is an associate professor and director of the Graduate School of Political Management at The George Washington University. She is the author of *Jockeying for the American Presidency: The Political Opportunism of Aspirants* (2010), and coeditor of *The Presidential Leadership Dilemma: Between the Constitution and a Political Party* (2013) and *Campaigning for President 2016: Strategy and Tactics* (2017). She has published articles in *Society, American Politics Research, Congress and the Presidency, Journal of Political Marketing,* and *Presidential Studies Quarterly.* In addition to presidential elections, political parties, and rhetorical leadership, she also writes about congressional incumbent scandals.

John P. Burke is the John G. McCullough Professor of Political Science at the University of Vermont. His most recent book is *Presidential Power: Theories and Dilemmas* (2016). He is also author of *Honest Broker? The National Security Advisor and Presidential Decision Making* (2009); *Becoming President: The Bush Transition 2000–2003* (2004); *The Institutional Presidency: Organizing and Managing the White House from FDR to Clinton* (2000); *Presidential Transitions: From Politics to Practice* (2000); *The Institutional Presidency* (1992); and *Bureaucratic Responsibility*

(1986). He is coauthor of *Advising Ike: The Memoirs of Attorney General Herbert Brownell* (1993) and *How Presidents Test Reality: Decisions on Vietnam, 1954 and 1965* (1989), which won the 1990 Richard E. Neustadt Award from the American Political Science Association for the best book on the presidency.

Matthew J. Dickinson is a professor of political science at Middlebury College. His blog on presidential power can be found at http://blogs.middlebury.edu/presidentialpower. He is the author of *Bitter Harvest: FDR, Presidential Power and the Growth of the Presidential Branch* (1999), coeditor of *Guardian of the Presidency: The Legacy of Richard E. Neustadt* (2007), and has published numerous articles on the presidency, Congress, and the executive branch. His current book manuscript, *Clerk or Leader? The President and the White House Staff: People, Positions and Processes, 1945–2016*, examines the growth of presidential staff in the post–World War II era.

George C. Edwards III is the University Distinguished Professor of Political Science at Texas A&M University and holds the Jordan Chair in Presidential Studies. He is also a Distinguished Fellow at the University of Oxford. He has written or edited twenty-five books on American politics. He is also editor of *Presidential Studies Quarterly* and general editor of the Oxford Handbook of American Politics series. Among his latest books are *On Deaf Ears: The Limits of the Bully Pulpit* (2003); *Why the Electoral College Is Bad for America* (2011); *Governing by Campaigning: The Politics of the Bush Presidency* (2007); *The Strategic President: Persuasion and Opportunity in Presidential Leadership* (2009); *Overreach: Leadership in the Obama Presidency* (2012); and *Predicting the Presidency: The Path to Successful Leadership* (2016). Edwards has served as president of the Presidency Research Group of the American Political Science Association, which has named its annual dissertation prize in his honor and awarded him its Career Service Award.

Marjorie Randon Hershey is a Professor and Associate Chair of Political Science at Indiana University. Her research is in the areas of U.S. political parties and political communication. She is the author of four books, one of which, *Party Politics in America* (2017) is now in its 17th edition. She has published articles in journals such as the *American Journal of Political Science*, the *Journal of Politics*, *Public Opinion Quarterly*, *Political Communication*, *Social Science Quarterly*, *Polity*, *The ANNALS*, *PS: Political Science and Politics*, as well as chapters in 27 books.

Marc Landy is a professor of political science at Boston College. He is the author of *American Government: Enduring Principles, Critical Choices* (fourth edition forthcoming) and coauthor of *Presidential Greatness* (2000, with Sidney M. Milkis). Other writings on the presidency include *Incrementalism v. Disjuncture: The President and American Political Development* (2015) and *Terror and the Executive* (2010). In addition to writing about the presidency, he also writes about federalism, public policy, and the environment. He is coauthor of *The Environmental Protection Agency: Asking the Wrong Questions: From Nixon to Clinton* (1994) and *Who's in Charge? Who Should Be?—The Role of the Federal Government in Megadisasters: Based on Lessons from Hurricane Katrina* (2009).

David E. Lewis is the William R. Kenan, Jr. Professor of Political Science at Vanderbilt University. He is the author of two books, *Presidents and the Politics of Agency Design* (2003) and *The Politics of Presidential Appointments: Political Control and Bureaucratic Performance* (2008). He has also published numerous articles on American politics, public administration, and management in journals such as the *American Journal of Political Science*, the *Journal of Politics*, the *British Journal of Political Science*, *Public Administration Review*, and *Presidential Studies Quarterly*. He is a member of the National Academy of Public Administration and serves on the editorial boards of *Presidential Studies Quarterly* and *Public Administration*.

Sidney M. Milkis is the White Burkett Miller Professor of the Department of Politics and a senior fellow at the Miller Center at the University of Virginia. His books include *The President and Parties: The Transformation of the American Party System since the New Deal* (1993); *Political Parties and Constitutional Government: Remaking American Democracy* (1999); *Presidential Greatness* (2000, with Marc Landy); *The American Presidency: Origins and Development, 1776–2014* (2016, with Michael Nelson); *Theodore Roosevelt, the Progressive Party, and the Transformation of American Democracy* (2009); and *Rivalry and Reform: The Modern Presidency, Social Movements, and the Transformation of American Democracy* (2018, with Daniel J. Tichenor). He is also coeditor of three volumes on twentieth-century political reform: *Progressivism and the New Democracy* (1999), *The New Deal and the Triumph of Liberalism* (2002), and *The Great Society and the High Tide of Liberalism* (2005).

Bruce Miroff is a professor of political science and a Collins Fellow at the State University of New York (SUNY) at Albany. He has published numerous articles and book chapters on the presidency, political leadership, American political development, and American political theory. He is the author of *Pragmatic Illusions: The Presidential Politics of John F. Kennedy* (1976), *Icons of Democracy: American Leaders as Heroes, Aristocrats, Dissenters, and Democrats* (1993), *The Liberals' Moment: The McGovern Insurgency and the Identity Crisis of the Democratic Party* (2007), and *Presidents on Political Ground: Leaders in Action and What They Face* (2016). In his youth, he wrote record reviews for *Rolling Stone*.

Terry M. Moe is the William Bennett Monroe Professor of Political Science and a senior fellow at the Hoover Institution. He has written extensively on political institutions, public bureaucracy, and the presidency. His articles and chapters include "The New Economics of Organization," "The Politicized Presidency," "The Politics of Bureaucratic Structure," "Presidents, Institutions, and Theory," "The Presidential Power of Unilateral Action," and "Power and Political Institutions." He is coauthor of *Relic: How Our Constitution Undermines Effective Government— and Why We Need a More Powerful Presidency* (2016) and has written volumes on the politics of public education, including *Politics, Markets, and America's Schools* (1990) and *Special Interest: Teachers Unions and America's Public Schools* (2011).

Andrew J. Polsky is the Ruth and Harold Newman Dean of the School of Arts & Sciences at Hunter College of the City University of New York (CUNY), and professor of political science at Hunter College and the Graduate Center, CUNY. He is author of *Elusive Victories: The American Presidency at War* (2012) and *The Rise of the Therapeutic State* (1991), and editor of *The Eisenhower Presidency: Lessons for the Twenty-First Century* (2015). A scholar of American political development and the presidency, his articles have appeared in such journals as *Perspectives on Politics, Studies in American Political Development, American Politics Research, Journal of Theoretical Politics, Polity*, and *Political Science Quarterly*. From 2005 to 2010, Polsky served as the editor of *Polity*.

Roger B. Porter is the IBM Professor of Business and Government at Harvard University. He is also a Senior Scholar at the Woodrow Wilson International Center for Scholars in Washington, D.C. He has spent more than eleven years serving as a senior economic advisor in the White House to Presidents Gerald R. Ford, Ronald Reagan, and George H. W. Bush. He has received presidential appointments from each of the last nine U.S. presidents. His books include *Presidential Decision Making: The Economic Policy Board* (1980), *The U.S.–U.S.S.R. Grain Agreement* (1984), and others that address a wide range of economic policy issues. His edited volumes include *Efficiency, Equity, and Legitimacy: The Multilateral Trading System at the Millennium* (2001) and *New Directions in Financial Services Regulation* (2011).

Paul J. Quirk holds the Phil Lind Chair in U.S. Politics and Representation at the University of British Columbia. He has published widely on the presidency, Congress, public opinion, and public policy. He has won the Louis Brownlow Book Award from the National Academy of Public Administration and the Aaron Wildavsky Enduring Achievement Award of the Public Policy Section from the American Political Science Association. In recent work on the presidency, he edited a special issue of *Presidencial Studies Quarterly* on "Presidents and Economic Governance in Hazardous Times," coauthored a chapter on "Triangulation: Positioning and Leadership in Clinton's Domestic Policy," and contributed a chapter titled "The Presidency: Donald Trump and the Question of Fitness" in *The Elections of 2016* (2017, edited by Michael Nelson).

Lyn Ragsdale is the Radoslav A. Tsanoff Professor of Public Affairs and Professor of Political Science at Rice University. She has published several books including *The American Nonvoter* (2017, with Jerrold G. Rusk) and *Vital Statistics on the Presidency* (fourth ed., 2014), as well as numerous articles on the American presidency and elections.

Andrew Rudalevige is the Thomas Brackett Reed Professor of Government at Bowdoin College and past president of the American Political Science Association's Presidents and Executive Politics section. His books include *The New Imperial Presidency: Renewing Presidential Power after Watergate* (2005); *Managing the President's Program* (2002), which won the APSA's Richard Neustadt Award for the best book on the presidency; the coauthored textbook *The Politics of the Presidency* (2016); and a series of edited volumes on the Bush and Obama administrations. He is a frequent contributor to the Monkey Cage, a *Washington Post* political science blog, and host of the American civics video series Founding Principles.

Stephen Skowronek is the Pelatiah Perit Professor of Political and Social Science at Yale University. His books include *The Politics Presidents Make: Leadership from John Adams to Bill Clinton* (1993) and *Presidential Leadership in Political Time* (2008). His most recent book is *The Policy State: An American Predicament* (2017) with Karen Orren.

Daniel J. Tichenor is the Philip H. Knight Chair of Political Science and Senior Scholar of the Wayne Morse Center for Law and Politics. He has published extensively on the presidency, social movements, public policy, immigration, race and ethnicity. His books include *Dividing Lines: The Politics of Immigration Control* (2001), *The Politics of International Migration* (2012), *A History of the U.S. Political System* (2009), *Debates on U.S. Immigration* (2012), and *Rivalry and Reform: Presidents, Social Movements and the Transformation of American Politics* (2018). He recently was named to the inaugural class of Andrew Carnegie Fellows, and is currently finishing a book on democracy and immigrant integration with grant support from the National Endowment for the Humanities.

Jeffrey K. Tulis teaches American politics and political theory at the University of Texas at Austin. His books include *The Constitutional Presidency* (2009, coedited with Joseph M. Bessette) and *The Limits of Constitutional Democracy* (2010, coedited with Stephen Macedo). In addition, *The Rhetorical Presidency* (2017) with a new Foreword and Afterword was published on its 30th anniversary in the Princeton Classics series. Most recently, he published *Legacies of Losing in American Politics* (2018, with Nicole Mellow).

David A. Yalof is the department head and a professor of political science at the University of Connecticut. His first book, *Pursuit of Justices: Presidential Politics and the Selection of Supreme Court Nominees* (1999), won the 1999 Richard E. Neustadt Award for best book on the presidency from the American Political Science Association's Presidency Research Group. More recently, he authored *Prosecution among Friends: Presidents, Attorneys General, and Executive Branch Wrongdoing* (2012). He is also coauthor of *The First Amendment and the Media in the Court of Public Opinion* (2002) and *The Future of the First Amendment* (2008). Yalof is currently completing a coauthored biography of Federal District Judge Harold R. Medina.

THE TWO CONSTITUTIONAL PRESIDENCIES

Jeffrey K. Tulis

The formal design of the presidency can be found in Article II of the Constitution. Yet, according to Jeffrey K. Tulis, two constitutional presidencies exist. One is the enduring, capital C version that the Framers invented at the Constitutional Convention of 1787, the formal provisions of which remain substantially unaltered. The other is the adapted, lowercase c constitution that Woodrow Wilson devised and that most presidents during the past century have followed. Sometimes the fit between the formal and informal constitutional presidencies is close—for example, in the months following the September 11, 2001, terrorist attacks on the United States. But, Tulis argues, the two constitutional presidencies usually are in tension. Both constitutions value "energy" in the presidency, but the exercise of popular rhetorical leadership that is proscribed by the Framers' Constitution is prescribed by Wilson's. As a result, Tulis concludes, "many of the dilemmas and frustrations of the modern presidency may be traced to the president's ambiguous constitutional station, a vantage place composed of conflicting elements." These dilemmas—and others—were never more apparent than during the first year of the Trump presidency.

The modern presidency is buffeted by two "constitutions." Presidential action continues to be constrained, and presidential behavior shaped, by the institutions created by the original Constitution. The core structures established in 1789 and debated during the founding era remain essentially unchanged. For the most part, later amendments to the Constitution have left intact the basic features of the executive, legislative, and judicial branches of government. Great questions, such as the merits of unity or plurality in the executive, have not been seriously reopened. Because most of the structure persists, it seems plausible that the theory on which the presidency was constructed remains relevant to its current functioning.[1]

Presidential and public understanding of the constitutional system, and of the president's place in it, has changed, however. This new understanding is the "second constitution," under which presidents attempt to govern. Central to this second constitution is a view of statecraft that is in tension with the original Constitution—indeed it is opposed to the Founders' understanding of the presidency's place in the political system. The second constitution, which puts a premium on active and continuous presidential leadership of popular opinion, is buttressed by several institutional, albeit extraconstitutional, developments. These include the proliferation of presidential primaries as a mode of selection and the emergence of the mass media as a pervasive force.[2]

Many of the dilemmas and frustrations of the modern presidency may be traced to the president's ambiguous constitutional station, a vantage place composed of conflicting elements. This chapter lays bare the theoretical core of each of the two constitutions to highlight those elements that are in tension between them.

To uncover the principles that underlie the original Constitution, I rely heavily on *The Federalist*. A set of papers justifying the Constitution, the text was written by three of the Constitution's most articulate proponents, Alexander Hamilton, James Madison, and John Jay. The purpose of this journey back to the Founders is not to point to their authority or to lament change; nor do I mean to imply that all the supporters of the Constitution agreed with each of their arguments. *The Federalist* does represent, however, the most coherent articulation of the implications of, and interconnections among, the principles and practices that were generally accepted when the Constitution was ratified.[3]

I explore the political thought of Woodrow Wilson to outline the principles of the second constitution. Wilson self-consciously attacked *The Federalist* in his writings; as president he tried to act according to the dictates of his reinterpretation of the American political system. Presidents have continued to follow his example, and presidential scholars tend to repeat his arguments. Most presidents have not thought through the issues Wilson discussed—they are too busy for that. But if pushed and questioned, modern presidents would probably (and occasionally do) justify their behavior with arguments that echo Wilson's. Just as *The Federalist* represents the deepest and most coherent articulation of understandings of the presidency held through the nineteenth century, Wilson offers the most comprehensive theory in support of contemporary impulses and practices.

THE FOUNDING PERSPECTIVE

Perhaps the most striking feature of the founding perspective, particularly in comparison with contemporary political analyses, is its synoptic character. The Founders' task was to create a whole government, one in which the executive would play an important part, but only a part. By contrast, contemporary scholars of American politics often study institutions individually and therefore tend to be partisans of "their institution" in its contests with other actors in American politics.[4] Presidency scholars often restrict their inquiries to the strategic concerns of presidents as they quest for power. Recovering the founding perspective provides a way to think about the systemic legitimacy and utility of presidential power as well. To uncover such a synoptic vision, one must range widely in search of the principles that guided or justified the Founders' view of the executive. Some of these principles are discussed most thoroughly in *The Federalist* in the context of other institutions, such as Congress or the judiciary.

The Founders' general and far-reaching institutional analysis was preceded by a more fundamental decision of enormous import. Federalists and Anti-Federalists alike sought a government devoted to limited ends. In contrast to polities that attempt to shape the souls of their citizenry and foster certain excellences or moral qualities by penetrating deeply into the "private" sphere, the Founders wanted their government to be limited to establishing and securing such a sphere. Politics would extend only to the tasks of protecting individual rights and fostering liberty for the exercise of those rights. Civic virtue would still be necessary, but it would be elicited from the people rather than imposed on them.

Proponents and critics of the Constitution agreed about the proper ends of government, but they disagreed over the best institutional means to secure them.[5] Some critics of the Constitution worried that its institutions would undermine its limited liberal ends. Although these kinds of arguments were settled politically by the Federalist victory, *The Federalist* concedes that they were not resolved fundamentally because they continued as problems built into the structure of American politics.

Is a vigorous executive consistent with the genius of republican government? Hasty readers of *The Federalist* think yes, unequivocally. Closer reading of *The Federalist* reveals a deeper ambivalence regarding the compatibility of executive power and republican freedom.[6]

Demagoguery

The Founders worried especially about the danger that a powerful executive might pose to the system if power were derived from the role of popular leader.[7] For most Federalists, "demagogue" and "popular leader" were synonyms, and nearly all references to popular leaders in their writings are pejorative. Demagoguery, combined with majority tyranny, was regarded as the peculiar vice to which democracies were susceptible. Although much historical evidence supported this insight, the Founders were made more acutely aware of the problem by the presence in their own midst of popular leaders such as Daniel Shays, who led an insurrection in Massachusetts. The Founders' preoccupation with demagoguery may appear today as quaint, yet it may be that we do not fear it today because the Founders were so successful in institutionally proscribing some forms of it.

The original Greek meaning of *demagogue* was simply "leader of the people," and the term was applied in premodern times to champions of the people's claim to rule as against that of aristocrats and monarchs. As James Ceaser pointed out, the term has been more characteristically applied to a certain quality of leadership—that which attempts to sway popular passions. Because most speech contains a mix of rational and passionate appeals, it is difficult to specify demagoguery with precision. But as Ceaser argued, one cannot ignore the phenomenon because it is difficult to define, suggesting that it possesses at least enough intuitive clarity that few would label Dwight Eisenhower, for example, a demagogue, whereas most would not hesitate to so label Joseph McCarthy. The main characteristic of demagoguery seems to be an excess of passionate appeals. Ceaser categorized demagogues according to the kinds of passions that are summoned, dividing these into "soft" and "hard" types.

The soft demagogue tends to flatter constituents "by claiming that they know what is best, and makes a point of claiming his closeness (to them) by manner or gesture."[8] Hard demagogues attempt to create or encourage divisions among the people to build and maintain their constituency. Typically, this sort of appeal uses extremist rhetoric that panders to fear. James Madison worried about the possibility of class appeals that would pit the poor against the wealthy. But the hard demagogue might appeal to a very different passion. "Excessive encouragement of morality and hope" might be employed to create a division between those alleged to be compassionate, moral, or progressive, and those thought insensitive, selfish, or backward. Hard demagogues may be of the right or the left.[9]

Demagogues can also be classified by their object, in which case the issue becomes more complicated. Demagoguery might be good if it were a means to a good end, such as preservation of a decent nation or successful prosecution of a just war. The difficulty is to ensure by institutional means that demagoguery would be used only for good ends and not simply to satisfy the overweening ambition of an immoral leader or potential tyrant. How are political structures created that permit demagoguery when appeals to passion are needed but proscribe it for normal politics?

The Founders did not have a straightforward answer to this problem, perhaps because there is no unproblematic institutional solution. Instead, they addressed it indirectly in two ways: they attempted both to narrow the range of acceptable demagogic appeals through the architectonic act of founding itself and to mitigate the effects of such appeals in the day-to-day conduct of governance through the particular institutions they created. The Founders did not choose to make provision for the institutional encouragement of demagoguery in time of crisis, refusing to adopt, for example, the Roman model of constitutional dictatorship for emergencies.[10] Behind their indirect approach may have been the thought that excessive ambition needs no institutional support and the faith that in extraordinary circumstances popular rhetoric, even forceful demagoguery, would gain legitimacy through the pressure of necessity.

Many references in *The Federalist* and in the ratification debates over the Constitution warn of demagogues of the hard variety who through divisive appeals would aim at tyranny. *The Federalist* literally begins and ends with this issue. In the final paper, Hamilton offered "a lesson of moderation to all sincere lovers of the Union [that] ought to put them on their guard against hazarding anarchy, civil war, a perpetual alienation of the states from each other, and perhaps the military despotism of a victorious demagogue."[11] The Founders' concern with hard demagoguery was not merely a rhetorical device designed to facilitate passage of the Constitution. It also reveals a concern to address the kinds of divisions and issues exploited by hard demagoguery. From this perspective, the founding can be understood as an attempt to settle the large issue of whether the one, few, or many ruled (in favor of the many "through" a constitution); to reconfirm the limited purposes of government (security, prosperity, and the protection of rights); and, thereby, to give effect to the distinction between public and private life. At the founding these large questions were still matters of political dispute. Hamilton argued that adopting the Constitution would settle these perennially divisive questions for Americans, replacing those questions with smaller, less contentious issues. Hamilton called this new American politics a politics of "administration," distinguishing it from the traditional politics of disputed ends. If politics was transformed and narrowed in this way, thought Hamilton, demagogues would be deprived of part of their once-powerful arsenal of rhetorical weapons because certain topics would be rendered illegitimate for public discussion. By constituting an American understanding of politics, the founding would also reconstitute the problem of demagoguery.[12]

If the overriding concern about demagoguery in the extraordinary period before the ratification of the Constitution was to prevent social disruption, division, and possibly tyranny, the concerns expressed through the Constitution for normal times were broader to create institutions that would be most likely to generate and execute good policy and resist bad policy. Underlying the institutional structures and powers the Constitution created are three principles designed to address this broad concern: representation, independence of the executive, and separation of powers.

Representation

As the Founders realized, the problem with any simple distinction between good and bad law is that it is difficult to provide clear criteria to distinguish the two in any particular instance. It will not do to suggest that in a democracy good legislation reflects the majority will. A majority may tyrannize a minority, violating its rights; and even a nontyrannical majority may be a foolish one, preferring policies that do not further its interests. These considerations lay behind the Founders' distrust of "direct" or "pure" democracy.[13]

Yet an alternative understanding—that legislation is good if it objectively furthers the limited ends of the polity—is also problematic. It is perhaps impossible to assess the "interests" of a nation without giving significant attention to what the citizenry considers its interests to be. This concern lay behind the Founders' animus toward monarchy and aristocracy.[14] Identifying and embodying the proper weight to be given popular opinion and its appropriate institutional reflections constitute one of the characteristic problems of democratic constitutionalism. The Founders' understanding of republicanism as representative government reveals this problem and the Constitution's attempted solution.

Practically, the Founders attempted to accommodate these two requisites of good government by four devices. First, they established popular election as the fundamental basis of the Constitution and of the government's legitimacy. They modified that requirement by allowing "indirect" selection for some institutions (for example, the Senate, Supreme Court, and presidency)—that is, selection by others who were themselves chosen by the people. With respect to the president, the Founders wanted to elicit the "sense of the people," but they feared an inability to do so if the people acted in a "collective capacity." They worried that the dynamics of mass politics would at best produce poorly qualified presidents and at worst open the door to demagoguery and regime instability. At the same time, the Founders wanted to give popular opinion a greater role in presidential selection than it would have if Congress chose the executive. The institutional solution to these concerns was the Electoral College, originally designed as a semiautonomous locus of decision for presidential selection and chosen by state legislatures at each election.[15]

Second, the Founders established differing lengths of tenure for officeholders in the major national institutions, which corresponded to the institutions' varying "proximity" to the people. House members were to face reelection every two years, making them more responsive to constituent pressure than members of the other national institutions. The president was given a four-year term, sufficient time, it was thought, to "contribute to the firmness of the executive" without justifying "any alarm for the public liberty."[16]

Third, the Founders derived the authority and formal power of the institutions and their officers ultimately from the people but immediately from the Constitution. The effect would be to insulate officials from day-to-day currents of public opinion, while allowing assertion of deeply felt and widely shared public opinion through constitutional amendment.

Fourth, the Founders envisioned that the extent of the nation itself would insulate governing officials from sudden shifts of public opinion. In his well-known arguments for an extended republic, Madison reasoned that large size would improve democracy by making the formation of majority factions difficult. But again, argued Madison, the extent of the territory and diversity of factions would not prevent the formation of a majority if the issue was an important one.[17]

The brakes on public opinion, not the provision for its influence, are what cause skepticism today.[18] Because popular leadership is so central to modern theories of the presidency, the rationale behind the Founders' distrust of "direct democracy" should be noted specifically. This issue was raised dramatically in *The Federalist* No. 49, in which Madison addressed Jefferson's suggestion that "whenever two of the three branches of government shall concur in [the] opinion . . . that a convention is necessary for altering the Constitution, *or correcting breaches of it,* a convention shall be called for the purpose." Madison recounted Jefferson's reasoning because the

Constitution was formed by the people, it rightfully ought to be modified by them. Madison admitted "that a constitutional road to the decision of the people ought to be marked out and kept open for great and extraordinary occasions." But he objected to bringing directly to the people disputes among the branches about the extent of their authority. In the normal course of governance, such disputes could be expected to arise fairly often. In our day they would include, for example, the war powers controversy, the impoundment controversy, and the issue of executive privilege.

Madison objected to recourse to "the people" on three basic grounds. First, popular appeals would imply "some defect" in the government: "Frequent appeals would, in great measure, deprive the government of that veneration which time bestows on everything, and without which perhaps the wisest and freest governments would not possess the requisite stability." *The Federalist* pointed to the institutional benefits of popular veneration—stability of government and the enhanced authority of its constitutional officers. Second, the tranquility of the society as a whole might be disturbed. Madison expressed the fear that an enterprising demagogue might reopen disputes over "great national questions" in a political context less favorable to their resolution than the Constitutional Convention.

Third, Madison voiced "the greatest objection of all" to frequent appeals to the people: "The decisions which would probably result from such appeals would not answer the purpose of maintaining the constitutional equilibrium of government." Chief executives might face political difficulties if frequent appeals to the people were permitted because other features of the office (its singularity, independence, and executive powers) would leave presidents at a rhetorical disadvantage in contests with the legislature. Presidents will be "generally the objects of jealousy and their administrations . . . liable to be discolored and rendered unpopular," Madison argued. "The Members of the legislatures on the other hand are numerous. . . . Their connections of blood, of friendship, and of acquaintance embrace a great proportion of the most influential part of society. The nature of their public trust implies a personal influence among the people."[19]

Madison realized that there may be circumstances "less adverse to the executive and judiciary departments." If the executive power were "in the hands of a peculiar favorite of the people . . . the public decision might be less swayed in favor of the [legislature]. But still it could never be expected to turn on the true merits of the question." The ultimate reason for the rejection of "frequent popular appeals" is that they would undermine *deliberation* and result in bad public policy:

> The *passions*, therefore, not the *reason*, of the public would sit in judgment. But it is the reason, alone, of the public, that ought to control and regulate the government. The passions ought to be controlled and regulated by the government.[20]

There are two frequent misunderstandings of the Founders' opinion on the deliberative function of representation. The first is that they naively believed that deliberation constituted the whole of legislative politics—that there would be no bargaining, logrolling, or nondeliberative rhetorical appeals. The discussions of

Congress in *The Federalist* Nos. 52 to 68 and in the Constitutional Convention debates reveal quite clearly that the Founders understood that the legislative process would involve a mixture of these elements. The founding task was to create an institutional context that made deliberation most likely, not to assume that it would occur "naturally" or, even in the best of legislatures, predominantly.[21]

The second common error, prevalent in leading historical accounts of the period, is to interpret the deliberative elements of the Founders' design as an attempt to rid the legislative councils of "common men" and replace them with "better sorts"—more educated and, above all, more propertied individuals.[22] Deliberation, in this view, is the by-product of the kind of person elected to office. The public's opinions are "refined and enlarged" because refined individuals do the governing. Although this view finds some support in *The Federalist* and was a worry of several Anti-Federalists, the Founders' Constitution placed much greater emphasis on the formal structures of the national institutions than on the background of office-holders.[23] Indeed, good character and high intelligence, they reasoned, would be of little help to the government if it resembled a direct democracy: "In all very numerous assemblies, of whatever characters composed, passion never fails to wrest the sceptre from reason. Had every Athenian citizen been a Socrates, every Athenian assembly would still have been a mob."[24]

The presidency was thus intended to be representative of the people, but not merely responsive to popular will. Drawn from the people through an election (albeit an indirect one), presidents were to be free enough from the daily shifts in public opinion that they could refine it and, paradoxically, better serve popular interests. Hamilton expressed well this element of the theory in a passage in which he linked the problem of representation to that of demagoguery:

> There are those who would be inclined to regard the servile pliancy of
> the executive to a prevailing current, either in the community or in the
> legislature, as its best recommendation. But such men entertain very crude
> notions, as well of the purposes for which government was instituted,
> as of the true means by which public happiness may be promoted. The
> republican principle demands that the deliberative sense of the community
> should govern the conduct of those to whom they intrust the management
> of their affairs; but it does not require an unqualified complaisance . . . to
> every transient impulse which the people may receive from the arts of men,
> who flatter their prejudices to betray their interests. . . . When occasions
> present themselves in which the interests of the people are at variance with
> their inclinations, it is the duty of the persons whom they have appointed
> to be the guardians of those interests to withstand the temporary delusion,
> in order to give them time and opportunity for more cool and sedate
> reflection.[25]

Independence of the Executive

To "withstand the temporary delusion" of popular opinion, the executive was made independent. The office would draw its authority from the Constitution rather than from another government branch. The Framers were led to this deci-sion from their knowledge of the states. According to John Marshall, the state governments (with the exception of New York's) lacked any structure "which could resist the wild projects of the moment, give the people an opportunity to reflect and allow the good sense of the nation time for exertion." As Madison stated at the convention, "Experience had proved a tendency in our governments to throw all power into the legislative vortex. The executives of the states are in general little more than Cyphers; the legislatures omnipotent."[26]

Independence from Congress was the immediate practical need, yet the need was based on the close connection between legislatures and popular opinion. Because insufficient independence from public opinion was the source of the concern about the legislatures, the Founders rejected James Wilson's arguments on behalf of pop-ular election as a means of making the president independent of Congress.

Executive independence created the conditions under which presidents would be most likely to adopt a different perspective from Congress on matters of public policy. Congress would be dominated by local factions that, according to plan, would give great weight to constituent opinion. The president, as Thomas Jefferson was to argue, was the only national officer "who commanded a view of the whole ground." Metaphorically, independence gave presidents their own space within, and their own angle of vision on, the polity. According to the founding theory, these constituent features of discretion are required by the twin activities of execut-ing the will of the legislature and leading a legislature to construct good laws to be executed, laws that would be responsive to the long-term needs of the nation.[27]

Separation of Powers

The constitutional role of the president in lawmaking raises the question of the meaning and purpose of separation of powers. What is the meaning of separation of power if power is shared among the branches of government? Clearly, legalists are wrong if they assume that the Founders wished to distinguish so carefully among executive, legislative, and judicial powers as to make each the exclusive preserve of a particular branch. However, such an error gives rise to another one.

Political scientists, following Richard Neustadt, have assumed that because powers were not divided according to the principle of "one branch, one function," the Founders made no principled distinction among kinds of power. Instead, according to Neustadt, they created "separate institutions sharing power."[28] The premise of that claim is that power is an entity that can be divided up to prevent any one branch from having enough to rule another. In this view, the sole purpose of separation of powers is to preserve liberty by preventing the arbitrary rule of any one center of power.

The Neustadt perspective finds some support both in the Founders' delibera-tions and in the Constitution. Much attention was given to making each branch "weighty" enough to resist encroachment by the others. Yet this "checks and bal-ances" view of separation of powers can be understood better in tandem with an alternative understanding of the concept powers were separated, and structures of each branch differentiated, to equip each branch to perform different tasks. Each branch would be superior (although not the sole power) in its own sphere and in its own way. The purpose of separation of powers was to make effective governance more likely.[29]

Ensuring the protection of liberty and individual rights was one element of effective governance as the Founders conceived it, but it was not the only one. Government also needed to ensure the security of the nation and to craft policies that reflected popular will.[30] These governmental objectives may conflict, for example, if popular opinion favors policies that violate rights. Separation of powers was thought to be an institutional way of accommodating the tensions among governmental objectives.

Table 1.1 presents a simplified view of the purposes behind the separation of powers. Note that the three objectives of government—popular will, popular rights, and self-preservation—are mixed twice in the Constitution. They are mixed among the branches and within each branch so that each objective is given

Table 1.1 ■ Separation of Powers		
Objectives (in order of priority)	Special qualities and functions (to be aimed at)	Structures and means
CONGRESS		
1. Popular will	Deliberation	a. Plurality
2. Popular rights		b. Proximity (frequent House elections)
3. Self-preservation		c. Bicameralism
		d. Competent powers
PRESIDENT		
1. Self-preservation	Energy and "steady administration of law"	a. Unity
2. Popular rights		b. Four-year term and reeligibility
3. Popular will		c. Competent powers
COURTS		
1. Popular rights	"Judgment, not will"	a. Small collegial body
		b. Life tenure
		c. Power linked to argument

priority in one branch. Congress and the president were to concern themselves with all three, but the priority of their concern differs, with self-preservation, or national security, of utmost concern to the president.

The term *separation of powers* has perhaps obstructed understanding of the extent to which different structures were designed to give each branch the special quality needed to secure its governmental objectives. Thus, although the Founders were not so naive as to expect that Congress would be simply "deliberative," they hoped its plural membership and bicameral structure would provide necessary, if not sufficient, conditions for deliberation to emerge. Similarly, the president's "energy," it was hoped, would be enhanced by unity, the prospect of reelection, and substantial discretion. As we all know, the Supreme Court does not simply "judge" dispassionately; it also makes policies and exercises will. But the Founders believed it made no sense to have a Court if it were intended to be just like a Congress. The judiciary was structured to make the dispassionate protection of rights more likely, if by no means certain.

The Founders differentiated powers as well as structures in the original design. These powers ("the executive power" vested in the president in Article II and "all legislative power herein granted" given to Congress in Article I) overlap and sometimes conflict. Yet both the legalists' view of power as "parchment distinction" and the political scientists' view of "separate institutions sharing power" provide inadequate guides to what happens and what the Founders thought *ought* to happen when powers collide. The Founders urged that "line drawing" among spheres of authority be the product of political conflict among the branches, not the result of dispassionate legal analysis. Contrary to more contemporary views, they did not believe that such conflict would lead to deadlock or stalemate.[31]

Consider the disputes that sometimes arise from claims of "executive privilege."[32] Presidents occasionally refuse to provide Congress with information that its members deem necessary to carry out their special functions. They usually justify assertions of executive privilege on the grounds of either national security or the need to maintain the conditions necessary for sound execution, including the unfettered canvassing of opinions.

Both Congress and the president have legitimate constitutional prerogatives at stake: Congress has a right to know, and the president has a need for secrecy. How does one discover whether in any particular instance the president's claim is more or less weighty than Congress's? The answer depends on the circumstances—for example, the importance of the particular piece of legislation in the congressional agenda versus the importance of the particular secret to the executive. There is no formula independent of political circumstance with which to weigh such competing institutional claims. The most knowledgeable observers of those political conflicts are the parties themselves: Congress and the president.

Each branch has weapons at its disposal to use against the other. Congress can threaten to hold up legislation or appointments important to presidents. Ultimately, it could impeach and convict them. For their part, presidents may continue to "stonewall"; they may veto bills or fail to support legislation of interest to their legislative opponents; they may delay political appointments; and they may put the issue to public test, even submitting to an impeachment inquiry for their own advantage. The lengths to which presidents and Congresses are willing to go were thought to be a rough measure of the importance of their respective constitutional claims. Nearly always, executive–legislative disputes are resolved at a relatively low stage of potential conflict. In 1981, for example, President Ronald Reagan ordered Interior Secretary James Watt to release information to a Senate committee after the committee had agreed to maintain confidentiality. The compromise was reached after public debate and "contempt of Congress" hearings were held.

This political process is dynamic. Viewed at particular moments, the system may appear deadlocked. Looked at over time, considerable movement becomes apparent. Similar scenarios could be constructed for the other issues over which congressional and presidential claims to authority conflict, such as the use of executive agreements in place of treaties, the deployment of military force, or the executive impoundment of appropriated monies.[33]

Although conflict may continue to be institutionally fostered or constrained in ways that were intended by the Founders, one still may wonder whether their broad objectives have been secured and whether their priorities should be ours. At the beginning of the twentieth century, Woodrow Wilson mounted an attack on the Founders' design, convinced that it had not achieved its objectives. More important, his attack resulted in a reordering of those objectives in the understandings that presidents have of their roles. His theory underlies the second constitution that buffets the presidency.

THE MODERN PERSPECTIVE

Woodrow Wilson's influential critique of *The Federalist* contains another synoptic vision. Yet his comprehensive reinterpretation of the constitutional order appears, at first glance, to be internally inconsistent. Between writing his classic dissertation, *Congressional Government,* in 1884 and publishing his well-known series of lectures, *Constitutional Government in the United States,* in 1908, Wilson shifted his position on important structural features of the constitutional system.

Early in his career Wilson depicted the House of Representatives as the potential motive force in American politics and urged reforms to make it more unified and energetic. He paid little attention to the presidency or judiciary. In later years he focused his attention on the presidency. In his early writings Wilson urged a plethora of constitutional amendments that were designed to emulate the British parliamentary system, including proposals to synchronize the terms of representatives and senators with that of the president and to require presidents to choose leaders of the majority party as cabinet secretaries. Wilson later abandoned formal amendment as a strategy, urging instead that the existing Constitution be reinterpreted to encompass his parliamentary views.

Wilson also altered his views at a deeper theoretical level. According to Christopher Wolfe, although the early Wilson held a traditional view of the Constitution, as a document whose meaning persists over time, the later Wilson adopted a historicist understanding, claiming that the meaning of the Constitution changed as a reflection of the prevailing thought of successive generations.[34]

As interesting as these shifts in Wilson's thought are, they all rest on an underlying critique of the American polity that Wilson maintained consistently throughout his career. Wilson's altered constitutional proposals—indeed, his altered understanding of constitutionalism itself—ought to be viewed as a series of strategic moves designed to remedy the same alleged systemic defects. Our task is to review Wilson's understanding of those defects and to outline the doctrine he developed to contend with them—a doctrine whose centerpiece would ultimately be the rhetorical presidency.

Wilson's doctrine counterpoises the Founders' understandings of demagoguery, representation, independence of the executive, and separation of powers. For clarity, I examine these principles in a slightly different order from before separation of powers, representation, independence of the executive, and demagoguery.

Separation of Powers

For Wilson, separation of powers was the central defect of American politics. He was the first and most sophisticated proponent of the now conventional argument that "separation of powers" is a synonym for "checks and balances"—that is, the negation of power by one branch over another. Yet Wilson's view was more sophisticated than its progeny because his ultimate indictment of the Founders' conception was a functionalist one. Wilson claimed that under the auspices of the Founders' view, formal and informal political institutions failed to promote true deliberation in the legislature and impeded energy in the executive.

Wilson characterized the Founders' understanding as "Newtonian," a yearning for equipoise and balance in a machinelike system:

> The admirable positions of the *Federalist* read like thoughtful applications of Montesquieu to the political needs and circumstances of America. They are full of the theory of checks and balances. The President is balanced off against Congress, Congress against the President, and each against the Court. . . . Politics is turned into mechanics under [Montesquieu's] touch. The theory of gravitation is supreme.[35]

The accuracy of Wilson's portrayal of the Founders may be questioned. He reasoned backward from the malfunctioning system as he found it to how they must have intended it. Wilson's depiction of the system, rather than his interpretation of the Founders' intentions, however, is of present concern. Rather than equipoise and balance, Wilson found a system dominated by Congress, with several attendant functional infirmities: major legislation frustrated by narrow-minded committees, lack of coordination and direction of policies, a general breakdown of deliberation, and an absence of leadership. Extraconstitutional institutions—boss-led political parties chief among them—had sprung up to assume the functions not performed by Congress or the president, but they had not performed them well. Wilson also acknowledged that the formal institutions had not always performed badly, that some prior Congresses (those of Webster and Clay) and some presidencies (those of Washington, Adams, Jefferson, Jackson, Lincoln, Roosevelt, and, surprisingly, Madison) had been examples of forceful leadership.[36]

These two strands of thought—the growth of extraconstitutional institutions and the periodic excellence of the constitutional structures—led Wilson to conclude that the Founders had mischaracterized their own system. The Founders' rhetoric was "Newtonian," but their constitutional structure, like all government, was actually "Darwinian." Wilson explained:

> The trouble with the Newtonian theory is that government is not a machine but a living thing. It falls, not under the theory of the universe, but under the theory of organic life. It is accountable to Darwin, not to Newton. It is modified by its environment, necessitated by its tasks, shaped to its functions by the sheer pressure of life.[37]

The Founders' doctrine had affected the working of the structure to the extent that the power of the political branches was interpreted mechanically and many of the structural features reflected the Newtonian yearning. A tension arose between the "organic" core of the system and the "mechanical" understanding of it by politicians and citizens. Thus "the constitutional structure of the government has hampered and limited [the president's] actions but it has not prevented [them.]" Wilson tried to resolve the tension between the understanding of American politics as Newtonian and its actual Darwinian character to make the evolution self-conscious and thereby more rational and effective.[38]

Wilson attacked the Founders for relying on mere "parchment barriers" to effectuate a separation of powers. This claim is an obvious distortion of founding views. In *Federalist* Nos. 47 and 48, the argument is precisely that the federal Constitution, unlike earlier state constitutions, would not rely primarily on parchment distinctions of power but on differentiation of institutional structures.[39] Through Wilson's discussion of parchment barriers, however, an important difference between his and the Founders' views of the same problem becomes visible. Both worried over the tendency of legislatures to dominate in republican systems.

To mitigate the danger posed by legislatures, the Founders had relied primarily on an independent president with an office structured to give its occupant the personal incentive and means to stand up to Congress when it exceeded its authority. These structural features included a nonlegislative mode of election, constitutionally fixed salary, qualified veto, four-year term, and indefinite reeligibility. Although the parchment powers of Congress and the president overlapped (contrary to Wilson's depiction of them), the demarcation of powers proper to each branch would result primarily from political interplay and conflict between the political branches rather than from a theoretical drawing of lines by the judiciary.[40]

Wilson offered a quite different view. First, he claimed that because of the inadequacy of mere parchment barriers, Congress, in the latter half of the nineteenth century, had encroached uncontested on the executive sphere. Second, he contended that when the president's institutional check was used, it took the form of a "negative"—prevention of a bad outcome rather than provision for a good one. In this view, separation of powers hindered efficient, coordinated, well-led policy.[41]

Wilson did not wish to bolster structures to thwart the legislature. He preferred that the president and Congress be fully integrated into, and implicated in, each other's activities. Rather than merely assail Congress, Wilson would tame or, as it were, domesticate it. Separation would be replaced by institutionally structured cooperation. Cooperation was especially necessary because presidents lacked the energy they needed, energy that could be provided only by policy backed by Congress and its majority. Although Congress had failed as a deliberative body, it could now be restored to its true function by presidential leadership that raised and defended crucial policies.

These latter two claims represent the major purposes of the Wilsonian theory: leadership and deliberation. Unlike the Founders, who saw these two functions in conflict, Wilson regarded them as dependent on each other. In "Leaderless Government" he stated,

> I take it for granted that when one is speaking of a representative legislature he means by an "efficient organization" an organization which provides for deliberate, and deliberative, action and which enables the nation to affix responsibility for what is done and what is not done. The Senate is deliberate enough; but it is hardly deliberative after its ancient and better manner. . . . The House of Representatives is neither deliberate nor deliberative. We have not forgotten that one of the most energetic of its recent Speakers thanked God, in his frankness, that the House was not a deliberative body. It has not the time for the leadership of argument. . . . For debate and leadership of that sort the House must have a party organization and discipline such as it has never had.[42]

It appears that the Founders and Wilson differed on the means to common ends. Both wanted "deliberation" and an "energetic" executive, but each proposed different constitutional arrangements to achieve those objectives. In fact, their differences went much deeper, for each theory defined deliberation and energy differently. These differences, hinted at in the previous quotation, will become clearer as we examine Wilson's reinterpretation of representation and independence of the executive.

Representation

In the discussion of the founding perspective, the competing requirements of popular consent and insulation from public opinion as a requisite of impartial judgment were canvassed. Woodrow Wilson gave much greater weight to the role of public opinion in the ordinary conduct of representative government than did the Founders. Some scholars have suggested that Wilson's rhetoric and the institutional practices he established (especially regarding the nomination of presidential candidates) are the major sources of contemporary efforts to create a more "participatory" democracy. However, Wilson's understanding of representation, like his views on separation of powers, was more sophisticated than that of his followers.[43]

Wilson categorically rejected the Burkean view that legislators are elected for their quality of judgment and position on a few issues and then left free to exercise that judgment:

> It used to be thought that legislation was an affair to be conducted by the few who were instructed for the benefit of the many who were uninstructed that statesmanship was a function of origination for which only trained and instructed men were fit. Those who actually conducted legislation and conducted affairs were rather whimsically chosen by Fortune to illustrate this theory, but such was the ruling thought in politics. The Sovereignty of the People, however . . . has created a very different practice. . . . It is a dignified proposition with us—is it not?—that as is the majority, so ought the government to be.[44]

Wilson did not think his view was equivalent to "direct democracy" or to subservience to public opinion (understood, as it often is today, as response to public opinion polls). He favored an interplay between representative and constituent that would, in fact, educate the constituent. This process differed, at least in theory, from the older attempts to "form" public opinion; it did not begin in the minds of the elite but in the hearts of the masses. Wilson called the process of fathoming the people's desires (often only vaguely known to the people until instructed) "interpretation." Interpretation was the core of leadership for him.[45] Before we explore its meaning further, it is useful to dwell on Wilson's notion of the desired interplay between the "leader–interpreter" and the people so that we may see how his understanding of deliberation differed from that of the Founders.

For the Founders, deliberation meant reasoning on the merits of policy. The character and content of deliberation would thus vary with the character of the policy at issue. In "normal" times, there would be squabbles among competing interests. Deliberation would occur to the extent that such interests were compelled to offer arguments and respond to those made by others. The arguments might be relatively crude, specialized, and technical, or they might involve matters of legal or constitutional propriety. But in none of these instances would they resemble the great debates over fundamental principles—for example, over the question of whether to promote interests in the first place. Great questions were the stuff of crisis politics, and the Founders placed much hope in securing the distinction between crisis and normal political life.

Wilson effaced the distinction between "crisis" and "normal" political argument:

> Crises give birth and a new growth to statesmanship because they are peculiarly periods of action . . . [and] also of unusual opportunity for gaining leadership and a controlling and guiding influence. . . . And we thus come upon the principle . . . that governmental forms will call to the work of the administration able minds and strong hearts constantly or infrequently, according as they do or do not afford at all times an opportunity of gaining and retaining a commanding authority and an undisputed leadership in the nation's councils.[46]

Wilson's lament that little deliberation took place in Congress was not that the merits of policies were left unexplored but rather that, because the discussions were not elevated to the level of major contests of principle, the public generally did not interest itself. True deliberation, he urged, would rivet the attention of press and public, whereas what substituted for it in his day were virtually secret contests of interest-based factions. Wilson rested this view on three observations. First, the congressional workload was parceled out to specialized standing committees, whose decisions usually were ratified by the respective houses without any general debate. Second, the arguments that did take place in committee were technical and structured by the "special pleadings" of interest groups, whose advocates adopted the model of legal litigation as their mode of discussion. As Wilson characterized committee debates,

> They have about them none of the searching, critical, illuminating character of the higher order of parliamentary debate, in which men are pitted against each other as equals, and urged to sharp contest and masterful strife by the inspiration of political principle and personal ambition, through the rivalry of parties and the competition of policies. They represent a joust between antagonistic interests, not a contest of principles.[47]

Finally, because debates were hidden away in committee, technical, and interest based, the public cared little about them. "The ordinary citizen cannot be induced to pay much heed to the details, or even the main principles of lawmaking," Wilson wrote, "unless something more interesting than the law itself be involved in the pending decision of the lawmaker." For the Founders this would not have been disturbing, but for Wilson the very heart of representative government was the principle of publicity: "The informing function of Congress should be preferred even to its legislative function." The informing function was to be preferred both as an end in itself and because the accountability of public officials required policies that were connected with one another and explained to the people. Argument from "principle" would connect policy and present constellations of policies as coherent wholes to be approved or disapproved by the people. "Principles, as statesmen conceive them, are threads to the labyrinth of circumstances."[48]

Wilson attacked separation of powers in an effort to improve leadership for the purpose of fostering deliberation. "Congress cannot, under our present system ... be effective for the instruction of public opinion, or the cleansing of political action." As mentioned at the outset of this section, Wilson first looked to Congress itself, specifically to its Speaker, for such leadership. Several years after the publication of *Congressional Government,* Wilson turned his attention to the president: "There is no trouble now about getting the president's speeches printed and read, every word," he wrote at the turn of the century.[49]

Independence of the Executive

The attempt to bring the president into more intimate contact with Congress and the people raises the question of the president's "independence." Wilson altered the meaning of this notion, which originally had been that the president's special authority came independently from the Constitution, not from Congress or the people. For the Founders, presidents' constitutional station afforded them the possibility and responsibility of taking a perspective on policy different from that of either Congress or the people. Wilson urged us to consider presidents as receiving their authority independently through a mandate from the people. For Wilson, presidents remained "special" because they were the only government officers with a national mandate.[50]

Political scientists today have difficulty finding mandates in election years, let alone between them, because of the great number of issues and the lack of public consensus on them. Wilson understood this problem and urged the leader to sift through the multifarious currents of opinion to find a core of issues that he believed reflected majority will even if the majority was not yet fully aware of it.

The leader's rhetoric could translate the people's felt desires into public policy. Wilson cited Daniel Webster as an example of such an interpreter of the public will:

> The nation lay as it were unconscious of its unity and purpose, and he called it into full consciousness. It could never again be anything less than what he said it was. It is at such moments and in the mouths of such interpreters that nations spring from age to age in their development.[51]

"Interpretation" involves two skills. First, the leader must understand the true majority sentiment underneath the contradictory positions of factions and the discordant views of the masses. Second, the leader must explain the people's true desires to them in a way that is easily comprehended and convincing.

Wilson's desire to raise politics to the level of rational disputation and his professed aim to have leaders educate the masses are contradictory. He acknowledged candidly that the power to command would require simplification of the arguments to accommodate the masses: "The arguments which induce popular action must always be broad and obvious arguments; only a very gross substance of concrete conception can make any impression on the minds of the masses."[52] Not only is argument simplified, but disseminating "information"—a common concern of contemporary democratic theory—is not the function of a deliberative leader, in Wilson's view:

> Men are not led by being told what they don't know. Persuasion is a force, but not information; and persuasion is accomplished by creeping into the confidence of those you would lead. . . . Mark the simplicity and directness of the arguments and ideas of true leaders. The motives which they urge are elemental; the morality which they seek to enforce is large and obvious; the policy they emphasize, purged of all subtlety.[53]

Demagoguery

Wilson's understanding of leadership raises again the problem of demagoguery. What distinguishes a leader–interpreter from a demagogue? Who is to make this distinction? The Founders feared there was no institutionally effective way to exclude the demagogue if popular oratory during "normal" times was encouraged. Indeed, the term *leader,* which appears a dozen times in *The Federalist,* is used disparagingly in all but one instance, and that one is a reference to leaders of the Revolution.[54]

Wilson was sensitive to this problem: "The most despotic of governments under the control of wise statesmen is preferable to the freest ruled by demagogues," he wrote. Wilson relied on two criteria to distinguish the demagogue from the leader, one based on the nature of the appeal, the other on the character of the leader. The demagogue appeals to "the momentary and whimsical popular mood, the transitory or popular passion," whereas the leader appeals to "true" and durable majority sentiment. The demagogue is motivated by the desire to augment personal power, and the leader is more interested in fostering the permanent interests of the community. "The one [trims] to the inclinations of the moment, the other [is] obedient to the permanent purposes of the public mind."[55]

Theoretically these distinctions present a number of difficulties. If popular opinion is the source of the leader's rhetoric, what basis apart from popular opinion is there to distinguish the "permanent" from the "transient"? If popular opinion is constantly evolving, what sense is there to the notion of "the permanent purposes of the public mind"? Yet the most serious difficulties are practical ones. Assuming it is theoretically possible to distinguish the leader from the demagogue, how is that distinction to be incorporated into the daily operation of political institutions? Wilson offered a threefold response to this query.

First, he claimed his doctrine contained an ethic that could be passed on to future leaders. Wilson hoped that politicians' altered understanding of what constituted success and fame could provide some security. He constantly pointed to British parliamentary practice, urging that long training in debate had produced generations of leaders and few demagogues. Indeed, Wilson had taught at Johns Hopkins, Bryn Mawr, Wesleyan, and Princeton, and at each of those institutions he established debating societies modeled on the Oxford Union.[56]

Second, Wilson placed some reliance on the public's ability to judge character:

> Men can scarcely be orators without that force of character, that readiness of resource, that cleverness of vision, that grasp of intellect, that courage of conviction, that correctness of purpose, and that instinct and capacity for leadership which are the eight horses that draw the triumphal chariot of every leader and ruler of freemen. We could not object to being ruled by such men.[57]

According to Wilson, the public need not appeal to a complex standard or theory to distinguish demagoguery from leadership, but could easily recognize "courage," "intelligence," and "correctness of purpose"—signs that the leader was not a demagogue. Wilson did not say why prior publics had fallen prey to enterprising demagogues, but the major difficulty with this second source of restraint is that public understanding of leaders' character would come from their oratory rather than from a history of their political activity or from direct contact with them. The public's understanding of character might be based solely on words.

Third, Wilson suggested that the natural conservatism of public opinion, its resistance to innovation that is not consonant with the speed and direction of its own movement, would afford still more safety:

> Practical leadership may not beckon to the slow masses of men from beyond some dim, unexplored space or some intervening chasm it must daily feel the *road* to the goal proposed, knowing that it is a slow, very slow, evolution to the wings, and that for the present, and for a very long future also, Society must *walk,* dependent upon practicable paths, incapable of scaling sudden heights.[58]

Wilson's assurances of security against demagogues may seem unsatisfactory because they did not adequately distinguish the polity in which he worked from others in which demagogues had prevailed, including some southern states in this country. However, his arguments should be considered as much for the theoretical direction and emphases that they implied as for the particular weaknesses they revealed. Wilson's doctrine stood on the premise that the need for more energy in the political system was greater than the risk incurred through the possibility of demagoguery.[59] His view represented a major shift, indeed a reversal, of the founding perspective. If Wilson's argument regarding demagoguery was strained or inadequate, it was a price he was willing to pay to remedy what he regarded as the Founders' inadequate provision for an energetic executive.

CONCLUSION

Both constitutions were designed to encourage and support an energetic president, but they differ over the legitimate sources and alleged virtues of popular leadership. For the Founders, presidents draw their energy from their authority, which rests on their independent constitutional position. For Woodrow Wilson and for presidents ever since, power and authority are conferred directly by the people. *The Federalist* and the Constitution proscribe popular leadership. Wilson prescribed it. Indeed, he urged the president to minister continually to the moods of the people as a preparation for action. The Founders' president was to look to the people, but less frequently, and to be judged by them, but usually after acting.

The second constitution gained legitimacy because presidents were thought to lack the resources necessary for the energy promised but not delivered by the first. The second constitution did not replace the first, however. Because many of the founding structures persist, while our understanding of the president's legitimate role has changed, the new view should be thought of as superimposed on the old, altering without obliterating the original structure.

Many commentators have noted the tendency of recent presidents to raise public expectations about what they can achieve. Indeed, public disenchantment with government altogether may stem largely from disappointment in presidential performance, inasmuch as the presidency is the most visible and important American political institution. Yet, rather than being the result of the personality traits of particular presidents, raised expectations are grounded in an institutional dilemma common to all modern presidents. Under the auspices of the second constitution, presidents must continually craft rhetoric that pleases their popular audience. Even though presidents are always in a position to promise more, the only additional resource they have to make good on their promises is public opinion itself. Because Congress retains the independent status conferred on it by the first Constitution, it can resist the president.

Naturally, presidents who are exceptionally popular or gifted as orators can overcome the resistance of the legislature. For the political system as a whole, this possibility is both good and bad. To the extent that the system requires periodic renewal through synoptic policies that reconstitute the political agenda, it is good. But the very qualities that are necessary to achieve such large-scale change tend to subvert the deliberative process, which makes unwise legislation or incoherent policy more likely.

Ronald Reagan's major political victories as president illustrate both sides of this systemic dilemma.[60] On the one hand, without the second constitution it would be difficult to imagine Reagan's success at winning tax reform legislation. His skillful coordination of a rhetorical and a legislative strategy overcame the resistance of thousands of lobbies that sought to preserve advantageous provisions of the existing tax code. Similarly, Social Security and other large policies that were initiated by Franklin D. Roosevelt during the New Deal might not have been possible without the second constitution.

On the other hand, Reagan's first budget victory in 1981 and the Strategic Defense Initiative (SDI, also known as Star Wars) illustrate how popular leadership can subvert the deliberative process or produce incoherent policy. The budget cuts of 1981 were secured with virtually no congressional debate. Among their effects was the gutting of virtually all of the Great Society programs initiated by President Lyndon B. Johnson, which themselves were the product of a popular campaign that circumvented the deliberative process.

When Congress does deliberate, as it has on SDI, the debate is often structured by contradictory forms of rhetoric, the product of the two constitutions. The arguments presidents make to the people are different from those they make to Congress. To the people, Reagan promised to strive for a new defense technology that would make nuclear deterrence obsolete. But to Congress, his administration argued that SDI was needed to supplement, not supplant, deterrence.[61] Each kind of argument can be used to impeach the other. President Jimmy Carter found himself in the same bind on energy policy. When he urged the American people to support his energy plan, Carter contended that it was necessary to remedy an existing crisis. But to Congress he argued that the same policy was necessary to forestall a crisis.[62]

The second constitution promises energy, which is said to be inadequately provided by the first. This suggests that the two constitutions fit together to form a more complete whole. Unfortunately, over the long run, the tendency of the second constitution to make extraordinary power routine undermines, rather than completes, the logic of the original Constitution. Garry Wills has described how presidents since John F. Kennedy have attempted to pit public opinion against their own executive establishment. Successors to a charismatic leader then inherit "a delegitimated set of procedures" and are themselves compelled "to go outside of procedures—further delegitimating the very office they [hold]."[63] In Reagan's case, this cycle was reinforced by an ideology opposed to big government. "In the present crisis," Reagan said at his first inaugural, "government is not the solution to our problem; government is the problem." Although fiascoes like the Iran-contra affair are not inevitable, they are made more likely by the logic and legitimacy of the second constitution.

It was hard to imagine that any leader would embrace the second constitution more than Reagan did, but President Bill Clinton surpassed him. According to George Edwards,

> The Clinton presidency is the ultimate example of the rhetorical presidency—a presidency based on a perpetual campaign to obtain the public's support and fed by public opinion polls, focus groups, and public relations memos. No president ever invested more in measuring, and attempting to mold, public opinion. [This administration] even polled voters on where it was best for the First Family to vacation. This is an administration that spent $18 million on ads in 1995, a nonelection year! And this is an administration that repeatedly interpreted its setbacks, whether in elections or health care reform, in terms of its failure to communicate rather than in terms of the quality of its initiatives or the strategy for governing. Reflecting his orientation in the White House, Bill Clinton declared that "the role of the President of the United States is message."[64]

The Clinton presidency was a roller coaster of political successes and failures. No doubt it will take scholars decades to make sense of Clinton's political choices and the public's reactions to them. No simple explanation can address how this president, who was the head of his political party when the Democrats were badly defeated in 1994, rebounded so decisively in 1996, or how he came to be impeached by the House in 1998 yet be acquitted by the Senate in 1999. A full analysis of these political undulations and their consequences for the polity would include, at a minimum, accounts of the president's character, his political acumen, the state of the economy and the world, and the actions of the Republican opposition. Without venturing to offer even the beginning of such an analysis, it may be helpful to suggest how the two constitutional presidencies may be a useful backdrop for a fuller narrative. The political dilemmas Clinton faced and the choices he made to contend with them are, at least in part, products of the uneasy conjunction of the two constitutions.

For example, the president's fidelity to the second constitution contributed to the most serious mistake that prompted the impeachment proceeding. Faced with an inquiry into his relationship with Monica Lewinsky, Clinton sought a rhetorical solution to his political difficulty. Oriented to the immediate demands of persuasion in a national plebiscite, Clinton relied on his bully pulpit. On the advice of his former pollster Dick Morris and friend and media adviser Harry Thomason, the president went on national television and forcefully denied that he had "sexual relations" with Lewinsky. That denial, more than the conduct it concealed, fueled congressional opposition and delegitimized his presidency in the eyes of many of his critics and even some of his allies.

Yet presidents are schooled by both constitutions even when they only consciously understand the second. President Carter discovered the Rose Garden strategy of retreating from public view when the demands of foreign policy placed him in a position to see the benefits of a political posture inherent to the first Constitution.[65] Similarly, President Clinton rediscovered the first Constitution as the nation taught itself the constitutional meaning of impeachment.

As the impeachment drama unfolded, Clinton was uncharacteristically mute. He let his lawyers and other surrogates do the talking about impeachment-related matters while he attended to the nation's other business. The nation's resurrection of a nineteenth-century constitutional anachronism, impeachment, placed the president in a position from which he could see the political benefit of acting like a nineteenth-century president. Because the animating charge of the political opposition was that Clinton had disgraced his office—whether through his sexual behavior or his subsequent deceptions and alleged perjury—the president's conduct during the formal proceedings became a rhetorical or dramaturgical refutation of the main charge against him. The one exception to this presidential style, so characteristic of the first Constitution, seemed to prove its significance. When the president emerged from the White House to lead congressional allies in a show of support immediately following the House vote, he was severely criticized for politicizing a constitutional process. Clinton's conscious and seemingly instinctive understanding of leadership conflicted with the model of statesmanship inherent to the constitutional order. After that misstep, the president attempted to recapture the advantages that the dignity of the office provided him.

Although political circumstance encouraged Clinton to rediscover the first Constitution, political crisis led George W. Bush to a more rhetorical presidency than would be his natural inclination.[66] Bush was not a gifted orator. Like his father, he had difficulty expressing himself, was prone to misstatement, and seemed unable to master the proper cadences of formal speech. Nevertheless, the terrorist attacks on New York and Washington, D.C., Bush's response to them in Afghanistan, and his subsequent war against Iraq required him to lead. In this array of circumstances and responsibilities, one can see both the promise and the pitfall of presidential leadership under the auspices of two constitutions. Bush's response to the 9/11 terrorist attacks shows how the president's traditional roles under the Constitution can be enhanced by modern rhetorical practices. His leadership of the nation into the war in Iraq reveals how the second constitution sometimes undermines the first.

In the wake of the terrorist attacks on the United States, Bush found it necessary to deliver a number of speeches to a grieving nation. Because it was proper for the president to do this, even under the first Constitution, his words gained in politically constructed authority what they lacked in natural grace. The Constitution, its norms, institutions, and traditions, elevated an ordinary speaker to a station from which he was able to deliver extraordinarily effective leadership.

By contrast, Bush's case for the war in Iraq did not respond to a widely felt crisis. Rather, the president tried to convince the nation that an unseen crisis existed. To do this he developed a public case for war that differed, at least in emphasis, from the real reasons that animated decision makers within the administration. The case for war that prevailed within the administration stood on three basic grounds: the threat from weapons of mass destruction, Iraq's support of terrorism, and the brutality of Iraq's totalitarian practices on its own people. Taken together, these three reasons were all grounded in the nature of the Iraqi regime and therefore were thought to necessitate regime change. Although all three were part of the public case for war,[67] the threat of weapons of mass destruction was the one the administration stressed. When it became apparent that there were no such weapons, the president's policy was, in effect, hoisted by its own rhetorical petard. Bush's credibility was undermined by the rhetorical choices he made to speedily gain popular support for the war and to pressure Congress to authorize the use of force. His "deception" was not, as many commentators alleged, an intentional effort to lie to Congress, to the United Nations, or to the American people. Instead, it was an effort to simplify a complex argument to make it more effective rhetorically.[68] The problem of credibility that hounded the Bush administration toward the end was not the president's personality or moral character. Rather, it was a by-product of a second constitution that lives in tension with the first.

President Barack Obama inherited both the worst economic crisis since the Great Depression and wars in Iraq and Afghanistan. Because he is such a gifted orator, because the nation needed a president to get it through a genuine crisis, and because Obama promised in his first presidential campaign to be a "transformational" leader, it was reasonable to expect that Obama would try to perfect the kind of rhetorical leadership that marked the administration of Franklin D. Roosevelt. He did not. To be sure, President Obama's first term, like FDR's, was marked by large and significant policy successes: an economic stimulus, banking regulation, auto bailouts, national health care reform, significant defeats for the Al Qaeda terrorist network, withdrawals from Iraq and Afghanistan, the end of "don't ask, don't tell" in the military, and an enhancement of legitimacy for gay marriage. But Obama did not offer a "new" New Deal, nor did he articulate a new grand strategy in foreign affairs. Instead of an overarching "public philosophy" he offered pragmatic responses to problems.[69] In many ways his leadership style reflected the norms of the first constitutional presidency more than the second. For example, when proposing a major reform of health care, he left the crafting of the legislation to Congress and did not mount a public speaking campaign to pressure legislators to adopt it or launch a subsequent speaking campaign to facilitate its implementation. As a series of concrete responses to practical problems, Obama's presidency was remarkably successful. Judging from the criticisms of progressive Democrats as well as conservative Republicans, however, one would have thought Obama a great disappointment. He was often criticized for a lack of popular leadership by friends as well as foes—for failure to be a rhetorical president.

Three years into his first term, Obama decided to follow the advice of his critics. He launched his bid for a second term while still in the midst of his first. Deploying the skills and tactics of electoral campaigns, Obama began to blend campaigning and governing in ways typical of the modern rhetorical presidency. He abandoned "post-partisanship" and became a partisan Democrat, albeit in a muted form compared with his political foes or presidential predecessors. Although this new leadership style pleased his party and helped him win reelection, Republican critics and many independent journalists seized the norms of the first constitution as their own and criticized Obama for being a "demagogue," as well as for pressuring Congress by appealing over its head to the people at large. For example, on the eve of his successful campaign to avoid the so-called "fiscal cliff" just before the new year of 2013, some senators accused the president of diminishing his office by giving a speech in which he criticized Congress generally and Republicans more specifically.[70]

How might President Obama have avoided the dilemma of being criticized from the vantage point of both of the two constitutions? Is there an alternative kind of presidential leadership to those made familiar by the first and second constitutions? There may be. Obama could have deployed the tools of the modern rhetorical presidency for a new kind of political purpose. Instead of trying to pressure or supplant the legislature, Obama might have diagnosed the failures of modern national politics and made a case for constitutional and institutional reform. Although he promised to be a post-partisan president in his first campaign, he never clearly explained what that meant, why it was required, or what it implied for the reform of our political institutions. Devoid of the familiar kind of "public philosophy" that marked the New Deal, Obama could only have become the transformational president he promised if he had changed our understanding of transformation itself. Instead of a public philosophy crafted to market a basket of public policies, Obama needed to articulate a new understanding of the constitutional order—of its infirmities and of the innovations needed for its repair. He needed to defend the kind of leadership in practice he enacted but never explained. He needed to show that the post-partisanship and pragmatism he heralded offered a political theory, not just a series of ad hoc responses. With pragmatism understood and explained as a theory of political reform, Obama might have created a third constitutional presidency.

Although Obama never consciously articulated a new understanding of leadership, he did instinctively resurrect the leadership style of George Washington to the extent that he renewed a sense of dignity in the nation's highest office. David Brooks wrote, in the early days of the Obama presidency, that contemporary American political culture suffered from an almost total absence of the understanding and practice of dignity. In the first year of the Obama presidency, a corrupt governor of Illinois fell from office in a manner completely lacking dignity or grace; a governor of South Carolina publicly humiliated his family and himself; and a governor of Alaska, according to Brooks, "aspire[d] to a high public role but [wa]s unfamiliar with the traits of equipoise and constancy, which are the sources of authority and trust."[71] But then there was Obama. "Whatever policy differences people may have with him, we can all agree the he exemplifies reticence, dispassion and the other traits associated with dignity. The cultural effects of his presidency are not yet clear, but they may surpass his policy impact. He may have [preserved] the concept of dignity for a new generation and [have] embodied a new set of rules for self-mastery."[72] Forrest McDonald's description of George Washington's most important and most subtle legacy may well describe Barack Obama: "he endowed the presidency with the capacity—and the awesome responsibility—to serve as the symbol of the nation, of what it is and what it can aspire to be."[73]

Obama's Washington-style dignity was most evident during the transition to the Donald Trump administration. Having campaigned hard against the new president and often expressed the view that Donald Trump lacked the skills and temperament to be president, during the transition Obama pivoted to a posture designed to facilitate an efficient and graceful transfer of power. Given a new president who campaigned on a platform to replace virtually all of the signature policies and achievements of the Obama presidency, the departing president seemed to trust his legacy to the manifest contrast between himself and his successor. In the waning days of his administration, Obama exemplified statesmanship for the nation and for his successor in a desperate hope that he could tutor and attenuate the proclivities of a demagogue or, at least, provide the citizenry a model against which to judge the new president.

Before Trump, America had never elected a demagogue. The only true demagogue who served as president was Andrew Johnson. But Johnson was not elected, and he served in a political order that opposed every one of his important initiatives, overruled his vetoes, impeached him, and drove him from office in disgrace.[74] President Trump was elected with a solid majority of Electoral votes, with his party in control of both houses of Congress and initially offering strong support, and a Supreme Court with a decisive seat open for his preferred candidate.

If President Trump continues to exercise the office in the same demagogic manner that he campaigned with he may actualize the Founders' nightmare scenario—a corrosive leader posing an existential threat to the constitutional order. Even Woodrow Wilson, who was more confident than the Founders that the American people would be unlikely to elect a demagogue, agreed with them on the range of serious dangers that demagogues pose for democratic sustenance—from a degradation of the political culture to autocracy.[75]

To be sure, some features of Trump's leadership style are not unprecedented. Many recent presidents have effaced the distinction between campaigning and governing. Many presidents have relied on their top campaign advisors as key counselors in governance. The techniques of campaigning have been brought into the White House as necessary instruments to advance policy agendas. Even specific or particular demagogic appeals are not new. Nevertheless, there is a big difference between importing the skills of campaigning and deploying a demagogic appeal to secure a specific objective, as all recent presidents have done, and demonstrating no understanding of governance other than a personal communion between the leader and his followers. All of Trump's recent predecessors toggled between the rhetorical presidency and the president's traditional Constitutional roles. There appears to be no toggle switch for Trump. One month into his term, Trump told reporters traveling with him to a rally in Florida, "Life is a campaign. Make America Great Again is a campaign. For me, [the presidency] is a campaign."[76]

The ascendance of Trump surprised most observers because during the campaign he made dozens of utterances and took dozens of actions any one of which would have sunk previous campaigns. Edmund Muskie, Howard Dean, Michael Dukakis, Gary Hart, John Edwards, and Rick Perry are just a few examples of politicians who stumbled and failed because of mistakes they made on the campaign trail. How was it possible for Trump to succeed given his proclivity to break any norm that got in his way, to say anything that came into his head no matter how crude or inappropriate? Trump proliferated his outrages, repeated his claims incessantly, and projected his vices onto his opponents. These techniques—proliferation, repetition, and projection—transformed what for other candidates would be gaffes or mistakes into the constitutive elements of his victory.

In a recent book, Michael Signer usefully interprets James Fenimore Cooper's essay on demagoguery to highlight certain features of the phenomenon. "As Cooper recognized, true demagogues meet four rules: (1) They fashion themselves as a man or woman of the common people, as opposed to the elites; (2) their politics depends on a powerful, visceral connection with the people that dramatically transcends ordinary political popularity; (3) they manipulate this connection, and the raging popularity it affords, for their own benefit and ambition; and (4) they threaten or outright break established rules of conduct, institutions, and even the law."[77] Jan-Werner Muller adds that demagogues nurture a powerful connection with their own supporters, and if such support is sufficient to win election, the faction supporting the demagogue is invested with the authority of the people as a whole. The enthusiasm of a faction is represented as the will of the people.[78]

Donald Trump amplified the power of a traditional demagogue to manipulate passion by turning traditional campaign vices into additional demagogic instruments. Faced with criticism for his gaffes, mistakes, and norm-breaking behavior, Trump not only refused to apologize: he instead reaffirmed his misstatements and uttered more of them. The effect of this strategy was to diminish or discount the harm to his campaign of any single mistake. Faced with fact-checking of his many untruths, Trump insisted on repeating them to the point that his followers believed them and the wider world became desensitized to the differences between truth and falsehood. Finally, Trump repeatedly accused his own opponents of his own vices. When he lied, he labeled his opponent the liar. When faced with a mountain of evidence of conflicts of interest, he painted his opponents as beholden to special interests. Faced with whistleblowers who revealed potentially illegal behavior by his staff, he labeled the reports themselves illegal because they were leaked. When investigations into his campaign's contacts with Russian officials mounted, he responded by accusing former President Obama of a Watergate-type crime. Through projection Trump was able to diminish the stature of his opponents, deflect attention from his own vices, and render disqualifying attributes as unremarkable. The effect of these demagogic innovations is the most extensive and troublesome degradation of presidential discourse in American history.[79]

NOTES

1. Notable structural changes in the Constitution are the Twelfth, Seventeenth, Twentieth, and Twenty-second Amendments, which deal, respectively, with change

in the Electoral College system, the election of senators, presidential succession, and presidential reeligibility. Although all are interesting, only the last seems manifestly inconsistent with the Founders' plan. For a defense of the relevance of the constitutional theory of the presidency to contemporary practice, see Joseph M. Bessette and Jeffrey Tulis, eds., *The Presidency in the Constitutional Order* (Baton Rouge: Louisiana State University Press, 1981); and Joseph M. Bessette and Jeffrey K. Tulis, *The Constitutional Presidency* (Baltimore: Johns Hopkins University Press, 2009). See also David K. Nichols, *The Myth of the Modern Presidency* (University Park: Pennsylvania State University Press, 1994).

2. James W. Ceaser, *Presidential Selection: Theory and Development* (Princeton, NJ: Princeton University Press, 1979); Nelson Polsby, *Consequences of Party Reform* (New York: Oxford University Press, 1983); Doris A. Graber, *Mass Media and American Politics,* 6th ed. (Washington, DC: CQ Press, 2001); David L. Paletz and Robert M. Entman, *Media, Power, Politics* (New York: Free Press, 1981); and Harvey C. Mansfield Jr., *America's Constitutional Soul* (Baltimore: Johns Hopkins University Press, 1991), chap. 12.

3. This essay does not reveal the Founders' personal and political motives except as they were self-consciously incorporated into the reasons offered for their Constitution. The Founders' views are treated on their own terms, as a constitutional theory; Hamilton's statement in the first number of *The Federalist* is taken seriously: "My motives must remain in the depository of my own breast. My arguments will be open to all and may be judged by all." James Madison, Alexander Hamilton, and John Jay, *The Federalist Papers,* ed. Clinton Rossiter (New York: New American Library, 1961), no. 1, 36. For a good discussion of the literature on the political motives of the founding fathers, see Erwin C. Hargrove and Michael Nelson, *Presidents, Politics, and Policy* (New York: Knopf, 1984), chap. 2.

4. The most influential study of the presidency is by Richard Neustadt. See *Presidential Power: The Politics of Leadership from FDR to Carter* (New York: Wiley, 1979), vi: "One must try to view the Presidency from over the President's shoulder, looking out and down with the perspective of his place."

5. Herbert J. Storing, *What the Anti-Federalists Were For* (Chicago: University of Chicago Press, 1981), 83n.

6. *The Federalist,* no. 70, 423.

7. In the first number, "Publius" warns "that of those men who have overturned the liberties of republics, the greatest number have begun their career by paying obsequious court to the people, commencing demagogues and ending tyrants." And in the last essay, "These judicious reflections contain a lesson of moderation to all the sincere lovers of the Union, and ought to put them upon their guard against hazarding anarchy, civil war, and perhaps the military despotism of a victorious demagogue, in the pursuit of what they are not likely to obtain, but from TIME and EXPERIENCE."

8. Ceaser, *Presidential Selection,* 12, 54–60, 166–167, 318–327. See also V. O. Key, *The Responsible Electorate* (New York: Random House, 1966), chap. 2; Stanley Kelley Jr., *Political Campaigning: Problems in Creating an Informed Electorate* (Washington, DC: Brookings Institution Press, 1960), 93; Pendleton E. Herring, *Presidential Leadership* (New York: Holt, Rinehart and Winston, 1940), 70; and *The Federalist,* no. 71, 432.

9. *The Federalist,* no. 10, 82; and Ceaser, *Presidential Selection,* 324.

10. Clinton Rossiter, *Constitutional Dictatorship: Crisis Government in the Modern Democracies* (Princeton, NJ: Princeton University Press, 1948), chap. 3.

11. *The Federalist,* no. 85, 527.

12. Harvey Flaumenhaft, "Hamilton's Administrative Republic and the American Presidency," in *The Presidency in the Constitutional Order,* ed. Bessette and Tulis, 65–114. The Civil War and turn-of-the-century progressive politics show that Hamilton's "administrative republic" has been punctuated with the sorts of crises and politics Hamilton sought to avoid.

13. *The Federalist,* no. 10, 77; no. 43, 276; no. 51, 323–325; no. 63, 384; and no. 73, 443. Moreover, the factual quest to find a "majority" may be no less contestable than is dispute over the merits of proposals. Contemporary political scientists provide ample support for the latter worry when they suggest that it is often both theoretically and practically impossible to discover a majority will—that is, to count it up—owing to the manifold differences of intensity of preferences and the plethora of possible hierarchies of preferences. Kenneth Arrow, *Social Choice and Individual Values* (New York: Wiley, 1963); and Benjamin I. Page, *Choices and Echoes in Presidential Elections* (Chicago: University of Chicago Press, 1978), chap. 2.

14. *The Federalist,* no. 39, 241; see also Martin Diamond, "Democracy and the Federalist: A Reconsideration of the Framers' Intent," *American Political Science Review* 53 (March 1959): 52–68.

15. *The Federalist,* no. 39, 241; no. 68, 412–423. See also James Ceaser, "Presidential Selection," in *The Presidency in the Constitutional Order,* ed. Bessette and Tulis, 234–282. Ironically, the Founders were proudest of this institutional creation; the Electoral College was their most original contrivance. Moreover, it escaped the censure of, and even won a good deal of praise from, antifederal opponents of the Constitution. Because electors were chosen by state legislatures for the sole purpose of selecting a president, the process was thought more democratic than potential alternatives, such as selection by Congress. Compare Nichols, *Myth of the Modern Presidency,* 39–45.

16. *The Federalist,* no. 72, 435. The empirical judgment that four years would serve the purpose of insulating the president is not as important for this discussion as the principle reflected in that choice, a principle that has fueled recent calls for a six-year term.

17. *The Federalist,* nos. 9 and 10.

18. Gordon Wood, *The Creation of the American Republic: 1776–1787* (New York: Norton, 1969); Michael Parenti, "The Constitution as an Elitist Document," in *How Democratic Is the Constitution?* ed. Robert Goldwin (Washington, DC: American Enterprise Institute, 1980), 39–58; and Charles Lindblom, *Politics and Markets* (New York: Basic Books, 1979), conclusion.

19. *The Federalist,* no. 49, 313–317.

20. Ibid., 317.

21. See *The Federalist,* no. 57; Joseph M. Bessette, "Deliberative Democracy," in *How Democratic Is the Constitution?* ed. Goldwin, 102–116; and Michael Malbin, "What Did the Founders Want Congress to Be—and Who Cares?" (paper presented at the annual meeting of the American Political Science Association, Denver, September 2, 1982). On the status of legislative deliberation today, see Joseph M. Bessette, *The Mild Voice of Reason: Deliberative Democracy and American National Government* (Chicago: University of Chicago Press, 1994); William Muir, *Legislature* (Chicago:

University of Chicago Press, 1982); and Arthur Maas, *Congress and the Common Good* (New York: Basic Books, 1983).

22. Wood, *Creation of the American Republic,* chap. 5; and Ceaser, *Presidential Selection,* 48.

23. *The Federalist,* no. 62; no. 63, 376–390; and Storing, *What the Anti-Federalists Were For,* chap. 7.

24. *The Federalist,* no. 55, 342.

25. *The Federalist,* no. 71, 432; Madison expresses almost the identical position in no. 63, where he stated,

    > As the cool and deliberate sense of the community, ought in all governments, and actually will in all free governments, ultimately prevail over the views of its rulers; so there are particular moments in public affairs when the people, stimulated by some irregular passion, or some illicit advantage, or misled by the artful misrepresentations of interested men, may call for measures which they themselves will afterwards be most ready to lament and condemn. In these critical moments how salutary will be [a Senate].

26. John Marshall, *Life of George Washington,* quoted in Charles Thatch, *The Creation of the Presidency* (1923; reprint, Baltimore: Johns Hopkins University Press, 1969), 51; and Max Farrand, ed., *The Records of the Federal Convention of 1787,* 4 vols. (New Haven, CT: Yale University Press, 1966), vol. 2, 35, 22, 32.

27. *The Federalist,* no. 68, 413; no. 71, 433; and no. 73, 442; see also Storing, "Introduction," in Thatch, *Creation of the Presidency,* vi–viii. Thomas Jefferson, "Inaugural Address," March 4, 1801, in *The Life and Writings of Thomas Jefferson,* ed. Adrienne Koch and William Peden (New York: Modern Library, 1944), 325.

28. Neustadt, *Presidential Power,* 26, 28–30, 170, 176, 204. See also James Sterling Young, *The Washington Community* (New York: Columbia University Press, 1964), 53. This insight has been the basis of numerous critiques of the American "pluralist" system, which, it is alleged, frustrates leadership as it forces politicians through a complicated political obstacle course. See also Jeffrey K. Tulis, "The President in the Political System: In Neustadt's Shadow," in *Presidential Power: Forging the Presidency for the Twenty-First Century,* ed. Robert Y. Shapiro, Martha Joynt Kumar, and Lawrence R. Jacobs (New York: Columbia University Press, 2000), 265–273.

29. Farrand, *Records,* vol. 1, 66–67; *The Federalist,* no. 47, 360–380; see also U.S. Congress, *Annals of Congress* (Washington, DC: Gales and Seaton, 1834), vol. 1, 384–412, 476–608. See generally Louis Fisher, *Constitutional Conflict between Congress and the President* (Princeton, NJ: Princeton University Press, 1985).

30. In many discussions of separation of powers today, the meaning of effectiveness is restricted to only one of these objectives—the implementation of policy that reflects popular will. See, for example, Donald Robinson, ed., *Reforming American Government* (Boulder, CO: Westview Press, 1985).

31. See, for example, Lloyd N. Cutler, "To Form a Government," *Foreign Affairs* 59 (Fall 1980): 126–143.

32. Gary J. Schmitt, "Executive Privilege: Presidential Power to Withhold Information from Congress," in *Presidency in the Constitutional Order,* ed. Bessette and Tulis, 154–194; and David Crockett, "Executive Privilege," in *The Constitutional Presidency,* ed. Bessette and Tulis, 203–228.

33. Richard Pious, *The American Presidency* (New York: Basic Books, 1979), 372–415; Gary J. Schmitt, "Separation of Powers: Introduction to the Study of Executive Agreements," *American Journal of Jurisprudence* 27 (1982): 114–138; and Louis

Fisher, *Presidential Spending Power* (Princeton, NJ: Princeton University Press, 1975), 147–201.

34. Woodrow Wilson, *Congressional Government: A Study in American Politics* (1884; reprint, Gloucester, MA: Peter Smith, 1973), preface to 15th printing, introduction; Wilson, *Constitutional Government in the United States* (New York: Columbia University Press, 1908); and Christopher Wolfe, "Woodrow Wilson: Interpreting the Constitution," *Review of Politics* 41 (January 1979): 131. See also Woodrow Wilson, "Cabinet Government in the United States," in *College and State,* ed. Ray Stannard Baker and William E. Dodd, 2 vols. (New York: Harper and Brothers, 1925), vol. 1, 19–42; Paul Eidelberg, *A Discourse on Statesmanship* (Urbana: University of Illinois Press, 1974), chaps. 8 and 9; Harry Clor, "Woodrow Wilson," in *American Political Thought,* ed. Morton J. Frisch and Richard G. Stevens (New York: Scribner, 1971); and Robert Eden, *Political Leadership and Nihilism* (Gainesville: University of Florida Press, 1984), chap. 1.

35. Wilson, *Constitutional Government,* 22, 56; and Wilson, "Leaderless Government," in *College and State,* ed. Baker and Dodd, 337.

36. Wilson, *Congressional Government,* 141, 149, 164, 195.

37. Wilson, *Constitutional Government,* 56.

38. Ibid., 60; see also Wilson, *Congressional Government,* 28, 30, 31, 187.

39. *The Federalist,* nos. 47 and 48, 300–313. Consider Madison's statement in *Federalist* no. 48, 308–309:

> Will it be sufficient to mark with precision, the boundaries of these departments in the Constitution of the government, and to trust to these parchment barriers against the encroaching spirit of power? This is the security which appears to have been principally relied upon by the compilers of most of the American Constitutions. But experience assures us that the efficacy of the provision has been greatly overrated; and that some more adequate defense is indispensably necessary for the more feeble against the more powerful members of the government. The legislative department is everywhere extending the sphere of its activity and drawing all power into its impetuous vortex.

40. Schmitt, "Executive Privilege."

41. Wilson, "Leaderless Government," 340, 357; Wilson, *Congressional Government,* 158, 201; and Wilson, "Cabinet Government," 24–25.

42. Wilson, "Leaderless Government," 346; at the time he wrote this, Wilson was thinking of leadership internal to the House, but he later came to see the president performing this same role. Wilson, *Constitutional Government,* 69–77; see also Wilson, *Congressional Government,* 76, 97–98.

43. Eidelberg, *Discourse on Statesmanship,* chaps. 8 and 9; and Ceaser, *Presidential Selection,* chap. 4, conclusion.

44. Woodrow Wilson, *Leaders of Men,* ed. T. H. Vail Motter (Princeton, NJ: Princeton University Press, 1952), 39. This is the manuscript of an oft-repeated lecture that Wilson delivered in the 1890s. See also Wilson, *Congressional Government,* 195, 214.

45. Wilson, *Leaders of Men,* 39; and Wilson, *Constitutional Government,* 49. See also Wilson, *Congressional Government,* 78, 136–137.

46. Wilson, "Cabinet Government," 34–35. See also Wilson, "Leaderless Government," 354; and Wilson, *Congressional Government,* 72, 136–137.

47. Wilson, *Congressional Government,* 69, 72.

48. Ibid., 72, 82, 197–198; Wilson, "Cabinet Government," 20, 28–32; and Wilson, *Leaders of Men,* 46.

49. Wilson, *Congressional Government,* 76, and preface to 15th printing, 22–23.

50. Ibid., 187.

51. Wilson, *Constitutional Government,* 49. Today the idea of a mandate as objective assessment of the will of the people has been fused with the idea of leader as interpreter. Presidents regularly appeal to the results of elections as legitimizing the policies they believe ought to reflect majority opinion. On the "false" claims to represent popular will, see Stanley Kelley Jr., *Interpreting Elections* (Princeton, NJ: Princeton University Press, 1984).

52. Wilson, *Leaders of Men,* 20, 26.

53. Ibid., 29.

54. I am indebted to Robert Eden for the point about *The Federalist.* See also Ceaser, *Presidential Selection,* 192–197.

55. Wilson, "Cabinet Government," 37; and Wilson, *Leaders of Men,* 45–46.

56. See, for example, Wilson, *Congressional Government,* 143–147.

57. Ibid., 144.

58. Wilson, *Leaders of Men,* 45.

59. Wilson, *Congressional Government,* 144.

60. I discuss this and other dilemmas more fully in *The Rhetorical Presidency* (Princeton, NJ: Princeton University Press, 1987; new ed., 2017). See also Jeffrey K. Tulis, "Revising the Rhetorical Presidency," in *Beyond the Rhetorical Presidency,* ed. Martin Medhurst (College Station: Texas A&M Press, 1996); and Jeffrey K. Tulis, "The Constitutional Presidency in American Political Development," in *The Constitution and the American Presidency,* ed. Martin Fausold and Alan Shank (Albany: State University of New York Press, 1991). For criticisms of these ideas along with my rejoinders, see Richard Ellis, ed., *Speaking to the People: The Rhetorical Presidency in Historical Perspective* (Amherst: University of Massachusetts Press, 1998); and Jeffrey Friedman and Shterna Friedman, eds., *Rethinking the Rhetorical Presidency* (London: Routledge, 2012).

61. Steven E. Miller and Stephen Van Evera, eds., *The Star Wars Controversy* (Princeton, NJ: Princeton University Press, 1986), preface.

62. Sanford Weiner and Aaron Wildavsky, "The Prophylactic Presidency," *Public Interest* 52 (Summer 1978): 1–18.

63. Garry Wills, "The Kennedy Imprisonment: The Prisoner of Charisma," *Atlantic Monthly,* January 1982, 34; and H. H. Gerth and C. Wright Mills, eds., *From Max Weber* (New York: Oxford University Press, 1958), 247–248.

64. George C. Edwards, "Campaigning Is Not Governing: Bill Clinton's Rhetorical Presidency," in *The Clinton Legacy,* ed. Colin Campbell and Bert A. Rockman (New York: Chatham House, 1999), 37. Clinton quoted in Elizabeth Drew, *Showdown: The Struggle between the Gingrich Congress and the Clinton White House* (New York: Simon and Schuster, 1996), 19.

65. Tulis, *Rhetorical Presidency,* 174–175.

66. For a firsthand account of the demands of rhetoric in the George W. Bush presidency, see John J. DiIulio, "The Hyper-Rhetorical Presidency," in Friedman and Friedman, eds., *Rethinking,* 106–115.

67. Deputy Secretary of Defense Paul Wolfowitz interview with Sam Tannenhaus, May 9, 2003, http://www.defenselink.mil/transcripts/2003/may2003.html.

68. See Nicole Mellow, "The Rhetorical Presidency and the Partisan Echo Chamber" in Friedman and Friedman eds., *Rethinking,* 158–162.

69. Jeffrey K. Tulis, "Plausible Futures," in *The Presidency in the Twenty-First Century*, ed. Charles W. Dunn (Lexington: University Press of Kentucky, 2011.) See also Rogers M. Smith, "The Constitutional Philosophy of Barack Obama: Democratic Pragmatism and Religious Commitment," *Social Science Quarterly* (December 2012) 93: 1251–71.

70. Transcript, Obama's New Year's Eve Remarks on the Fiscal Cliff. *Washington Post,* December 31, 2013, http://articles.washingtonpost.com/2012-12-31/politics/36104248_1_tax-hike-tax-credits-fiscal-cliff (accessed January 2, 2012); see also James Ceaser, "The Changing Face of Barack Obama's Leadership," in Carol MacNamara and Melanie M. Marlowe, eds., *The Obama Presidency in the Constitutional Order* (Lanham, MD: Rowman and Littlefield, 2011). I respond to Ceaser in "*The Rhetorical Presidency* in Retrospect," in Friedman and Friedman eds., *Rethinking,* 272–277.

71. David Brooks, "In Search of Dignity," *New York Times,* July 7, 2009, A23.

72. Ibid.

73. Forrest McDonald, "Today's Indispensable Man," in *Patriot Sage: George Washington and the American Political Tradition,* ed. Gary L. Gregg II and Matthew Spalding (Wilmington, DE: ISI Books, 1999), 37.

74. Jeffrey K. Tulis and Nicole Mellow, *Legacies of Losing in American Politics* (Chicago: University of Chicago Press, 2018), chap. 3.

75. See Terri Bimes and Stephen Skowronek, "Woodrow Wilson's Critique of Popular Leadership: Reassessing the Modern-Traditional Divide in Presidential History," *Polity* 29, no. 1 (Autumn 1996): 27–63.

76. Lindsey Bever, "'Demonic Activity Was Palpable' at Trump's Rally, Pastor Says," *Washington Post,* February 22, 2017. "One advisor calls political rallies the president's 'oxygen,'" https://www.washingtonpost.com/news/acts-of-faith/wp/2017/02/22/demonic-activity-palpable-at-president-trumps-rally-pastor-says/?tid=sm_fb&utm_term=.e09de89c9308 (accessed February 25, 2017).

77. Michael Signer, *Demagogue: The Fight to Save Democracy From Its Worst Enemies* (New York: St. Martin's, 2009) p. 35, citing James Fenimore Cooper, *The American Democrat* (Indianapolis, IN: Liberty Classics, 1931 reprint; orig. publ. 1838).

78. Jan-Werner Muller, *What Is Populism?* (Philadelphia: University of Pennsylvania Press, 2016).

79. See William E. Connolly, *Aspirational Fascism: The Struggle for Multifaceted Democracy Under Trumpism* (Minneapolis, MN: University of Minnesota Press, 2017).

STUDYING THE PRESIDENCY

Why Presidents Need Political Scientists

Lyn Ragsdale

Political scientists study the presidency, but even before Donald Trump took office presidents generally have not been interested in learning what they have to teach. That's too bad, argues Lyn Ragsdale, because most presidents could learn a great deal. Employing a variety of perspectives and methods, political scientists have uncovered several general patterns in the presidency. Some of these have to do with presidential imagery—for example, "People respond to presidents more through emotions than through rational calculations about the government's performance or presidents' positions on issues." Other generalizations ("Cabinet government does not work") concern the presidential institution. Ragsdale finds that presidents who are ignorant of what political scientists know often make avoidable, sometimes serious mistakes.

American presidents are surrounded by experts. Economists show presidents how to study budgets, inflation figures, and unemployment rates. Domestic policy analysts tell presidents about the details of proposals on civil rights, health care reform, Social Security, and education. Military, foreign relations, and intelligence experts inform presidents about the capabilities of military hardware, defense strategies, international diplomacy, and covert operations. On occasion, historians remind presidents about what past chief executives have accomplished. After six months in office, President Barack Obama met with a group of nine historians and asked them to reflect on how several of his predecessors had succeeded and failed in tackling key national problems.[1] But political scientists are rarely asked to the White House to instruct presidents about the presidency. Since President Bill Clinton's first term, a team of political scientists has run the White House Transition Project, which offers systematic advice to new presidents' transition teams about specific offices in the White House and the executive departments and what to do and not do when making cabinet and other appointments.[2] Although incoming administrations typically have embraced the Transition Project, the Trump administration bypassed these experts, preferring to run the transition not in Washington, D.C., but from Trump Tower in New York. No matter how much an incoming administration relies on the Transition Project, once the transition is complete, political scientists are much less known to American presidents. Few presidents seem ever to have taken a course on the presidency; some seem to have failed one. Presidents typically presume that by virtue of being in office they must know the job's ins and outs. Yet political scientists understand the presidency in a way that other experts cannot. Presidents could benefit from studying the presidency.

This chapter considers what political scientists know about the presidency and what presidents themselves should know. First, two central features of the modern office—imagery and institution—are outlined.[3] Second, several generalizations about the presidency that are related to its imagery and institution are addressed. These generalizations describe what usually happens in the office and outline regular patterns that are difficult for presidents to avoid and equally difficult for them to modify. Third, several episodes of presidential mistakes are examined that might have been avoided had presidents studied the office more carefully. Finally, the issue of what presidents can learn from how political scientists study the presidency is reexamined.

IMAGERY AND INSTITUTION

The first thing presidents need to know about the presidency is that it has two major dimensions: imagery and institution. The main image of the presidency is of the president, speaking with a clear lone voice, governing the country. The institution is the complex organization of people that surrounds the president, helps to make presidential decisions, and structures relations with other institutions, such as Congress, the media, the bureaucracy, and the courts.

These two features of the presidency appeared around the beginning of the twentieth century.[4] Image and institution emerged through a philosophical shift from presidential restraint to presidential activism. As proponents of activism, Theodore Roosevelt (1901–1909) and Woodrow Wilson (1913–1921) argued that presidents have the ability to do anything on behalf of the people that does not directly violate the Constitution. Activism thus relies on two concepts, both of which forge the presidential image. First, presidents can do "anything"—they are to be active policymakers and problem solvers. Second, presidents do so on behalf of the people—they are, in Theodore Roosevelt's words, "stewards of the people." The institution is needed to carry out the responsibilities assumed by presidents in the new imagery. The one demands the other.

Neither of these features of the presidency existed in the nineteenth century when presidents operated under notions of restraint—they exercised only those powers specified in the Constitution and existing laws. As a rule, presidents were neither seen nor heard. George Washington, Thomas Jefferson, Andrew Jackson, James Polk, and Abraham Lincoln aside, presidents before the twentieth century either did not take active roles in policymaking and public leadership or were unsuccessful when they did so; both arenas were thus left to Congress. For modern presidents the key is to understand more specifically what the image and the institution are like.

On Imagery

The image of the presidency is the single executive image: The president is the most powerful, most important person in the government and in the nation. As the only official elected by the entire country, presidents represent the people. They profess compassion for the average American and passion for the American dream. They are the nation's principal problem solvers, the ones who identify its most daunting challenges and offer solutions. They press their leadership to ensure that the proposed solutions become law. In times of crisis, they single-handedly protect the nation. The image of the president is thus of a person who is omnicompetent (able to do all things) and omnipresent (working everywhere).

An image is a simplification. It is one's mental picture of an object, a product, a situation, or, in this case, a political office. The image usually magnifies certain features while glossing over other relevant details. Reality is typically checked against the image more than the other way around. For example, if you have an image of the perfect cat—big, white, and fluffy—then you are unlikely to enjoy cats who do not match this image. If a scrawny, black, matted feline wanders by, you are much less likely to adopt a new image of the perfect cat to accommodate it. The single executive image is a simplification of both the presidency and American politics. It personalizes the office by embodying all its units, staff, and decisions in one person—the president. In the mind's eye of the nation, the president is the person who matters most. American politics is presidential politics. Many people's recollections of American politics are dominated by the day Truman dropped the bomb, the day John Kennedy was shot, the day Richard Nixon resigned, the day Barack Obama announced the killing of Osama Bin Laden, the day after day that Jimmy Carter could not free the hostages in Iran. People often simplify their views of both the presidency and American politics by focusing on the exploits of one person.

To be sure, people are aware that the government is immensely more complex than this—Congress is a powerful and, at times, dominant branch; the bureaucracy seems to do whatever it wants; the Supreme Court announces decisions that tell the rest of the government what to do. Yet citizens look at this assemblage as if it were the scrawny cat. It does not fit their presidential image of the government. Similarly, when they find that presidents appear to be in over their heads with national economic difficulties, dissension within their own party in Congress, or civil wars abroad, they do not modify the single executive image to fit the harsh (and very typical) presidential circumstance. Instead, they revise their opinions of the incumbent chief executive, who comes out the loser in public opinion polls.

Sources of the Single Executive Image. The single executive image arises from three sources: the public, the press, and presidents themselves. Citizens are keenly interested in political figures as individuals, and presidents are the political figures they know best. The political scientist Fred Greenstein observed that people draw on the president as an important cognitive aid to simplify and ultimately understand politics.[5] Many Americans pay little attention to politics, but the one person they do know something about is the president. Many can recall the most trivial details about presidents, from their taste in food—whether it is President Obama's taste for arugula or President Clinton's affinity for McDonald's—to the names of the family pets: Fala (Franklin Roosevelt), King Timahoe (Nixon), Millie (George H. W. Bush), Socks the Cat (Clinton), Barney (George W. Bush), and Bo and Sunny (Barack Obama). Several "first pets" have become celebrities in their own right, with Millie "writing" a best-selling book and Bo and Sunny routinely "posting" on their Facebook page. Indeed, when Donald Trump took office a mild controversy ensued because Trump had no dog or cat and was unlikely to get one. This was the first time in more than 100 years that no presidential pet would wander the White House lawn. Thus people simplify the complex operations of government by concentrating on the actions of a single player—the president.

The media help produce the ubiquity of president-watching among the public. The most important national story that the press reports, day in and day out, is about the president. A Pew Research Center study of news coverage during the first 100 days in office for presidents George W. Bush, Clinton, and Obama showed that well over 30 percent of the stories were about their leadership skills and style.[6] During his first 100 days in office, Donald Trump not only was covered more often than his predecessors but also was the central speaker in 65 percent of White House news stories.[7] The press then is fascinated with presidents as individuals—what they say, where they go, whom they meet. It is not clear which fascination came first—that of the public or that of the press. Much press coverage has become known as the "body watch."[8] Reporters watch the president's every move just in case, as Ronald Reagan put it, the "awful awful" happens. As one television news executive producer observed, "We cover the president expecting he will die."[9] When George W. Bush choked on a pretzel while watching a football game and momentarily passed out, it became international news. The body watch carries with it a vivid irony. Especially since the Kennedy assassination, the press assumes, probably correctly, that people want to know if a president becomes ill, is injured, or is killed. Yet on most days, nothing catastrophic happens. So the body watch captures the ordinary aspects of the president's life. Otherwise mundane activities, such as taking a morning walk, jogging, playing golf, eating at a restaurant, and boating, become news as part of the body watch. Sometimes, the White House goes to great lengths to prevent cameras from capturing aspects of the president's routine. Although reporters were allowed to cover Donald Trump dining at his Mar-a-Lago resort in Florida, they were forbidden from recording the president playing golf there or at his other properties in an attempt to rebuff reports that Trump spent too much time on the golf course.[10] In addition, only when problems arise among members of the White House staff do viewers and readers learn about some of the more than 1,000 people who work within the presidency. Most often the president stands alone in daily press coverage.

This press focus on the president was underscored the evening of President Clinton's fourth State of the Union address on February 4, 1997, the same evening a civil jury returned a verdict against former football star O. J. Simpson in the deaths of Simpson's wife and her friend. The television networks had a major decision to make—whether to follow the president or follow the arguably more sensational and dramatic story about Simpson. Consistent with the emphasis on presidential media, the broadcasters decided to cover the president. As Frank Sesno, the Washington Bureau chief for CNN, stated, "If it comes down to it, we go with the president. We don't interrupt the president of the United States."[11]

The press focus on the presidency reinforces the image of the president as omnipresent and omnicompetent. Presidents work to portray particular images of themselves. Many of these images first emerge during the election campaign as the candidates attempt to distinguish themselves from each other and often from the current occupant of the White House. Candidates portray themselves as smart when the predecessor or opponent is depicted as dumb. They portray themselves as energetic, hardworking, and eager for change when the predecessor is shown as lethargic. The personal image of a president also develops while he or she is in office. Some aspects of this image are built quite intentionally by the White House, such as the notion of the smart, calm, family-oriented Barack Obama. Other aspects are shaped more unwittingly through selective media coverage of the president's daily activities, such as Gerald Ford's being typecast as a bumbler after he slipped on ice and hit several errant golf balls. Whether crafted intentionally or occurring accidentally, a president's personal image is measured continually against the single executive image.

How to Study Presidential Imagery. How, then, should presidents study the single executive image so that they can use it most effectively? Presidents may think they know something about imagery from the campaign. It is tempting for them to believe that as long as they stick with what worked then, they will have no problems once in office. But converting campaign imagery into presidential imagery is trickier than many candidates-turned-presidents imagine.

Campaign imagery carries with it a large amount of puffery. Candidates compete to appear as the most convincing omnicompetent player. They make outlandish promises, such as to wipe out a multi-trillion-dollar deficit, to impose no new taxes, to implement secret plans to end the war in Vietnam, and to reduce dramatically the role of the federal government in American society. Campaigns operate according to their own laws of physics: almost no promise or accusation is ever too incredible; almost no number of promises or accusations is ever too many. Campaign physics also provides some room for ambiguity and fine-tuning during the exceedingly long election season. Candidates can make sweeping commitments but say that the details have not been fully worked out. Or they can say that a proposal has been misunderstood by the media or misrepresented by the opposition.

Campaign imagery is certainly related to the single executive image and derives many of its features from presidential imagery. But the laws of campaign physics do not apply in office. The media now focus not just on the promises made, but also on the promises kept. Sweeping commitments must be converted into detailed plans. If presidents back away from promises, compromise them, postpone them, or break them, they violate presidential imagery because the single executive image suggests that presidents keep their promises and act in the best interest of the nation in doing so. When George H. W. Bush broke his "read my lips: no new taxes" campaign promise, he later lamented that it was the worst mistake of his presidency. In contrast, when Dwight Eisenhower made good on his campaign pledge to "go to Korea" and bring the warring parties to the peace table, he was heralded as a hero, even though the war ended with the borders unchanged from where they were when the war began three years earlier. Presidents must be constantly aware of the comparison between what was promised during the campaign and what is undertaken in office. As a candidate, Donald Trump confidently promised, "You're going to have such great health care at a tiny fraction of the cost. And it's going to be so easy."[12] In office, he observed that "nobody knew health care could be so complicated" and congressional Republicans were unable to "repeal and replace" the Affordable Care Act passed during the Obama administration.[13] This campaign–office comparison is only one part of the much larger comparison between presidents' personal images and the single executive image. Throughout their terms, all presidents endure a gap between the two images that can never be fully closed. The size of the gap depends on how well presidents present themselves as living up to the single executive image. Part of the gap involves the extent to which campaign promises are kept. But other dimensions include demonstrations of power, success, and American pride.

The wider the image gap, the more the media will depict the president as omnipresent but not omnicompetent. As one example, the failed Bay of Pigs invasion in April 1961—a CIA-directed attempt by Cuban exiles to oust the Communist government of Fidel Castro—opened President Kennedy, whose administration approved the attempt, to charges of reckless youth, arrogance, and incompetent decision making. Yet the closer a president's personal image comes to the omnicompetence and omnipresence expected in the single executive image, the less likely the president will end up looking like the scrawny cat. During the Cuban missile crisis in October 1961, when the Soviet Union tried to install missiles in Cuba that were pointed at the United States, Kennedy was praised for his acumen in invoking a naval blockade of the island, as well as for the tough yet calm manner in which he did so. Similarly, after George W. Bush, wearing a full pilot suit and helmet, landed in a navy fighter plane on the aircraft carrier *USS Lincoln* on May 2, 2003, he tried to embody the single executive image of a leader by boldly proclaiming that the military effort in Iraq had ended while a banner in the background proclaimed

"Mission Accomplished." As the war and U.S. involvement continued for another five years, people frequently recalled the aircraft carrier moment. Consequently, the gap between Bush's image and the single executive image loomed large. In contrast, immediately after the September 11, 2001, terrorist attacks, Bush made a trip to Ground Zero in New York City to visit the search and rescue teams working at the World Trade Center site. Standing alongside firemen and the American flag, Bush told those assembled that "America today is on bended knee, in prayer for the people whose lives were lost here, for the workers who work here, for the families who mourn."[14] Bush was touted as being caring, sensitive, and bold—all the things required by the single executive image. Thus presidents can study the dimensions of the single executive image to recognize how their personal images will be evaluated by journalists, politicians, and the public.

On the Institution

Although the public, the press, and presidents are at least somewhat familiar with presidential imagery, none of them, not even presidents, are well acquainted with the presidential institution. During the campaign, candidates do not think much about the presidency as an institution; instead, it is a prize to win. They are most likely to invoke imagery that defies the institution: they will do numerous things single-handedly, they will succeed with Congress and the bureaucracy where their predecessors have failed, and they will bring peace to the world and prosperity to the nation. When he took office, Donald Trump may have been surprised to learn the full extent of what he had inherited: a complex organization consisting of forty-two separate offices, more than 1,800 employees, and an annual budget of more than $600 million, officially named the Executive Office of the President (EOP). Outgoing president Barack Obama was undoubtedly more familiar with the organization and also more aware of his limited abilities to change its size and shape. Despite the declared intentions of Presidents Reagan, Clinton, and George W. Bush to streamline the EOP, none had any real success. The number of employees and the budget of the EOP during Clinton's first term looked remarkably similar to those observed during both Bush administrations. The total executive staff averaged 1,727 people under George H. W. Bush, 1,620 under Clinton, and 1,704 during George W. Bush's term. It crept up by roughly 100 people under Obama to 1,870 employees.[15] The first Trump budget offered a similarly sized EOP.

An institution is an organization of people established to carry out a set of functions. Institutions include schools, corporations, police departments, legislatures, and courts. A peculiar characteristic of an institution is that it acts independently of the people within it. An institution establishes regular patterns of behavior for its members to follow, including divisions of labor (specialization) and standard operating procedures (rules about how things are done). These patterns are followed regardless of who holds positions in the institution, even at the very top.

The contemporary presidency is an institution. It is an organization of people who carry out an array of policy, public, and political functions for which the president is responsible. The presidential institution is no small family business. It operates with a division of labor—offices within the White House specialize in foreign, domestic, and economic policy; the budget; press relations; public appearances; congressional liaison; and group affairs. Through the years the institution has developed standard operating procedures to devise budgets, write and reject legislation, and invoke vetoes. These procedures change only modestly from one president to another. The presidential institution makes many decisions on behalf of the president that the president knows little about.

Not only is the presidential institution elaborate, it is also decentralized. The decentralization means that there is a proliferation of offices, many of which have roughly equal status and the ability to direct, if not determine, presidential decisions. There is less top-down authority in the presidency than one might expect. It is difficult for the president or his senior staff to effectively monitor or even establish the direction for all the work that is done on his behalf. The political scientist Alfred de Grazia remarked, "On a normal issue that comes before the 'President' some dozens of persons are involved. It might be presumptuous to say that more of a collectivity is engaged than when the same type of issue would come before the Congress; but it would be equally presumptuous to say that fewer persons were taken up with the matter."[16]

Institutional Responsibilities. Regardless of who is president, the presidential institution exists to handle three sets of responsibilities: policy issues, political targets, and the daily workload. First, units in the EOP handle three broad policy domains: national security, the economy, and domestic affairs. Because each category is so encompassing, several units, each with slightly different jurisdictions, share responsibility for each domain and often compete to exercise their expertise and their control of presidents' ultimate decisions. To make matters even more complicated for presidents, many of the units that have the greatest authority over a particular policy area are not within the EOP but instead are in the departments and agencies of the federal bureaucracy. For example, the National Security Council, the national security adviser, the National Security Council staff, the secretaries of state and defense, the Joint Chiefs of Staff, the director of the Central Intelligence Agency, and in some cases the secretary of Homeland Security all participate in making national security decisions. Only the first three are in the EOP.

Second, units in the EOP target political players and other political institutions for presidential persuasion. The job of these units is to convince their targets that what the president wants is what they should want. For example, the Office of Legislative Affairs targets Congress and is the focal point for White House lobbying activities on Capitol Hill. In addition, the White House Press Office targets the press through, among other things, the daily briefing by the press secretary. The Office of Public Liaison and Intergovernmental Affairs targets interest groups, at times pressuring them to support the president's proposals and at other times organizing their support as part of a larger White House lobbying campaign.

Third, key units in the White House—the Office of Administration and the Office of Management and Budget (OMB)—are assigned certain high-volume tasks to ease the presidential workload. The Office of Administration follows routine, computerized procedures for hiring White House and other personnel. The OMB is the largest, and arguably the most active, presidential office; it is involved in the preparation of presidents' budgets, sending legislation to Congress, determining whether presidents should sign or veto bills passed by Congress, and reviewing thousands of administrative regulations. The OMB's procedures purposely remove presidents from, rather than involve them in, as much daily presidential business as possible.

How to Study the Institution. On entering office, many presidents delight in announcing bold plans to rearrange many of the units within the presidential institution—subtract some, add others. Other presidents proclaim that they will dramatically cut the size and budget of the institution. They do so believing that the presidential institution is a personal organization—one that each president can shape and reshape. To some extent, they are right. Presidents do cut units from the EOP, usually under the guise of getting rid of a holdover from the previous administration. These cuts are more than offset by additions that place the president's own stamp on the EOP. Most of the changes presidents make are at the edges of the presidential institution. For example, George W. Bush ended three EOP offices that Bill Clinton had started: the President's Council on Sustainable Development, the Office of Women's Initiatives and Outreach, and the President's Critical Infrastructure Protection Board. But he replaced them with specialty offices of his own: the White House Office of Faith-Based and Community Initiatives, the Office of Strategic Initiatives, the Office of Homeland Security, USA Freedom Corps, the Office of Global Communications, and the Privacy and Civil Liberties Oversight Board. Upon taking office, Barack Obama expanded the EOP to include the new Council on Women and Girls. In 2017, Donald Trump created the White House National Trade Council to highlight U.S. trade negotiations and industrial capabilities, distinct from the Office of the United States Trade Representative, a part of the EOP since 1963. Still in the first year of the Trump presidency, the Trade Council has not been particularly important on trade policy.[17]

In addition, at the beginning of each president's term there is a grand arrival of new people who scramble for office space following the mass exodus of the previous administration. This rapid turnover leads some observers to suggest that there is no institution at all—instead, just a large staff personally serving a president. But the institution does not grind to a halt every four to eight years. Perhaps nothing better underscores the continuity of the institution than a story about President Nixon's last day in office. On the afternoon that Nixon was to announce his resignation, a congressional staffer phoned the White House and inquired whether several minor pieces of legislation were "in accordance with the president's program."[18] There was no functioning president, nor was there a presidential program that afternoon, but the presidential institution continued to operate—the staffer got an answer. The institution has a fair number of employees who are career civil servants, especially in the OMB, and who thus stay on from one president to the next. In addition, the vast array of White House procedures concerning budgeting, legislation, and personnel remain intact. At best, then, the presidential institution is only a quasi-personal organization.

It is also a quasi-formal one. Incoming presidents have less ability to change the size and shape of the institution than they might think. The size, structures, and procedures of the White House breed continuity that is difficult to end. Presidents cannot do without the functions that the EOP provides. Only one president in the twentieth century was able to reduce significantly the number of White House employees. In the aftermath of Watergate, Gerald Ford decreased the EOP by 67 percent—from 5,751 employees in 1974 to 1,910 employees in 1975—by eliminating some offices and councils that had been established during the Nixon years. But he reduced the size of neither the White House Office (the unit closest to the president) nor the OMB. Indeed, both increased slightly. In addition, Ford's personnel cutbacks in 1975 were countered by large increases in expenditures during 1975 and 1976 especially for the White House Office and the OMB. Although Ronald Reagan touted his desire to shrink the size of the federal government, the EOP diminished by little more than 100 people in his first term and by only 76 people in his second term. The overall size crept back up during the George H. W. Bush years. Thus presidents who study the size and shape of the institution learn that the presidency has a life of its own that is quite independent of the people within it, even the president. At a luncheon with former presidents Carter, George H. W. Bush, and Clinton designed to welcome Barack Obama to the Oval Office, George W. Bush reflected that "all of us who have served in this office understand that the office itself transcends the individual."[19]

GENERALIZATIONS ABOUT PRESIDENTIAL IMAGERY

What can political scientists tell presidents about image and institution?

Principles of Image Making

Political scientists offer four empirical generalizations about presidential image making.

1. Through their speeches, presidents present themselves as representatives of the people and as moral and religious leaders. Their own words typically portray them as nonpartisan leaders who work alone in the government without the aid of staff, members of Congress, or other executive officials.[20]

2. Public opinion polls show that the public most consistently expects presidents to place the country's interest ahead of politics, be intelligent, exercise sound judgment in a crisis, take firm stands on issues, get the job done, and be concerned about the average citizen.[21]

3. In addition, public opinion polls indicate that people respond to presidents more through emotions than through rational calculations about the government's performance or presidents' positions on issues.[22]

4. Early press coverage, which deals with family stories and future policy plans, is more favorable than subsequent press coverage.[23]

Taken together, these generalizations suggest that the single executive image endures in presidents' own words, public impressions, and press coverage. In their speeches, presidents offer the country the single executive image. They sponsor the dual notions of presidential omnicompetence and omnipresence. They suggest that they alone are linked to the American people, above politics, beyond party, and touched by God. Gerald Ford revealed his connection to the American people on assuming office:

> I will be the President of black, brown, red, and white Americans, of old
> and young, of women's liberationists and male chauvinists and all the rest
> of us in-between, of the poor and the rich, of native sons and new refugees,
> of those who work at lathes or at desks or in mines or in the fields, of
> Christians, Jews, Moslems, Buddhists, and atheists, if there really are any
> atheists after what we have all been through.[24]

Similarly, the public judges presidents according to the single executive image. As a Nixon aide wrote, "Presidents are measured against an ideal that's a combination of leading man, God, father, hero, pope, king. . . . They want him to be . . . someone to be held up to their children as a model; someone to be cherished by themselves as a revered member of the family."[25]

Early press coverage also reinforces the single executive image by depicting the president as a person of the people (complete with family, furniture, and daily routines) with bold new plans to lead the nation forward. Political scientists Michael Grossman and Martha Kumar found in a study of newspaper, television, and magazine coverage of presidents from 1953 to 1978 that, during the early part of the term, reporters are most attentive to human interest stories about the president. Indeed, a Ford White House official predicted that the first stories about the incoming Carter administration would be personality stories about the president: "First, who is Jimmy Carter? What is his personality? Does he get mad? Does he golf? Does he fish in a pond? How do you find out who somebody is? You look at his friends, his habits, his manner, his character, his personality."[26]

Taking the generalizations together, political scientists reveal two features of the presidential imagery. First, the single executive image rests on symbolism—the president symbolizes the nation, its people, and its government. There is a symbolic equivalence between the president and the public, with the two blurring together as one in presidents' speeches and in media coverage of the office. Presidents frequently use the pronoun *we* to refer to themselves and the American people.[27] As noted previously, human interest news reports depict the president as one of the people. The symbolism is emotionally, not rationally, based. Ordinary citizens, who are often inattentive to government and politically unorganized, find it difficult to obtain tangible benefits from a president, unlike a major industry requesting relief from a regulation or an interest group seeking legislation. Instead, people seek "quiescence" in politics—reassurance that everything is all right or at least that someone is in charge.

People, then, may well be less concerned about what presidents do than how they make them feel. These emotions help to explain the otherwise ironic situations in which presidential failure garners public support. As one example, Kennedy's popularity rose ten points after the ill-fated Bay of Pigs invasion of Cuba in 1961. Had people judged the decision rationally, based on costs and benefits, their response would have been to disapprove of the president's performance. Instead the president benefited in the short term, because people sought quiescence that the "bad guys" were being challenged, no matter what the outcome of the challenge was.

Without studying the presidency, presidents may neglect this emotionally based symbolic connection and expect the American public to evaluate their proposals and achievements on their policy merits. In so doing they confuse objective accomplishment with perceived triumph. Bill Clinton was frustrated, for example, that his numerous legislative successes in 1993 were not accompanied by high public approval ratings. By 1995 Clinton recognized that presidential success is in the eyes of the beholders. In the aftermath of the 1994 midterm congressional elections, in which Republicans gained majorities in both houses of Congress for the first time in forty years, Clinton and the Republican leadership played a tumultuous game of brinkmanship by failing to reach a budget agreement and ultimately shutting down the government for several weeks. Although such deadlock could hardly be deemed an objective success, Clinton gained the upper hand by casting the Republicans as the culprits. His perceived victory boosted his popularity ratings. Following the single executive image, presidents must shape a visceral political experience through telling folksy stories, witnessing human tragedies and triumphs, and offering examples of old-fashioned American values. Presidents who try to behave differently will find the public otherwise engaged.

Second, the single executive image is false. Although the image is a very real part of the American body politic, it is an exaggeration and distortion of grand proportions. The president does not single-handedly lead the people and govern the country. The president may be the single most powerful individual in the country, but Congress as a body is at least as powerful as the president. Presidents surely hold a unique position in the government, but they are not alone, either in the presidential institution or in the larger government. Barack Obama was reminded of the power of Congress when in summer 2011, nearing a historic debt and spending deal with Speaker of the House John Boehner, Obama attempted to pressure Boehner for more tax increases, but Boehner, livid that Obama would push him further, refused to return the president's phone call and the deal collapsed.[28]

In two ways the falsehood of the single executive image may perplex presidents who have not adequately studied the presidency. Some presidents fail to see the falsehood. Instead, they act as though they are singularly powerful, flouting regular consultation with Congress and defying laws that prevent unilateral presidential action. In an interview with David Frost after resigning the presidency, Richard Nixon was asked about a president's breaking the law in the best interests of the nation. Nixon responded, "Well, when the President does it, that means that it is not illegal."[29] This was a contorted extension of the single executive image into a claim that the president can do no wrong.

Other presidents who know the image to be false risk pointing out the falsehood at their own peril. Jimmy Carter tried on several occasions to downplay people's expectations by suggesting that he was only one man and could not do it all. Although he was right, the public did not recognize that their expectations were unrealistic. Instead, they judged Carter a failure for not living up to them. Presidents must both recognize the falsehood and live with it, just as they must recognize the symbolic connection between the president and the public and do what they can to capitalize on both.

Closing the Image Gap

What can presidents do to capitalize on the single executive image? Political scientists offer four generalizations. (The numbering of these statements continues in sequence from the earlier discussion.)

5.   Short successful wars, sudden international crises, and significant diplomatic efforts temporarily improve the president's public approval rating.[30]

6.   Major nationally televised addresses also temporarily improve public approval.[31]

7.   Protracted wars, domestic riots, public protests and demonstrations, and declining economic conditions diminish public approval.[32]

8.   During the course of their terms, presidents face a decline in public approval.[33]

The size of the image gap that presidents endure between their personal images and the single executive image bears directly on presidents' public support—the wider the gap, the lower the public approval rating. Political scientists have recognized two aspects of the image gap: (1) the short-term events, activities, and circumstances that narrow or widen it; and (2) the long-term pattern of public approval during a president's term as it relates to the gap.

In the Short Term. Presidents have a fair degree of control over some ventures that work to their advantage in closing the image gap, such as emergency military interventions, dramatic diplomatic efforts, and well-timed major television addresses. Presidents also face some circumstances beyond their control, such as international crises like the fall of the Berlin Wall and the collapse of the Soviet Union, which may work to their advantage. Whether presidents have control or not, a rally of national support typically takes place. After the terrorist attacks on September 11, 2001, George W. Bush's approval rating soared from 51 percent to 85 percent and peaked at 89 percent. Barack Obama's approval rating increased ten percentage points in a single month after the killing of Osama Bin Laden, rising from 46 percent in April 2011 to 57 percent in May 2011. Consistent with the emotional basis of public approval, presidents receive all but unconditional support for actions that place the United States in a clear-cut good-versus-evil, us-against-them position or that envelop the actions or positions of the administration in patriotic trappings.

But other sudden and unforeseen events or conditions at home—such as urban riots, skyrocketing consumer prices, or plummeting job prospects—may leave the public wondering what the president will do. Many of these exigencies will tarnish the president's reputation in relation to the single executive image. The single executive image suggests that presidents are responsible even for things that they cannot predict and over which they have no immediate control. Yet for the very reason that presidents can neither predict nor control what will happen, they are unable to capitalize on these events and conditions. The us-against-them focus changes; it is no longer the United States as a whole against foreign foes. Instead, it is more likely that presidents portray their side as "us" and the opposition as "them," thereby ensuring domestic controversy rather than a popular mandate about how the issues should be handled. George W. Bush's approval rating dropped nearly ten percentage points overnight, from 48 percent to 39 percent, following Hurricane Katrina because many Americans felt the government's response to the calamity was inadequate.

Generalizations 5, 6, and 7 taken together—the mix of the controlled and the uncontrollable, the presidential rallying of public support, and the public questioning of presidential action—imply that presidents must engage in domestic, foreign, and economic policymaking. The single executive image demands attention to all three policy spheres. Although presidents are likely to get less credit in domestic than in foreign affairs because the public rally feature is absent, they may come up short politically if they emphasize foreign over domestic initiatives. For example, because President George W. Bush limited his domestic agenda in order to focus on Iraq, he left himself open to charges of not caring sufficiently about the consequences of Hurricane Katrina on New Orleans. The opposite is also true: it is unwise for presidents to develop high-profile domestic agendas and make short shrift of foreign policy. By doing so, they defy the symbolic importance of acting as the leader of the nation to the world and do not show skills of crisis management, both of which are expected parts of the single executive image. President Clinton initially appeared hesitant in foreign and military affairs, but when criticism about the perceived hesitation mounted, he began to act more decisively. Finally, although economic bad news widens the image gap, economic good news closes it. Even though presidents have limited control over what happens in the economy, they are credited with being economic wizards if the economy is robust. As President Carter observed, "When things go bad you get entirely too much blame. And I have to admit that when things go good, you get entirely too much credit."[34]

In the Long Run. Political scientists have also observed an overall pattern to the shifts in public approval across presidents' terms: approval starts high in the first year, slides during the second and third years, and then rebounds slightly in the fourth year. This pattern denotes three distinct phases to public approval across the term: a honeymoon in some portion of the first year; a period of disillusionment in the middle of the term, when the image gap is at its widest; and a phase of forgiveness at the term's end, when people recognize to some degree that the image is just that and that the president was not so bad after all.

This long-term pattern is one that seems to be an inviolate canon of the office: what starts high must decline. The three phases vary considerably in intensity and duration by president, but the overall pattern is obvious. From Franklin Roosevelt, who was president when public opinion polling first began, to Ronald Reagan, only one president—Dwight Eisenhower—escaped the pattern. Eisenhower's first-term popularity started high and stayed high, although the pattern of decline did occur in his second term. Even presidents who were typically viewed as popular presidents, such as Roosevelt and Reagan, nonetheless witnessed the downward pattern during their times in office. George W. Bush also experienced a classic, if precipitous, decline in approval. Despite surging in the aftermath of 9/11 Bush's approval rating dropped throughout his first term and continued to do so during his second term, reaching a historic low of 25 percent during much of 2008. As unpopular as Bush was, even he experienced the forgiveness phase: his approval rating rose from 25 percent at the time of the November elections to 34 percent as he left office. The cycle began anew with Barack Obama, who entered office with a 68 percent approval rating. By September 2011, his approval was at an all-time low of 37 percent, but rebounded to nearly 50 percent during the 2012 reelection period.

Presidents George H. W. Bush and Bill Clinton appear as exceptions to the overall pattern of decline. Neither followed the three phases of support, and it is unclear that future presidents will return to them. Instead, the elder Bush and Clinton faced sharp peaks and valleys in their popularity timed to specific events and presidential actions with little, if any, trend across their terms. Bush's approval started relatively high, soared, and then plummeted. He began office with 69 percent of the American public approving of his job in office. His popularity peaked at 89 percent in February 1991 during the Persian Gulf War, the highest ever recorded for any president. During the war, he had effectively moved his personal image toward the single executive image, getting high marks for exercising good judgment in a crisis and engaging in a large, short, successful military encounter. After the war, there was an expectation on Capitol Hill, in the media, and among many Americans that the president would convert this wave of public support into public deeds, notably with regard to the sluggish economy. Instead, longtime Bush strategist and secretary of state James Baker snapped to reporters, "When you're at 90 percent, you can do what you damn well please." Bush left the impression that he was not willing to do anything about the weak economy or to try to understand the average American's plight. As the economy continued to sour, Bush's image gap widened. His approval sunk to 29 percent by the summer of 1992, a free fall of sixty percentage points in sixteen months. George H. W. Bush not only achieved the highest approval rating of any president but also incurred the sharpest drop in approval of any president in the shortest period of time.

Clinton's first-term approval started modestly, dropped immediately on taking office, and then rose steadily after the midterm, something no other president has achieved. Clinton began office with 58 percent of Americans approving of his performance in office, but this rating fell sharply to 37 percent by June 1993. Just six months into Clinton's term, his approval ratings had dropped by just over twenty percentage points after bruising battles with Congress over gays in the military, health care reform, and the budget. His ratings remained in the low

40-percent range throughout 1994 and did not break 50 percent again until April 1995. Thereafter, Clinton's approval ratings rose consistently, hitting 60 percent by the end of his first term. During this time, the president appeared to successfully act as the nation's problem solver, consistent with the single executive image, as the White House struck deals with the new Republican-controlled Congress over the budget and welfare reform.

Clinton's second term was marked by still higher ratings in the midst of an impeachment proceeding in the House and a trial in the Senate on charges related to his affair with former White House intern Monica Lewinsky. Clinton's approval rating peaked at 73 percent in December 1998 just after the House voted to impeach him. His ratings remained high during the Senate trial and then, in the months after the Senate failed to convict him, declined somewhat to an average of 60 percent. The public, apparently dismayed by the highly partisan nature of the impeachment process, expressed support for Clinton with strong approval ratings, which then returned to more normal levels as the president returned to more normal business.

Donald Trump also began his presidency without the typical honeymoon phase. At eight months in office, only 36 percent of Americans approved of his performance in office.[35] The historic level of early public disapproval was rooted in Americans' concerns about Trump's character—his temperament and inexperience.[36] By contrast, the average job approval rating at the eight-month mark for presidents from Truman through Obama was 62 percent. Only Gerald Ford had ratings similar to Trump at the eight-month mark—38 percent of Americans approved of Ford's job performance after he pardoned Richard Nixon and the American-backed government of South Vietnam fell to communist North Vietnam after more than a decade of war.

In general, three factors appear to be pushing presidents into a new era of volatile relations with the public in which quick swings in approval may occur within the honeymoon disillusionment forgiveness sequence. First, the frequency of public opinion polls has increased dramatically. Although American politics has run on public opinion polls for decades, the sheer number of polls and the number of organizations conducting them has never been higher. Polling organizations that used to poll once a month now poll once a week. During periods of presidential crisis, whether related to wars, sex scandals, or critical mistakes, pollsters conduct surveys two to three times a week. On any given news day, several polls may be released by different polling companies and news organizations. In a critical period of the Clinton–Lewinsky scandal in August 1998 when Lewinsky testified before independent counsel Kenneth Starr's grand jury about the nature of her relationship with Clinton, the Gallup Organization conducted separate surveys on August 7, 10, 18, 20, and 21 to monitor any moment-to-moment Clinton approval shifts, which began at 64 percent in the August 7 poll, peaked at 66 percent in the August 18 poll, and dropped slightly to 62 percent by the August 21 poll. The frequency of polling places inordinate attention on *any* approval shift. Even though many of these changes are likely to be within the margin of error of the survey, they are not reported this way.[37] Instead, it appears that the wind has shifted, even if only slightly.

Second, presidents and their advisers have expressly developed political and policy strategies with these omnipresent polls in mind. Although presidents have kept an eye on the polls since the early days of opinion polling, the extent to which presidents have become pollsters is notably more vivid and intense. Dick Morris, one-time polling adviser to President Clinton, commented, "The icons of the past relied on political instinct. Now presidents can use scientific polls and focus groups." Of equal importance, Morris contended that the polls enable a president to take positions that maintain his popularity because "an elected executive—whether president, governor, or mayor—needs a popular majority every day in his term. When [his ratings dip] below 50 percent, he is functionally out of office."[38]

Third, presidential news is more instantaneous and comprehensive than in the past. Presidents have long been the single most covered news figure in American politics, but the growth of the twenty-four-hour news day through CNN, the Internet, and social media has greatly accelerated this visibility. This moment-to-moment monitoring of presidential actions and reactions means that presidential failures and successes receive far more microscopic treatment than they once did. Not only the failures and successes but also the depth and length of the treatment become a part of what shifts public approval with swifter reactions and sharper peaks and valleys. All-encompassing presidential news became even more dramatic with Donald Trump, who touted his frequent use of Twitter as a way to communicate directly with the public, bypassing the press. Trump tweeted: "My use of social media is not Presidential—it's MODERN DAY PRESIDENTIAL" (emphasis in the original).[39] The tweets became important pieces of presidential news as White House staff, other politicians, and political commentators offered interpretations of the 280-character content. These three factors—more polls taken faster, presidents as pollsters, and all-day news—set up a cycle of presidential action–news–polls–presidential action with a pace that is much faster than when Harry Truman said, "I don't read the polls because they don't mean much." The new metric used to judge a president's job in office may well be how effectively the administration responds to these crises. If presidents encounter a major problem that goes unaddressed, then popularity ratings may be in free fall. If they move effectively to deal with the crisis, they should expect significant increases in approval. Presidents must play the crises with the single executive image in full view or risk appearing ineffectual.

GENERALIZATIONS ABOUT THE PRESIDENTIAL INSTITUTION

In addition to image, political scientists have examined the presidential institution. They have done so by looking inward to the makeup of the organization and outward to the relations that the presidency has with other institutions, especially Congress, the media, and departments and agencies in the federal bureaucracy.

Inside the Institution

Political scientists offer three generalizations about the internal workings of the presidential institution.

1. Hierarchical staff systems with a single chief of staff are generally more successful than more collegial systems in which every top adviser reports directly to the president.[40]

2. Presidents' own rhetoric to the contrary, cabinet government does not work.[41]

3. Presidents are not solely in charge of the 1,800 people who are employed in the EOP.[42]

In the early weeks after the election, many presidents-elect attempt to wrap their fledgling administrations in democratic expectations. They promise that, unlike past administrations, theirs will be run with great openness. As a symbol of such openness, presidents often promise to take great personal care in the daily running of the White House by granting access to divergent staff voices. As another symbol, presidents announce that the cabinet will meet frequently as a source of information, inspiration, and advice. Neither promise is kept for long.

Why are the promises so quickly abandoned? Political scientists observe that the presidential institution is too large for any of them to be kept. Several recent presidents have learned the hard way that collegial staff configurations lead to presidential overload. To give numerous staff members direct access to the president places a considerable burden on the president to keep abreast of the many major and minor issues being monitored by staff members, not to mention the task of resolving numerous major and minor personality and turf clashes within the staff.

For example, President Ford began his administration with a collegial staff system of nine people reporting directly to him, a spokes-of-the-wheel arrangement with advisers at the rim of the wheel and the president at its hub. Ford soon became bogged down in the collegiality and turned to a hierarchical arrangement, naming Donald Rumsfeld as his chief of staff. Other staff members then filtered information and advice through Rumsfeld rather than going directly to Ford. Dick Cheney, then Ford's second chief of staff and later George W. Bush's vice president, was reminded of the collegial approach at a White House staff party. He received a bicycle wheel mounted on a board with each of its spokes mangled and twisted. A plaque below read, "The spokes of the wheel: a rare form of management artistry as conceived by Don Rumsfeld and modified by Dick Cheney." Cheney left the wheel and a note on his desk as a gift to the incoming adviser to Jimmy Carter, Hamilton Jordan. The note read, "Dear Ham. Beware the spokes of the wheel."[43] But the Carter administration replayed the Ford administration's mistake. It, too, adopted a collegial staff system, which it later abandoned in favor of a more hierarchical one. In Cheney's words, "Someone has to be in charge."[44] The hierarchical approach places a chief of staff between the president and other staff members so that the president will be less overwhelmed by policy and personnel details. Adopting the hierarchical approach does not give presidents any more control over the entire White House apparatus, which remains large and unwieldy, but it does give them more control over the top echelon of the organization, to which they have immediate access. Presidents since Carter have all invested in the hierarchical model. Upon taking office, Donald Trump announced that his chief of staff, Reince Priebus, would have co-equal status with chief strategist and senior counselor Stephen Bannon. This sharing of leadership quickly devolved into a faction-riddled White House. After just seven months in the post, Priebus resigned and was replaced by retired General John Kelly, who insisted on having sole control over staff time, energy, and access to the president. Soon Bannon was fired and the hierarchical model returned.

Presidents also find cabinet government to be unworkable. It is cumbersome and unproductive to meet with the cabinet as a whole, let alone to rely on its collective judgment. The cabinet is a body of unequals—some cabinet members enjoy considerably greater access to presidents than do others. In addition, many members of the cabinet are chosen for political reasons—to be a cross-section of the American populace—rather than for their policy expertise. Finally, cabinet members frequently adopt departmental outlooks rather than the more global outlook that might make cabinet government possible. Presidents soon realize that the cabinet is one of the few organizations of government for which the whole is less than the sum of the parts.

The need for coordination at the top and the limited role of the cabinet are symptoms of the internal complexity that marks the presidential institution. Political scientists have uncovered considerable evidence of that complexity as the presidential institution acts independently of the president or the president acts as only one of many players in the institution. For example, although President Kennedy was involved in the decision that gave American approval to the plot by the South Vietnamese military to overthrow President Diem in 1963, the American ambassador to South Vietnam, Henry Cabot Lodge, had considerable control over the matter.[45] Institutional complexity also permits presidents to hide in the labyrinth of the presidential institution and deny their involvement in schemes that may have backfired, gone awry, or skirted the law. The evidence now suggests that President Reagan knew of the arms-for-hostages agreement with Iran and the channeling of money to the Nicaraguan contra rebels that constituted the Iran-contra affair, but he safely hid his involvement through the "plausible deniability" afforded him by the presidential institution. His national security advisers, first Robert McFarlane and then Adm. John Poindexter, and National Security Council staff members, including Oliver North, acted as screens for the president. They suggested that they had made the decisions without the president's full knowledge, thereby allowing the president to deny any involvement.[46]

Interinstitutional Relations

Political scientists offer presidents generalizations about White House relations with other institutions. The first generalization pertains to what is known about relations between the White House and the departments and agencies of the executive branch; the others describe relations between the White House and Congress.

1. Efforts to politicize the bureaucracy and bureaucratize the White House have only a limited effect on presidents' success in policy implementation.[47]

2. Presidents who establish their legislative agendas early—in the first three to six months of their terms—are more successful at getting specific agenda items passed than are those who wait.[48]

3. The higher presidents' level of legislative activity (that is, the more pieces of legislation on which they take positions), the lower the legislative success. Conversely, the lower the activity, the more successful is the president.[49]

4. Presidential addresses and public approval increase presidents' success in Congress. In turn, presidential success in Congress improves public approval.[50]

Bureaucratic Relations. Many presidents and many citizens are under the misguided impression that the president is the chief executive—the head of the departments and agencies of the executive branch. Nothing could be further from the truth. As Harry Truman complained, "I thought I was the president, but when it comes to these bureaucrats, I can't do a damn thing." In many ways, presidents are satellites of the executive branch. They and their administrations do not share in the values of the various departments and agencies, they operate under different timetables, and they do not know or serve as advocates for clients of the bureaucracy, whether farmers, welfare mothers, or some other group.

In that realization, presidents have attempted three strategies to win the hearts and minds of 3 million bureaucrats. Presidents Lyndon Johnson and Nixon adopted one strategy—namely, to bring as many decisions about policy implementation as possible into the White House. The Johnson administration created the Office of Economic Opportunity (OEO) in the White House to fight the War on Poverty. The result was a disaster. OEO failed to coordinate community-based poverty programs adequately, leaving many without supervision and leaving the War on Poverty as a whole to flounder. The Nixon administration brought a variety of implementation functions into the White House. Yet the resulting increase in the White House staff was not sufficient to alter bureaucratic patterns of thinking and procedures, especially in the areas of health, welfare, and poverty, over which Nixon sought the greatest control.

President Reagan promoted a second strategy: to groom people for positions in the bureaucracy who espoused the president's philosophy. This strategy met with early success, but as Reagan's term waned so did the strategy. After a year or two, many Reagan recruits returned to the private sector to make more money. In addition, when President George H. W. Bush arrived at the White House with a less firmly defined ideological outlook than Reagan's, hiring people who fit the presidential outlook became difficult. The approach returned with George W. Bush, especially at the Justice Department, where seven U.S. attorneys who were considered to be insufficiently interested in pursuing cases against Democrats were dismissed. In a January 2005 memo to Attorney General John Ashcroft, Kyle Sampson, the Department of Justice's counsel, described the U.S. attorneys who would not be fired: "The vast majority of U.S. Attorneys, 80–85 percent, are doing a great job, are loyal Bushies."[51]

A third strategy, known as administrative clearance, began during the Nixon administration, greatly expanded under Carter, and was heavily relied on by the Reagan White House. It involved the OMB's approval of the rules and regulations proposed by departments and agencies. During the Reagan years, the clearance process had a significant effect on the proposed regulations of several agencies, notably the Environmental Protection Agency and the Departments of Housing and Urban Development, Education, and Energy, all of which Reagan disliked. Some agencies refused even to submit certain regulations to the OMB for fear they would be shot down. Similarly, many regulations that the OMB rejected were never resubmitted.[52]

Administrative clearance shows the greatest promise for putting the presidency into the executive branch loop. It is the first institutionalized effort presidents have made to rein in the bureaucracy. By comparison, the other two strategies were decidedly ad hoc. The OMB has established procedures to investigate administrative rules and regulations and acts as a watchdog for the rest of the government. It determines whether rules proposed by a department or an agency in the executive branch are consistent with White House criteria. If they are, the rules are designated as "consistent without change." If they are not, the rules are returned to the agency in one of two ways. First, the OMB may issue a "prompt letter" designating the rules as "consistent with change." This requires the agency that has proposed the rule to act on the specific modifications requested by the OMB in the prompt letter. Second, the OMB may issue a "return letter," which asserts that the rule has failed to meet OMB standards. More than 70 percent of agency rules submitted during the George W. Bush administration were deemed "consistent with change" and required modifications based on OMB instructions.[53] As might be expected, because of the institutional nature of the clearance process, presidents have little personal involvement and essentially trust the OMB to do what the presidents want.

Congressional Relations. Political scientists have uncovered important lessons for presidents working with Congress. First, presidents must not clutter the legislative agenda with lots of big issues or even lots of small ones. Nor must presidents meet Congress on its own terms, because its agenda is always burdened with large and small issues. Instead, presidents benefit by presenting Congress with a small list of big-ticket items that spell out what the president wants.

Second, presidents must adjust to two kinds of presidential time that dictate many of their most important legislative strategies: electoral time and organizational time. Electoral time is a highly compressed four-year cycle that is geared toward the upcoming election. The electoral clock ticks fast and loudly. As one White House aide put it, "You should subtract one year for the reelection campaign, another six months for the midterms, six months for the start-up, six months for the closing, and another month or two for an occasional vacation. That leaves you with a two-year presidential term."[54] In contrast, many Washington politicians—those elected, those appointed, and those hired—have long time frames for action. Their clocks tick slowly. They have careers—at least a decade but most likely two—in which to finish what they start. Many members of Congress, although they must look toward the next election, enjoy safe seats that ensure their political longevity. Most people in Washington are there to stay. Presidents come and go. The contrast between the two contrasting political time clocks was made clear after the failure of Republican efforts to pass health care legislation in the summer of 2017. Senate Majority Leader Mitch McConnell (R-KY) chided Trump for having "excessive expectations about how quickly things happen in the democratic process" and "setting too many artificial deadlines unrelated to the reality of the legislature."[55] Trump angrily responded in a tweet: "Mitch, get back to work and put Repeal and Replace, Tax Reform & Cuts and a great infrastructure Bill on my desk for signing. You can do it!"[56] Organizational time is the slower pace at which the White House apparatus gathers information, follows existing procedures, and makes decisions. It reflects the start-up-and-slow-down rhythm of the presidency. Organizational time is at its slowest early in the term, when staff members are just beginning to understand their jobs. It may speed up later in the term as people, including the president, learn the ropes.

Although electoral and organizational time run at opposite speeds, they are linked closely in two ways. In one way, electoral time helps to create the slower organizational time. Because electoral time forces presidents to act in a hurry and to keep acting, it creates a need for a large presidential institution to carry on the action. In such a compressed time frame, it is impossible for presidents and just a few close advisers to develop agendas, see them through Congress, and have the executive branch implement them. They must draw on a presidential institution that operates on its own slow time schedule, made even slower by the coming and going of presidents every four or eight years.

In another way, the joining of electoral and organizational time poses a dilemma for presidents. What is the best time for presidents to put forward their legislative agenda during their terms? Electoral time says the best time to act is early in the term. Organizational time urges presidents to act later, when people are more settled into their jobs. Most presidents and their staffs acknowledge that electoral time takes precedence over organizational time. The organization must try to catch up with demands in the political arena. Electoral time allows presidents to use the single executive image most dramatically if they "hit the ground running" by presenting major policy initiatives to Congress with great public fanfare in the first months of the first year of their terms. "It's definitely a race," stated a Carter aide. "The first months are the starting line. If you don't get off the blocks fast, you'll lose the race."[57] Yet hitting the ground running is neither easy nor fun. Presidents often stumble in their first months in office and delay their legislative goals. The presidential institution may not be ready to go. Like any large organization, it needs time to work properly. It may even need more organizational time than many institutions because its flow of operation is interrupted every four to eight years by the arrival of a new president and new staff members. The Nixon administration fell into such a trap postponing the announcement of a welfare reform plan. A Nixon aide lamented, "We gave our opponents a great deal of time to fight the Family Assistance Plan. They had at least six months to prepare before the initial announcement. Then, because we were late, the program bogged down in congressional committee. We gave them too many chances to hit us."[58]

In addition, if a president has already encountered volatile public reactions (as discussed previously), then hitting the ground running may not be possible for political as well as organizational reasons. In the absence of a honeymoon period early in the president's term, there is little reason to expect that a major controversial policy initiative is going to sail through Congress.

Finally, the presidential image and the presidential institution intertwine in the legislative process. Presidential addresses and public approval increase presidents' success in Congress on passing various pieces of proposed legislation. Obama used presidential addresses, campaign-style trips across the country, and public support to win a protracted legislative fight over his health care reform bill. In turn, presidential success in Congress increases public approval. These relationships take place within a larger political–economic context. Presidential success in Congress is shaped by the size of the president's party, the year in the term (the later in the term, the less likely the president's position is to prevail), economic circumstances, and international conflicts.[59]

PRESIDENTIAL MISTAKES

The fifteen generalizations about imagery and institution embody much of what political scientists know about the presidency. Presidents, like everyone else, make mistakes. But many of them could be avoided if presidents carefully observed these generalizations and the broader discussions of imagery and institution from which they derive.

Presidents' mistakes can be defined as situations in which presidents adopt courses of action that bring about the opposite of what they want or significantly less than what they want. To be sure, mistakes are not always clear-cut. For example, when President Truman fired Gen. Douglas MacArthur for insubordination at the height of an offensive against the Chinese during the Korean War, Truman incurred tremendous political opposition, especially when MacArthur returned to the United States to a hero's welcome. But the decision was not necessarily a military mistake because MacArthur was pushing for a much wider war with China. Truman replaced MacArthur with Gen. Matthew Ridgway, who was able to correct some of MacArthur's tactical excesses. There are, however, numerous instances in which mistakes are not subject to multiple interpretations. Presidents make mistakes on imagery, on institutional relations, and on the combination of the two.

Mistaken Images

Image mistakes involve the president's failure to live up to some central aspect of the single executive image. Many of these mistakes relate to the president as a person. They often involve small things, such as haircuts, walks on the beach, pets, and trips to the grocery store, because the single executive image depends on the symbolic connection between the president and the American public. People understand the connection best when it is based on activities in daily life that they share with the president. Everyone gets a haircut; everyone goes to the grocery store. As planes reportedly waited on nearby runways at Los Angeles International Airport, President Clinton paid $200 for a haircut by a Beverly Hills stylist aboard *Air Force One*. In a grocery store, President George H. W. Bush was revealed as being unaware of how price scanners worked, indicating that he had not done his own shopping in many years. President Nixon walked on the beach near his home in San Clemente, California, in a tie and dress shoes, looking stiff and uncomfortable. President Johnson played with his pet beagles, Him and Her, by pulling them up by their long floppy ears, outraging dog lovers. Because such image mistakes typically leave the president looking out of touch with average citizens, the gap between the personal image and the single executive image grows. But these mistakes can also center on much larger issues. In his first months in office, Donald Trump haphazardly tampered with the single executive image. With the lowest approval rating of any president since polling began, he has made no effort to improve those poll numbers by appealing to the entire nation through the single executive image. He has eschewed non-controversial, feel-good public appearances in favor of campaign rallies and fundraisers. One of the most vivid clashes between his approach and the single executive image came when he spoke in the aftermath of a white supremacist rally in Charlottesville, Virginia, in August 2017, which left one counter protestor dead and many injured. Trump stated that there was "blame on both sides."[60] This led to a firestorm of criticism against Trump for implicitly siding with the neo-Nazis. The single executive image asserts moral values as a part of presidential leadership, while Trump's statement seemed to put on an even plane white supremacists and those opposed to them. Image mistakes may also involve the president as a policymaker—breaking a promise, not doing what the single executive image demands under certain policy circumstances, or attempting to revise the image itself. President George W. Bush made image mistakes when he repeatedly suggested not only that Saddam Hussein was aiding Al Qaeda and thus was linked to the terrorist attacks on September 11, 2001, but also that Hussein possessed weapons of mass destruction. No evidence supported either claim. This not only weakened Bush's credibility and thus created significant image problems for him, but also had major policy consequences in defining the impetus for the Iraq War.

As may be imagined, the second type of image mistake is more likely than the first to harm presidents. Although the personal mistakes cause momentary embarrassment and for a time draw considerable press attention, the press and the public soon tire of the topic and move on to something else. The policy mistakes tend to have longer-range consequences and thus are more apt to characterize the failures of an administration.

Institutional Mistakes

Presidents are also prone to mistakes when they fail to address various institutional constraints adequately. Such mistakes involve relations in the White House and relations between the White House and other institutions, such as Congress, the Supreme Court, or a department or an agency in the executive bureaucracy.

Within the institution, presidents frequently fail to acknowledge tensions between units that share similar jurisdictions. Several presidents have let animosity fester between the national security adviser and the secretary of state on matters of diplomacy.[61] Information leaks are common occurrences as units within the White House compete with each other to make decisions to their own advantage. In-house scandals or embarrassments also erupt because too many people are going in too many directions to be monitored adequately by the chief of staff or other staff members, let alone the president. Indeed, many of these instances have involved the chiefs of staff themselves, ranging from charges against Eisenhower's chief of staff, Sherman Adams, that he improperly accepted gifts, to those leveled against George H. W. Bush's chief of staff, John Sununu, for using government planes and cars for personal use. Many internal institutional mistakes prompt the question, "Who is minding the store?" And the answer often is, "No one." The mistakes are reflections of the complexity of the presidential institution and the limits to presidents' control over it.

Presidents also make mistakes in relations between the presidency and other institutions. At the base of many of these mistakes is the recent presidential tendency to run against Congress. Presidents charge that Congress is unwieldy, irresponsible, and unable to do what the country needs. Although this tactic may play well with the folks back home, it does not play well with the people on Capitol Hill who will support or oppose presidential legislative priorities. President Reagan's ill-fated nomination of Robert Bork to the Supreme Court in 1987 revealed several dimensions of interinstitutional mistakes. Although the Reagan administration had been in office for six years, it violated several basic principles of the presidential institution during the nomination battle that lasted for three and one-half months and ended with the Senate's defeat of Bork by the largest margin in history—forty-two to fifty-eight. The Reagan people disregarded fundamental institutional constraints surrounding the nomination of Bork, an activist conservative: the Senate was solidly Democratic; it was late in Reagan's term; his popularity had slipped; Congress had been angered by the disclosures of the Iran-contra scandal; and several senators, notably Senate Judiciary Committee chair Joseph Biden, were running for president. Institutional miscalculations continued when the Reagan strategists pinned their hopes for victory on southern Democratic senators but did not conduct an aggressive lobbying campaign—either publicly or privately—for Bork until well after the swing senators had been pressured by their constituents not to back Bork. They also gave up a critical timing advantage when Reagan announced the nomination in July. The Senate adjourned for its summer recess in July, and Biden did not call for hearings on the nomination until September. Had the Reagan people anticipated Biden's move, they could have delayed the president's own announcement of the nomination until after the Senate reconvened. This would have prevented Bork's opponents from mobilizing during July and August. Interinstitutional mistakes occur with Congress when presidents fail to take into account its composition, the link between presidential success and public approval, and the idea of timing issues in such a way as to gain the upper hand.

Image–Institution Mistakes

Presidents also make mistakes that join lapses in imagery with those in institutional relations. Presidents may choose a course of action that widens their image gap. The gap then leaves space for other institutions to gain strategic advantages. President Clinton's attempt to end the forty-eight-year-old ban on gay men and lesbians in the military in 1993 is an example of this kind of image–institution mistake.

Clinton made a campaign promise to end the ban and reiterated the pledge as president-elect. At first glance, one might argue that Clinton did exactly what the single executive image demands. At the earliest possible opportunity—even before being sworn in—he announced that he would issue an executive order lifting the ban. Surely this is the kind of swift, bold action the single executive image requires.

But the single executive image also dictates boundaries within which such swift actions must be taken. They must be done with average Americans in mind and in such a way that citizens either will not be aroused or will be unified. Instead, Clinton chose a highly controversial issue that tapped, among other things, homophobic prejudice both in and out of the military. In doing so, he pushed away his own main agenda item, summarized in his campaign headquarters as "it's the economy, stupid." Nor did the Clinton team lay any rhetorical or public opinion groundwork for the decision. The apt comparison between lifting the gay ban and Truman's executive order desegregating the military was left to several members of Congress and gay rights leaders to make. Furthermore, Clinton announced the decision at a time when few other administration decisions were being made. Indeed, this was the Clinton strategy. The president would look strong lifting the ban early with one stroke of the pen while more intricate plans were being developed for the economic programs at the core of Clinton's agenda. Yet the absence of other presidential news allowed the press to focus intense coverage on the matter of gays in the military rather than on the more typical stories of the new First Family moving into the White House and the president's plans for the future. As a result, a public uproar ensued and Clinton lost much of his honeymoon support.

In an attempt to ameliorate the issue, Secretary of Defense Les Aspin announced that he would review the ban and make recommendations to the president in six months. The Clinton people hoped this would be a cooling-off period during which the controversy would diminish. Yet their timing decision set off a series of institutional machinations. Members of the armed forces and members of Congress, especially the Joint Chiefs of Staff and Senate Armed Services Committee chair Sam Nunn, now had a full opportunity to organize against Clinton's proposal. The Joint Chiefs had threatened in November to resign en masse if an executive order not to their liking was forthcoming. Nunn held hearings and visited a submarine to dramatize the close quarters in which sailors, in particular, lived. The Joint Chiefs and Nunn were able to define the issue around their own alternatives. A compromise policy—"Don't ask, don't tell"—was ultimately worked out that permitted gay men and lesbians to serve in the military but not openly to acknowledge their sexual orientation. The ban had been modified but not lifted. Thus Clinton began his term with a wide image gap and also allowed two competing institutions—the military and Congress—to define an issue in such a way that the president had to acquiesce to them rather than the other way around.

It is not always the case that presidential mistakes permit other institutions to achieve their goals at the expense of the president. President Clinton's mistakes during the Lewinsky scandal created an immense image gap—he was deceptive when addressing the American people about the affair, he offered a tortured defense of his actions based on a narrow definition of sexual relations, and he did not offer an unequivocal apology for his actions until quite late. These actions were well out of sync with the single executive image, which would expect presidents to be family oriented, honest, and contrite. But two factors saved Clinton from his own mistakes. First, the American public viewed the mistakes as personal in nature. And the public believed they already knew a good deal about this personal side of Clinton, given that rumors about his sexual exploits flew as early as the 1992 campaign. The public knew this in 1992 when they elected Clinton, and they knew it in 1996 when they reelected him, indicating that these matters were not as important as policy matters in defining the importance and visibility of the single executive image. On policy matters, Clinton scored high marks and little gap appeared to exist between his presidential image and the single executive image. The economy was booming, the deficit was gone, Social Security was saved, and welfare reform was in place.

Second, the prosecution of Clinton by independent counsel Kenneth Starr and the impeachment proceedings in the House appeared to be highly partisan. The House, in particular, seemed heedlessly out of step with public opinion. The closer the House moved toward impeachment, the higher went Clinton's approval ratings. In a rather loud statement of dissent to the House, the public indicated in an array of polls that Clinton's transgressions were of a personal nature and did not warrant removal from office. House Republicans created an image gap of their own, appearing to go after the president for their own political gains. Thus, not all mistakes are equal. Even sensational ones may not spell presidential failure if the presidential missteps are not policy related and other institutions make their own even more heedless miscalculations.

President George W. Bush made significant image and institutional mistakes in the aftermath of Hurricane Katrina. On August 29, 2005, the day the hurricane made its second, more devastating landfall, Bush interrupted his vacation at his Texas ranch to fly to Arizona for a small birthday party for Republican senator John McCain. The next day he flew on to San Diego to commemorate the sixtieth anniversary of V-J Day, marking the end of the war against Japan in World War II. For those two days, he appeared to be preoccupied not with the storm and its impact, but with other ceremonial and political duties. On August 31, with 80 percent of New Orleans flooded from levees broken by the storm surge, Bush finally cut his vacation short. En route to Washington, he flew over the flooded area of the Gulf coast but did not land. This decision compounded the initial image problem. After first appearing not to care about the situation, he then appeared to avoid direct involvement in its solution.

Not until September 2, five days after the hurricane hit, did Bush visit the region. When he did so, he praised Federal Emergency Management Agency head

Michael Brown: "Brownie, you are doing one heck of a job." But it was clear to many Americans watching around-the-clock coverage of the devastation in New Orleans that Brown's management of the recovery effort was seriously flawed. Brown himself did not know for two days that people were stranded at the New Orleans Convention Center, even though it had been reported on all the major news networks. Numerous mix-ups occurred among federal, state, and local agencies, and 47 percent of Americans blamed President Bush directly for the failures of aid and assistance. Institutional breakdowns, then, seemed just as apparent as the image problems. Not only was there a wide image gap as Bush tended to other business while thousands died in the hurricane's wake, but also there were significant institutional failures with little coordination from the White House. Mindful of these mistakes, President Obama made a concerted effort to offer a caring image and also used the White House to cut through bureaucratic red tape in the aftermath of Hurricane Sandy, which devastated the New Jersey and New York coastlines in 2012. The picture of a concerned president meeting with Governor Chris Christie of New Jersey was widely reported, as was Christie's comment that "it's been very good working with the president and his administration. It's been wonderful."[62]

CONCLUSION: PRESIDENTS AND POLITICAL SCIENTISTS

Is it possible that, if President Clinton had a political scientist position in the White House Office or even the cabinet advising him on the nature of the presidency, the issue of gays in the military would have been resolved in a manner more in keeping with what the White House wanted? Could the Reagan administration have saved the Bork nomination? Could President George H. W. Bush have translated public support into domestic policies after the Persian Gulf War? Political scientists are no more omniscient than presidents or their primary advisers. They would not get it right all of the time. But they have knowledge quite different from that offered by presidents' other advisers, knowledge that is pertinent to every decision that presidents make—namely, how the presidency operates.

Presidents have three main types of advisers. Policy advisers lay out various domestic and international policy problems that presidents may wish to address or may have to address. They also develop positions and programs for presidents to offer as solutions. Economic advisers spell out various options on how to keep the economy robust, how to make the good times return, and how to cut or add to the federal budget. Political advisers consider the politics of a decision—how it will play with the public, how the press will cast the issue, and how other politicians will respond. Political advisers then devise strategies to sell presidents' decisions with these political considerations in mind.

Missing are advisers skilled in telling presidents about the office they hold. Although each type of adviser teaches presidents a good deal about what they need to know to work in the White House, none of them is an expert on the presidency.

The generalizations from political science research are not lessons that the other advisers would fully know. Even political advisers, who may be aware of some of the generalizations, such as those on public opinion, are typically not schooled in the presidency per se. Because many political advisers began their stint with the president during the campaign, they often have an electoral framework in mind that is much narrower than that offered by political scientists.

What presidents need is a fourth set of advisers—presidency advisers. Nor will it do to hire only those political scientists who view the presidency from a single perspective or advocate but one method. The generalizations about imagery and institution are a mix of qualitative and quantitative findings. Conclusions about different types of White House staff systems, cabinet government, and the limits to presidents' control of the EOP and the bureaucracy are drawn largely from qualitative accounts. Conclusions about presidential success in Congress, presidential approval, and presidential speeches are drawn primarily from quantitative studies.

The generalizations also reveal the perspectives that political scientists adopt. Studies of presidential dealings with Congress and the public typically adopt the perspective of presidential power. Presidents must persuade members of Congress and the public to give them what they want. Accounts of the relations between presidents and their advisers, cabinet members, and the bureaucracy incorporate historical descriptions, interpretations of the power of presidents, and institutional analyses.

Thus political scientists' understanding of the presidency rests on an accumulation of knowledge that cuts across methods and perspectives. Effective presidency advisers must have studied the office from several perspectives and must be knowledgeable about work using qualitative and quantitative methods. This permits them to understand the full scope of the office and its two central dimensions of imagery and institution. How presidents can succeed at using imagery and the institution is one of the main lessons political scientists offer in studying the presidency.

NOTES

1. Kenneth Walsh, "Obama's Secret Dinner with Presidential Historians," *U.S. News and World Report,* July 15, 2009, http://www.usnews.com/news/obama/articles/2009/07/15/obamas-secret-dinner-with-presidential-historians.
2. White House Transition Project, http://whitehousetransitionproject.org.
3. For more details on these two concepts, see Lyn Ragsdale, *Presidential Politics* (Boston: Houghton Mifflin, 1993).
4. Jeffrey Tulis, *The Rhetorical Presidency* (New Haven, CT: Yale University Press, 1987).
5. Fred Greenstein, "What the President Means to Americans," in *Choosing the President,* ed. James David Barber (Englewood Cliffs, NJ: Prentice Hall, 1974), 144.
6. "Media Metric: Obama's 100 Days of Press," Pew Research Center Publications, April 28, 2009, http://pewresearch.org/pubs/1206/media-coverage-of-obama-100-days.
7. Thomas Patterson, "News Coverage of Donald Trump's First 100 Days," Shorenstein Center on Media, Politics, and Public Policy, Harvard University, May 18, 2017, https://shorensteincenter.org/news-coverage-donald-trumps-first-100-days/.

8. Michael Grossman and Martha Kumar, *Portraying the President* (Baltimore: Johns Hopkins University Press, 1981).

9. Herbert Gans, *Deciding What's News* (New York: Pantheon, 1979), 145.

10. Deborah Berry, "Black Plastic Covers Windows, Blocking Reporters' Views of Trump Golfing," *USA Today,* February 11, 2017, https://www.usatoday.com/story/news/politics/onpolitics/2017/02/11/black-plastic-covers-windows-blocking-reporters-views-trump-golfing/97787920/.

11. "Clinton vs. O. J.: Fate Lets Networks, Viewers Off Hook," *Arizona Daily Star,* February 5, 1997, A-12.

12. Ed Rogers, "Lessons Learned from Failure on Repeal and Replace," *Washington Post,* July 18, 2017, https://www.washingtonpost.com/blogs/post-partisan/wp/2017/07/18/lessons-learned-from-failure-on-repeal-and-replace/?utm_term=.ee10712bee6d.

13. Kevin Liptak, "Trump: 'Nobody Knew Health Care Could Be so Complicated,'" CNN, February 28, 2017, http://www.cnn.com/2017/02/27/politics/trump-health-care-complicated/index.html

14. Rick Hampson, "New York Might Not Be as Inviting as It Once Was," *USA Today,* http://www.usatoday.com/educate/election04/article16.htm.

15. Office of Personnel Management, "Data, Analysis & Documentation: Employment & Trends," http://www.opm.gov/feddata/html/empt.asp.

16. Alfred de Grazia, "The Myth of the President," in *The Presidency,* ed. Aaron Wildavsky (Boston: Little, Brown, 1969), 50.

17. Allan Smith, "The Man Who Was Supposed to Be Integral to Trump's Economic Policy Appears to Be Losing Influence," *Business Insider,* April 24, 2017, http://www.businessinsider.com/peter-navarro-trump-administration-2017-4.

18. Hugh Heclo, "Introduction: The Presidential Illusion," in *The Illusion of Presidential Government,* ed. Hugh Heclo and Lester Salamon (Boulder, CO: Westview Press, 1981), 3.

19. "Obama Hails 'Extraordinary Gathering,'" Associated Press, January 1, 2009, http://www.msnbc.msn.com/id/28535240/?GT1=43001.

20. Barbara Hinckley, *The Symbolic Presidency* (New York: Routledge, 1990); Roderick Hart, *The Sound of Leadership* (Chicago: University of Chicago Press, 1987); Tulis, *The Rhetorical Presidency.*

21. George C. Edwards III, *The Public Presidency* (New York: St. Martin's Press, 1983), 196; Stephen Wayne, "Expectations of the President," in *The President and the Public,* ed. Doris Graber (Philadelphia: Institute for the Study of Human Issues, 1982), 17–39.

22. Lyn Ragsdale, "Strong Feelings: Emotional Responses to Presidents," *Political Behavior* 13 (March 1991): 33–65; Greenstein, "What the President Means to Americans," 144–145.

23. Grossman and Kumar, *Portraying the President.*

24. "Remarks upon Taking the Oath of Office," *Public Papers of the Presidents, Gerald R. Ford, 1974* (Washington, DC: U.S. Government Printing Office, 1975), 1.

25. Quoted in Michael Novak, *Choosing Our King* (New York: Macmillan, 1974), 44.

26. Grossman and Kumar, *Portraying the President,* 275–276.

27. Hinckley, *The Symbolic Presidency.*

28. Bob Woodward, *The Price of Politics* (New York: Simon and Schuster, 2012).

29. *New York Times,* May 21, 1977, A1.

30. Paul Brace and Barbara Hinckley, *Follow the Leader: Opinion Polls and Modern Presidents* (New York: Basic Books, 1992).

31. Lyn Ragsdale, "The Politics of Presidential Speechmaking," *American Political Science Review* 78 (December 1984): 971–984.

32. Ibid.; Samuel Kernell, "Explaining Presidential Popularity," *American Political Science Review* 72 (June 1978): 506–522; Charles Ostrom and Dennis Simon, "Promise and Performance: A Dynamic Model of Presidential Popularity," *American Political Science Review* 79 (June 1985): 334–358.

33. John Mueller, "Presidential Popularity from Truman to Johnson," *American Political Science Review* 64 (March 1970): 18–34; James Stimson, "Public Support for American Presidents: A Cyclical Model," *Public Opinion Quarterly* 40 (Spring 1976): 1–21; Brace and Hinckley, *Follow the Leader.*

34. Quoted in Godfrey Hodgson, *All Things to All Men: The False Promise of the Modern American Presidency* (New York: Simon and Schuster, 1980), 25.

35. http://www.gallup.com/poll/203198/presidential-approval-ratings-donald-trump .aspx.

36. http://www.gallup.com/poll/214091/trump-disapproval-rooted-character-con cerns.aspx?g_source=position7&g_medium=related&g_campaign=tiles.

37. Sampling error is created in selecting a group of people from the general popula- tion. This error depends on the size of the sample taken and usually is three to four percentage points on most national public opinion surveys. This means that for a given poll result, say 62 percent approval, and a margin of error of three percentage points, the true value of approval falls within the range of 59 percent to 65 percent.

38. Dick Morris, *The New Prince* (Los Angeles: Renaissance Books, 1999).

39. https://twitter.com/realdonaldtrump/status/881281755017355264

40. Samuel Kernell and Samuel Popkin, eds., *Chief of Staff* (Berkeley: University of California Press, 1986).

41. Richard Fenno, *The President's Cabinet* (New York: Vintage Books, 1959).

42. John Burke, *The Institutional Presidency* (Baltimore: Johns Hopkins University Press, 1992); Bradley Patterson Jr., *The Ring of Power* (New York: Basic Books, 1988); Karen Hult, "Advising the President," in *Researching the Presidency,* ed. George C. Edwards, John Kessel, and Bert Rockman (Pittsburgh, PA: University of Pittsburgh Press, 1993), 111–160.

43. Quoted in James Pfiffner, *The Strategic Presidency* (Chicago: Dorsey Press, 1988), 29.

44. Ibid.

45. See Ragsdale, *Presidential Politics,* 191–196.

46. George Shultz, *Turmoil and Triumph: My Years as Secretary of State* (New York: Scribner, 1993).

47. Richard Nathan, *The Administrative Presidency* (New York: Wiley, 1983).

48. Paul Light, *The President's Agenda* (Baltimore: Johns Hopkins University Press, 1982).

49. Ostrom and Simon, "Promise and Performance."

50. Brace and Hinckley, *Follow the Leader;* Lyn Ragsdale, "Disconnected Politics: The President and the Public," in *Understanding Public Opinion,* ed. Barbara Norrander and Clyde Wilcox (Washington, DC: CQ Press, 1996).

51. Allegra Hartley, "Timeline: How the U.S. Attorneys Were Fired," *U.S. News & World Report,* March 21, 2007, http://www.usnews.com/usnews/news/articles/070321attorn eys-timeline.htm.

52. Ragsdale, *Presidential Politics*, 239.
53. Lyn Ragsdale, *Vital Statistics on the Presidency,* 3rd ed. (Washington, DC: CQ Press, 2009), 317.
54. Quoted in Light, *The President's Agenda,* 17.
55. Ryan Nobles, "McConnell Criticizes Trump's 'Excessive Expectations,'" CNN, August 8, 2017, http://www.cnn.com/2017/08/08/politics/mitch-mcconnell-excessive-expectations/index.html.
56. https://twitter.com/realdonaldtrump/status/895686351529672704
57. Ibid., 43.
58. Ibid.
59. Ostrom and Simon, "Promise and Performance."
60. Jordan Fabian and Jonathan Easley, "Trump Defiant: 'Blame on Both Sides' in Charlottesville," *The Hill*, August 15, 2017, http://thehill.com/homenews/administration/346668-trump-there-were-two-violent-sides-in-charlottesville.
61. For example, a feud that developed in the Carter administration between Secretary of State Cyrus Vance and National Security Adviser Zbigniew Brzezinski affected the ill-fated helicopter rescue attempt of the American hostages held in Iran.
62. Linda Feldman, "Two Reasons the Obama-Christie Photo Op Is Worth Its Weight," *Christian Science Monitor,* October 31, 2012, http://www.csmonitor.com/USA/DC-Decoder/2012/1031/Two-reasons-the-Obama-Christie-photo-op-in-N.J.-is-worth-its-weight.

3

THE DEVELOPMENT OF PRESIDENTIAL POWER

Conservative Insurgency and Constitutional Construction[1]

Stephen Skowronek

Modern conservatives have embraced an understanding of the presidency's constitutional authority called the "unitary executive." Because the unitary executive, as understood by its defenders, has untrammeled authority in many areas previously thought to lie at the intersection of the presidency and Congress, the courts, and the bureaucracy, even Democratic presidents such as Barack Obama have embraced aspects of it in practice while claiming to reject it in theory. As Stephen Skowronek argues, the unitary executive is the latest in a series of constitutional constructions of the office, all of which have claimed to be consistent with the intentions of the Constitution's Framers. In this chapter he appraises the unitary executive construction in terms of its predecessors: Hamiltonian, Jeffersonian, Jacksonian, and, most influential of all, progressive.

The American Constitution was designed to render political change slow and difficult, and that has put it at odds with the various insurgencies that have, from time to time, swept over it. Indeed, few things about America's political development are more impressive than the ingenuity of empowered movements in confounding the checks and balances that thwart their ambitions, and nothing has proven more consequential for American government over time than the ideas and institutions they have conjured to ease those constraints. The underlying political dynamic was noted long ago. Early in the nineteenth century, Virginia theorist John Taylor of Caroline complained of a proclivity to "stretch constitutions" by "construction," that is, "to interpret them . . . according the temporal interest of the predominant sect."[2] Taylor saw constitutional constraints on programmatic change giving way before a "machine called inference," a machine that works by "conceding principles, and then construing them away."[3]

The American presidency as we know it today is one of the chief products of the political machinery of constitutional inference. Time and again the office has proven indispensable to the ambitions of newly empowered political movements, and each has brought to it a distinctive set of legitimating ideas and institutional resources to help break through the obstacles in their path. Looking back with contemporary eyes, the value of the presidency in the promotion of programmatic change seems obvious. But the attraction of insurgents to this office is, in fact, one of the great paradoxes of American constitutional design. The Framers feared leaders of the sort who would agitate the people on behalf of one political program or another, and they created the presidency in large part to check popular enthusiasms. Their assumptions in separating executive and legislative powers were that Congress, with its vast repository of expressed constitutional powers and its close proximity to the people, was the branch most likely to catch a fever for change, and that a properly constituted executive would serve to stabilize the affairs of state. The division of powers, the provision for indirect presidential elections, the formal charge to "preserve, protect and defend the Constitution," the veto power—all marked the presidency as a counterweight to impulsive legislative majorities and a prod to a more deliberative stance in national affairs.[4] It might be said that the Framers anticipated moments like the mid-1860s, under President Andrew Johnson, and the mid-1990s, under President Bill Clinton, when congressional insurgents flush with power and emboldened by a radical vision of new possibilities squandered precious time and energy trying to weaken and circumvent an uncooperative occupant of the White House. What they did not anticipate was that handicapping the legislative branch in the enactment of popular mandates and reconstructive programs would spur the development of alternative instrumentalities designed to work through the executive. The unintended effect of their constitutional divisions has been to direct proponents of programmatic action to elaborate upon the endowments of the presidency and to refashion that counterweight to insurgency into its cutting edge.

This chapter traces these successive constructions of presidential power through to the latest formulation, the conservative insurgency's "unitary executive." Work on this construction accelerated through the 1970s and 1980s, during the transition from progressive to conservative dominance of the national agenda. Conservative legal scholars took up the doctrinal challenge of redeploying presidential power, and in the 1990s they emerged with a fully elaborated constitutional theory. After

2001 aggressive, self-conscious advocacy of the unitary theory in the administration of George W. Bush put a fine point on its practical implications.[5] Much has been written about this theory in recent decades, but virtually all of the discussion has been among legal scholars. Seeking to adjudicate the constitutional merits of the case, they have debated the soundness of the theory's claims as an interpretation of texts and precedents.[6] The objective here is different. It is to situate the theory in the long line of insurgent constructions and to address it more directly as a political instrument and a developmental phenomenon.

The guiding assumption of this analysis is that a new construction of the presidency gains currency when it facilitates the release of governmental power for new political purposes. I do not mean to suggest that reckoning with construction in this way disposes of the constitutional claims of the unitary theory, or of any other theory for that matter. A developmental analysis raises a different issue: whether the advance of presidential power is rendered legitimate simply by supplying constitutional warrants for it. Nor do I mean to suggest that the claims advanced by the unitary theory on behalf of presidential prerogative are likely to appeal only to conservative presidents. President Barack Obama exercised powers stretched wide by the theory even though he expressed reservations about it in his initial bid for office.[7] I contextualize the unitary theory in order to highlight the latest twist in a ratchet pattern of development. I want to consider the practical political problems that conservative insurgents of the 1970s and 1980s confronted in venting their ambitions, the sequence of prior constructions on which their response to those problems was built, and the cumulative effects of construction on constitutional constraints.

The power of ideas is registered, first and foremost, in ideas about power. Those who have sought, time and again, to make American government a more efficient vehicle for their transformative ambitions have understood that implicitly. And yet, as constructions of power superimpose themselves one on another, each implicated in the next, standards of control tend to drift, and as plausible premises for action accumulate, calling power to account becomes more difficult. The phalanx of legal scholars debating the claims of the unitary executive is indicative not only of the high political stakes at issue, but also of the high premium to be paid in the twenty-first century for a coherent theory of American government. A developmental perspective might be useful here because advocates of the unitary theory offer to restore coherence by reaching back to the eighteenth century. They propose to recover basic principles of our government's design and to strip away extraneous presumptions upon which modern forms of power were built up. The sequence of change is very much at issue in this construction. The question is whether, at this late date, a long reach back to the original idea offers the safest way forward.

A NEW FORMALISM

From a developmental point of view, it seems reasonable to suppose that conservative insurgents were prompted to recast the case for presidential power because the received construction interfered with the pursuit of their ambitions. What those limitations might have been, however, is not readily apparent. American progressives already had spent the better part of the twentieth century relaxing constraints on the American executive. Dismissive of what they called "Constitution worship" for its blind attachment to the governing arrangements of an earlier day, and impatient with what they perceived as the rigid formalities of a written text, progressive reformers advanced a pragmatic, capacious, and famously open-ended theory of national power.[8] With that theory, they proceeded to reconstruct institutional relationships throughout American government around presidential initiative and administrative capacity. For all appearances, "presidential government" was a done deal by the mid-1960s.[9]

Equally curious is that conservatives of the late twentieth century would take up advocacy of a cause that had left conservatives anxious and defensive only a few decades earlier.[10] In the later years of progressive dominance, American conservatives were still cuing off a hallowed Whig tradition of hostility to presidential aggrandizement and executive pretension; opposition to progressive political priorities went hand in hand with skepticism toward the progressives' construction of a "modern" presidency. The conservatives of the 1950s and 1960s were formalists who eschewed the pragmatism and experimentation of progressive reform and upheld constitutional arrangements that the shift to presidential government threatened. A diverse array of conservative analysts—James Burnham, Willmoore Kendall, Alfred de Grazia, and James Buchanan—countered the higher-order aggregations of the progressives' new system of rule by repairing to the original design of American government and expounding upon the congressional and local prerogatives it harbored.[11] The theory of the unitary executive promotes exactly what that earlier generation of conservatives resisted. It is a brief for the president to act as the exclusive manager of all matters that fall within the purview of the instrumentalities of the executive branch. By that premise, contemporary conservatives have sought to limit prerogatives long claimed by the other branches over administrative instruments, procedures, and personnel; to tap the vast repositories of power accumulated in the modern executive establishment; and to expand the capacities of the president to set policy and adjudicate disputes unilaterally. The construction is recognizably "conservative" in its insistence that all governmental powers are located within and contained by the text and formal arrangements of the Constitution; the effect, however, is to advance the case for presidential direction. The theory cuts off the operations of the modern presidency from progressive argumentation on behalf of experimentation with governmental design and preempts further elaboration of the pragmatic approach to institutional development.

There are now different strands of the unitary theory, and advocates of one do not necessarily endorse all the propositions of another. They do, however, move out from a common core. All proceed upon an elaboration of the principle of the separation of powers, most especially upon the Constitution's grant of independent powers to the president.[12] Of particular importance is the Constitution's vesting of "the executive power" in a single officer, the president, as that is read to imply expansive authority and exclusive responsibility. When the distinctly unqualified wording of Article II's vesting clause is figured into other presidential powers derived from the oath of office, the commander in chief clause, and the take care clause, the domain of unfettered action can be broadened along any number of fronts—for example, in interpreting and executing the law, in conducting foreign relations, and in the control of military affairs. The theory can be invoked to justify unilateral war-making powers for the president. It can be used to expand presidential discretion with signing statements that defend executive prerogatives against possible infringement by specific parts of legislation being enacted into law. Even in its more modest forms, the theory undercuts administrative arrangements designed to secure the independence of prosecutors, regulators, inspectors, accountants, forecasters, personnel officers, scientists, and the like. It discounts the notion of objective, disinterested administration in service to the government as a whole and advances in its place the ideal of an administration run in strict accordance with the president's priorities. The central claim is that the Constitution mandates an integrated and hierarchical administration—a unified executive branch—in which all officers performing executive business are subordinate to the president, accountable to his interpretations of their charge, and removable at his discretion. The formal reasoning authorizes the president to capitalize on all that the historical development of national power has created while leaving to others the Constitution's most rudimentary and combative instruments: term limits and quadrennial elections, congressional control of the purse and Senate review of appointments, and judicial intervention and the threat of impeachment.

The unitary theory serves as an interesting window into developmental processes precisely because there is no simple way of characterizing its relationship to positions advanced in the recent past. Whereas advocates of presidential power in the early twentieth century revamped American government in general, and the presidency in particular, in a concerted "revolt against formalism,"[13] this new advocacy rests on strict adherence to constitutional stricture. Moreover, though conservatives have consistently adhered to formalism, the new formalism no longer counters presidential empowerment. On the contrary, it is deployed as a vehicle for more aggressively asserting the president's independence and freedom of action. The latest construction reinvigorates the traditional conservative case for returning to an original understanding of the Constitution's distribution of powers, but it jettisons traditional conservative reservations about the modern presidency, and it extends the progressive paradigm of presidency-centered government while jettisoning the distinctly progressive premises on which it was built. The result is an arresting recombination of the historical elements in play—a new marriage of formalism with presidentialism, of originalism with unilateralism.

EARLY CONSTRUCTIONS

Constitutional construction is a constrained process. The text of the document cannot be ignored, nor can advocates of a new dispensation afford to have their interpretation of it dismissed out of hand as implausible. Notwithstanding the shifts over time in the standards employed, and the distensions produced over the long haul, constructions of presidential power are likely to succeed to the extent that their premises appear in the course of events as familiar, sensible, even restorative.

Arresting as it may be as a new amalgam, the construction of presidential power advanced by insurgent conservatives was hardly unfamiliar. Advocates of the unitary theory have a long, if contentious, history on which to draw. During the Washington administration, Alexander Hamilton ventured that when the Framers of the Constitution vested "the Executive Power" in the president, they had in mind a well-established model of what those powers encompassed. It followed that the clauses of Article II should be read expansively in light of what the "general theory and practice" of other nations at the time considered the executive's "natural" domain, and that presidential powers were limited only narrowly by the qualifications stipulated in the rest of the document.[14] This argument was reworked at the height of the Progressive movement by Theodore Roosevelt in his "stewardship theory" of the presidency.[15] Drawing upon Hamilton's broad reading of the vesting clause and celebrating what he called the "Jackson-Lincoln" school of presidential practice, Roosevelt asserted that the American president was free to do anything on behalf of the nation except what the Constitution and the laws explicitly proscribed.[16] The companion notion of "departmentalism" also has a long and distinguished pedigree. It holds that the presidency, as a separate and equal branch of government, cannot be subordinated to interpretations of the Constitution and the laws proffered by the coordinate branches but must remain free to interpret both by its own lights in the fulfillment of its executive responsibilities.[17] The common feature of this family of arguments is that they assess the constitutional distribution of powers from the president's perspective. Today's unitary theorists have elaborated this perspective in the form of a lawyer's brief: they have highlighted its doctrinal underpinnings, generalized their application, and drawn out their contemporary implications. The additional rigor has also prompted them to discriminate among historical expressions of the argument. For example, Steven Calabresi, who has done more than any other contemporary scholar to flesh out the theory, rejects Roosevelt's stewardship notions as overblown and unsupported by a strict reading of the Constitution.[18] But when he and his collaborators surveyed presidential history, they found that claims consistent with a more disciplined presentation of the unitary theory have been voiced by virtually all incumbents of the office—the mediocre as well as the great, the failed as well as the successful. Though it is hardly surprising that presidents have sought all along to maximize their power within the constitutional system, the unitary theorists are not out to surprise. On the contrary, the strength of their case for presidential power in contemporary American government hinges on the claim that it is really nothing new.

To a large extent, they are correct. The theory of the unitary executive is new less for what it adds to prior arguments for presidential power than for what it does away with. Indeed, for all that is familiar in this construction of presidential power and for all the scholarly discipline that has been brought to bear on its articulation in recent years, it is easy to lose sight of what is missing. On inspection, however, this is the first time since the Founding that a political movement has elaborated upon the powers of the presidency without at the same time inventing some new mechanisms to pace the exercise of those powers and ensure their accountability. Put another way, the familiarity of the formal arguments on which this construction rests obscures the extent to which past insurgencies relied upon the development of extraconstitutional innovations to resolve the riddle of empowerment and control. Presidential power expanded historically alongside political and institutional improvisations that externalized its purview and collectivized its responsibilities. The power that the unitary theory seeks to capitalize upon formally by recovering the internal logic of the original design was built up over the decades by advocates assiduously reworking the foundations of that power and reorienting its operations.

Previously, presidential empowerment in America has been accompanied by insurgent campaigns to democratize the government. That is to say, new power claims by the president were accommodated by the political movements that supported them in alternative governing arrangements designed to surround and regulate the release of that power from outside the Constitution proper. The Jeffersonians, Jacksonians, and progressives, though markedly different from one another in their immediate programmatic objectives, each coupled enthusiasm for a more expansive reading of executive prerogatives with innovations designed to render the exercise of power more broadly based and cooperative. Until recently, unity has been a *political* ideal directed at *interbranch* relations and achieved through the organization and mobilization of the polity at large; hitherto, insurgent movements have sought political solutions to what they perceived to be the constitutional *problem* of separation. Formal checks and balances were eased in the past by the creation of auxiliary institutions and informal controls that sought at once to foster institutional collaboration and to make the representation of public opinion more continuous and effective. Prior insurgencies have, to be sure, interpreted presidential power permissively, but they were not content to let the Constitution alone dictate its design or legitimate its development.

Thomas Jefferson's conception of presidential power proved in practice to be no less expansive than Hamilton's.[19] But there was a crucial difference between them. Whereas Hamilton sought to lodge presidential prerogatives in Article II of the Constitution, Jefferson sought to extricate presidential strength from the constitutional text and anchor it instead in externalized expressions of public opinion.[20] By claiming ground beyond the Constitution, Jefferson's construction was in some ways less constrained than Hamilton's, and yet its scope was kept circumstantial and subject to the judgments of others. For Jefferson, extraordinary assertions of presidential power could be justified as a collective act of popular will, a mandate from the people, a populist intervention.[21] By implication, these interventions would extend no further than the people's collective action and political indulgence would take them. Checks and balances would be left intact as security against the impositions of individuals and factions who had less than overwhelming popular support.

Jefferson's construction of presidential power was reflected institutionally in innovations that played to the political strengths of his movement. The formation of the Republican Party, the ratification of the Twelfth Amendment, the designation of the congressional caucus as the presidential nominating body, the selection of state electors in accordance with the national party ticket—each repositioned the office in the governmental system at large and constructed new foundations for its operation. All served extra-constitutional causes such as popular mobilization, political coordination, and institutional cooperation.[22] With these innovations, Jefferson swept the field of his political opponents, secured his party's control of all the elected branches, reconstructed national political priorities, and exercised prerogatives that dwarfed those of his Federalist predecessors. But there was more than license in the new arrangements, and they left Jefferson's successors to labor under their constraints. Once the insurgents were safely ensconced in power, the auxiliary instruments they instituted to express the public will strengthened the position of Congress in governmental affairs and saddled presidents with norms that were deeply suspicious of the formal appurtenances of executive power.[23]

The Jacksonian construction of the presidency extended the Jeffersonian ideal of an office empowered through popular mobilization and institutional coordination, but the mechanisms deployed were different. In the course of their struggle for power, the Jacksonians would reject the trappings of political control of the executive by Congress and find the ideal of a single party of national consensus unwieldy. Pressing his political priorities upon a nation more sprawling and more varied in its interests, Andrew Jackson encountered stiffer resistance to his designs than Jefferson had, and his claims to a popular mandate for independent action grew correspondingly sharper.[24] When push came to shove, Jackson embraced the political divisions his policies were creating, proclaimed the presidency superior to Congress as an agency of democratic expression, and set about mobilizing majorities on the electoral battlefield sufficient to gain control of Congress and secure deference to his will. His constitutional assertions fueled the organization and integration of rival mass-based parties designed to compete for power at all levels.

Jackson created a presidency more fully extricated from congressional domination and more fully supported in its popular connection. His followers saw to it that it was also more fully integrated into state and local politics. The characteristic institutional forms of the post-Jackson period—the party convention for nominating candidates and the spoils system of political rotation and partisan appointment to administrative positions—paced the greater strength of the Jacksonian presidency with more disciplined instruments of collective oversight. As the party convention took candidate selection and programmatic commitments out of the hands of Congress, it lodged them more firmly in a national coalition of local party machines. The spoils system, in turn, bolstered congressional support for the executive by transforming the bureaucracy into a jobs program for the local party workforce. Whereas the party of Jefferson had articulated an accord among elites at the center of power and delivered it to the periphery, these new parties generated power from the bottom up; their candidates were, like Jackson, to deliver to the center an accord hammered out by local and regional aggregations of interest.[25] This new construction was motivated even more clearly than the Jeffersonian one by perception of the Constitution's inadequacies. Martin Van Buren, the leading theoretician of the new design, candidly addressed it to defects in the selection procedure that he deemed responsible for the failure to resolve the election of 1824 on democratic principles.[26] Once in place, the new party-based system went far toward upending the original scheme of checks and balances. But it did not endorse the separation of powers as the alternative.[27] As a practical matter, it joined the president more tightly to others. Together, the party convention and the spoils system created a near-perfect community of interests for the release, control, and direction of presidential power. Fortifying the president with an organized base of popular support outside the constitutional apparatus created a less insular office. The new arrangements made it easier for the chief executive to forge a concert of interests with fellow partisans in the other branches. At the same time, it raised the political risks of his acting alone.

The party-based presidency reached its zenith during the Civil War under the insurgent Republicans. Eyeing the enormous war machine mobilized under Abraham Lincoln to contest the meaning of the Constitution, New York state senator A. H. Bailey, speaking at a Republican county convention, neatly summed up the prevailing premises: "He has no army, no navy, no resources of any kind except what the people give him. In a word, he is powerless, unless the people stand at his back and uphold his hands."[28] As Bailey saw it, "The Republican organization, in all its principles, in all its practices, and by all its members, is committed to the preservation of the Union, and to the overthrow of the Rebellion. It is the power of the State and the power of the Nation."[29]

THE PROGRESSIVE CONSTRUCTION

Well before the Jackson insurgency began, the congressional nominating caucus that had empowered Jefferson had become "King Caucus," a suspect body whose selections had become tantamount to election and whose operations were seen to compromise the independence of state and national officers alike.[30] By the time the progressive insurgency began, the party convention that had empowered the mid-nineteenth-century presidents had become the plaything of state and local "bosses" who held the executive branch hostage to the patronage demands of their local organizations.[31] The irritation expressed by later generations about the arrangements improvised by their predecessors reflected the bargain implicit in the development of presidential power: checks and balances were eased in exchange for shifting presidential accountability onto less formal and more collective foundations operating alongside the formal constitutional design.

The third, progressive, iteration of this dynamic proved to be more sustained, more broad-ranging, and more systemic in its consequences than its Jeffersonian and Jacksonian precursors. Successive waves of progressive reform extending over the first two-thirds of the twentieth century expanded the domain of national action, constructed an extensive administrative apparatus for intervention at home and abroad, and concentrated power in the presidency on a scale that dwarfs nineteenth-century precedents. This concerted shift toward national, executive, and presidential power marked a pivotal turn in American political development. If nothing else, decades of progressive advocacy on behalf of a more presidency-centered government have lent a commonsense plausibility to the claims for presidential authority recently advanced by conservatives through their unitary theory. By the same token, however, now that the progressive construction of presidential power has been superseded by a fourth, its place in the sequence of constructions begs to be reassessed.

On inspection, progressive advocacy of presidential power has more in common with nineteenth-century advocacy than with the new conservative advocacy. The greater investment progressives made in presidential power was not underwritten by greater faith in the Constitution; their faith was placed instead in the development of new forms of authority, in alternative means of representation, in the common purposes of "the public," and in expanded standards of democratic rule. It is little wonder that Theodore Roosevelt's "stewardship theory" of the presidency makes unitary theorists uneasy. Just as surely as Roosevelt's invocation of the "Jackson-Lincoln school" indicated his preference for an expansive reading of the president's constitutional powers, it also indicated his interest in new modes of democratic expression. His notion of presidential stewardship combined elements of both. The theory was part of Roosevelt's larger conception of the presidency as a "bully pulpit" for mobilizing the public. It was promulgated in the midst of an insurgent political campaign that reached out to newly organized national interests and offered to develop federal powers so as to address their new concerns in new ways. Acknowledging at the climax of his 1912 bid that the enhanced powers to be claimed in modern America by the nation's "steward" would require new forms of accountability, Roosevelt radicalized his commitment to democracy and endorsed the notion of a popular recall of presidents who had lost the confidence of the people.[32] Considering progressive thought more broadly indicates something similar. Like the Jeffersonians and the Jacksonians, progressive reformers sought at once to empower the presidency and to open it up to more broad-ranging influences. Like the Jeffersonians and Jacksonians, their idea was not just to bolster the executive, but also to envelop it in a new community of national interests. Like the Jeffersonians and Jacksonians, the objective was an office that would be less self-contained, more fully democratized, and more outwardly directed in its orientation. The progressives were emboldened to rethink formal constitutional divisions and protections because they were confident in the new mechanisms they were devising to distill the public interest, promote political cooperation, and induce elite collaboration.

This is not to deny that the progressive departure was radical. The progressives broke with the nineteenth-century reliance on party mechanisms for easing constitutional constraints and for balancing presidential empowerment with collective control. As the centerpiece of the received construction, party power struck early-twentieth-century reformers as the central problem to be overcome. Progressives saw the party machines as increasingly indifferent to the interdependencies of industrial society; party competition appeared to them to perpetuate outmoded conflicts and submerge the common interests upon which a new national government might foster greater social cohesion. More pointedly, the progressives wanted to recast the institutional bond between president and Congress around an expandable bureaucracy capable of reconciling national economic interests and tying them to a national purpose, and that ambition placed them at odds with mechanisms of government previously developed to hold the president accountable to state and local concerns.[33] Mounting a sharp critique of the principal instruments of

Jacksonian democracy, the reformers worked to displace the selection of candidates by party conventions with a primary system, and they sought to displace the politicized bureaucracies created by spoils appointments with more capable administrative units. Their primary system was to unleash the entrepreneurial skills of individual leaders and render political coalitions more responsive to opinion at large; their meritocracy was to advance stabilizing values such as professional competence, expert management, and administrative integrity.[34]

At the same time, the progressives unleashed a critique of the Constitution that was more direct, explicit, and sweeping than anything the Jeffersonians or the Jacksonians had contemplated.[35] There was much for these critics to admire in the Framers: realism, nationalism, reconstructive instincts, and leadership of public opinion. Rather than defer, however, they proposed to emulate their forefathers with a "new" nationalism, one that would overthrow what they now regarded as "the monarchy of the Constitution."[36] Their legal realism turned all theories of the state, including the Framers' theories, into just so many "justifications or rationalizations of groups in power or seeking power—the special pleadings of races, religions, classes [o]n behalf of their special situations."[37] Their political realism described all institutional arrangements, including the Framers' arrangements, as contingent expressions of the power of interests.[38] Realism in both forms served progressive purposes by upending unreflected premises about government carried over from an earlier day and by legitimating experimentation with alternative arrangements. The progressives wanted to strip discussions of power of their constitutional pretenses so as to force the defenders of established arrangements to engage in a pragmatic, open-ended, and explicitly political debate over what the largest interest, "the public interest," demanded. More radically still, they wanted to locate the public interest itself in the evolving concerns of an "organic" society. The progressives conjured a "living" constitution, one continuously attentive to the interests of the public and operated as the protean instrument of democratic will.[39]

Finally, the progressives seized upon the possibility of constructing a *presidential* democracy: they singled out the chief executive as the instrument around which to build their new national polity. Parties were too decentralized; courts were too tied to precedent; Congress was too cumbersome and beholden to special interests. Only the presidency had the national vision to articulate the public's evolving interests and the wherewithal to act upon them with dispatch. The progressives put the president to work accordingly. They constructed an office in which incumbents would be incentivized to assume political leadership of the nation on an ongoing basis. Each was individually charged to test his skills in keeping national opinion mobilized behind great public purposes and to overcome thereby the constitutional obstacles in its path. As Woodrow Wilson saw it, presidents would make their proposals irresistible to Congress insofar as they reached out to the people directly, articulated their common concerns, and garnered their support.[40] As Henry Jones Ford wrote, the work of the presidency was "the work of the people, breaking through the constitutional form."[41] Like Theodore Roosevelt, Henry Jones Ford took Jackson and Lincoln as models for this new presidency, and it may be a fair summary of the progressives' vision to observe that a constitution in which every president does what Jackson and Lincoln did would hardly be a constitution at all. To speak of theirs as a "broad" construction is to diminish their ambition. As Charles Beard described "the changing spirit of the Constitution," Roosevelt's declaration of a presidential stewardship was not a new constitutional doctrine. It was the liberation of national statesmanship from tired doctrinal disputes, a way of breaking American politics free from debates between "finely spun theories about strict and liberal interpretations of the Constitution."[42] Similarly, Herbert Croly touted the rise of Roosevelt as a release from the narrow-mindedness of "government by lawyers"[43] and an acknowledgment "that the national principle involve[s] a continual process of internal reformation."[44]

To this extent at least, latter-day charges that the progressives eviscerated constitutional restraints, exacerbated political agitation, and sanctioned demagoguery all have a ring of truth.[45] And yet, the self-regarding "personal president" that critics in our day have found emergent in the shortfall could not have been further from their intent.[46] The progressives' designs may appear naïve to us today; the mechanisms they developed to regulate the new forms of power they were generating may be scored in retrospect as inadequate and unreliable. But progressive reform held in its sights a magnetic and catalytic presidency, an office that would operate to attract interests throughout the government and society and align them for concerted national action.

True to this vision, progressives gave far more attention to the new political and institutional mechanisms that they wanted to animate and surround the presidency than they did to defining the scope of its powers. They conditioned the legitimacy of their new order on the creation of a more engaged citizenry, on opening the operations of government to new forms of publicity, on elevating administrative power on the ground of "neutral competence." They worried about the political resources of "the public," about how to facilitate its adjustment to new conditions and to mobilize its opinions. They sought objective indicators of the "public interest" and cultivated independent authorities to articulate it. Even ardent neo-Hamiltonians, who were eager to concentrate national power in new hierarchically controlled administrative bodies, sought legitimating anchors external to the Constitution itself. Most famous in this regard was Croly's effort to tie Hamiltonian means to Jeffersonian ends by specifying a substantive precept—the social and economic amelioration of the circumstances of the common man—that would direct the exercise of power and subordinate it to a purpose in which all Americans could be expected to concur.[47]

The institutions the progressives built expressed this faith in a discernible public interest outside of government, and they never flagged in their efforts to enhance the authority of those institutions or to bring them to bear more directly on the government. While weakening the role of party organizations in presidential selection and ejecting the local parties from their pivotal coordinating role in national administration, they generated an extensive "parastate" apparatus[48]—universities, graduate schools, think tanks, professional associations, information clearinghouses, journals of national opinion—all with an eye to infusing national political power with what they thought would be true and reliable distillations of the interests of the whole. Their new bureaucracies were to recruit from these institutions and to speak to the interests of the public by cultivating an independent voice in government.

Administrative authority would stem from the interests of all in technical expertise and professional judgment, in the objective distillation of "the facts" from the situation at hand, and in the production of services attractive to new groups in the polity at large.

Progressives who came of age after World War I had fewer illusions about the consensus to be found for these designs in unvarnished public opinion, but they were no less confident in their ability to distill the public interest independently. They augmented their outreach with efforts to tap the potential of group representation and pluralistic participation. Charles Merriam, a champion of academic political science who served Franklin Roosevelt on his Committee on Administrative Management and on his National Resources Planning Board, proposed an ongoing mobilization of "the political prudence of the community"[49] in the policymaking process. The assembled wisdom of the nation was to circumscribe governmental power and infuse it with "the facts essential to intelligent national government."[50] In part, this was just an extension of the progressives' faith in expertise, of their zeal for deploying in government the resources of the nation's new universities and graduate schools and for consummating a marriage of power with positivism. But, on inspection, Merriam's offensive on behalf of the prudential authority of the public was remarkably multifaceted. It was addressed to the limits of science as well as the limits of formal governmental authority. He insisted on representation for "all phases of opinion," for he saw that confidence in progressive government would come to hinge on the public's perceptions of "the impartiality of the *prudentes* who [were] brought together."[51] He envisioned integrating and coordinating mechanisms that would tap "the wisdom reached by the few more skilled and experienced" while remaining sensitive to the "general level of judgment and insight reached by the mass of the community itself."[52] Merriam's efforts to surround formal power with extraconstitutional authority filled out a burgeoning potpourri of progressive prescriptions: civic education for the common man, clearing houses to collect and make public information from all sources, data analysis by specialists, advice from neutral experts, forecasting by independent administrators, outreach to national interest groups and professional associations, and representation for diverse communities.

Important aspects of the new balance being struck between presidential empowerment and collective control can be found in the institutional capstone of the progressive presidency, the Executive Office of the President (EOP). Though it tagged the president with new responsibilities for planning and forecasting and bolstered the institution of the presidency with new resources for policy development and administrative oversight, the EOP was less an instrument of unitary command and control than an instrument of institutional coordination and collective action. Its offices were designed to serve interbranch relations, not just the president.[53] They anticipated a new governmental partnership, a partnership built on assurances to Congress that executive actions and recommendations were grounded in shared purposes as well as in the best managerial practices, the latest forecasting instruments, and the most reliable data. President Harry Truman was initially wary of the formation of the National Security Council and the Council of Economic Advisers within the EOP because he perceived the elevation of professional managers and expert advisers to positions of authority within the presidency as a constraint on his constitutional prerogatives.[54] But it was precisely by means of this technocratic interposition on behalf of "enlightened administration" that the progressive presidency was to meet other centers of power on common ground and solicit their cooperation.

The progressive construction tilted radically in the direction of "presidential government," but, as Richard Neustadt astutely pointed out in 1960, presidents in this new order were well advised not to depend on the Constitution for the powers needed to fulfill their newfound responsibilities. As Neustadt saw it, the "separation of powers" was illusory; this was a system of "separate institutions *sharing* powers."[55] *Presidential Power,* the last of the great progressive tracts, described an office engrossed in interactions with others outside its own sphere and an officer newly charged to orchestrate the far-flung interests of the whole. The progressive president was less a constitutional figure wielding formal power within a specified domain than a political entrepreneur out to bridge different authorities and to induce among them a concert of action.

THE UNITARY EXECUTIVE AS THEORY

By the 1970s progressives had begun to turn on their own handiwork. True to their conception of the modern presidency as a collective instrument of democratic control, they renounced incumbents for what they had come to perceive as overwrought pretensions to imperial rule, they condemned new forms of privilege that had developed behind the façade of a public interest in the administrative state, and they recoiled at the egocentric scramble of modern election campaigns.[56] "Power invested, promise unfulfilled" was their summary judgment of the twentieth century's great experiment in presidency-centered government.[57] Echoes from conservative voices of the 1950s can be heard in these criticisms. Acknowledging that something had gone wrong, disillusioned progressives looked back to the Constitution with keen appreciation for their theories' unintended consequences, with new concern for the derangement of modern practices, and with heightened anxiety about executive power.[58]

But as the progressives were recoiling and the intellectual foundations of their "modern" presidency were foundering, another political movement began to rework the case for presidential power. Given past episodes, it is no surprise that these new advocates proved impatient with checks and balances. Like all insurgencies, this one sought to unleash the presidency against reigning political priorities, to break through the thicket of institutions that had grown up around them, and to reconfigure American government to advance their own commitments. The only curious thing was the indifference of these new insurgents to the challenge of inventing alternative machinery to surround presidential power and call it to account, machinery that might justify easing checks and balances with superior forms of external supervision, institutional coordination, and collective control.

Their premise cut hard the other way. It was that everything needed to justify further indulgence of presidential prerogatives was to be found in "the text, structure, and ratification history of the Constitution."[59]

During the 1970s and 1980s, the progressives' insistence that modern governance find a way to marry a concentration of power in the executive with new mechanisms for calling that power to account fell by the wayside. The debate on all sides came to focus on original understandings of presidential power and how to get right with the Constitution. Whatever its intellectual merits, this debate has left the contemporary critics of presidential power at a practical disadvantage. They may have a strong argument that the expansion of presidential power has been a misguided departure from constitutional understandings, but coming up with a scheme that will reverse course and reinvigorate the original system of checks and balances is a tall order, especially as governance challenges of the sort that prompted latter-day developments continue to mount apace.[60] For their part, constitutional advocates of sweeping presidential powers have not been asking for a reversal of course but for a formal codification and further extension of what the long history of agitation on behalf of the presidency has actually produced. Not the least of the attractions of the unitary theory is the constitutional sanction it projects back upon accumulated historical practices. It sorts through the far-flung innovations that institutional development of the executive branch has brought in its train and aligns those most favorable to presidential prerogative and independence with first principles and immutable standards. Unlike the progressives, who historicized the Constitution, subsumed it within the stream of national development, and urged the polity to continue experimenting with alternative governing arrangements, the new conservatives have disavowed risky experiments and advanced presidential control over the modern executive establishment on what would appear to be the most secure ground possible. They purport only to reaffirm and restore the interior logic of our government's founding document.

To bring theoretical coherence to the advance of presidential power, the unitary theorists push the dispositive action backward in time to the years prior to the inauguration of George Washington. By elevating the significance of the prehistory of the office, they counter the notion that the powers of the modern presidency are an invention of latter-day reformers. Their principal claim is that those powers have been there all along and that they only need to be recovered, restored, and reasserted in their true and original significance.[61] To this end, the new construction scouts European developments in the theory and practice of executive power leading up to the American Revolution.[62] The theory does not ignore the clear rejection of the European executive in the Declaration of Independence and the constitutions of the post-Revolutionary period; rather, it dwells on the deliberate reintroduction of independent executive authority into American government in the new Constitution of 1787.

The unitary executive comes to rest on a particular interpretation of this initial developmental sequence. The reasoning is clear if not uncontroversial: that the Constitutional Convention broke decisively with the unorthodox principles of executive organization ushered in by the American Revolution and that, in ratifying the Constitution, the people endorsed a design that reaffirmed more traditional understandings of executive authority. Put more sharply, in repudiating their post-Revolutionary experiments in collective control of the executive power, the American people allegedly repudiated all but the rudimentary forms of collective control that survived the convention and foreclosed any future experimentation along those lines.[63] By implication, the efforts of every subsequent generation to rework those arrangements and qualify the president's unilateral control of executive power stand discredited as a betrayal of the intent of the American people at their most authoritative moment. By extension, contemporary derangements of power do not stem from some latter-day extension of the president's reach in government but from misguided improvisations that have sought to renegotiate the office's original mandate. All told, it is not the powers of the presidency that have developed over time, only illegitimate constraints on those powers.[64]

Americans are accustomed to hearing appeals to the text and structure of the Constitution as the sole authority defining the extent of presidential power. These appeals have been associated all along with resistance to those who have sought to alter the basis of presidential action. This was Henry Clay's appeal against the pretensions of Andrew Jackson[65] and William Howard Taft's appeal against the pretensions of Theodore Roosevelt.[66] Clay and Taft both rejected populist trumps to constitutional strictures; both rejected the notion of an "undefined residuum"[67] of presidential power; both sought to hold the powers and duties of the chief executive to a stringent textual standard. But Clay and Taft were both trounced by the reform movements they opposed, movements that extended the reach of the presidency by altering the foundations of its legitimacy. Therein sits a glaring complication in recent invocations of formalism on behalf of presidential power: it turns the long sequence of development since the ratification of the Constitution into a scheme of bait and switch. When powers that swelled on the promise of superseding constitutional divisions with more democratic forms of control are recaptured, contained, and defended by the Constitution alone, collective claims on those powers are abruptly curtailed. Or, to put it another way, when all extraconstitutional interventions are rendered superfluous, the expanded resources of the modern presidency are redeployed on behalf of the personal form of rule which the institutional innovations of all previous reformers were at pains to qualify.

To be sure, in reworking the case for presidential power, each of America's great insurgencies has pulled forward prior advances while discarding the legitimating qualifications that no longer served its purposes. In this regard, the conservative's unitary theory was no different than any other. Much as the progressives scooped the Jackson–Lincoln model from its party-based constraints, contemporary conservatives have scooped the progressive model. Their return to the Constitution expands the domain of unilateral action by exploiting the progressive legacy of national power, administrative capacity, and executive management. Everything else, however, is left behind. As it scoops up the progressive legacy of presidency-centered government, the unitary theory marginalizes the extraconstitutional mechanisms that the progressives had relied upon to surround and regulate a presidency-centered system. Public opinion, pluralism, publicity, openness, empiricism, science, technical expertise, professionalism, administrative independence, freedom of information—all the operating norms and intermediary authorities on which the progressives pegged their faith in a "modern" presidency—are called into question by this appeal back to the formalities of the Constitution. While disillusioned progressives were lamenting the inadequacy of these old nostrums and calling for new forms of institutional restraint, insurgent conservatives were busy crafting an alternative that would render those nostrums irrelevant and further experimentation with constraints unduly intrusive.

THE UNITARY EXECUTIVE AS POLITICS

To leave it at that, however, is to ignore the political paradox at the heart of this construction. On the face of it, the theory of the unitary executive would appear to be as politically self-limiting today as it was in the time of Hamilton. As a rarefied legal brief for the president's unilateral claims to rule, it is not clear why anyone besides the president would support it. If new constructions of presidential power rise to prominence on the heels of major reform insurgencies, how are we to credit a construction so indifferent to matters of collective control? How does an ideologically charged political movement maximize its leverage in a democratic polity by enclosing power within an exclusively presidential domain?

Answers to these questions are to be found in the peculiar circumstances in which the conservative insurgency gestated. In the 1970s suspicion of the sprawling bureaucratic state spawned by the progressives, anger at the progressives' repudiation of the Vietnam War, resistance to the progressives' penchant for market regulations, and rejection of their social and cultural permissiveness all came together in a formidable political tide. Richard Nixon's reelection landslide in 1972 amply demonstrated the potential of this new coalition to dominate presidential contests. And yet, in the short run at least, any hope of its gaining control of Congress appeared a pipe dream. American politics entered into a long period in which conservatives were on the offensive ideologically but unable to consolidate their hold on national power. Shorn of an interbranch consensus on foreign and economic policy and faced with the stubborn persistence of divided government, they could anticipate little but frustration for their new national majority.

Context drives theory-building as much as principle. The alterations conservative intellectuals made in the ideational foundations of presidential power followed directly from the political circumstances they were facing. The return to formalism in defense of expansive presidential prerogatives facilitated programmatic action in the absence of an overarching political consensus; a unitary executive promised to ease the way to the political reconstruction of a divided polity.[68] The quest for unity, which since the time of Jefferson had prompted political solutions to the problem of constitutional divisions, now prompted a constitutional solution to the problem of political divisions.

Like all previous constructions, this one played to the political strengths of the insurgent movement behind it. Conservatives could not but notice that the progressives' main stipulation for the release of presidential power—a clear public voice—had come to present a daunting standard. In effect, they seized upon the instrument in hand—a presidency-centered government—to advance an alternative. The new construction sought unity in the executive because there was little prospect of institutional collaboration or political cooperation across the branches. It demanded strict administrative subordination to the will of the president because the ideal of administration in service to government as a whole had grown hollow. It was cast as a lawyer's brief because the new insurgents, unlike previous ones, saw no final victory on the horizon; they anticipated a future of ongoing political division, institutional confrontation, and, ultimately, judicial intervention.[69]

The political context also offered something of a democratic defense for the conservatives' assault on collective control, and it was on this count perhaps that the legacy of progressivism was most deeply implicated. It is not just that the presidency-centered government built by the progressives made it easier to imagine incumbents resourceful enough to reconstruct priorities on their own. At least as important was the fact that progressives had raised the political profile of presidents, foisting them on the public and charging them to act as spearheads of a "continual process of internal reformation." Most important of all was the fact that the progressives' reconstruction of American government had fallen short by its own standards of democracy. With the exposure of interest group control of the progressives' bureaucratic networks, the idea of "enlightened administration" lay exposed.[70] The stage was set for another great reversal, another redirection of presidential power against the auxiliary instruments that had previously justified it. A populist attack on the power of overbearing intellectuals, independent media, and irresponsible bureaucrats was now of a piece with the traditional demand of all insurgencies to reclaim government for the people. It justified the release of presidential power within the executive branch as a restoration of responsibility and accountability in government. All the conservatives needed to do to tap the cause of democracy was to constitutionalize the public voice, to tie the notion that the president is the only officer in American government who represents the nation as a whole more closely to the notion that the selection of the president had become, in effect, the only credible expression of the public's will. Once the public voice was fused more tightly to the will of the incumbent, extraconstitutional controls could be rejected as inconsistent with democratic accountability, and the vast repository of discretionary authority over policy accumulated in the executive branch could be made the exclusive province of the incumbent.

The Nixon administration anticipated at a practical level what the new theory would soon seek to elevate as a standard of rule. Although he was quick to remind his critics of precedents from his progressive predecessors for everything he sought to do, President Nixon was also acutely aware of the very different circumstances in which he was invoking them: he was acting in a government otherwise controlled by his political opponents; there was no cohesive national sentiment on which to base expansive claims to power; his was a "silent" majority. Faced with these circumstances and emboldened by his lopsided victory in 1972, Nixon tapped the historical development of presidency-centered government to sharpen the argument for presidential independence and to press forward on his own with a transformation of American government and politics. Using many of the tools already available, he worked to undercut institutions put in place to foster interbranch collaboration and collective control. The statutory offices of the EOP were downgraded by compromising their neutrality and negating their promise of cooperative action.[71] At the same time, the president enhanced his own governing capacities. He concentrated resources in the White House Office itself and extended the political supervision of the White House deeper into the permanent bureaucracy.[72] When asked what was to prevent a president so empowered from overreaching, Nixon invoked the retroactive sanction of voters: "A President has to come up before the electorate."[73] Here then was a clear road map showing how to move away from the idea of governing more collectively *through* the presidency toward the idea of governing more exclusively *within* the presidency.

The key assertions in what would become the unitary theory of the executive circulated through the conservative movement in the tumultuous years between the precipitous collapse of the Nixon presidency at the hands of the political enemies he so feared and the capitulation of George H. W. Bush to a Democratic Congress on the signal conservative issue of taxes in the budget agreement of 1990. In this period of persistent political division and stiff institutional resistance to the conservative turn, arguments were elaborated in and around the White House for the firmer subordination of executive power to presidential will. The Ford presidency, installed by appointment rather than election, directed administration insiders to new consideration of the formal powers of the executive and how they might be sustained in the face of a suspicious and resurgent Congress.[74] The basic ideas were already in place by the time Rep. Richard Cheney instigated the minority report of the congressional investigation into the Iran-contra affair.[75] Terry Eastland responded to the perceived capitulation of George H. W. Bush to Congress by broadening and sharpening the case for independent executive action.[76] The subsequent extension of the conservative movement through the national legal establishment disseminated these arguments and linked them to potent political and intellectual networks.[77] When the contested election of 2000 robbed George W. Bush of a popular endorsement for his ambitious political agenda, a theory was ready at hand to shift the ground for programmatic action further onto the formal vesting of power, and legal counsel in the White House and Justice Department provided the necessary applications. The new dispensation was encapsulated rhetorically in 2008 when an interviewer asked Vice President Cheney about the tide of public opinion rising against Bush administration war policies. His quick retort—"So?"[78]—was a pointed rejection of the assumption of informal, external claims on the exercise of presidential power.

Had the programmatic ambitions of the conservative insurgency not met such stubborn resistance for so long, it would be harder to credit its heavy investment in the exclusivity of presidential control. As it is, the unitary theory has become a high-stakes gamble that leaves movement priorities no more secure than the next election. More awkward still is the theory's pretension to upholding constitutional intent, for its personalization of executive powers now threatens to render the whole of modern American government more volatile.[79] When the notion of a presidential stewardship is stripped of progressive provisions for collective oversight by the nation's *prudentes,* when the notion of a politicized bureaucracy is stripped of Jacksonian provisions for collective oversight by locally based parties, when the notion of a concert of power is stripped of Jeffersonian provisions for collective oversight by Congress, when the extraconstitutional ballast for presidential government is all stripped away and the idea is formalized as fundamental law, the original value of stability in government is all but eclipsed. It is this confounding of constitutional ideals in the name of restoring constitutional principles that alerts us, in the final analysis, to just how distorting the cumulative effects of construction have become.

THE POWER NEXT TIME

The ideological impetus behind a new construction of presidential power is incidental to its long-term significance. Though candidate Obama rejected the unitary theory, President Obama selectively incorporated practices it serves to authorize. Though President Donald Trump is no conservative stalwart, he has nonetheless embraced unilateralism to erase much of Obama's legacy. This chapter has taken a broad view of the politics of construction. It has situated the unitary theory within the long sequence of prior constructions and considered the dynamics that have driven that sequence forward. In thinking about where things stand today and about how best to move ahead, the critical issue is not whether the theory of the unitary executive is right or wrong, but how, and with what consequence, ideas about presidential power have traveled through time.

The turning points in the politics of construction have each been marked by widespread disillusionment with the extraconstitutional mechanisms for collective oversight previously put in place to ease the system of checks and balances and empower the president. The congressional caucus eventually became "King Caucus"; local party leaders eventually became the "bosses"; enlightened administrators eventually became petty bureaucrats presiding despotically over independent fiefdoms. All told, the various supplemental devices improvised to qualify presidential empowerment were eventually recast as intolerable blockages to programmatic change. The fact that insurgent movements have expended great energy displacing those devices and renouncing the norms they supported is, if nothing else, an indication that their significance historically has been more than merely cosmetic.

Gutting the mechanisms devised by the prior construction to keep presidential power accountable is part and parcel of the broader repudiation of older political priorities conveyed by new reform movements. Breaking prior restraints appears in the course of events as a democratic act, a confirmation of the capacity of the people to remake their government for a new day. But each insurgency has also built on its predecessor's handiwork, selectively appropriating and transposing the case for enhanced presidential power. The result is a ratcheting up of claims; presidential power leapfrogs constraints by expanding on the back of newly established baselines. The Jacksonians elaborated upon the Jeffersonian idea of empowerment through a mandate from the people so as to dispense with the extraconstitutional mechanisms the Jeffersonians had put in place to secure presidential deference to the authority of Congress. The progressives elaborated upon the Jacksonian idea of the superiority of the presidency as an instrument for representing the public interest so as to dispense with the extraconstitutional mechanisms the Jacksonians had put in place to secure presidential deference to local party organizations. Conservatives have recently elaborated on the progressives' notion of presidency-centered government so as to dispense with the extraconstitutional mechanisms the progressives had put in place to ensure presidential deference to the nation's *prudentes*. Power accumulates through these selective appropriations because there is much that is familiar in the new ideas being advanced; the familiar ideas lend plausibility to the new and ease the discarding of the rest. Progressive opposition to the unitary theory, like Federalist opposition to Jefferson, has been compromised from the get-go by its own deep complicity in the construction of a more expansive presidency.

Constitutional construction is an American political tradition—perhaps *the* American political tradition. It is at the core of the successful adaptation of American government to the changing circumstances of its operation. But in the case of the presidency, as in other aspects of constitutional government where construction has been piled upon construction, the interpretive standards grow increasingly opaque. Little seems certain or secure when a presidency-centered system of government built on the rejection of formalism and originalism is consolidated in the name of formalism and originalism, or when the fruits of democracy's claims against limits are redeployed to limit democracy's claims. Coming up with new ideas for the deployment of presidential power is now a lot easier than coming up with new ideas about how to hold that power to account.

It may seem odd in such a circumstance to caution against a rush back to the safety of the Constitution, but that is exactly what a developmental analysis does. The sequence of change has altered quite profoundly the practical meaning of any return to original principles. A developmental analysis suggests that contemporary advocates who claim the Constitution as safe, familiar, and wholly adequate ground on which to venture a further expansion of executive prerogatives are, in fact, elevating a form of personal power that is neither restorative nor well anchored. By the same token, a developmental analysis suggests that contemporary critics of presidential power are unlikely to get very far with their own appeal back to the Constitution. Ever since the rise of parties in the nineteenth century, democratic reformers have been seeking ways to ease checks and balances, and the mechanisms they have developed have so altered the operations of American government that reaching back to the formal rules of mutual containment and urging Congress to reclaim its rightful role hardly seems a practical option.

Development is a stern taskmaster. Hard as it may be, the work of inventing supplemental systems of control—democratic forms of accountability operating alongside the formal apparatus of the Constitution and capable of keeping pace with the expanding reach of presidency—cannot be abandoned. A developmental analysis tells us that the informal political mechanisms improvised in one period to enhance the accountability of a newly empowered executive are unlikely to suffice in the next. It also assures us that, unlike the mechanisms of the Constitution, these less formal improvisations can be replaced when they no longer serve their purpose. Above all else, a developmental analysis should caution us not to mistake the apparent exhaustion of the supplements on hand for the absence of any need for supplements. There is no substitute for the invention of new and effective responses to the riddle of empowerment and control.[80] The time has long past when reclaiming the wisdom of the Framers was a straightforward proposition. If nothing else, the return to formal constitutional debates over the scope of presidential power has shown us that. The surer path to a secure future is one that follows the example of the institution builders who transformed American government in the nineteenth and twentieth centuries. They did not resist new claims of presidential power, but neither did they accept them before staking out fresh claims of their own.

NOTES

1. The original version of this paper was published as "The Conservative Insurgency and Presidential Power: A Developmental Perspective on the Unitary Executive," *Harvard Law Review* 122 (June 2009): 2070–2103. The paper has been altered for this volume.
2. John Taylor, *Construction Construed and Constitutions Vindicated* (New York: Da Capo Press, [1820] 1970), 23.
3. Ibid.
4. Clinton Rossiter, ed., *The Federalist* no. 48 (New York: Penguin, 1999), 306; Charles Rossiter, ed., *The Federalist* no. 71 (New York: Penguin, 1999), 432. On enduring tensions in relations between presidents and political movements, see Sidney M. Milkis, "The President in the Vanguard: Lyndon Johnson and the Civil Rights Insurgency," in *Formative Acts: American Politics in the Making,* ed. Stephen Skowronek and Matthew Glassman (Philadelphia: University of Pennsylvania Press, 2007), 269; Elizabeth Sanders, "Presidents and Social Movements: A Logic and Preliminary Results," in Skowronek and Glassman, eds., *Formative Acts,* 223; Daniel J. Tichenor, "Leaders, Citizenship Movements, and the Politics Rivalries Make," in Skowronek and Glassman, eds., *Formative Acts,* 241.
5. See John P. MacKenzie, *Absolute Power: How the Unitary Executive Theory Is Undermining the Constitution* (New York: Century Foundation Press, 2008), 1–4, 31–62; James P. Pfiffner, *Power Play: The Bush Presidency and the Constitution* (Washington, DC: Brookings Institute Press, 2008); Steven E. Schier, "George W. Bush and Washington Governance: Effective Use of a Self-Limiting Style," *The Forum* 6, no. 2 (2008), http://www.bepress.com/forum/v016/iss2/art2/.
6. See, e.g., MacKenzie, *Absolute Power,* 5–11; Curtis A. Bradley and Martin S. Flaherty, "Executive Power Essentialism and Foreign Affairs," *Michigan Law Review* 102, no. 4 (2004): 545–688; A. Michael Froomkin, "The Imperial Presidency's New Vestments," *Northwestern University Law Review* 88, no. 4 (1994): 1346; A. Michael Froomkin, "Still Naked After All These Words," *Northwestern University Law Review* 88 (1994): 1420; Lawrence Lessig and Cass R. Sunstein, "The President and the Administration," *Columbia Law Review* 94, no. 1 (1994): 1–123; Kevin M. Stack, "The President's Statutory Powers to Administer the Laws," *Columbia Law Review* 106, no. 2 (2006): 263–323; Louis Fisher, Jack Rakove, John Yoo, and Gordon Silverstein, "The Imperial Presidency and the Founding," discussion at the University of California, Berkeley, September 19, 2008, video available at http://www.youtube.com/watch?v=w1qGDeAZ9-w.

7. By the same token, after Obama took office some conservatives began to distance themselves from the theory's broad claims of presidential prerogative. See http://m .motherjones.com/mojo/2012/11/john-yoo-american-enterprise-institute-execu tive-power.

8. On the Progressives' critique of constitutional rigidities and the rejection of "Constitution worship," see, for example, Herbert Croly, *The Promise of American Life*, ed. Arthur M. Schlesinger Jr. (Cambridge, MA: Belknap Press of Harvard University Press, 1965), 200; and Woodrow Wilson, *Congressional Government*, ed. Peter Smith (Cleveland, OH: World Publishing, 1973), 215.

9. James MacGregor Burns, *Presidential Government* (Boston: Houghton Mifflin, 1965), 309–351.

10. On this oft-noted reversal, see, for example, James Risen, "The Executive Power Awaiting the Next President," *New York Times,* June 22, 2008, § 4 (Week in Review), 4; Sam Tanenhaus, "Sidebar: When Reining in an Imperial President Was the Conservatives' Cause," *New York Times,* June 22, 2008, § 4 (Week in Review), 4.

11. See James Burnham, *Congress and the American Tradition* (Eastford, CT: Martino Fine Books, [1959] 2011); Alfred de Grazia, *Republic in Crisis: Congress against the Executive Force* (Carmel, NY: Federal Legal Publications, 1965); Willmoore Kendall, "The Two Majorities," *Midwest Journal of Political Science* 4, no. 4 (1960): 317–345; G. Patrick Lynch, "Protecting Individual Rights through a Federal System: James Buchanan's View of Federalism," *Publius* 34 (Fall 2004): 153.

12. See, e.g., Steven G. Calabresi, "Some Normative Arguments for the Unitary Executive," *Arkansas Law Review* 48, no. 23 (1995): 45–70; Steven G. Calabresi, "The Vesting Clauses as Power Grants," *Northwestern University Law Review* 88 (Summer 1994): 1377; Steven G. Calabresi and Saikrishna B. Prakash, "The President's Power to Execute the Laws," *Yale Law Journal* 104 (December 1994): 541, 570–599; Steven G. Calabresi and Kevin H. Rhodes, "The Structural Constitution: Unitary Executive, Plural Judiciary," *Harvard Law Review* 105, no. 6 (1992): 1153–1216; see also John Yoo, *The Powers of War and Peace: The Constitution and Foreign Affairs after 9/11* (Chicago: University of Chicago Press, 2005); John Yoo, *War by Other Means: An Insider's Account of the War on Terror* (New York: Atlantic Monthly Press, 2006).

13. See generally Morton G. White, *Social Thought in America: The Revolt against Formalism* (New York: Viking, 1949).

14. See Alexander Hamilton, *Pacificus, No. 1* (June 29, 1793), reprinted in *Classics of American Political and Constitutional Thought,* vol. 1, ed. Scott J. Hammond, Kevin R. Hardwick, and Howard L. Lubert (Indianapolis, IN: Hackett Publishing, 2007), 634, 636.

15. William H. Harbaugh, "The Constitution of the Theodore Roosevelt Presidency and the Progressive Era," in *The Constitution and the American Presidency,* ed. Martin L. Fausold and Alan Shank (New York: SUNY Press, 1991), 63, 67; see ibid., 66–68.

16. *Theodore Roosevelt, An Autobiography* (New York: Da Capo Press, 1985), 380; ibid., 371–372, 379–380.

17. See Keith E. Whittington, *Political Foundations of Judicial Supremacy: The Presidency, the Supreme Court, and Constitutional Leadership in U.S. History* (Princeton, NJ: Princeton University Press, 2007), xi, 14–18; Walter F. Murphy, "Who Shall Interpret? The Quest for the Ultimate Constitutional Interpreter," *The Review of Politics* 48, no. 3 (1986): 401, 411–412.

18. Steven Calabresi and Christopher Yoo, *The Unitary Executive* (New Haven, CT: Yale University Press, 2010), 245.

19. See, e.g., Henry Adams, *History of the United States of America during the Administrations of Jefferson and Madison* (Upper Saddle River, NJ: Prentice Hall, [1891] 1963), 78.

20. See Jeremy D. Bailey, *Thomas Jefferson and Executive Power* (New York: Cambridge University Press, 2007), 18.

21. See Bruce Ackerman, *The Failure of the Founding Fathers* (Cambridge, MA: Harvard University Press, 2005), 5–6, 9, 22; Sidney M. Milkis and Michael Nelson, *The American Presidency: Origins and Development 1776–2002* (Washington, DC: CQ Press, 2003), 103.

22. For a discussion of the nominating caucus, see M. Ostrogorski, "The Rise and Fall of the Nominating Caucus, Legislative and Congressional," *American History Review* 5, no. 2 (1899): 253, 263–264. Ostrogorski may exaggerate the efficiency of this system, but he nicely captures contemporary understandings of its departure from original constitutional assumptions. See also C. S. Thompson, "An Essay on the Rise and Fall of the Congressional Caucus as a Machine for Nominating Candidates for the Presidency" (New Haven, CT: Yale University, 1902); William G. Morgan, "The Decline of the Congressional Nominating Caucus," *Tennessee Historical Quarterly* 24 (1965): 245.

23. See Wilfred E. Binkley, *President and Congress* (New York: Vintage, 1962), 67–80; James Ceaser, *Presidential Selection: Theory and Development* (Princeton, NJ: Princeton University Press, 1979), 101–106, 118–119; Richard P. McCormick, *The Presidential Game* (New York: Oxford University Press, 1982), 76–163.

24. See Stephen Skowronek, *The Politics Presidents Make* (Cambridge, MA: Belknap Press, 1997), 130–154.

25. See McCormick, *The Presidential Game,* 164–206; Milkis and Nelson, *The American Presidency,* 130; Martin Shefter, "Party, Bureaucracy, and Political Change in the United States," in *Political Parties,* ed. Louis Maisel and Joseph Cooper (Washington DC: CQ Press, 1978), 211, 218–225.

26. See Gerald Leonard, "Party as a 'Political Safeguard of Federalism': Martin Van Buren and the Constitutional Theory of Party Politics," *Rutgers Law Review* 54 (Fall 2001): 244–276.

27. See Leonard D. White, *The Jacksonians: A Study in Administrative History, 1829–1861* (New York: Macmillan, 1954), 558.

28. Senator A. H. Bailey, Speech at the Republic Party Convention Held at Rome, New York, September 26, 1862, in "Proceedings of the Republican Party Convention Held at Rome, New York," *Utica Morning Herald,* September 27, 1862, 5. Available online at http://digital.library.cornell.edu/cgi/t/text/text-idx?c=nys;idno=nys592.

29. "Proceedings of the Republican Party Convention," 11.

30. With the eclipse of the Federalist Party as a serious competitor in presidential elections, the caucus nomination became, de facto, a selection of the next president. See sources cited in note 22.

31. See, e.g., Matthew Josephson, *The Politicos, 1865–1896* (New York: Harcourt, Brace, 1938), 3–315; E. E. Schattschneider, *Party Government* (New York: Rinehart and Co., 1942), 170–186.

32. Sidney M. Milkis, *Theodore Roosevelt, the Progressive Party, and the Transformation of American Democracy* (Lawrence: University Press of Kansas, 2009); Sidney

M. Milkis and Daniel J. Tichenor, "'Direct Democracy' and Social Justice: The Progressive Party Campaign of 1912," *Studies in American Political Development* 8, no. 2 (1994): 282, 289–298.

33. See Eldon J. Eisenach, *The Lost Promise of Progressivism* (Lawrence: University Press of Kansas, 1994), 8–47; Marc Stears, *Progressives, Pluralists, and the Problems of the State: Ideologies of Reform in the United States and Britain, 1909–1926* (New York: Oxford University Press, 2002), 52–87.

34. See Sidney M. Milkis, *The President and the Parties: The Transformation of the American Party System since the New Deal* (New York: Oxford University Press, 1993), 98–124; see also Stephen Skowronek, *Building a New American State: The Expansion of National Administrative Capacities 1877–1900* (Cambridge: Cambridge University Press, 1982).

35. See, e.g., Charles A. Beard, *An Economic Interpretation of the Constitution of the United States* (New York: Free Press, [1913] 1935), original 913; J. Allen Smith, *The Spirit of American Government,* ed. Cushing Strout (Cambridge, MA: Belknap Press of Harvard University, 1965); Wilson, *Congressional Government.*

36. Herbert Croly, *Progressive Democracy* (New Brunswick, NJ: Transaction, [1914] 1998), 145–148; see also Eisenach, *The Lost Promise of Progressivism,* 73, 216, n. 56 (quoting Croly).

37. Charles E. Merriam, *New Aspects of Politics,* 3rd ed. (Chicago: University of Chicago Press, 1970), 58.

38. See Beard, *An Economic Interpretation of the Constitution of the United States.*

39. See Howard Gillman, "The Collapse of Constitutional Originalism and the Rise of the Notion of the 'Living Constitution' in the Course of American State-Building," *Studies in American Political Development* 11 (Fall 1997): 191.

40. Woodrow Wilson, *Constitutional Government in the United States* (New Brunswick, NJ: Transaction, 1908), 68–71.

41. Henry James Ford, *The Rise and Growth of American Politics* (New York: Macmillan, 1898), 292–293.

42. Charles A. Beard, *American Government and Politics,* 5th ed. (New York: Macmillan, [1910] 1930), 100.

43. Croly, *The Promise of American Life,* 136.

44. Ibid., 168.

45. See James W. Ceaser, Glen E. Thurow, Jeffrey Tulis, and Joseph M. Bessette, "The Rise of the Rhetorical Presidency," in *Rethinking the Presidency,* ed. Thomas Cronin (Boston: Little, Brown, 1982), 243–246.

46. See generally Theodore J. Lowi, *The Personal President: Power Invested, Promise Unfulfilled* (Ithaca, NY: Cornell University Press, 1985).

47. Croly, *The Promise of American Life,* 213–214.

48. The notion of "parastate" institutions comes from Eldon Eisenach. See Eisenach, *The Lost Promise of Progressivism,* 18. See also Donald T. Critchlow, "Think Tanks, Antistatism, and Democracy: The Nonpartisan Ideal and Policy Research in the United States, 1913–1987," in *The State and Social Investigation in Britain and the United States,* ed. Michael J. Lacey and Mary O. Furner (New York: Cambridge University Press, 1993), 279; Michael J. Lacey, "The World of the Bureaus: Government and the Positivist Project in the Late Nineteenth Century," in Lacey and Furner, eds., *The State and Social Investigation,* 127. See generally Lacey and Furner, eds., *The State and Social Investigation.*

49. Charles E. Merriam, "Political Prudence" in Merriam, *New Aspects of Politics,* 3rd ed. (Chicago: University of Chicago Press, 1970), 246.

50. Ibid., 254.

51. Ibid., 258.

52. Ibid., 262.

53. See, for example, the retrospective assessment of original purpose in Don K. Price and Rocco C. Siciliano, "Revitalizing the Executive Office of the President," in Cronin, ed., *Rethinking the Presidency,* 305, 305–307, as well as the argument that the EOP should be structured to encourage institutional cooperation in Hugh Heclo, "OMB and Neutral Competence," in *The Managerial Presidency,* 2nd ed., ed. James P. Pfiffner (College Station: Texas A&M University Press, 1999), 131. Also, J. Bradford De Long, "Keynesianism, Pennsylvania Avenue Style: Some Economic Consequences of the Employment Act of 1946," *Journal of Economic Perspectives* 10 (Summer 1996): 50.

54. See John Hart, *The Presidential Branch: From Washington to Clinton,* 2nd ed. (Chatham, NJ: Chatham House, 1995), 52–53, 68–69; Stephen Hess, *Organizing the Presidency* (Washington, DC: Brookings Institution, 1976), 53–55.

55. Richard Neustadt, *Presidential Power: The Politics of Leadership* (New York: John Wiley and Sons, 1960), 33.

56. See generally Theodore J. Lowi, *The End of Liberalism: Ideology, Policy, and the Crisis of Public Authority* (New York: W. W. Norton, 1969); Milkis, *The President and the Parties;* Arthur M. Schlesinger Jr., *The Imperial Presidency* (New York: Popular Library, 1973).

57. Lowi, *The Personal President;* see also Arthur M. Schlesinger Jr., *Journals, 1952–2000* (New York: Penguin Press, 2007), 260.

58. See generally Louis Fisher, *Presidential War Power,* 2nd ed. (Lawrence: University Press of Kansas, 2004); Milkis, *The President and the Parties;* Jeffrey K. Tulis, *The Rhetorical Presidency* (Princeton, NJ: Princeton University Press, 1982).

59. Yoo, *The Powers of War and Peace,* 5.

60. Andrew Rudalevige, *The New Imperial Presidency: Renewing Presidential Power after Watergate* (Ann Arbor: University of Michigan Press, 2005), 211–285.

61. In a similar spirit, see David K. Nichols, *The Myth of the Modern Presidency* (University Park: Pennsylvania State University Press, 1994).

62. See Harvey C. Mansfield Jr., *Taming the Prince: The Ambivalence of Modern Executive Power* (New York: Free Press, 1989); Forrest McDonald, *The American Presidency: An Intellectual History* (Lawrence: University Press of Kansas, 1994), 9–97; Nichols, *The Myth of the Modern Presidency,* 139–161; see also Benjamin A. Kleinerman, "Can the Prince Really Be Tamed? Executive Prerogative, Popular Apathy, and the Constitutional Frame in Locke's Second Treatise," *American Political Science Review* 101 (May 2007): 209; Sheldon S. Wolin, "Executive Liberation," *Studies in American Political Development* 6, no. 1 (1992): 211, 211–216 (reviewing Mansfield, *Taming the Prince*).

63. Steven Calabresi and Christopher Yoo, *The Unitary Executive* (New Haven, CT: Yale University Press, 2010), 30–36; see also Yoo, *The Powers of War and Peace,* 30–142 (discussing these early developments with respect to the president's foreign affairs power).

64. See Hadley Arkes, "On the Moral Standing of the President as an Interpreter of the Constitution: Some Reflections on Our Current 'Crises,'" *PS* 20, no. 3 (1987): 637.

65. *Register of Debates in Congress* 10 (December 1833): 84–85 (statement of Sen. Henry Clay); Richard J. Ellis and Stephen Kirk, "Presidential Mandates in the Nineteenth Century: Conceptual Change and Institutional Development," *Studies in American Political Development* 9, no. 1 (1995): 117, 152–153.

66. William Howard Taft, *Our Chief Magistrate and His Powers* (New York: Columbia University Press, 1916).

67. Ibid., 140.

68. Instructive on this point is Daryl J. Levinson and Richard H. Pildes, "Separation of Parties, Not Powers," *Harvard Law Review* 119, no. 8 (2006): 2311.

69. See, e.g., Phillip J. Cooper, *By Order of the President: The Use and Abuse of Executive Direct Action* (Lawrence: University Press of Kansas, 2002), 201–203 (describing the Reagan administration's strategic thinking about signing statements).

70. See Lowi, *The End of Liberalism.*

71. See, e.g., Hugh Heclo, *A Government of Strangers* (Washington, DC: Brookings Institution Press, 1977), 78–80.

72. See generally Richard P. Nathan, *The Administrative Presidency* (New York: John Wiley and Sons, 1983); Richard P. Nathan, *The Plot that Failed* (New York: John Wiley and Sons, 1975). Note the Nixon-era breakpoints in the organization history as reviewed in Hart, *The Presidential Branch,* 1–147; see also Heclo, *A Government of Strangers,* 13, 75; and Karen M. Hult and Charles E. Walcott, *Empowering the White House* (Lawrence: University Press of Kansas, 2004), 166–172.

73. Christopher H. Pyle and Richard M. Pious, *The President, Congress, and the Constitution* (New York: Free Press, 1984), 74 (quoting interview by David Frost with Richard Nixon [May 19, 1977]).

74. See generally James Mann, *The Rise of the Vulcans: The History of Bush's War Cabinet* (New York: Penguin, 2004) (exploring the formative years of some Bush administration officials in the Nixon and Ford administrations).

75. See Minority Report, in *Report of the Congressional Committees Investigating the Iran-Contra Affair,* H.R. Rep. No. 100–433, S. Rep. No. 100–216 (1987).

76. See Terry Eastland, *Energy in the Executive: The Case for the Strong Presidency* (New York: Free Press, 1992); see also L. Gordon Crovitz and Jeremy A. Rabkin, eds., *The Fettered Presidency: Legal Constraints on the Executive Branch* (Washington, DC: American Enterprise Institute, 1989) (responding to the frustrations of the late years of the Reagan administration).

77. See generally Steven M. Teles, *The Rise of the Conservative Legal Movement* (Princeton, NJ: Princeton University Press, 2008).

78. Interview by Martha Raddatz with Richard Cheney, vice president of the United States, in Muscat, Oman, March 19, 2008, ABC News, http://abcnews.go.com/politics/story?id=4481568.

79. See Jeremy D. Bailey, "The New Unitary Executive and Democratic Theory: The Problem of Alexander Hamilton," *American Political Science Review* 102, no. 4 (2008): 453.

80. Bruce Ackerman sketches a new set of institutional arrangements to restore accountability to the post-progressive presidency in *The Decline and Fall of the American Republic;* Eric Posner and Adrian Vermeule argue, in contrast, that although the Constitution does not control the president and never has, the political controls on hand are sufficient to hold it accountable. (See *The Executive Unbound: After the Madisonian Republic.*)

THE PRESIDENCY IN HISTORY

Leading from the Eye of the Storm

Sidney M. Milkis and Marc Landy

Although they were written more than two centuries ago, America's founding documents, the Declaration of Independence (1776) and the Constitution (1787), have consistently remained the touchstones of American political development. What keeps these documents relevant, argue Marc Landy and Sidney M. Milkis, are the occasional "refoundings" that certain presidents have wrought in how Americans interpret and apply the documents in changing times. Four presidents in particular—Thomas Jefferson, Andrew Jackson, Abraham Lincoln, and Franklin Roosevelt—each initiated a constitutional refounding by waging a "conservative revolution," which Landy and Milkis define as "a new constitutional teaching, albeit one steeped in the American political tradition."

To properly place the presidency in the context of American political development, three questions are paramount. First, and most fundamentally, how have presidents understood the meaning of executive power and what have been the critical controversies with other branches over conflicting interpretations of that meaning? Second, what role has the president played in the critical episodes that have transformed the American political and constitutional order? Finally, in what ways does the contemporary presidency differ from, and in what ways does it remain the same as, the office envisaged by the Framers?

PRESIDENTIAL POWER AND CONSTITUTIONAL REFOUNDINGS

The president is both the embodiment of the national government and the country's leading political figure. In a sense, this has always been so. In their effort to establish self-government on a grand scale, the architects of the Constitution created the need for such a figure. Alexander Hamilton praised Article II for the way it summoned individuals of great ambition to the office. "The love of fame, the ruling passion of the noblest minds," he wrote in *The Federalist* No. 72, will "prompt a man to plan and undertake extensive and arduous enterprises for the public benefit."[1]

Hamilton's constitutional justification for granting the president sweeping discretionary power rested in the distinction between how the Constitution vests authority in the legislature and how it vests power in the executive. Article I, Hamilton pointed out, states that "all legislative Powers herein granted shall be vested in a Congress of the United States," while Article II does not restrict executive power in that way: "The executive Power shall be vested in a President of the United States of America." The absence of the words "herein granted," he argued, meant that the executive power is both wide ranging and vested exclusively in the president, "subject only to the exceptions and qualifications expressed in the Constitution." This constitutional language, Hamilton insisted, merely confirmed the nature of executive power, which was indispensable to the success of a large and diverse republic.[2]

George Washington put this broad understanding of executive power into practice, establishing a precedent that presidents have followed ever since. In 1793 Washington issued the Neutrality Proclamation, which announced that the United States would not join in the hostilities then taking place between France and Great Britain. Thomas Jefferson and James Madison considered Washington's unilateral executive action to be unconstitutional. A declaration of neutrality was, in effect, a declaration that there should be no war—a decision that rightfully belonged to Congress. To claim that such action was constitutional, Madison argued, was to imply that the executive had a legislative power. Such an argument was "in theory an absurdity—in practice a tyranny."[3]

Hamilton dismissed Madison's view and insisted that in the absence of a declaration of war by Congress the executive had full authority to proclaim and enforce American neutrality. Executive power, he insisted, included the president's duty to take all actions needed to preserve the nation's security unless specifically precluded from doing so by the Constitution. Although political scientists and constitutional scholars are still debating this broad question, Washington did declare neutrality, Congress did not contradict him, the country remained at peace, and the power of the president to act unilaterally in emergency circumstances was affirmed.

Much of the conflict between Congress and the president, which has erupted repeatedly in the course of American history, stems from the broad reading of executive power that many presidents have claimed as their own. Jefferson's purchase of Louisiana, which seemed to defy his opposition to executive aggrandizement;

Lincoln's suspension of habeas corpus; Franklin D. Roosevelt's prewar provision of military aid to Great Britain and the Soviet Union; Ronald Reagan's sale of arms to Iran and provision of arms to the Nicaraguan contras; George W. Bush's authorization of unwarranted electronic surveillance; and Barack Obama's efforts to protect large numbers of undocumented immigrants from deportation are prominent examples of actions by presidents who exercised their prerogative in the face of considerable opposition from Congress.

Indeed, support for a sweeping executive power can be found among both defenders and opponents of the Constitution. Hamilton spoke for the Federalists' interpretation of the Constitution, which emphasized that the president is the principal "guardian of the people's interests." As he wrote in *The Federalist Papers,* "when occasions present themselves in which the interests of the people are at variance with their inclinations," the president has the "duty . . . to withstand the temporary delusion in order to give them time and opportunity for cool and sedate reflection."[4] But even the Anti-Federalists, most of whom considered Hamilton's formula for executive guardianship a recipe for despotism, acknowledged the important role the president would play in holding together a large and diverse society. Their hope was that the president would nurture a sense of patriotism, a vital principle of self-government that would be hard to establish in a large republic. In the words of the Federal Farmer, "In every large collection of people there must be a 'first man,'" a "visible point serving as a common center of government, towards which to draw their eyes and attachment."[5] George Washington, recognized widely by Federalists and Anti-Federalists alike as the "first man in America," made perhaps his most important contribution to the presidency by serving as this "visible point" of attachment.[6]

Thomas Jefferson developed this idea of "first citizen" into a more capacious view of popular leadership. During his presidency he argued that the executive was justified in operating outside the law as long as it provided the people with standards for judging its actions. Indeed, when linked securely to popular opinion, the executive would embody American democracy. As Jefferson stated in his first inaugural address, only the president could "command a view of the whole ground" and thus deserved the people's "support against the errors of others, who may condemn what they would not if seen in all its parts."[7]

In short, the essence of the so-called modern presidency, which most scholars associate with the deployment of national administrative power in the name of the people, was there from the beginning. Both Hamilton and Jefferson—the great rivals for the constitutional soul of the American people—prescribed an executive who, when circumstances dictated, could act beyond the law. And even Hamilton, who, as Jeffrey Tulis claims, appeared to "proscribe popular leadership," recognized that the Constitution's celebration of "We, the People" would subject the president to the court of public opinion.[8] As he wrote in defending the unitary, or one-person, executive,

> The plurality of the executive tends to deprive the people of the two greatest securities they can have for the faithful exercise of any delegated power, *first,* the restraints of public opinion, which lose their efficacy [to] censure . . . on

account of the uncertainty on whom it ought to fall; and *second,* the
opportunity of discovering with facility and clearness the misconduct of
the person they trust, in order either to their removal from office or to their
actual punishment in cases which admit of it.[9]

Significantly, it was Hamilton's mentor, Washington, who ensured that the
president had the right to speak directly to the people by issuing a Thanksgiving
Proclamation, not to Congress, but to the people directly. Indeed, in the face of the
bitter partisanship aroused by the Neutrality Proclamation, Hamilton and his political allies organized a series of mass meetings throughout the country to generate
public support for the president's policy.[10]

That the seeds of the modern presidency were there from the start casts doubt
on the notion that the presidency, as James Sterling Young has claimed, originally
was meant to restrict itself to the constitutional obligation, stated explicitly in
the oath of office, "to preserve, protect, and defend the Constitution."[11] Stephen
Skowronek's view of the office is more complex and paradoxical but also more
credible. Those elected president swear both "to preserve, protect, and defend the
Constitution," which requires them to affirm the existing order of things, and
"to execute the office of the President of the United States," which presupposes
their independent intervention in political affairs. This dual obligation creates a
strong executive, but one in the grips of a dilemma: it is "a governing institution
inherently hostile to inherited governing arrangements."[12] As an institution that
bridles against order, Skowronek argues, the executive summons not the guardians of ordered liberty whom Hamilton prized, but rather the ambitious characters
Lincoln describes in his Lyceum Address: they are members of the "family of the
lion, or tribe of the eagle," who disdain the well-worn path of constitutional government (or any existing path) and seek to use executive power to remake politics
and government in their own image. This is true of not just "reconstructive presidents" (who create enduring governing regimes) and "preemptive presidents" (who
seek to operate independently of the reigning political order), but also those "loyal
sons" who express allegiance to a regime's founder. All presidents, even regime loyalists, are intent on "shattering order."[13]

Yet throughout history presidents have been restrained by constitutional norms,
the separation and division of powers, and political parties. Some presidents, in
fact, have strongly resisted allegiance to the prevailing regime, not to "shatter" the
existing order but to moderate its excesses in the name of constitutional sobriety.
Despite the temptation to expand executive power unduly, presidents who have
defined themselves as institutional conservatives—most notably, Grover Cleveland,
William Howard Taft, Calvin Coolidge, and Dwight Eisenhower—deserve careful attention, if for no other reason than their critical warnings about the perils
of executive aggrandizement. It is especially important to consider these alarms
today—a time when recent presidents have broken free of constitutional and partisan constraints.

Even presidents who have left the most indelible marks on the American political order have not simply engaged in "creative destruction." They exerted leadership
during major episodes of American political development that were truly conservative

revolutions. These "refoundings" required presidents to think constitutionally: to interpret the meaning of the Declaration of Independence, the Constitution, and the relationship between the two for their own time. Lincoln's call for a joining of the principles of the Declaration and the Constitution in a form that condemned slavery to extinction is the most famous. But all of America's most consequential presidents—Jefferson, Jackson, Lincoln, and Franklin D. Roosevelt—have justified regime change in terms of fundamental principles and constitutional norms.

Beyond rhetoric, America's refoundings have been collective engagements. Presidents have been at the center of the storm, but they have not created new regimes on their own. Perhaps most important, regime building has required extraordinary party leadership. To be sure, political parties have not always constrained presidential ambition. Indeed, all of the presidents who instigated regime change were either founders or refounders of political parties. In important respects, as Skowronek suggests, these reconstructive presidents used their parties to remake American politics in their own image. But extraordinary party leadership serves mostly to highlight the collective nature of great political transformations. Political parties have kept presidents faithful to broader interests, even as, episodically, they have given presidents the political strength to embark on ambitious projects of national reform. Moreover, prior to the New Deal, none of the programs that formed the core of a new political regime called for a substantial expansion of executive power.

To dismiss the conventional view of the modern presidency is not to deny that distinctively modern attributes mark the contemporary executive. One such feature involves the decline of the idea of limited constitutional government during the course of the twentieth century. The first to question the idea of limits on the ends and means of government were the Progressives. Theodore Roosevelt, in particular, was dismissive of "parchment barriers" that stood in the way of implementing the people's will. The New Deal prescribed a new understanding of rights that erased many of the traditional impediments to deploying the federal government in the public's service. The use of the federal government by the Great Society to dismantle the ramparts of Jim Crow–style racial segregation further embellished centralized administration. The "steward of the public welfare," as Theodore Roosevelt famously described the modern executive, became the principal object of the public's heightened expectations about what the national government could and should accomplish.

Another characteristic that defines the contemporary presidency is the executive aggrandizement that has followed from the nation's being on a war footing since the start of World War II. Previously, wars were of limited duration and military mobilization was followed by demobilization. As commander in chief, the president has power and responsibilities that expand drastically in time of war. The Cold War lasted from the end of World War II to the late 1980s. The War on Terror began in earnest in 2001 and showed no signs of abating, even as the Obama administration wound down the country's military missions in Iraq and Afghanistan. The iconoclastic mogul Donald Trump's improbable and startling ride to the White House was propelled by an "America First" message that promised to disengage the United States from many of its international entanglements, most notably its "obsolete" commitment to NATO, and to vastly reduce, if not end, the nation's military presence in Afghanistan and Iraq. Yet President Trump abandoned much of this neo-isolationist platform during his first year in office, declaring that he "strongly supported NATO," authorizing the secretary of defense to intensify the war in Afghanistan, and maintaining American troops in Iraq.[14]

The final part of this chapter examines how the president's essential, uneasy place in the American constitutional order has been transformed by the expanded reach of federal public policy and by the permanent war footing on which the country has been placed. The rise of an executive-centered administrative state has strengthened the national government's capacity to ameliorate massive economic dislocations at home and to protect the "homeland" from international terrorism. At the same time, this development has weakened constitutional constraints on presidents and aroused "populist" assaults from the right and the left that have sharpened political conflict and rattled national resolve.

DEMOCRATIZING THE CONSTITUTIONAL PRESIDENCY

Washington and John Adams were republicans. They acknowledged that the people were the ultimate source of authority, but they believed that the preservation of liberty required checks on popular rule. Jefferson was a democrat. He believed that the primary defense of liberty was not constitutional checks and balances, but majority rule. In response to questions posed by the French encyclopedist Jean Baptiste Meusnier, Jefferson proudly replied, "This . . . [is] a country where the will of the majority is the law, and ought to be the law."[15]

Thomas Jefferson began and Andrew Jackson completed a major reinterpretation of the meaning of executive power. Their view of the president as the tribune of the people was an essential component of the conservative revolutions they wrought.

Jefferson's View of the Presidency

As Washington understood, the manners adopted by the president are extremely important because they tell the public how it should envisage "the first man." To emphasize the democratic aspect of the presidency, Jefferson jettisoned the presidential coach and rode his own horse. He ignored distinctions of rank at official functions. He dressed in ordinary attire.

But Jefferson's revision of the presidency was more about substance than style. As Jeremy Bailey has demonstrated, Jefferson accepted the expansive view of presidential power put forth by Hamilton but added three critical elements, each of which promoted its democratic aspect. First, the president unifies and thereby embodies the will of the nation. In Jefferson's mind the president was not just the "first man" but, as the only government official elected by the nation as a whole, he was also the instrument of the national will. Second, although Jefferson agreed with Hamilton and Washington that the president must sometimes act outside the law, or even against it, to serve the public good, he insisted that the president must be held accountable for doing so. Once the emergency had passed, it was the president's duty to submit to the people's judgment. Indeed, Jefferson believed that such accountability extended to all presidential actions. Third, the president had to provide a basis for this accountability by explaining to the people what he was proposing to do and why it was in their best interest. Such declarations provided the people with the information and standards of evaluation they needed to judge him adequately.[16]

As the author of the Declaration of Independence, Jefferson relied, not surprisingly, on declarations to explain his views to the people. His first declaration as president was his first inaugural address, which remains his most important presidential utterance. Although the address is most famous for its conciliatory statement that "we are all republicans, we are all federalists," its greatest importance lies in the clear declaration of how Jefferson conceived of his office and what he pledged to accomplish through it. Unlike his predecessors, whose inaugural addresses were perfunctory, Jefferson used his to lay out what he took to be the essential principles of government—"those which ought to shape its administration." He listed fourteen such principles, including three that lie at the heart of democratic government: equal justice for all, free and fair elections, and majority rule. Jefferson admitted that he would make errors of judgment in his fervent efforts to promote democracy, but he also warned that others would misjudge his rightful efforts because their "position will not command a view of the whole ground." Thus, Jefferson implied that only the president, by virtue of his election by the whole nation, commands such a view and can speak authentically for the people as a whole.[17] Jefferson's statement of principles also provided the people with a checklist against which to judge his performance. Because they understood what he intended to do, they could decide whether he succeeded or failed.

Unlike Hamilton, Jefferson never claimed that the vesting clause of Article II gave him sweeping powers; he simply acted as if it did. Lincoln would later assert that the oath of office required him to act against the letter of the Constitution in order to preserve it. Jefferson offered no explicit constitutional rationale for his actions. The most momentous act of his presidency was the Louisiana Purchase, which he admitted, privately at least, was unconstitutional.[18] The Constitution makes no provision for the acquisition and incorporation of new territory. But Jefferson purchased the vast Louisiana territory anyway. John Quincy Adams and others argued that the enormity of the land acquired amounted to a full-fledged "dissolution and recomposition" of the Republic and therefore required a constitutional amendment.[19] Jefferson seemed to agree, but he stopped calling for an amendment after receiving reports that Napoleon Bonaparte was having second thoughts about the deal. Jefferson feared that the prolonged amendment process would give the French ruler time to renege.[20]

Instead, Jefferson relied on a declaration in his second inaugural address to defend the merits of the Louisiana Purchase. The Purchase's great expansion of territory would not endanger the Republic because the federative principle embodied in the Constitution—the idea of a large republic divided into sovereign states—would prevent any such threat. Jefferson borrowed from Madison's *The Federalist* No. 10 to argue that "the larger our association the less will it be shaken by local passions." He also argued that national security dictated the Purchase: "Is it not better that the opposite bank of the Mississippi should be settled by our own brethren and children than by strangers of another family? With which should we be most likely to live in harmony and friendly intercourse?"[21] Unlike Washington and, later, Lincoln, Jefferson chose not to defend his right to take this fateful action but instead defended the action itself. It would then be up to the people to determine whether his extraconstitutional action merited their censure.

Jackson's View of the Presidency

Andrew Jackson viewed himself as a disciple of Jefferson, but he expanded Jefferson's understanding of executive power in vital ways. Most importantly, he reconciled Jefferson's democratic understanding of the executive with Washington's conception of the president as defender of the Union. Although Jefferson had invoked national security as a rationale for the Louisiana Purchase, he never renounced the states' rights convictions that, prior to his presidency, had impelled him to draft the Kentucky Resolutions. In his mind the Constitution was a compact among the states that left each state considerable power to resist dictates from the national government. Thus the Kentucky Resolutions urged the states to find some means to challenge the odious Alien and Sedition Acts that Congress passed during the Adams administration.[22]

Jackson shared Jefferson's preference for decentralized government, but he also showed greater respect for his oath of office. When South Carolina claimed the right to nullify a tariff bill that Congress had passed and he had signed, Jackson issued a proclamation stating that no state could defy a legitimate act of Congress and that he would suppress this act of rebellion.[23] Lincoln's successful resistance to secession would have been far more difficult but for the precedent Jackson established.

Jackson's defense of limited government also relied on energetic executive action. He turned the veto power into a potent democratic weapon. With few exceptions, previous presidents, including Jefferson, had used the veto only when they determined that Congress had acted unconstitutionally. Jackson extended its use to include any legislation that he opposed. He vetoed more bills than all six previous presidents combined. His rationale was that since, like Jefferson, he saw himself as the embodiment of the will of the people, he was entitled, even obligated, to use his powers of office to serve that will to the fullest extent possible. The Constitution placed no conditions on the president's use of the veto. Therefore, Jackson's democratic duty was to use it whenever doing so was to the people's benefit.[24]

Conservative Revolutions

Both Jefferson and Jackson placed their democratic understanding of executive power at the service of the conservative revolutions they led. Their radical commitment to majority rule was tempered by a conservative understanding of the proper role of government in a regime dedicated to inalienable individual rights. Jefferson was acutely aware that the greatest threat to those rights was posed by government. It was therefore of critical importance that the president spearhead the campaign to defeat initiatives to enhance the power of the central government, regardless of how benign the purposes of those initiatives might be. Indeed, the most dangerous government encroachments were those that promised to enhance the lives of the people, because they had the greatest seductive power.

A great deal of Jefferson's presidency aimed at repealing Federalist policies that he believed had undermined liberty. By the end of Jefferson's first year in office, Congress had abolished all internal taxes, including the tax on spirits that had sparked the Whiskey Rebellion. Tariffs and the sale of public lands thus became the sole sources of federal revenue, and Congress dedicated a good portion of those funds to paying off the federal debt, further reducing the monies available to fund government activities. Despite this vast reduction in available revenue, Congress reduced spending so much that the government ran a surplus during seven of Jefferson's eight years in office.[25]

Because of Jefferson's commitment to the "federative principle," the Louisiana Purchase did not lead to an aggrandizement of national power. As the habitable portions of the vast territory became populated, the settlers were encouraged to organize territorial governments as a first step to acquiring statehood. An "empire of liberty," the president believed, would be created, consisting of state governments that would resist any effort by the federal government to expand its power.[26]

Paradoxically, Jackson's strengthening of executive power coincided with a renewed commitment to Jefferson's assault on centralized power. In the intervening years between their administrations, many limits on federal activity had been relaxed. A second Bank of the United States had been established, and financial support for public improvements had increased. Jackson vetoed the bill to recharter the national bank, arguing that it served to entrench economic privilege and was detrimental to the well-being of ordinary people.[27] He adopted a literal interpretation of the Constitution's commerce clause and was therefore willing to fund only those public improvements that were unambiguously interstate in character. Jackson vetoed Congress's appropriation for the Maysville Road because, even though it was part of the interstate Wilderness Road, the Maysville portion fell entirely within the Commonwealth of Kentucky.[28]

The Jacksonian era was more than Jefferson redux. Jackson launched a conservative revolution of his own, the key to which was his political party. Jefferson was the first president to serve simultaneously as party leader. Indeed, the Republican Party that he and Madison created was indispensable to his election and to his program of limited government. But Jefferson, like most of the Founding generation, detested political parties. He hoped that, after it succeeded in restoring constitutional balance, the Republican Party would wither away. For the most part it did. With the demise of the Federalists, one-party rule evolved into no-party rule. In 1820 James Monroe ran for reelection unopposed. The definition of "Republican" became so capacious as to include the son of a Federalist president, John Quincy Adams, whose commitment to an activist federal government was much more akin to Hamilton's than to his adopted party's own founder, Jefferson.

Strongly influenced by Martin Van Buren, Jackson came to see that a Jeffersonian restoration would require a new form of politics. A political party was not a one-time remedy to a one-time problem. The temptation to use government to support economic privilege was ineradicable. The less vigilant and informed the public, the greater the advantages that would accrue to the privilege seekers. Only an active political party could maintain the ongoing level of public concern and mobilization necessary to keep government neutral in the competition for scarce economic goods. To accentuate their commitment to popular political involvement as the key to thwarting the despotism of the rich, Jeffersonian Republicans who were rallied by Jackson and Van Buren gave themselves a new name: the Democrats.

The key to the development of the Democratic Party was the so-called spoils system. The Jacksonian Democrats argued that the government belonged to the people, and therefore no one should consider public office to be an entitlement.[29] The people gave the offices, and the people could take them away. As instruments of the people, the Democrats would award government posts to those who subjected themselves to party discipline and remove them from office if they failed to obey such discipline. Thus the system both promoted popular participation by encouraging the hope of gaining office and promoted democratic accountability by enabling party leaders to remove those who failed to do the people's bidding.

The spoils system also sustained the decentralized nature of party politics. When state and local party leaders demanded offices as their reward for rallying voters to the national ticket in congressional and presidential elections, even powerful presidents were not inclined to refuse them. Moreover, to keep their jobs, many federal officeholders, particularly those who served in the widely scattered customhouses and post offices, were required to return part of their salaries to the local party organization that sponsored their office, to do party work, and to "vote right" on Election Day. In this way, decentralized Jacksonian parties imitated the "federative principle" of the government, with lines of authority reaching up and down from the local to the state to the national party. This highly decentralized and mobilized party system provided a connection between the ordinary citizen and the various levels of government that had been absent in the years of no-party rule.

Thus the presidency emerged from the era of Jefferson and Jackson newly empowered. Jefferson's and Jackson's efforts regarding the Louisiana Purchase and nullification, respectively, showed that they would not retreat from Washington's assertion that the president wielded emergency powers. Furthermore, their understanding of themselves as instruments of the popular will caused them to expand the scope of presidential leadership. They would serve as legislative leaders, fighting for new laws that served the public interest and, in Jackson's case, vetoing those that did not. And they would be party leaders, mobilizing and disciplining the collective efforts on which the success of their democratically inspired efforts depended. But this expansion of presidential power was constrained by the end it was meant to serve: limited constitutional government. Both Jefferson and Jackson saw limited government as the essential safeguard of liberty. Their commitment to small government, reinforced by decentralized parties, was the most important check on presidential power because it constrained any excesses of personal ambition that might arise among Jackson's successors.

LINCOLN AND THE CIVIL WAR REFOUNDING

The Civil War refounding is perhaps the most important of America's political transformations. For the leadership he displayed in fostering what he famously termed a "new birth of freedom," Abraham Lincoln won the lasting esteem of the American people as one of their finest presidents. Scholars have shared this celebration of Lincoln's statesmanship. Yet during his rise to power and throughout his presidency, Lincoln was subjected to ridicule, and even as he gained respect for navigating the uncharted waters of emancipation and a full-scale domestic rebellion, he was frequently charged with being a despot. Even Lincoln's greatest champions have granted that he went beyond the normal bounds of presidential power during the Civil War. Lincoln's bold actions, however, like Jefferson's and Jackson's, did not expand executive power enduringly. Although he espoused a more positive understanding of liberty than these two predecessors, the reform program that Lincoln championed was still bounded tightly by the nation's long-standing commitment to natural rights, limited government, and administrative decentralization.

Indeed, Lincoln was highly critical of the expansion of presidential power wrought by Jackson and his Democratic successors. His invocation of "the family of the lion" and the "tribe of the eagle" in the 1838 Lyceum Address can only be understood as an attack on the Democratic Party's aggrandizement of executive power in peacetime. This was not merely a rhetorical flourish. In the mid-1840s, Lincoln's devotion to settled, standing law informed his opposition to Jackson's protégé, James K. Polk, for initiating and prosecuting the war with Mexico. As a Whig member of the House of Representatives, Lincoln argued that the Constitution gave the "war making power to Congress" and that "the will of the people should produce its own result without examining executive influence."[30]

Nor did Lincoln give any indication that he had abandoned his Whig principles during his rise to political prominence in the Republican Party during the 1850s. To the contrary, as he stated in the Lyceum Address, Lincoln feared that the slavery controversy had made greater the danger of demagogy. "It thirsts and burns for distinction," he said of executive ambition, "and if possible, it will have it, whether at the expense of emancipating the slaves, or enslaving free people."[31] The Republican Party that Lincoln represented in the 1860 presidential election consisted mostly of former Whigs who, like Lincoln, were dedicated to undoing the Jacksonians' expansion of executive power.

Lincoln's rise to power—unlike that of Jefferson, the celebrated author of the Declaration, and Jackson, whose initial fame was born of military glory—was tied inextricably to partisan loyalty and maneuver. Close attachment to his party constrained, even frustrated, Lincoln at times. Just the same, his partisanship provided an indispensable connection to political allies around the country. In no small measure, Lincoln's success stemmed from his extraordinary party leadership. His involvement in party politics both reinforced the conservative nature of the Civil

War refounding and ensured that his stewardship, as remarkable as it was, did not expand presidential power in a way that would survive in peacetime.

Lincoln, the Slavery Controversy, and the Constitution

The challenge for Lincoln and the Republican Party in trying to resolve the slavery controversy was to find a constitutional path between the Abolitionists, who celebrated the Declaration's claim that "all men were created equal," and southern leaders such as Chief Justice Roger Taney—the author of the notorious *Dred Scott* decision—who believed that the Constitution sanctified slavery as a right of property. Just as the fiery abolitionist William Lloyd Garrison condemned the Constitution as "a covenant with death and an agreement with hell," so did slave hounds such as Taney and even the more moderate Democratic senator from Illinois, Stephen Douglas, wish to confine the freedoms of the Declaration to whites. Lincoln and the GOP sought to escape this conundrum by forging a dynamic relationship between the Declaration and the Constitution that provided opportunities to fulfill America's creed constitutionally as soon as practical circumstances allowed.

A national debate over slavery exploded with the enactment of the 1854 Kansas-Nebraska Act. Sponsored by Douglas, Lincoln's main political rival, and supported by Democratic president Franklin Pierce, the act repealed the Missouri Compromise of 1820 and gave the Kansas and Nebraska territories a choice about whether to allow slavery. Although it passed Congress because of Pierce's heavy-handed use of patronage, it was justified publicly as a logical extension of the Democrats' commitment to local self-government because the voters of each territory would decide whether they should enter the Union as a free or slave state. In his debates with Lincoln during the 1858 Illinois Senate race, Douglas justified northern Democrats' defense of "popular sovereignty" on the grounds that the United States had been "formed on the principle of diversity in the local institutions and laws, and not on that of uniformity . . . [e]ach locality having different interests, a different climate, and different surroundings, required different laws, local policy, and local institutions, adopted to the wants of the locality."[32]

Born of local protest meetings aroused by the Kansas-Nebraska Act, the new Republican Party insisted that Douglas's position defiled the Declaration. Lincoln mocked the idea that "if one man would enslave another, no third man should object," insisting that it was the height of hypocrisy to call that position "popular sovereignty." Proclaiming his "reverence for the constitution and laws," Lincoln conceded that the national government had no power to interfere with slavery where it already existed. But he was unwilling to tolerate extending it to the territories, which would undermine the moral foundation of American constitutional government. Drawing on a verse from the Bible's Book of Proverbs—"A word fitly spoken is like apples of gold in pictures of silver"—Lincoln praised the Declaration's principle of "liberty to all" as the essence of American political life. "The assertion of this principle, at the time," he added, "was the word 'fitly spoken' which has proven an 'apple of gold' to us. The Union, and the Constitution, are the pictures of silver, subsequently framed around it. The picture was made, not to conceal, or destroy the apple, but to adorn and preserve it."[33]

Lincoln and the Republicans claimed that they, not the Democrats, were the rightful heirs of Thomas Jefferson because, in tolerating the expansion of slavery by linking popular sovereignty with the infamous Kansas-Nebraska Act, the Democrats had forsaken their Jeffersonian heritage. Indeed, Lincoln insisted that Jefferson had given form to the Framers' opposition to the expansion of slavery into the territories by drafting the Northwest Ordinance of 1787, which banned slavery in the five states—Ohio, Michigan, Indiana, Wisconsin, and Illinois—that composed the Northwest Territory. Prohibiting slavery's expansion into the territories, therefore, was true to the principles of the Declaration, as well as to the proper understanding of the Constitution. Equally important, with the enactment of the Missouri Compromise, which prohibited slavery from expanding into the northern part of the Louisiana Territory, this policy became a public doctrine shared by a majority of Americans. Lincoln wanted to restore the Missouri Compromise, not only for the sake of the Union but also for the "sacred right of self-government" and the "restoration of national faith."

The honor Lincoln bestowed on Jefferson was limited, however. He emulated his old foe, Jackson, in believing that the Constitution drew a sharp line between states' rights, which were constitutional, and nullification, which was not. By the time of Lincoln's inauguration, South Carolina and six other southern states—Georgia, Alabama, Mississippi, Florida, Louisiana, and Texas—had seceded. Following Jackson's example, Lincoln used his inaugural address to pronounce the secessionist movement as treasonous: "I hold that in contemplation of universal law and of the Constitution of the Union of these states is perpetual . . . , that no state upon its own mere notion can lawfully get out of the Union." Lincoln declared that he would defend and preserve the Union by enforcing federal laws in all the states, just as the Constitution enjoined him to do.[34]

Moreover, Lincoln reinterpreted the Declaration to invest the Union with a moral—even religious—purpose that gave rise to a new, more positive understanding of liberty. As Daniel Walker Howe has observed, Lincoln's Gettysburg Address transmuted "the proposition that all men are created equal [into] a positive goal for political action, not simply a pre-political state that government should preserve by inaction."[35] The authors of the Declaration, Lincoln maintained, "did not mean to assert the obvious untruth, that all were actually enjoying that equality, nor yet, that they were about to confer it immediately upon them. They meant simply to declare the *right,* so that *enforcement* of it might follow as fast as circumstances should permit." The principles of the Declaration, therefore, were to be "constantly looked to, constantly labored for, and even though never perfectly attained, constantly approximated."[36]

Lincoln gave more concrete expression to this new view of liberty in his address to the special session of Congress that convened on July 4, 1861. The Union's struggle, he told Congress, was to maintain that "form and substance of government, whose leading object is, to elevate the conditions of men—to lift artificial weights from all shoulders—to clear the paths of laudable pursuit for all—to afford all, an unfettered start, and a fair chance in the race of life."[37]

The Great American Crisis and Lincoln's Wartime Measures

Lincoln's greatest challenge and opportunity was to stay faithful to this purpose in the face of the most dangerous emergency the country has ever faced. His artful joining of the Declaration and Constitution seemed to promise a moderate position toward slavery and a limited role for the president in resolving the issue. As the *Chicago Tribune* editorialized in boosting Lincoln for president early in 1860, "He has the radicalism which a keen insight into the meaning of the anti-slavery conflict is sure to give; but, coupled with it, that constitutional conservatism which could never fail in proper respect for existing institutions and laws, and which would never precipitate or sanction innovations more destructive than the abuses that they seek to correct."[38] Yet the outbreak of Civil War led Lincoln to suspend his constitutional conservatism. As soon as secession became violent and irrevocable, he believed, his oath to uphold the Constitution allowed—even compelled—him to take extraordinary measures, including emancipating the slaves, in order to restore the Union.

From the day after the rebels bombarded Fort Sumter on April 12, 1861, until Congress convened on July 4, everything that Lincoln did to protect the Union and prosecute the war was done on his own authority. Some of his actions, such as mobilizing 75,000 state militia, were clearly within the proper bounds of the president's constitutional authority. Yet Lincoln went well beyond these bounds. Hoping to bring the insurrection to a speedy end, he ordered a naval blockade of the southern coast, enlarged the army and navy (adding 18,000 men to the navy and 22,000 to the army), and suspended the writ of habeas corpus in northern and border states, where rebellious activity was high. This suspension empowered government officials who were acting under the president's authority to make arrests without warrant for offenses undefined in the laws without having to answer for their actions before the regular courts.

Many of Lincoln's measures raised grave doubts about the constitutionality of his prosecution of the war. His unauthorized enlargement of the military seemed to disregard blatantly Congress's clear constitutional power "to raise and support Armies." The president's critics also argued that because the power to suspend the writ of habeas corpus during a national emergency appears in Article I of the Constitution, which defines the authority of the legislature, the right to exercise the power belongs to Congress. Moreover, Lincoln claimed sweeping powers not only to arrest and detain those who were suspected of rebellious activity, but also to try them before military tribunals. Lincoln was the first president to authorize the use of these tribunals, which operated outside the rules of evidence and other codes of judicial conduct governing civilian courts.

Lincoln's conception of the president's responsibility to suppress treasonous activity justified both the suspension of habeas corpus and the establishment of martial law in many areas of the country. Indeed, as the Civil War progressed, Lincoln proclaimed even more comprehensive powers for the military authorities, without any apparent thought of seeking congressional authorization. For example, on September 24, 1862, he issued an executive order declaring that all rebels and insurgents and all persons who discouraged enlistment in the Union army, resisted the draft, or engaged in any disloyal practice were subject to martial law and to trial by either a court-martial, which observes rules of evidence similar to those observed by civilian courts, or a military tribunal. This order provoked sharp controversy in the North. It added to the unrest aroused by the draft, which was imposed for the first time during the Civil War. In July 1863 draft riots broke out in New York City, sparking the greatest civil disorder in the nation's history, save for the Civil War itself. Yet resistance to the draft only served to convince Lincoln that military justice and the suspension of habeas corpus were necessary, not only where the war was being fought but also in some peaceful regions of the country.

Lincoln did not assume these extraordinary powers lightly, but only when he believed that his oath of office gave him no choice. As he wrote in an 1864 letter to the Kentucky newspaper editor Albert G. Hodges, domestic rebellion imposed on him an obligation to use "every dispensable means" to "preserve the nation, of which the Constitution was the organic law." It was senseless, Lincoln argued, to obey legal niceties while the very foundation of the law was threatened:

> Was it possible to lose the nation and yet preserve the Constitution? By general law, life and limb must be protected, yet often a limb must be amputated to save a life; but a life is never wisely given to save a limb. It felt that measures otherwise unconstitutional might become lawful by becoming indispensable to the preservation of the nation.[39]

Not surprisingly, the severity of Lincoln's war measures prompted charges of "military dictatorship," even from some Republicans, and has remained the source of considerable debate and controversy. The distinguished presidential scholar Clinton Rossiter described Lincoln's conduct as a "constitutional dictatorship," an apparent contradiction in terms that was meant to capture Lincoln's impressive, if not fully persuasive argument that constitutional government has an unqualified power of self-preservation and that this power was centered in the office of the president. Although Lincoln's use of power during this supreme crisis was eminently defensible, Rossiter warned, it might set a damaging precedent. "If Lincoln could calmly assert: 'I conceive that I may, in an emergency, do things on a military ground which cannot constitutionally be done by Congress,'" Rossiter concluded, then "some future President less democratic and less patriotic might assert the same thing."[40]

Lincoln as Party Leader

Lincoln's crisis presidency was not undertaken *uno solo,* as Rossiter claims. Instead, it was linked to an understanding of the country's constitutional heritage and to a political party dedicated to upholding that heritage. As president-elect, Lincoln strongly resisted any compromise of his party's campaign pledge to prevent the expansion of slavery in the territories. When word leaked that Congress was considering Kentucky senator John J. Crittenden's plan to extend slavery into the Southwest, Lincoln intervened to defeat it. To surrender, under threat, what Lincoln defined as the Republican bedrock would betray those voters who supported the party in the 1860 election. Republicans in Congress agreed. William

H. Seward, the former governor of New York, who was Lincoln's chief rival for the Republican presidential nomination, instigated talk of a negotiated settlement, but not a single Republican legislator voted for the Crittenden plan.[41]

Once in office, Lincoln attended to party-building measures that would "bring to life the political philosophy the Republican Party espoused." In the nineteenth century, patronage was central to the task of transforming a political party into an effective instrument of national unity. Lincoln removed Democrats from practically every appointed office they held, and he took full advantage of the enormous growth of government demanded by the war to amplify the effect of patronage appointments. The president prudently distributed these positions to supporters of the leading Republicans in the cabinet and Congress. By letting his fellow partisans who represented the competing Republican factions influence patronage, Lincoln ensured that a range of party opinions would be heard. Equally important, joining patronage to the objective of Republican unity inserted party loyalists into every level of government. These political friends included scores of Republican newspaper editors, who were awarded government publishing contracts and positions in government offices. "Editors seem to be in great favor with the party in power," the *Baltimore Evening Patriot* noted, "a larger number of the fraternity having received appointments at its hands than probably under any administration."[42]

In selecting and managing his cabinet, Lincoln also displayed a studied attention to party unity. He appointed Seward as secretary of state not merely to assuage a disappointed rival but also because Seward was a gradualist who prescribed patient acceptance of slavery until the ineluctable advance of nationalism and commercialism gradually extinguished it. Just as Seward represented former Whigs' respect for constitutional formalism, so Salmon Chase of Ohio, whom Lincoln named as secretary of the Treasury, stood for the more vigorous antislavery position in the party. Like Lincoln, Chase viewed the Declaration of Independence as the guiding light of the Constitution. But Chase was more committed than Lincoln to accelerating emancipation, even at the price of weakening constitutional forms. His appointment to the cabinet gave radical Republicans greater confidence that the president's resolve to prevent the expansion of slavery would not waver.

The presence of Seward and Chase created a contest in the cabinet. As each side struggled for Lincoln's favor, the administration risked being paralyzed by continuous bickering between competing party factions. But this was a risk that Lincoln was willing to take to ensure that diverse elements of the newly formed Republican Party would feel included in the administration's counsels. When the tension between Seward and Chase became the center of a great cabinet crisis in late 1862, Lincoln managed the dispute masterfully, maintaining the loyalty of both statesmen and the constituencies they represented. "Lincoln's cabinet represented an ever uneasy alliance, which is why it required so much of his attention," Eric McKitrick wrote. "But in the very process of managing it he was, in effect, at the same time managing the party and fashioning it into a powerful instrument for waging war."[43]

That Lincoln skillfully made the Union's war effort a collective endeavor helps explain the strong support that Congress gave to his controversial emergency actions after the attack on Fort Sumter. In upholding the legality of these actions, the Supreme Court, in the Prize Cases, drew attention to legislation Congress passed on July 13, 1861, to ratify Lincoln's orders.[44] The Court's decision supported Lincoln's claim that his conduct was justified not only by the threat the southern rebellion posed to the public safety, but also by his expectation that Congress eventually would approve what he did. As Lincoln said in his special message to Congress on July 4, 1861, "These measures, whether strictly legal or not, were ventured upon under what appeared to be a popular demand and a public necessity, trusting then as now, that Congress would ratify them. It is believed that nothing has been done beyond the constitutional competency of Congress."[45] The one exception in Congress's expression of support concerned Lincoln's suspension of habeas corpus. But when Congress finally did act in 1863, it created arrangements to supplement (not replace) those that Lincoln had put in place.[46]

In the final analysis, Lincoln's party leadership succeeded because, in spite of the important differences that divided Republicans, they shared a commitment to free-soil principles. Even the Committee on the Conduct of War, the oversight body formed by Congress in January 1862 that is often portrayed as a thorn in Lincoln's side, served the president's ultimate objective of crushing the southern rebellion and abolishing slavery. Lincoln did not cooperate directly with the radical Republicans who controlled this committee, and he sometimes resisted their most zealous abolitionist tendencies. Nonetheless, he allowed his secretary of war, Edwin Stanton, to collaborate with its members in pressuring recalcitrant Union generals, especially George B. McClellan, whose cautiousness in battle and indifference to emancipation frustrated the president.[47]

Lincoln the Emancipator

The importance of Lincoln's party leadership, and its effect on the Constitution, is revealed most clearly in the struggle for emancipation. His issuance of the Emancipation Proclamation on January 1, 1863, appeared to place the abolition of slavery alongside the restoration of the Union as the primary objectives of the war. But the proclamation was a more limited, cautious measure than some Radical Republicans had hoped it would be. It did not emancipate the slaves everywhere; in fact, Lincoln earlier had voided the declarations of two of his generals freeing slaves in captured territory. Instead, Lincoln, who based the proclamation solely on the "war power" and regarded it as a "fit and necessary war measure for suppressing rebellion," abolished slavery only in the unconquered parts of the Confederacy. Significantly, the proclamation also declared that the door was open for African Americans "to be received into the armed forces of the United States."[48] Nearly 200,000 former slaves became Union soldiers, disrupting the South's labor force and converting part of that force into a northern military asset.

Although the Emancipation Proclamation became a critical part of Union war strategy, it neither condemned slavery as immoral nor guaranteed that it would be abolished after the war. Lincoln vetoed the Wade-Davis Bill of 1864, which included sweeping emancipation and Reconstruction measures that he believed the federal government had no constitutional authority to impose on the states. Yet the president realized that to return the emancipated African Americans to slavery would betray the core principle of the Republican Party. When urged to do so by some northern Democrats, who argued that coupling emancipation with restoration of the Union was a stumbling block to peace negotiations with the Confederacy, Lincoln countered that "as a matter of policy, to announce such a purpose, would ruin the Union cause itself."[49] Thus Lincoln's Reconstruction policy, which he announced in December 1863, offered a pardon and amnesty to any white southerner who took an oath of allegiance not only to the Union, but also to all of the administration's wartime policies concerning slavery and emancipation.

Emancipation thereby became, as Lincoln had urged in the Gettysburg Address, an end as well as a means of Union victory. But for this cause to become the foundation of a conservative revolution—a true refounding—it had to be endorsed by a popular election and accomplished through regular constitutional procedures. Jefferson and Jackson were content to oversee a fundamental reinterpretation of constitutional principles. Lincoln, seeking to reconcile popular government with devotion to law, worked to achieve abolition by constitutional amendment. In 1864 he took the lead in persuading the Republican National Convention to adopt a platform pledging that, because slavery was "hostile to the principles of republican government, justice and national safety," the GOP would accomplish its "utter and complete extirpation from the soil of the Republic."[50] In stark contrast, the Democratic candidate, the reluctant General McClellan, opposed the Emancipation Proclamation and wanted the Union to continue fighting only until the presecession status quo could be restored.

Reelected in 1864 by large majorities, Lincoln and other Republican leaders moved to enact the Thirteenth Amendment—the Emancipation Amendment—which the president considered the keystone of the party platform. Lincoln played a critical part in the complicated congressional maneuvers, "intervening more directly in the legislative process than at any other point in his presidency."[51] Once the amendment passed, Congress sent it to Lincoln for his signature. The Constitution does not require presidents to sign constitutional amendments, but legislative leaders somehow forgot that Lincoln's endorsement was not needed.[52] This oversight testifies to the importance of Lincoln as a party leader. That the amendment, which was ratified in 1865, was drafted as a pastiche of the Northwest Ordinance must have given Lincoln special satisfaction because he had been pointing to the earlier document since 1854 as an expression of the Framers' hostility to slavery. Just as surely, the Thirteenth Amendment vindicated Lincoln and his fellow partisans' position that the Republicans, not the Democrats, were the true heirs of Jeffersonian democracy.

Lincoln's disregard for legal constraints on the war power, therefore, went hand in hand with a deep and abiding commitment to the principles and institutions of the Constitution. In his case, popular leadership did not leave a legacy of military dictatorship. Instead, it was dedicated to a conservative revolution—a new constitutional teaching, albeit one steeped in the American political tradition. The Thirteenth Amendment transformed America's scripture, the Declaration of Independence, into a formal constitutional obligation. That obligation was extended by the Fourteenth Amendment, ratified in 1868, which granted all Americans the "privileges and immunities of citizens of the United States," "due process," and "equal protection of the laws." The Fifteenth Amendment, added in 1870, proclaimed that the "right of citizens of the United States to vote shall not be abridged by the United States or any State on account of race, color, or previous condition of servitude."

The three Civil War amendments changed the course of constitutional development and expanded government's obligation to protect the rights of the common citizen. But the political order formed by Lincoln and the Republican Party did not seek to remove all limits on presidential power. Even during the war, Lincoln did not forsake the Whig view of executive power that he had defended in the 1830s and 1840s. Consistent with this view, which most Republicans embraced, Lincoln denied that the president could veto bills merely because he disagreed with them. Only legislation, like the Wade-Davis Bill, that he regarded as unconstitutional would be returned to Congress.[53] He deferred almost entirely to Congress on matters unrelated to the war, "contributing little more than his signature" when Republican lawmakers "created a Department of Agriculture, established land grant colleges, passed the Homestead Act (to encourage western settlement), instituted the national income tax, and erected the legislative framework that would lead to the construction of a transcontinental railroad."[54] As the postwar Republican reformer Carl Schurz wrote of Lincoln,

> With scrupulous care he endeavored, even under the most trying circumstances, to remain strictly within the constitutional limits of his authority; and whenever the boundary become indistinct, or when the dangers of the situation forced him to cross it, he was equally careful to mark his acts as exceptional measures, justifiable only by the imperative necessities of the civil war, so that they might not pass into history as precedents for similar acts in time of peace.[55]

The powers that Lincoln was willing to accumulate as commander in chief during the Civil War freed him to use the executive office energetically. But Lincoln's assassination and his replacement as president by the bigoted Andrew Johnson severely limited the Civil War refounding. The failure of Reconstruction was also attributable to the Republicans' principled opposition to centralized power. That fear formed a critical backdrop to the notorious "Compromise of 1877," which enabled white majorities in southern states to enact segregation laws that prevented the enforcement of the Fourteenth and Fifteenth Amendments and denied African Americans a full share of citizenship. This debased form of local self-determination severely constrained presidential power for the rest of the nineteenth century, so much so that the self-styled modern reformers who emerged at the end of the nineteenth century overwhelmingly viewed party politics as an obstacle to their ambition to construct an executive-centered "modern" state on American soil.

THE NEW DEAL AND THE CONSOLIDATION OF MODERN EXECUTIVE POWER

Like the other presidents who animated America's refoundings, Franklin D. Roosevelt left more than a record of achievement; he also left a constitutional legacy. The New Deal constitutional order consolidated political developments that led to the rise of mass democracy and the expansion of national administrative power. The relationship between state and society would henceforth be negotiated in critical ways by the "modern presidency," a Progressive Era innovation that FDR and his New Deal political allies grafted onto the traditions of natural rights and limited constitutional government that had dominated the polity since the beginning of the nineteenth century. Roosevelt's leadership, like Jefferson's, Jackson's, and Lincoln's, was an indispensable ingredient in a conservative revolution. But the New Deal was the first refounding dedicated to expanding national administrative power and to placing the presidency at the heart of its approach to politics and government. After Roosevelt, this new understanding of executive responsibilities led even conservative Republican presidents to embrace the powers and responsibilities of modern executive leadership.

Redefining the Social Contract

Roosevelt first spoke of the need to modernize elements of the old faith in his Commonwealth Club address, delivered during the 1932 campaign. His theme was that the time had come—indeed, it had come three decades earlier—to recognize the "new terms of the old social contract." It was necessary to rewrite the social contract, FDR argued, to take account of a national economy remade by industrial capitalism and concentrated economic power. This new contract would establish countervailing power in the form of a stronger national state, lest the United States steer "a steady course toward economic oligarchy." Protection of the national welfare must shift from the private citizen to the government. As FDR put it, "The day of enlightened administration has come."[56]

Yet FDR acknowledged that the creation of a national state with expansive supervisory powers would be a "long, slow task." He was sensitive to the uneasy fit between energetic central government and the Constitution. It was imperative, therefore, that the New Deal be informed by a public philosophy in which the new concept of state power would be carefully interwoven with earlier conceptions of American government. The task of modern government, FDR announced, was to assist the development of an "economic declaration of rights, an economic constitutional order."[57] The traditional emphasis in American politics on individual self-reliance—"rugged individualism," as Herbert Hoover put it—must give way to a new understanding of the social contract, in which government guaranteed individual men and women protection from the uncertainties of the marketplace. Government-provided security was to be the new self-evident truth of American political life.

Defending progressive reform in terms of an economic constitutional order was a critical development in the advent of an executive-centered administrative state. Theodore Roosevelt and Woodrow Wilson had anticipated many elements of this argument, but FDR was the first to advocate an ongoing supervisory role for the government that linked this new social contract to constitutional principles. Although Roosevelt's triumph was aided greatly by the economic exigencies of the Great Depression, his deft reinterpretation of the American constitutional tradition was no less important. This reinterpretation went beyond Wilson's New Freedom, which honored decentralized party practices and emphasized initiatives such as antitrust policy and reform activity in the states. FDR's eye was fixed more on his cousin Theodore, who expressed an alternative progressive understanding that envisioned a dominant president serving as the "steward of the public welfare." Theodore Roosevelt's Progressive Party crusade of 1912, which celebrated social justice and the president as the agent of an unvarnished majoritarianism, made an especially strong impression on FDR and his Brains Trust.[58]

FDR called his philosophy "liberalism" rather than "progressivism." He meant to signify that the New Deal would expand rather than subvert the natural rights tradition embedded in the Declaration of Independence. As Roosevelt made clear in the Commonwealth Club address, this new understanding of rights required both a return to and a redefinition of the Declaration, a document in which "rulers were accorded power, and the people consented to that power on consideration that they be accorded certain rights. The task of statesmanship has always been the redefinition of these rights in terms of a changing and growing social order. New conditions impose new requirements upon government and those who conduct government."[59]

Roosevelt reaffirmed the principles of the Commonwealth Club address throughout his presidency. Like Lincoln, FDR believed that this new understanding of the Constitution had to be sanctified by a popular election. He made the "economic constitutional order" the principal message of his first reelection bid in 1936, the decisive triumph that established for a generation the Democratic Party, recast in the New Deal image, as the majority party in American politics. Just as the 1860 and 1864 Republican platforms had celebrated the Declaration as the nation's scripture, so was the 1936 platform, drafted by FDR, written in the cadence of the Declaration, emphasizing the need for a fundamental reconsideration of rights. As the platform claimed with respect to the 1935 Social Security Act: "We hold this truth to be self evident—that government in a modern civilization has certain inescapable obligations to its citizens," among which is the responsibility "to erect a structure of economic security for [its] people, making sure that this benefit shall keep step with the ever increasing capacity of America to provide a high standard of living for all its citizens."[60]

The new idea of rights—for all intents and purposes, a second Declaration—was not forgotten during World War II. Instead, it became a central rhetorical theme in mobilizing public support for America's participation in the struggle. Roosevelt's Four Freedoms speech, which summoned support for the 1941 Lend-Lease Act, also engaged Congress and the people in a debate about America's role in the world. To the traditional freedoms of speech and religion, Roosevelt added the "freedom from fear," dedicated to "a world-wide reduction of armaments to such a point and in such a fashion that no nation will be in a position to commit an act of physical aggression against any neighbor," and the "freedom from want," the commitment "to economic understandings which will secure to every nation a healthy peacetime life for its inhabitants."[61] The four freedoms soon became, as David Kennedy has written, "a shorthand for America's war aim." More to the point, "they could be taken . . . as a charter for the New Deal itself."[62]

The New Deal Constitutional Program

Roosevelt's redefinition of the social contract had an important influence on laws and institutional change. Historians have generally divided FDR's first term into two periods, each identified by a flurry of legislative activity lasting approximately 100 days. The first period (1933–1934) was a response to FDR's call for "bold, persistent experimentation" to meet the great emergency at hand. Among these measures were the Emergency Banking Relief Bill and other legislation establishing the Public Works Administration, the Agricultural Adjustment Administration, and the National Recovery Administration.[63] The second period (1935–1936) brought laws such as the Social Security Act and the National Labor Relations Act that converted emergency programs into ongoing obligations of the national government, beyond the vagaries of public opinion and the reach of elections and party politics. As one New Dealer observed hopefully, "We may assume the nature of the problems of American life are such as not to permit any political party for any length of time to abandon most of the collective functions which are now being exercised."[64]

During his second term, FDR pursued a program to thoroughly reconstruct the institutions and practices of constitutional government in the United States. This program—the Third New Deal—was pursued with the understanding that programmatic rights such as Social Security and collective bargaining would not amount to much unless new institutional arrangements were established that would reorganize the institutions and redistribute the powers of government.[65] The program included three extremely controversial initiatives: the Executive Reorganization Act, the centerpiece of the program, announced in January 1937; the "court packing" plan, proposed a few weeks later; and the so-called purge campaign, attempted during the 1938 Democratic primary elections. These measures' common objective was to strengthen national administrative power. They marked an effort to transform a decentralized polity, dominated by local parties and court rulings that supported property and states' rights, into a more centralized, even bureaucratic, form of democracy that could deliver the goods championed by New Dealers.[66]

Although the New Deal constitutional program was hostile to localized parties, national partisanship was central to the task of "state building." Indeed, Roosevelt and his New Deal allies recognized that the Democratic Party was a critical means to the creation of the administrative constitution they envisioned. New Deal programmatic rights attracted new groups and interests, such as union members, African Americans, and Jews, who became the key constituencies of the new, more programmatic party. Moreover, Roosevelt viewed partisan maneuvers such as the purge campaign as part of a broader endeavor to transform the Democrats into a national, executive-centered party. In fact, the Third New Deal, especially the administrative reform program, which proposed to significantly expand presidential staff support and greatly extend presidential authority over the executive branch, became at FDR's urging a major focus of party responsibility. The purge campaign focused on conservative Democrats, mostly from border and southern states, who had opposed the executive reorganization and court-packing plans.[67]

Roosevelt suffered damaging political defeats in his pursuit of the Third New Deal, galvanizing opposition that contributed to the heavy losses the Democrats sustained in the 1938 congressional election. The court-packing plan in particular served as a lightning rod for FDR's political enemies, spurring a resurgence of congressional independence and the formation of a bipartisan "conservative coalition." The new alliance of Republicans and southern Democrats blocked nearly every major presidential reform initiative from 1937 until the mid-1960s.

Nevertheless, the New Deal did not come to an end in 1938, as many historians and political scientists have claimed. Starting in 1939, FDR rebounded from the defeats he suffered during the first two years of his tempestuous second term and managed to consolidate and institutionalize a political order that reshaped significantly the dynamics of American constitutional government. First, having failed to get his 1937 administrative reform program through Congress, Roosevelt orchestrated the passage of a compromise bill, the Executive Reorganization Act of 1939. Its enactment led to the creation of the Executive Office of the President, including important staff agencies such as the White House Office and the Bureau of the Budget, and enhancing the president's capacity to manage the expanding activities of the executive branch. Consequently, the presidency was no longer merely an office; it was an institution that presidents and their appointees could use to short-circuit the separation of powers. In sum, administrative reforms carried out during the latter part of FDR's second term tended to ratify a process in which public expectations and institutional arrangements established the president, rather than Congress or the political parties, as the principal agent of American democracy.

Second, Roosevelt ran an extraordinary third-term campaign, starting in earnest in the summer of 1938. By then it was clear that FDR's effort to purge conservative Democrats from Congress in a dozen primary contests and replace them with "100% New Dealers" would fail. In contrast to the purge campaign, the bid for a third term was hidden from public view, but it was no less energetic and was perhaps better organized. FDR's shattering of the two-term tradition ratified the subordination of party politics to executive administration. As one aide put it, FDR had "pistol whipped" Democratic Party chieftains into nominating him for a third term and accepting as his running mate Henry Wallace, a militant liberal with virtually no organized support in the Democratic organization. Roosevelt's victory in 1940 ameliorated the bitter defeats the administration suffered during the 1938 elections.

Roosevelt's election to a third term gave him the opportunity to ensure that the New Deal constitutional order would endure. He was able to push through and administer the 1940 Ramspeck Act, which gave him the authority to extend civil service protection to some 200,000 New Deal loyalists who had come to Washington as emergency personnel during his first term to staff the fledgling welfare state. Moreover, Roosevelt remained in the White House to command the nation during World War II. Woodrow Wilson had put business leaders such as Bernard Baruch in charge of industrial mobilization during World War I; in contrast, FDR staffed key wartime positions with New Dealers. With loyalists such as Chester Bowles, who headed the Office of Price Administration, organizing industrial mobilization, "Dr. Win the War" never truly eclipsed "Dr. New Deal." Rather, the New Deal and war effort were melded in such a way as to establish irrevocably the government's responsibility for the welfare of the American people. This synergy was evident in the enactment of the 1944 GI Bill, which entitled veterans to home and business loans, unemployment compensation, and subsidies for education and training.[68]

The Administrative Constitution and Presidential Power

Roosevelt's role in the New Deal refounding surpassed the role played by previous presidents in conservative revolutions. After Roosevelt was elected to a fourth term, death brought his extraordinary stewardship of the nation to an end in April 1945. As Barry Karl has written, FDR's death "set off tremors of disbelief. Caesar was dead." And "whether one feared him as a tyrant or worshipped him as a God," an America without Roosevelt seemed inconceivable.[69] To assure that there would be no more Roosevelts, Republicans and southern Democrats enacted a constitutional amendment that limited future presidents to two terms, the only formal constitutional change that followed in the wake of FDR's path-breaking leadership.

But the New Deal refounding transformed American politics. FDR's constitutional teaching led to a redefinition of the social contract—a new understanding of rights—that caused most Americans to expect that the federal government, with the president in the lead, would remain active in domestic and world affairs. Although Roosevelt bequeathed a stronger executive to his successors than did Jefferson, Jackson, or Lincoln, he did not craft the modern presidency as an imperial office. As a conservative revolution that grafted an activist public philosophy and national administrative apparatus onto a rights-based constitutional system, the New Deal created new obstacles to presidential ambitions. Soon viewed as entitlements, New Deal programs became autonomous islands of power that would constrain presidents no less than natural rights philosophy and localized parties once had. As Martha Derthick has written, the architects of the Social Security program "sought to foreclose the opposition of future generations by committing them irrevocably to a program that promises benefits by rights. . . . In that sense they designed social security to be uncontrollable."[70]

Dwight Eisenhower, the first Republican elected after the New Deal revolution, acknowledged that the new understanding of rights had become an established part of modern American government. When his conservative brother Edgar criticized him privately for carrying on FDR's liberal policies, the president replied bluntly, "Should any political party attempt to abolish social security and eliminate labor law and farm programs, you should not hear of that party again in our political history."[71] In the wake of the New Deal, Oscar Handlin wrote soon after Ike left office, "Eisenhower made palatable to most Republicans the social welfare legislation of the preceding two decades. In the 1950s, the New Deal ceased to be an active political issue and became an accepted part of the American past."[72] Eisenhower also bestowed bipartisan legitimacy on the liberal internationalism practiced by Roosevelt and Harry Truman. He was contemptuous of Republicans—notably, Robert Taft, his main rival for the party's presidential nomination in 1952—who wanted the United States to withdraw into isolation from world affairs.

"Freedom from fear" and "freedom from want"—elaborated as the "Second Bill of Rights"—were not incorporated in a formal constitutional program. Indeed, Roosevelt and most New Dealers were skeptical about the benefits of formal constitutional change. To transform the new understanding of rights into a formal document would deny New Dealers the discretion to administer programs prudently and instead would bind the "economic constitutional order" in a legal straightjacket. Committed to an administrative constitution, the New Deal revolution sought to emancipate the national government from the demands of formal constitutionalism. "The Constitution," FDR insisted in his address celebrating its 150th anniversary, "was not a Lawyers' Contract."[73] It had to be remade so that constitutional policy displaced constitutional obligation.

In the end, however, the administrative constitution did not create the sort of national state that Roosevelt and the architects of the modern presidency had hoped for. Roosevelt's reforms left most New Deal programs exposed to interference not only by Congress and the courts, but also by the interest groups that formed to protect these programs. By the 1970s New Deal liberalism would be condemned as "interest group liberalism," an indictment that inadvertently helped resuscitate conservatism.[74] In the 1980s a serious challenge to the administrative state was mounted by a popular president who was determined to prove that the New Deal had not, after all, "sucked out the meaning of the old slogans of opposition to government activity."[75]

THE POST-NEW DEAL PRESIDENT: THE DISPERSION OF STEWARDSHIP

The national administrative state, forged on the anvil of the New Deal, has remained the dominant reality of American government and politics ever since its creation. "Freedom from want" is still at the core of American domestic policy, and "freedom from fear" remains the dominant principle of American foreign policy. But after FDR, the president's ability to control the administrative state was constrained by Congress, the courts, and a complex maze of private groups representing an ever more diverse set of interests and ideologies. Post–New Deal Democratic presidents from Truman to Barack Obama have enthusiastically embraced the stewardship model of the American presidency, whose roots go back to Jefferson and Jackson and were embellished by the Roosevelts. But FDR's success in expanding the notion of rights and institutionalizing ambitious interventionist policies within the administrative state deprived his successors of their exclusive claim to be the steward of the people. The expanded rights understanding and the enlarged demands of various segments of society for government aid that were born in the New Deal also strengthened the stewardship claims of Congress and the courts. For example, one of the greatest of all postwar policy changes, school desegregation, was initiated by the Supreme Court. Another extremely important innovation, the development of national environmental policy, was initiated by Congress.

The post–New Deal Republican presidents who preceded Ronald Reagan—Eisenhower, Richard Nixon, and Gerald Ford—performed the stewardship role with less enthusiasm than their Democratic counterparts, but pressure from the Supreme Court and Congress pushed them to adopt it. Thus, it was Eisenhower who sent troops to Little Rock to enforce the Supreme Court's desegregation edict. It was Nixon who established the Environmental Protection Agency to enforce the landmark antipollution laws that Congress passed in the early 1970s. Fearful that the Democrats would defeat him for reelection by outbidding his domestic reform agenda, Nixon went so far as to advocate a guaranteed national income and an expanded affirmative action program.

Theodore Lowi coined the term "interest group liberalism" to describe how private associations and their allies in Congress and the bureaucracy exploited New Deal policies to seize control of specific policy realms. Organized labor gained control of labor policy, farmers of farm policy, and advocates for the poor of the War on Poverty. The president had very little say about how these sectors were governed. He lost control of them to the tight-knit coalitions of members of Congress, permanent civil servants, and lobbyists that formed around each domain of public policy.

In the 1970s new political associations, claiming to be "public interest groups," were able to exploit the rights-endowing aspects of judicial and congressional actions to exert considerable leverage in the new policy realms of civil rights, the environment, disability, and consumer protection. This variant of interest group liberalism also featured the tripartite alliance of members of Congress (and their staffs), bureaucrats, and lobbyists, but its powerful rights orientation also privileged judges and their clerks. Thus, the project of programmatic rights that FDR pioneered flourished in the second half of the twentieth century but morphed into a structure and a set of legal and political dynamics that deprived the president of power to control and direct it.[76]

The Reagan "Revolution"

Not until 1980 was a serious challenge mounted to the rights-endowing interest group liberal expansion of the New Deal political order. In that year, Ronald Reagan was elected president. The central message of his campaign was that "government is the problem." He promised to reduce big government and the tax burdens needed to sustain it. His rhetoric was replete with examples of how the private sector was both more efficient and humane than the public sector and that the discipline and liberty associated with markets was to be highly prized, especially as compared with the straightjacket imposed by government bureaucracy. "The important thing," Hugh Heclo has written, "is not that Reagan said anything fundamentally new," but rather that in the political context created by the New Deal and the Great Society, "Reagan continued to uphold something old."[77]

In Reagan's first year in office, his challenge to big government and the interest groups that sustained it scored two major successes. The Professional Air Traffic Controllers Organization (PATCO), one of the very few unions to endorse Reagan, naturally expected to benefit from his victory. When he refused to accept PATCO's contract terms, its members went on strike, fully expecting him to use the disruption they were causing to commercial aviation as an excuse to settle. Instead, Reagan fired them and hired a whole new team of air traffic controllers. No accidents occurred. The strikers were utterly defeated and many never recovered their jobs. This stunning victory for the president was taken by the unions and the public at large as a mark of Reagan's seriousness about resisting both the coercive power of unions and demands for increased spending.

The Republicans gained control of the Senate as well as the presidency in 1980, but the Democrats retained control of the House of Representatives, the more powerful of the two chambers with respect to revenue matters. It thus appeared that Reagan would have little success cutting spending. To do so, he reversed the typical conservative program of cutting taxes only after cutting spending. Instead, he proposed major tax cuts, knowing that most of the spending cuts he proposed had no chance of being enacted. He dared the House to resist the popular idea of tax reduction and was willing to accept the enormous deficits that would result from cutting revenue but not spending. The House did as he hoped, and Reagan happily accepted the resulting deficit. His bet was that the surge in economic activity spurred by the cuts would eventually reduce the deficit. More important, the sheer size of the deficit would act as a deterrent to any new expensive Democratic policy initiatives. He was proved right on both counts.

Reagan's attack on big government did not constitute a refounding in the same sense as those accomplished by Jefferson, Jackson, Lincoln, and FDR. Unlike Roosevelt, Reagan failed to capitalize on his personal popularity to further his broader political ends. He squandered his one great opportunity to create the enduring electoral and congressional Republican majority that would have been required to sustain his revolution. FDR had used his 1936 reelection bid to mobilize support for the entire Democratic ticket. By contrast, Reagan's 1984 campaign was ostentatiously nonpartisan and devoid of serious political content. The theme was "Morning in America," as if, by some obscure diurnal logic, the Democrats could be made to endorse the darkness. The Republicans failed to take control of the House, picking up just fourteen additional seats, and lost two seats in the Senate, presaging the Democratic takeover in 1986. When the Republicans finally gained control of the House and the Senate in 1994, they did so in the middle of the term of Democratic president Bill Clinton, who was reelected in 1996. In the three decades from 1980 to 2010, the Republicans enjoyed undivided control of the presidency and Congress only during the middle four years of George W. Bush's presidency. The Democrats then regained control of Congress in 2006 and took undivided control of the presidency and Congress in 2008.

Despite Reagan's partisan shortcomings, something profound happened as a result of his presidency. A decided shift in public philosophy took place. Reagan's mantra that "government is the problem" clearly resonated in enduring ways. Not since the 1920s had there been such enthusiasm among policymakers and the public at large for free markets and such widespread denigration of government. The greatest complement to Reagan was the extent to which Clinton abetted the turn toward freer markets both practically and rhetorically. In his 1992 campaign, Clinton stated famously that he would "end Welfare as we know it." He did not fulfill this pledge immediately, but after suffering a humiliating defeat to expand the right to health care and seeing his party suffer terrible losses in 1994, Clinton acknowledged that the "era of big government is over." He then kept his 1992 campaign pledge by signing the 1996 Welfare Reform Act, which not only imposed stringent work requirements on welfare recipients, but also ended all welfare payments to recipients after five years. This law was the only real retrenchment of the welfare state that took place in the wake of the Reagan "revolution." Just as Eisenhower bestowed a form of bipartisan legitimacy on the New Deal, so did Clinton advance a renascent conservatism.

Clinton also joined Presidents Reagan and George H. W. Bush in perpetuating and expanding the deregulation of various sectors of the economy that had begun under President Ford. The Ford administration persuaded Congress to deregulate airlines and trucking, and it initiated action by the Supreme Court that led to the divestiture of the AT&T telephone monopoly. Under Reagan, Congress deregulated the savings and loan industry. Under George H. W. Bush, Congress exempted wholesale electricity generators from constraints imposed by one of the key New Deal regulatory statutes, the Public Utility Holding Company Act. In 1999, under Clinton, Congress repealed anticompetitive provisions of another New Deal regulatory stalwart, the Glass-Steagall Act of 1933. The Gramm-Leach-Bliley Financial Services Modernization Act repealed Glass-Steagall's prohibition against commercial banks offering investment and insurance services.[78] As a result, what had been three separate markets—investment banking, commercial banking, and insurance—now became a single, largely unfettered financial services market. The leaders of both parties fought aggressively to open up markets and to constrain federal spending.[79]

Optimism about market competition, as important as it was, did not undermine the essential contours of the New Deal. The welfare program that was eliminated in 1996—Aid to Families with Dependent Children—was never established firmly as an entitlement. All the New Deal programs that were—Social Security, Medicare, and veterans' benefits—remained firmly in place. In 2003 President George W. Bush—who styled himself as a Reagan disciple—joined with a Republican Congress to pass the largest expansion of entitlement spending since the inception of Medicare when it extended that program to include the provision of prescription drugs. Moreover, in alliance with a liberal icon, Massachusetts senator Edward Kennedy, Bush invoked the right to education in supporting the most important school reform since the Great Society, the No Child Left Behind Act, which dramatically transformed and expanded the role of the federal government in elementary and secondary education. After a brief flirtation with abolishing subsidies, the farm program returned to its former high levels of price supports.

In the end, the Reagan–Clinton–Bush embrace of free markets was selective. It applied to economic regulatory policy and to only one segment of aid to the dispossessed. Otherwise, the rights-based programs of interest group liberalism survived unscathed—indeed, they were expanded in important ways. Thus Reagan's efforts stopped well short of the refoundings undertaken by Jefferson, Lincoln, and FDR. The New Deal was reinterpreted only marginally. There was no broad-scale redefinition of the meaning of constitutional rights allied to the formation of an enduring partisan majority. The limits of the Reagan "revolution" appeared to confirm how New Deal programmatic rights and regulations had won the allegiance not just of bureaucrats and interest groups, but also of individuals. As Hugh Heclo concludes, Reagan's attack on government as a bureaucratic nightmare was "a partial truth masquerading as the whole. Government also grew to do things that people, in all their variegated ways, really wanted done."[80]

Continual War–Continual War Powers

The greatest and most enduring change in the nature and functioning of the modern presidency has taken place in the realm of foreign policy. Prior to World War II, the United States returned to a peace footing after a war ended. It did not do so after World War II. Throughout the postwar era, military budgets burgeoned, large numbers of men remained in uniform, and fear of a major, probably nuclear conflagration remained omnipresent. Cold war is an apt metaphor for the manner in which the United States and the Soviet Union remained poised for war, provoked each other, and fought small wars through surrogates. Never have two such powerful rivals engaged in such elaborate war preparations and goaded each other so frequently and aggressively without ever going to war.

The Cold War changed the concept of commander in chief. The president did not lead a nation into war but presided over military, quasi-military, and diplomatic activities that were geared toward both maintaining an armed peace and gaining competitive advantage over a dreaded rival. In recognition of the inherent manpower inferiority of the United States compared with the Soviets, a crucial aspect of Cold War strategy was to maintain technological superiority. This required massive expenditures, creating the largest peacetime budgets in history. It also necessitated the creation of an extensive and intricate web of relations between the federal government and the many and varied actors involved in the arms race. Eisenhower coined the term "military industrial complex" to describe this new set of relationships, but given the centrality of scientific, engineering, and operations research to the enterprise, he might well have called it the "military–industrial–university–consulting firm complex."

Harry Truman presided over an important government reorganization effort geared toward providing the president with institutional arrangements capable of coping with such massive yet delicate responsibilities. The United States had fought World War II with only the crudest tools for coordinating the activities of the various branches of the armed forces and the civilian departments that also were involved. The 1947 National Security Act reorganized government to provide the president with a better purchase on the management of war making, be it hot or cold. The War Department and Navy Department were grouped in a single Department of Defense under the secretary of defense, along with the newly created Air Force Department.[81] The 1947 act also created the Central Intelligence Agency to serve as the main provider and processor of civilian intelligence. And it established the National Security Council (NSC). The council was composed of the president, vice president, secretary of state, secretary of defense, and other members (such as the director of the Central Intelligence Agency), who met at the White House to discuss long-term problems and handle more immediate national security crises. An initially small NSC staff was hired to coordinate foreign policy materials from other agencies for the president.

Although both the Department of Defense and the NSC were established to improve interagency coordination and cooperation, they also became important sources of rivalry and discord. Over time the NSC staff grew in size, and many presidents came to rely heavily on its director, the national security adviser, to distill the disparate and often conflicting information and advice emanating from the Department of Defense, the State Department, the CIA, and other agencies with intelligence, military, and diplomatic responsibilities. In many administrations, the national security adviser attained a level of status and influence on a par with the secretary of defense and the secretary of state and used that stature to introduce his or her own initiatives and opinions. Coping with the three-way competition between these senior advisers has proven to be among the president's most serious challenges. The national administrative state's efforts to uphold "freedom from fear" have woven as complex a web of bureaucratic entanglements and rivalries as did its efforts to champion "freedom from want."

CONCLUSION: PRESIDENTIAL POWER AND AMERICAN DEMOCRACY

Presidents have been at the center of American political development. They have conveyed a coherent understanding of constitutional change and infused energy into party organizations that have gained them political strength to embark on ambitious projects of national reform. Various refoundings have placed the presidency at the eye of the political storm, but the resolution of these constitutional episodes also has set boundaries on executive authority. By enmeshing the president in a constitutional order dedicated to states' rights and localized parties, those who adhered to Jeffersonian principles hoped to avoid the unified and energetic executive envisioned by Hamilton. Jacksonian Democrats sought to strengthen the executive as the "tribune of the people," but this was accomplished by hitching presidential leadership to a party that enforced collective responsibility for principles that were hostile to centralized power. Jackson's celebrated veto of the bill to recharter the national bank signified that the president's veto power, originally envisioned by the Federalists as a check on democracy, was now an important weapon in the battle to promote equality through limited government. As the failure of Reconstruction showed, even the Civil War refounding did not alter the essential characteristics of a decentralized constitutional order. Rather, Lincoln and the Republican Party gave new life to Whig principles that celebrated natural rights, private property, and legislative supremacy.

The New Deal was the first refounding to place executive power at the center of its reform program. But in forging an alliance between rights and national administration, Roosevelt and his New Deal allies did not abolish the obstacles to a centralized state. The defeats Roosevelt suffered during the Third New Deal did not prevent him from strengthening executive administration. Abetted by the exigencies of World War II, FDR's plans for consolidating the modern presidency were successful. But clothed in the garb of constitutional sobriety, opponents of the New Deal were able to preserve the independence of the courts and Congress to influence the details of administration. The American people came to support executive action in the name of the greater security that New Dealers championed: FDR's "freedom from want" and "freedom from fear." But this support for domestic entitlements and relief from foreign threats did not translate into firm acceptance of executive dominion. Roosevelt himself was somewhat diffident in his support of centralized administration. The New Deal redefinition of rights, he insisted throughout the court-packing ordeal, did not require reducing the constitutional powers of the courts, as Theodore Roosevelt and his Progressive followers had prescribed. The problem was not the Constitution, FDR argued, but "the manner in which it had been interpreted."[82]

The United States and its leaders are still struggling to come to terms with the legacy of the New Deal. Although the development of the modern presidency does not preclude future refoundings, an executive-centered administrative state appeared to encourage pragmatic responses and bureaucratic solutions to global problems such as the economy, climate change, and homeland security that diminished somewhat the constitutional struggles that gave rise to previous conservative revolutions. To be sure, the nation's efforts to cope with the threat of terrorism, massive demographic shifts that followed from immigration reform in the mid-1960s, and the economic dislocations of a global economy require presidents to face imposing new challenges that require innovative solutions. But the War on Terror and the Great Recession led to actions during the presidencies of George W. Bush and Barack Obama that tended to further extend and elaborate, rather than depart from, the New Deal state.[83] In calling for the creation of a new executive department, President Bush directly linked the cause of homeland security to the 1947 National Security Act, asking Congress to form "a single permanent department with an overriding and urgent mission: securing the homeland of America, and protecting the American people."[84] President Obama formally eschewed the term *War on Terror;* nevertheless, he pursued a "surge" strategy in Afghanistan and expanded deployment of Special Forces and armed drones in counterterrorism missions—policies that resembled more than contrasted with those of his successor. Even after United States soldiers killed Osama bin Laden and began disengaging from Iraq and Afghanistan, Obama began taking measures toward the end of his first term to embed his administration's Overseas Contingency Operation in the national security apparatus, with the expectation that "targeted killings" would continue for at least another decade.[85]

Similarly, Obama not only continued the emergency measures that the Bush administration had undertaken in its final days to meet the worst economic crisis since the Great Depression, but he also worked with large Democratic majorities in the House and Senate to achieve important domestic reforms. The enactment of a major financial reform bill, which was dedicated to protecting consumers against abuses by credit card and mortgage lenders, and the vast expansion of health care provisions conformed to the idea, born of the New Deal, that the federal government had an obligation to protect individual men and women from the abuses of big business and the uncertainties of the marketplace. Obama's ambitious domestic program, especially the Patient Protection and Affordable Care Act, sharply divided Democrats and Republicans and contributed to the GOP's dramatic gains in the 2010 congressional elections. But the president and his party rebounded to win a bitterly contested but decisive victory in 2012.

Yet, the ongoing partisan rancor that reverberated through Obama's second term and the 2016 election raised serious doubts that his major programmatic advances would become ongoing obligations of the national government. Indeed, the election of a president and Congress in 2016 determined, as one advisor to the Trump campaign put it, to "erase" Obama's presidency posed severe challenges, not only to Obama's legacy but also to the very foundation of the rights-based national state spawned by the New Deal.[86] Many pundits and scholars viewed Trump, the first president without any experience in public office, as the object of a cult of personality who might not survive a full term in office, let alone leave an enduring imprint on the Republican Party, whose leaders he scorned, and the country. Yet Trump's America First slogan—and his promise to Make America Great Again— resonated powerfully among blue-collar, religiously devout, and non-urban whites who were frightened about demographic and social change forging an American State to which they no longer feel an allegiance.[87]

Seeking to discredit the threat of Trump's "movement" to the pragmatic policy state, President Obama warned the nation during the 2016 campaign that the complexity of problems facing America required an experienced and steady hand. Proclaiming that he did not think "there's ever been someone so qualified to hold this office," Obama pleaded with Americans to place their faith in the first woman nominated by a major political party, the former First Lady, Senator from New York, and Secretary of State, Hillary Clinton. Clinton's pioneering yet baggage-laden campaign well depicted the strengths and vulnerabilities of the existing political order. Like Obama, Clinton argued that the country should dismiss the grandiose promises and despondent narratives of a man who had never held public office. Trump's retort, roared during his acceptance of the Republican Party's nomination, was that only an outsider who had long jousted with the "establishment" could truly reform a "rigged system." "Nobody knows the system better than me," Trump claimed, "which is why I alone can fix it."[88]

One year into the Trump presidency, such braggadocio had become the stuff of ridicule by scholars, pundits, and detractors on both sides of the partisan divide. Trump had failed to translate any of his promises into legislation: "Obamacare" was still the law of the land, and no "big, beautiful" wall had been built on the border with Mexico to end undocumented immigration. Although a unified Republican Congress did pass a massive tax reform bill toward the end of 2017, Trump had the lowest public approval ratings for a president's first year in modern history.[89] Yet often overlooked among the disappointments and recriminations of Trump's frenzied beginning was his administration's aggressive and deliberate assault on the Liberal state. From the beginning, Trump forcefully—and sometimes successfully—took aim at the programmatic achievements of his predecessor. Throughout his first year, the White House and executive departments issued a blizzard of executive initiatives that refashioned, or seriously disrupted, government commitments in critical policy arenas such as immigration, climate change, foreign trade, criminal justice, civil rights, and health care policy.[90]

Although Trump's America First program had been compromised by the exigencies of international events, especially the perpetual War on Terror, he made clear in a combative speech before the United Nations in September 2017 that he still was committed to it. The president remained determined, he told the delegates, to depart from Obama's "disastrous" free trade agreements, notably the Trans-Pacific Partnership trade deal, which his administration abandoned soon after occupying the White House; and he cast scorn on the Obama administration's diplomacy in dealing with authoritarian regimes, especially Iran and North Korea. Claiming that the international nuclear deal Obama struck with Iran was an "embarrassment," the president strongly hinted that his administration would pull out of it. Derisively referring to North Korean dictator Kim Jong Un, who was aggressively presiding over an expanding nuclear arsenal, as "rocket man," Trump warned that to protect the United States and her allies in the region it might be necessary to "totally destroy" a nation of twenty-five million people. Whether such pugilistic rhetoric would prove to be an effective tactic in dealing with two countries that George W. Bush once decried as composing an "axis of evil" remains to be seen. But such a bombastic posture, amplified by harsh social media tweets, unsettled allies abroad and unnerved advocates of diplomacy, including Trump's Secretary of State Rex Tillerson, at home.[91]

In pursuing such an aggressive domestic and foreign policy during his first tumultuous year in office, Trump may mark a troubling culmination of, rather than a departure from, the New Deal administrative state. The aggrandizement of the executive and the decline of party politics that it has wrought has encouraged each new president to exploit the full splendor of the office at the expense of responsible public debate and resolution. Caught between the Scylla of bureaucratic indifference and the Charybdis of the public's demand for new rights, the presidency has evolved, or degenerated, into a plebiscitary form of politics that mocks the New Deal concept of "enlightened administration" and exposes citizens to public figures who exploit their impatience with the difficult tasks of sustaining a healthy constitutional democracy. The view that the system is rigged against the American people is more pronounced among Republicans than Democrats; but as the surprising insurgency of the self-style democratic socialist, Bernie Sanders, in the 2016 Democratic primaries made clear, this message resonates on the Left as well, especially among young people. That the Democrats won the popular vote and witnessed what looked to them like the devastating intervention of the FBI in the campaign only fanned the flames of their discontent with America's governing institutions.

As the stormy Clinton, Bush, and Obama presidencies had illustrated, the New Deal freed the executive from formal constitutional forms and political parties, but it did so at the cost of subjecting it to fractious politics within Washington and volatile public opinion outside it. Once the foundation of pragmatic centrism, the administrative state now embroils the country in high-stakes policy controversies that diminish the integrity of the Congress and the states, weaken the system of checks and balances, and erode citizens' trust in the competence and fairness of the national government. Trump's ascension, as unexpected as it has been, is understandable in this new institutional context.

NOTES

1. Alexander Hamilton, James Madison, and John Jay, *The Federalist Papers* (New York: New American Library, 1961), no. 72, 437.
2. Harold C. Syrett, ed., *The Papers of Alexander Hamilton* (New York: Columbia University Press, 1969), vol. 8, 38–39.
3. *Letters of Pacificus and Helvidius on the Proclamation of Neutrality of 1793* (Washington, DC: Gideon, 1845), 53–64.
4. Hamilton, Madison, and Jay, *Federalist Papers,* no. 71, 432.
5. "Letters from the Federal Farmer, I," in *The Antifederalists,* ed. Cecilia M. Kenyon (Indianapolis: Bobbs-Merrill, 1966), 204.
6. Even as he lamented the "aristocratical" tendencies of the delegates who attended the Constitutional Convention in Philadelphia, the Anti-Federalist Federal Farmer acknowledged that Virginia made a "very respectable appointment, and placed at the head of it, the first man in America." Ibid., 204.
7. Thomas Jefferson, "First Inaugural Address, March 4, 1801," in *The Portable Thomas Jefferson,* ed. Merrill D. Peterson (New York: Viking Press, 1975), 294. On Jefferson's view of the relationship between executive power and popular rule, see Jeremy Bailey, *Thomas Jefferson and Executive Power* (New York: Cambridge University Press, 2007).
8. Jeffrey Tulis, *The Rhetorical Presidency* (Princeton: Princeton University Press, 1987).
9. Hamilton, Madison, and Jay, *Federalist Papers,* no. 70, 428–429 (emphasis in original).
10. Gary J. Schmitt, "President Washington's Neutrality Proclamation," in *The Constitutional Presidency,* ed. Joseph Bessette and Jeffrey Tulis (Baltimore: Johns Hopkins University Press, 2009).
11. James Sterling Young, "Power and Purpose in *The Politics Presidents Make," Polity* 28, no. 3 (1995): 509–516.
12. Stephen Skowronek, *The Politics Presidents Make: Leadership from John Adams to Bill Clinton* (Cambridge, MA: Harvard University Press, 1997), 20.
13. Ibid., chaps. 1–3.
14. Mark Landler, "From 'America First' to a More Conventional View of U.S. Diplomacy," *New York Times,* March 1, 2017, https://www.nytimes.com/2017/03/01/us/politics/national-security-foreign-policy-white-house.html.
15. Thomas Jefferson, "Answers to de Meusnier Questions, 1786," in *The Writings of Thomas Jefferson,* 20 vols., ed. Andrew A. Lipscomb and Albert Ellery Bergh (Washington, DC: Thomas Jefferson Memorial Association, 1903–1904), vol. 17 (memorial edition), 85.
16. Bailey, *Thomas Jefferson and Executive Power,* 9–10.
17. Jefferson, "First Inaugural Address," 290–295.
18. Thomas Jefferson, letters to James Madison, July 1803 and August 24, 1803, in *The Republic of Letters,* ed. James Morton Smith (New York: Norton, 1995), 1269–1271.

19. John Quincy Adams, *Memoirs of John Quincy Adams,* ed. Charles Francis Adams (New York: AMS Press, 1970), vol. 5, 401. Cited by Bailey, *Thomas Jefferson and Executive Power,* 192.

20. Thomas Jefferson, letter to James Madison, August 18, 1803, in Smith, *Republic of Letters,* 1278. Cited in Bailey, *Thomas Jefferson and Executive Power,* 180.

21. Thomas Jefferson, "Second Inaugural Address," Bartleby.com, http://www.bartleby.com/124/pres17.html.

22. Thomas Jefferson, "The Kentucky Resolutions of 1798," adopted by the Kentucky legislature on November 10, 1798, http://www.constitution.org/cons/kent1798.htm.

23. Andrew Jackson, "Proclamation Regarding Nullification, December 10, 1832," Yale Law School, Lillian Goldman Law Library, http://avalon.law.yale.edu/19th_century/jack01.asp.

24. Robert Remini, *Andrew Jackson and the Bank War* (New York: Norton, 1967), 81.

25. Leonard White, *The Jeffersonians: A Study in Administrative History, 1801–1829* (New York: MacMillan, 1956), 213–214, 267.

26. Thomas Jefferson, letter to James Madison, April 27, 1809, in Lipscomb and Bergh, eds., *Writings of Thomas Jefferson,* vol. 12, 277.

27. "President Jackson's Veto Message Regarding the Bank of the United States, July 10, 1832," Yale Law School, Lillian Goldman Law Library, http://avalon.law.yale.edu/19th_century/ajvet001.asp.

28. Robert Remini, *Andrew Jackson* (New York: HarperCollins, 1966), 145–146.

29. Andrew Jackson, "First Annual Message to Congress, December 8, 1829," The American Presidency Project, http://www.presidency.ucsb.edu/ws/index.php?pid=29471.

30. Edward S. Corwin, *The President: Office and Powers, 1787–1957,* 4th ed. (New York: New York University Press, 1957), 451.

31. J. B. McClure, ed., *Abraham Lincoln's Speeches* (Chicago: Rhodes and McClure, 1891), 21–22.

32. Robert W. Johannsen, ed., *The Lincoln-Douglas Debates of 1858* (New York: Oxford University Press, 1965), 126–127.

33. Ibid., 131–132. Undated fragment written in early 1861 in *New Letters and Papers of Lincoln,* ed. Paul N. Angle (Boston: Houghton Mifflin, 1930), 241–242. Lincoln's reference is to Proverbs 25: 11.

34. Abraham Lincoln, "First Inaugural Address, March 4, 1861," in *The Political Thought of Abraham Lincoln,* ed. Richard N. Current (Indianapolis, IN: Bobbs-Merrill, 1967), 171–172.

35. David Walker Howe, *The Political Culture of American Whigs* (Chicago: University of Chicago Press, 1979), 292.

36. Current, *Political Thought of Abraham Lincoln,* 88–89 (emphasis in original).

37. Ibid., 187–188.

38. *Chicago Tribune,* February 18, 1860, in *Abraham Lincoln: A Press Portrait,* ed. Herbert Mitgang (Athens: University of Georgia Press, 1989), 153.

39. "Abraham Lincoln's Letter to Albert G. Hodges," in *The Evolving Presidency: Addresses, Cases, Essays, Letters, Reports, Resolutions, Transcripts, and Other Landmark Documents, 1787–1998,* ed. Michael Nelson (Washington, DC: CQ Press, 1999), 70–74.

40. Clinton L. Rossiter, *Constitutional Dictatorship* (Princeton, NJ: Princeton University Press, 1948); see also L. Gerald Bursey, "Abraham Lincoln," in *Popular Images of*

American Presidents, ed. William C. Spragens (New York: Greenwood Press, 1988), 77–85.

41. Philip Shaw Paludan, *The Presidency of Abraham Lincoln* (Lawrence: University Press of Kansas, 1994), 33.
42. Ibid.
43. Eric McKitrick, "Party Building and the Union and Confederate War Efforts," in *The American Party System: Stages of Development,* ed. William Nisbet Chambers and Walter Dean Burnham (London: Oxford University Press, 1975), 131.
44. *Prize Cases,* 67 Black 635 (1863).
45. James D. Richardson, ed., *Messages and Papers of the Presidents,* 20 vols. (New York: Bureau of National Literature, 1897), vol. 7, 3225.
46. Bursey, "Abraham Lincoln," 82.
47. Paludan, *Presidency of Abraham Lincoln,* 104–105.
48. Richardson, *Messages and Papers of the Presidents,* vol. 7, 3359.
49. Abraham Lincoln, letter to Charles D. Robinson, August 7, 1864, in *The Collected Works of Abraham Lincoln,* 9 vols., ed. Roy P. Basler (New Brunswick, NJ: Rutgers University Press, 1953), vol. 7, 499–500. At the urging of the abolitionist Frederick Douglass, Lincoln did not send the letter to Robinson. Douglass objected to the final sentence of the draft letter that added, "If Jefferson Davis wishes . . . to know what I would do if he were to offer peace and reunion, saying nothing about slavery, let him try me." "It would be given a broader meaning than you intend to convey," Douglass warned, and be taken as "a complete surrender of your anti-slavery policy." In the face of continuing pressure to retreat on his position, with the strong support of anti-slavery activists, Lincoln continued to express the moral and practical reasons why he could not go back on the Emancipation Proclamation. Eric Foner, *Fiery Trial: Abraham Lincoln and American Slavery* (New York: Norton, 2010), 305–306.
50. James M. McPherson, *Abraham Lincoln and the Second American Revolution* (New York: Oxford University Press, 1991), 86.
51. Eric Foner, *The Fiery Trial,* 312.
52. Paludan, *Presidency of Abraham Lincoln,* 297–302.
53. Lincoln took this position in refusing to veto a bill that reduced fees paid to the marshal for the District of Columbia; see Basler, *Collective Works of Abraham Lincoln,* vol. 7, 414–415.
54. Matthew Crenson and Benjamin Ginsberg, *Presidential Power: Unchecked and Unbalanced* (New York: Norton, 2007), 101.
55. Carl Schurz, "Abraham Lincoln," in *Abraham Lincoln,* ed. Carl Schurz (New York: Chautauqua, 1891), 72.
56. *The Papers and Addresses of Franklin D. Roosevelt,* 13 vols., ed. Samuel I. Rosenman (New York: Random House, 1938–1950), vol. 1, 751–752.
57. *The Papers and Addresses of Franklin D. Roosevelt,* vol. 1, 756.
58. Sidney M. Milkis, *Theodore Roosevelt, the Progressive Party and the Transformation of American Democracy* (Lawrence: University Press of Kansas, 2009).
59. Ibid., 756.
60. "Democratic Platform of 1936," in *National Party Platforms,* ed. Donald Bruce Johnson (Urbana: University of Illinois Press, 1978), 360.
61. Roosevelt, *Public Papers and Addresses,* vol. 9, 671–672.

62. David M. Kennedy, *Freedom from Fear: The American People in Depression and War, 1929–1945* (New York: Oxford University Press, 1999), 469–470.

63. The Works Progress Administration (WPA) was not created during the first 100 days; it was established in January 1935 as the successor to the New Deal's Federal Emergency Relief Agency. Thus the WPA was set during the interregnum between the First and Second New Deals, but its organization and policies were characteristic of the emergence of legislation of the former period. See William Leuchtenburg, *Franklin D. Roosevelt and the New Deal, 1932–1940* (New York: Harper and Row, 1963), chaps. 6 and 7.

64. Joseph Harris, "Outline for a New York Conference, April 8, 1936," in *Papers of the President's Committee on Administrative Management* (Hyde Park, NY: Franklin D. Roosevelt Library).

65. For an overview and critique of the work on the Third New Deal, see John W. Jeffries, "A Third New Deal? Liberal Policy and the American State, 1937–1945," *Journal of Policy History* 8, no. 4 (1996): 387–409; and Sidney M. Milkis, *The President and the Parties: The Transformation of the American Party System since the New Deal* (New York: Oxford University Press, 1993), chaps. 5 and 6.

66. Stephen Skowronek, *Building a New American State: The Expansion of National Administrative Capacities, 1887–1920* (Cambridge: Cambridge University Press, 1982).

67. For a more complete account of New Deal party politics, see Milkis, *The President and the Parties,* chaps. 1–4.

68. Ronald Story, "The New Deal and Higher Education," in *The New Deal and the Triumph of Liberalism,* ed. Sidney M. Milkis and Jerome M. Mileur (Amherst: University of Massachusetts Press, 2002); and Suzanne Mettler, *Soldiers to Citizens: The GI Bill and the Making of the Greatest Generation* (New York: Oxford University Press, 2005).

69. Barry Karl, *The Uneasy State: The United States from 1915 to 1945* (Chicago: University of Chicago Press, 1983), 223.

70. Martha Derthick, *Policymaking for Social Security* (Washington, DC: Brookings Institution, 1983), 417.

71. Quoted in William E. Leuchtenburg, *In the Shadow of FDR: From Harry Truman to Ronald Reagan,* rev. ed. (Ithaca, NY: Cornell University Press, 1985), 49.

72. Oscar Handlin, "The Eisenhower Administration: A Self-Portrait," *Atlantic Monthly,* November 1963, 68.

73. Roosevelt, *Public Papers and Addresses,* vol. 6, 357–367.

74. Theodore Lowi, *The End of Liberalism: The Second Republic of the United States,* 2nd ed. (New York: Norton, 1979).

75. Harris, "Outline for a New York Conference."

76. R. Shep Melnick, "The Courts, Congress, and Programmatic Rights," in *Remaking American Politics,* ed. Richard A. Harris and Sidney M. Milkis (Boulder, CO: Westview Press, 1989).

77. Hugh Heclo, "Ronald Reagan and the American Public Philosophy," in *The Reagan Presidency: Pragmatic Conservatism and Its Legacies,* ed. Elliot Brownlee and Hugh Davis Graham (Lawrence: University Press of Kansas, 2003), 23.

78. Public Law 106–102, 113 Stat. 1338, enacted November 12, 1999, is an act of the 106th U.S. Congress.

79. For a comprehensive discussion and analysis of various Reagan and Clinton deregulation efforts, see Marc Landy, Martin Levin, and Martin Shapiro, eds., *Creating Competitive Markets: The Politics and Economics of Regulatory Reform* (Washington, DC: Brookings Institution, 2007).

80. Heclo, "Ronald Reagan and American Public Philosophy," 34.

81. Each of the three branches maintained their own service secretaries. In 1949, the act was amended to give the secretary of defense more power over the individual services and their secretaries.

82. The conversations concerning the court-packing plan between FDR and his attorney general, Homer Cummings, recorded in the latter's diary, offer important clues to FDR's views on the New Deal constitutional program. See the *Diaries of Homer Stille Cummings,* December 26, 1936, no. 6, 185–194, Homer Cummings Papers, Manuscript Department, Alderman Library, University of Virginia.

83. Jeffrey Tulis, "Plausible Futures," in *The Presidency in the Twenty-First Century*, ed. Charles Dunn (Lexington: University Press of Kentucky, 2011).

84. George W. Bush, Address to the Nation, June 6, 2002, The White House, http://georgewbush-whitehouse.archives.gov/news/releases/2002/06/20020606-8.html.

85. Greg Miller, "Plan for Hunting Terrorists Signals U.S. Intends to Keep Adding Names to Kill Lists," *Washington Post,* October 23, 2012, http://articles.washingtonpost.com/2012–10–23/world/35500278_1_drone-campaign-obama-administration-matrix.

86. Evan Osnos, "President Trump's First Term," *The New Yorker*, September 26, 2016, https://www.newyorker.com/magazine/2016/09/26/president-trumps-first-term.

87. Ronald Brownstein, "The Clinton Conundrum." *The Atlantic*, https://www.theatlantic.com/politics/archive/2015/04/the-clinton-conundrum/431949/.

88. Donald Trump's full remarks available in "Full Text: Donald Trump 2016 RNC Draft Speech Transcript," July 21, 2016, *Politico*, http://www.politico.com/story/2016/07/full-transcript-donald-trump-nomination-acceptance-speech-at-rnc-225974.

89. According to the average of several polls calibrated by Real Clear Politics, 39.9 percent of those surveyed approved of Trump's performance, while 55 percent disapproved. Using data from Gallup, we calculate that no president's first eight months in office has, on average, been viewed so unfavorably; see https://www.realclearpolitics.com/epolls/other/president_trump_job_approval-6179.html; http://www.gallup.com/poll/116677/presidential-approval-ratings-gallup-historical-statistics-trends.aspx.

90. For a detailed account of Trump's disruptive first year, see Sidney M. Milkis and Nicholas Jacobs, "'I Alone Can Fix It': Donald Trump, the Administrative Presidency, and Hazards of Executive-Centered Partisanship," *Forum,* vol. 15, issue 3 (November 2017), https://www.degruyter.com/view/j/for.2017.15.issue-3/for-2017-0037/for-2017-0037.xml; and Michael Nelson, "Donald Trump's First Year: Decreasing Influence Without Increasing Effectiveness," in *Trump's First Year*, ed. Michael Nelson (Charlottesville: University of Virginia Press, 2018).

91. David Nakamura and Ann Gearon, "Trump Defends America First Policy at U.N.," *Washington Post*, September 19, 2017, https://www.washingtonpost.com/politics/trump-defends-america-first-foreign-policy-at-un-threatens-to-totally-destroy-north-korea/2017/09/19/33162080-9d62-11e7-9083-fbfddf6804c2_story.html?utm_term=.7e775eb8a512.

5

PRESIDENTIAL COMPETENCE

Paul J. Quirk

The skills of political leadership that a president requires are a recurring theme of modern presidential scholarship. Most students of political skill have dwelt on techniques such as bargaining, persuasion, rhetoric, and management. Paul J. Quirk approaches the subject differently, asking, "What must a president know?" Quirk rejects, as impossibly demanding, a "self-reliant" model patterned after Franklin Roosevelt. Yet he also rejects a "minimalist" model that was initially associated with Ronald Reagan and later adopted by George W. Bush. Instead, Quirk proposes a "strategic competence" model of the kind practiced, at least part of the time, by presidents John Kennedy, Gerald Ford, George H. W. Bush, Bill Clinton, and Barack Obama. On this view, presidents do not need to know everything, but they must make strategic choices about what to know. From this perspective, Donald Trump has operated in previously uncharted territory, often ignoring the requirements for any of these models.

In this chapter I address a simple, yet frequently overlooked question about the presidency: What must the president know? To serve the country effectively and achieve political success, must presidents have deep knowledge of the issues and processes of government? Or can they rely on other officials—especially the cabinet and White House staff—to provide nearly all of the relevant expertise? Considering the enormous complexity of modern government, is the president's direct, personal knowledge even relevant?

This chapter explores this question in two parts. In the first part, using evidence on presidents from Franklin Roosevelt to Ronald Reagan, I identify three competing conceptions of the president's personal tasks and expertise—that is, of presidential competence. I criticize two of these conceptions—one of them modeled on Roosevelt and more orthodox; the other associated with Reagan. I then offer a third conception, based on a notion of "strategic competence," and discuss its requirements in three major areas of presidential activity. Second, I test the usefulness of the analysis by assessing the performance of the five presidents who followed Reagan: George H. W. Bush, Bill Clinton, George W. Bush, Barack Obama, and Donald Trump.

THE SELF-RELIANT PRESIDENCY

Most commentary on the presidency assumes a concept of the president's personal tasks that borders on the heroic. Stated simply, the president must strive to be self-reliant and personally bear a large share of the burden of governing. He or (in the future) she must therefore meet intellectual requirements that are correspondingly rigorous.

The classic argument for the self-reliant presidency is presented in Richard Neustadt's *Presidential Power*.[1] In arguing for an enlarged concept of the presidential role, Neustadt stressed that the president's political interests, and therefore his perspective on decisions, are unique. Only the president has political stakes that arguably correspond with the national interest. Thus a president's chances for success depend on what he can do for himself: his direct involvement in decisions, his personal reputation and skill, his control over subordinates.[2] In this spirit, students of the presidency have often held up Franklin Roosevelt as the exemplary modern president. A perfect "active-positive," in James David Barber's typology of presidential personalities, Roosevelt made strenuous efforts to ensure his thorough understanding of issues and thus increase his control.[3] For example, he often set up competing channels of information and advice. He also looked outside the government for people who could offer additional perspectives.[4] The ideal president, in this view, has a consuming passion for control and thus for information.

This image of the president—as one who makes the major decisions himself, depends on others only in lesser matters, and firmly controls his subordinates—is attractive to most citizens, and presidents seek to project that appearance. But the notion of the self-reliant presidency overlooks the realities of modern government. Even for Roosevelt, self-reliance had costs. In a generally admiring description of his administrative practices, Arthur Schlesinger Jr. concedes that his methods hampered performance in some respects. Roosevelt's creation of unstructured, competitive relations among subordinates caused "confusion and exasperation on the operating level"; it was "nerve-wracking and often positively demoralizing." Because Roosevelt reserved so many decisions for himself, he could not make all of them promptly, and aides often had to contend with troublesome delays.[5]

In later administrations the weaknesses of the self-reliant presidency have emerged clearly. Presidents who have aspired to self-reliance have ended up leaving serious responsibilities badly neglected. Lyndon Johnson, another president with prodigious energy and a need for control, gravitated naturally to the self-reliant approach.[6] Eventually, however, he directed his efforts narrowly and obsessively to the Vietnam War. Meeting daily with the officers in charge, Johnson directed military operations from the Oval Office, at times selecting specific bombing targets. He essentially set aside every other area of presidential concern. In all likelihood, the military officers themselves, guided by the president's civilian subordinates, would have made the military decisions at least as well as Johnson, and probably better. Moreover, his direct operational control of military strategy may have impaired Johnson's ability to take a broader, "presidential" perspective on the war. Johnson illustrates a tendency for self-reliance to become an end in itself.

Jimmy Carter, although less psychologically driven than Johnson, preferred self-reliance as a matter of conviction. It led him toward another kind of narrowness. From the first month in office, Carter signaled his intention to be thoroughly involved, completely informed, and prompt. "Unless there's a holocaust," he told the staff, "I'll take care of everything the same day it comes in." Thus he spent long hours daily poring over stacks of memoranda and took thick briefing books with him for weekends at Camp David. Initially, he even checked arithmetic in budget documents. Later he complained mildly about the number of long memoranda he had to read, but he still made no genuine effort to curb the flow.[7] Carter's extreme attention to detail cannot have contributed more than very marginally to the quality of his administration's decisions. Yet it took his attention from other, more essential tasks. Carter was criticized as having failed to articulate the broad themes or ideals that would give his presidency a sense of purpose—a natural oversight for a president who was wallowing in detail. He certainly neglected the task of nurturing relationships with other leaders in Washington.[8] The main defect of the self-reliant presidency, however, is none of these particular risks; rather, it is the physical impossibility of carrying it out. Perhaps Roosevelt, an extraordinary individual who served when government was still relatively manageable, could achieve an approximation of the ideal. But the larger and more complex government has become, the more presidents have been forced to depend on the judgments of others. Today, any important policy question produces enough proposals, studies, and advocacy papers to keep a policymaker who seeks to master it all fully occupied. In any remotely literal sense, presidential self-reliance is inconceivable.

THE MINIMALIST PRESIDENCY

A second approach to presidential competence rejects the heroic demands of self-reliance altogether. In this approach the president requires little or no understanding of specific issues and problems and instead can mainly rely on subordinates to deal with them. This "minimalist" approach commands attention both because the Reagan administration relied explicitly on such an approach and because, in certain respects, George W. Bush followed in Reagan's footsteps.

Minimalism does not imply a passive conception of the presidency as an institution, like that of some nineteenth-century American presidents, who subscribed to the Whig theory of government.[9] With the help of an activist White House staff and the various agencies of the Executive Office of the President, a minimalist president can exercise power as expansively as any. Nor does minimalism describe the "hidden-hand" leadership ascribed to Dwight Eisenhower.[10] Long viewed as a passive president, Eisenhower sometimes exercised considerable influence behind the scenes.

The first modern minimalist president was Ronald Reagan, whose administration flatly rejected the self-reliant approach and its cognitive and intellectual demands on the president. President Reagan's role in decision making, his spokesmen said during the first year, would be that of a "chairman of the board." He would personally establish the general policies and goals of his administration, select cabinet and other personnel who shared his commitments, and then delegate broad authority to them so that they could work out the particulars.[11]

Fundamentally, the limited role for the president was designed to accommodate Reagan's work habits—especially his distaste for reading memoranda or sitting through lengthy discussions—and to answer critics who questioned his intellectual ability to serve as president. By expounding a minimalist theory, the Reagan White House was able to defend the president's factual lapses and inaccuracies as harmless. It is a "fantasy of the press," said the communications director, David Gergen, that an occasional "blooper" in a news conference has any importance.[12]

But the administration presented this minimalist conception not only as an accommodation to Reagan's limitations, but as a sensible way for any president to operate. It has at least one claim to be taken seriously: unlike self-reliance, minimalism is at least attainable. For several reasons, however, the minimalist presidency has serious deficiencies as a general model. Nor did it work well even in Reagan's case.

Chairman-of-the-board notions notwithstanding, a minimalist president and his administration are likely to have difficulties reaching decisions that serve the president's fundamental goals. Most obvious is that the president's subordinates may have their own agendas. Unless the president is fairly attentive, he will have trouble knowing when an ostensibly loyal subordinate is mainly serving some other constituency. The strategy makes selecting genuinely responsive senior officials exceptionally critical.[13]

But just as important, a minimalist president—or rather, the sort of president who would adopt a minimalist approach—is likely to overestimate his capabilities and judgment. Having neglected the complexities of policy issues over the course of a political career, he would fail to appreciate careful analysis. At least in politics, few people place a high value on discussion or analysis more sophisticated than their own habitual mode of thought.

That President Reagan showed no particular humility about his ability to make policy judgments was most apparent in his decisions about budgets, taxes, and the federal deficit.[14] In late 1981 Reagan's main economic policymakers—Office of Management and Budget (OMB) director David Stockman, Secretary of the Treasury Donald Regan, and White House chief of staff James Baker—recommended unanimously that the president propose a modest tax increase to keep the budget deficit to an acceptable level. But Reagan rejected their recommendation. As a result, the presidential budget was so far in deficit that it was dismissed out of hand even by the Republican Senate, and the president ended up accepting a package of "revenue enhancements" that Congress virtually forced on him.

Moreover, even if a minimalist president is willing to delegate authority and accept advice, his aides and cabinet members may have difficulty making up for his limitations. As they compete for the president's favor, they take cues from his rhetoric and descend to his level of argument. Advocates emerge for almost any policy the president is inclined to support. Such imitation apparently produced the scandals in the Environmental Protection Agency that embarrassed Reagan during his first term and led to the removal of numerous high-level officials. These officials, including the administrator of the agency, Anne Gorsuch Burford, interpreted Reagan's sweeping antiregulatory rhetoric to mean that, requirements of the law notwithstanding, they should hardly regulate at all.

The effect of Reagan's relaxed approach to policy decisions on the quality of debate in his administration is illustrated by a White House meeting on the defense budget in September 1981, recounted in Stockman's revealing memoir.[15] The OMB was proposing a moderate reduction in the planned growth of defense spending—still giving the Pentagon an inflation-adjusted increase of 52 percent over five years and 92 percent of its original request. In a presentation that Stockman calls "a masterpiece of obfuscation," Secretary of Defense Caspar Weinberger compared American and Soviet capabilities as if the OMB were refusing to endorse any increase. Almost all of his comparisons, displayed in elaborate charts, concerned weapons categories that Stockman was not trying to cut. The secretary concluded his presentation by showing a cartoon depicting the OMB's version of the defense budget as "a four-eyed wimp who looked like Woody Allen, carrying a tiny rifle." In the end, Weinberger got his way.

Finally, if a president openly delegates decisions and takes subordinates' advice, the press will criticize him for it. Because the public likes presidents who seem in command, it makes good copy for a reporter to charge that aides are assuming the president's job—even when that may be a sensible adaptation to the president's personal limitations. The press sometimes challenged Reagan to demonstrate his involvement in decisions. During summit meetings with Soviet president Mikhail Gorbachev, Reagan took his chances negotiating one-to-one on arms control, a subject of daunting complexity for any president.[16] It is certainly possible for a minimalist president to resist the temptations and pressures to overstep his capability and impose his own ill-informed decisions, and instead to rely on subordinates to tell him what to do. But such deference to subordinates would require a self-effacing personality—rare among successful politicians—and a willingness to face questioning about who is "the real president." Such a strategy would also make the president exceptionally dependent on his senior aides and cabinet members, who would have extraordinary opportunity to shape the president's goals and agenda according to their own preferences.

Neither self-reliance nor minimalism therefore offers a plausible general route to presidential competence. The question is whether another possible model exists that corrects the defects of both—making feasible demands on the president yet allowing for competent performance.

STRATEGIC COMPETENCE

The third conception of presidential competence, set forth in the rest of this chapter, lies between the two extremes of minimalism and self-reliance. But it is not a mere compromise between those extremes. It is based on a notion of *strategic competence.*

The argument is that to perform competently, presidents must have a workable strategy for achieving competence. This strategy must take into account three basic elements of the president's situation.

1. The president's time, energy, and talent, and thus his capacity for direct, personal competence, are scarce resources. Choices must be made concerning what things a president will attempt to know. Delegation is necessary.

2. Depending on the task (for example, deciding issues or promoting policies), the president's ability to substitute the judgment and expertise of others for his own and still get satisfactory results varies considerably. Delegation works better for some tasks than for others.

3. The success of such substitutions will depend on a relatively small number of presidential actions and decisions concerning the selection of subordinates, the general instructions they are given, and the president's interactions with them. How well delegation works depends on how it is done.

Achieving competent performance, then, can be viewed as a problem of allocating resources. The president's personal abilities and time to use them are the scarce resources. For each task, the possibilities and requirements for effective delegation determine how much of these resources should be used and how they should be employed.

In the rest of this section, I spell out the implications of strategic competence in three major areas of presidential activity: policy decisions, policy processes, and policy promotion. The approach demands realistic levels of attention and expertise and yet permits competent performance in each of these areas.

Policy Decisions

When it comes to substantive issues, vast presidential ignorance is simply inevitable. No one understands more than a few significant issues very well. Fortunately, presidents can get by—that is, control subordinates reasonably well and minimize the risk of serious policy mistakes—on far less than a thorough mastery. Some prior preparation, however, is required. And presidents lacking that preparation are likely to have difficulty.

As a matter of course, each president has a general outlook or philosophy of government. His principal aides must share that outlook or represent a variety of views roughly centered on it. The main requirement beyond this is for the president to be familiar enough with the substantive policy debates in each major area to recognize the signs of responsible argument. This familiarity includes having enough exposure to the work of policy analysts and experts in each area to know, if only in general terms, how they reach conclusions and the contribution they make. The point is not that the president will then be able to work through all the facts and arguments about an issue, evaluate them properly, and reach a sound, independent conclusion—that is ruled out if only by lack of time. As he evaluates policy advice, however, such a substantively aware president will at least be able to tell which of his subordinates are making sense. Whatever the subject at hand, the president will be able to judge whether an advocate is bringing to bear the relevant kinds of evidence, considerations, and arguments and citing appropriate authorities.

One can observe the importance of this ability by comparing two—in some respects similar—episodes. Both John F. Kennedy in 1963 and Ronald Reagan in 1981 proposed large, controversial reductions of the individual income tax, each in some sense unorthodox. But in the role played by respectable economic opinion, the two cases could not be more different.

Kennedy brought to bear Keynesian economics, which by then had been the dominant school of professional economic thought for nearly three decades. The Kennedy administration took office when the economy was in a deep recession. From the beginning, Walter Heller, a leading academic economist and the chair of Kennedy's Council of Economic Advisers (CEA), had sought tax reductions to promote economic growth—the appropriate Keynesian response, even though it might increase the federal deficit. Already aware of the rationale for stimulation, Kennedy did not require persuasion on the economic merits, but he did have political reservations. "I understand the case for a tax cut," he told Heller, "but it doesn't fit my call for sacrifice." Nor did it fit the economic views of Congress or the general public, both of which remained faithful on the whole to the traditional belief in an annually balanced budget. But the CEA continued lobbying, and Kennedy—first partially, later completely—went along. Finally, in 1963, Kennedy proposed to reduce income taxes substantially.

The novelty of this proposal, with the economy already recovering and the budget in deficit, alarmed traditionalists. "What can those people in Washington be thinking about?" asked former president Eisenhower in a magazine article. "Why would they deliberately do this to our country?" Congress, which also had doubts, moved slowly but eventually passed the tax cut in 1964. The Keynesian deficits proved right for the time: the tax cut stimulated enough economic activity that revenues, instead of declining, actually increased.[17]

Aside from being a tax cut and being radical, Reagan's proposal bore little resemblance to Kennedy's. Pushed through Congress in the summer of 1981, it represented an explicit break with mainstream economic thinking, both liberal and conservative. The bill embodied the ideas of a small fringe group of economists whose views the conservative Republican economist Herbert Stein dismissed in the *Wall Street Journal* as "punk supply-side economics." In selling the bill to Congress, which was submissive in the aftermath of Reagan's landslide election, the administration made bold, unsupported claims. Despite tax-rate reductions of 25 percent in a three-year period, it promised that the bill would so stimulate investment that revenues would increase and deficits decline. This resembled the claims for the Kennedy bill except that, under the prevailing conditions, nothing in conventional economic models or empirical estimates remotely justified the optimistic predictions. Senate Republican leader Howard Baker, a reluctant supporter, termed the bill "a riverboat gamble." Within a year, policymakers faced deficits in the $200 billion range—twice what they had considered intolerable a short time earlier and enough, nearly all agreed, to damage the economy severely.[18] A president with any sophistication about economic policy would have dismissed the wild claims made for the tax cuts. He would have been aware that mainstream economists had developed responsible, empirically grounded methods for estimating the effects of tax policies. President Reagan presumably knew that most economists did not endorse his proposal. But he had never paid enough attention to serious economic debate to appreciate the difference between ideological faith and empirical evidence.

None of this is to suggest that presidents should set aside their ideologies and defer to ideologically neutral experts. Gerald Ford, another conservative president, had a strong belief in free markets and assembled a cabinet and staff largely of individuals who shared that perspective. Yet Ford also insisted that sound professional analysis underlie his decisions and took pains to consider a variety of views. Ford's conservatism shaped the policies of his administration, which held down government spending, stressed controlling inflation more than reducing unemployment, and started the process of economic deregulation.[19] In much the same way, Reagan achieved both conservative goals (cutting tax rates and reducing the tax system's distortion of private economic decisions) and some liberal ones (tax relief for low-income people) in the historic Tax Reform Act of 1986. The president's proposal embodied the consensual judgment among experts both inside and outside of government that the proliferation of credits, exemptions, and deductions in the federal tax code was harmful to the economy.[20] Adequate policy expertise cannot be acquired in a hurry. A president needs to have been, over the years, the kind of politician who participates responsibly in decision making and debate and who does his homework. This means occasionally taking the time to read some of the policy documents (such as congressional hearing testimony and committee reports) that are prepared especially for politicians and their staff. Such documents respect the limits of a politician's expertise and tolerance for detail yet provide a fairly rigorous education.

Policy Processes

In addition to policy issues, presidents must be competent in the processes of policymaking.[21] Most presidential policy decisions are based on advice from several agencies or advisory groups in the executive branch, each with different responsibilities and a different point of view. To be useful to the president, the advice must be brought together in a timely, intelligible way, with proper attention given to all the significant viewpoints and considerations. Unfortunately, complex organizational and group decision processes like these have a notorious capacity to produce self-defeating or morally unacceptable results. The specific ways in which they go awry are numerous, but in general terms there are three major threats: intelligence failures, in which critical information is filtered out at lower organizational levels (sometimes because subordinates think the president would be upset by or disagree with it);[22] groupthink, in which a decision-making group commits itself to a course of action prematurely and adheres to it because of social pressures to conform;[23] and noncoordination, which may occur in formulating advice, in handling interdependent issues, or in carrying out decisions.[24] Many of the frustrations of the Carter administration resulted from its failure to organize decision processes with sufficient care and skill. Carter's original energy proposals, which affected numerous federal programs, were formulated by a single drafting group under the direction of Secretary of Energy James Schlesinger. The group worked in secrecy and isolation, as well as under severe time pressure, which the president had imposed. The resulting proposals had serious flaws that, combined with resentment of the secrecy, led to a fiasco in Congress. Such problems were typical of the Carter administration. Its system of interagency task forces for domestic policymaking generally was chaotic and not well controlled by the White House.[25] Moreover, the White House itself lacked effective coordination.[26] In foreign policy, the major criticisms of the Carter administration concerned its propensity for vacillation and incoherence. These tendencies resulted largely from its failure to manage the conflict between the national security adviser, Zbigniew Brzezinski, and Secretary of State Cyrus Vance. Despite their different approaches to foreign policy, neither their respective roles nor the administration's foreign policy doctrines were ever adequately clear.[27] The problem was caused in part by Carter's failure to insist that Brzezinski stay within the limits of his assigned role.

In short, serious presidential failures will often result not from individual ignorance—the president's or his advisers'—but from an administration's collective failure to maintain reliable processes for decision. But what must a president know to avoid this danger, and how can he learn it?

The effort to design the best possible organization for presidential coordination of the executive branch is exceedingly complex and uncertain—fundamentally, it's a matter of hard trade-offs and guesses, not elegant solutions. Rather than adopt any one organizational plan, a president needs to have a high degree of process sensibility. He should be generally conversant with the risks and impediments to effective decision making and strongly committed to avoiding them. He should recognize the potentially decisive effects of structure, procedures, and leadership methods. And he should be prepared to assign these matters a high priority. In short, the president should treat organization and procedure as difficult matters of vital importance.

The main operational requirements are straightforward. One or more of the president's top-level staff should be a process specialist—someone with experience managing large organizations, ideally the White House itself, and whose role is defined primarily as a manager and guardian of the decision process, not as an adviser on politics and policy.[28] Certainly, one such person should be the president's chief of staff; others, lower in rank, are needed to manage each major area of policy. A suitable person for each of these roles is one who is sophisticated about the problems of organizational design and the subtleties of human relationships. The president should invest such a person with the support and authority needed to impose a decision-making structure and help him or her insist that everyone adhere to it. Because any organizational arrangement will have weaknesses, some of them unexpected, the president and other senior officials must give the decision-making process continual attention, monitoring its performance and making adjustments.

Finally, if any of this is to work, the president also must be willing to discipline his own participation in decision making. A well-managed, reliable decision-making process sometimes requires the president to perform, so to speak, unnatural acts. In the heat of debate about a major decision, taking the trouble to enforce general plans about structures and roles does not come naturally. Senior officials inevitably will try to bypass established procedures—asking for more control of a certain issue or ignoring channels to give the president direct advice. To enforce the procedures appears to distract from urgent decisions. In any case, the president's temptation is to react according to the substantive outcome he thinks he prefers: if an official who is supposed to be a neutral coordinator has a viewpoint the president likes, let him or her be heard; if an agency will make trouble over a decision that the president expects to support, let them stay out of it. Presidents are also tempted to attend primarily to those issues that most interest them, that they understand best, or that they see as promising satisfying results—all of which may fail to reflect their relative importance.

On important decisions that require intensive discussion—decisions in major foreign policy crises, for example—the requirements for presidential self-restraint are even more unnatural. To avoid serious mistakes, it is crucial not to suppress disagreement or close off debate prematurely. Thus it is important for the president to assume a neutral stance until the time comes to decide. According to psychologist Irving Janis's study of the Kennedy administration's disastrous decision to invade Cuba via the Bay of Pigs, the president unwittingly inhibited debate by his tone and manner of asking questions, which made it obvious that he believed, or wanted to believe, the invasion would work.[29] The president must restrain tendencies that are perfectly normal: to form opinions, especially optimistic ones, before all the evidence is in, and then to want others to relieve his anxiety by agreeing. He must have a strong process sensibility, if only because without it, he will lack the motivation to do his own part.

The performance of Reagan and his aides in organization and policy management was mixed. In establishing effective advisory systems, especially at the outset of the administration, they did well. The administration's principal device for making policy decisions, a system of "cabinet councils," was planned and run largely by Chief of Staff James Baker, who had a knack for organization and previous experience in the Ford administration.[30] Each cabinet council was a subcommittee of the full cabinet, staffed by the White House and chaired by a cabinet member or sometimes the president. The system generally worked well in blending departmental and White House perspectives and reaching decisions in a timely manner, and it kept cabinet members attuned to the president's goals. Inevitably, adjustments were made with the passage of time. The White House Legislative Strategy Group ended up making many of the decisions. Among the cabinet councils, the one assigned to coordinate economic policy, chaired by Treasury Secretary Regan, assumed a broad jurisdiction. To a degree, Reagan played his part in making these arrangements work. He enforced roles—removing a secretary of state, Alexander Haig, who was prone to exceed the limits of his charter—and invested the chief of staff with the authority to run an orderly process.

Nevertheless, the Reagan administration often failed to make decisions through a reasonably sound, deliberate process. One difficulty was that some of the officials Reagan selected to manage decision making lacked the appropriate skills or disposition for the task. In 1985 he allowed an exhausted Baker and an ambitious Regan to switch jobs. Although Regan by then had plenty of experience, he was less suited than Baker to the coordinating role of a chief of staff, and he soon came under attack for surrounding himself with weak subordinates and seeking to dominate the decision process. Until the appointment of Frank Carlucci in December 1986, the administration went through four undistinguished national security advisers— one of them, William Clark, a longtime associate of Reagan's with minimal experience in foreign policy.

On many occasions an even more important source of difficulty was the conduct of the president himself. Instead of exercising self-restraint and fostering discussion, Reagan gave his impulses free rein. He ignored bad news and reacted angrily to unwelcome advice.[31] His role in decisions was unpredictable. Reagan's announcement in March 1983 of the effort to develop a "Star Wars" missile defense system was made, as John Steinbruner says, "without prior staff work or technical definition . . . [and] rather astonished professional security bureaucracies throughout the world."[32] During the 1986 summit meeting with Mikhail Gorbachev in Reykjavik, Iceland, Reagan again acted without prior staff work when he tentatively accepted a surprise Soviet proposal to do away with long-range nuclear weapons—a utopian notion that ignored the vast superiority of Soviet conventional forces and was soon disavowed by the administration.

Finally, a lack of concern for the integrity of the decision process figured prominently in the Iran-contra scandal that emerged in late 1986, a disaster for U.S. foreign policy and the worst political crisis of the Reagan presidency. The secret arms sales to Iran were vehemently opposed by Secretary of State George Shultz and Secretary of Defense Caspar Weinberger, who wrote on his copy of the White House memorandum proposing the plan that it was "almost too absurd for comment." To get around their resistance, the White House largely excluded Shultz and Weinberger from further discussions and carried out the sales, in some degree, without their knowledge. Moreover, to escape the normal congressional oversight of covert activities, the transfers were handled directly by the staff of the National Security Council, designed as an advisory unit, instead of the Department of Defense (DOD) or the Central Intelligence Agency (CIA). In short, the White House deprived itself of the advice of the two principal cabinet members in foreign policy, the congressional leadership on intelligence matters, and the operational staff of DOD and the CIA—any of whom would have been likely to point out, aside from other serious objections, that the weapons transfers almost inevitably would become public.

Policy Promotion

Good policy decisions, carefully made, are not enough. Presidents also need competence in policy promotion—the ability to get things done in Washington and especially in Congress.[33] For no other major presidential task is the necessary knowledge more complicated or esoteric. Nevertheless, it is also a task in which delegation can largely substitute for the president's own judgment and thus one in which strategic competence places a modest burden on the president.

To promote his policies effectively, a president must make good decisions on complex, highly uncertain problems of strategy and tactics. Which presidential policy goals are politically feasible and which must be deferred? With which groups or congressional leaders should coalitions be formed? When resistance is met, should the president stand firm, perhaps taking the issue to the public, or should he compromise? In all these matters what is the proper timing? Such decisions call for a form of political expertise that has several related elements (all of them different from those involved in winning elections): a solid knowledge of the main coalitions, influence relationships, and rivalries among groups and individuals in Washington; personal acquaintance with a considerable number of important or well-informed individuals; and a fine-grained, practical understanding of how the political institutions work. Clearly, this expertise can be acquired only through substantial and recent experience in Washington. Its lack, however, need not pose much difficulty for a president. Like any technical skill, which in a sense it is, the necessary expertise can easily be hired; the president must only see his need for it.

Because a government as complex as that of the United States has a multitude of jobs that require political skill, people with the requisite experience in policy promotion abound. Many of them (to state the matter politely) would be willing to serve in the White House, and by just asking around a president can get readings on their reputations for effectiveness. Most important, having hired experienced Washington operatives, a president can delegate to them the critical judgments about feasibility, strategy, and political technique. It is not that such judgments are clear-cut, but unlike questions of policy, in these matters the boundary between the realm of expertise and that of values and ideology is easy to discern. Political strategy, in the narrow sense of how to realize policy objectives to the greatest possible extent, is ideologically neutral. It is even nonpartisan: Republican and Democratic presidents attempt to influence Congress in much the same ways.[34] In any case, a political expert's performance in the White House can be measured primarily by short-term results, that is, by how well the administration's policy goals are being achieved.

Both the value and the necessity of delegating policy promotion emerge from a comparison of Carter and Reagan—two presidents who had no prior Washington experience. If there was a single, root cause of the Carter administration's failure (underlying even its mismanagement of decision making), it was the president's refusal to recruit people with successful experience in Washington politics for top advisory and political jobs in the White House.

One of Carter's more unfortunate choices was that of Frank Moore to direct legislative liaison. Although he had held the same job in Georgia when Carter was governor, Moore had no experience in Washington and came to be regarded in Congress as out of his depth. Among Moore's initial staff, which consisted mostly of Georgians, two of the five professionals had worked neither in Congress nor as lobbyists. In organizing them, Moore chose a plan that had been opposed by the former Democratic liaison officials who had been asked for advice. Instead of using the conventional division by chambers and major congressional groups, Moore assigned each of his lobbyists an area of policy. This kept them from developing the stable relationships with individual members of Congress that would enhance trust, and it ignored the straightforward consideration that not all the issues in which the lobbyists specialized would be actively considered at the same time.[35] The Carter administration's reputed incompetence in dealing with Congress could have been predicted: the best of the many Georgians on Carter's staff were able and effective, but others were not, and collectively they lacked the local knowledge to operate skillfully in Washington.[36] Given this widely condemned failure of his immediate predecessor, it is not surprising that President Reagan avoided the same mistake. But it is still impressive how thoroughly he applied the lesson, even setting aside sectarian considerations for some of the top White House positions. James Baker, who was responsible mainly for political operations during the first term, had been a Ford administration appointee and campaign manager for Reagan's main opponent for the 1980 Republican nomination, George H. W. Bush. Baker was also considered too moderate for a high-level position by many of Reagan's conservative supporters. The congressional liaison director, Max Friedersdorf, was another mainstream Republican, who had worked on congressional relations for Nixon and Ford.[37] In short, the political strategy for policy promotion by which the "Reagan revolution" was pushed through Congress in 1981 was devised and executed by hired hands who were latecomers, at most, to Reaganism. Some change in personnel occurred in subsequent years, including the job switch by Baker and Regan, but the organization and management of this function were essentially stable.[38]

Although the task of formulating strategy for policy promotion can be delegated, much of the hard work cannot. Nothing can draw attention to a proposal and stimulate active public support like a well-presented speech by the president. Furthermore, certain votes are available in Congress if the president makes the necessary phone calls or meets with the right members. The latter task is often tedious, however, if not somewhat demeaning—pleading for support, repeating the same pitch over and over, and promising favors to some while evading requests from others. Presidents therefore often neglect this duty, a source of frustration for their staffs. Carter "went all over the country for two years asking everybody he saw to vote for him," his press secretary complained, "but he doesn't like to call up a Congressman and ask for his support on a bill."[39] Reagan, in contrast, spared no personal effort to pass his program. During the debate on funding for the MX missile in 1985, he had face-to-face meetings with more than 200 members of Congress and followed up with dozens of phone calls. In 1986, when House Republicans felt they were being ignored in negotiations on tax reform, he went to Capitol Hill to make amends. In the end, a president's effectiveness in lobbying and making speeches depends very much on his basic skills in persuasive communication. A lack of such skills cannot be made up by presidential aides, nor can it be overcome to any great extent by on-the-job learning.

THE POSSIBILITY OF COMPETENCE

Presidential competence, then, is not impossible. The requirements of knowledge and effort on the president's part are manageable—but only if the president has a strategy for competence that puts his own limited resources to use where they are most needed.

With regard to knowledge for making *policy decisions,* the president needs to have given serious attention to public policy, in one or more prior roles, and thus be able to recognize the elements of responsible advocacy. The inauguration is too late to begin learning about policy. On the other hand, reading stacks of policy memoranda—whether as president or beforehand—is neither necessary nor even productive. To maintain an effective *policy process,* the president need not draw the boxes and arrows of organization charts. He needs to have a strong process sensibility—that is, a clear sense of the need for careful and self-conscious management of decision making and a willingness to discipline his own participation. Finally, the president must know enough to avail himself of the assistance of persons experienced in *policy promotion* in Washington, and especially in dealing with Congress—whether they have been longtime supporters or not. Then he must largely follow their advice and do the often tedious work they ask of him.

Such competence does not ensure that presidents will always make good decisions or act in effective ways from their own standpoint—let alone that those decisions and actions will always have the intended results. But it will help avoid costly mistakes and give a president the greatest chances for success.

PRESIDENTIAL COMPETENCE FROM GEORGE H. W. BUSH TO DONALD TRUMP

The requirements for strategic competence help to account for the successes and failures of the five presidents who followed Reagan—George H. W. Bush, Bill Clinton, George W. Bush, Barack Obama, and Donald Trump. The experience of these presidents provides ample support for the central notions of strategic competence—in particular, the impossibility of self-reliance, the inadequacy of minimalism, and the importance of the president's prior preparation, process sensibility, self-discipline, and strategic use of his own talents.

George H. W. Bush: Failing Self-Discipline

Political commentators often refer to George H. W. Bush as a failed president, mostly because he was defeated for reelection.[40] His defeat, however, did not reflect adversely on his competence as president. In 1991, with the economy in a recession, Bush refused to support a stimulative tax cut or spending increase, a stance later portrayed by Democratic opponent Bill Clinton as showing indifference to the nation's economic distress. In fact, Bush followed the advice of most economists, who argued that recovery was already underway and warned that increasing an already oversized budget deficit would do harm in the long run.[41] Unfortunately for Bush, the weak economy hung on through most of 1992, eroded his public support, and was central to his defeat in the election.[42] Politically, Bush's economic competence mostly benefited his Democratic successor, who had the advantage of a sound economic recovery.

Yet Bush's political difficulties also stemmed from his own deficiencies in strategic competence. To be sure, he was generally well versed in public policy. He appointed an experienced cabinet and staff and used orderly decision processes.[43] He drew on his extensive personal contacts to help advance his policies in Congress.

Bush fell short of strategic competence, however, in one important respect. Instead of disciplining his participation in decision making, he allowed personal predilections to shape advisory processes and determine decisions. In particular, Bush had little patience for dealing with domestic policy. With a Democratic Congress, political circumstances did not favor major domestic achievements, and Bush's extensive experience in foreign policy as a former U.S. envoy to China and CIA director led him to prefer his international responsibilities. Instead of working within the political constraints, Bush openly disdained his domestic role.[44] He offered no legislative agenda in his first year, and ignored the few administration officials who tried to advance innovative conservative domestic initiatives.[45] Added to the weak economy, Bush's lack of a domestic agenda was an effective issue for the Democrats in the 1992 campaign. Bush was reduced to promising that in a second term he would replace his White House staff and work mainly on domestic problems. He did not get the chance.

Bill Clinton: Learning on the Job

Bill Clinton's presidency was marked by both success and failure. Although Clinton achieved major policy successes on deficit reduction and the North American Free Trade Agreement, he experienced costly defeats on gay rights and health care reform. He suffered a crushing partisan defeat in the 1994 congressional elections, but then bounced back to win reelection in 1996. In his second term, he balanced the federal budget and presided over a booming economy. In the central crisis of his presidency, Clinton was impeached by the House on charges of perjury and obstruction of justice in the Monica Lewinsky scandal, but then he was acquitted on a mostly partisan vote in the Senate trial.[46]

Two points are crucial to understanding Clinton's performance. First, he had good luck with the economy. Although his economic policies generally received reasonably high marks from economists, he also had the good fortune to enter office at the beginning of a major, technology-induced economic boom.[47] He enjoyed sustained popularity on the strength of a prolonged stretch of economic growth. Second, he learned from his early strategic mistakes.

In many respects, Clinton was a conspicuously gifted political leader.[48] From the outset of his presidency, he showed an extraordinary grasp of policy issues. He performed with energy and skill in promoting his policies and was an exceptionally effective public speaker.

With respect to management of decision processes, however, Clinton began abysmally and got his bearings only later. His first chief of staff, Thomas "Mack" McLarty, was an Arkansas businessman who was out of his element in White House politics, and many staff members were young people from the campaign with minimal professional experience of any kind.[49] Dominated by liberals, the early staff included few of the centrist Democrats for whom Clinton had been a spokesman before the 1992 campaign.[50] The decision-making process in the early Clinton White House was haphazard, without much explicit management or structure.[51] In some areas, Clinton practiced a form of self-reliance, making up for the lack of structured advisory processes by indulging in long-winded discussions with the staff.[52] As a result, he effectively ignored other important areas, especially foreign policy. In separate episodes, the administration announced major policy changes on Bosnia and Cuba without the president having been apprised of them.[53] In an episode that undermined the main element of his domestic program, Clinton put his wife, Hillary Clinton, and academic policy analyst Ira Magaziner—neither with experience in executive branch policymaking—in charge of developing his 1993 health care reform plan. They came up with a proposal that sank under the weight of its massive costs and bureaucratic complexity.[54] The inexperienced and ideologically unbalanced staff contributed to a legion of political difficulties in Clinton's first two years and a disastrous Democratic defeat in the 1994 congressional elections.

By the beginning of his second year, however, Clinton had come to understand the costs of careless management and began to bring order and a more moderate direction to the decision-making process.[55] Clinton found an experienced Washington hand and skilled manager to run the White House: Leon Panetta, OMB director and former chair of the House Budget Committee. In addition, he brought in David Gergen, a former Republican White House aide, to consult on strategy.

After he reformed his decision-making methods, Clinton was generally skillful and effective. Paying more attention to foreign policy, he undertook successful military interventions in Bosnia, Haiti, and Serbia. In 1995, Clinton won a political showdown with congressional Republicans over their Contract with America and, especially, the budget.[56] In his second term, Clinton worked with the Republicans to balance the budget while fending off their attacks on Medicare and Social Security. In the end, the grave questions about Clinton raised by the Monica Lewinsky scandal concerned character, not competence.

George W. Bush: Careless Delegation

Although George W. Bush was the son of one president, his approach to the office had more in common with that of a different president, Ronald Reagan. Like Reagan, Bush was a minimalist, who made only modest investments of personal effort in decision making and management. But his version of minimalism differed from Reagan's in two respects. On one hand, Bush was more willing than Reagan to defer to subordinates. On the other hand, Bush's subordinates reflected a narrower range of the political spectrum. The combination was often disastrous.

Bush's resort to a chair-of-the-board, minimalist strategy was essentially required by his limited interest in substantive issues of government and policy.[57] In his six years as governor of Texas, Bush rarely dealt with issues in much depth.[58] During the 2000 campaign, he displayed unfamiliarity with major issues.[59] As president, therefore, he was highly dependent on his advisors.

Early in his first term, Bush appeared to escape the pitfalls of the minimalist approach. His vice president—Dick Cheney—his cabinet, and his White House staff were undeniably capable and experienced.[60] Senior political counselor Karl Rove and communications director Karen Hughes were experienced political hands, and the chief of staff, Andrew Card, had been deputy chief of staff in the earlier Bush administration. Card faithfully adopted the honest-broker role in policy deliberations. Bush appointed an academic with modest governmental experience, Condoleezza Rice, as national security adviser.[61] But Secretary of State Colin Powell and Secretary of Defense Donald Rumsfeld both had had distinguished Washington careers.

Bush allowed subordinates to define the direction of his administration. Indeed, Cheney ran the transition process while Bush waited in the wings at his Texas ranch. After the inauguration, Bush delegated critical decisions with little direction.[62] He met with his budget team for a total of five hours to make all the decisions for his first budget proposal.[63] In general, domestic policy was divided between Cheney, who focused on economic issues, and Rove, the main pipeline to the Christian right, who focused on social issues.

Predictably, Bush's heavy reliance on subordinates led to media criticism and pressure for the president to take on more personal responsibility. Regarding Cheney's extraordinary power, the joke circulated that Bush was "a heartbeat away from the presidency." To counter this image, the White House put out dubious accounts of Bush's deep engagement in policy making,[64] all based on unverifiable reports of private meetings.[65] Nevertheless, unlike with Reagan, there were no reports of Bush overruling his advisers, barring options they wanted to consider, or catching them off guard with an unexpected decision. On the whole, Bush appeared comfortable in the limited role of a minimalist president.[66]

Well into his first year as president, the Bush-style minimalist presidency appeared to be working. But it eventually contributed to serious difficulties and a failed, if not calamitous, presidency.[67] His methods had three problematic consequences for his performance. First, Bush allowed hardline conservative senior officials, especially Cheney, to manipulate advisory processes and capture control of his administration. Cheney promoted a hard-right agenda on a wide range of domestic, foreign policy, and constitutional issues.[68] Bush thus lurched away from the centrist, "compassionate conservative" posture of his presidential campaign.[69] Second, Bush's approach enabled advisers to abandon formal advisory processes and seriously neglect substantive deliberation.[70] Instead of compensating for the president's lack of interest in substantive policy deliberation, Bush's advisers often took cues from it.[71] Independent reports by former senior officials portrayed a lack of concern for the substantive merits of policy decisions. "On social policy and related issues," said an analytically inclined former staffer, "the lack of even basic policy knowledge, and the only casual interest in knowing more, was somewhat breathtaking."[72] After Treasury Secretary Paul O'Neill was forced out of the administration in 2003, he described Bush's indifference to economic analysis of decisions about taxes and the budget.[73] In fact, the Bush administration pushed a series of tax cuts that drove long-term budget deficits to alarming levels.[74] The Bush domestic team confirmed the tendency for White House decision making to mimic a minimalist president's style of thinking.[75]

Third, Bush's methods permitted his administration's foreign-policy-making process to be dominated by advocates of an even narrower ideological perspective. Most of the central figures in Bush's foreign policy apparatus—Cheney, Rice, Defense Secretary Donald Rumsfeld, and Deputy Secretary Paul Wolfowitz—held a highly distinctive, neoconservative view of the world, shared by only a fraction of the foreign-policy community. From the start, administration neoconservatives favored an aggressive, unilateralist foreign policy; unwavering support for Israel; and, at the first opportunity, war with Iraq to remove Saddam Hussein from power.[76] Even conventional conservatives such as Secretary of State Powell were marginalized. A strategically competent president would have maintained a more balanced foreign policy advisory process.

In 2003 Bush, Cheney, and Rumsfeld led the nation into a costly and unnecessary war in Iraq, which they also mismanaged in multiple ways.[77] They acted on dubious assumptions about the need for the war and the prospects for success and overlooked contrary evidence. Perhaps unintentionally, they put pressure on military and intelligence agencies to confirm their beliefs. In the most notorious mistake, they asserted repeatedly and with complete certitude that Iraq possessed major stockpiles of chemical and biological weapons, had an active program to develop nuclear weapons, and constituted an imminent threat to the United States.[78] At a crucial meeting leading up to the invasion, Bush asked CIA director George Tenet for his final assessment of the case for Iraq's possessing weapons of mass destruction. Tenet called it "a slam dunk."[79] A competent president would have asked hard questions about the evidence, but Bush settled for the sports metaphor. As subsequent investigations found, the evidence was ludicrously weak, consisting largely of unsupported claims by Iraqi defectors who were currying favor with American officials.[80]

The Bush administration made additional costly misjudgments, mostly reflecting wishful thinking, on a variety of crucial matters about the war—from the troop levels needed, to the severity of sectarian conflict, to the prospects for a rapid transition to self-government in Iraq, among others. On all these issues, the administration's doctrinaire approach distorted the intelligence it received.[81] In the final two years of his presidency—following the collapse of his public support and the Democratic sweep in the 2006 midterm congressional elections—Bush made important changes. He replaced Rumsfeld with the moderate and experienced Robert Gates as secretary of defense, reduced Cheney's influence, and restored procedural regularity to White House decision making.[82] Bush's policymaking became less driven by ideology and wishful thinking. He changed course in Iraq, using a 2007 "surge" in troop levels to help improve the security situation there and prepare for an eventual withdrawal of American troops. In the financial crisis that developed in fall 2008, Bush swallowed his ideological objections to government intervention and helped pass a $750 billion financial rescue package. From the standpoint of rescuing Bush's presidency, however, the learning came too late.

Barack Obama: The Limits of Competence

Barack Obama entered the White House in 2009 amid the most threatening national conditions that had faced any president since Franklin Roosevelt during the Great Depression.[83] American troops were fighting in Iraq and Afghanistan. The nation's economy was sinking rapidly into the worst recession in seventy years, propelled downward by a collapse of the credit markets. In his first two years, Obama performed competently. He had major successes in effecting policy change and substantial success in resuscitating the economy. After Republicans took control of the House and picked up six Senate seats in the 2010 midterm elections, however, a new level of polarized conflict and partisan gridlock made American government virtually unworkable. Even after his solid reelection victory in 2012, Obama sometimes faced a struggle just to avoid calamitous governmental failure.

Despite limited prior experience in Washington, Obama arrived in the White House with ample sophistication about policy to permit strategic competence in policymaking. After catapulting to national prominence with a celebrated 2004 Democratic convention speech, Obama had spent four years in the Senate, mostly campaigning for president. But he had done his homework on public policy throughout his prior career. His speeches as an Illinois state senator were noted for in-depth treatment of policy issues. During the 2008 televised presidential debates, Obama gave specific, informed answers to questions about national issues. He discussed a range of issues accurately and in detail in his first press conference, only two weeks after the inauguration.[84] Obama demonstrated a well-developed process sensibility and appreciation for the value of Washington experience. In an unusual investment of time for a presidential candidate, he quietly worked on plans for his presidency with an unannounced transition team during the last two months of the campaign.

After the election, Obama quickly named a chief of staff, Rahm Emanuel, who had an extraordinary range of Washington experience as both deputy chief of staff in the Clinton White House and a member of the House Democratic leadership. The selection promised competent staff leadership for White House management, political strategy, and policy promotion. Obama's appointees to top economic and foreign policy positions—Lawrence Summers as director of the National Economic Council, Timothy Geithner as secretary of the Treasury, Hillary Clinton as secretary of state, Robert Gates as secretary of defense, and James Jones as national security adviser, among others—were notable for diverse views, distinguished credentials, and high-level experience in national government.[85]

With respect to structure, Obama designated White House "czars" to coordinate policy for energy and climate change, health care reform, and urban affairs, and he created new staff positions to coordinate technology and management-performance policies. He appointed Vice President Joe Biden to oversee the massive economic stimulus program. In describing his plans for the decision-making process, Obama cited the danger of groupthink and promised that he would make decisions on the basis of vigorous debate between advisers with strong views.[86] In a careful analysis of his decision-making processes on four major issues, James Pfiffner found that Obama, unlike Bush, largely followed through on his stated organizational plans.[87] He heard vigorous debate on each issue.

Obama also disciplined his own participation in decision making. He was highly engaged in major decisions but relied on his appointees and executive branch experts to present the issues and arguments. When military leaders proposed to send additional troops to Afghanistan, Obama, who had campaigned on winding down the war, was initially skeptical. But he listened to a full-scale debate among his military and foreign-policy advisers and approved the troop increase.[88] Although Obama never abandoned the deliberative process, neither did he simply ratify the majority view of his advisers. In his decision to authorize the risky military raid into Pakistan that succeeded in killing Osama Bin Laden, for example, he overruled a more cautious majority view. Finally, he avoided premature expressions of his personal views that would tend to bias subordinates' advice. In short, Obama's management of decision-making processes met the requirements of strategic competence.

In general, Obama did his part to promote his policies. To build support for his $800 billion economic stimulus package, he met with numerous Republican as well as Democratic members of Congress. Exploiting his early popularity, with public approval ratings above 60 percent, he traveled around the country every week, visiting places hard hit by the economic crisis to make the case for his proposals. On other issues, Obama went on speaking tours, gave televised speeches, made visits to Congress, or met face-to-face with Republican congressional leaders. On the health care reform bill, Obama was by many accounts too deferential to Congress and tolerant of delay, especially in the slow-moving Senate. But the approach reflected a conscious strategy of allowing Congress to take the lead on health care, in contrast with Clinton's unsuccessful, opposite strategy sixteen years earlier. After House Democrats criticized his approach as too passive, Obama joined the fray with a more assertive and ultimately successful approach.

The main objections to Obama's efforts at policy promotion concerned these and other matters of strategy. Two issues of strategy resulted from commitments he made during the 2008 campaign. First, he promised to bring "change" to Washington, in large part by restoring a greater degree of bipartisan cooperation.[89] In Obama's first months in office, he bent over backward trying to build bipartisan coalitions in Congress. Unfortunately, the severe partisan conflict that had developed by the time he became president was not the result of misunderstanding that could be overcome through friendly gestures. It was grounded in long-term trends in regional partisan alignments, the media, and electoral politics.[90] As the result of these trends, statistical analyses show, centrists had almost disappeared from both congressional parties, and Republicans in particular had become more ideologically extreme.[91]

Obama's efforts to cultivate Republican support failed almost completely. Congress passed his stimulus package without a single Republican vote in the House and with the votes of only the three most moderate Republicans in the Senate, barely enough to avoid a filibuster. Democrats complained that Obama made costly policy concessions to the Republicans and received nothing in return but partisan criticism. The episode led Obama to warn that eventually he would run out of patience for such results. "I am the eternal optimist," he remarked. "But I am not a sap."[92]

In the view of many liberals, however, Obama was exactly that—making major concessions to Republicans on health care, financial reform, stimulus measures, and tax policy without receiving significant concessions or support in return. In the transition to his second term, Obama deferred to Republican criticism of his first choice of successor to Hillary Clinton as secretary of state, Susan Rice. He also named a former Republican senator, Chuck Hagel, as his nominee for secretary of defense, only to encounter strong Republican opposition to Hagel. Liberal economist Paul Krugman has blamed Obama's deference to Republicans—especially his failure to push for a much larger stimulus program—for the disappointing pace of the economic recovery.[93] The liberal criticism of Obama's strategy is, however, speculative. If Obama had taken stronger liberal positions, he might merely have lost support from the small group of centrists, prompted even more intense or more effective Republican resistance, and accomplished less.[94]

In the second issue regarding his strategy, Obama, despite the onset of a severe economic crisis in the middle of the 2008 campaign, refused to scale back his ambitious agenda of policy reforms. In addition to dealing with the economy and trying to wind down two wars, Obama began his presidency in 2009 with plans for major initiatives on health care, financial regulation, education, immigration, energy, and climate change. Critics argued that he was biting off more than he or Congress could chew and that he should postpone domestic reforms and concentrate on the economy. In rebuttal, Emanuel remarked that the administration did not want to "waste a good crisis," suggesting that the need for economic stimulus would enhance support for worthy programs.[95] In fact, Congress in 2009 and 2010 passed landmark measures to rescue the auto industry, reform health care, and strengthen regulation of banking and financial services.

Some have argued that enacting health care reform, in particular, entailed heavy political costs for Obama and the Democrats.[96] By the time the Affordable Care Act was signed into law in March 2010, it had become moderately unpopular. Republicans campaigned on promises to repeal it in every election from 2010 to 2016.[97] But when the 2016 elections finally handed Republicans unified control of the presidency and both houses of Congress, they proved unable to agree on a measure to replace it. In the long run, "Obamacare" may be the centerpiece of Obama's legacy. In short, Obama's major strategic choices were defensible and arguably successful in both policy and political terms.

In the end, however, the Obama presidency points to the profound difficulties that face even a generally competent president in a period of exceptionally intense and often destructive partisan conflict. Obama's major first-term policy achievements all occurred during the first two years of his first term, during which the

Democrats controlled both houses of Congress. Under the conditions of divided party control that shaped his last six years—and with the Republican congressional leadership often unable even to secure the cooperation of their own party's most conservative wing—Congress exhibited a level of dysfunction that no amount of presidential competence could have overcome. The president and congressional leaders struggled merely to keep the government open and avoid a potentially cata-strophic decision to default on the government's debt, and the three Congresses of that period were the three least productive Congresses of the modern era.

Donald Trump: Refusing to Learn

In the first year of his term, Donald Trump's presidency differed from all of the others discussed in this chapter. Trump did not attempt any of the major approaches to competent leadership employed by previous presidents—ranging from prior learning and prodigious personal effort, to wholesale delegation to qualified sub-ordinates, to the calculated combination of delegation and personal engagement that I have called "strategic competence." With only occasional, partial exceptions, he met none of the requirements for strategic competence. Rather, Trump in effect rejected the basic assumption—never before challenged in the modern era—of the need for specialized skills and highly informed decisions for a successful presidency. His presidency was an experiment in substituting the skills and methods that he had learned during his business and entertainment-industry career and in the 2016 presidential campaign for those normally associated with presidential leadership. As of the fall of 2017, the experiment by any plausible standard was an abject failure.

Throughout the campaign, it was apparent that for Trump to perform com-petently as president would be, at best, a major challenge. From the standpoint of prior experience and knowledge of government, he was perhaps the least pre-pared major party candidate in American history.[98] He was the first who had never held public office of any kind. Far from being generally familiar with sophisticated policy argument in a wide range of areas—one of the prerequisites for strategic competence—he apparently had less awareness of issues or policies than many lay people. In published transcripts of interviews with the editorial boards of both the *Washington Post* and the *New York Times*, he displayed wildly incorrect factual beliefs about multiple rudimentary matters of government and policy—leaving the reporters and editors incredulous.[99] His main prior involvement in political debate had been as the leading promoter of Obama birtherism, the scurrilous conspiracy theory that President Obama had not been born in the United States. Unlike many business executives and even some entertainers, Trump had never served on a major expert commission, advised policymakers on issues of national policy, or been a leading spokesperson for a significant public-policy initiative.

Nor did Trump have any experience with the process or management issues that face a president. He had neither participated in nor observed from a position of proximity presidential decision making, the management of the Executive Branch, or the promotion of policy change in Washington. He had been the chief executive of a moderately large, privately held business enterprise, engaged mainly in real estate development and franchising of hotels, resorts, and casinos. He managed the enterprise in a manner that generally met the requirements of such a business—relying on a highly informal top-management group consisting mainly of family members and a few personally loyal hired managers.[100] Given the limitations of his knowledge and experience, for Trump to serve competently as president, he would have had more to learn, and would have been forced to rely more heavily on experienced advisers, than any other modern occupant of the office. As discussed earlier in the chapter, there would have been, at best, serious risks of that approach.

Unfortunately, Trump had more permanent and ultimately disabling barriers to competent performance in his fundamental dispositions and personality. His lack of knowledge about matters of government during the campaign reflected an absence of any curiosity about such information, or even willingness to take it seriously.[101] His policy positions were evidently selected for how they played at campaign rallies, without regard for feasibility or substantive soundness. In his signature campaign commitment, he promised, dubiously, to build a wall along the border with Mexico and added, absurdly, that Mexico would pay for it. He suddenly dropped that promise in order to facilitate a planned meeting with the president of Mexico, and then reinstated it just as suddenly when campaign supporters called him out. His feel-good economic proposals were rejected by every one of the 35 ideologically diverse economists surveyed by the University of Chicago.[102] He dismissed scientific findings, economic analysis, bipartisan consensus, and even Republican doctrines on issues such as climate change, immigration, trade, military alliances, and other subjects. After winning the election, Trump generally declined to sit for the president's daily intelligence briefings, which he pronounced boring and unnecessary, and he rejected the agencies' highly confident finding that the Russian government had sought to help Trump win the 2016 election. Far from working to get up to speed on policy, Trump largely ignored specific information or expert opinion about policy and made whatever claims or promises he found rhetorically appealing at the time he made them.[103]

Trump's attitude toward policy information, however, was just one facet of his deeply problematic personality.[104] He told falsehoods with prodigious frequency, even when they could be immediately exposed through readily available video evidence. He expressed wildly exaggerated estimates of his abilities and power, declaring, "I know more about ISIS than the generals do" and (in reference to various national problems) "I alone can fix it." He was prone to destructive rage and obsessed with punishing anyone who criticized him—even when the targets of his attacks would receive most of the sympathy. He needed constant praise and spent much of his time watching *Fox News* or reading staff-curated collections of favorable news coverage in order to find it. Although many mental-health professionals were wary of attempting a diagnosis without benefit of a formal examination, those who offered opinions almost uniformly agreed that Trump exhibited a particular, dysfunctional mental-health condition—narcissistic personality.[105] Meanwhile, pundits and journalists debated whether Trump was aware of his falsehoods or simply deluded, as well as about whether his aggressive attacks were conscious strategies to rally his base or impulsive behavior that he could not control.[106]

To an extent that cannot be defined less than a year into his presidency, Trump also entered office with another major barrier to successful performance: several members of his campaign—including campaign chairman Paul Manafort, foreign-policy adviser Michael Flynn, Trump's son Donald Jr., and his son-in-law Jared Kushner—had questionable contacts with persons associated with the Russian government.[107] News reports suggested that some of these contacts may have involved illegal business dealings, collusion in Russian efforts to influence the election, or both. Trump was not yet implicated in these activities.[108] At this stage, it is still possible that no definitive evidence of serious misconduct will emerge. What is already clear, however, is that multiple individuals close to Trump repeatedly failed to disclose numerous and extensive contacts with Russians, when legally required to do so, and that Trump has been alarmed, angered, and massively distracted by the congressional and FBI investigations into these matters. As will be seen below, his responses to the investigations only harmed his cause. It may eventually emerge that the campaign's connections with Russia, or the subsequent efforts to cover up those connections, doomed Trump's presidency before it began.

Finally, Trump faced a highly distinctive and difficult challenge in that not only did he lack ties to any network of experienced Republican or conservative advisers and managers, able to serve in staff or other appointive positions, but many of the individuals otherwise eligible for such roles had strongly opposed him, often in sharply disparaging terms, during the nomination campaign. One group of fifty former Republican foreign-policy officials signed a widely reported public letter declaring him unfit for the presidency.[109] Trump was not one to forgive and forget such insults, even if those who made them wanted his forgiveness. Other potential staffers and appointees might have served in another Republican administration but perceived too much risk to their careers in signing on with the Trump administration. Compared with most incoming presidents, therefore, Trump had to deal with a depleted talent pool of potential appointees.[110]

Through the transition and first year of his presidency, Trump proved, if anything, less competent and more dangerous than even most of his pre-election critics might have expected. Rather than pivoting to a more presidential approach—recruiting and relying on some of the better-qualified advisers and managers who would have been willing to serve—Trump acted on his own uninformed, self-obsessed, and often reckless impulses to an extent that few commentators had anticipated.

In staffing and organizing the White House, Trump frequently ignored generally accepted notions of sound practice that had developed through the experience of previous presidents.[111] Initially, he appointed New Jersey governor Chris Christie to head his transition team. But before the Inauguration, Trump, reportedly offended by Christie's promotion of some of his own aides for high-level positions, fired him as transition chief and threw out all of the plans, research, and lists of potential appointees that he had developed. Trump thus entered the White House with minimal planning or preparation.

His staffing of the White House flew in the face of recognized sound practice in several respects. He appointed Reince Priebus as chief of staff and Steve Bannon as senior advisor for political strategy. Priebus had never held public office, legislative or executive, but had been chair of the Republican National Committee (RNC). Although he could serve as a bridge to mainstream Republicans, he had no direct experience with policymaking or administration, let alone coordinating the White House. In any case, Trump held an abiding and undisguised distrust of Priebus for his lack of support at certain stages of the nomination contest. There was never a chance that Trump would give Priebus the authority to create and maintain orderly decision processes. Bannon, the chief executive of the alt-right Breitbart News website and a leading adviser to Trump's campaign, had no experience in government either, but was adept at fashioning rhetorical and policy appeals to Trump's right-wing populist constituency. In addition to their lack of experience, Priebus and Bannon had radically opposed views about the direction of the administration. Few commentators had much optimism about their ability to work together.

At the same time, Trump appointed a third individual with no government experience, his 36-year-old businessman son-in-law Jared Kushner, to another senior advisor position, and gave him possibly the most diverse substantive policy jurisdiction ever seen in the White House. Kushner had lead responsibility for the Arab–Israeli conflict, governmental efficiency reforms, criminal justice reform, and the opioid crisis. Trump's daughter Ivanka also occupied an office in the White House. Other White House positions were distributed among several, frequently warring factions. Few observers, if any, expected this staffing to produce an effective White House operation.[112]

Trump's first-year cabinet and subcabinet appointments also represented sharp departures from accepted practice. The cabinet appointments heavily emphasized business people and campaign contributors. Most appointees had little or no experience relevant to their agencies—except, in a few cases, as opponents of their agencies' central missions. Most of them were extremely wealthy. Economists, scientists, and other experts were notable for their absence. Unlike any previous president, Trump made no nominations for a large majority of the roughly 200 top subcabinet positions—the assistant secretaries, undersecretaries, and other senior administration posts. Although he suggested that most of these jobs were unnecessary, they are in fact central to an agency's effective performance and to a presidential administration's ability to control it.

An area of relative strength in Trump's appointments was his foreign policy and national security team. His initial choice for national security adviser, the hardline anti-Islamic promoter of conspiracy theories General Michael Flynn, alarmed commentators. But Flynn resigned within two weeks of his appointment over his false denial of ties to Russia, and Trump then appointed a highly respected general with extensive Washington and foreign-policy experience, H. R. McMaster. Secretary of State Rex Tillerson, the former chief executive of Exxon-Mobil, was qualified only by his leadership of a major international business. Tillerson also isolated himself from and worked to dismantle the professional expertise of the State Department. But Secretary of Defense James Mattis was a distinguished military leader with a deep understanding of national security issues.[113] Collectively, the national security team was experienced, accomplished, and determined to maintain the United States' long-term international commitments and preserve the country's strategic alliances.

Despite serious deficiencies of the White House and agency personnel, the truly debilitating weakness of Trump's presidency was his own undisciplined and reckless conduct. Trump made decisions on the spur of the moment, without information or qualified advice, even on sensitive issues of foreign policy. In his speech at a major meeting of the North Atlantic Treaty Organization (NATO), for example, he caught his national security team off guard by pointedly omitting the expected reaffirmation of the alliance's mutual defense commitments—an omission that not only offended allies but potentially encouraged Russian aggression.[114] Secretary Mattis rushed to publicly affirm the American commitment, but the damage had been done to both the United States' and NATO's credibility. During a visit to Saudi Arabia, Trump casually gave his strong endorsement of Saudi complaints against Qatar; with the president's implied support, a Saudi-led multi-country coalition imposed an economic boycott on Qatar, critically threatening an important American military ally in the region. Again, Trump's national security team was forced to try to rescue the situation.

In another rude surprise for national-security officialdom, Trump tweeted a declaration that the U.S. military would no longer permit service by transgender personnel—even though an estimated several thousand transgender individuals had been providing valued service, without significant difficulties, for many years. The legal effect of an order conveyed by a tweet from the president, with no accompanying formal document, was highly uncertain. The message also gave no guidance on the handling of transgender persons who were currently serving. The Defense Department, openly irritated, essentially nullified the order, at least temporarily, announcing that there would be no change in policy until further notice. Secretaries Tillerson and Mattis also worked hard, with limited success, to prevent Trump from pulling out of the Iranian nuclear agreement, which Trump was eager to do if only because it had been signed by President Obama.

In dealing with North Korea's threatening testing of nuclear weapons and ballistic missiles, Trump exchanged a series of public, cataclysmic threats with the similarly volatile North Korean leader Kim Jong-un. All but explicitly, Trump threatened a nuclear attack on a country that had unpredictable, reckless leadership and that was already able to impose vast harm, at least with conventional weapons, on an American ally, South Korea. In a characteristic, over-the-top insult, Trump derided Kim as "little rocket man." When Secretary of State Tillerson announced that he had established contact with North Korea and intended to pursue negotiations, Trump tweeted that Tillerson was wasting his time and implied his preference for a military solution. Horrified critics from all parts of the political spectrum denounced Trump's conduct as risking the start of World War III. In the midst of this conflict, Trump reportedly told a meeting of his national security advisers that he wanted a 10-fold increase in American nuclear arms. The demand prompted Tillerson in conversation after the meeting to call Trump a "f***ing moron."[115]

On the domestic front, Trump's lack of self-discipline and orderly processes was manifested both in substantive policymaking and in efforts at policy promotion.[116] In his first days in office, he issued a "travel ban," targeting seven Islamic countries, without consulting the Departments of Justice or Homeland Security. He called for a repeal of the Affordable Care Act ("Obamacare"), while providing no assistance in developing a workable substitute health care policy. As House and Senate Republicans struggled to develop bills that they could pass, Trump casually changed positions on basic strategy multiple times (for example, on whether to enact the needed replacement policy immediately or at a future date), and issued substantive demands that no Republican health care policy could conceivably achieve (for example, that no one would lose health coverage). Republican legislators came away from a strategy meeting at the White House complaining that Trump knew nothing about how health care worked or the provisions of the bill he was pushing. After successfully pressuring House Republicans to pass a repeal bill that cut coverage for millions and would give Democratic opponents strong ammunition in the midterm elections, Trump called the bill "mean" and urged the Senate to improve it—in effect, sharply criticizing the House members who had supported him. When Senate Republicans proved unable to pass a repeal bill, Trump publicly questioned whether Majority Leader Mitch McConnell should keep his position. The incoherent policymaking and unsteady leadership were more-or-less duplicated in each major area of Trump's domestic agenda—immigration (and the border wall), infrastructure, and tax reform. By the end of the year, only a major tax bill—primarily tax cuts for corporations and the wealthy—had been enacted.

In what could ultimately bring about a premature end to his presidency, Trump exhibited the same reckless, uncalculating conduct in dealing with the ongoing investigations about Russian election interference, possible collusion by his campaign, and possible efforts to cover up illegal conduct. Trump repeatedly and consistently rejected the intelligence community's highly confident finding— accepted by all other leading Republicans—that Russia had used a variety of means to influence the campaign in his favor. (The finding did not suggest that the Russian interference had swung the election.) Most important, Trump in private meetings pressed FBI director James Comey to announce that he was not a target of the investigation and to drop the case against former National Security Adviser Flynn.[117] When Comey did not comply, Trump found a flimsy pretext and ordered him fired. Dropping the pretext, however, he explained in a sit-down interview with NBC News anchor Lester Holt that he had indeed fired Comey precisely to block the Russia investigation. As some commentators noted, a good legal argument could be made that Trump had confessed on national television to obstruction of justice.[118] Instead of ending the investigation, the firing led the Justice Department to appoint a special counsel, Robert Mueller, to take it over and expand it.[119]

As of the fall of his first year in office, Trump's presidency was in disarray. He had had one undeniable major success—appointing and gaining Senate confirmation for a well-qualified conservative Supreme Court justice, Neil Gorsuch. His administration had also reversed or rescinded hundreds of Obama administration regulations. Most of these actions, however, faced serious legal challenges and would not become effective for several years, if ever. The most tangible positive effect of the Trump presidency was a sharp decline in illegal immigration from Mexico. If nothing else, the administration's aggressive efforts to deport undocumented persons had deterred large numbers of them from entering the country.

But Trump and the Republican Congress had struggled to pass just a single important piece of legislation, the tax bill. Apart from that, Trump's entire legislative agenda was dead for the year. His staffing and appointments, along with his chaotic management, had yielded a clear sort of failure—early departures from the administration—in greater numbers than those of any prior president. In particular, the top two White House staff appointees—Priebus and Bannon—were both dismissed within six months. A press secretary (Sean Spicer) and communications director (Anthony Scaramucci) had also left, along with several other White House staff. One cabinet secretary (Tom Price) had resigned over improper use of government funds to hire private jets for personal travel, several others were vulnerable to similar charges, and another top adviser (Carl Icahn) resigned over charges that he had recommended policies that would benefit himself financially. Trump had called his Attorney General Jeff Sessions weak and disappointing for his recusing himself from the Russia investigation, and yet had not removed him.

With most appointive positions remaining vacant, the departments and agencies lacked the leadership to do more than routine business. When the administration faced its first domestic crisis—a hurricane that left the entire island of Puerto Rico (a U.S. territory) devastated—Trump personally was slow to take notice and the Federal Emergency Management Agency (FEMA) was unprepared to organize the delivery of vital assistance. Weeks after the hurricane most of the island was still without power, much of the population lacked safe water, and officials were battling against the spread of disease.

In one promising development, the replacement for Priebus as chief of staff—General John Kelly—had some success in establishing orderly processes in the White House. But Kelly did not claim to have any control over Trump himself, who continued to spend much of his time visiting his business properties, playing golf, watching *Fox News,* and tweeting commentary. He persisted in prosecuting various conflicts—over his defense of "alt-right" and white supremacist protesters in Charlottesville, Virginia; his demands for punishment of National Football League players who "took a knee," in protest, during the National Anthem; and his nearly daily, unsupported allegations of "fake news" against mainstream news media, among many others.

In early October, Trump publicly disparaged Secretary Tillerson, who, when asked by a reporter, did not immediately deny his "moron" remark. At the same time, he engaged in an ugly media fight with the Republican chairman of the Foreign Relations Committee and one of his first Senate supporters, Bob Corker, who had already announced that he would not run for reelection in 2018. In an on-camera interview, Corker, speaking slowly and deliberately when asked about Trump's troubled relationship with Tillerson, said that "Secretary Tillerson, Secretary Mattis, and Chief of Staff Kelly are those people that help separate our country from chaos," a ringing vote of no-confidence in Trump himself. Trump went on a Twitter rampage against "liddle Bob Corker." Corker then elaborated on his views in another interview, adding that the White House was in effect "an adult day care center" preoccupied with controlling Trump; that Trump's reckless behavior could lead to World War III; and that many Senate Republicans, though afraid to speak out, shared his views. Sources close to Trump expressed alarm that he was becoming more unstable and out of control and that his presidency was unraveling.[120]

Assessments of presidential low points, as well as high points, are often overblown. It was possible in late 2017 that the Trump presidency was damaged beyond repair—conceivably leading to Trump's removal or resignation from office. But it was also possible that he would rebound, take lessons from his first-year troubles, reboot his relations with congressional Republicans, and end up a moderately successful president. The central obstacle to such a turnaround was that his first-year failures were far more deep-seated than the various deficiencies of strategic competence that we have observed in other presidents.

NOTES

1. Richard E. Neustadt, *Presidential Power: The Politics of Leadership* (New York: Wiley, 1960).
2. Ibid., chap. 7.
3. James David Barber, *The Presidential Character: Predicting Performance in the White House,* 2nd ed. (Englewood Cliffs, NJ: Prentice Hall, 1977).
4. Arthur M. Schlesinger Jr., "Roosevelt as Administrator," in *Bureaucratic Power in National Politics,* 2nd ed., ed. Francis E. Rourke (Boston: Little, Brown, 1972), 126–138.
5. Ibid., 132–133, 137.
6. On Johnson's personality and his presidency, see Doris Kearns, *Lyndon Johnson and the American Dream* (New York: Harper and Row, 1976).
7. James Fallows, "The Passionless Presidency," *Atlantic Monthly,* May 1979, 33–48.
8. See Nelson W. Polsby, *The Consequences of Party Reform* (New York: Oxford University Press, 1983), 108–109.
9. See James L. Sundquist, *The Decline and Resurgence of Congress* (Washington, DC: Brookings Institution Press, 1981), chap. 2.
10. Fred I. Greenstein, *The Hidden-Hand Presidency: Eisenhower as Leader* (New York: Basic Books, 1982).
11. Dick Kirschten, "White House Strategy," *National Journal,* February 21, 1981, 300–303.
12. Quoted in "The Presidency and the Press Corps," by John Herbers, *New York Times Magazine,* May 9, 1982, 45ff.
13. G. Calvin Mackenzie, *The In-and-Outers: Presidential Appointees and Transient Government in Washington* (Baltimore: Johns Hopkins University Press, 1987).
14. Erwin C. Hargrove, *The President as Leader: Appealing to the Better Angels of Our Nature* (Lawrence: University Press of Kansas, 1999), chap. 6.
15. David A. Stockman, *The Triumph of Politics: How the Reagan Revolution Failed* (New York: Harper and Row, 1986), 276–295.
16. Fred I. Greenstein, *The Presidential Difference: Leadership Style from FDR to Clinton* (Princeton: Princeton University Press, 2001), chap. 10.
17. Arthur M. Schlesinger Jr., *A Thousand Days: John F. Kennedy in the White House* (Boston: Houghton Mifflin, 1965), 628–630, 1002–1008.
18. William Greider, "The Education of David Stockman," *Atlantic Monthly,* December 1981, 27ff.
19. See A. James Reichley, *Conservatives in an Age of Change: The Nixon and Ford Administrations* (Washington, DC: Brookings Institution Press, 1981), chap. 18; Roger Porter, *Presidential Decision Making: The Economic Policy Board* (New York: Cambridge University Press, 1980), chap. 3; and Martha Derthick and Paul J. Quirk,

The Politics of Deregulation (Washington, DC: Brookings Institution Press, 1985), chap. 2.

20. Timothy B. Clark, "Strange Bedfellows," *National Journal,* February 2, 1985. For a penetrating study of the politics of taxation, see John F. Witte, *The Politics and Development of the Federal Income Tax* (Madison: University of Wisconsin Press, 1985).

21. The president's task in managing decision making is more difficult than that of chief executives in some of the parliamentary democracies because they have more elaborate and better institutionalized coordinating machinery. See Colin Campbell and George J. Szablowski, *The Super-Bureaucrats: Structure and Behavior in Central Agencies* (New York: New York University Press, 1979). For insightful analyses of the influences on presidential ability to use information effectively, see John P. Burke and Fred I. Greenstein, *How Presidents Test Reality: Decisions on Vietnam, 1954 and 1965* (New York: Russell Sage Foundation, 1989); and Bert A. Rockman, "Organizing the White House: On a West Wing and a Prayer," *Journal of Managerial Issues* 5 (Winter 1993): 453–464.

22. Harold Wilensky, *Organizational Intelligence: Knowledge and Policy in Government and Industry* (New York: Basic Books, 1967).

23. Irving Janis, *Victims of Groupthink: A Psychological Study of Foreign-Policy Decisions and Fiascoes* (Boston: Houghton Mifflin, 1972).

24. Fundamentally, all organization theory concerns the problem of coordination. See Anthony Downs, *Inside Bureaucracy* (Boston: Little, Brown, 1967), chap. 11; and Jay R. Galbraith, *Organization Design* (Reading, MA: Addison-Wesley, 1977). Problems of coordination in the executive branch are emphasized in I. M. Destler, *Making Foreign Economic Policy* (Washington, DC: Brookings Institution Press, 1980). For a general treatment of presidential staffing and organization, see James P. Pfiffner, *The Strategic Presidency: Hitting the Ground Running,* 2nd ed. (Lawrence: University Press of Kansas, 1996).

25. Lester M. Salamon, "The Presidency and Domestic Policy Formulation," in *The Illusion of Presidential Government,* ed. Hugh Heclo and Lester Salamon (Boulder, CO: Westview Press, 1982), 177–212.

26. For this and other Reagan–Carter comparisons, see John H. Kessel, "The Structures of the Reagan White House" (paper presented at the annual meeting of the American Political Science Association, Chicago, September 1–4, 1983). More generally on Carter, however, see Kessel, "The Structures of the Carter White House," *American Journal of Political Science* 22 (August 1983).

27. See Cyrus Vance, *Hard Choices: Critical Years in America's Foreign Policy* (New York: Simon and Schuster, 1983); and Zbigniew Brzezinski, *Power and Principle: Memoirs of the National Security Advisor, 1977–1981* (New York: Farrar, Straus and Giroux, 1983).

28. Alexander George, "The Case for Multiple Advocacy in Making Foreign Policy," *American Political Science Review* 66 (September 1972): 751–785; see also George, *Presidential Decision Making: The Effective Use of Information and Advice* (Boulder, CO: Westview Press, 1980).

29. Janis, *Victims of Groupthink,* chap. 2.

30. James P. Pfiffner, "White House Staff versus the Cabinet: Centripetal and Centrifugal Roles," *Presidential Studies Quarterly* 16 (Fall 1986): 666–690.

31. See Stockman, *Triumph of Politics;* and Laurence I. Barrett, *Gambling with History: Reagan in the White House* (New York: Penguin Books, 1984), esp. 174.

32. John D. Steinbrunner, "Security Policy," in *The New Direction in American Politics,* ed. John E. Chubb and Paul E. Peterson (Washington, DC: Brookings Institution Press, 1985), 351.

33. See Barbara Kellerman, *The Political Presidency* (New York: Oxford University Press, 1984); and Mark A. Peterson, *Legislating Together: The White House and Capitol Hill from Eisenhower to Reagan* (Cambridge, MA: Harvard University Press, 1990).

34. For a historical treatment and analysis of organization for White House liaison, see Stephen J. Wayne, *The Legislative Presidency* (New York: Harper and Row, 1978).

35. Eric L. Davis, "Legislative Liaison in the Carter Administration," *Political Science Quarterly* 95 (Summer 1979): 287–302. Eventually, organization of the staff by issues was dropped.

36. Polsby, *Consequences of Party Reform,* 105–114.

37. Dick Kirschten, "Second Term Legislative Strategy Shifts to Foreign Policy and Defense Issues," *National Journal,* March 30, 1985, 696–699.

38. Samuel Kernell, *Going Public: New Strategies of Presidential Leadership,* 3rd ed. (Washington, DC: CQ Press, 1997); and Theodore J. Lowi, *The Personal President: Power Invested, Promise Unfulfilled* (Ithaca, NY: Cornell University Press, 1985).

39. Quoted in Polsby, *Consequences of Party Reform,* 109.

40. On the Bush presidency, see Colin Campbell and Bert A. Rockman, eds., *The Bush Presidency: First Appraisals* (Chatham, NJ: Chatham House, 1991); and Ryan J. Barilleaux and Mary E. Stuckey, eds., *Leadership and the Bush Presidency: Prudence or Drift in an Era of Change?* (Westport, CT: Greenwood Press, 1992).

41. See Paul J. Quirk and Bruce Nesmith, "Explaining Deadlock: Domestic Policymaking in the Bush Presidency," in *New Perspectives on American Politics,* ed. Lawrence C. Dodd and Calvin Jillson (Washington, DC: CQ Press, 1994), 200–201.

42. See Paul J. Quirk and Jon K. Dalager, "The Election: A 'New Democrat' and a New Kind of Presidential Campaign," in *The Elections of 1992,* ed. Michael Nelson (Washington, DC: CQ Press, 1993), 57–88.

43. Richard Cohen, "The Gloves Are Off," *National Journal,* October 14, 1989, 2508–2512; and "Mr. Consensus," *Time,* August 21, 1989, 17–22.

44. Robert Shogun, *The Riddle of Power: Presidential Leadership from Truman to Bush* (New York: Penguin Books, 1982), chap. 10.

45. Quirk, "Domestic Policy," 69–92.

46. Burt Solomon, "White House Notebook: Bush Plays Down Domestic Policy in Coasting towards Reelection," *National Journal,* March 30, 1991, 752–753.

47. William D. Nordhaus, "The Story of a Bubble," *New York Review of Books,* January 15, 2004, http://www.nybooks.com/articles/16878.

48. Fred I. Greenstein, *The Presidential Difference: Leadership Style from FDR to Clinton* (Princeton, NJ: Princeton University Press, 2001), chap. 12.

49. Colin Campbell, "Management in a Sandbox: Why the Clinton Administration Failed to Cope with Gridlock," in *The Clinton Presidency: First Appraisals,* ed. Colin Campbell and Bert A. Rockman (Chatham, NJ: Chatham House, 1995), 51–87.

50. Fred Barnes, "Neoconned," *New Republic,* January 25, 1993, 14–16.

51. Burt Solomon, "Crisscrossed with Connections . . . West Wing Is a Networker's Dream," *National Journal,* January 15, 1994, 256–257.

52. Elizabeth Drew, *On the Edge: The Clinton Presidency* (New York: Simon and Schuster, 1994).

53. On Clinton's lack of attention to foreign policy, see Larry Berman and Emily O. Goldman, "Clinton's Foreign Policy at Midterm," in Campbell and Rockman, eds., *Clinton Presidency: First Appraisals,* 290–324.

54. Paul J. Quirk and Joseph Hinchliffe, "Domestic Policy: The Trials of a Centrist Democrat," in Campbell and Rockman, eds., *Clinton Presidency: First Appraisals,* 262–289; Theda Skocpol, *Boomerang* (New York: Norton, 1996), 10; and Lawrence R. Jacobs and Robert Y. Shapiro, *Politicians Don't Pander: Political Leadership, Public Opinion, and American Politics* (Chicago: University of Chicago Press, 2000), chap. 2.

55. Julie Kosterlitz, "Changing of the Guard," *National Journal,* March 6, 1993, 575; and Burt Solomon, "Boomers in Charge," *National Journal,* June 19, 1993, 1472.

56. Elizabeth Drew, *Showdown: The Struggle between the Gingrich Congress and the Clinton White House* (New York: Simon and Schuster, 1996).

57. For a fuller discussion of Bush's prior experience, see Paul J. Quirk and Sean C. Matheson, "The Presidency: The Election and the Prospects for Leadership," in *The Elections of 2000,* ed. Michael Nelson (Washington, DC: CQ Press, 2001), chap. 7.

58. Dan Balz and Terry M. Neal, "Bush as President: Questions, Clues, and Contradiction," *Washington Post,* October 22, 2000, A1.

59. At a campaign appearance, for example, Bush attacked the Democratic ticket for wanting the federal government to control Social Security, "like it's some kind of federal program." It is the largest federal domestic program and is fully administered by the federal government. *Slate,* "Complete Bushisms," March 20, 2009, http://www.slate.com/articles/news_and_politics/bushisms/2000/03/the_complete_bushisms.html.

60. Richard L. Berke, "Bush Shapes His Presidency with Sharp Eye on Father's," *New York Times,* March 28, 2001, A1.

61. Rice had been a member of the staff of the National Security Council in the George H. W. Bush administration. Karen DeYoung and Steven Mufson, "Leaner and Less Visible NSC: Reorganization Will Emphasize Defense, Global Economics," *Washington Post,* February 10, 2001, A1.

62. Ron Suskind, *The Price of Loyalty: George W. Bush, the White House, and the Education of Paul O'Neill* (New York: Simon and Schuster, 2004), chap. 1.

63. Richard L. Berke, "Bush Is Providing Corporate Model for White House," *New York Times,* March 11, 2001, A1.

64. Jane Perlez, David E. Sanger, and Thom Shanker, "A Nation Challenged: The Advisers; from Many Voices, One Battle Strategy," *New York Times,* September 23, 2001, A1.

65. Howard Kurtz, "What Bush Said and When He Said It," *Washington Post,* October 1, 2001, C1.

66. Balz and Neal, "Bush as President."

67. For a balanced assessment of the Bush presidency, see Robert Maranto, Tom Lansford, and Jeremy Johnson, eds., *Judging Bush* (Palo Alto, CA: Stanford University Press, 2009), especially chap. 1. For the widespread negative assessment, see Robert S. McElvaine, "HNN Poll: 61% of Historians Rate the Bush Presidency Worst," April 1, 2008, http://hnn.us/articles/48916.html.

68. Shirley Anne Warshaw, "The Cheneyization of the Bush Administration," in Maranto et al., eds., *Judging Bush,* chap. 3; James P. Pfiffner, "President Bush and the Use of Executive Power," in Maranto et al., eds., *Judging Bush,* chap. 4; Pfiffner, *Power Play:*

The Bush Presidency and the Constitution (Washington, DC: Brookings Institution Press, 2008); Michael Nelson, "Richard Cheney and the Power of the Modern Vice Presidency," in *Ambition and Division: Legacies of the George W. Bush Presidency,* ed. Steven E. Schier (Pittsburgh, PA: University of Pittsburgh Press, 2009).

69. Dana Milbank and Ellen Nakashima, "Bush Team Has 'Right' Credentials: Conservative Picks Seen Eclipsing Even Reagan's," *Washington Post,* March 25, 2001, A1; Richard Stevenson, "Political Memo: Bush's Moves to Assure Right Ignite Storm on Left," *New York Times,* April 8, 2001, A22; and Juliet Eilperin, "For GOP House Moderates a Season of Discontent," *Washington Post,* July 22, 2001, A6; Paul Pierson and Jacob S. Hacker, *Off Center: The Republican Revolution and the Erosion of American Democracy* (New Haven, CT: Yale University Press, 2005). For the major exception to Bush's rightward drift, see Frederick Hess and Patrick McGuinn, "Bush's Great Society: No Child Left Behind," in Maranto et al., eds., *Judging Bush,* chap. 9.

70. Karen Hult, David B. Cohen, and Charles Walcott, "The Bush White House and Bureaucracy," in Maranto et al., eds., *Judging Bush,* chap. 7; James P. Pfiffner, "Decision Making in the Bush White House," *Presidential Studies Quarterly* 39, no. 2 (June), 363–383.

71. Gary Mucciaroni and Paul J. Quirk, "Deliberations of a 'Compassionate Conservative': George W. Bush's Domestic Presidency," in *The George W. Bush Presidency: Appraisals and Prospects,* ed. Colin Campbell and Bert A. Rockman (Washington, DC: CQ Press, 2003), chap. 7.

72. Ron Suskind, "Why Are These Men Laughing?," *Esquire,* January 2003, 96–105 (quote on 99). The staffer was political scientist John DiIulio, who briefly headed Bush's Office of Faith-Based Initiatives.

73. Suskind, *Price of Loyalty,* 116–118.

74. Jeffrey E. Cohen and Costas Panagopoulos, "George W. Bush and Economic Policy: A Study in Irony," in Maranto et al., eds., *Judging Bush,* chap. 10.

75. Associated Press, "Experts Decry Bush Science Policies," *USA Today,* February 2, 2005, http://www.usatoday.com/news/washington/2005-02-20-bush-science_x.htm.

76. Lawrence Korb and Laura Conley, "Forging an American Empire," in Maranto et al., eds., *Judging Bush,* chap. 13; Suskind, *Price of Loyalty;* and Richard A. Clarke, *Against All Enemies: Inside America's War on Terror* (New York: Free Press, 2004).

77. Thomas E. Ricks, *Fiasco: The American Military Adventure in Iraq* (New York: Penguin Press, 2006).

78. U.S. Senate, Report of the Select Committee on Intelligence on the U.S. Intelligence Community's Prewar Assessments on Iraq, 108th Congress, 2nd Session, Senate Report 108–301, July 9, 2004.

79. Bob Woodward, *Plan of Attack* (New York: Simon and Schuster Paperbacks, 2004), 247–250.

80. U.S. Senate, Report of the Select Committee on Intelligence.

81. Ibid., 272–285; Thomas Powers, "How Bush Got It Wrong," *New York Review of Books,* September 23, 2004, http://www.nybooks.com/articles/article-preview?article_id=17413.

82. Hult, Cohen, and Walcott, "The Bush White House and Bureaucracy."

83. Paul J. Quirk and Bruce Nesmith, "The Presidency: The Unexpected Competence of the Barack Obama Administration," in *The Elections of 2008,* ed. Michael Nelson (Washington, DC: CQ Press, 2009), chap. 4.

84. Fred I. Greenstein, "The Leadership Style of Barack Obama: An Early Assessment," *The Forum* 7, no. 1 (2009), article 6.

85. Quirk and Nesmith, "The Presidency: Unexpected Competence."

86. Greenstein, "The Leadership Style of Barack Obama: Early Assessment."

87. Pffifner, "Decision Making in the Obama White House."

88. Helene Cooper and Eric Schmitt, "White House Debate Led to Plan to Widen Afghan Effort," *New York Times,* March 27, 2009, http://www.nytimes.com/2009/03/28/us/politics/28prexy.html?_r=1&scp=1&sq=obama%20afghanistan&st=cse.

89. Quirk and Nesmith, "The Presidency: Unexpected Competence."

90. Richard Fleisher and Jon R. Bond, "The Shrinking Middle in the U.S. Congress," *British Journal of Political Science* 34, no. 3 (July 2004): 429–451.

91. Keith T. Poole and Howard Rosenthal, "The Polarization of the Congressional Parties," Voteview.com, http://voteview.com/political_polarization.asp. Northern Democrats—the core of the liberal wing of the Democratic Party—have almost exactly the same average ideological score that they had in the early 1970s, the low point of polarization.

92. William Schneider, "For Divided Congress, Making Up Is Hard to Do," *National Journal,* February 28, 2009, http://www.nationaljournal.com.

93. Paul Krugman and Robin Wells, "Getting Away with It," *New York Review of Books,* July 12, 2012, http://www.nybooks.com/articles/archives/2012/jul/12/getting-away-it/? pagination=false.

94. Republicans have generally denied that Obama made serious efforts to win Republican support.

95. Jonathan Rauch, "Is Obama Repeating Bush's Mistakes?" *National Journal,* March 28, 2009, http://www.nationaljournal.com.

96. George Edwards, *Overreach: Leadership in the Obama Presidency* (Princeton, NJ: Princeton University Press, 2012).

97. Voters in the midterm elections disapproved of the reform by a 49–42 margin. However, polls have also indicated that about a third of the voters who disapproved felt that the bill was "not liberal enough" rather than "too liberal." There has never been a strong majority in support of simply repealing the reform or replacing it with a Republican approach. See "Health Policy," Polling Report, http://www.pollingreport.com/health.htm.

98. On Trump's qualifications for the presidency, see Paul J. Quirk, "The Presidency: Donald Trump and the Question of Fitness," in Michael Nelson, ed., *The Elections of 2016* (Washington, DC: CQ Press, 2017), chap. 8.

99. Chris Cillizza, "Donald Trump's Interview with the Washington Post is Totally Bananas," *Washington Post,* March 22, 2016, https://www.washingtonpost.com/news/the-fix/wp/2016/03/22/donald-trumps-interview-with-the-washington-post-is-totally-bananas/?utm_term=.795322fa1cbf; "Highlights from Our Interview with Donald Trump on Foreign Policy," *New York Times,* March 26, 2016, https://www.nytimes.com/2016/03/27/us/politics/donald-trump-interview-highlights.html.

100. James P. Pfiffner, "Organizing the Trump Presidency," prepared for presentation at the American Political Science Association Annual Meeting, San Francisco, September 2017.

101. See Quirk, "Donald Trump and the Question of Fitness," 202–203.

102. Justin Wolfers, "Why Most Economists Are So Worried about Trump," *New York Times*, January 11, 2017, https://www.nytimes.com/2017/01/11/upshot/why-most-economists-are-so-worried-about-trump.html.

103. See also, Michael Nelson, "Donald Trump's First Year: Decreasing Influence without Increasing Effectiveness," in *Crucible: The President's First Year*, eds. Michael Nelson, Stefanie Georgakis Abbott, and Jeffrey L. Chidester (Charlottesville: University of Virginia Press, 2018).

104. Quirk, "Donald Trump and the Question of Fitness," 203–205; Brandy Lee, ed., *The Dangerous Case of Donald Trump: 27 Psychiatrists and Mental Health Experts Assess a President* (New York: St. Martin's Press, 2017).

105. Lee, ed., *Dangerous Case of Donald Trump.*

106. Nate Silver, "The Media Needs to Stop Rationalizing Trump's Behavior," *FiveThirtyEight*, September 30, 2017, https://fivethirtyeight.com/features/the-media-needs-to-stop-rationalizing-president-trumps-behavior/.

107. Nelson, "Donald Trump's First Year," pp. 16–53.

108. Matt Apuzzo and Michael S. Schmidt, "Hoping to Have Trump Cleared, Legal Team Eases Resistance to Inquiry," *New York Times*, October 7, 2017, https://www.nytimes.com/2017/10/07/us/politics/trump-russia-legal.html.

109. Eric Bradner, Elise Labott, and Dana Bash, "50 GOP National Security Experts Oppose Trump," CNN, August 8, 2016, http://www.cnn.com/2016/08/08/politics/republican-national-security-letter-donald-trump-election-2016/index.html.

110. Pfiffner, "Organizing the Trump Presidency."

111. Ibid.

112. Ibid.

113. H. R. McMaster, *Dereliction of Duty: Johnson, McNamara, the Joint Chiefs of Staff, and the Lies That Led to Vietnam* (New York: Harper Perennial, 1998).

114. Nelson, "Donald Trump's First Year."

115. Fred Kaplan, "Trump's Nuclear Meltdown," *Slate*, October 11, 2017, http://www.slate.com/articles/news_and_politics/war_stories/2017/10/now_we_know_why_rex_tillerson_called_donald_trump_a_moron.html.

116. Nelson, "Donald Trump's First Year."

117. According to Comey, Trump was indeed not a direct target of the investigation at the time. But the FBI does not make such announcements, partly because investigations often expand to new targets.

118. Barry H. Berke, Noah Bookbinder, and Norman Eisen, "Did President Trump Obstruct Justice? *Brookings Institution*, October 10, 2017, https://www.brookings.edu/blog/fixgov/2017/10/10/did-president-trump-obstruct-justice/.

119. As of October 2017, there were strong indications that Flynn and Manafort would be indicted. There was as yet no clear indication that Trump, personally, was a target of Mueller's investigation, and Trump's legal team was reportedly pushing for its speedy conclusion.

120. Gabriel Sherman, "'I Hate Everyone in the White House': Trump Seethes as Advisers Fear the President is 'Unraveling,'" *Vanity Fair*, October 11, 2017, https://www.vanityfair.com/news/2017/10/donald-trump-is-unraveling-white-house-advisers.

6

THE PSYCHOLOGICAL PRESIDENCY

Michael Nelson

Several delegates to the Constitutional Convention of 1787 noted during the first week of debate that to invest power in a unitary office was to invest power in one person. Not until James David Barber wrote *The Presidential Character*, however, was a systematic effort made to explore the psychological conse- quences of that important truism. Michael Nelson examines this influential book, along with another that Barber wrote about the voters' contributions to the "psychological presidency," *The Pulse of Politics.* Although Nelson finds Barber's theories wanting (the healthiest of Barber's character types, for example, are not always successful presidents), he praises Barber for draw- ing scholars' attention to the psychological aspects of the presidency and for encouraging political journalists to do the same in their coverage of presiden- tial campaigns.

The United States elects its president every four years, which makes it unusual among democratic nations. During several presidential election campaigns in the 1970s and 1980s, *Time* magazine ran a story about James David Barber, which makes him equally singular among political scientists. The two quadrennial oddi- ties were not unrelated.

The first *Time* article, which appeared in the June 19, 1972, issue, was about Barber's just-published book, *The Presidential Character: Predicting Performance in the White House,* in which he argued that presidents could be divided into four psychological types: "active–positive," "active–negative," "passive–positive," and "passive–negative." What's more, according to Barber via *Time,* by taking "a hard look at men before they reach the White House," voters could tell in advance what candidates would be like if elected: healthily "ambitious out of exuberance," like the active–positives; pathologically "ambitious out of anxiety," like the active–negatives; "compliant and other-directed," like the passive–positives; or "dutiful and self-denying," like the passive–negatives. In the 1972 election, Barber told *Time,* the choice was between an active–positive, George McGovern, and a psychologically defective active–negative, Richard M. Nixon.[1]

Nixon won the election, but Barber's early insights into Nixon's personality won notoriety for both him and his theory, especially in the wake of Watergate. So prominent had Barber become by 1976 that White House correspondent Hugh Sidey used his entire "Presidency" column in the October 4 issue of *Time* to tell readers that Barber was refusing to type candidates Gerald R. Ford and Jimmy Carter this time around. "Barber is deep into an academic study of this election and its participants, and he is pledged to restraint until it is over," Sidey reported solemnly.[2] Actually, more than a year before, Barber had told *U.S. News & World Report* that he considered Ford an active–positive.[3] Carter, who read Barber's book twice when it came out, was left to tell the *Washington Post* that active–positive is "what I would like to be. That's what I hope I prove to be."[4] And so Carter would be, wrote Barber in a special postelection column for *Time.*[5]

The 1980 election campaign witnessed the appearance of another Barber book, *The Pulse of Politics: Electing Presidents in the Media Age,* and, in honor of the occasion, two *Time* articles. This was all to the good because the first, a Sidey column in March, offered more gush than information: "The first words encountered in the new book by Duke's Professor James David Barber are stunning: 'A revolution in presidential politics is under way.' . . . Barber has made political history before."[6] A more substantive piece in the magazine's May 19 "Nation" section described the new book's cycle theory of presidential elections. According to Barber, ever since 1900 steady four-year beats in the public's psychological mood, or "pulse," have caused a recurring alternation among elections of "conflict," "conscience," and "conciliation." *Time* went on to stress, although not explain, Barber's view of the importance of the mass media, both as a reinforcer of this cycle and as a potential mechanism for helping the nation to break out of it.[7]

In subsequent years Barber, who died in 2004, wrote for and was written about in numerous other national publications. But it was *Time*'s infatuation with Barber that brought him a level of fame that comes rarely to political scientists. For Barber, fame came at some cost. Although widely known, his ideas were little understood. The media's cursory treatment made them appear superficial or even foolish—instantly appealing to the naïve, instantly odious to the thoughtful. Partly as a result, Barber's reputation in the intellectual community as an *homme sérieux* suffered. In the backrooms and corridors of scholarly gatherings, one heard "journalistic" and "popularizer," the ultimate academic epithets, muttered along with his name. Indeed, in a 1991 assessment of contemporary scholarly research on the presidency, Paul Quirk observed of the whole field of presidential psychology that "researchers seem to have kept their distance from the subject as if to avoid guilt by association" with Barber.[8]

This situation remains in need of remedy. Barber's theories may be seriously flawed, but they are serious theories. For all their limitations—some of them self-confessed—they offer one of the most significant contributions a scholar can make: an unfamiliar but useful way of looking at a familiar subject that we no longer see very clearly. In Barber's case, the familiar thing is the American presidency, and the unfamiliar way of looking at it is through the lenses of psychology.

PSYCHOLOGICAL PERSPECTIVES ON THE PRESIDENCY

Constitutional Perspectives

To look at politics in general, or the American presidency in particular, from a psychological perspective is nothing new. Although deprived of the insights of modern psychology, the Framers of the Constitution constructed their plan of government on a foundation of Hobbesian assumptions about what motivates *homo politicus*. (They called what they were doing moral philosophy, not psychology.) James Madison and most of his colleagues at the Constitutional Convention assumed that "men are instruments of their desires"; that "one such desire is the desire for power"; and that "if unrestrained by external checks, any individual or group of individuals will tyrannize over others."[9] Because the Framers believed these things, a basic tenet of their political philosophy was that the government they were designing should be a "government of laws and not of men." Not just psychology but history and experience had taught them to associate liberty with law and tyranny with rulers who depart from law, as George III and his colonial governors had.

In the end the convention yielded to those who urged, on grounds of "energy" in the executive, that the Constitution lodge the powers of the executive branch in a single person: the president.[10] There are several reasons why the delegates were willing to put aside their doubts and inject such a powerful dose of individual character into the new plan of government. One is the Framers' certain knowledge that George Washington would be the first president. They knew that Washington aroused powerful and, from the standpoint of winning the nation's support for the new government, vital psychological responses from the people. As Seymour Martin Lipset has shown, Washington was a classic example of what sociologist Max Weber called a charismatic leader, a man "treated [by the people] as endowed with supernatural, superhuman, or at least specifically exceptional powers or qualities."[11] Marcus Cunliffe noted:

> Babies were being christened after him as early as 1775, and while he was still President, his countrymen paid to see him in waxwork effigy. To his

admirers he was "godlike Washington," and his detractors complained
to one another that he was looked upon as a "demigod" whom it was
treasonous to criticize. "Oh Washington!" declared Ezra Stiles of Yale (in
a sermon of 1783). "How I do love thy name! How have I often adored
and blessed thy God, for creating and forming thee the great ornament of
human kind!"[12]

Just as Washington's "gift of grace" would legitimize the new government, the
Framers believed, so would his personal character ensure its republican nature. The
powers of the president in the Constitution "are full great," wrote Pierce Butler, a
convention delegate from South Carolina, to a British kinsman,

> and greater than I was disposed to make them. Nor, entre nous, do I believe
> they would have been so great had not many of the delegates cast their eyes
> towards General Washington as President; and shaped their Ideas of the
> Powers to be given to a President, by their opinions of his Virtue.[13]

The Framers were not so naïve or shortsighted as to invest everything in
Washington. To protect the nation from power-mad tyrants after he left office, they
provided that the election of the president, whether by electors or members of the
House of Representatives, would involve selection by peers—personal acquain-
tances of the candidates who could screen out those of defective character. And
even if someone of low character slipped through the net and became president,
the Framers believed that they had structured the office to protect the nation from
harm. "The founders' deliberation over the provision for indefinite reeligibility,"
Jeffrey Tulis has shown, "illustrates how they believed self-interest could sometimes
be elevated."[14] As Alexander Hamilton argued in *The Federalist,* whether presidents
are motivated by "avarice," "ambition," or "the love of fame," they will behave
responsibly to secure reelection to the office that allows that desire to be fulfilled.[15]
Underlying this confidence was the assurance that in a relatively slow-paced world,
mad or wicked presidents could do only so much damage before corrective action
could remove them. As John Jay explained, "So far as the fear of punishment and
disgrace can operate, that motive to good behavior is amply afforded by the article
on the subject of impeachment."[16]

Scholarly Perspectives

The Framers' decision to inject personality into the presidency was a conscious
one. But it was made for reasons that eventually ceased to pertain. The destructive
powers at a modern president's disposal are ultimate and swift. The impeachment
process now seems uncertain and slow. Peer review never took hold in the Electoral
College. The rise of the national mass media, later joined by various forms of digital
media, has made the president's personality all the more pervasive. In sum, most of
the Framers' carefully conceived defenses against a president of defective character
are gone.

Clearly, then, a sophisticated psychological perspective on the presidency was overdue in the late 1960s, when Barber began offering one in a series of articles and papers that culminated in *The Presidential Character*.[17] Presidential scholars had long taken it as axiomatic that the American presidency is an institution shaped in some measure by the personalities of individual presidents. But rarely had the literature of personality theory been brought to bear, in large part because scholars of the post–Franklin D. Roosevelt era no longer seemed to share the Framers' reservations about human nature, at least as far as the presidency was concerned. Instead, historians and political scientists exalted not only presidential power, but also presidents who are ambitious for power. Richard Neustadt's influential book *Presidential Power,* published in 1960, was typical in this regard:

> The contributions that a president can make to government are indispensable. Assuming that he knows what power is and wants it, those contributions cannot help but be forthcoming in some measure as by-products of his search for personal influence.[18]

As Erwin Hargrove reflected in post-Vietnam, post-Watergate 1974, this line of reasoning was the source of startling deficiencies in scholarly understandings of the office: "We had assumed that ideological purpose was sufficient to purify the drive for power, but we forgot the importance of character."[19]

Scholars also had recognized for some time that Americans' attitudes about the presidency, like presidents' actions, are psychologically as well as politically rooted. Studies of schoolchildren indicated that they first come into political awareness by learning of, and feeling warmly toward, the president. As adults, they rally to the president's support, both when they inaugurate a new one and in times of crisis.[20] Popular nationalistic emotions, which in constitutional monarchies are directed toward the king or queen, are deflected in American society onto the president. Again, however, scholars' awareness of these psychological forces manifested itself more in casual observations (Dwight D. Eisenhower was a "father figure"; the "public mood" is fickle) than in systematic investigation.

The presidencies of John F. Kennedy, Lyndon B. Johnson, and Richard Nixon altered this scholarly quiescence. Surveys taken shortly after the Kennedy assassination recorded the startling depth of the feelings that Americans have about the presidency. A large share of the population experienced symptoms classically associated with grief over the death of a loved one. Historical evidence suggests that the public has responded similarly to the deaths of all sitting presidents, young or old, popular or not, whether by murder or natural causes.[21]

If Kennedy's death illustrated the deep psychological ties of the public to the presidency, the experiences of his immediate successors showed even more clearly the importance of psychology in understanding the connection between president and presidency. Johnson, the peace candidate who rigidly pursued a self-defeating policy of war, and Nixon, who promised "lowered voices" only to angrily turn political disagreements into personal crises, seemed to project their personalities onto policy in ways that were both obvious and destructive. The events of the 1960s and 1970s brought students of the presidency up short. As they paused to consider the "psychological presidency," they found Barber standing at the ready with the foundation and first floor of a full-blown theory.

JAMES DAVID BARBER AND THE PSYCHOLOGICAL PRESIDENCY

Barber's theory offers a model of the presidency as an institution shaped largely by the psychological mix between the personalities of individual presidents and the public's deep feelings about the office. It also proposes methods of predicting what those personalities and feelings are likely to be in particular circumstances. These considerations govern *The Presidential Character* and *The Pulse of Politics,* books that will be examined in turn. The question of how we can become masters of our own and of the presidency's psychological fate is also treated in these books, but it receives fuller exposition in other works by Barber.

Presidential Psychology

> The primary danger of the Nixon administration will be that the President will grasp some line of policy or method of operation and pursue it in spite of its failure. . . . How will Nixon respond to challenges to the morality of his regime, to charges of scandal and/or corruption? First such charges strike a raw nerve, not only from the Checkers business, but also from deep within the personality in which the demands of the superego are so harsh and hard. . . . The first impulse will be to hush it up, to conceal it, bring down the blinds. If it breaks open and Nixon cannot avoid commenting on it, there is a real setup here for another crisis.

James David Barber was more than a little proud of that prediction, mainly because he made it in a talk he gave at Stanford University on January 19, 1969, the eve of Nixon's first inauguration. It was among the earliest in a series of speeches, papers, and articles whose purpose was to explain his theory of presidential personality and how to predict it, always with his forecast for Nixon's future prominently, and thus riskily, displayed. The theory received its fullest statement in *The Presidential Character.*

Character, in Barber's usage, is not quite a synonym for "personality," but it comes close.[22] To be sure, a politician's psychological constitution includes two other components: an adolescence-born *worldview,* which Barber defines as "primary, politically relevant beliefs, particularly his conceptions of social causality, human nature, and the central moral conflicts of the time"; and *style,* or a "habitual way of performing three central political roles: rhetoric, personal relations, and homework," which develops in early adulthood. But clearly Barber considered character, which forms in childhood and shapes the later development of style and worldview, to be "the most important thing to know about a president or candidate." As he defined the term, "character is the way the President orients himself toward life—not for the moment, but enduringly." It "grows out of the child's experiments in relating to parents, brothers and sisters, and peers at play and in school, as well as to his own body and the objects around it." Through these experiences, the child—and thus the adult to be—arrives subconsciously at a deep and private understanding of his or her fundamental worth.

For some, this process results in high self-esteem, the vital ingredient for psychological health and political productiveness. Others must search outside themselves for evidence of worth that at best will be a partial substitute. Depending on the source and nature of their limited self-esteem, Barber suggested, they will concentrate their search in one of three areas: the affection from others that compliant and agreeable behavior brings, the sense of usefulness that comes from performing a widely respected duty, or the deference attendant with dominance and control over other people. Because politics is a vocation rich in opportunities to find all three of these things—affection from cheering crowds and devoted aides, usefulness from public service in a civic cause, dominance through official power—it is not surprising that some insecure people are attracted to a political career.

This makes for a problem, Barber argued. If public officials, especially presidents, use their office to compensate for private doubts and demons, it follows that they will not always use it to serve public purposes. Affection seekers will be so concerned with preserving the goodwill of those around them that they seldom will challenge the status quo or otherwise rock the boat. The duty-doers will be similarly hidebound, although in their case inactivity will result from the feeling that to be useful they must be diligent guardians of time-honored practices and procedures. Passive presidents of both kinds may provide the nation with "breathing spells, times of recovery in our frantic political life," or even "a refreshing hopefulness and at least some sense of sharing and caring." Still, in Barber's view, their main effect is to "divert popular attention from the hard realities of politics," thus leaving the country to "drift." And "what passive presidents ignore, active presidents inherit."[23]

Power-driven presidents pose the greatest danger. They will seek their psychological compensation not in inaction, but in intense efforts to maintain or extend their personal sense of domination and control through public channels. When things are going well for power-driven presidents and they feel they have the upper hand over their political opponents, problems may not arise. But when matters cease to go their way, as eventually will happen in a democratic system, the power-driven president's response almost certainly will take destructive forms, including rigid defensiveness and aggression against opponents. Only those with high self-esteem will be secure enough to lead as democratic political leaders should lead, with persuasion and flexibility as well as action and initiative.

Perhaps more important than the theoretical underpinnings of Barber's character analysis is the practical purpose that animates *The Presidential Character:* to help citizens choose their presidents wisely. The book's first words heralded this purpose:

> When a citizen votes for a presidential candidate he makes, in effect, a prediction. He chooses from among the contenders the one he thinks

(or feels, or guesses) would be the best president. . . . This book is meant to help citizens and those who advise them cut through the confusion and get at some clear criteria for choosing presidents.

How, though, in the heat and haste of a presidential election, with candidates notably unwilling to bare their souls for psychological inspection, are we to find out what they are really like? Easy enough, argues Barber. To answer the complex question of what motivates a political leader, just answer two simpler questions in its stead: active or passive? ("How much energy does the man invest in his presidency?") and positive or negative? ("Relatively speaking, does he seem to experience his political life as happy or sad, enjoyable or discouraging, positive or negative in its main effect?").

According to Barber, the four possible combinations of answers to these two questions turn out to be almost synonymous with the four psychological strategies that people use to enhance self-esteem. The *active–positives* are the healthy ones in the group. Their high sense of self-worth enables them to work hard at politics, enjoy what they do, and thus be fairly good at it. Of the four eighteenth- and nineteenth-century presidents and the sixteen twentieth-century presidents whom Barber typed, he placed Thomas Jefferson, Franklin D. Roosevelt, Harry S. Truman, Kennedy, Ford, Carter, George H. W. Bush, and Bill Clinton in this category. The *passive–positives* (James Madison, William H. Taft, Warren G. Harding, Ronald Reagan) are the affection seekers. Although not especially hardworking, they enjoy their time in office. The *passive–negatives* (Washington, Calvin Coolidge, Eisenhower) neither work nor play; it is duty, not pleasure or zest, that gets them into politics. Finally, there are the power-seeking *active–negatives,* who compulsively and with little satisfaction throw themselves into their presidential chores.

In Barber's view, active–negative presidents John Adams, Woodrow Wilson, Herbert Hoover, Lyndon Johnson, and Richard Nixon all shared one important personality-rooted quality: they persisted in disastrous courses of action (Adams's repressive Alien and Sedition Acts, Wilson's League of Nations battle, Hoover's depression policy, Johnson's Vietnam, Nixon's Watergate) because to have conceded error would have been to lose their sense of control, something their psychological constitutions would not allow them to do. Table 6.1 summarizes Barber's four types and his categorizations of individual presidents.

Not surprisingly, *The Presidential Character* was extremely controversial when it came out in 1972. Many argued that Barber's theory was too simple, that his four types did not begin to cover the range of human complexity. At one level, this criticism is as trivial as it is true. In spelling out his theory, Barber stated clearly that "we are talking about tendencies, broad directions; no individual man exactly fits a category." He offered his character typology as a method for sizing up potential presidents, not for diagnosing and treating them. In the midst of image-laden election campaigns, a reasonably accurate shorthand device is about all we can hope for. The real question, then, is whether Barber's shorthand device is reasonably accurate.

Table 6.1 ■ Barber's Character Typology, with Presidents Categorized According to Type		
Energy directed toward the presidency	**Affect toward the presidency**	
	Positive	**Negative**
Active	Thomas Jefferson Franklin Roosevelt Harry Truman John Kennedy Gerald Ford Jimmy Carter George H. W. Bush Bill Clinton	John Adams Woodrow Wilson Herbert Hoover Lyndon Johnson Richard Nixon
	"consistency between much activity and the enjoyment of it, indicating relatively high self-esteem and relative success in relating to the environment. . . . shows an orientation to productiveness as a value and an ability to use his styles flexibly, adaptively."	"activity has a compulsive quality, as if the man were trying to make up for something or escape from anxiety into hard work. . . . seems ambitious, striving upward, power-seeking. . . . stance toward the environment is aggressive and has a problem in managing his aggressive feelings."
Passive	James Madison William Taft Warren Harding Ronald Reagan	George Washington Calvin Coolidge Dwight Eisenhower
	"receptive, compliant, other-directed character whose life is a search for affection as a reward for being agreeable and cooperative. . . . low self-esteem (on grounds of being unlovable)."	"low self-esteem based on a sense of uselessness . . . in politics because they think they ought to be. . . . tendency is to withdraw, to escape from the conflict and uncertainty of politics by emphasizing vague principles (especially prohibitions) and procedural arrangements."

Sources: Barber's discussions of all presidents but Clinton are in *The Presidential Character: Predicting Performance in the White House,* 4th ed. (Englewood Cliffs, NJ: Prentice Hall, 1992). Clinton is characterized by Barber in Doyle McManus, "Key Challenges Await Clinton," *Los Angeles Times,* January 20, 1993, A6. See also James David Barber, "Predicting Hope with Clinton at Helm," *Raleigh News and Observer,* January 17, 1993.

Barber's intellectual defense of his typology's soundness, quoted in full, is not altogether comforting:

> Why might we expect these two simple dimensions [active–passive, positive–negative] to outline the main character types? Because they stand for two central features of anyone's orientation toward life. In nearly every study of personality, some form of the active–passive contrast is critical; the general tendency to act or be acted upon is evident in such concepts as dominance-submission, extraversion-introversion, aggression-timidity, attack-defense, fight-flight, engagement-withdrawal, approach-avoidance. In every life we sense quickly the general energy output of the people we deal with. Similarly we catch on fairly quickly to the affect dimension— whether the person seems to be optimistic or pessimistic, hopeful or skeptical, happy or sad. The two baselines are clear and they are also independent of one another: all of us know people who are very active but seem discouraged, others who are quite passive but seem happy, and so forth. The activity baseline refers to what one does, the affect baseline to how one feels about what one does. Both are crude clues to character. They are leads into four basic character patterns long familiar in psychological research.[24]

In the library copy of *The Presidential Character* from which I copied this long passage, there is a handwritten note in the margin: "Footnote, man!" But there is no footnote to relevant psychological literature, here or anywhere else in the book. Casual readers might take this to mean that none was necessary, and they would be right if Barber's types really were "long familiar in psychological research" and "appeared in nearly every study of personality."[25] But they are not and they do not. As Alexander George has pointed out, personality theory itself is a "quagmire" in which "the term 'character' in practice is applied loosely and means many different things."[26] Barber's real defense of his typology—it works; look at Nixon—is not to be dismissed, but one wishes he had explained better why he thinks it works.[27]

Barber's typology also has been criticized for not being simple enough, at least not for purposes of accurate preelection application. Where, exactly, is one to look to discover whether deep down candidate Jones is the energetic, buoyant person her image makers say she is? Barber was quite right to warn analysts away from their usual hunting ground—the candidate's recent performance in other high offices. These offices "are all much more restrictive than the Presidency is, much more set by institutional requirements,"[28] and thus much less fertile cultures for psychopathologies to grow in. This was Barber's only real mention of what might be considered a third, equally important component of the psychological presidency: the rarefied, courtlike atmosphere—described first and best in George Reedy's *The Twilight of the Presidency*[29]—that surrounds presidents and allows those whose psychological constitutions so move them to seal themselves off from harsh political realities.

Barber's alternative to performance-based analysis—namely, a study of the candidate's "first independent political success," or FIPS, during which he or she developed a personal formula for success in politics—is not very helpful either. How, for example, is one to tell which IPS was first? According to Barber's appropriately broad definition of *political*, Johnson's first success was not his election to Congress, but his work as a student assistant to his college's president. Hoover's was his incumbency as student body treasurer at Stanford. Sorting through a candidate's life with the thoroughness necessary to determine his or her FIPS may or may not be an essential task. But it is clearly not a straightforward one.

Further difficulties arise from the unevenness of the evidence about presidents that is available when they are still candidates or even while they are in office. Clinton's behavior as president, for example, persuaded Fred Greenstein that he (and Barber) had been wrong in their initial assessment of his character. "The ever-smiling, hyperactive Clinton has all of the outward signs of an active–positive character," Greenstein wrote near the end of Clinton's second term. "Yet his actions, particularly in the Monica Lewinsky affair, reveal him to be as emotionally deficient as any active–negative president."[30] Similarly, Greenstein's immersion in the Eisenhower papers, which did not become available until long after the president left office, allowed him to demonstrate that Ike was an active rather than a passive president. Eisenhower's public passivity represented a leadership strategy of reassurance; in truth, Greenstein found, he pursued a vigorous behind-the-scenes, "hidden-hand presidency."[31]

Some scholars question not only the scientific basis or practical applicability of Barber's psychological theory of presidential behavior, but also the importance of psychological explanation itself. Psychology appears to be almost everything to Barber, as this statement from his research design for *The Presidential Character* reveals:

> What is de-emphasized in this scheme? Everything which does not lend itself to the production of potentially testable generalizations about presidential behavior. Thus we shall be less concerned with the substance or content of particular issues . . . less concern[ed] for distant phenomena, such as relationships among other political actors affecting events without much reference to the president, public opinion, broad economic or historical trends, etc.—except insofar as these enter into the president's own approach to decision-making.[32]

But is personality all that matters? Provocative though Barber's theory may be, it seems to unravel in the application. A "healthy" political personality turns out to be no guarantee of presidential success. Barber classed Ford, Carter, and Bush early in their presidencies as active–positives, for example. Carter, in fact, seemed to take flexibility—a virtue characteristic of active–positives—to such an extreme that it approached vacillation and inconsistency, almost as if in reading *The Presidential Character* he had learned its lessons too well.

Nor, as Table 6.2 shows, does Barber's notion of psychological unsuitability seem to correspond to failure in office. The ranks of the most successful presidents in five recent surveys by scholars include some whom Barber classified as active–positives (Jefferson, Truman, Kennedy, and Franklin Roosevelt), but also several active–negatives (Wilson, Lyndon Johnson, and John Adams), and others whom Barber labeled passive–negative (Washington and Eisenhower) or passive–positive (Reagan).[33] The most perverse result of classifying presidents by this standard involves Abraham Lincoln, whom Jeffrey Tulis, correctly applying Barber's theory, found to be an active–negative.[34]

Hargrove found the active–positive category equally unhelpful because it is too broad:

> Active–positive presidents vary so as individuals that the category lacks the capacity to analyze and explain actions of presidential leadership. A schema that puts Franklin Roosevelt and Jimmy Carter in the same cell tells us that they shared high self-esteem and the capacity to learn and adapt to circumstances, but it says nothing about the great differences in political skill between them or the psychological bases for such differences.[35]

One could raise similar doubts about categories that lump together Harding and Reagan (passive–positive) or Coolidge and Eisenhower (passive–negative).

Clearly, personality is not all that matters in the presidency. As Tulis noted, Lincoln's behavior as president can be explained much better by his political philosophy and leadership skills than by his personality. Similarly, one need not resort to psychology to explain the failures of active–negatives Hoover and, in the latter

Table 6.2 ■ "Great" Presidents and Barber's Character Typology		
	Positive	**Negative**
Active	Thomas Jefferson	John Adams
	Franklin Roosevelt	Woodrow Wilson
	Harry Truman	Lyndon Johnson
	John F. Kennedy	[Abraham Lincoln]
Passive	Ronald Reagan	George Washington
		Dwight Eisenhower

Note: For purposes of this table, a "great" president is defined as one who ranked among the first ten in at least one of these five polls of scholars: Steve Neal, "Our Best and Worst Presidents," *Chicago Tribune Magazine*, January 10, 1982, 9–18; Robert K. Murray and Tim H. Blessing, *Greatness in the White House: Rating the Presidents, Washington through Carter* (University Park: Pennsylvania State University Press, 1988); David L. Porter, letter to author, January 15, 1982; Arthur M. Schlesinger Jr., "The Ultimate Approval Rating," *New York Times Magazine*, December 15, 1996, 47–51; and "C-Span 2009 Historians' Presidential Leadership Survey," http://www.c-span.org/Presidential>Survey/Overall-Ranking.aspx. Four others who achieved this ranking (Andrew Jackson, James K. Polk, Theodore Roosevelt, and William McKinley) are not included because Barber did not classify them according to his typology. Lincoln's name is bracketed because Jeffrey Tulis classified him using Barber's typology.

years of his presidency, Lyndon Johnson. Hoover's unbending opposition to instituting massive federal relief in the face of the Great Depression may have stemmed more from ideological convictions than psychological rigidity. Johnson's refusal to change his administration's policy in Vietnam could be interpreted as the action of a self-styled consensus leader trying to steer a moderate course between hawks who wanted full-scale military involvement and doves who wanted unilateral withdrawal.[36] These presidents' actions were ineffective but not necessarily irrational.

Theoretical and practical criticisms such as these are important, and they do not exhaust the list. Observer bias is another. Because Barber's published writings provide no clear checklist of criteria by which to type candidates, subjectivity is absolutely inherent. But the criticisms should not blind us to his major contributions in *The Presidential Character:* a concentration (albeit excessive) on the importance of presidential personality in explaining presidential behavior, a sensitivity to the role of personality as a variable (power does not always corrupt, nor does the office always "make the man"), and a boldness in approaching the problems voters face in predicting what kind of president a candidate will be if elected.

Public Psychology

The second side of the psychological presidency—the public's side—was Barber's concern in *The Pulse of Politics: Electing Presidents in the Media Age.* The book is about elections, those occasions when, because citizens are deciding who will fill the presidency, they presumably feel (presidential deaths aside) their emotional attachment to the office most deeply. Again Barber presented a typology. The public's election moods come in three varieties, he argued: *conflict* ("we itch for adventure, . . . [a] blood-and-guts political contest"), *conscience* ("the call goes out for a revival of social conscience, the restoration of the constitutional covenant"), and *conciliation* ("the public yearns for solace, for domestic tranquility").[37] In this book the types appear in recurring order as well, over a twelve-year cycle: a conflict election, followed by a conscience election, and then a conciliation election.

Barber's question in *The Pulse of Politics*—what is "the swirl of emotions" with which Americans surround the presidency?—is as important and original as the questions he posed in *The Presidential Character.* But again, his answer is as puzzling as it is provocative. Although Barber's theory applies only to American presidential elections since 1900, he seemed convinced that the psychological "pulse" has been beating deeply, if softly, in all humankind for all time. Barber discovered conflict, conscience, and conciliation in the "old sagas" of ancient peoples and in "the psychological paradigm that dominates the modern age: the *ego,* instrument for coping with the struggles of the external world [conflict]; the *superego,* warning against harmful violations [conscience]; the *id,* longing after the thrill and ease of sexual satisfaction [conciliation]." He found this primordial pulse firmly reinforced in American history. Conflict is reflected in our emphasis on the war story ("In isolated America, the war-makers repeatedly confronted the special problem of arousing the martial spirit against distant enemies. . . . Thus our history vibrates with *talk* about war"). Conscience is displayed in America's sense of itself as an instrument of divine providence ("Our conscience has never been satisfied by government as a mere practical arrangement"). Conciliation shows up in our efforts to live with each other in a heterogeneous "nation of nationalities." In the early twentieth century, Barber argued, these three themes became the controlling force in the political psychology of the American electorate, so controlling that every presidential election since the conflict of 1900 has fit its place within the cycle: conscience in 1904, conciliation in 1908, conflict again in 1912, and so on. What caused the pulse to start beating so strongly, he feels, was the rise of national mass media.

The modern newspaper came first, just before the turn of the century: "In a remarkable historical conjunction, the sudden surge into mass popularity of the American daily newspaper coincided with the Spanish-American War." Because war stories sold papers, daily journalists also wrote about "politics as war"—that is, as conflict. In the early 1900s, national mass circulation magazines arrived on the scene, taking their cues from the Progressive movement reformers who dominated the politics of that period. "The 'muckrakers'—actually positive thinkers out to build America, not destroy reputations"—wrote about "politics as a moral enterprise," an enterprise of conscience. Then came the broadcast media—radio in the 1920s and television in the 1950s. What set them apart was their commercial need to reach not just a wide audience, but the widest possible audience. "Broadcasting aimed to please, wrapping politics in fun and games . . . conveying with unmatched reach and power its core message of conciliation."

As for the cyclic pulse, the recurring appearance of the three public moods in the same order, Barber suggested that the dynamic is internal: each type of public mood generates the next. After a conflict election ("a battle for power . . . a rousing call to arms"), a reaction sets in. Conscience calls for "the cleansing of the temple of democracy." But "the troubles do not go away," and four years later "the public yearns for solace," or conciliation. After another four years, Barber claimed, "the time for a fight will come around again," and so on.

In *The Pulse of Politics,* difficulties arise not in applying the theory (a calendar will do: if it's 2020 this must be a conflict election), but in the theory itself. Barber needed an even more secure intellectual foundation for the cyclic pulse than for the character typology because this time he not only classified all presidential elections into three types, but also asserted that they recur in a fixed order. Once again, however, one finds no footnotes. If Barber grounded his theory in scholarly sources, then it is impossible to tell—and hard to imagine—what they are. Nor does the theory stand up sturdily under its own weight. It would be unfair to expect Barber to have anticipated the rise of talk radio and cable television, much less the internet and social media. But in the broadcast era in which he wrote, why didn't the rise of radio and television, both of them agents of conciliation, produce more conciliating elections after they became our dominant political media? Perhaps that is why some of the "postdictions" to which Barber's theory leads are as questionable as they are easy to make. Did conflict really typify the civil, substantive 2008 election involving Arizona senator John McCain and Sen. Barack Obama of Illinois, or conscience the mutually disdainful contest between President Obama and Massachusetts governor Mitt Romney in 2012? Would anyone describe the brutal, mean-spirited campaign that pitted the celebrity businessman Donald Trump against former secretary of state Hillary Clinton in 2016 as one of conciliation?

The most interesting criticism pertinent to Barber's pulse theory, however, was made in 1972 by a political scientist concerned with the public's presidential psychology, which he described as a "climate of expectations" that "shifts and changes." This scholar wrote,

> Wars, depressions, and other national events contribute to that change, but there is also a rough cycle, from an emphasis on action (which begins to look too "political") to an emphasis on legitimacy (the moral uplift of which creates its own strains) to an emphasis on reassurance and rest (which comes to seem like drift) and back to action again. One need not be astrological about it.

A year earlier the same scholar had written that although "the mystic could see the series . . . marching in fateful repetition beginning in 1900 . . . the pattern is too astrological to be convincing." Careful readers will recognize the identity between the cycles of action–legitimacy–reassurance and conflict–conscience–conciliation. Clever ones will realize that both passages were written by James David Barber.[38]

Person, Public Mood, and the Psychological Presidency

A good deal about the public's political psychology, in fact, is sprinkled through *The Presidential Character,* and the more of it one discovers, the more puzzling things get. Most significant is the brief concluding chapter, "Presidential Character and the Moods of the Eighth Decade" (reprinted in the three subsequent editions of the book, most recently in 1992), which contains Barber's bold suggestion of a close fit between the two sides of his model. For each type of public psychological climate, Barber posited a "resonant" type of presidential personality. This seems to be a central point in his theory of the presidency. "Much of what [a president] is remembered for," he wrote, "will depend on the fit between the dominant forces in his character and the dominant feelings in his constituency." Furthermore, "the dangers of discord in that resonance are severe."[39]

What is the precise nature of this fit? When the public cry is for action (conflict), Barber argued, "it comes through loudest to the active–negative type, whose inner struggle between aggression and control resonates with the popular plea for toughness. . . . [The active–negative's] temptation to stand and fight receives wide support from the culture." In the public's reassurance (conciliation) mood, he wrote, "they want a friend," a passive–positive. As for the "appeal for a moral cleansing of the Presidency," or legitimacy (conscience), Barber suggested that it "resonates with the passive–negative character in its emphasis on *not* doing certain things." This leaves the active–positive, Barber's president for all seasons.[40] Blessed with a "character firmly rooted in self-recognition and self-love," Barber's "active–positive can not only *perform* lovingly or aggressively or with detachment, he can *feel* those ways."[41]

What Barber first offered in *The Presidential Character,* then, was the foundation for a model of the psychological presidency that was not only two-sided but integrated as well, one in which the "tuning, the resonance—or lack of it" between the public's "climate of expectations" and the president's personality "sets in motion the dynamic of his Presidency." Barber concentrated on the personality half of his model in *The Presidential Character,* then filled in the other half—the public's—in *The Pulse of Politics.* And this is where his work becomes especially puzzling. Most authors, when they complete a multivolume opus, trumpet their accomplishment. Barber did not. In fact, one finds in *The Pulse of Politics* no mention at all of presidential character, of public climates of expectations, or of "the resonance—or lack of it"—between them.[42]

At first blush, this seems doubly strange because there is a strong surface fit between the halves of Barber's model. As Table 6.3 indicates, in the twenty-three twentieth-century elections after Theodore Roosevelt's in 1904 (Barber did not type twentieth-century presidents before Taft or after Clinton), presidential character and public mood resonated sixteen times. The exceptions—active–negative Wilson's election in the conscience year of 1916, passive–negative Coolidge's in conflictual 1924, active–negative Hoover's in the conscience election of 1928, passive–negative Eisenhower's in the conciliating election of 1956, active–negative Johnson's in conscience-oriented 1964, active–negative Nixon's in conciliating 1968, and passive–positive Reagan's in conflict-dominated 1984—perhaps could be explained by successful campaign image management, an argument that would also support Barber's view of the media's power in presidential politics. In that case, a test of Barber's model would be: Did these "inappropriate" presidents lose the public's support when people found out what they were really like after the election? In every presidency but those of Coolidge, Eisenhower, and Reagan, the answer would have been yes.

On closer inspection, however, it also turns out that in every case but these, the presidents whose administrations were unsuccessful were active–negatives. But, Barber tells us, active–negative presidents fail for reasons that have nothing to do with the public mood. As for the model's overall success rate of sixteen out of twenty-three, it includes ten elections that were won by active–positives who, he says, resonate with every public mood. A good hand in draw poker is seldom a good hand in Texas Hold 'Em; Barber's success rate in the elections not won by active–positives was just six of thirteen. In conscience elections, only once did a representative of the resonant type (passive–negative) win, while purportedly less suitable active–negatives won three times.

Barber's Prescriptions

In *The Presidential Character* and *The Pulse of Politics* Barber developed a suggestive and relatively complete model of the psychological presidency. Why he failed even to acknowledge the connection between the theories in each book, much less present them as a unified whole, is unclear. Perhaps he feared that the lack of fit between his mood and personality types—the public and presidential components—would have distracted critics from his larger points.

In any event, the theoretical and predictive elements of Barber's approach to the presidency are sufficiently provocative as to warrant him a hearing for his prescriptions

Table 6.3 ■ Resonance of Character Type and Public Mood in Presidential Elections, 1908–1996				
Election			Winning presidential candidate	
Year	Public mood	"Resonant" character types	Name	Character type
1908	Conciliation	Passive–positive (Active–positive)	Taft	Passive–positive
1912	Conflict	Active–negative (Active–positive)	Wilson	Active–negative
1916	Conscience	Passive–negative (Active–positive)	Wilson	Active–negative
1920	Conciliation	Passive–positive (Active–positive)	Harding	Passive–positive
1924	Conflict	Active–negative (Active–positive)	Coolidge	Passive–negative
1928	Conscience	Passive–negative (Active–positive)	Hoover	Active–negative
1932	Conciliation	Passive–positive (Active–positive)	Roosevelt	Active–positive
1936	Conflict	Active–negative (Active–positive)	Roosevelt	Active–positive
1940	Conscience	Passive–negative (Active–positive)	Roosevelt	Active–positive
1944	Conciliation	Passive–positive (Active–positive)	Roosevelt	Active–positive
1948	Conflict	Active–negative (Active–positive)	Truman	Active–positive
1952	Conscience	Passive–negative (Active–positive)	Eisenhower	Passive–negative
1956	Conciliation	Passive–positive (Active–positive)	Eisenhower	Passive–negative
1960	Conflict	Active–negative (Active–positive)	Kennedy	Active–positive

Election			Winning presidential candidate	
Year	Public mood	"Resonant" character types	Name	Character type
1964	Conscience	Passive–negative (Active–positive)	Johnson	Active–negative
1968	Conciliation	Passive–positive (Active–positive)	Nixon	Active–negative
1972	Conflict	Active–negative (Active–positive)	Nixon	Active–negative
1976	Conscience	Passive–negative (Active–positive)	Carter	Active–positive
1980	Conciliation	Passive–positive (Active–positive)	Reagan	Passive–positive
1984	Conflict	Active–negative (Active–positive)	Reagan	Passive–positive
1988	Conscience	Passive–negative (Active–positive)	Bush	Active–positive
1992	Conciliation	Passive–positive (Active–positive)	Clinton	Active–positive
1996	Conflict	Active–negative (Active–positive)	Clinton	Active–positive

Sources: Compiled by the author; data from James David Barber, *The Presidential Character: Predicting Performance in the White House* (Englewood Cliffs, NJ: Prentice Hall, 1972, 1977, 1985, 1992) and *The Pulse of Politics: Electing Presidents in the Media Age* (New York: Norton, 1980).

for change. Barber's primary goal for the psychological presidency was that it be "depsychopathologized." He wanted to keep active–negatives out of the White House and put healthy active–positives in. He wanted the public to become the master of its own political fate, breaking out of its electoral mood cycle, which is essentially a cycle of psychological dependency. Freed of their inner chains, the president and the public, Barber claimed, will be able to forge a "creative politics" or "politics of persuasion," as he variously dubbed it. Just what this kind of politics would be like is not clear, but apparently it would involve greater sensitivity on the part of both presidents and citizens to the ideas of the other.[43]

It will not surprise readers to learn that Barber, by and large, dismissed constitutional reform as a method for achieving his goals. After all, if the presidency is as shaped by psychological forces as he said it is, then institutional tinkering will be, almost by definition, beside the point.[44] Change, to be effective, will have to come in the hearts and minds of the people—in the information they get about politics, the way they think about that information, and the way they feel about what they think. Because of this, Barber argued, the central agent of change will have to be the most pervasive—namely, media journalism, especially its coverage of presidential elections.[45] Even the advent of digital and social media has not displaced news organizations as the main drivers of political communication.

It is in his prescriptive writings that Barber was on the most solid ground and that his answers were as good as his questions. Unlike many media critics, he did not assume imperiously that the sole purpose of newspapers, magazines, and television is to elevate the masses. Barber recognized that the media are made up of commercial enterprises that must sell papers and attract viewers, readers, and listeners. He recognized, too, that the basic format of news coverage is the story, not the scholarly treatise. Barber's singular contribution was his argument that the media can improve the way they do all of these things at the same time, and that better election stories will attract bigger audiences in more enlightening ways.

The first key to better stories, Barber argued, is greater attention to the candidates. Election coverage that ignores the motivations, developmental histories, and basic beliefs of its protagonists is as lifeless as dramas or novels would be if they neglected these crucial human attributes. Such coverage is also uninformative. Elections, after all, present the voters with choices among people, and, as Barber showed, the kinds of people the candidates are influences the kinds of presidents they would be. Good journalism, according to Barber, would "focus on the person as embodying his historical development, playing out a character born and bred in another place, connecting an old identity with a new persona—the stuff of intriguing drama from Joseph in Egypt on down. That can be done explicitly in biographical stories."[46]

Barber was commendably diffident; he did not expect reporters to master and apply his own character typology. But he did want them to search the candidates' lives for patterns of behavior, particularly the rigidity that characterizes active–negatives. (Of all behavior patterns, rigidity, he believed, "is probably the easiest one to spot and the most dangerous one to elect.")[47] With public interest ever high in "people" stories and in psychology, Barber probably was right to think that this kind of reporting would not only inform readers but engage their interest as well.

As *Washington Post* editors Leonard Downie and Robert Kaiser point out, press coverage of recent elections has sometimes tried to fulfill Barber's expectations.[48] During the nomination stage of the 1988 campaign, the "character" issue drove two Democratic candidates from the field, much to the relief of most political leaders and (eventually) most voters. Former senator Gary Hart's extramarital escapades, which were revealed by the *Miami Herald,* were politically harmful less because of his moral weakness than because of the recklessness the incidents illuminated in his character. Serious doubts also were raised about Sen. Joseph Biden's intellectual and personal depth when the press discovered that he had lied to voters about his success in school and then tried to pass off stories from an autobiographical speech by a British politician as events drawn from his own life. As for the Republican nominee in 1988, George H. W. Bush, he triumphed in part because he was able to lay to rest the so-called wimp factor—that is, the suspicion that he was too weak to be a successful president.

Coverage of the character issue took a different and, from Barber's perspective, lamentable turn in the 1990s. Moral, not psychological, character became the media's obsession. In 1992 Clinton's truthfulness and fidelity were called into question when an Arkansas acquaintance, Gennifer Flowers, publicly charged that she and Clinton had engaged in a long-standing extramarital affair while he was governor. Clinton denied the charge but conceded that he and his wife had endured some marital problems in the past. Soon after, letters in Clinton's own hand were published suggesting that he had dodged the draft during the Vietnam War. In contrast to their strong response to the candidates whose psychological character was questioned in 1988, however, voters overcame their doubts about Clinton's moral character and elected him—an active–positive, in Barber's reckoning[49]— as president. Coverage of the 1996 election, which matched two well-established figures, the incumbent Clinton and the long-familiar Senate Republican leader Robert Dole, was less character centered than its recent predecessors. But in 1998 Clinton's affair with former White House intern Monica Lewinsky dominated the national agenda.

In campaigning for their parties' presidential nominations in 2000, Al Gore and George W. Bush each worked hard to persuade the voters that he was a leader of strong moral character. Gore emphasized that he was a family man who regarded Clinton's affair with Lewinsky as "inexcusable." Bush did his best to inoculate himself against character charges by admitting long before the first vote was cast that he had been morally lax as a younger man. He regularly ended campaign speeches by raising his hand skyward and declaring, "Should I be fortunate enough to win, when I put my hand upon the Bible, I will swear to uphold the dignity and honor of the office." The *Post* "printed book-length series of articles about the lives and careers of both men."[50]

Character concerns of the psychological sort went a long way toward determining the outcome of the 2000 general election. Gore carried into the campaign a reputation as an aggressive, experienced, and skillful debater, a reputation Bush lacked. Yet Bush ended up benefiting considerably more from their three nationally televised debates than Gore did. In the first debate, Gore treated his opponent with disdain, often speaking condescendingly when it was his turn and sighing and grimacing while Bush spoke. Chastened by the adverse public response, Gore was deferential, almost obsequious during the second debate. He hit his stride in the third debate, but the inconsistency of his behavior from one debate to the next fed voters' doubts about who Gore really was. Bush was not strongly impressive in any of the debates, but voters saw the same man in all three of them. Gore, who entered the debate season leading Bush by around five percentage points in the polls, left it trailing by five points.[51]

Although neither Bush nor Kerry made character a major issue in any form in 2004, their supporters did. Documentary filmmaker Michael Moore's *Fahrenheit 9/11,* an election year box-office hit, portrayed Bush sometimes as stupid, sometimes as evil, but always as a man of dangerously defective character. Kerry's character came under assault from a new political group called Swift Boat Veterans for Truth. In television commercials, the group attacked Kerry's record as a swift boat commander in the Vietnam War, sowing doubts about his truthfulness and courage. The character of John McCain and Barack Obama was also emphasized by their supporters in 2008, but in a more positive way. McCain's heroic "grace under pressure" as a prisoner of war in North Vietnam and Obama's reflective search for identity and meaning as the son of a white American mother and a black Kenyan father became much-celebrated features of their candidacies for president. In 2012 Romney campaigned as a morally upright family man, while Democrats attacked him for being insensitive during his years in business to the interests of workers and communities and, beyond that, somehow "weird."

Donald Trump's election in 2016 raised questions of character in all its forms. Morally, he seemed bankrupt to some voters. Most astonishing, in a video-recorded 2005 conversation with *Access Hollywood* host Billy Bush that became public in October 2016, Trump bragged that when he saw beautiful women, "I just start kissing them. . . . And when you're a star, they let you do it. They let you do it. . . . Grab 'em by the p***y. You can do anything."[52] Yet other voters accepted that Trump's characterization of his opponent, Hillary Clinton, as "Crooked Hillary" made her morally worse. One in five Trump voters cast their ballots for him despite agreeing that he was not "honest and trustworthy." Another one-fifth of his supporters put aside their doubts about his psychological character even though they thought he lacked "the temperament to serve effectively as president."[53]

By July 2017, the six-month mark in Trump's presidency, nearly sixty thousand self-identified "mental health professionals" had signed a petition declaring that "Trump manifests a serious mental illness" and "should be removed from office" under the disability provisions of the Twenty-fifth Amendment.[54] In August, Republican senator Bob Corker said that Trump "has not yet been able to demonstrate the stability, nor some of the competence, that he needs."[55] He later accused Trump of "volatility," of "heading towards World War III," and of needing to be contained by aides" every single day at the White House" in a kind of "adult day care center."[56] In October, Yale psychiatry professor Bandy Lee and more than two dozen colleagues published *The Dangerous Case of Donald Trump.* Lee had already warned that Trump's "severe emotional impediments" pose "a grave threat to international security."[57] Other contributors to the book assessed Trump as being pathologically hedonistic, narcissistic, or sociopathic, among other diagnoses.[58]

Engaging readers' interest was Barber's final key to better journalism. What voters need in order to make decisions is the same as what they want—namely, information about who the candidates are and what they believe. According to a study of network evening news coverage of the 1972 election campaign, which Barber cited, almost as much time was devoted to the polls, strategies, rallies, and other "horse-race" elements of the election as to the candidates' personal qualifications and issue stands combined. The trend toward horse-race coverage has only accelerated since then. As Barber noted, "The viewer tuning in for facts to guide his choice would, therefore, have to pick his political nuggets from a great gravel pile of political irrelevancy."[59] Critics who doubt the public's interest in long, fleshed-out stories about what candidates think, what they are like, and what great problems they would face as president would do well to check a half-century of ratings for CBS's *60 Minutes.*

An electorate whose latent but powerful interest in politics is engaged by the media will become an informed electorate because it wants to, not because it is supposed to. This was Barber's strong belief. So sensible a statement of the problem was this, and so attractive a vision of its solution, that one can forgive him for cluttering it with types and terminologies.

NOTES

1. "Candidate on the Couch," *Time,* June 19, 1972, 15–17; James David Barber, *The Presidential Character: Predicting Performance in the White House* (Englewood Cliffs, NJ: Prentice Hall, 1972); a second edition was published in 1977, a third edition in 1985, and a fourth edition in 1992. Unless otherwise indicated, the quotations cited in this essay appear in all four editions, with page numbers drawn from the first edition.
2. Hugh Sidey, "The Active-Positive Searching," *Time,* October 4, 1976, 23.
3. "After Eight Months in Office—How Ford Rates Now," *U.S. News & World Report,* April 28, 1975, 28.
4. David S. Broder, "Carter Would Like to Be an 'Active Positive,'" *Washington Post,* July 16, 1976, A12.
5. James David Barber, "An Active-Positive Character," *Time,* January 3, 1977, 17.
6. Hugh Sidey, "'A Revolution Is Under Way,'" *Time,* March 31, 1980, 20.
7. "Cycle Races," *Time,* May 19, 1980, 29.
8. Paul J. Quirk, "What Do We Know and How Do We Know It? Research on the Presidency," in *Political Science: Looking to the Future,* vol. 4, ed. William J. Crotty and Alan D. Monroe (Evanston, IL: Northwestern University Press, 1991), 52. Psychologists, on the other hand, have been paying more attention to the presidency. See, for example, Dean Keith Simonton, *Why Presidents Succeed: A Political Psychology of Leadership* (New Haven, CT: Yale University Press, 1987); and Harold M. Zullow, Gabriele Oettingen, Christopher Peterson, and Martin E. P. Seligman, "Pessimistic Explanatory Style in the Historical Record," *American Psychologist* 43 (September 1988): 673–681.
9. Robert A. Dahl, *A Preface to Democratic Theory* (Chicago: University of Chicago Press, 1956), 6–8.
10. The phrase is Alexander Hamilton's. See Alexander Hamilton, James Madison, and John Jay, *The Federalist Papers,* edited and with an introduction by Clinton Rossiter (New York: New American Library, 1961), no. 70, 423.
11. Seymour Martin Lipset, *The First New Nation* (New York: Basic Books, 1963), chap. 1; and Max Weber, *The Theory of Social and Economic Organization* (New York: Oxford University Press, 1947), 358.
12. Marcus Cunliffe, *George Washington: Man and Monument* (New York: New American Library, 1958), 15. See also Richard Brookhiser, *Founding Father: Rediscovering George Washington* (New York: Free Press, 1996).
13. Max Farrand, *The Records of the Federal Conventions of 1787,* 4 vols. (New Haven, CT: Yale University Press, 1966), vol. 1, 65.

14. Jeffrey Tulis, "On Presidential Character," in *The Presidency in the Constitutional Order,* ed. Jeffrey Tulis and Joseph M. Bessette (Baton Rouge: Louisiana State University Press, 1981), 287.

15. *The Federalist,* nos. 71 and 72, 431–440.

16. Ibid., no. 64, 396.

17. See, for example, James David Barber, "Adult Identity and Presidential Style: The Rhetorical Emphasis," *Daedalus* 97 (Summer 1968): 938–968; Barber, "Classifying and Predicting Presidential Styles: Two 'Weak' Presidents," *Journal of Social Issues* 24 (July 1968): 51–80; Barber, "The President and His Friends" (paper presented at the annual meeting of the American Political Science Association, New York, September 1969); and Barber, "The Interplay of Presidential Character and Style: A Paradigm and Five Illustrations," in *A Source Book for the Study of Personality and Politics,* ed. Fred I. Greenstein and Michael Lerner (Chicago: Markham, 1971), 383–408.

18. Richard E. Neustadt, *Presidential Power: The Politics of Leadership* (New York: Wiley, 1960), 185.

19. Erwin C. Hargrove, *The Power of the Modern Presidency* (New York: Knopf, 1974), 33.

20. See, for example, Fred I. Greenstein, *Children and Politics* (New Haven, CT: Yale University Press, 1965); and John E. Mueller, *War, Presidents, and Public Opinion* (New York: Wiley, 1973).

21. Paul B. Sheatsley and Jacob J. Feldman, "The Assassination of President Kennedy: Public Reactions," *Public Opinion Quarterly* 28 (Summer 1964): 189–215. See also Michael Nelson, "Evaluating the Presidency," in *The Presidency and the Political System,* 8th ed., ed. Michael Nelson (Washington, DC: CQ Press, 2006), 1–27.

22. Unless otherwise indicated, all quotes from Barber in this section are from *The Presidential Character,* chap. 1.

23. Ibid., 145, 206. In later writings, Barber's assessment of presidential passivity grew more harsh. A passive–positive, for example, "may . . . preside over the cruelest of regimes." *Presidential Character,* 3rd ed., 529–530.

24. Barber, *Presidential Character,* 12.

25. Thirteen years after *The Presidential Character* was first published, in an appendix to the third edition, Barber described a variety of works to show that his character types "are not a product of one author's fevered imagination," but rather keep "popping up in study after study." In truth, most of the cited works are not scholarly studies of psychological character at all, nor are they claimed to be by their authors.

26. Alexander George, "Assessing Presidential Character," *World Politics* 26 (January 1974): 234–282.

27. Ibid. George argued that Nixon's behavior was not of a kind that Barber's theory would lead one to predict.

28. Barber, *Presidential Character,* 99.

29. George Reedy, *The Twilight of the Presidency* (New York: New American Library, 1970). See also Bruce Buchanan, *The Presidential Experience: What the Office Does to the Man* (Englewood Cliffs, NJ: Prentice Hall, 1978).

30. Fred I. Greenstein, *The Presidential Difference: Leadership Style from FDR to Clinton* (New York: Free Press, 2000), 3.

31. Fred I. Greenstein, *The Hidden-Hand Presidency* (New York: Basic Books, 1982).

32. James David Barber, "Coding Scheme for Presidential Biographies," January 1968, mimeographed, 3.

33. The surveys are reported in Steve Neal, "Our Best and Worst Presidents," *Chicago Tribune Magazine,* January 10, 1982, 9–18; Robert K. Murray and Tim H. Blessing, *Greatness in the White House: Rating the Presidents, Washington through Carter* (University Park: Pennsylvania State University Press, 1988); David L. Porter, letter to author, January 15, 1982; Arthur M. Schlesinger Jr., "The Ultimate Approval Rating," *New York Times Magazine,* December 15, 1996, 47–51; and "C-Span 2009 Historians' Presidential Leadership Survey," http://www.c-span.org/PresidentialSurvey/Overall-Ranking.aspx.

34. Tulis, "On Presidential Character."

35. Erwin C. Hargrove, "Presidential Personality and Leadership Style," in *Researching the Presidency: Vital Questions, New Approaches,* ed. George C. Edwards III, John H. Kessel, and Bert Rockman (Pittsburgh, PA: University of Pittsburgh Press, 1993), 96.

36. Erwin C. Hargrove, "Presidential Personality and Revisionist Views of the Presidency," *Midwest Journal of Political Science* 17 (November 1973): 819–836.

37. James David Barber, *The Pulse of Politics: Electing Presidents in the Media Age* (New York: Norton, 1980). Unless otherwise indicated, all quotes from Barber in this section are from chapters 1 and 2.

38. The first quote appears in *Presidential Character,* 9; the second in "Interplay of Presidential Character and Style," n2.

39. Barber, *Presidential Character,* 446.

40. Ibid., 446, 448, 451.

41. Ibid., 243.

42. Barber did draw a connection between the public's desire for conciliation and its choice of a passive–positive in the 1980 election: "Sometimes people want a fighter in the White House and sometimes a saint. But the time comes when all we want is a friend, a pal, a guy to reassure us that the story is going to come out all right. In 1980, that need found just the right promise in Ronald Reagan, the smiling American." James David Barber, "Reagan's Sheer Personal Likability Faces Its Sternest Test," *Washington Post,* January 20, 1981, 8.

43. James David Barber, "Tone-Deaf in the Oval Office," *Saturday Review/World,* January 12, 1974, 10–14.

44. James David Barber, "The Presidency after Watergate," *World,* July 31, 1973, 16–19.

45. Barber, *Pulse of Politics,* chap. 15. For other statements of his views on how the press should cover politics and the presidency, see James David Barber, ed., *Race for the Presidency: The Media and the Nominating Process* (Englewood Cliffs, NJ: Prentice Hall, 1978), chaps. 5–7; Barber, "Not Quite the *New York Times:* What Network News Should Be," *Washington Monthly,* September 1979, 14–21; and Barber, *Politics by Humans: Research on American Political Leadership* (Durham, NC: Duke University Press, 1988), chaps. 17–18.

46. Barber, *Race for the Presidency,* 145.

47. Ibid., 171, 162–164.

48. Leonard Downie Jr. and Robert G. Kaiser, *The News about the News: American Journalism in Peril* (New York: Knopf, 2002), 36.

49. James David Barber, "Predicting Hope with Clinton at Helm," *Raleigh News and Observer,* January 17, 1993. For a different view of Clinton, one that offers examples

of "the driven investments of energy" characteristic of active–negatives, see Stanley A. Renshon, "A Preliminary Assessment of the Clinton Presidency: Character, Leadership and Performance," *Political Psychology* 15 (June 1994): 331–394.

50. Downie and Kaiser, *News about the News,* 36.

51. Barber, *Race for the Presidency,* 174, 182–183.

52. David A. Farenthold, "Trump Recorded Having Extremely Lewd Conversation about Women in 2005," *Washington Post,* October 8, 2016.

53. "Exit Polls," CNN, http://edition.cnn.com/election/results/exit-polls/national/president.

54. John Gartner, "Mental Health Professionals Declare Trump Is Mentally Ill and Must Be Removed," Change.org, n.d., https://www.change.org/p/trump-is-mentally-ill-and-must-be-removed.

55. Austin Wright, "Corker: Trump Hasn't Shown Stability or Competence," *Politico*, August 17, 2017, http://www.politico.com/story/2017/08/17/trump-bob-corker-charlottesville-response-241751.

56. See Chapter 6, notes 24 and 25.

57. Sharon Begley, "Democrats in Congress Explore Creating an Expert Panel on Trump's Mental Health," *Scientific American*, August 16, 2017, https://www.scientificamerican.com/article/democrats-in-congress-explore-creating-an-expert-panel-on-trump-rsquo-s-mental-health/.

58. Bandy Lee, *The Dangerous Case of Donald Trump: 27 Psychiatrists and Mental Health Experts Assess a President* (New York: Thomas Dunne, 2017).

59. Michael Nelson, "The Election: Ordinary Politics, Extraordinary Outcome," in *The Elections of 2000,* ed. Michael Nelson (Washington, DC: CQ Press, 2001), 78–79.

THE PRESIDENCY AND THE NOMINATING PROCESS

Aspirants, Parties, and Selections

Lara M. Brown

"I don't care who does the electing so long as I do the nominating."

—William M. Tweed, Tammany Hall political boss[1]

The Constitution was written in the hope that political parties would not arise. For better (mostly) and worse (partially), parties did form, in part for the purpose of contesting presidential elections. That meant developing methods for parties to nominate their candidates, and over the years those methods have evolved from closed caucuses of each party's members of Congress to national conventions that assembled party leaders from every state to a mixed system of primaries and conventions to the current system of primaries-based nominations in which conventions are mostly coronation ceremonies for the winners. As Lara M. Brown argues, the transition from one nominating process to the next often has occurred because aspirants for a party's nomination lost in a way that struck them as being unfair—and many others agreed. Their typical response was to try to open up the process in some way, and sometimes, especially after the nominations of 1828 and 1968, they were enormously successful.

Over many hours on many days during the summer of 1787, the delegates to the Constitutional Convention argued in circles about how presidents should be selected.[2] Wrestling with the novelty of designing an elected executive, the Framers debated numerous selection methods and their likely political ramifications. Along with stipulating the length of the executive's term and eligibility for reelection, the proposals put forward varied widely on the question of who should choose the president: the national legislature, state executives, the people, or some other newly defined constituency. Nearly all of the delegates aspired to craft procedures that would safeguard the executive's independence; prevent "cabal, intrigue, and corruption"; and elevate "characters preeminent for ability and virtue" to the presidency. But few agreed on the best way to achieve these goals.[3] As James Madison explained in late July, "There are objections agst. every mode [of presidential selection] that had been, or perhaps can be proposed."[4]

It was not until September 4 that a compromise plan began to take shape. Slightly amending a previously discussed alternative, the Brearly Committee[5] suggested a method that rested on presidential electors casting ballots in their respective states.[6] The person earning the most electoral votes, so long as that number was a majority, would become the president, and the person garnering the second-largest number of votes would become the vice president. After further consideration on September 6 and 7, the convention approved a modified version of this "electoral college" recommendation, which also specified that the House of Representatives (voting by state delegation) would break electoral vote ties and make the final decision if none of the candidates earned a majority of the ballots. In sum, the Framers imagined that there would either be a clear choice for president who would effortlessly receive a majority of the electoral ballots (like George Washington), or a two-step process in which the electors would split their votes among a handful of candidates[7] and then from that group, the House would select the president. Hence, in most instances, the Electoral College would perform the nominating function. Even though this presidential selection compromise was, as Alexander Hamilton noted during ratification, "almost the only part of the [constitutional] system . . . which has escaped without severe censure, or which has received the slightest mark of approbation from its opponents,"[8] it did not operate in practice in the way that the Framers envisioned.

Aside from the double-balloting problem, which was remedied in 1804 by the Twelfth Amendment,[9] the absence from the Constitution of a formal nomination method created an institutional void that enterprising presidential candidates have exploited ever since. This chapter explores the role played by candidate agency in the development of the presidential nomination process. More specifically, it argues that since the first competitive election in 1796, presidential aspirants have sought to use political parties to bypass House election and win the necessary votes in the Electoral College. Accordingly, the nomination process has become the province of the parties and the subject of recurring political contention. As John H. Aldrich explained, "The standard line that anyone can grow up to be president may be true, but it is true only if one grows up to be a major party nominee."[10] As such, the key question regarding the executive that the Framers debated (who should choose the president) persists—only now this debate has been remanded to the parties. Thus Boss Tweed's reputed remark about who does the nominating pinpoints well what underlies the changes observed in the parties: everyone wants to do the nominating.

Over the years aspirants ardently desiring the nomination have not only pursued the support of their fellow partisans, but also sought to change their party's rules to advantage their candidacies. Somewhat predictably, these aspirants often sought rule changes that would "open up" the process, and, by this means, undermine whatever group of partisans controlled the nomination at that time. These aspirants' efforts have combined to make the modern nominating system more democratic than it has ever been. Still, few observers are satisfied with some of the other features that now mark the nomination process, such as the front-loading of primaries and caucuses toward the beginning of the election year. Further, as Richard M. Pious perceptively observed, "Those who emerge with nominations lack national executive experience, a situation that rarely occurs in other nations."[11] Before analyzing the political tensions associated with the modern presidential nomination process, this chapter traces the intricate partisan history of the changes in the process.

THE FIRST ELECTIONS AND THE TWELFTH AMENDMENT

When the Constitution was drafted in Philadelphia, all the delegates assumed that the president of the Constitutional Convention, George Washington, would become the nation's first president. Although Washington remained "disinterested" in the presidency during the struggle for ratification, once the Constitution was adopted and the electors met for balloting, "all knew that Washington would be the winner."[12] In actual fact, Washington's status was such that he twice earned the unanimous vote of the electors, serving two terms without contest. Still, there were early clues that requiring each elector to cast ballots for "two persons"[13] for president might become a problem. As early as January 1789, Alexander Hamilton noted in a letter to James Wilson that "every body is aware of that defect in the constitution which renders it possible that the man intended for Vice President may in fact turn up President." Hamilton then suggested that the Federalists would "be prudent to throw away a few votes say 7 or 8" from the candidate meant to be vice president, John Adams, to ensure that Washington (not Adams) ended up as president.[14] In 1792 Hamilton was again tasked with managing the Federalists' electoral votes, which were secure for Washington but uncertain for Adams. Although Adams defeated his primary rival, George Clinton, the vice presidential balloting was closer than expected (77–50), which again suggested that partisan maneuvering was a key ingredient in determining the electoral vote tally.[15] Said another way, long before Washington declined to stand for a third term, aspirants had come to understand that disinterestedly awaiting notice from Congress about the Electoral College's final balloting was a surefire way to lose not only a presidential nomination, but also the election. Thus the presidential game had not only nurtured, but would now require, political parties.[16]

Although there was little doubt about John Adams receiving the Federalists' presidential nomination in their first "quasi-caucus"[17] meeting in 1796, there was some ambiguity among Republicans about their presidential choice that election year. Thomas Jefferson had been actively engaged with James Madison in building an opposition party since 1791, but he had resigned from Washington's cabinet in 1794 and returned to private life. In the months leading up to the election, Jefferson had also written letters petitioning Madison to take up the mantle of their party.[18] Yet, as Joseph J. Ellis noted, "by the spring of 1796, whether [Jefferson] knew it or not, he had become the standard bearer for the Republican party."[19] In sum, in this first contested election, political elites were nearly as unified about the choices of their respective party nominees as the presidential electors had been about Washington in the previous two contests. The Electoral College, however, did not function so smoothly this time. When the votes were counted, the double balloting for president and vice president resulted in the two parties' opposing nominees having to serve together. Adams was made the president and Jefferson the vice president. The vice presidential nominees (Thomas Pinckney and Aaron Burr) had come in third and fourth, respectively, in the voting.

The political situation was made worse in 1800, when Jefferson tied with his Republican vice presidential running mate, Aaron Burr, in the Electoral College and the decision devolved to the House of Representatives. Because he did not always agree with the Republicans, Burr was preferred over Jefferson by many Federalists in the House. As a result, a stalemate ensued and "for five grueling days, the legislators suffered through thirty-five ballots" and neither candidate earned a majority.[20] On the thirty-sixth ballot, a representative from Delaware, inundated with letters from Hamilton about Burr's unfitness for the presidency, withdrew his vote for Burr, and Jefferson secured the majority. In addition to this deadlock, prior to the electoral vote, the Federalist Party had fractured over its nominee. Even though Adams was the incumbent, the Federalists' congressional caucus nominated both him and Charles Cotesworth Pinckney "without giving preference to one or the other for president."[21] Hamilton had long been convinced that Adams was neither likely to win the Electoral College nor the best choice for the presidency. In October 1800 he wrote a pamphlet criticizing Adams's character and leadership, and promoting Pinckney for president. Although Federalist electors remained committed to Adams, his total vote was only one more than Pinckney's: 65–64. More generally, the 1800 election confirmed two truths about the presidential selection method. First, in a partisan atmosphere, double balloting for president and vice president allowed for too much mischief making, and, second, if parties wanted to win the presidency, they needed to select their nominees before the electors cast their ballots.

Unsurprisingly, before the next presidential election commenced in earnest, the Twelfth Amendment to the Constitution passed Congress and was ratified by the states. The amendment required electors to cast distinct ballots for president and vice president and reduced from five to three the number of candidates who would be considered in a contingent House election. Although the amendment fixed the "defect," it also advantaged the Republican Party. Donald Lutz and colleagues incisively depicted the partisan politics of the amendment:

> Federalists strongly opposed the amendment . . . [in part because it] violated the general principle of minority rights. Federalists were quite frank about the fact that under the conditions of the new amendment, they would no longer have a chance to elect a Federalist vice president . . . [and] the amendment, true to Federalist protestations in Congress, accelerated the demise of the Federalist Party. The Federalists might have elected a vice president in one or both of the next two elections and thus, kept the party alive as a force in national politics to provide alternatives to Republican policies.[22]

Beyond this, the amendment's construction—codifying "party tickets" and reducing the field of candidates eligible for House election—was an acknowledgement that the American system would have political parties.[23] Said another way, the amendment made the Electoral College the arena of interparty competition and the parties the arena for aspirants to fight for a nomination.

NATIONAL PARTY ELITES AND KING CAUCUS

Although Federalist members of Congress had met and nominated Adams and Pinckney in 1796, it was not until 1800 that both political parties used congressional caucuses to select their presidential and vice presidential nominees. This process, which later earned the epithet "King Caucus" because of its closed nature and insular selections, involved congressional partisans voting by secret ballot for their party's nominees at a meeting scheduled during the election year. Although the caucus system persisted until 1824, there was no election in which both parties were able to hold caucuses untarnished by some factional strife. Hence, almost from its inception, the process was a failure. It lasted as long as it did because during most of this period, the anemic (at times, nonexistent) competition between the two political parties discouraged institutional innovation. Further, the greatly elevated political stature of both Jefferson and Madison among Republican elites in Washington bolstered the system's validity. Still, King Caucus enjoyed only tenuous legitimacy during its reign.

In 1804 the Republicans had their most successful caucus of the period. Meeting in late February, they renominated Jefferson by acclamation and overwhelmingly agreed to replace Vice President Aaron Burr on the ticket with George Clinton. The Federalist Party, still in disarray after the "Revolution of 1800," did not hold a formal caucus. On July 11 Burr fatally shot Hamilton in a duel, which depressed further the Federalists' feeble presidential election efforts. Jefferson easily won a second term. Although James Madison had some opposition for the presidential nomination in 1808 from George Clinton and James Monroe, he won eighty-three of the eighty-nine votes in the caucus. This unity, however, was not all that it seemed. Forty percent of Republican congressional members protested the caucus with their absence, and despite having been renominated for vice president, Clinton had wanted the presidential nomination. As a result, Clinton "publicly denounced the caucus," and "Pro-Clinton newspapers in New York launched attacks on Madison."[24] The Federalists officially decided on their nominees in August, but only about twenty-five attended the caucus. Additionally, some broke from the party to support Monroe, while others backed Clinton. Madison won the presidency and Clinton the vice presidency, but Clinton also received six presidential votes from New York electors. In 1812 the factional split grew among Republicans. Even though Madison garnered eighty-two votes for his renomination, only 83 of the party's 178 members of Congress attended the caucus. Further, Republicans from many of the northern states chose to back George Clinton's nephew, New York lieutenant governor DeWitt Clinton. When the Federalists met in September, they failed to field a presidential nominee, choosing instead to back the defecting Republican, Clinton.

When Madison stepped aside after two terms, the problems with the congressional caucus nominating process became more pronounced. In November 1815 Aaron Burr wrote to his son-in-law, South Carolina governor Joseph Alston, and captured the pervasive cynicism that attended King Caucus and one-party governance by the Republicans:

> A congressional caucus will, in the course of the ensuing month, nominate James Monroe for President of the United States, and will call on all good republicans to support the nomination. Whether we consider the measure itself, the character and talents of the man, or the state whence he comes, this nomination is equally exceptional and odious. I have often heard your opinion of these congressional nominations. They are hostile to all freedom and independence of suffrage. A certain junto of actual and factitious Virginians, having possession of the government for twenty-four years, consider the United States as their property, and by bawling "Support the Administration," have so long succeeded in duping the republican public. . . . The moment is extremely auspicious for breaking down this degrading system."[25]

Republicans had a difficult time persuading congressional members to attend their party's caucuses in 1816 and 1820. In fact, in 1816, when only 58 of the 141 members showed up, they decided to call a second meeting. Although 114 members attended this second caucus, they only narrowly approved Monroe's nomination (65–54). In 1820, with only about one-quarter of the 191 members attending, Republicans made no nominations.[26] Federalists did not hold a formal congressional caucus in 1816, and by 1820 the Federalist Party no longer really existed.

The election of 1824 was a watershed. The Republican Party divided among the several leaders who were aspiring to the presidency. William Crawford, who had challenged Monroe in 1816 and earned fifty-four caucus votes, was thought the favorite until he had a major stroke that "left him partially paralyzed, speechless, and almost sightless."[27] When his supporters engineered the congressional caucus to deliver him the presidential nomination, the other aspirants—John Quincy Adams, Henry Clay, and Andrew Jackson—were outraged. Publicly disputing its legitimacy, they derided the system as "undemocratic" and pushed for a more "open" presidential nominating process. In a showcase of their support outside of Washington, these aspirants' allies across the country began promoting them in newspaper editorials and at public rallies. As early as 1822, Jackson's friends in the Tennessee State Legislature passed a resolution endorsing his candidacy.[28] By 1828 state legislative endorsements were being acquired by both Adams and Jackson in lieu of securing a formal party nomination. Hence, 1828, despite consisting mostly of hyperbole about the "corrupt bargain" (the presumed deal that had awarded Speaker Henry Clay the secretary of state position in return for his securing the contingent House vote for president for Adams), became a critical year of transition. The Republican Party split into National Republicans and Democratic Republicans, and state party leaders became an essential constituency of presidential aspirants. Significantly, this courting of state party leaders to accumulate state legislative endorsements presaged what would arrive by 1832: state party delegations choosing nominees at national conventions.

STATE PARTY LEADERS AND NATIONAL CONVENTIONS

The American political landscape of the 1830s little resembled the one from 1800. Not only had the country expanded from sixteen to twenty-four states, but most states had reformed their suffrage laws, doing away with property requirements and enfranchising all white men. Further, by 1832 every state but South Carolina selected its presidential electors by popular vote.[29] Jackson's election in 1828 had also changed the political culture. As Walter A. McDougall colorfully described,

> At Jackson's inauguration Washington City teemed with Democratic "Hurra Boys" waving hickory sticks, federal job-seekers, panhandlers, laborers, and immigrants. . . . What had happened? Elite scions of Puritans, New Yorkers, Quakers, and southern planters along the east coast had always assumed their settled notions of liberty, hierarchy, law, and order would gradually spread west and tame the frontier. Instead, it seemed the rollicking frontier had spread east and conquered the nation![30]

In short, republicanism had given way to democracy, and with it the parties had become mass-based political organizations. Since Jackson had won the White House on the shoulders of many state party leaders and owed nothing to Washington "insiders," when "Jacksonians from New Hampshire proposed the Democratic convention of 1832 . . . the president and his advisers jumped at the opportunity."[31]

Even though state parties had regularly held conventions to nominate candidates for local office, the first national convention to nominate a presidential candidate was held by the Anti-Masonic Party in 1831. When the Democrats convened their first meeting in 1832, they passed a rule that presidential nominees had to win at least a two-thirds majority of the delegates; they also awarded the vice presidential nomination to Martin Van Buren, who envisioned and then helped to build a mass-based political party.[32] National Republicans held their own national convention and bestowed their presidential nomination on Henry Clay. By 1836 national party conventions had become the place where presidential nominations happened.

The national convention system "was a democratic leap forward."[33] Not only were these conventions more "representative in character" of the country, but they also unified the party's leaders and "concentrated the party's strength behind a single ticket."[34] Overall, national party conventions opened the presidential nomination process to state-based party elites and institutionalized the two-party system. That said, the nearly 140-year era of national conventions had three phases of elite participation and party leadership: national, state and local bosses, and post-Progressives.

National Party Leadership, 1832–1864

Prior to the Civil War, partisan competition was mostly between the Democrats and the Whigs, who replaced National Republicans. With the country still expanding and tensions increasing on the issue of slavery, both parties' national leaders aimed to present voters with balanced tickets (one politician from a slave state and one from a free state). Although many thought the new nominating process would empower state party leaders, presidential selection at these early conventions remained in the hands of the national party leaders. For instance, in 1844 Democratic aspirant James K. Polk's convention managers were only able to wrest the nomination from Martin Van Buren because Andrew Jackson's opinion was decisive.[35] Among Whigs, Henry Clay's political maneuvers concentrated the attention of the delegates in most nearly every election. During this period Clay sought the presidential nomination three times and won twice (1832 and 1844); he also turned down the vice presidential nomination once (1840). In sum, although these national party conventions engaged state party leaders, the presidential nomination game continued to be dominated by national insiders.

When the Whig Party dissolved in the mid-1850s, some measure of national elite control went with it.[36] In 1854 the Republican Party was founded by state political leaders in Ripon, Wisconsin—far away from Washington. As a result, Abraham Lincoln's nomination in 1860 and his managers' efforts to defeat several better-known party leaders marked something of a transition between the old system of lining up behind national "insiders" and the new process, which involved bargaining with state and local powerbrokers (party bosses). In 1864 Lincoln's maneuvering was again impressive. Working behind the scenes, he managed to secure "the selection of pro-Union governor Andrew Johnson of Union-occupied

Tennessee—a lifelong Democrat—as the vice presidential candidate."[37] To be sure, this was not the last time that an incumbent president had his way with convention delegates, but in an important way it was the first time that a president felt the need to flatter the delegates to achieve his aim.

State and Local Boss Party Leadership, 1868–1916

When political observers think of old-style party conventions, they most often think of those from the era of powerful party bosses and the proverbial smoke-filled back room. These party conventions not only remain a source of fascination, but in their day they attracted thousands of attendees.[38] The unscripted speeches, incomplete platform planks, and uncertain roll call votes frequently turned the meetings into political theater. Presidential aspirant William McKinley put on a masterful performance in 1892, orchestrating an "on deck" position that helped him win the 1896 nomination.[39] Gilded Age conventions were full of both substance and spectacle.

What these conventions did not provide were participatory opportunities for rank-and-file partisans in the presidential nomination process. Nearly all of the delegates were elected officials and party bosses who presided over state or city party organizations that could deliver votes by the thousands to their preferred candidates. As Morton Keller shrewdly described, "The politicos of the Gilded Age were half feudal chieftains, half-sophisticated organizers of men and money. They differed from their pre-War counterparts in the scale of their operations and the degree to which an organizational model—an industrial one—superseded the more democratic, voluntaristic party culture of the past."[40] These party bosses were powerful because at the national level, the parties were basically tied. As George Mayer explained, "The fact that most states supported either one party or the other left the settlement of Presidential elections to the three states that possessed a genuine two-party structure: New York, New Jersey, and Indiana. . . . These states decided four of the five Presidential Elections during this period [1876–1892]."[41] This meant that presidential aspirants needed these bosses to secure not only their party's nomination, but also the election. Hence, neither presidents nor aspirants could win by "going over the heads" of the party bosses and appealing directly to the people. In return, from the candidates they supported, the bosses wanted federal pork and patronage to keep their machines running smoothly.

Repulsed by the corruption in government and the strong-arm tactics of the parties, reformers sought to dismantle the machines. By the mid-1890s, these reformers, many of whom identified as progressives, had begun making their mark. Several states had started mandating voter registration and instituting secret ballots. Two years after President James Garfield's assassination at the hands of a Republican office seeker, the federal government passed the Pendleton Act, initiating civil service reform and diminishing the patronage powers of the presidency. Tired of owing fealty to state party politicians, many of the aspirants at the turn of the nineteenth century took stock of the changes occurring and started looking for ways to win presidential nominations without the bosses. In 1896 William McKinley found one such route. Rather than compete with Thomas Reed and

William Allison for the favor of the party bosses, McKinley courted southern Republican delegates, who had mostly been neglected because the Republicans were likely to lose these states in the general election. These votes (all 191½) put McKinley over the top at the convention and allowed him more freedom from the bosses during his presidency.[42] The other key reform of this period was the use of primary elections to select national convention delegates. In 1901 Florida's legislature enacted the first primary statute. Progressive Wisconsin governor Robert La Follette pushed through his state's law in 1905, requiring national convention delegates to be directly elected. Soon after, Pennsylvania followed suit with a new law that further required that "each candidate for delegate to a national convention have printed beside his name on the official primary ballot the name of the presidential candidate he would support at the convention."[43] On the heels of these laws, the push to establish presidential preference primaries flourished in a number of other states. Unsurprisingly, presidential aspirant Woodrow Wilson, not a favorite of the party bosses, also encouraged the adoption of primaries. By the time of Wilson's nearly unanimous renomination in 1916, presidential primary elections were held in twenty-six states.

Progressives also gained traction among Republicans. In the wake of their fractious 1912 convention, during which the party delegates had renominated incumbent president William Howard Taft over former president Theodore Roosevelt, progressives got the Republicans to change the party's delegate allocation formula. Taft had used McKinley's trick of accumulating the votes of southern delegates to win the nomination, which had angered the northern and western progressives. With this change, the South lost seventy-eight delegate seats, which helped progressives secure for Charles Evans Hughes the 1916 Republican presidential nomination.[44] Despite these modest compositional changes to the national conventions and the increasing trend away from party-boss-backed presidential candidates, state party leaders continued to dominate the presidential selection process. Simply put, the primary laws had not brought the "democracy" to the system that many believed they would. There were a number of reasons for this. Since the delegates were not typically bound to vote for a specific candidate, many were able to be persuaded either before or during the convention proceedings. Primaries were also expensive for states to run, and when the Great Depression hit, few states saw them as necessary expenditures. Further, turnout was often low in primary elections, and party bosses were able to win these contests to become national convention delegates. Nevertheless, party conventions were not quite the same after the decline of the progressives.

Post-Progressives Party Leadership, 1920–1968

Although many states repealed their primary election statutes during the 1920s and 1930s, the parties and the presidential selection process did not revert to the prior system. As governor of New York, Franklin Roosevelt reformed his state party and took on the Tammany Hall bosses in New York City. Taking the civil service reform ethic to a new level, he encouraged a more "professional" approach to Democratic Party politics. His road to the nomination in 1932, like those of

McKinley and Taft, ran through the South and away from the party bosses in the North and the Midwest.[45] Once president, he pushed Democrats to repeal the two-thirds nominating rule, which meant that he would no longer need boss-controlled delegates to support his renomination. Even though his efforts undermined many of the state party leaders and old-time party bosses, they also tended to entrench a new group of professional party "administrators."[46] Hence, reforms aimed at opening up the system to rank-and-file partisans in the electorate had again not met with expectations.

After World War II, primary elections experienced a revival. Enterprising aspirants, aware that "the party leadership was not enthusiastic about their candidacies, entered the primaries to try to generate a bandwagon effect."[47] For instance, in 1952 Republican presidential draftee Dwight Eisenhower, who had not yet agreed to run, bested the conservative faction's candidate, Robert Taft, in the New Hampshire primary and left no doubt among the delegates about his popular appeal.[48] In 1960 Democratic aspirant John F. Kennedy, a Catholic, showed he was electable with his strong performance in primaries, especially in Protestant West Virginia. Hence primaries became vehicles in which candidates could demonstrate their electoral viability to the convention delegates. Still, as was true throughout the entire national party convention period, party insiders remained influential. Whether these insiders were national leaders, state and local bosses, or professional elites, the one thing they were not was rank-and-file partisans. Thus, even though the presidential nomination process was far more open than it had been in the days of King Caucus, it was not democratic. For the next change to occur, another crisis of legitimacy was required.

THE 1968 TURNING POINT AND THE MCGOVERN–FRASER REFORMS

The political legitimacy of state delegates voting on presidential nominations at national party conventions was shattered at the Democratic National Convention in 1968. That year it was expected that Lyndon Johnson would win the Democratic Party's renomination and run again for president. But as protests grew over the Vietnam War, Johnson's political fortunes sank, and on March 31 he announced that he would not seek reelection. With Johnson's blessing, Vice President Hubert Humphrey entered the contest, running against Robert Kennedy and Eugene McCarthy. Humphrey did not enter any primaries.[49] As Marty Cohen and colleagues described his strategy, "Humphrey, who inherited responsibility for Johnson's war policies, had no wish to confront [antiwar activists] in a popular election. . . . Humphrey even avoided giving speeches in states that were holding primaries."[50]

Despite ignoring these nominating contests, Humphrey trounced McCarthy in delegate votes (1,759¼–601) on the first presidential ballot at the Democratic convention in Chicago that August. Antiwar activists protested all week, and on the night of the nomination, "the worst violence of the convention broke out downtown, and television screens carried pictures of phalanxes of Chicago police advancing on demonstrators."[51] Inside the hall, the delegates were almost as unruly. When Senator Abraham Ribicoff nominated George McGovern (who entered the race after Kennedy was assassinated), he remarked that "with George McGovern as president of the United States we wouldn't have to have Gestapo tactics in the streets of Chicago."[52] Chicago mayor Richard Daley responded from the convention floor with a string of obscenities.[53] Humphrey's nomination was the final blow of a heated factional dispute between party "regulars" and "reformers." The reformers, who supported McCarthy and McGovern, challenged the credentials of party delegates in fifteen states. The reformers lost nearly every vote, but they won some important concessions. Not only would the unit rule, which allowed a majority of a state delegation to cast the votes of the entire delegation, be eliminated "at every level of party activity leading up to and including the 1972 convention,"[54] but also a reform commission would be established to consider and propose new nomination rules. McGovern was made the chair of this commission.

The McGovern–Fraser Commission (Representative Donald Fraser took over after McGovern stepped aside to run for president in 1972) issued "eighteen guidelines to be met by the states in the delegate-selection process."[55] Among the more important recommendations were those requiring the states to (1) limit the number of delegates named by the state party committee to 10 percent; (2) ensure that delegates were chosen in the same calendar year as the convention; (3) give public notice about each step in the delegate selection process; (4) include women, minorities, and young people as delegates "in reasonable relationship"[56] to the proportion in the state's population; and (5) use proportional representation to award pledged delegates to candidates in primaries and caucuses. All eighteen guidelines were approved by the Democratic National Committee and were included in the 1972 "call to convention." States were required to implement these guidelines if they wanted their delegates' credentials to be upheld and the delegates seated at the national convention.

In succeeding years several states adopted presidential primaries to ensure that the composition of the state's convention delegation would not be challenged as violating the "fair reflection rule." By 1980 both the number of states holding primaries and the percentage of delegates awarded in these contests nearly doubled.[57] After the 1980 election, the Democratic rules were altered again to codify the window on the calendar for holding nominating contests, establish a threshold percentage of the vote for earning delegates, and create a new group of delegates who could change their votes at any time. Members of this group were called superdelegates or PLEOs (party leaders and elected officials).

Throughout most of the 1970s and 1980s, Democrats had majorities in the state legislatures across the country, and, as a result, many of the changes that were made to state laws to meet the new Democratic requirements ended up affecting the Republicans as well. In every election since 1992, both parties have held primaries in about thirty-five states and selected about 75 percent of their convention delegates through these contests. Still, Republicans maintain some differences (no affirmative action, no PLEOs, and, until 2012, most states awarded delegates using winner-take-all, not proportional representation).[58] The widespread changes to the delegate selection process in the states also changed the national party conventions.

Since the process is now effectively over when a candidate has earned a majority of the delegate votes in the nominating contests (usually sometime in April), the presidential nomination roll call vote at the national convention has lost its excitement. Beyond this, most recent presidential aspirants have announced their vice presidential choices a week or more before the convention in an attempt to dominate the preconvention media coverage. In other words, national party conventions, which used to be deliberative bodies, are now mostly "four-day public relations spectacles, during which the nominees present themselves to the American electorate."[59] That said, few would argue that conventions have no purpose. In addition to their formal functions of approving a party platform and ratifying the party's presidential and vice presidential nominees, and their informal functions of unifying the party faithful, they help the parties connect with the American public. As John Sides and colleagues explained, "Campaign strategists have three goals at the convention: tell voters what the past four years have been about, identify how the current candidates are different, and offer a vision for the country."[60] In these respects, national conventions are no longer for party insiders.

Yet when one considers some of the demographic changes of the party delegates, this notion that conventions are no longer for party insiders is not as evident as one might expect. In 1968 the average percentage of women delegates at the two national conventions was fifteen, and in 2008 it was forty-one. But while the Democrats have increased their percentage of African American delegates (from 5 percent to 23 percent), the Republicans have remained the same (2 percent). More generally, the percentage of those with a college degree has increased at both conventions, and the percentage attending their first convention has decreased. In addition, the issue stances of the delegates on matters such as the role of government, free trade, and abortion have also grown more polarized over time.[61] In short, the recent reforms, like some of the previous changes, served mostly to alter the identity of the party insiders. That said, given that the independent choices of the delegates no longer matter because they are now bound to the votes of their state primaries, these demographic changes may not be relevant in terms of determining the openness of the current system. In essence, the identity of the insiders may not matter if insiders no longer have any power.

More broadly, the effects of the 1968 Democratic convention and the reforms that followed were significant. As Cohen and colleagues summarized, "Through all previous party history, most delegates to party nominating conventions were effectively controlled by party insiders . . . [but after the reforms] voters, not party insiders, were in charge."[62] Although a scholarly debate presently exists over whether or not party insiders have regained control,[63] all analysts agree that the reforms transformed the modern system into one that is unlike any that has come before.

THE MODERN NOMINATING SYSTEM

With fifty states, the District of Columbia, and five U.S. territories now holding primaries or caucuses to select national convention delegates, the most noticeable feature of the modern system is its complexity.[64] Along with the other major feature, a dynamic known as front-loading, this complexity makes the modern system teem with normative ambiguity. What states should go first? What type of nominating contest should states use? How open to independent voters and voters of the other party should these convention delegate selection contests be? How should states award delegates to candidates—proportionally or winner-take-all; at-large or by district?[65] Although some questions, such as whether states should receive delegates proportional to their electoral votes or in relation to their party loyalty in the last election, have always existed, the more open and extensive nature of today's process has functioned to bring more of these questions to the fore.

By and large the national parties have either left these questions to the states or been powerless to genuinely enforce their preferences. As might be expected, aspirants have tended to take positions that served their candidacies. This was vividly on display in early 2016 when the aspirants who crashed the two parties' nomination contests, Bernie Sanders and Donald Trump, described the rules that worked against their candidacies as "rigged."[66] Ironically, had the parties swapped rules—that is, if the Democrats used "winner-take-all" and the Republicans used "proportional representation" for delegate allocation—it is likely that Sanders would have fallen to Hillary Clinton sooner than he did and Trump would have lost after a contested delegate fight on the convention floor.[67] Hence recent reforms may have made the system more open, but it may not have made it better. After reviewing the modern system's central features (complexity and front-loading), this section considers their effects on the "invisible primary"[68] and the presidential candidates. As will be evident, striking the optimal balance in the nominating process between rank-and-file participation and leadership influence is no easy task. The debate about who should choose the president that stymied the Framers persists in today's parties.

As suggested above, the system's complexity stems from the fact that it now runs through every state, federal district, and territory in the country. Consequently, the election laws concerning contest type, contest date, candidate qualifications, filing deadlines, and voter absentee provisions vary widely. Simply put, any serious aspirant must employ a crew of election lawyers to stay atop these myriad rules and evaluate their strategic implications. As Dan Balz and Haynes Johnson wrote about the 2008 contest, "The Obama campaign concluded early on that investing in the caucus states could pay big [delegate] dividends. . . . Jeff Berman, a lawyer who oversaw Obama's delegate operations . . . assembled a group of seventy-five lawyers to research the rules governing primaries and caucuses in all of the states. . . . The rules assured a virtual stalemate between two evenly balanced candidates."[69] In addition to state laws, there are also federal statutes, especially the Bipartisan Campaign Finance Reform Act, and party rules that can change between elections. Further, the nominating calendar that marks the sequence of the contests rarely remains constant.[70] For instance, New Hampshire, aiming to protect its "first primary in the nation" status, did not decide on a date for its 2012 contest until November 2, 2011. In sum, today's presidential nomination game is an ever-moving target.

Along these lines, front-loading is "the process by which the primary calendar has become characterized by an increasing number of primaries held and percentage of delegates selected in the early portion of the nomination calendar."[71] This dynamic occurs because the states want to garner attention from candidates and the media and be influential in selecting a party's presidential nominee. Before each election the national parties establish a contest "window," a range of dates in which the states are expected to schedule their nominating contests. Although the national parties exempt a few states (in the past only Iowa and New Hampshire, but recently Nevada and South Carolina as well), other states not complying with this window risk losing convention delegates.[72] As a result, states often swarm opening day. In 2016 both political parties agreed to open the window on the first Tuesday in March. Fourteen states and one territory held contests that day.[73] This was down from 2008, when on the first open day (February 5) twenty-four states held contests. Still, the changing calendar involving many states (and delegates) acted as a barrier to those candidates who lacked either widespread name recognition or substantial war chests.

Aside from the calendar chaos, front-loading has been shown to have several effects on the nomination itself.[74] Front-loading often increases the cost of elections, stretches the length of the campaign, compresses the decisive time frame, amplifies any media momentum, and depresses turnout in the states that come later in the process.[75] These trends have led to what some believe is a less deliberative process because the voting tends to be over nearly as quickly as it begins. Front-loading further helps those aspirants who lead the public opinion polls amass elite endorsements, receive plentiful media coverage, and raise large sums during the invisible primary.[76] These front runners are able to win so many delegates so rapidly that an underdog has no real mathematical chance to accrue a majority of delegates once the contests are underway. As Andrew E. Busch and William G. Mayer noted, "Of all the candidates who have been nominated since 1980, *every one* of them can plausibly be regarded as, if not *the* front-runner, at least one of the top-tier candidates."[77] Together, complexity and front-loading affect not only how the election plays out, but also who wins.

The Invisible Primary

Although a presidential nomination is formalized at a national party convention, the nominating process no longer centers on that delegate meeting. To be sure, most of it never really did. In times past, it only culminated—in one last pitched battle—at the convention. In other words, because earlier delegates had operated more as trustees (doing what they thought was best) and were not bound to popular votes, it was difficult for any party or politician to guarantee the convention's outcome. Even incumbent presidents found it sometimes challenging to ensure a convention's result. In each election, party insiders hoped for smooth proceedings and solid nomination choices that would bring unity, not division. But everyone also understood that "politics is the art of the possible," and one could not know whether a fellow partisan might sense an opportunity for himself or herself that would upset the collective party's plans.

This uncertainty masked the fact that the "invisible primary," which Cohen and colleagues neatly described as a "long-running and widely inclusive series of interactions of party members with candidates and each other,"[78] has long been part of the nominating process. History also reveals that this "national conversation" had often lasted for six years, not two. Typically, successful aspirants started running for the nomination more than one full presidential election before they won it.[79] Still, prior to the McGovern–Fraser reforms, the most visible politicking occurred during the national conventions. After the reforms this politicking occurred during the invisible primary—that is, before the contests. Hence, nominating campaigns seem as though they now last longer, but what has really changed is the visibility of the invisible primary. In fact, given the tremendous advances in communication and travel over the last century, there is the possibility that this "long-running and widely inclusive" conversation may be cycling through potential nominees faster than it once did, meaning that aspirants may not need five to six years to court their fellow partisans and win a party's nomination. Of course, this increased visibility may come with higher costs to the aspirants of time and money than in the past. But whether the time frame is longer or shorter and the costs are more or less, one thing appears constant: aspirants are driving the changes in the presidential nominating system and "their motors are rarely, if ever, in neutral."[80]

The Presidential Candidates

A presidential nomination process needs to consider more than inputs (who votes). It should also consider outputs (presidential nominees). Since 1972 there has been a fair amount of concern not only over the types of candidates who have run, but also over those who have secured a nomination, such as Jimmy Carter, Ronald Reagan, and Donald Trump. Most of the winners were the front runners at the start of the nominating contests, but there are some questions about what characteristics made them front runners in the first place and whether these qualities are ones that may lead to a successful presidency.

To answer these questions, it is helpful to reconsider the challenges aspirants face in the modern nominating process. First, given the complexity of the process, no serious aspirant can run without a large staff and an ability to raise millions for the campaign. Second, given the dynamic of front-loading, one's nationwide campaign must be built nearly everywhere simultaneously. Serious aspirants focus on winning the early states, but they do not ignore the later states. Any candidate who believes that the media momentum after winning Iowa or New Hampshire will carry him or her through the rest of the contests is almost certain to lose, as Mike Huckabee did in 2008 and Rick Santorum did in 2012. Media momentum solves money problems, but it cannot make up for a field program and dedicated volunteers on the ground.

In sum, aspirants must devote substantial time to their presidential campaigns. Running for president is now a full-time, unpaid job. It is no wonder many front-running candidates have had personal fortunes valued in the millions. In fact, John Kerry may not have won the Democratic nomination in 2004 had he not been able to take out a $6 million loan against his Beacon Hill home to sink into his Iowa efforts. And Donald Trump may not have made it to June without being able to loan his campaign nearly $44 million.[81] But, most importantly, their wealth allows them to not work while they run for president. Most Americans—even most politicians—do not have the luxury of committing several years of their life to a risky goal without worrying about the cost of living. Although the constitutional requirements to be president are broadly inclusive,[82] the informal requirements are profoundly exclusive.

Front runners have three other traits worth noting. First, few recent party nominees, excluding incumbent presidents and vice presidents, have had much political experience in Washington. In the last eleven elections, the previous or then-current position of the twelve party nominees who were not presidents or vice presidents was either that of governor (six), senator (five), or businessman (one).[83] Further, five of the seven incumbent presidents had been governors. Second, candidates' overall political experience has declined. Before the Civil War, major party nominees on average had sought and held about eleven political positions and served a total of about twenty-one years in political office. Between 1972 and 2008, major party nominees on average had sought and held about eight positions and served a total of about sixteen years in political office.[84] And these averages seem likely to keep declining. Donald Trump had contemplated seeking elected office in the past but never done so until his successful run in 2016. Hillary Clinton sought one position (senator) and held two (senator and secretary of state) for a total of twelve years. Mitt Romney sought three positions (senator, governor, and president) and held one (governor) for a total of four years prior to winning the Republican nomination in 2012. These most recent nominees' averages amount to two positions sought and held and five years of total service.

Lastly, recent front runners have tended to have been known for their ability to emotionally connect with partisan voters. As political "outsiders" (Carter in 1976, G. W. Bush in 2000, and Trump in 2016) or good communicators (Reagan in 1980, Bill Clinton in 1992, and Obama in 2008) who captured the electorate's hearts, rather than their minds, these aspirants made ample use of talk show programs like *The Daily Show* and *The View*, partisan news outlets like *Daily Kos* and *Breitbart*, and social media platforms, like Facebook and Twitter. In each instance, these candidates sought to move around the traditional news media and connect directly with voters. In doing so, they were able to campaign on both wedge and valence issues, ignoring legitimate policy debates and the tough questions real journalists are inclined to ask. In combination, these traits and tactics suggest that the modern nomination process may now favor precisely those candidates the Framers had hoped to exclude through the Electoral College—those with "talents for low intrigue, and the little arts of popularity."[85] Still, American history abounds with examples of party nominees who might also be considered to have fit this bill, including Horace Greely in 1872, William Jennings Bryan in 1896, and Wendell Willkie in 1940. Thus, as Robert E. DiClerico and Eric M. Uslander pointed out, "There seems to be a compulsion to look back to the 'good old days' and assume that the pre-reform conventions of party leaders were really wiser . . . [but] 'unreformed' conventions gave us . . . the eminently qualified but politically disastrous Herbert Hoover."[86] The normative questions that run rife through the modern presidential nominating system do not have clear answers. It is true that more people are involved than ever before, yet it is also true that the widely varying state contest laws are far worse in terms of delivering representational equality than the Electoral College. Further, because the states do not all vote on one day and because the number of candidates declines precipitously after Iowa, the "democracy" that exists is not that meaningful. More aspirants also now run for president. But the quality of the recent crop of candidates (millionaires, media figures, and political dilettantes) is not necessarily reassuring, especially when one considers the gravity of the issues with which a president must contend. In short, there is a troubling sense that the presidential nominating process has devolved into something more akin to *Dancing with the Stars* or *Survivor* than *60 Minutes,* where entertainment matters more than education. Still, the notion of again restricting the process to only party insiders—especially now that party insiders, convention delegates, and those running the parties are more ideologically extreme than in the past—does not seem to be appropriate. Thus the modern presidential nominating system appears every bit as nonsensical now as it did in earlier times.[87]

CONCLUSION

The presidential nomination process has undergone a major transformation over the course of American history. What began with a small group of political elites informally agreeing on whose turn it was to reach for the ship of state's helm has become a complex, highly competitive and demanding process, involving a surfeit of rules, millions of dollars, and many thousands of people. Exploiting the opportunities in their environment and seeking to advantage their presidential nomination prospects, aspirants drove these changes in the parties and the political system. Their countless combined individual efforts have made the modern nominating system more democratic than it has ever been. Still, few are satisfied with the process. Considering that the most significant changes have occurred in the wake of some crisis of legitimacy over the system's selected nominee (Crawford in 1824 and Humphrey in 1968), it seems unlikely that there will be any large procedural overhauls in the modern nominating system until such a moment again occurs.

When it does—as at some point it most likely will—one imagines that the centuries-long trend toward more openness and greater levels of participation will continue. Said another way, it seems more likely that the next reforms will attempt to correct the enormous inequities that attend today's nomination calendar. Of course, reforming the system toward either a one-day national primary or a few days of rotating regional primaries[88] is likely to only amplify the concerns of candidate quality associated with today's system. In other words, the complexity and the frontloading are only likely to become worse under either one of these reform proposals. Thus the debate that began with the Framers at the Constitutional Convention about who should choose the president is sure to endure as long as the Republic lasts.

NOTES

1. Rumored to have been said by "Boss" Tweed, this quote captures the importance of the presidential nomination process. For further discussion, see Robert E. DiClerico and Eric M. Uslaner, *Few Are Chosen: Problems in Presidential Selection* (New York: McGraw-Hill, 1984), 37.

2. Forrest McDonald, *Novus Ordo Seclorum: The Intellectual Origins of the Constitution* (Lawrence: University of Kansas Press, 1985); William G. Mayer, "What the Founders Intended: Another Look at the Origins of the American Presidential Selection Process," in *The Making of the Presidential Candidates 2008,* ed. William G. Mayer (New York: Rowman and Littlefield, 2008); Gordon Lloyd, "Establishing the Electoral College and the Presidency," Major Themes at the Constitutional Convention, Teaching American History, http://teachingamericanhistory.org/convention/themes/8.html.

3. Alexander Hamilton, *The Federalist: A Commentary on the Constitution of the United States by Alexander Hamilton, John Jay, and James Madison,* ed. Robert Scigliano (New York: Modern Library, 2001), no. 68, 434–439.

4. Max Farrand, ed., *The Records of the Federal Convention of 1787,* vol. II (New Haven, CT: Yale University Press, 1966), 109.

5. Convention delegate David Brearly was the chair of this committee, and as such it is often referred to by his name (see http://www.teachingamericanhistory.org/convention/delegates/brearly.html). That said, this committee was sometimes also called the Committee of Eleven or the Committee on Postponed Matters.

6. Article II, Section 1 of the Constitution reads that "each State shall appoint, in such manner as the Legislature may direct," which meant that the states could decide the method of selecting their electors.

7. As will be discussed shortly, the Twelfth Amendment reduced the number of candidates from five to three.

8. Hamilton, *The Federalist* no. 68, 434–439.

9. Mayer, "What the Founders Intended," 225, 227.

10. John Aldrich, *Before the Convention: Strategies and Choices in Presidential Nomination Campaigns* (Chicago: University of Chicago Press, 1980), 5.

11. Richard M. Pious, "The Presidency and the Nominating Process," in *The Presidency and the Political System,* 9th ed., ed. Michael Nelson (Washington, DC: CQ Press, 2009), 189; see also Lara M. Brown, *Jockeying for the American Presidency: The Political Opportunism of Aspirants* (Amherst, NY: Cambria Press, 2010).

12. John Ferling, *The Ascent of George Washington: The Hidden Political Genius of an American Icon* (New York: Bloomsbury Press), 272, 274; also see ibid., 272–275.

13. Article II, Section 1 of the Constitution originally had electors voting for "two persons."

14. Joanne Freeman, ed., *Hamilton: Writings* (New York: Library of America), 513–515.

15. Ron Chernow, *Alexander Hamilton* (New York: Penguin Press), 419–424.

16. Richard P. McCormick, *The Presidential Game: The Origins of American Presidential Politics* (New York: Oxford University Press, 1982); Roy E. Nichols, *The Invention of the American Political Parties: A Study of Political Improvisation* (New York: Free Press, 1972).

17. Nichols, *The Invention of the American Political Parties,* 192.

18. Brown, *Jockeying for the American Presidency,* 119–129.

19. Joseph J. Ellis, *American Sphinx: The Character of Thomas Jefferson* (New York: Vintage Books, 1998), 189.

20. Chernow, *Alexander Hamilton,* 636.

21. Congressional Quarterly, *Presidential Elections, 1789–2000* (Washington, DC: CQ Press, 2002), 20.

22. Donald Lutz, Philip Abbott, Barbara Allen, and Russell Hansen, "The Electoral College in Historical and Philosophical Perspective," in *Choosing a President: The Electoral College and Beyond,* ed. Paul D. Schumaker and Burdett Loomis (New York: Chatham House, 2002), 37–38.

23. For further discussion of the partisan consequences of the Twelfth Amendment, see Lutz et al., "The Electoral College in Historical and Philosophical Perspective," 38–40.

24. Congressional Quarterly, *Presidential Elections,* 22.

25. H. W. Brands, *Andrew Jackson: His Life and Times* (New York: Doubleday Press, 2005), 313.

26. Congressional Quarterly, *Presidential Elections,* 24.

27. Robert V. Remini, *John Quincy Adams* (New York: Henry Holt and Company, Times Books, 2002), 66.

28. Brown, *Jockeying for the American Presidency,* 131.

29. All states used the popular vote to select electors with the exception of Maryland, which used the at-large, winner-take-all method; see Congressional Quarterly, *Presidential Elections,* 160–161.

30. Walter A. McDougall, *Throes of Democracy: The American Civil War Era, 1829–1877* (New York: HarperCollins, 2008), xxvi.

31. Congressional Quarterly, *Presidential Elections,* 25–26.

32. Robert V. Remini, *The Election of Andrew Jackson* (Philadelphia: J. B. Lippincott Co., 1963), 18–19.

33. Ibid., 27.

34. Eugene H. Roseboom, *A History of Presidential Elections* (New York: Macmillan, 1970), 106.

35. Brown, *Jockeying for the American Presidency,* 7.

36. Nichols, *The Invention of the American Political Parties,* 380–381.

37. Congressional Quarterly, *Presidential Elections,* 35.

38. It was estimated that 18,000 attended the 1880 Republican National Convention in Chicago.

39. Brown, *Jockeying for the American Presidency,* 172–173.

40. Morton Keller, *America's Three Regimes: A New Political History* (New York: Oxford University Press, 2007), 139.

41. George H. Mayer, *The Republican Party, 1854–1966,* 2nd ed. (New York: Oxford University Press, 1967), 172.

42. Wayne H. Morgan, *William McKinley and His America,* rev. ed. (Kent, OH: Kent State University Press, 2003), 146–147.

43. Congressional Quarterly, *National Party Conventions, 1831–2000* (Washington, DC: CQ Press, 2002), 12.

44. Ibid., 86.

45. Kenneth S. Davis, *FDR: The New York Years, 1928–1933* (New York: Random House, 1985), 248.

46. Sean Savage, *Roosevelt: The Party Leader, 1932–1945* (Louisville: University of Kentucky Press, 1991), 6, 9.

47. Congressional Quarterly, *National Party Conventions,* 15.

48. Marty Cohen, David Karol, Hans Noel, and John Zaller, *The Party Decides: Presidential Nominations before and after Reform* (Chicago: University of Chicago Press), 133.

49. Fourteen states and the District of Columbia held primaries that year. Humphrey's name was on the District of Columbia's ballot, but this was done by local party officials.

50. Cohen et al., *The Party Decides,* 157.

51. Congressional Quarterly, *National Party Conventions,* 127.

52. Ibid., 127.

53. Peggy McCarthy, "Ribicoff and Daley Head to Head," *New York Times,* August 25, 1996, http://www.nytimes.com/1996/08/25/nyregion/ribicoff-and-daley-head-to-head.html.

54. Congressional Quarterly, *National Party Conventions,* 127.

55. Ibid., 130.

56. Ibid., 130.

57. L. Sandy Maisel and Mark D. Brewer, *Parties and Elections in America: The Electoral Process,* 6th ed. (New York: Rowman & Littlefield, 2012), 242, table 8.1.

58. For further discussion, see Cohen et al., *The Party Decides,* 161.

59. John Sides, Daron Shaw, Matt Grossman, and Keena Lipsitz, *Campaigns and Elections: Rules, Reality, Strategy, Choice* (New York: W. W. Norton & Company), 226.

60. Ibid., 227.

61. Karlyn Bowman and Andrew Rugg, "AEI Special Report: Delegates at National Conventions, 1968–2008," American Enterprise Institute, August 27, 2012, http://www.aei.org/article/politics-and-public-opinion/polls/delegates-at-national-conventions-1968–2008/.

62. Cohen et al., *The Party Decides,* 158.

63. For instance, Cohen et al., in *The Party Decides* argue that parties are strong and control presidential nominations. Brown in *Jockeying for the American Presidency* argues that parties and candidates are sometimes both strong and sometimes both weak; thus who wins the nomination battle is more contingent on time and opportunity, but candidates are driving the presidential nomination process, not parties.

64. Barbara Norrander, *The Imperfect Primary: Oddities, Biases, and Strengths of U.S. Presidential Nomination Politics* (New York: Routledge, 2010).

65. A good overview of the different types of nominating contests is available online at http://www.thegreenpapers.com/Definitions.html#Prim.

66. Albert Hunt, "Trump and Sanders, Please Stop Whining," *Chicago Tribune,* April 20, 2016, http://www.chicagotribune.com/news/opinion/commentary/ct-donald-trump-bernie-sanders-rigged-delegates-20160420-story.html.

67. Nate Silver, "Donald Trump Would Be Easy to Stop under Democratic Rules," FiveThirtyEight.com, March 6, 2016, https://fivethirtyeight.com/features/donald-trump-would-be-easy-to-stop-under-democratic-rules/; Daniel Nichanian, "Clinton's Delegate Lead Would Triple under GOP Rules," FiveThirtyEight.com, April 28, 2016, https://fivethirtyeight.com/features/clintons-delegate-lead-would-triple-under-gop-rules/.

68. Journalist Arthur Hadley coined this phrase, which refers to the campaign period before the contests get underway. See Arthur T. Hadley, *The Invisible Primary* (Englewood Cliffs, NJ: Prentice Hall, 1976).

69. Dan Balz and Hayes Johnson, *The Battle for America 2008: The Story of an Extraordinary Election* (New York: Viking, 2009), 182–185.

70. Political scientist Josh Putnam posted a "marked-up" version of the 2012 calendar on his Web site that is well worth viewing; see http://frontloading.blogspot .com/p/2012-presidential-primary-calendar_26.html.

71. Andrew Busch, "The Reemergence of the Iowa Caucus: A New Trend, an Aberration, or a Useful Reminder?" in Mayer, ed., *The Making of the Presidential Candidates 2008.*

72. For discussion of the politics surrounding the penalized states in 2008, see Lara M. Brown, "A High Speed Chase: Presidential Aspirants and the Nomination Process," in *Understanding the Presidency,* ed. James P. Pfiffner and Roger H. Davidson (New York: Pearson, 2012).

73. Eleven states (Alabama, Arkansas, Colorado, Georgia, Massachusetts, Minnesota, Oklahoma, Tennessee, Texas, Vermont, and Virginia) held nominating contests for both parties; Alaska, North Dakota, and Wyoming each held a Republican caucus; and American Samoa held a Democratic caucus.

74. William G. Mayer and Andrew E. Busch, *The Front-Loading Problem in Presidential Nominations* (Washington, DC: Brookings Institution Press, 2004) and William G. Mayer, "The Basic Dynamics of the Contemporary Nomination Process: An Expanded View," in *The Making of the Presidential Candidates 2004,* ed. William G. Mayer (Lanham, MD: Rowman and Littlefield, 2004).

75. For further discussion on front-loading, see Lara M. Brown, "A High Speed Chase."

76. See Mayer and Busch, *Front-Loading Problem.* See also Mayer, "The Basic Dynamics," 1–43; 83–132; Nelson W. Polsby and Aaron Wildavsky, *Presidential Elections: Strategies and Structures of American Politics,* 11th ed. (Lanham, MD: Rowman and Littlefield, 2004), 89–115; Stephen J. Wayne, *The Road to the White House 2004: The Politics of Presidential Elections* (Belmont, CA: Wadsworth/ Thomson Learning, 2004), 103–158; Michael J. Goff, *The Money Primary: The New Politics of the Early Presidential Nomination Process* (Lanham, MD: Rowman and Littlefield, 2004); and Cohen et al., *The Party Decides.*

77. Busch and Mayer, *Front-Loading Problem;* and Mayer, "The Basic Dynamics," 23.

78. Cohen et al., *The Party Decides,* 102

79. Brown, *Jockeying for the American Presidency,* 27.

80. Ibid., 17.

81. John Sommers, "Trump's Primary Run Financed by $44 Million in Loans," *Reuters,* May 21, 2016, http://www.newsweek.com/trump-loaned-campaign-44-million-462217.

82. According to the Constitution, one need only be at least thirty-five years of age, a natural-born citizen, and a resident of the United States for fourteen years. The Twenty-second Amendment also set a term limit on the office, which means that no person may be elected more than twice to the presidency or have held the office for more than ten years.

83. The 2016 Democratic nominee Hillary Clinton had served as a senator prior to serving as secretary of state.

84. Brown, *Jockeying for the American Presidency,* 102.

85. Hamilton, *The Federalist* no. 68, 434–439.

86. DiClerico and Uslaner, *Few Are Chosen,* 174.

87. DiClerico and Uslaner, *Few Are Chosen,* included a quote from a *Washington Post* editor that addressed this: "I absolutely agree with those who point out that the 'reformed' system, with its marathon primaries and its nit-picking financing rules, is crazy. But I always thought the old system was pretty crazy too, as we have a crazy system, reformed and unregenerate" (p. 174).

88. Caroline J. Tolbert and David P. Redlawsk, "Reforming Presidential Nominations: Rotating State Primaries or a National Primary?" Political Science at Iowa Research Online, 2009, http://ir.uiowa.edu/polisci_pubs/86.

THE FAULTY PREMISES OF THE ELECTORAL COLLEGE

George C. Edwards III

Political parties control the nomination of presidential candidates, but the Constitution spells out how the president will be chosen from among these nominees. Few issues vexed the delegates to the Constitutional Convention more than presidential selection. The method they eventually came up with— after rejecting proposals to have the president chosen by Congress, the people, or even the state governors—was the Electoral College. Modern supporters of the Electoral College defend it with arguments that, according to George C. Edwards III, are unpersuasive and inaccurate on their own terms and that neglect the foundational democratic principle of political equality. Noting that, among other problems with the Electoral College, both George W. Bush in 2000 and Donald Trump in 2016 were elected president despite losing the national popular vote, Edwards argues instead for a system of direct election of the president.

In the 2016 presidential election, Hillary Clinton won nearly 3 million more votes than Donald Trump. Nevertheless, Trump won the election and became president. His Electoral College victory in the face of popular vote defeat, the second such occurrence in the last five elections, raises once again the question of how we select the chief executive.

Political equality lies at the core of democratic theory. Robert Dahl, the leading democratic theorist, includes equality in voting as a central standard for a democratic process: "Every member must have an equal and effective opportunity to vote, and all votes must be counted as equal,"[1] Indeed, it is difficult to imagine a definition of democracy that does not include equality in voting as a central standard.

Because political equality is a central standard for democratic government, we must evaluate any current or proposed mechanism for selecting the president against it. A popular misconception is that electoral votes simply aggregate popular votes. In reality, the electoral vote regularly deviates from the popular will as expressed in the popular vote—sometimes merely in curious ways, usually by strengthening the victory margin of the popular vote leader, but at other times in such a way as to deny the presidency to the people's preferred candidate.

The percentage of electoral votes received by a candidate nationwide rarely coincides with the candidate's percentage of the national popular vote for several reasons, the most important of which is the winner-take-all (or unit-vote) system.[2] All states except Maine and Nebraska have a winner-take-all system in which they award *every* electoral vote to the candidate who receives the most popular votes in that state. In effect, the system assigns to the winner the votes of the people who voted *against* the winner.

The operation of the winner-take-all system effectively disenfranchises voters who support losing candidates in each state. In the 2000 presidential election, nearly 3 million people voted for Al Gore in Florida. Because George W. Bush won 537 more votes than Gore, however, he received all of Florida's electoral votes. A candidate can win some states by very narrow margins, lose other states by large margins (as Bush did by more than 1 million votes in California and New York in 2000), and so win the electoral vote while losing the popular vote. Because there is no way to aggregate votes across states, the votes for candidates who do not finish first in a state play no role in the outcome of the election.

African Americans, who are the nation's most distinctive minority group, are disproportionately concentrated in the Deep South. They rarely vote for the Republican candidates who win the states in that region. Thus, their votes are wasted because they are never added up across the country. It is not surprising that presidential candidates have generally ignored these voters in their campaigns.[3] In a multi-candidate contest such as the ones in 1992, 1996, 2000, and 2016, the winner-take-all system may suppress the votes of the majority as well as the minority. In 1996 less than a majority of voters decided how the electoral votes of twenty-six states would be cast. In 2000 pluralities rather than majorities determined the allocation of electoral votes in eight states, including Florida and Ohio. In 2016, pluralities decided the electoral votes in fourteen states. In each case, less than half the voters determined how *all* of their state's electoral votes were cast.

One result of these distorting factors is that there is typically a substantial disparity in almost all elections between the share of the national popular vote a candidate receives and that candidate's percentage of the electoral vote. In 1876, 1888, 2000, 2016, and, arguably, 1960,[4] the candidate who finished second in the popular vote won the election.

The unit-vote system also allows even small third parties to siphon more votes from one major-party candidate than the other and thus determine the outcome in a state, as Ralph Nader did in both Florida and New Hampshire in 2000. Indeed, by taking more votes from Gore than from Bush, Nader determined the outcome of the entire election. The results distorted the preferences of the voters because the preferred candidate in both Florida and New Hampshire in a two-person race was Al Gore, not George W. Bush, who ultimately won the states.

If no candidate wins a majority of the electoral votes, as happened in 1800 and 1824, the House of Representatives chooses the president. In such an election, each state's House delegation receives one vote, which would allow the seven smallest states, with a population of about 5 million, to outvote the six largest states, with a population of about 123 million. It is virtually impossible to find any defenders of this constitutional provision, which is the most egregious violation of democratic principles in American government.

The Electoral College violates political equality. It is not a neutral counting device. Instead, it favors some citizens over others, depending solely upon the state in which they live. The Electoral College is not just an archaic mechanism for counting the votes; it is also an institution that aggregates popular votes in an inherently unequal manner.

What good reason is there to continue such a system in an advanced democratic nation in which the ideal of popular choice is the most deeply ingrained principle of government?

CONSTITUTIONAL CONSISTENCY

Some defenders of the Electoral College argue that its violations of majority rule are just an example of several constitutional provisions that require supermajorities to take action.[5] For example, it takes the votes of two-thirds of the senators present to ratify a treaty. The Framers designed all such provisions, however, to allow minorities to *prevent* an action. The Electoral College is different. It allows a minority to *take* an action—that is, to select the president. As such, it is the only device of its kind in the Constitution. Thus, the Electoral College does not prevent tyranny of the majority. Instead, it provides the potential for tyranny of the minority.

DEFENDING INTERESTS

One common justification for the Electoral College and its violations of political equality is that it protects important interests that a system of direct election by the people would overlook or even harm. Advocates argue that allocating electoral votes by state, with states casting their votes as units, ensures that presidential candidates will be attentive to and protective of states' interests, especially the interests of states with small populations. Most supporters of the Electoral College also maintain that it is an essential bulwark of federalism and that electing the president directly would undermine the federal system.[6]

On their face, such claims seem far-fetched. In practice, candidates allocate proportionately more campaign stops and advertisements to competitive and large states than to small ones.[7] Because these justifications for the Electoral College are so common, however, we must investigate them more systematically. (It is illuminating—and frustrating—that advocates of the Electoral College virtually never offer systematic evidence to support their claims.)

Proponents of the view that one of the major advantages of the Electoral College is that it forces candidates to be more attentive to and protective of state interests, especially the interests of states with small populations, base their argument on the premises that (1) states have interests as states, (2) these interests require protection, and (3) interests in states with smaller populations both require and deserve special protection from federal laws.

State Interests

States do not have coherent, unified interests. Even the smallest state has substantial diversity within it. No state includes just one point of view. That is why Alaska may have a Republican governor and one or more Democratic senators, and why "California, New York, and Massachusetts, among the bluest of states, often elect Republican governors. As historian Jack Rakove argues, "States have no interest, as states, in the election of the president; only citizens do." He adds:

> The winner-take-all rule might make sense if states really embodied
> coherent, unified interests and communities, but of course they do not.
> What does Chicago share with Galena, except that they both are in Illinois;
> Palo Alto with Lodi in California; Northern Virginia with Madison's home
> in Orange County; or Hamilton, N.Y., with Alexander Hamilton's old
> haunts in lower Manhattan?[8]

James Madison, recognizing how diverse each states is, opposed counting the presidential vote by state (as in the unit rule) and hoped that, at the least, votes would be counted by district within states. Disaggregating the statewide vote and allowing districts within states to support the same candidate would encourage cohesiveness in the country and counter the centrifugal tendencies of regionalism.[9] Moreover, Madison did not want candidates to make appeals to special interests. As he proclaimed at the Constitutional Convention, "Local considerations must give way to the general interest"—even on slavery.[10]

Judith Best, who is perhaps the most diligent defender of the Electoral College, recognizes that heterogeneity exists within states but nevertheless argues that the citizens of each state share a common interest in managing their state's resources, including roads, parks, schools, local taxes, and the like. True enough. She also argues that these interests are as important as or more important than the characteristics people in a state share with people in other states, such as race, gender, religion, and ethnicity.[11] Many women, blacks, Hispanics, farmers, and members of other groups would be surprised to hear that local roads and parks are more important to their lives than the place they occupy in the economic and social structure of the country.

Equally important, Best makes a series of either logically or empirically incorrect statements about the relation between community interests and the election of the president. First, she confuses local communities with states. Her examples are largely of local, not state, issues, even though the policies of local governments vary widely within each state. Second, she argues that the president must be responsive to state interests to be elected and that candidates must "build [the] broadest possible coalitions of local interests" to win.[12] No evidence exists to support these assertions, and Best provides none. "State interest" is a dubious concept. Best cannot offer a single example of such an interest.

Do presidents focus on local interests when building their electoral coalitions? They do not. As we will see, candidates ignore most of the country in their campaigns, and they do not focus on local interests where they do campaign. Similarly, nowhere in the vast literature on voting in presidential elections has any scholar found that voters choose candidates on the basis of their stands on state and local issues. Indeed, candidates avoid such issues because they do not want to be seen by the rest of the country as pandering to special interests. In addition, once elected, the president has little to do with the issues that Best raises as examples of the shared interests of members of communities. There is no reason, and certainly no imperative, to campaign on these issues.

The Need for Protection

The Constitution places many constraints on the actions a simple majority can take. Minorities have fundamental rights to organize, communicate, and participate in the political process. The Senate greatly overrepresents small states and, within that chamber, the filibuster is a powerful extraconstitutional tool for thwarting majorities. Moreover, much more than a simple majority is required to overcome minority opposition by changing the Constitution.

With these powerful checks on simple majorities already in place, do some minority rights or interests require additional protection from national majorities? If so, are these minorities concentrated in certain geographic areas? (Because it allocates electoral votes on the basis of geography, the Electoral College protects only geographically concentrated interests.) Does anything justify awarding interests in certain geographic locations—namely, small states—additional protections in the form of extra representation in the electoral system that citizens in other states do not enjoy?[13]

Two of the most important authors of the Constitution, James Wilson and James Madison, understood well both the diversity of state interests and the need to protect minorities that are embodied in the Constitution. They saw little need to confer additional power to small states through the Electoral College. "Can we forget for whom we are forming a government?" Wilson asked. "Is it for *men,* or for the imaginary beings called *States?*"[14] Madison declared that experience had shown no danger of state interests being harmed by a national majority[15] and that "the President is to act for the *people* not for *States.*"[16] Congress, whose members are elected by districts and states, is designed to be responsive to constituency interests. The president, as Madison pointed out, is supposed to take a broader view. When advocates of the Electoral College express concern that direct election of the president would suppress local interests in favor of the national interest, they are in effect endorsing a presidency that is responsive to parochial interests in a system that already offers minority interests extraordinary access to policymakers and opportunities to thwart policies they oppose.

Interestingly, supporters of the Electoral College almost never specify what geographically concentrated rights or interests need special protection through the Electoral College. They certainly have not developed a general principle to justify additional protections for some interests rather than others. So let us do our own analysis of the distribution of interests in the United States.

The Interests of Small States

Do the states with small populations that receive special consideration in the Electoral College have common interests to protect? In the Constitutional Convention, Madison pointed out that it was not necessary to protect small states from large ones because the large ones—Virginia, Massachusetts, and Pennsylvania—had such different economic, religious, and other interests. Their size did not constitute a common interest. Indeed, rivalry was more likely to occur among large states than coalition.[17] Madison was prescient. The great political battles of American history—in Congress and in presidential elections—have been fought by opposing ideological and economic interests, not by small states and large states.

A brief look at the fifteen states with the fewest electoral votes (that is, three, four, or five) shows that they are quite diverse.[18] Maine, Vermont, New Hampshire, and Rhode Island are in New England; Delaware and West Virginia are in the Middle Atlantic region; North and South Dakota, Montana, and Nebraska are in the Great Plains; New Mexico is in the Southwest; and Wyoming and Idaho are in the Rocky Mountain region. Alaska and Hawaii are regions unto themselves.

Some of these states have high average levels of income and education, and others have considerably lower levels. Some are quite liberal and others are very conservative, and their policies and levels of taxation reflect these differences. Several of the states are primarily urban, but many others are rural. They represent a great diversity of core economic interests, including agriculture, mining, chemicals, tourism, and energy. Even their agricultural interests are quite diverse, ranging from grain and dairy products to hogs and sheep. In sum, small states do not share common interests. It is not surprising that their representatives do not vote as a bloc in Congress and that their citizens do not vote as a bloc for president.

Even if small states share little in common, are there some interests that occur only in states with small populations? Not many. The first interest that may come to mind is agriculture, with visions of small farmers tilling small plots of soil in small states. But most farmers live in states with large populations. The market value of the agricultural production of California, Texas, Florida, and Illinois alone substantially exceeds that of all seventeen of the smallest states combined.[19] For that matter, agriculture does not lack for powerful champions, especially in Congress, which has taken the lead in providing benefits, principally in the form of subsidies, for farmers. Rather than competing to give farmers more benefits, presidents of both parties have attempted to restrain congressional spending on agriculture. The Electoral College has not turned presidents into champions of rural America.

It is difficult to identify interests that are centered in a few small states. Even if we could, however, the question remains whether these few interests out of the literally thousands of interests in the United States deserve special protection. What principle would support such a view? Why should those who produce wheat and hogs have more say in electing the president than those who produce vegetables, citrus, and beef? Is not the Senate's disproportionate representation of states in which wheat and hogs are produced enough to protect these interests? There is simply no evidence that interests like these deserve or require additional protection from the electoral system.

ATTENTION TO STATE INTERESTS

As we have seen, a core justification for the Electoral College and its violations of political equality is that allocating electoral votes by state forces candidates to pay attention to state-based interests in general and the interests of small states in particular. In their enthusiasm for the status quo, some advocates go further and claim that, under the Electoral College, "all states are 'battlegrounds'" in the presidential election.[20]

Although defenders of the Electoral College almost never specify what interests the Electoral College is protecting, they nevertheless argue that candidates would ignore these interests if the president were chosen in a direct popular election. They base this argument on the premise that candidates appeal directly to state interests and give disproportionate attention to those of small states.

Do presidential candidates focus on state-level interests in their campaigns? Do they devote a larger percentage of their campaign efforts to small states than they would if the president were elected directly? To answer these questions, we need to see what candidates actually do and whether there is evidence that the Electoral College encourages candidates to be more attentive to small states. If candidates are not more oriented to small states and the interests within them than we would expect in a system of direct election, then we have reason to reject one of the principal justifications for the Electoral College's violation of political equality.

Candidates' Speeches

One prominent way that a candidate could attend to the interests of a state is by addressing them in speeches to that state's voters. What do candidates actually say when they campaign in the various states?

The presidential election of 2000 provides an excellent test of the hypothesis that the Electoral College motivates candidates to focus on state-based interests. Because the outcome in every single state that year was crucial to the outcome of this extraordinarily close election, each candidate had the maximum incentive to appeal to state interests. Nevertheless, neither George W. Bush nor Al Gore focused on state interests in their speeches, and they certainly did not focus on small state interests.[21] Was the presidential election of 2000 unique in this way? Apparently not. A study of the campaign speeches of Bill Clinton and Robert Dole during the 1996 campaign found that they also did not focus their speeches on local interests.[22]

Candidates' Visits[23]

The most direct means for candidates to appeal to voters is to visit their states and address them directly. Modern transportation has made it relatively easy for candidates to crisscross the nation in search of votes. Proponents of the Electoral College argue that one of its principal advantages is that it forces candidates to pay attention to small states that would otherwise be neglected in a national election and to build a broad national coalition by appealing to voters in every region.

During the presidential general election of 2012, the major party presidential candidates visited just three of the twenty-five smallest states (including the District of Columbia): New Hampshire, Nevada, and Iowa. Barack Obama visited only eight states during the entire general election, and Mitt Romney visited only ten. The states the candidates did visit were competitive states, especially large competitive states such as Florida and Ohio.

The emphasis on campaigning in swing states is not unusual.[24] In 2016, no presidential candidate visited any of the ten smallest states. Of the twenty-five smallest, they visited only seven. Once again, they focused their attention on large competitive states.

In addition to its failure to encourage candidates to visit small states, the Electoral College provides incentives to ignore many larger states during the general election. In 2012 the candidates never campaigned in California, Texas, New York, or Illinois, four of the five largest states. In 2016, Hillary Clinton made one stop in Illinois and Donald Trump visited Texas twice.

In the course of overlooking most states, candidates also avoid entire regions of the country. Democrats have little incentive to campaign in the heavily Republican Great Plains and Deep South, and Republicans have little incentive to visit the West Coast and most of Democratic New England.

In sum, the Electoral College provides no incentive for candidates to pay attention to small states and take their cases directly to their citizens. Indeed, it is difficult to imagine how presidential candidates could be less attentive to small states than they already are. Candidates are not fools. They go where the Electoral College makes them go, and it makes them go to competitive states, especially large competitive states. They ignore most small states; in fact, they ignore most of the country.

Candidates' Advertising

Candidates reach most voters through television advertising. Technology makes it easy to place ads in any media market in the nation at short notice. Do candidates operating under the Electoral College compensate for their lack of visits to small or noncompetitive states by advertising there?

No. Some voters are bombarded with television advertising; others see none at all. In 2016, 99 percent of the advertising was done in fourteen battleground states, which included only 35 percent of the population.[25] Similarly, in the 2012 general election, almost all the advertising by the Democrats and Republicans occurred in the swing states.[26] Focusing advertising on competitive states is nothing new.[27] Thus, as in the case of candidate visits, the idea that the Electoral College forces candidates to take their cases to small states and build coalitions from all regions of the country is erroneous.

In sum, the fundamental justification of the Electoral College—that it forces candidates to be attentive to particular state interests, especially those concentrated in small states—is based on a faulty premise. In reality, the Electoral College discourages candidates from paying attention to small states and to much of the rest of the country as well.

PRESERVING FEDERALISM

One of the most serious assertions by those opposed to abolishing the Electoral College and instituting direct popular election of the president is that doing so would undermine the federal nature of the constitutional system. Defenders of the Electoral College base this assertion on the premise that the Electoral College is a key underpinning of federalism. In truth, it is unclear what federalism has to do with the presidency, the one elective part of the government that is designed to represent the nation as a whole rather than as an amalgam of states and districts. Federalism is certainly an important component of the constitutional system, but does federalism need the Electoral College to maintain it?

A Federal Principle?

The Founders did not design the Electoral College on the federal principle. The Electoral College does not enhance the power or sovereignty of the states. Moreover, the Founders expected electors to exercise their individual discretion when casting their votes. They did not expect electors to vote as part of any state bloc. No delegate at the Constitutional Convention referred to the Electoral College as an element of the federal system or even as important to the overall structure of the Constitution.

Similarly, the Founders did not regard the Electoral College as a means of implementing the Connecticut Compromise, which created a House of Representatives apportioned according to population and a Senate in which each state has two seats. The allocation of two electoral votes to each state corresponding to its Senate representation was not to further federalism. Instead, the extra votes were to serve as a corrective for large state power. The federative principle would have required that these extra electors be organized like the Senate as a separate body with an independent voice in the choice of the president.

The Electoral College was not designed to protect state interests. If it were, the Founders would have insisted that state legislatures choose electors, who would be agents of the state governments. But they did not do so. Indeed, the Electoral College was "an anti-states-rights device," designed to keep the election of the president away from state politicians.[28]

Essential for Federalism?

Even if the Electoral College was not designed as an aspect of federalism, is it essential for preserving federalism? We have already seen that the Electoral College does not cause presidential candidates to devote attention to the states as states in general or to small states in particular. Neither the existence nor the powers and responsibilities of state governments depend in any way on the existence of the Electoral College. If it were abolished, states would have the same rights and duties they have now. Federalism is deeply embodied in congressional elections, in which two senators represent each state just because it is a state and in which members of the House are elected from districts within states. Direct election of the president would not alter these federalism-sustaining aspects of the constitutional structure. A leading expert on federalism, Neal Peirce, has said it best: "The vitality of federalism rests chiefly on the constitutionally mandated system of congressional representation and the will and capacity of state and local governments to address compelling problems, not on the hocus-pocus of an eighteenth-century vote count system."[29]

Greater National Control of the Electoral Process?

Occasionally, a defender of the Electoral College laments the prospect that direct election of the president would foster greater national control of the electoral process. But this has already occurred. The Fifteenth, Eighteenth, Nineteenth, Twenty-third, Twenty-fourth, and Twenty-sixth Amendments to the Constitution all expanded the electorate. Federal, not state, law effectively determines most rules of voter eligibility, and in the wake of the vote-counting debacle in Florida in the 2000 election, federal law dictates the rules for voter registration, voter access to the polls, counting votes, correcting voters' errors on their ballots, resolving challenges to a citizen's right to vote, and ensuring that voting systems have minimal rates of error. The federal government also provides aid to states to improve their voting machinery and registration lists.

Federal standards are here to stay—within the framework of the Electoral College. Moreover, Americans and their elected representatives overwhelmingly support these laws and constitutional amendments. If anything, the enormous disparity in ballot designs across the states, many of which are needlessly complex, makes a strong case for greater uniformity.[30] The Caltech/MIT Voting Technology Project concluded that 4 to 6 million votes were lost in the 2000 election as a result of problems with ballots, voting equipment, and registration databases.[31] As President George W. Bush said when he signed the Help America Vote Act of 2002, "The administration of elections is primarily a state and local responsibility. The fairness of all elections, however, is a national priority."[32]

PROTECTING NON-STATE-BASED MINORITY INTERESTS

Some observers claim that the Electoral College ensures a "proper distribution" of the vote, in which the winning candidate receives majority support across social strata, thus protecting minority interests.[33] This claim is nonsense. In 2016 Donald Trump won a smaller percentage than Hillary Clinton of the votes of women; African Americans, Hispanics, and Asian Americans; voters ages eighteen to forty-four; members of labor unions; those with less than $50,000 annual household income; college graduates and those with postgraduate educations; Jews; liberals and moderates; urbanites; or those living in the East and the West.

In 2000 George W. Bush did not win a larger percentage than Al Gore of the votes of women, African Americans, Hispanics, and Asian Americans; voters aged eighteen to twenty-nine or those aged sixty-five or older; the poor; members of labor unions; those with less than $50,000 of household income; those with a high school education or less and those with postgraduate education; Catholics, Jews, and Muslims; liberals and moderates; urbanites; or those living in the East and West.[34]

It strains credulity to claim that Trump's or Bush's votes represented concurrent majorities across the major strata of American society. What actually happened in 2000 and 2016 was that the Electoral College imposed a candidate supported by white male Protestants—the dominant social group in the country—over the objections not only of a plurality of all voters, but also of most "minority" interests in the country. This antidemocratic outcome is precisely the opposite of what defenders of the Electoral College claim for the system.

WHY NOT ELECT EVERYONE BY THE SAME RULES?

A common refrain by advocates of the Electoral College goes something like this: "If you insist on majority—or at least plurality—rule, why don't you insist on abolishing the Senate, in which seats are allocated to states rather than people?" The answer is straightforward. The Founders designed the Senate explicitly to represent states and the interests within them. The presidency is designed to do something quite different. The president is supposed to rise above parochial interests and represent the entire nation. Perhaps the most compelling argument that the president should be elected by direct popular vote is that the president and vice president are the only national officials in the country who represent the people as a whole and that the candidate who wins the most votes best approximates the choice of the people.

Similarly, some defenders of the Electoral College ask, "If you are so concerned that the people choose the president, what about all the nonelected judges and other officials in government? Shouldn't we elect them as well?" Of course not. It is not feasible to elect department heads and other executive officials, no matter how the president is selected. The issue is not electing additional officials. The issue is letting a plurality of voters elect the president who nominates judges and executive officials.

ADVANTAGE OF DIRECT ELECTION

It is difficult to see whose interests the Electoral College protects. Rather than protecting the interests of states and minorities, it reduces the incentives for people to vote in states that are safe for the locally dominant party's candidate. It also weakens the incentive for either the majority or minority party to attempt to persuade citizens to go to the polls and support its national ticket. Under the Electoral College, it makes no sense for candidates to allocate scarce resources to states they either cannot win or are certain to win, in which case the size of their victory is irrelevant.

Candidates would be much more attentive to small states and minorities with direct election than they are with the Electoral College. Because every vote counts in a direct election, candidates would have an incentive to appeal to all voters and not just those strategically located in swing states.[35] An extra vote in Massachusetts or Texas would count as much as one in Michigan or Florida.

Presidential and vice presidential candidate Robert Dole explained that, under direct election, candidates also would have to pay attention to areas within states that are now ignored because they are safe for one party or the other. Thus "the voters in the majority of States would receive greater attention and the objective of federalism would be served better."[36]

With these incentives candidates would find it easy to spread their attention more evenly across the country. Because the cost of advertising is mainly a function of market size, it does not cost more to reach 10,000 voters in Wyoming than it does to reach the same number of voters in a neighborhood in Queens or Los Angeles. Actually, it may cost less to reach voters in smaller communities because larger markets tend to run out of commercial time, increasing the price of advertising.[37] Politicians know this, even if advocates of the Electoral College do not. That is why, in the election of 2000, the candidates "devoted nearly as much advertising to Yakima as in Seattle, as much to Traverse City as to Flint, as much to Wausau as to Milwaukee" when they campaigned within states.[38]

Direct election of the president also would provide the incentive for candidates to encourage all of their supporters, no matter where they live, to go to the polls, because under direct election, every vote counts. Conversely, under the Electoral College, it does not matter how many votes a candidate receives in a state as long as the number of votes surpasses that any opponent receives. The goal is to win states, not voters. As Douglas Bailey, the media manager of the 1976 Ford–Dole campaign, put it, "There is a vast population [outside urban areas], with every vote counting, that you cannot ignore in a direct election."[39]

It is possible, but by no means certain, that some candidates would find it more cost-effective under direct election to mobilize votes in urban areas or to visit urban areas where they would receive free television coverage reaching large audiences. Such actions would do nothing to undermine the argument against the Electoral

College, however. Small states cannot be worse off than they are now, because under the Electoral College, candidates rarely visit or campaign there. Direct election of the president cannot diminish campaign efforts that do not exist. Instead, direct election would provide increased incentives for candidates to campaign in most small states, as well as increased incentives to campaign in many large and medium-sized states. Direct election would disperse campaign efforts rather than deprive small states of them.

Direct election, unlike the Electoral College, thus encourages citizens to participate in elections and candidates to take their campaigns to these citizens, enhancing our civic life. Direct election would increase voter turnout and stimulate party-building efforts in the weaker party, especially in less competitive states.

Some critics of direct election mistakenly claim that it would splinter the two-party system. Their criticism is based on the premise that direct election would require a runoff between the two leading candidates. But it would not. Under the Electoral College, victorious presidential candidates—including, most recently, John F. Kennedy (1960), Richard Nixon (1968), Bill Clinton (1992 and 1996), George W. Bush (2000), and Donald Trump (2016)—have received less than a majority of the national popular vote about 40 percent of the time since 1824, and there is no relation between the vote they received and their later success in, say, dealing with Congress. Some of our strongest presidents, including James K. Polk, Abraham Lincoln, Grover Cleveland, Woodrow Wilson, Harry S. Truman, and Kennedy, received a plurality, but not a majority, of the popular vote.

Nor is the Electoral College the basis of the two-party system. Single-member districts and plurality election are, and the nation would be one electoral district under direct election. Thus direct election would not splinter the party system.

By contrast, direct election would protect the country from the mischief of third parties. The Electoral College's unit rule encourages third parties, especially those with a regional base, because by winning a few states they may deny either major-party candidate a majority of the electoral vote. Such a result was certainly the goal of Strom Thurmond in 1948 and George Wallace in 1968. Imagine giving these racist candidates leverage to negotiate with the leading candidates before the electoral votes were officially cast. Moreover, even without winning any states, Ralph Nader inadvertently distorted the vote and determined the outcome of the 2000 election.

CONCLUSION

In 2000 Republican George W. Bush was elected despite losing the national popular vote by more than 539,000 votes. In 2016, Donald Trump won the presidency despite running nearly 3 million votes behind Hillary Clinton in the popular vote. A shift of 59,300 votes in Ohio in 2004 would have elected Democrat John Kerry over George W. Bush, despite Bush's margin of nearly 3 million votes nationwide. In 2012 Republican Mitt Romney could have won the popular vote by a similar margin and still lost the election.

A core justification offered by defenders of the Electoral College and its violations of political equality is that it is necessary to protect important interests that would be overlooked or harmed by a system of direct election of the president. Yet such claims are based on faulty premises. States—including those with small populations—do not embody coherent, unified interests and communities, and they have little need for protection. Even if they did, the Electoral College does not provide it. Contrary to the claims of the institution's supporters, candidates do not pay attention to small states. The Electoral College distorts the presidential campaign so that candidates ignore many large and most small states and devote most of their attention to a few competitive states.

The Electoral College is also not a bastion of federalism. It is not based on federative principles and is not essential for the continuance of a healthy federal system. As former Senate majority leader and Republican presidential nominee Robert Dole put it, direct election is "commonsense federalism."[40]

NOTES

1. Robert A. Dahl, *On Democracy* (New Haven, CT: Yale University Press, 2000), 37. See also Robert A. Dahl, *Democracy and Its Critics* (New Haven, CT: Yale University Press, 1989), 110.

2. See George C. Edwards III, *Why the Electoral College Is Bad for America,* 2nd ed. (New Haven, CT: Yale University Press, 2011), chap. 3.

3. Darshan J. Goux and David A. Hopkins, "The Empirical Implications of Electoral College Reform," *American Politics Research* 36 (November 2008): 860–864.

4. For a discussion of the 1960 election, see Edwards, *Why the Electoral College Is Bad for America,* 2nd ed., 67–70.

5. See, for example, Tara Ross, *Enlightened Democracy: The Case for the Electoral College* (Los Angeles: World Ahead, 2004).

6. Ross, *Enlightened Democracy,* 53; Judith A. Best, *The Choice of the People? Debating the Electoral College* (Lanham, MD: Rowman and Littlefield, 1996), 55; William C. Kimberling, "The Electoral College," May 1992, http://www.fec.gov/pdf/eleccoll.pdf; James R. Stoner Jr., "Federalism, the States, and the Electoral College," in *Securing Democracy: Why We Have an Electoral College,* ed. Gary L. Gregg (Wilmington, DE: ISI Books, 2001), 51–52.

7. Raymond Tatalovich, "Electoral Votes and Presidential Campaign Trails, 1932–1976," *American Politics Quarterly* 7 (October 1979): 489–497; Scott C. James and Brian L. Lawson, "The Political Economy of Voting Rights Enforcement in America's Gilded Age: Electoral College Competition, Partisan Commitment, and the Federal Election Law," *American Political Science Review* 93 (March 1999): 115–131; Daron R. Shaw, "The Methods behind the Madness: Presidential Electoral College Strategies, 1988–1996," *Journal of Politics* 61 (November 1999): 893–913; Daron R. Shaw, *The Race to 270* (Chicago: University of Chicago Press, 2007).

8. Jack Rakove, "The Accidental Electors," *New York Times,* December 19, 2000, A35.

9. James Madison to George Hay, August 23, 1823. In *The Writings of James Madison,* vol. 9, ed. Gaillard Hunt (New York: G. P. Putnam's Sons, 1900–1910), 47–55.

10. Max Farrand, ed., *The Records of the Federal Convention of 1787,* rev. ed., vol. 2 (New Haven, CT: Yale University Press, 1966), 111.

11. Best, *Choice of the People?*, 37.

12. Ibid., 35.

13. See Robert A. Dahl, *How Democratic Is the American Constitution?* (New Haven, CT: Yale University Press, 2001), 50–53, 84.

14. Max Farrand, ed., *The Records of the Federal Convention of 1787*, rev. ed., vol. 1 (New Haven, CT: Yale University Press, 1966), 483.

15. Farrand, *Records of the Federal Convention of 1787*, vol. 1, 447–449.

16. Farrand, *Records of the Federal Convention of 1787*, vol. 2, 403.

17. Farrand, *Records of the Federal Convention of 1787*, vol. 1, 447–449.

18. I have omitted Washington, D.C., from this analysis because it is limited to the number of electoral votes of the least populous state and is not overrepresented in the Electoral College.

19. U.S. Department of Agriculture, *2007 Census of Agriculture,* vol. 1, chap. 2, table 2, 294–310. (This census occurs every five years.)

20. Ross, *Enlightened Democracy,* 41, 87; Michael M. Uhlman, "Creating Constitutional Majorities: The Electoral College after 2000," in Gregg, ed., *Securing Democracy,* 106; Paul A. Rahe, "Moderating the Political Impulse," in Gregg, ed., *Securing Democracy,* 63.

21. Edwards, *Why the Electoral College Is Bad for America,* 2nd ed., 122–124.

22. The speeches are provided by the *Annenberg/Pew Archive of Presidential Campaign Discourse* (CD-ROM), 2000. The results are reported in Edwards, *Why the Electoral College Is Bad for America,* 2nd ed., 124.

23. The author collected the data for 2000–2016. The data for 2000 and 2008 are reported in Edwards, *Why the Electoral College Is Bad for America,* 2nd ed., 3–6, 124–128.

24. Stanley Kelley Jr., "The Presidential Campaign," in *The Presidential Election and Transition 1960–1961,* ed. Paul T. David (Washington, DC: Brookings Institution, 1961), 70–72; Daron R. Shaw, "The Effect of TV Ads and Candidate Appearances on Statewide Presidential Votes, 1988–96," *American Political Science Review* 93 (June 1999): 359–360; Edwards, *Why the Electoral College Is Bad for America,* 2nd ed., 124–132. See also Larry M. Bartels, "Resource Allocation in a Presidential Campaign," *Journal of Politics* 47 (August 1985): 928–936; Steven J. Brams and Morton D. Davis, "The 3/2's Rule in Presidential Campaigning," *American Political Science Review* 68 (March 1974): 113–134; Claude S. Colantoni, Terrence J. Levasque, and Peter C. Ordeshook, "Campaign Resource Allocation under the Electoral College," *American Political Science Review* 69 (March 1975): 142–154; Steven J. Brams and Morton D. Davis, "Comment on 'Campaign Resource Allocations under the Electoral College,'" *American Political Science Review* 69 (March 1975): 155–156.

25. Nonprofit Vote and US Elections Project, *America Goes to the Polls 2016* (Nonprofit Vote and US Elections Project, 2017), 12–13.

26. "Mad Money: TV Ads in the 2012 Presidential Campaign," *Washington Post,* November 14, 2012, http://www.washingtonpost.com/wp-srv/special/politics/track-presidential-campaign-ads-2012/.

27. Edwards, *Why the Electoral College Is Bad for America,* 2nd ed., 132–139; "Testimony of Hon. Hubert H. Humphrey, U.S. Senator from the State of Minnesota," *The Electoral College and Direct Election: Hearings before the Committee on the Judiciary,*

United States Senate, January 27, February 1, 2, 7, and 10, 1977, 95th Congress, 1st sess., 25, 35; "Testimony of Douglas Bailey," *The Electoral College and Direct Election: Hearings before the Subcommittee on the Constitution of the Committee on the Judiciary, Supplement, United States Senate,* July 20, 22, 28, and August 2, 1977, 95th Congress, 1st sess., 267, 258–273; as well as the testimony at the same hearings by Sen. Robert Dole ("Testimony of Hon. Robert Dole, U.S. Senator from the State of Kansas," *The Electoral College and Direct Election: Hearings before the Subcommittee on the Constitution of the Committee on the Judiciary, Supplement,* 30), who also stressed the campaign distortions created by the Electoral College. See also Bartels, "Resource Allocation in a Presidential Campaign"; Shaw, "The Effect of TV Ads"; Shaw, *Race to 270,* chap. 4.

28. Martin Diamond, *The Electoral College and the American Idea of Democracy* (Washington, DC: American Enterprise Institute, 1977), 4.

29. Twentieth Century Fund, *Winner Take All* (New York: Holmes and Meier, 1978), chap. 6.

30. See Richard G. Niemi and Paul S. Herrnson, "Beyond the Butterfly: The Complexity of U.S. Ballots," *Perspectives on Politics* 1 (June 2003): 317–326.

31. Caltech/MIT Voting Technology Project, *Voting: What Is, What Could Be,* 2001, http://vote.caltech.edu/content/voting-what-what-could-be.

32. Remarks of President George W. Bush at signing ceremony for the Help America Vote Act of 2002, October 29, 2002, American Presidency Project, http://www.presidency.ucsb.edu/youtubeclip.php?clipid=73161&admin=43.

33. Ross, *Enlightened Democracy,* 41, 87, 109, 142, 170, 182, 187, 188; Uhlman, "Creating Constitutional Majorities"; Rahe, "Moderating the Political Impulse"; Best, *Choice of the People?,* 14, 21, 23–24, 27, 36–37.

34. Voter News Service Exit Polls; Gallup News Service, "Candidate Support by Subgroup," News Release, November 6, 2000 (based on six-day average, October 31–November 5, 2000).

35. See Eric R. A. N. Smithy and Peverill Squire, "Direct Election of the President and the Power of the States," *Western Political Quarterly* 40 (March 1987): 29–44.

36. *Electoral College and Direct Election,* 40.

37. Goux and Hopkins, "The Empirical Implications of Electoral College Reform."

38. Michael Hagen, Richard Johnston, and Kathleen Hall Jamieson, "Effects of the 2000 Presidential Campaign" (paper delivered at the annual meeting of the American Political Science Association, August 29–September 1, 2002), 3.

39. Quoted in U.S. Congress, Senate, Committee on the Judiciary, *Report on Direct Popular Election of the President and Vice President of the United States,* 95th Congress, 1st sess., 1967, 124.

40. Electoral College and Direct Election, 39.

9

THE PRESIDENTIAL SPECTACLE

Bruce Miroff

To govern successfully, presidents have always needed support from the public. What is new in the modern presidency is how hard they work to achieve it. As Bruce Miroff argues, the modern president not only responds to popular demands and passions, but also actively reaches out to shape them. The president does so in speeches and in symbol-laden events, which Miroff, borrowing from the language of cultural anthropology, calls "spectacles." Understood properly, for example, Barack Obama's 2012 reelection campaign resembled nothing so much as a professional wrestling match, in which the audience (the majority of voters) was gratified by the sight of the fighting good guy (President Obama) overpowering the rich, teetotaling bad guy (Republican nominee Mitt Romney). In prosecuting the post–9/11 war against terrorism and the war against Iraq, George W. Bush even adopted the costume of a good guy, dressing sometimes in military garb, which previous commanders in chief almost never have done. Neither came close to emulating Donald Trump, however, for an "all-spectacle-all-the-time" presidency.

Leadership in the modern presidency is enacted as a spectacle. Presidents' concern for their public image can be traced all the way back to George Washington, but the emergence first of television and now of social media has necessitated a more consuming concern for the management of presidential appearances. In communicating with the public and seeking its support, the White House strives to present the president as a winning, indeed a spectacular, character.

Scholars have extensively studied the nuances of presidential rhetoric and the effects of presidential persuasion on behalf of legislation.[1] The presidential spectacle includes these but is more encompassing, involving a large array of verbal and visual gestures that emanate from the White House on a daily basis. At stake in the spectacle is a critical and contested subject: the identity of the president. With so many partisan and media critics poised to disparage and diminish the president's character, the White House devotes considerable resources to portraying the president's identity in shining terms.

Beginning in the administration of John F. Kennedy, the first television president, chief executives have varied enormously in the nature and effectiveness of their spectacles. Only a few have been masters of spectacle, and some have tried to resist its demands in order to concentrate on the substance of their office's responsibilities. But none have been as attuned to spectacle as Donald J. Trump. The early months of Trump's presidency have been all-spectacle-all-the-time.

THE PRESIDENCY AS SPECTACLE

A spectacle is a kind of symbolic event, one in which particular details stand for broader and deeper meanings. What differentiates a spectacle from other kinds of symbolic events is the centrality of character and action. A spectacle presents intriguing and often dominating characters not in static poses, but through actions that establish their public identities.

Spectacle implies a clear division between actors and spectators. As Daniel Dayan and Elihu Katz have noted, a spectacle possesses "a narrowness of focus, a limited set of appropriate responses, and . . . a minimal level of interaction. What there is to see is very clearly exhibited; spectacle implies a distinction between the roles of performers and audience."[2] A spectacle does not permit the audience to interrupt the action and redirect its meaning. Spectators can become absorbed in a spectacle or can find it unconvincing, but they cannot become performers. A spectacle is not designed for mass participation; it is not a democratic event.

Perhaps the most distinctive characteristic of a spectacle is that the actions that constitute it are meaningful not for what they achieve, but for what they signify. Actions in a spectacle are gestures rather than means to an end. What is important is that they be understandable and impressive to the spectators. Roland Barthes illustrates this distinction between gestures and means in his classic discussion of professional wrestling as a spectacle. Barthes shows that professional wrestling is completely unlike professional boxing. Boxing is a form of competition, a contest of skill in a situation of uncertainty. What counts is the outcome, and because that is in doubt, we can wager on it. But in professional wrestling, the outcome is preordained; it would be senseless to bet on who is going to win. What matters in professional wrestling are the gestures made during the match, gestures by performers portraying distinctive characters, gestures that carry moral significance. In a typical match, an evil character threatens a good character, knocks him down on the canvas, and abuses him with dirty tricks, but he ultimately loses when the good character rises up to exact a just revenge.[3]

It may seem odd to approach the presidency through an analogy with boxing and wrestling—but let us pursue it for a moment. Much of what presidents do is analogous to what boxers do: they engage in contests of power and policy with other political actors, contests in which the outcomes are uncertain. But a growing amount of presidential activity is akin to pro wrestling. The contemporary presidency is presented by the White House (with the collaboration of the media) as a series of spectacles in which a larger-than-life main character and a supporting team engage in emblematic bouts with immoral or dangerous adversaries.

A number of contemporary developments have converged to foster the rise of spectacle in the modern presidency. The mass media have become its principal vehicle. As they focus more of their coverage on presidents than on any other person or institution in American life, the media keep presidents constantly before the public and give them unmatched opportunities to display their leadership qualities. Television provides the view most amenable to spectacle; by favoring the visual and the dramatic, it promotes stories with simple plotlines over complex analyses of causes and consequences. But other media are not fundamentally different. Twitter, for example, allows the White House to write its own headlines without having to provide any details to back them up.

Spectacle has also been fostered by the president's rise to primacy in the American political system. A political order originally centered on institutions has given way, especially in the public mind, to a political order that centers on the person of the president. Theodore Lowi wrote, "Since the president has become the embodiment of government, it seems perfectly normal for millions upon millions of Americans to concentrate their hopes and fears directly and personally upon him."[4]

To understand the modern presidency as a form of spectacle, we must consider the presentation of presidents as spectacular characters, the role of their teams as supporting performers, and the arrangement of gestures that convey the meaning of their actions to the audience.

A contemporary president is, to borrow a phrase from Guy Debord, "the spectacular representation of a living human being."[5] An enormous amount of attention is paid to the president as a public character; every deed, quality, and even foible is regarded as fascinating and important. The American public may not learn the details of policy formulation, but they know that Gerald Ford bumps his head on helicopter door frames, that Ronald Reagan likes jellybeans, that Bill Clinton enjoys hanging out with Hollywood celebrities, and that Barack Obama prides himself on his basketball skills. In a spectacle, a president's character possesses intrinsic as well as symbolic value; it is to be appreciated for its own sake. The spectators do not press presidents to specify what economic or social benefits they are providing, nor do they closely inquire into the truthfulness of the claims presidents make. (To the extent that they do evaluate the president in such terms, they step outside the terms of the spectacle.) The president's featured qualities are presented as benefits in themselves. Thus John Kennedy's glamour casts his whole era in a romanticized glow, and Reagan's amiability relieves the grim national mood that had developed under his predecessors.

The president's character must be not only appealing in itself, but also magnified by the spectacle. The spectacle makes the president appear exceptionally decisive, tough, courageous, prescient, or prudent. Whether the president is in fact all or any of these things is obscured. What matters is that he or she is presented as having these qualities in magnitudes far beyond what ordinary citizens can imagine themselves to possess. The president must appear confident and masterful before spectators whose very position as onlookers denies them the possibility of mastery.[6]

The presidential qualities most likely to be magnified will be those that contrast dramatically with the attributes that drew criticism to the previous president. Reagan, following a president perceived as weak, was featured in spectacles that highlighted his potency. George H. W. Bush, succeeding a president notorious for his disengagement from the workings of his own administration, was featured in spectacles of hands-on management. Clinton, supplanting a president who seemed disengaged from the economic problems of ordinary Americans, began his administration with spectacles of populist intimacy. George W. Bush, replacing a president notorious for personal indiscipline and staff disorder, organized a corporate-style White House where meetings ran on time and business attire was required in the Oval Office. Obama, coming after a president disparaged as intellectually incurious and ideologically stubborn, emphasized his openness to dialogue and pragmatism. Trump, following a president criticized for excessive deliberation and caution, has disdained the need for expert knowledge and dismissed the risks in impulsive decision-making.

Presidents are the principal figures in presidential spectacles, but they have the help of aides and advisers. The star performer is surrounded by a team. Members of the president's team can, through the supporting parts they play, enhance or detract from the spectacle's effect on the audience. For a president's team to enhance the spectacles, its members should project attractive qualities that either resemble the featured attributes of the president or make up for the president's perceived deficiencies. A team will diminish presidential spectacles if its members project qualities that underscore the president's weaknesses.

A performance team, Erving Goffman has shown, contains "a set of individuals whose intimate cooperation is required if a given projected definition of the situation is to be maintained."[7] The team can disrupt presidential spectacles in a number of ways. A member of the team can call too much attention to himself or herself, upstaging the president. This was one of the disruptive practices that made the Reagan White House eager to be rid of Secretary of State Alexander Haig, and it was at the core of the short-lived tenure as communications director of Anthony Scaramucci in the Trump White House. A team member can give away important secrets to the audience; Budget Director David Stockman's famous confessions about supply-side economics to a reporter for the *Atlantic* jeopardized the mystique of economic innovation that the Reagan administration had created in 1981. Worst of all, a member of the team can, inadvertently, discredit the central meanings that a presidential spectacle has been designed to establish. The revelations of Budget

Director Bert Lance's questionable banking practices deflated the lofty moral tone established at the beginning of the Carter presidency.

The audience watching a presidential spectacle, the White House hopes, is as impressed by gestures as by results. Indeed, the gestures are sometimes preferable to the results. Thus a "show" of force by the president is preferable to the death and destruction that are the results of force. The ways in which the invasion of Grenada in 1983, the bombing of Libya in 1986, and the seizing of the Panamanian dictator Manuel Noriega in 1990 were portrayed to the American public suggest an eagerness in the White House to present the image of military toughness but not the casualties from military conflict—even when they are the enemy's casualties.

Gestures overshadow results in a presidential spectacle. They also overshadow facts. But facts are not obliterated. They remain present; they are needed, in a sense, to nurture the gestures. Without real events, presidential spectacles would not be impressive; they would seem contrived, mere pseudoevents. Some of the facts that emerge in the course of an event, however, might discredit its presentation as spectacle. Therefore, a successful spectacle, such as Reagan's "liberation" of Grenada, must be more powerful than any of the facts on which it draws. Rising above contradictory or disconfirming details, the spectacle must transfigure the more pliant facts and make them carriers of its most spectacular gestures.

Presidential spectacles are seldom pure spectacles in the sense that a wrestling match can be a pure spectacle. Although they may involve a good deal of advance planning and careful calculation of gestures, they cannot be completely scripted in advance. Unexpected and unpredictable events will occur during a presidential spectacle. If the White House is fortunate and skillful, it can capitalize on some of those events by using them to enhance the spectacle. If the White House is not so lucky or talented, such events can detract from, or even undermine, the spectacle.

Also unlike wrestling or other pure spectacles, the presidential variety often has more than one audience. Its primary purpose is to construct meanings for the American public. But it also can direct messages to those whom the White House has identified as its foes or the sources of its problems. In 1981, when Reagan fired the air traffic controllers of the Professional Air Traffic Controllers Organization (PATCO) because they engaged in an illegal strike, he presented to the public the spectacle of a tough, determined president who would uphold the law and, unlike his predecessor, would not be pushed around by grasping interest groups. The spectacle also conveyed to organized labor that the White House knew how to feed popular skepticism about unions and could make things difficult for a labor movement that became too assertive.

As the PATCO firing shows, some presidential spectacles retain important policy dimensions. Nonetheless, spectacle production and policy production are fundamentally different: Spectacle deploys gestures to enhance the president's image, while policymaking employs means to solve problems affecting others. As the cases of Obama and Trump suggest, a balance between spectacle and policy can be difficult to achieve. A president can pay a political price for focusing on policy while slighting spectacle; but the political price can also be high when a dramatic spectacle cannot conceal the weaknesses of presidential policies.

THE TRIUMPH OF SPECTACLE: RONALD REAGAN

The Reagan presidency was a triumph of spectacle. In the realm of substantive policy, it was marked by striking failures, as well as significant successes. But even the most egregious of the failures—public exposure of the disastrous covert policy of selling arms to Iran and diverting some of the profits to the Nicaraguan contras—proved to be only a temporary blow to the political fortunes of the most spectacular president in decades. With the help of two heartwarming summits with Soviet leader Mikhail Gorbachev, Reagan recovered from the Iran-contra debacle and left office near the peak of his popularity. His presidency, for the most part, floated above its flawed processes and failed policies, secure in the brilliant glow of its successful spectacles.

The basis of this success was the character of Ronald Reagan. His previous career in movies and television made him comfortable with and adept at spectacles; he moved easily from one kind to another.[8] Reagan presented to his audience a multifaceted character, funny yet powerful, ordinary yet heroic, individual yet representative. His was a character richer even than John F. Kennedy's in mythic resonance.

Coming into office after Jimmy Carter, a president who was widely perceived as weak, Reagan as a spectacle character projected potency. His administration featured a number of spectacles in which Reagan displayed his decisiveness, forcefulness, and will to prevail. The image of masculine toughness was played up repeatedly. The American people saw a president who, even though in his seventies, rode horses and exercised vigorously, a president who liked to quote (and thereby identify himself with) movie tough guys such as Clint Eastwood and Sylvester Stallone. Yet Reagan's strength was balanced nicely by his amiability; his aggressiveness was rendered benign by his characteristic one-line quips. The warm grin took the edge off the toughness, removed any intimations of callousness or violence.

The power of Reagan's character rested not only on its intrinsic attractiveness, but also on its symbolic appeal. The spectacle specialists who worked for Reagan seized on the idea of making him an emblem for the American identity. In a June 1984 memo, White House aide Richard Darman sketched a reelection strategy that revolved around the president's mythic role: "Paint RR as the personification of all that is right with or heroized by America. Leave Mondale in a position where an attack on Reagan is tantamount to an attack on America's idealized image of itself."[9] Having come into office at a time of considerable anxiety, with many Americans uncertain about the economy, their future, and the country itself, Reagan was an immensely reassuring character. He had not been marked by the shocks of recent U.S. history—and he denied that those shocks had meaning. He told Americans that the Vietnam War was noble rather than appalling, that Watergate was forgotten, that racial conflict was a thing of the distant past, and that the U.S. economy still offered the American dream to any aspiring individual. Reagan (the character) and America (the country) were presented in the spectacles of the Reagan presidency as timeless, above the decay of aging and the difficulties of history.

The Reagan team assumed special importance because Reagan ran what Lou Cannon has called "the delegated presidency."[10] As the public knew, Reagan's team members carried on most of the business of the executive branch; his own work habits were decidedly relaxed. Reagan's team did not contain many performers who reinforced the president's character, as Kennedy's youthful, energetic New Frontiersmen had. But it featured several figures whose spectacle role was to compensate for Reagan's deficiencies or to carry on his mission with a greater air of vigor than the amiable president usually conveyed.

David Stockman was the most publicized supporting player in the first months of 1981. His image in the media was formidable. *Newsweek,* for example, marveled at how "his buzz-saw intellect has helped him stage a series of bravura performances before Congress" and acclaimed him "the Reagan Administration's boy wonder."[11] There was spectacle appeal in the sight of the nation's youngest budget director serving as the right arm of the nation's oldest chief executive. More important, Stockman's appearance as the master of budget numbers compensated for a president who was notoriously uninterested in data. Stockman faded in spectacle value after his disastrous confession in fall 1981 that budget numbers had been doctored to show the results the administration wanted.

Secretary of Defense Caspar Weinberger became the administration's most visible Cold War hard-liner. As the tireless spokesperson and unbudging champion of a soaring defense budget, he was a handy symbol for the Reagan military buildup. Nicholas Lemann noted that although "Weinberger's predecessor, Harold Brown, devoted himself almost completely to management, Weinberger . . . operated more and more on the theatrical side."[12] His grim, hawk-like visage was as much a reminder of the Soviet threat as the alarming, book-length reports on the Russian behemoth that his Defense Department issued every year.

The Reagan presidency benefited not only from a spectacular main character and a useful team but also from talent and good fortune in enacting spectacle gestures. The Reagan years were sprinkled with events—the PATCO strike, the Geneva summit, the Libyan bombing, and others—whose significance lay primarily in their spectacle value. The most striking Reagan spectacle of all was the invasion of Grenada. As the archetypal presidential spectacle, Grenada deserves a close look.

Reagan ordered American forces to invade the island of Grenada in October 1983. Relations had become tense between the Reagan administration and the Marxist regime of Grenada's Maurice Bishop. When Bishop was overthrown and murdered by a clique of more militant Marxists, the Reagan administration began to consider military action. It was urged to invade by the Organization of Eastern Caribbean States, composed of Grenada's island neighbors. And it had a pretext for action in ensuring the safety of the Americans—most of them medical students—on the island. Once the decision to invade was made, U.S. troops landed in force, evacuated most of the students, and seized the island after encountering brief but unexpectedly stiff resistance. Reagan administration officials announced that, in the course of securing the island, U.S. forces had discovered large caches of military supplies and documents indicating that Cuba planned to turn Grenada into a base for the export of communist revolution and terror.

The details that eventually came to light cast doubt on the Reagan administration's claims of a threat to the American students and a buildup of "sophisticated" Cuban weaponry in Grenada. Beyond such details, there was the sheer incongruity between the importance bestowed on Grenada by the Reagan administration and the insignificance of the danger it posed. Grenada is a tiny island, with a population of 100,000, a land area of 133 square miles, and an economy whose exports totaled $19 million in 1981.[13] That U.S. troops could secure it was never in question; as Richard Gabriel has noted, "In terms of actual combat forces, the U.S. outnumbered the island's defenders approximately ten to one."[14] Grenada's importance did not derive from the military, political, and economic implications of America's actions, but from its value as a spectacle.

What was this spectacle about? Its meaning was articulated by a triumphant President Reagan: "Our days of weakness are over. Our military forces are back on their feet and standing tall."[15] Reagan, even more than the American military, came across in the media as "standing tall" in Grenada.

The spectacle actually began with the president on a weekend golfing vacation in Augusta, Georgia. His vacation was interrupted first by planning for an invasion of Grenada and then by news that the U.S. Marine barracks in Beirut had been bombed. Once the news of the Grenada landings replaced the tragedy in Beirut on the front page and television screen, the golfing angle proved to be an apt beginning for a spectacle. It was used to dramatize the ability of a relaxed and genial president to rise to a grave challenge. And it supplied the White House with an unusual backdrop for photographs which depicted the president in charge, with members of his team by his side.[16]

Pictures of the president as decision maker were particularly effective because pictures from Grenada itself were lacking; the Reagan administration had barred the American press from covering the invasion. This move outraged the press but was extremely useful to the spectacle, which would have been subverted by pictures of dead bodies or civilian casualties or by independent sources of information with which congressional critics could raise unpleasant questions.

The initial meaning of the Grenada spectacle was established by Reagan in his announcement of the invasion. The enemy was suitably evil: "a brutal group of leftist thugs."[17] America's objectives were purely moral—to protect the lives of innocent people on the island, namely American medical students, and to restore democracy to the people of Grenada. And the actions taken were unmistakably forceful: "The United States had no choice but to act strongly and decisively."[18]

But the spectacle of Grenada soon expanded beyond this initial definition. The evacuation of the medical students provided one of those unanticipated occurrences that heighten the power of spectacle. When several of the students kissed the airport tarmac to express their relief and joy at returning to American soil, the resulting pictures on television and in the newspapers were better than anything the administration could have orchestrated. They provided the spectacle with historical as well as emotional resonance. Here was a second hostage crisis—but where Carter had been helpless to release captive Americans from Iran, Reagan had swiftly come to the rescue.

Rescue of the students quickly took second place, however, to a new theme: the claim that U.S. forces had uncovered and uprooted a hidden Soviet–Cuban base for adventurism and terrorism. In his nationally televised address, Reagan did not ignore the Iran analogy: "The nightmare of our hostages in Iran must never be repeated."[19] But he stressed the greater drama of defeating a sinister communist plot. "Grenada, we were told, was a friendly island paradise for tourism. Well, it wasn't. It was a Soviet–Cuban colony being readied as a major military bastion to export terror and undermine democracy. We got there just in time."[20] Grenada was turning out to be an even better spectacle for Reagan: he had rescued not only the students, but the people of all the Americas as well.

As the spectacle expanded and grew more heroic, public approval increased. The president's standing in the polls went up. *Time* reported that "a post-invasion poll taken by the *Washington Post* and ABC News showed that 63% of Americans approve the way Reagan is handling the presidency, the highest level in two years, and attributed his gain largely to the Grenada intervention."[21] Congressional critics, although skeptical of many of the claims the administration made, began to stifle their doubts and chime in with endorsements in accordance with the polls. An unnamed White House aide, quoted in *Newsweek,* drew the obvious lesson: "You can scream and shout and gnash your teeth all you want, but the folks out there like it. It was done right and done with dispatch."[22]

In its final gestures, the Grenada spectacle actually commemorated itself. Reagan invited the medical students to the White House and, predictably, basked in their praise and cheers. The Pentagon contributed its symbolic share, awarding some 8,000 medals for the Grenada operation—more than the number of American troops that had set foot on the island. In actuality, Gabriel has shown, "the operation was marred by a number of military failures."[23] Yet these were obscured by the triumphant appearances of the spectacle.

That the spectacle of Grenada was more potent and would prove more lasting in its effects than any disconfirming facts was observed at the time by Anthony Lewis. Reagan "knew the facts would come out eventually," wrote Lewis. "But if that day could be postponed, it might make a great political difference. People would be left with their first impression that this was a decisive President fighting communism."[24] Grenada became for most Americans a highlight of Reagan's first term. Insignificant in military or diplomatic terms, as spectacle it was one of the most successful acts of the Reagan presidency.

A POSTMODERN SPECTACLE: BILL CLINTON

Reagan's successor, George H. W. Bush, had two disparate spectacles: a masterful spectacle in global affairs and an inept spectacle on the home front. The man who defeated him, Bill Clinton, had many more than two, for Clinton's was a postmodern spectacle. A postmodern spectacle, previously more familiar in popular culture than in presidential politics, features fleeting images and fractured continuity, surfaces without depths, personae rather than personalities. Characters in a post-modern spectacle succeed not by capturing the lasting admiration or trust of their audience, but by artfully personifying the changing fashions that fascinate it.

Depictions of Clinton by close observers in the media tended to agree on his shape-shifting presidential performance but to differ about whether it should evoke moral indignation or neutral evaluation. One caustic Clinton watcher, *New York Times* columnist Maureen Dowd, called the president "the man of a thousand faces."[25] Other commentators preferred cool, postmodern terms such as *makeover* and *reinvention,* the same words used to describe a diva of contemporary pop culture, Madonna.[26]

Clinton's presidency had important elements of constancy, including the successful economic course he first charted in 1993 and his underlying attachment to government as a potentially positive force in society. The frequent changes of course during Clinton's two terms owed as much to the formidable political constraints he faced as to the opportunities for spectacle he seized.[27] Moreover, historical precedents for Clinton's "mongrel politics" may be found in the administrations of presidents such as Woodrow Wilson and Richard Nixon, who also were accused of opportunistic borrowing from ideological adversaries in eras when the opposition party set the reigning terms of political discourse.[28] Nonetheless, Clinton's repeated redefinitions of himself and his presidency made these predecessors seem almost static by comparison. Sometimes awkwardly, sometimes nimbly, Clinton pirouetted across the presidential stage as no one before him.

Clinton's first two years in office were largely a failure of spectacle. The promising populist intimacy he displayed in the 1992 campaign quickly gave way to a spectacle of Washington elitism: social life among the rich and famous (including an infamous $200 haircut by a Beverly Hills stylist) and politics among the entrenched and arrogant (the cozy alliance with the Democratic congressional leadership). The new president seemed simultaneously immature (the undisciplined decision delayer aided by a youthful and inexperienced White House staff) and old-fashioned (the big-government liberal with his bureaucratic scheme to reform the health care system). The crushing rebukes that Clinton suffered in 1994—the failure of his health care plan even to reach the floor of either house of Congress and the Republican takeover of both houses in the midterm elections—showed how little he had impressed his audience. Yet a postmodern irony was at work for Clinton—his defeats freed him. Not having to implement a large-scale health care plan, Clinton was able to dance away from the liberal label. Not having to tie himself to his party's congressional leadership in a bid for legislative achievement, he was able to shift his policy stances opportunely to capitalize on the excesses of the new Republican agenda.

In his first two years, Clinton lacked an important ingredient of many presidential spectacles: a dramatic foil. Bush had Manuel Noriega and Saddam Hussein, but the post–Cold War world was too uninteresting to most Americans to supply foreign leaders ripe for demonization. (That would change after September 11, 2001.) The hidden blessing of the 1994 elections for Clinton was that they provided him with a domestic foil of suitably dramatic proportions: Speaker of the House Newt Gingrich. Gingrich was often compared to Clinton—and the comparison worked mostly in Clinton's favor. Shedding the reputation of liberalism, Clinton pronounced himself a nonideological centrist saving the country from Gingrich's conservative extremism. Before, Clinton had talked and shown off too much in public; now, in comparison to the grandiose garrulousness of Gingrich, he seemed almost reticent—and certainly more mature. Attacked as too soft in his first two years, Clinton could turn the image of compassion into a strength by attacking a foil who proposed to reduce spending for seniors on Medicare and to place the children of welfare mothers in orphanages. Lampooned as spineless in his first two years, Clinton could display his backbone by winning the budget showdown with Gingrich and the Republicans in the winter of 1995–1996.[29]

In a postmodern spectacle, a president can try on a variety of styles without being committed to any one of them. As the 1996 election season commenced (and as Gingrich fled the spotlight after his budget defeat), Clinton executed another nimble pirouette by emulating the patron saint of modern Republicans, Ronald Reagan. Clinton's advisers had him watch Reagan videotapes to study "the Gipper's bearing, his aura of command."[30] His campaign team found a model for 1996 in the 1984 Reagan theme of "Morning in America," in which a sunny president capitalized on peace and prosperity while floating serenely above divisive issues. Clinton's postmodern appropriation of Reagan imagery helped to block the Republicans from achieving their goal of a unified party government that would fulfill Reagan's ideological dreams.

Clinton's postmodern spectacle shaped the public's impressions of his team. With a man of uncertain character in the White House, strong women in the cabinet drew special attention: Attorney General Janet Reno at the outset of his first term, Secretary of State Madeleine Albright at the outset of his second. But no members of Clinton's cabinet or staff played as important a supporting role in his spectacle as his wife, Hillary, and his vice president, Al Gore. Hillary Rodham Clinton appeared as an updated, postfeminist version of Eleanor Roosevelt, a principled liberal goad pressing against her husband's pragmatic instincts. Like Eleanor, she was a hero to the liberal Democratic faithful and a despised symbol of radicalism to conservative Republican foes. Al Gore's spectacle role was to be the stable and stolid sidekick to the quicksilver president. Even his much-satirized reputation as boring was reassuring when counterpoised to a president who sometimes appeared all too eager to charm and seduce his audience.

A postmodern spectacle is best crafted by postmodern spectacle specialists. When Clinton's presidential image began taking a beating, he turned for help to image makers who previously had worked for Republicans but who were as ideologically unanchored as he was. In 1993 Clinton responded to plunging poll ratings by hiring David Gergen, the White House communications chief during Reagan's first term. But the amiable Gergen was unable to reposition Clinton as a centrist nearly so effectively as did Dick Morris, Clinton's image consultant after the 1994 electoral debacle. Morris had worked before for Clinton but also for conservative Republicans such as Senate Majority Leader Trent Lott. As a *Newsweek* story described him, Morris "was a classic mercenary—demonic, brilliant, principle-free."[31] It was Morris's insight, as much as Clinton's, that rhetoric and gesture, supported by the power of the veto, could turn a presidency seemingly moribund after 1994 into a triumphant one in 1996.

The remarkable prosperity the nation enjoyed during Clinton's second term purchased an unusual stretch of calm (some called it lethargy) for his administration—until the Monica Lewinsky storm threatened to wreck it in early 1998. Americans of all political persuasions were appalled by Clinton's sexual escapades and dishonest explanations in the Lewinsky affair. But for Clinton haters on the right, long infuriated by the successful spectacles of a character who symbolized (for them) the 1960s culture they despised, the Lewinsky scandal produced a thrill of self-confirmation. See, they proclaimed, his soul *is* the moral wasteland we always said it was. The unwillingness of most Americans to concur with conservative Republicans that Clinton's moral failures necessitated his ouster from the presidency only made his impeachment and conviction more urgent for the right. If strong support for Clinton in the polls indicated that the public was following him down the path toward moral hollowness, then removing him became a crusade for the nation's soul, an exorcism of the moral rot jeopardizing the meaning of the Republic.

But the moralistic fulminations of the right were no match for the power of spectacle. It was not spectacle alone that saved the Clinton presidency. Clinton was protected by prosperity and by Americans' preference for his centrist policies over the conservative alternatives. He was aided, too, by the inclination of most Americans to draw a line between public rectitude and private freedom. Nonetheless, Clinton's eventual acquittal by the Senate owed much to spectacle. To be sure, his own spectacle performance in the Year of Lewinsky was hardly his best. Perhaps no role suited Clinton so little as that of repentant sinner. But he was blessed by even worse performances from his adversaries. Just as Newt Gingrich had been necessary to resuscitate Clinton from the political disaster of 1994, so was Kenneth Starr, the independent counsel in hot pursuit of the president, essential to his rescue from the personal disaster of 1998. Starr's self-righteous moralism disturbed most Americans more than Clinton's self-serving narcissism.

In the end, the shallowness of the postmodern spectacle that had characterized the Clinton presidency from the start supplied an ironic benefit in the Lewinsky scandal. Had Clinton possessed a stable, respected character, revelations of secret behavior that violated that character might have startled the public and shrunk its approval of his performance in office. His standing in the polls might have plummeted, as President Reagan's did after the disclosure that his administration was selling arms to terrorists. But because a majority of Americans had long believed, according to the polls, that Clinton was not very honest or trustworthy, his misbehavior in the Lewinsky affair came as less of a shock and was diluted quickly by frequent reminders of his administration's popular achievements and agenda. Postmodern spectacle is not about character, at least not in a traditional sense; it is about delivering what the audience desires at the moment. Personality, political talent, and a keen instinct for survival made Bill Clinton the master of postmodern spectacle.

THE SOURING OF SPECTACLE: GEORGE W. BUSH

George W. Bush scored the highest Gallup approval rating in history after the terrorist attacks on September 11, 2001—and the highest Gallup disapproval rating ever during his final year in office. Bush's was a spectacle that soared briefly, then soured worse than that of even his most beleaguered predecessors.[32]

Although Bush promised the novelty of "compassionate conservatism" during the 2000 campaign, his administration's original agenda mainly followed the familiar priorities of the Republican right. But Bush's conservatism ran deeper than his policy prescriptions. In its characters, its styles, and its gestures, the Bush administration was determined to reach back past the postmodern spectacle of Bill Clinton and restore the faded glories of contemporary conservatism.

One fund of recycled images and themes upon which Bush drew was the Reagan spectacle. As a presidential character, Bush enjoyed many affinities with Reagan. He presented himself as a Reagan-style nonpolitician whose optimism and bonhomie would brighten a harsh and demoralizing political environment. His principal policy prescriptions for the nation—tax cuts and a missile defense system—also recycled Reaganesque themes and gestures. Recycled images and themes from his father's administration were equally evident in the early months of Bush's presidency and were especially useful as emblems of the new president's "compassionate" side. Like his father, "W" trumpeted his conciliatory stance toward congressional opponents and set out to be an "education president."

On September 11, 2001, when Al Qaeda terrorists killed thousands of Americans in a twisted spectacle of their own by piloting hijacked airliners into the World Trade Center and the Pentagon, Bush was given the chance to stage a more original and politically potent spectacle. The recycled conservative became the warrior president, Clumsy in his first public responses to the horror of September 11, 2001, Bush quickly hit his stride in what would be remembered as iconic moments of his presidency: his visit with rescue workers at Ground Zero in New York and his impressive speech to Congress on September 20, which struck a delicate balance between a forceful response to terrorism, a compassionate response to tragedy, and a teaching of tolerance toward followers of the Islamic faith.

After the initial success of the military campaign against Al Qaeda and the Taliban regime that harbored it in Afghanistan, the delicate balance in Bush's approach to September 11 gave way to a spectacle of muscular globalism. In his State of the Union address in January 2002, the commander in chief previewed an expansion of the War on Terror to combat an "axis of evil" composed of North Korea, Iran, and especially Iraq.[33] Signaling the intention to topple the regime of Saddam Hussein in Iraq, the phrase gestured toward the spectacular completion by the son of the mission in which the father, it now seemed, had sadly fallen short. The speech began the buildup to the war against Iraq that was launched a year later, as the Bush administration mustered its political and rhetorical resources to portray Saddam's regime, with its alleged weapons of mass destruction and ties to Al Qaeda, as a sinister threat to American security.

The war in Iraq was far more serious and deadly than Reagan's invasion of Grenada, and Bush's spectacle specialists were on the lookout for even more gripping gestures that would display a president "standing tall." As Elisabeth Bumiller noted in the *New York Times*, "The Bush administration, going far beyond the foundations in stagecraft set by the Reagan White House, is using the powers of television and technology like never before."[34]

Copiloting an S-3B Viking onto the deck of the aircraft carrier *Abraham Lincoln* on May 1, 2003, President Bush starred in what was instantly recognized as a new classic of presidential spectacles; the press quickly dubbed it Bush's *Top Gun* affair, recalling the Tom Cruise movie. The White House used the carrier as its stage to announce that major combat operations in Iraq were over; a banner over the president's head was emblazoned, "Mission Accomplished." Every detail of the event was meticulously planned for how it would look on television and in newspaper photos. The landing of the Viking at sea highlighted the degree of risk, with the fighter jet brought to a halt by the last of the four cables that catch planes on the carrier deck. Members of the *Lincoln* crew were garbed in varied but coordinated shirt colors as they surrounded the president—reminiscent of a football halftime ceremony. At the center of this massive stage was President Bush, who played his part with evident relish. *New York Times* columnist Maureen Dowd described the moment: "He flashed that famous all-American grin as he swaggered around the deck of the aircraft carrier in his olive flight suit, ejection harness between his legs, helmet tucked under his arm, awe-struck crew crowding around."[35]

Through these gestures, Bush's spectacle specialists implanted his image as a warrior president while eliding the realities on the ground in Iraq. Adhering to the tradition of civilian control of the military, Bush's predecessors had generally eschewed military garb. But his choice of martial clothing on the *Abraham Lincoln* and at subsequent appearances with soldiers deployed to Iraq played up his oneness with the American armed forces. The tailhook landing on the carrier suggested that Bush, as copilot, was willing to share some of the risks to which his decisions as commander in chief exposed American troops. No matter how controversial the war in Iraq might be, the one aspect of it that aroused consensus among Americans was the steadfast courage of the armed forces. Amalgamating himself with the troops through warrior spectacles, Bush signified that this virtue was his, too.

Viewers of Bush's dramatic flight to the *Abraham Lincoln* had witnessed what appeared to be a risky jet landing at sea. Later it was revealed by the press that the aircraft carrier was close to San Diego and could have been reached by helicopter; in fact, the ship had sailed a bit farther out into the Pacific so that the California coastline would not be visible on television.[36] The president also was derided later on for the "Mission Accomplished" banner, the sentiment of which turned out to be wildly premature.

Although the premises with which Bush had taken the nation to war in Iraq were soon shown to be false, his 9/11 image as America's protector against terrorists and his identification through spectacle with American troops were formidable assets when he faced the voters in 2004. At the hands of the president's campaign managers (some of whom had designed his Iraq spectacles), John Kerry, a decorated war hero in Vietnam, was re-created as a foreign policy weakling compared with George W. Bush, who had avoided Vietnam but had become a spectacle warrior.

Yet if Bush's spectacle specialists had hoped to portray the invasion and occupation of Iraq as an adventure tale, by the time of Bush's reelection, it was beginning to turn into a horror story instead. The "bad guys" in Iraq, with their suicide bombings and beheadings, perpetrated such sickening violence that Americans began to wonder what had happened to the Bush administration's prediction that Iraqis would greet U.S. forces as liberators. Even worse for the Bush spectacle was horror on the American side. American guards at the Abu Ghraib prison abused and sexually humiliated Iraqi prisoners. Meanwhile, American troops, many left poorly protected due to insufficient armor, were subjected to grievous wounds from insurgent explosive devices in Iraq, and when they were shipped home, they were housed in shabby medical facilities. Most Americans continued to perceive the troops as virtuous, but it was increasingly difficult to find virtue in the civilian leaders who had sent them into such a hell.

September 11, 2001, was an unexpected event that allowed Bush's spectacle to soar. Hurricane Katrina in 2005 was an equally unexpected event that compounded Bush's failures in Iraq and soured his presidency for the remainder of his term. The hurricane that devastated New Orleans and the Gulf Coast was among the worst natural disasters in American history. It was also a political disaster for the Bush presidency. Television, the tool of presidential spectacle, now savagely undermined it. Heart-wrenching pictures of hurricane victims, most of them poor and black, were powerful as well for what was absent: the federal rescue effort that could have saved many. Irate media commentators suggested that the president had abandoned his people.

President Bush's personal role in the Hurricane Katrina story contributed to that message. On vacation when the hurricane struck the Gulf Coast, Bush was urged by his top political adviser, Karl Rove, to fly over New Orleans and survey the damage. But unlike his "Mission Accomplished" landing, this was no *Top Gun* immersion in the thick of action. Photos of Bush soaring high above New Orleans in the comfort and safety of *Air Force One,* his press secretary Scott McClellan later observed, fostered "an image of a callous, unconcerned president."[37] Accompanying stories of incompetence on the part of Bush's subordinates in response to the hurricane, the pictures suggested a president who poorly comprehended what was happening either at home or abroad.

Bush's team made its own contributions to the souring of his spectacle. The hapless supporting player in the Hurricane Katrina story was Michael Brown, the lightweight head of the Federal Emergency Management Agency. Leading roles in the Iraq fiasco were played by administration heavyweights, especially Vice President Dick Cheney and Secretary of Defense Donald Rumsfeld. Both Cheney and Rumsfeld became notorious in the media for the arrogance with which they wielded power and dismissed criticism. Cheney was prone to cheery pronouncements about Iraq that had no connection to events on the ground, as when he proclaimed that the insurgency was in its "last throes" just before it reached new depths of violence. Rumsfeld was inclined to disparage discontent in the military's ranks, replying to one soldier who bemoaned the lack of armor for trucks, "You go to war with the army you have, not the army you might want."[38] Bush eventually dumped Rumsfeld, but he could not fire the vice president, whom some satirists compared to Darth Vader.

By his final months in office, Bush's spectacle had become so sour that the president was nearly ignored by the media. As the extraordinary election contest between Barack Obama and John McCain took center stage in 2008, Bush seemed more spectator than performer. A small and unexpected occurrence during the president's last visit to Iraq in December 2008 encapsulated the fate of his spectacle. Infuriated by what had happened to his country after Bush invaded it, an Iraqi journalist threw both of his shoes (a gesture of extreme contempt in his culture) at the American president during a news conference. At the heyday of his spectacle, aboard the *Abraham Lincoln,* Bush had emulated Reagan in "standing tall" as a warrior. Now, he was reduced to ducking footwear.[39]

SPECTACLE AND RATIONALITY: BARACK OBAMA

Shortly after President Barack Obama and the Democratic Party took a "shellacking" in the 2010 congressional elections, Obama told a journalist that he had been too preoccupied with enacting legislation at the expense of connecting to the American public: "the symbols and gestures—what people see coming out of this office— are at least as important as the policies we put forward."[40] A year and a half later, amid the 2012 campaign, he returned to the theme in a television interview: "The mistake of my first term . . . was thinking that this job was just about getting the policy right. And that's important. But the nature of this office is also to tell a story to the American people that gives them a sense of unity and purpose and opti- mism, especially during tough times."[41] Obama's words are unusual in a dual sense: seldom before has a president openly acknowledged the power of spectacle—and seldom before has a president candidly acknowledged his own shortfall in using this power.

Anyone witnessing Obama's remarkable campaign for the presidency in 2008 would never have predicted this shortfall. Obama's was one of the most spec- tacular runs for the presidency in American history. The historic audacity of a black man aiming for and then capturing the White House was a spectacle all by itself. But Obama's rhetorical gifts and golden smile captivated millions, as vast throngs assembled along the campaign trail to be energized by his message of hope and change. Of what other presidential candidate could it be said that his cam- paign oratory could be remixed as song? But when will.i.am of the Black-Eyed Peas assembled an all-star cast of musicians and actors to transform Obama's "Yes We Can" speech in an early primary into a music video, it swiftly went viral and became an anthem for the candidate's young supporters.

Once in office, however, President Obama focused intently on the primacy of policy to the neglect of spectacle. Situating himself, as Stephen Skowronek has observed, in the Progressive tradition, the new president operated under the assumption that "good policy" alone could transform the nation.[42] Bill Clinton had demonstrated that small-bore policies could make for smart symbolic politics. But Obama was after large-scale legislative victories in economic recovery, financial regulatory reform, health care reform, and alternative energy.

The hallmark of Obama's approach to his job was rationality and expertise applied to problem solving. His was a serious and substantive approach to politics— but one that cut against the requirements of spectacle. The protracted, unseemly process of congressional action and the complex, highly technical details of the legislation that resulted were so often arcane that few outside the Washington elite could follow the action. In the midst of shepherding several history-making bills to passage, Obama was unable to communicate their public meaning. Spectacle thrives on narrative simplicity—and Obama's rational style of policymaking was anything but simple.

Obama's critics rushed to fill the vacuum of narrative simplicity, enacting potent spectacle gestures of condemnation. Eschewing the "policy-wonk" discourse of the president and his administration's technocrats, Obama's opponents seized on elemental motifs of birth and death. A bizarre "birther" meme, whose most prominent champion was Donald Trump, spread through the Internet and subsequently received extensive coverage in the "mainstream media" to the effect that Obama was an illegitimate president because he had not proved that he was born in the United States. A small clause in the president's vast health care bill providing for physician recommendations on end-of-life care was transformed by former vice presidential candidate Sarah Palin into the chilling claim that "Obamacare" would create "death panels," with government bureaucrats deciding whether elderly patients with serious illnesses would be allowed to live.[43] The most important counter-spectacle to the Obama presidency was the Tea Party movement that emerged only a few months into his administration. If Obama's presidency suggested that the United States had passed a tipping point and become a multiracial and multicultural nation nurtured by supportive public policies, the Tea Party harked back to a mythical founding in which all of the Founders were of native stock and individual liberty, rather than any progressive concept of active government, was the nation's true creed.[44]

The one arena of presidential spectacle in which Obama clearly prevailed during his first term was international affairs. The most satisfying moment for the public in Obama's first term was the killing of Osama bin Laden in his Pakistani hideout by U.S. Navy Seals. In contrast to the byzantine Washington processes through which a policy-oriented president had to navigate, killing bin Laden was a direct, forceful, decisive executive action, carried out in the name of justice but with a strong emotional edge of righteous revenge. Unfortunately for Obama, the gains he reaped in the polls from bin Laden's death were short-lived; the public's attention soon shifted back to the grim economic crisis at home in which the president's current actions hardly appeared so successful.

Against this bleak domestic backdrop, observers began to view Obama as a spectacle character in terms radically at odds with his campaign image in 2008. Many journalists, who had been fascinated by Obama's electrifying persona during the campaign, now depicted the president as an aloof, even chilly figure, unable to stir public excitement because he had become so "professorial." Taken aback by the diminution of "hope" and the halting progress in "change," many of the president's ardent supporters became dejected and failed to turn out for the midterm congressional elections that dealt a terrible blow to his legislative prospects. Only Obama's most strident opponents continued to perceive him in the White House as they had characterized him during the campaign: as an alien figure, more socialist than liberal, more European than American, more of a threat to than an embodiment of the American Dream.

Although it proved difficult for Obama to alter the impression of coldness on his own, he was the beneficiary of reflected warmth from those close to him. Most important in this regard was the glow of his family, especially his wife, Michelle. Considerably more popular than her husband according to the polls, Michelle Obama tackled everyday problems, from childhood obesity to the travails of military families, with energy and charm. A more subtle contributor to the task of lightening up the president's image was Vice President Joe Biden. With his notorious penchant for verbal gaffes, Biden generally failed to gain the respect that he deserved as one of the president's most seasoned and savvy advisers. But the vice president's unvarnished persona brought a down-to-earth touch to an administration otherwise prone to lofty atmospherics. No one accused Joe Biden, with his working-class roots and associations, of acting like a haughty lecturer talking down to his students. Biden was the perfect companion for the president in an early photo op outing to Ray's Hell Burger, a small D.C.-area eatery.[45]

Even if Obama had enacted warmer spectacle gestures during his first term, the depth and persistence of the economic crisis would have remained an obstacle to public approval. Unrelenting statistics—and images—of joblessness and home foreclosures haunted the White House as a large majority of Americans repeatedly told pollsters that the country was heading in the wrong direction. George W. Bush continued to receive more of the blame for economic bad news than Obama, but a cheerless nation could hardly be expected to be enthusiastic about reelecting its president. Entering the 2012 campaign, Republicans, who had effectively contributed to Obama's feckless reputation as economic manager by obstructing most of his plans for recovery, understandably entertained high hopes of making him a one-term president.

The elections of 2012 proved to be a rude awakening for the GOP. During his first three years in office, the president, in his successes and especially his shortfalls, had commanded the attention, while his Republican adversaries had only been seen out of the corner of the public's eye. Now, much like Bill Clinton once he was blessed with Newt Gingrich as a foil, Barack Obama looked a lot better to many of his doubters when he was sized up against the Republican nominee for president, Mitt Romney. It is hard to imagine an opponent who had less of a chance to draw support away from Obama's base of women, minorities, and young voters. In the simple terms of spectacle, Romney was squarely of the rich, making Obama, despite his own actual affluence, symbolically middle class. With his fixation on the "job creators" at the top of the economic ladder, Romney turned the president into the champion of a vast majority who are not employers, especially the "47 percent" whom Romney famously disparaged, including soldiers and retirees, because they receive checks from the government. The Obama of his first three White House years may have seemed distant and chilly, but Romney came across as so sober and stiff that by contrast the president appeared positively on fire.

Obama's surprisingly comfortable margin of victory owed as much to his renewed energy and passion as to his rival's abundant shortcomings. Once more in a campaign rather than a policymaking context, he found his groove again. Some of the magical appeal of 2008 returned to the Obama spectacle: even if his original supporters were not so starry-eyed this time around, they proved no less ready to donate their money and volunteer their time. The president adopted a more com-bative persona than he had four years earlier. The earnest rhetoric of unity and bipartisanship gave way to the feisty phrases of a populist and partisan.

As Obama's second term commenced, however, the president again became mired in a stalemate with congressional Republicans. He soon decided that he would no longer be stymied by Republican obstructionism and vigorously grasped the instruments of unilateral executive action. In domestic areas such as climate and immigration policy, and especially in foreign affairs, Obama became the auda-cious president in his final two years that he had previewed in his initial run for the office. At least for his supporters, his executive actions produced some heartwarm-ing spectacles. For example, having broken with the archaic Cold War policy of isolating Cuba, Obama followed up the resumption of diplomatic relations with the island nation with a visit in the spring of 2016. During his stay in Havana, his televised message about democratic change thrilled Cubans who had never before heard such words on their government-controlled channels.[46]

Still, Obama remained a rationalist in his second term, only intermittently attentive to media demands for presidential spectacle. When a flood of migrant children from Central America crossed into Texas in the summer of 2014, creating a sudden crisis at the border, a presidential inspection trip to the "disaster area" was the expected response. But Obama balked at this convention. "I'm not interested in photo ops," he told reporters. "I'm interested in solving the problem. There is nothing taking place down there that I am not intimately aware of and briefed on."[47] No doubt the president was correct from the perspective of policymaking. But by rejecting the terms of the spectacle, he opened himself to criticism that he was uncaring in the face of suffering. With predictable hyperbole, Republicans pounced, declaring this to be Obama's "Katrina moment." For their part, journal-ists were puzzled that the photo op, a standard gesture in the White House media playbook, was so readily jettisoned.

ALL-SPECTACLE-ALL-THE-TIME: DONALD TRUMP

White House aides called him "no drama Obama" because the president insisted on a steady and calm administration. Succeeding Obama, Donald Trump is his opposite: all-spectacle-all-the-time. Critics of candidate Trump charged that he did not have any qualifications to be president. But he did have at least one: a career built on spectacle.

How did a flamboyant billionaire with a brand that screams luxury make him-self into a champion of the working class? During the 2012 presidential campaign, Democrats had effectively defined Romney as an exploitative and heartless pluto-crat. But they had no success hanging a similar label on Trump in 2016. Whereas Romney touted the "job creators" in business, Trump pitched his appeal to the class and racial resentments of white workers. He was no novice in targeting this part of the conservative base; through prior spectacles he had already cultivated it.

Consider his stint as part-owner of World Wrestling Entertainment, including his simulated body-slam of the WWE's Vince McMahon before a howling stadium crowd.[48] Or consider his role as impresario of the Miss Universe pageant.[49] These were not entertainment spectacles for the educated classes, those whom Trump delighted in disparaging as "politically correct." Instead, they connected him to a working-class audience that no other candidate in 2016 could reach. One cannot imagine a Hillary Clinton or Bernie Sanders, a Jeb Bush or Ted Cruz, as the host of wrestling matches or beauty contests.

The signature events of Trump's presidential campaign were his rallies. For the thousands in attendance and for millions of followers watching on television, these rallies functioned as outlets for fervor and fury. In some respects, they resembled rock concerts: the star performer in the spotlight, the fans garbed in Make America Great Again hats and T-shirts, the crowds aggressively chanting favorite lines, especially "Build the Wall" and "Lock Her Up." The deeper motif of Trump rallies lay in what Roland Barthes had recognized in the spectacle of professional wrestling: a symbolic battle between good and evil in which a hero encounters the standard bearer of a corrupt elite and gains victory for the long-suffering mass.

Some observers speculated that Trump would "pivot" once he entered office, leaving behind the angry tone of his campaign and becoming more "presidential" in bearing and serious about public policy. But the spectacle of his presidency has been continuous with the spectacle of his campaign. Obsessed with his own image, Trump has remained fixated on spectacle while displaying little interest in the substance of his administration's policy agenda. As political scientist Daniel Drezner bluntly put it, "The president certainly does not seem to have any bright ideas. Or any coherent ideas, for that matter. . . . [W]hat stands out is Trump's complete inability to grasp any policy ideas."[50]

A media feedback loop has been central to Trump's daily presidential spectacle. First, the president absorbs news coverage about himself and his administration, primarily by spending hours watching cable television shows in the early morning.[51] Then, he comments furiously on Twitter about what he has just seen and heard, generating a fresh slew of media stories. The loop continues with another round of Trump tweets. The president's favorite cable shows—*Morning Joe* and *Fox and Friends*—have been boosters of his image. But when the hosts of *Morning Joe,* Joe Scarborough and Mika Brzezinski, became increasingly critical of Trump, he responded with a savage tweet about "Psycho Joe" and "low IQ Crazy Mika."[52]

Uncomfortable with such traditional venues for presidential communication as press conferences and written speeches, Trump loves Twitter, which he has found ideal for boasts, blasts at opponents, and repetition of stock phrases such as "FAKE NEWS." He casts himself as a Twitter pacesetter, announcing that "my use of social media is not Presidential—it's MODERN DAY PRESIDENTIAL."[53] Obama actually was the first president to use Twitter, but he employed it chiefly to send routine messages to his supporters, seldom making news with his tweets.[54] Firing off multiple tweets nearly every day, Trump keeps the media's focus on his presidency continually churning, playing to his fans and infuriating his foes. Through his use of Twitter, and the controversies that he sets off, he has increased the volume of media coverage for himself beyond that of his predecessors. Yet the spiteful tone of many Trump tweets has sometimes proved self-sabotaging; some of his supporters have told reporters that they wish he would not tweet so often.

Presidential spectacles often operate by pitting the chief executive against a widely disliked foil. Even after defeating her, Trump continued his denigration of "Crooked Hillary." But his principal foil as president has been the news media, which polling data has shown is not trusted by a majority of Americans. Trump has declared rhetorical war on mainstream journalists, whom he has called "the enemy of the people." With leading media outlets calling him out for lying, failing to repudiate hate groups, fumbling policies, and presiding over a chaotic White House, the president has struck back with a string of invectives aimed at news organizations that attract his ire. In tweeting about "the Fake News of CNN, NBC, ABC, CBS, washpost or nytimes,"[55] Trump insists that the truth about himself and his administration can only be obtained by turning to media cheerleaders on the right, especially Fox News and Breitbart.

The Trump team has played a part in the presidential spectacle unlike any predecessor. Hardly earning a reputation for collaboration or competence, the team's members have stood out as an oddball cast of characters, resembling their boss in how easily they are satirized. Presidential strategist Steve Bannon, the "nationalist" link to the alt-right until he was fired, was portrayed on *Saturday Night Live* as the Grim Reaper. Communications counselor Kellyanne Conway swiftly became notorious for her loopy defenses of Trump's falsehoods, coining the phrase "alternative facts" to justify whatever the White House claimed. The ten-day tenure of communications director Anthony (the Mooch) Scaramucci set new White House standards for vulgar language and in-house brawling. Initially, Trump's daughter Ivanka and son-in-law Jared Kushner supplied a rare touch of class to this crew, but increasingly they have been depicted by critics as enablers of the president's crude behavior.

With his appointments and policies relating to hot-button issues such as racial conflict, immigration, and climate change, Trump clearly has played to the white working-class base that was the key to his election. For economic policy, however, his spectacle has obscured what he actually put in place: plutocracy in the guise of populism. During his campaign, Trump tarred his opponents as tools of plutocracy, first associating Republican rival Ted Cruz and later Democratic opponent Hillary Clinton with Goldman Sachs, the premier firm and symbol of Wall Street. In office, Trump staffed his economic policy apparatus with Goldman Sachs alumni, including his chief economic adviser (Gary Cohn) and secretary of the treasury (Steven Mnuchin). To regulate Wall Street, he picked a Wall Street lawyer (Jay Clayton) among whose major clients had been Goldman Sachs. When big money is at stake, Trump's base is found in the quiet boardrooms of the financial elite, worlds away from the fiery spectacles of his rallies.[56]

Counter-spectacles have been as prominent for Trump as they were for Obama. Starting almost immediately after his election, a self-styled Resistance (a name redolent of World War II European anti-fascism) has mounted widespread protests against the president and his policies. The Women's March assemblages across the nation the day after the Inauguration were, collectively, the largest mass protests in American history. Even more threatening to Trump's future has been the simmering specter of the Russia scandal. The still-unanswered questions of whether his campaign colluded with Russian intelligence agents to defeat Hillary Clinton and whether his White House continues to cover up this crime have generated a puzzle reminiscent of a Cold War spy tale. Lurking ominously in the background has been an archetypal villain: Russian president Vladimir Putin. Doggedly pursuing evidence that could either indict or exonerate Trump have been two lawmen: an FBI director, James Comey, whom the president fired, and a special counsel, Robert Mueller, whose legal powers may threaten the president's own.

Even though President Trump continues to deride the media for "fake news," it has not flagged in non-stop coverage of his spectacle. As Paul Farhi wrote in *The Washington Post*, "the cable networks, in particular, have devoted so much time and attention to President Trump in his first six months in office that they have little time or interest in covering much else."[57] Yet the president's declining numbers in the polls suggest that the ubiquity of his spectacle has not translated into its success. Nonstop spectacles are exhausting. When leading media publications breathlessly announce "breaking news" about the president several times a day, many of these stories come to seem like more of the same. More damaging, a shrinking percentage of "spectators" (only a quarter of the public in an August 2017 CNN poll) say they believe what the Trump White House is presenting.[58] Lacking governing experience or policy substance as qualifications for the presidency, candidate Trump offered himself as the hero of a spectacle that would revive the nation. If that spectacle falls flat, President Trump has almost nothing else to offer.

CONCLUSION

It is tempting to blame the growth of spectacle on individual presidents, their calculating advisers, and compliant journalists. It is more accurate, however, to attribute the growth of spectacle to larger, structural forces: the extreme personalization of the modern presidency, the excessive expectations of the president that most Americans have, and the media coverage that fixes on presidents and treats American politics largely as a report of their adventures. Indeed, presidential spectacles can be linked to a culture of consumption in which spectacle is the predominant form that relates the few to the many. Spectacle, then, is more a structural feature of the contemporary presidency than a strategy of deception adopted by particular presidents.

Judged by the standard of American democratic values, the promotion of gesture over accomplishment, the obfuscation of executive responsibility, and the encouragement to citizens' passivity that have typified many past presidential spectacles are troubling. Yet spectacles have become so much a part of the modern presidency, expected by the media and readily grasped by the public, that they cannot be neglected even in the communication of high-minded goals. Ideally, a president serious about the substance of public policy would effectively communicate the desirability of his or her agenda through an appealing spectacle, but finding a balance between policy and spectacle is not easy. Barack Obama was plenty serious but conceded that too often he was neglectful of the "symbols and gestures" of spectacle. Donald Trump's experience so far suggests the consequences when symbols and gestures replace substance.

NOTES

1. A short list of seminal books on presidential communication includes the follow-ing: Jeffrey K. Tulis, *The Rhetorical Presidency* (Princeton, NJ: Princeton University Press, 1987); Samuel Kernell, *Going Public: New Strategies of Presidential Leadership*, 3rd ed. (Washington, DC: CQ Press, 1997); Lawrence R. Jacobs and Robert Y. Shapiro, *Politicians Don't Pander: Political Manipulation and the Loss of Democratic Responsiveness* (Chicago: University of Chicago Press, 2000); George C. Edwards III, *On Deaf Ears: The Limits of the Bully Pulpit* (New Haven, CT: Yale University Press, 2003); Brandice Canes-Wrone, *Who Leads Whom? Presidents, Policy, and the Public* (Chicago: University of Chicago Press, 2005); and Jeffrey E. Cohen, *The Presidency in the Era of 24-Hour News* (Princeton, NJ: Princeton University Press, 2008).

2. Daniel Dayan and Elihu Katz, "Electronic Ceremonies: Television Performs a Royal Wedding," in *On Signs,* ed. Marshall Blonsky (Baltimore: Johns Hopkins University Press, 1985), 16.

3. Roland Barthes, *Mythologies* (New York: Hill and Wang, 1972), 15–25.

4. Theodore J. Lowi, *The Personal President* (Ithaca, NY: Cornell University Press, 1985), 96.

5. Guy Debord, *Society of the Spectacle* (Detroit: Black and Red, 1983), para. 60.

6. On the confidence of the public personality and the anxiety of his audience, see Richard Sennett, *The Fall of Public Man* (New York: Knopf, 1977).

7. Erving Goffman, *The Presentation of Self in Everyday Life* (Garden City, NY: Anchor Books, 1959), 104.

8. See Michael Rogin, *Ronald Reagan, the Movie, and Other Episodes in Political Demonology* (Berkeley: University of California Press, 1987), 1–43.

9. Quoted in ibid., 100.

10. Lou Cannon, *Reagan* (New York: Putnam, 1982), 371–401.

11. "Meet David Stockman," *Newsweek,* February 16, 1981.

12. Nicholas Lemann, "The Peacetime War," *Atlantic,* October 1984, 88.

13. "From Bad to Worse for U.S. in Grenada," *U.S. News & World Report,* October 31, 1983.

14. Richard A. Gabriel, *Military Incompetence: Why the American Military Doesn't Win* (New York: Hill and Wang, 1985), 154.

15. Quoted in "Fare Well, Grenada," *Time,* December 26, 1983.

16. Francis X. Clines, "Days of Crisis for President: Golf, a Tragedy and Secrets," *New York Times,* October 26, 1983.

17. "Remarks of the President and Prime Minister Eugenia Charles of Dominica Announcing the Deployment of United States Forces in Grenada," October 25, 1983, http://www.reagan.utexas.edu/archives/speeches/1983.

18. Ibid.

19. Ibid.

20. "Address to the Nation on Events in Lebanon and Grenada," October 27, 1983, http://www.reagan.utexas.edu/archives/speeches/1983.

21. "Getting Back to Normal," *Time,* November 21, 1983.

22. "'We Will Not Be Intimidated,'" *Newsweek,* November 14, 1983.

23. Gabriel, *Military Incompetence,* 186.

24. Anthony Lewis, "What Was He Hiding?" *New York Times,* October 31, 1983.

25. Maureen Dowd, "Bubba Don't Preach," *New York Times,* February 9, 1997.
26. Howard Fineman and Bill Turque, "How He Got His Groove," *Newsweek,* September 2, 1996; and Garry Wills, "The Clinton Principle," *New York Times Magazine,* January 19, 1997.
27. See Bert A. Rockman, "Leadership Style and the Clinton Presidency," in *The Clinton Presidency: First Appraisals,* ed. Colin Campbell and Bert A. Rockman (Chatham, NJ: Chatham House, 1996), 325–362.
28. Stephen Skowronek, *The Politics Presidents Make: Leadership from John Adams to Bill Clinton* (Cambridge, MA: Harvard University Press, 1997), 447–464.
29. Elizabeth Drew, *Showdown: The Struggle between the Gingrich Congress and the Clinton White House* (New York: Simon and Schuster, 1996).
30. Fineman and Turque, "How He Got His Groove."
31. Evan Thomas et al., "Victory March," *Newsweek,* November 18, 1996.
32. "Bush's 69% Job Disapproval Rating Highest in Gallup History," April 22, 2008, http://www.gallup.com/poll/106741/bushs-69-job-disapproval-rating-highest-gallup -history.aspx.
33. "Bush State of the Union Address," January 29, 2002, CNN, http://edition.cnn .com/2002/ALLPOLITICS/01/29/bush.speech.txt/.
34. Elisabeth Bumiller, "Keepers of Bush Image Lift Stagecraft to New Heights," *New York Times,* May 16, 2003.
35. Maureen Dowd, *Bushworld: Enter at Your Own Risk* (New York: Putnam's, 2004), 356. For details about the carrier event, see David E. Sanger, "In Full Flight Regalia, the President Enjoys a 'Top Gun' Moment," *New York Times,* May 2, 2003.
36. Paul Krugman, "Man on Horseback," *New York Times,* May 6, 2003.
37. Scott McClellan, *What Happened? Inside the Bush White House and Washington's Culture of Deception* (New York: Public Affairs, 2008), 274.
38. Quoted in Frank Rich, *The Greatest Story Ever Sold: The Decline and Fall of Truth in Bush's America* (New York: Penguin Books, 2007), 177, 156–157.
39. Sudarsan Raghavan and Dan Eggen, "Shoe-Throwing Mars Bush's Baghdad Trip," *Washington Post,* December 15, 2008.
40. Ron Suskind, *Confidence Men: Wall Street, Washington, and the Education of a President* (New York: HarperCollins, 2011), 482.
41. Lindsey Boerma, "Obama Reflects on His Biggest Mistake as President," CBS News. com, July 12, 2012, http://www.cbsnews.com/8301-503544_162-57471351- 503544/obama-reflects-on-his-biggest-mistake-as-president/.
42. Stephen Skowronek, *Presidential Leadership in Political Time: Reprise and Reappraisal,* 2nd ed. (Lawrence: University Press of Kansas, 2011), 185.
43. Sarah Palin, "Statement on the Current Health Care Debate," Palin's Facebook page, August 7, 2009.
44. See Jill Lepore, *The Whites of Their Eyes: The Tea Party's Revolution and the Battle over American History* (Princeton, NJ: Princeton University Press, 2010).
45. Jonathan Martin, "Obama, Biden Share Burgers," *Politico,* May 5, 2009, http://www .politico.com/news/stories/0509/22123.html.
46. Nick Miroff, "A Family in Havana is Enthralled and Heartened by Obama's Call for Change," *Washington Post,* March 22, 2016.
47. Linda Feldman, "Obama's No-Win Situation on Border Crisis," *Christian Science Monitor,* July 10, 2014.

48. Aaron Oster, "Donald Trump and WWE: How the Road to the White House Began at 'Wrestle Mania,'" *Rolling Stone*, February 1, 2016.

49. Judy Bachrach, "What's Behind Donald Trump's Obsession with Beauty Pageants?" *Vanity Fair*, January 13, 2016.

50. Daniel W. Drezner, "The Marketplace of Ideas Is Killing the Trump Administration," *Washington Post*, August 2, 2017.

51. Elaine Godfrey, "Trump's TV Obsession Is a First," *The Atlantic*, April 3, 2017.

52. Jessica Estepa and David Jackson, "President Trump Hurls Crude New Insults at 'Morning Joe' Hosts," *USA Today*, June 30, 2017.

53. Twitter.com/realDonaldTrump, July 1, 2017.

54. Juliet Eilperin, "Here's How the First President of the Social Media Age Has Chosen to Connect with Americans," *Washington Post*, May 27, 2015.

55. Trump quoted in Glenn Thrush, "Trump Defends Twitter Use as Aides Urge Him to Cut Back," *New York Times*, August 4, 2017.

56. Matt Egan, "Trump Hires Yet Another Goldman Sachs Banker," CNN, March 15, 2017.

57. Paul Farhi, "On Cable, 'All Trump, All the Time' Isn't Going Away—the Networks Are Addicted," *Washington Post*, August 11, 2017.

58. Jennifer Agiesta, "Trump at 200 Days: Declining Approval amid Widespread Mistrust," CNN, August 8, 2017.

THE PRESIDENT
AND THE MEDIA

The Case of Donald Trump

Marjorie Randon Hershey

The relationship between the presidency and the news media is at times cooperative and at other times adversarial. But it has always been symbiotic—because each draws on the same source of legitimacy. Presidents can reach the American people only through the media: newspapers, magazines, radio, network television, cable television, and, more recently, multiple forms of Web-based communication. The news media need the president to speak words and take actions that will provide interesting content to their audiences. As Marjorie Randon Hershey shows, these constant elements in the presidency–media relationship can be seen in Donald Trump's presidency, often in heightened form.

Before becoming president, Thomas Jefferson was a big fan of the media. He wrote, "Our citizens may be deceived for awhile, and have been deceived; but as long as the presses can be protected, we may trust to them for light."[1] Time in the White House apparently changed his mind: he later contended, "Nothing can now be believed which is seen in a newspaper. Truth itself becomes suspicious by being put into that polluted vehicle."[2]

Many presidents would probably side with the later Jefferson. But although they might wish it were otherwise, presidents absolutely need media coverage. Without it, they lose one of their primary means of influencing action in Congress and protecting their own popularity. The media need presidents as well, but for different reasons. Journalists' aim is not to enhance presidents' popularity but to find audiences for media outlets, and news about presidents is a major draw for viewers, listeners, and readers. In short, presidents have a symbiotic relationship with the media: they depend on one another. Yet because presidents and journalists have different priorities, their relationship tends to be combative and often hostile.

This chapter explains why presidents' interactions with journalists are so intense, conflict-filled, and also fundamental to a democracy. Then I will examine the tensions in President Donald Trump's relationship with media, and illustrate the relationship by looking at media treatment of Trump's connections with the Russian government.

PRESIDENTS NEED (FAVORABLE) MEDIA COVERAGE

The Constitution created a presidency with limited powers and, as a result, few tools for playing a regular, long-term role in policymaking.[3] At times, events combined with personalities—think of Abraham Lincoln's response to the South's rebellion in 1860 and Franklin D. Roosevelt's actions to combat the Great Depression— to increase the scope of presidential powers. The presidency grew as the federal government greatly expanded in the 1900s. But even now, with presidents able to wield much greater policy heft and institutional resources,[4] their influence over the policy agenda is not automatic or assured.[5] Presidents still depend heavily on their persuasive skills to deal with other elected and appointed officials[6] and their ability to marshal public support.[7] These are interrelated: when presidents are seen as having strong public support, they are better positioned to persuade other officials to back their proposals.

To generate that support, they must rely extensively on the news media.[8] Presidents rarely get to speak directly to members of the public. Most citizens see a president only through various forms of media. So presidents seek favorable media coverage in order to generate public approval. They may do this in many ways: for instance, by claiming they have a public "mandate" to pursue certain policies, which Congress and journalists ought to respect.[9] Neutral coverage is good; friendly coverage is better.

MEDIA NEED PRESIDENTS TO DRAW AUDIENCES

In turn, media need presidents. Journalism has always been a competitive business, especially in recent decades as the media industry has become much more fragmented.[10] Media outlets must have audiences to survive. Big media outlets are private businesses, which earn money by selling access to their audiences to advertisers. Even bloggers are more likely to keep going if they can generate enough readers.

As a result, journalists have long defined "news" in terms of the characteristics most likely to attract an audience. Millions of events happen every day. Media don't have the space or time, and viewers don't have the interest, to attend to them all; they must choose. So media people choose to cover events that attract audiences. This produces a particular definition of "news." News is something immediate— a change from what usually happens. News requires drama, conflict, threat, or fear—similar to the types of stories that attract ratings on entertainment media. News is something we can personalize; journalists report about unemployment by opening with the story of one individual who has been laid off, because that interests audiences more than the impersonal concept of "unemployment."

This definition of news, focusing on what will draw an audience rather than what might be considered important using other criteria, has costs. Ongoing institutional patterns, such as the economic policies that affect job prospects, student loan interest rates, and college tuition costs, affect our lives more than does a celebrity's car crash or even a terrorist attack. But startling breaks in the normal pattern make headlines, whereas the fundamental forces that structure our choices are not normally seen as "news."[11] The immediate, the dramatic, the conflict-filled, and the unusual bring audiences, and therefore advertisers' money, to media outlets. Reports about structural unemployment and the Federal Reserve do not. One observer offers this comparison: "It's why there are ice cream parlors and no broccoli parlors."[12]

Presidents have high news value; they are the ice cream parlors while the Federal Reserve is the broccoli parlor. As Herbert Gans wrote, "Unlike other people who get into the news only when they are involved in unusual, innovative, or dramatic activities, [the president] is the only individual whose routine activities are deemed newsworthy."[13] Why? The president is an individual, whereas the other major figures of the federal government—Congress, the bureaucracy, and the judiciary—are institutions with large numbers of legislators, employees, and judges. A story about a person, especially a familiar individual such as the president, draws people's attention more easily than a story about congressional committees or legislative oversight.[14] Presidents deal with dramatic matters every day. Theirs is the hand that controls the nuclear codes. Their elevation to the presidency means that a sizable part of the population considers them interesting and important. Americans have bought millions of books in recent decades about presidents' political maneuvering and personal relationships.[15] For all these reasons, media coverage focuses on the president more than on any other individual in American politics.[16]

Presidents typically invest major effort into influencing the nature of their coverage. They hire communications directors and press secretaries. They urge other members of the administration to speak to reporters on the president's behalf, while trying to snuff leaks of information the president doesn't want publicized. The volume and tone of their coverage can affect their electability and public approval because many Americans are too little interested in politics to seek out alternative sources of political information.[17]

Yet the media spotlight can become uncomfortably hot. Especially in these polarized times, commentators and bloggers can build a lucrative following by stoking hostile reactions to a president's decisions. Journalists' focus on drama and conflict often leads them to look for disputes between presidents and congressional leaders, strains among White House staffers, and problems in a president's personal life. The extensive leaks from within the Donald Trump administration attracted massive coverage, not necessarily because media people wanted to damage Trump but rather because the leaked information attracted readers—and Trump's condemnation of those leaks attracted even more.[18]

The relationships between presidents and the media are complicated and contentious. Presidents want reporters to highlight a president's accomplishments, help get his or her policies passed, and write stories that will promote the president's reelection. They want journalists to downplay the strategic and partisan maneuvering of presidential politics and to emphasize instead the president's successes and popularity.[19] Journalists, on the other hand, know that audiences love to read about strategic and partisan maneuvering. In addition, the idea that reporters serve as a vital watchdog on government, rather than as a mouthpiece for the current administration, retains a powerful hold over those who work for the mainstream media.[20] As *New York Times* executive editor Dean Baquet put it, "journalism is holding powerful people to account."[21] When presidents and the media are tightly bound by their mutual needs but pursue different objectives, conflict is inevitable.

Donald Trump has dealt with these conflicts differently from other recent presidents. Although he has fought to keep himself constantly at the center of media attention, he has also cultivated an unusually poisonous relationship with mainstream news media. That has helped him sustain his support among his media-hostile Republican base. But it also has contributed to his record-low public approval ratings and inability to achieve his legislative priorities.

THE SPECIAL CASE OF PRESIDENT DONALD TRUMP

For decades before his 2016 presidential run, Trump had a close but ambivalent relationship with journalists. As the owner of his family's large real estate development company, he aimed to create a brand; the Trump name would project such success and great wealth that clients would fight to be associated with it. To build this brand, he needed a lot of favorable publicity. That wouldn't be easy to obtain, because the company's business record was spotted by bankruptcies, charges of failing to pay subcontractors, and other stains. So Trump worked hard to develop relationships with journalists in his home city of New York, especially among the tabloid press. He cajoled them, flattered them, threatened them, and even pretended to be a public relations staffer for himself to gain the kind of coverage that would enhance his brand's reputation.[22]

Trump furthered this goal by hosting a long-running reality TV show, *The Apprentice,* in which he projected power and business acumen. The *Times*'s Dean Baquet assessed Trump as "a complicated guy. It would be a mistake for people to say this is just a guy who wants to kill all reporters. This is a guy who also lives—and has died on occasion—by the press. . . . This is a guy [who] writes handwritten notes to reporters. But it's also a guy who has said some of the most vile things about journalists of any politician of his generation."[23]

Trump's circumstances changed when he contemplated running for the Republican presidential nomination in 2016. Because much of the conservative Republican base has long distrusted the mainstream media,[24] Trump found obvious benefits in boasting of a hostile relationship with mainstream journalists. Picking fights with the elite media could convince Republican voters that Trump was on their side. It would also inoculate prospective supporters against media mentions of his scant political experience and frequent misstatements of facts. And the aggressive approach had little downside; the marked drop of public trust in the media since the 1970s, especially among Republicans, led more readers and viewers to discount mediated portrayals of campaigns and presidents.[25]

Trump's campaign blasts against CNN, the *New York Times,* the *Washington Post,* and other mainstream media were very well received at large rallies of his supporters. The candidate typically enclosed reporters in a conspicuous area and called on his audiences to jeer at them, labeling the media "totally dishonest" and "scum." At times he encouraged audiences to threaten reporters with violence. Trump tweeted in mid-August 2016 that "if the disgusting and corrupt media covered me honestly and didn't put false meaning into the words I say, I would be beating Hillary by 20%." His supporters at these rallies often responded to his media attacks with standing ovations.[26]

Trump's assaults on the media escalated after he was elected president. Beginning in mid-December 2016, he posted on Twitter that CNN and other media outlets were reporting "fake news." After that post, which was well received by Trump fans, the president tweeted about "fake news" as many times as he did about his proposed border wall to stop illegal immigration, NAFTA, other trade matters, and veterans' issues combined.[27] His tweets particularly reviled media accounts of public opinion polls, which showed him to be unusually unpopular for a new president. On February 6, 2017, for instance, Trump tweeted, "Any negative polls are fake news, just like the CNN, ABC, NBC polls in the election."

Just a month into his term, President Trump went beyond charging that news reports were wrong, or even intentionally incorrect. He claimed that the mainstream media were the "enemy," guilty of subverting the public trust. On February 17, he posted, "The FAKE NEWS media (failing @nytimes, @NBCNews, @ABC, @CBS, @CNN) is not my enemy, it is the enemy of the American People!" After facing widespread criticism for his claim that protesters at a white supremacist rally in Charlottesville, Virginia, were as much to blame as were the neo-Nazi and KKK marchers, Trump stated at a campaign stop that the "sick" and "really, really dishonest" media were responsible for "trying to take away our history and our heritage."[28]

Trump went beyond spoken criticism. He took the unusual step of banning some mainstream media outlets (including the *Post* and the *Times*) from White House press conferences while inviting right-wing outlets such as Breitbart News to ask questions.[29] He threatened to propose legislation making it easier for public figures to sue news organizations for libel.[30] Some Trump supporters in the media, including a conservative radio talk show host, went so far as to urge people to plant false information and documents with mainstream media outlets about Trump's links with Russia and then "out" them as false information. At least some of these efforts were identified by journalists, vetted, and not reported.[31]

Perhaps the most extreme example of Trump's antagonistic relationship with the media came from former FBI director James Comey's testimony before a congressional committee. According to Comey, Trump suggested imprisoning reporters who publish classified information. "Suggesting that the government should prosecute journalists for the publication of classified information is very menacing, and I think that's exactly what they intend," said Martin Baron, the *Washington Post*'s executive editor. "It's an act of intimidation."[32]

Trump defended his actions by alleging that he had been treated more unfairly than any other politician in American history.[33] But his treatment of journalists drew pushback even from within his own party. In mid-summer 2017, for example, Trump retweeted an old video clip of himself taking part in a staged professional wrestling match, in which his opponent's head was replaced by the CNN logo. In the clip, Trump slams "CNN" to the canvas and pretends to batter its head repeatedly. The retweet closes with the hashtags #FraudNewsCNN and #FNN, for "fraud news network." Republican Senator Ben Sasse accused the president of "weaponizing distrust" toward the news media.[34] Trump's opponents blasted him for seeming to encourage violence against journalists, as well as behaving in a manner unbecoming a president. Trump's supporters claimed that the media brought the attack on themselves by reporting criticisms of the president.

In addition, in interviews and speeches, candidate and then President Trump demonstrated an unprecedented disregard for facts. The Pulitzer Prize–winning fact-checker PolitiFact reported that only 17 percent of the president's statements could be verified as true or mostly true, whereas fully 69 percent were mostly false, false, or "pants on fire," the site's rating for statements that are both false and ridiculous. Among these statements were that the United States is the highest-taxed nation in the world (it is actually in the bottom third), that the "real" unemployment rate was 42 percent (he later lowered that to 23 percent, which was also several times too high), that blacks were responsible for 81 percent of white homicides (the FBI's statistics said less than 15 percent), and that Barack Obama and Hillary Clinton founded the Islamic radical terrorist group ISIS.[35]

Trump's looseness with facts posed serious questions for mainstream journalists. For a profession that has long maintained norms of impartiality and professionalism, is it responsible to publicize statements known to be false, accompanied only by a brief rebuttal from an opposition political figure? Or does such a presentation imply that the statement and the rebuttal are equally valid? It took more than a year of such misstatements before most mainstream reporters were willing to call out the untruths without having to find an anti-Trump source willing to be quoted as doing so.[36] As one mainstream media reporter stated, "I think the media has struggled to cover the dark side of the Trump phenomenon because political reporters do not have experience covering a major political figure who is both openly racist and—let's be honest—an extremely entertaining politician."[37]

In short, President Trump's self-acknowledged "war on the media" and his toxic relationship with mainstream media were clearly more antagonistic than was the case for other recent presidents.[38] Although they might dream of bashing the media, most presidents (and Trump himself as a real estate developer) acknowledge the benefits of accommodating and trying to use the mainstream press. Why has Trump taken such a different approach?

During the crowded Republican presidential nominating season, Trump's attacks on the media kept him in the headlines and helped distinguish him from other, more experienced Republican candidates.[39] His war with the media also distracted public attention from President Trump's apparent failures, such as the lack of progress on his stated goal of repealing and replacing Obamacare (the Affordable Care Act).[40] The fact that Republicans controlled both the presidency and both houses of Congress might have otherwise made it hard for Trump voters to understand why more of his promises weren't being fulfilled.

Many Trump supporters preferred to believe their candidate rather than the media sources they regarded as prejudiced against him. After one of the many battles between President Trump and CNN, a July 2017 poll found that 89 percent of Republicans said they trusted President Trump more than CNN, while 91 percent of Democrats trusted CNN more than the president. Independents (by 15 percentage points) and all respondents (by 7 percentage points) trusted CNN over Trump.[41] In such a polarized atmosphere, President Trump could count on his base to disregard news coming from sources other than pro-Trump outlets.

Trump's media relations were not entirely unconventional. Like other chief executives, he used a succession of press secretaries to put forward his policies to the mainstream press, although he "inserted himself into the White House's press operations in an unprecedented fashion for a president."[42] His successive communications directors kept trying to spin the news in the president's favor.[43] The president occasionally sought to improve his fraught relationships with mainstream media outlets. For example, he granted an exclusive interview to the *New York Times*—the newspaper he always referred to as the "failing *New York Times*," and which had just disclosed damaging e-mails between his eldest son and Russian operatives—at the height of *Times* coverage of this scandal.

Like previous presidents, Trump sought to benefit from changes in media technology. Early in American history, presidents and party leaders established newspapers to report political developments with their own preferred slant.[44] More recent presidents have worked to communicate directly with viewers through broadcast addresses so they could control the story they wanted to tell.[45] In the 1930s, early in the broadcast era, President Franklin D. Roosevelt used the relatively new medium of radio to hold "Fireside Chats" transmitted directly to large audiences.[46] His successors relied mostly on television. Barack Obama innovated with YouTube and the White House website.[47] Trump, in turn, made heavy use of Twitter.

TRUMP AND SOCIAL MEDIA

For presidents and other politicians, social media platforms such as Facebook and Twitter provide a great advantage: they allow political figures to speak directly to citizens who choose to listen, with no editor or journalist serving as gatekeeper. When Twitter was founded and Facebook opened to the general public in 2006, candidates and elected officials jumped on board. Twitter became a particularly important medium for political postings. On Election Day 2016, for instance, Twitter was the most frequent source of breaking news; more than 40 million election-related tweets were sent that day.[48]

Barack Obama used his daily presence on Twitter to build support for his policies. But Trump took tweeting to a new level. He had used Twitter for years, but when he ran for president, it became an alternative communications channel with which he could circumvent the mainstream news media and address his supporters directly. As Trump tweeted in June 2017: "The Fake News Media hates when I use what has turned out to be my very powerful Social Media – over 100 million people![49] I can go around them." His tweets have often been amplified by coverage in the mainstream press because they are immediate, dramatic, and full of conflict: in short, they meet the prevailing definition of "news." One analyst wrote that Twitter is an ideal medium for Trump as a candidate and president: "Mr. Trump expertly exploits journalists' unwavering attention to their Twitter feeds, their competitive spirit and their ingrained journalistic conventions—chiefly, that what the president says is inherently newsworthy. . . . Mr. Trump overwhelms the media with boatloads of what was once a rare commodity: access. He creates impressions faster than journalists can check them. By the time they turn up the facts, the news cycle has moved on to his next missive, leaving less time (and reader attention) for the stories Mr. Trump does not highlight on his feed.'"[50]

With his multiple daily tweets, Trump attempts what any president hopes to achieve: to frame an event, a policy, or a proposal in a way that strengthens his support among target audiences. Although Trump's following on Twitter was not unprecedented (Obama had a Twitter following of 92 million), Trump attracted many more followers than most other political figures; by mid-2017 Twitter listed him as having 33.1 million followers, compared with 16.7 million for Hillary Clinton and 816,000 for Paul Ryan, the Speaker of the House.[51] His numbers were thought to be greatly inflated by the presence of "bots," or automated systems of response that can produce huge numbers of responses to an online stimulus.[52] Even so, Trump's audience was bigger than the combined total of the *New York Times,* the *Washington Post,* the *Wall Street Journal,* and *USA Today.* In fact, Trump's Twitter followers almost equal the total number of daily subscribers to all U.S. newspapers (including their online subscriptions).[53]

As president, Trump used Twitter very differently from his predecessor (see Figure 10.1)—and about twice as frequently.[54] Obama's tweets referred mainly to policy issues; two-thirds promoted his administration's priorities, and they usually contained factual data or linked to reports on the issue in question. For example, "The economy added 242,000 jobs in February – a record-breaking six straight years of private-sector job growth" (March 4, 2016). Notice the references to specific data. In contrast, only about three in ten of Trump tweets dealt with policies of any kind. And while Obama policy tweets were heavy on details, Trump's tended toward broader and less specific language, such as these: "The American dream is back. We're going to create an environment for small business like we haven't had in many, many decades!" (January 30, 2017) and "Great numbers on the economy. All of our work, including the passage of many bills & regulation killing Executive Orders, now kicking in!" (June 11, 2017).

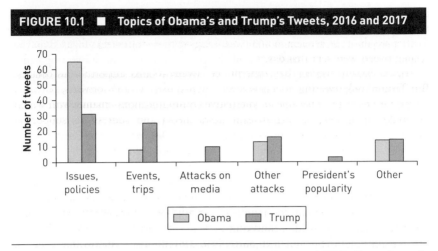

FIGURE 10.1 ■ Topics of Obama's and Trump's Tweets, 2016 and 2017

Note: Includes tweets from February 1–August 31 in 2016 for Obama, and 2017 for Trump. See end-note 54 for details.

In their tweets about policy issues, Trump focused on different issues than Obama did. The largest portion of Obama's tweets (21 percent) referred to judicial activity. Obama had nominated federal appeals court judge Merrick Garland to fill a vacant seat on the Supreme Court. The Republican Senate majority refused even to consider the nomination, thus leaving the Court without a tie-breaking ninth justice for over a year. Obama frequently used Twitter to urge the Senate, or to ask citizens to urge the Senate, to confirm Garland. All of Obama's "attack tweets" (13 percent of all tweets) focused on policy, criticizing Republican Senate leaders, though rarely by name, for refusing to consider Garland's nomination. Here is an example: "Senate leaders are continuing to obstruct a fair hearing for Judge Garland – help put the pressure on" (May 17, 2016). Because the seat was still open when Trump became president, he also had the chance to nominate a new justice, but this was the focus of only five of his 1,290 tweets during this time, presumably because his nominee was quickly confirmed by a slim Senate majority.

The second most frequent topic of Obama's policy-oriented tweets was climate change and energy; about 16 percent had to do with this issue. Another 10 percent referred to the economy. The remaining policy issues cited in at least twenty of Obama's tweets were guns and crime, women's rights, energy, and LGBT rights. Health care ran slightly behind. For Trump, the top three topics were foreign policy and defense (10.5 percent of all tweets), the economy (7 percent), and health care (5 percent). Immigration and guns and crime were mentioned much less often. Trump never tweeted about women's, LGBT, or African American rights or labor issues.

By tweeting so seldom about policy issues, President Trump lost a major opportunity to communicate with citizens about the policies his administration claimed to be promoting. In an especially vivid example, the White House announced that it would devote the month of June 2017 to four specific administration priorities:

energy, infrastructure, technology, and workforce development. As *Washington Post* reporter Philip Bump showed, it appears that President Trump didn't get the memo. Just 7 percent of the president's 163 tweets during those four weeks focused on the "topic of the week." The high point of the president's on-message tweeting came during "Infrastructure Week," when 19 percent of his tweets were on that subject. But during Workforce Development Week, only 6 percent of the president's tweets referred to that theme, none at all did on technology during Technology Week, and only 8 percent on energy did during Energy Week.[55] Instead, during Infrastructure Week Trump tweeted criticisms of his own Justice Department, and during Made in America Week he tweeted that he had the power to pardon himself if indicted by a special prosecutor.[56]

If not his policy proposals, then what *did* President Trump tweet about? A quarter of his tweets announced events happening at the White House or on his trips. These tended to follow a pattern, beginning with "I had the great honor of meeting with ____ today" or "Just landed in ____," or "Thanks to the people of ____ for a great visit!", accompanied by an official photo. In contrast, only 8 percent of Obama's tweets dealt with events or trips.

The Trump tweets that attracted the most media and public attention, however, were those in which he attacked another individual or a group; these constituted more than a quarter of his total. The individual targets of his attacks ranged from Arnold Schwarzenegger, who succeeded Trump as the host of *The Apprentice,* to the mayor of London in the wake of a terrorist attack: "At least 7 dead and 48 wounded in terror attack and Mayor of London says there is 'no reason to be alarmed!'" (June 4, 2017). His opponent in the 2016 election, former Secretary of State Hillary Clinton, came in for frequent criticism, even though the election had long been over. An example: "HillaryClinton can illegally get the questions to the Debate & delete 33,000 emails but my son Don is being scorned by the Fake News Media?" July 16, 2017). Even many of the Trump tweets ostensibly concerned with a policy issue also attacked other political actors. On health care, for instance, Trump posted, "Next week the Senate is going to vote on legislation to save Americans from the ObamaCare DISASTER!" (July 15, 2017).

Many of these attack posts contained explicit or implied threats. After Trump's executive order banning immigrants from several Muslim-majority nations was stayed by a federal judge, the president tweeted, "The opinion of this so-called judge, which essentially takes law-enforcement away from our country, is ridiculous and will be overturned!" (February 4, 2017). Two days earlier, Trump had threatened a major university: "If U.C. Berkeley does not allow free speech and practices violence on innocent people with a different point of view – NO FEDERAL FUNDS?" (February 2, 2017). Critics of these posts complained that the president showed little respect for the limits of presidential power and the central principle of separation of powers.[57]

A large minority of these attack tweets criticized the mainstream news media, or what the president preferred to call "fake news." In two remarkable tweetstorms on this topic, Trump set his sights on CNN and MSNBC's *Morning Joe.* The retweet of the clip purporting to show Trump punching a figure whose head had been replaced with the label "CNN" was widely disseminated.[58] The network traced the original tweet to an individual with a record of racist and anti-Semitic posts.[59]

At around the same time, Trump responded to criticisms of his administration by the hosts of the news and talk show *Morning Joe,* Joe Scarborough and Mika Brzezinski, with a series of tweets calling them "psycho" and "crazy." He claimed Brzezinski had tried unsuccessfully to befriend Trump at a private event while she was "bleeding badly from a face lift." Increasingly, Trump's tweets attacked Republican leaders of Congress.

These tweets outraged not only Trump opponents but also several of his supporters. Several high-profile Republicans in Congress begged Trump to stop demeaning himself and the office.[60] The president's proclivity for tabloid feuds distracted public attention from his administration's policy efforts at a time when the Republican pledge to repeal and replace Obamacare was facing a very tight battle in Congress. One reporter described the president's tweets as "a surreal dispute featuring allegations of extortion, dueling tweets and low-rent insults that has little precedent in recent political history. With major policy battles over health care and taxation looming, Mr. Trump has devoted several days to squabbling with the stars of MSNBC's 'Morning Joe.'"[61]

These attack tweets had one advantage for Trump: as with the president's more general criticisms of the media, they generated considerable support from Trump's political base. His retweet of the CNN wrestling clip was one of his most retweeted posts ever. The policy-related post that was most frequently retweeted—in which Trump asked the House of Representatives to pass a bill increasing accountability by the Veterans Administration—gained substantially less attention from followers.[62] Trump could justifiably conclude, then, that his strongest supporters were stimulated more by his harsh attacks than by the policy issues he mentioned.

The disadvantage of this approach was that the large numbers of Americans who were not solidly in Trump's camp might view his attack tweets as inappropriate departures from the usual tone of presidential communications. In a poll in early July 2017, just 7 percent of respondents described Trump's tweets as "presidential."[63] The president tweeted in response: "My use of social media is not Presidential – it's MODERN DAY PRESIDENTIAL." But after he had been in office for six months, two-thirds of poll respondents disapproved of the president's use of Twitter.[64] The harsh and sometimes poisonous tone of his tweets displeased a large majority of citizens and several leading members of Congress, whose support would be needed to pass his administration's policies. These attack tweets also stepped on his administration's efforts to highlight those policies. In short, Trump's reliance on this recent change in media technology, which permitted him to communicate directly with tens of millions of Americans, may have pleased his most devoted followers but did little to advance his policy agenda. His tweets' content represented a lost opportunity to promote his administration's issue stands.

A CASE STUDY OF TRUMP AND THE MEDIA: THE RUSSIAN CONNECTION

One of the most bizarre episodes in a highly unconventional presidency was continuing coverage of the charges that Donald Trump's presidential campaign colluded to some degree with the government of Russia. Russian agents were found to have attacked the computer systems of the Democratic National Committee and several state governments in order to disrupt the 2016 election and defeat Democratic presidential candidate Hillary Clinton. To millennials, this may sound like an odd but minor impropriety. In historical context, it has greater significance.

For most of the twentieth century, the United States and Russia (then the Soviet Union) were bitter opponents in a "cold war" (defined by threats and espionage but little actual fighting). Until the recent rise of Al Qaeda, ISIS, and other terrorist groups, the Soviet Union was seen as the United States' greatest enemy.[65] Republican politicians in particular led periods of anti-Soviet outrage during the 1920s, the 1950s, and the 1980s.[66] At these times, even the suspicion of cooperating with Soviet interests was enough to destroy the careers of State Department officials, film scriptwriters, and others who were accused of having communist sympathies.

When the Soviet Union imploded in 1991, relations with Russia softened. The new Russian government seemed to be moving toward democracy, at least for a time, and its large population and desire for foreign investment gave Russia the appearance of a thriving business opportunity for American firms. That didn't last. Russian leader Vladimir Putin soon strengthened his iron grip on power. Under his leadership, Russia annexed Crimea, invaded Ukraine, and intervened militarily in Syria and other conflict zones. Amid widespread accusations of vote-rigging in Russian elections and harsh punishment of dissenters, hopes for democracy in Russia faded.

Yet Donald Trump held a more optimistic view of Putin's Russia. He told CNN talk show host Larry King in 2007 that Putin was "doing a great job" in rebuilding Russia.[67] As a presidential candidate in 2016, Trump publicly praised Putin's leadership. When reminded that the Russian leader had murdered opponents and journalists, Trump responded, "He's running his country, and at least he's a leader. Unlike what we have in this country."[68] Some journalists, seeking to explain Trump's unusual fondness for Putin, wondered publicly whether Trump was trying to protect and expand his business interests in Russia, though his refusal to release his income tax returns made it difficult to verify the extent of Trump's financial holdings in that nation.[69] But Trump's son told a real estate conference in 2008 that, "in terms of high-end product influx into the US, Russians make up a pretty disproportionate cross-section of a lot of our assets. . . . We see a lot of money pouring in from Russia."[70]

American intelligence agencies uncovered evidence that since the early 2000s the Russian government had used cyberattacks to try to undermine election results in France, Austria, Germany, and other democracies.[71] In June 2016, the news hit home. The *Washington Post* broke the story that agents working for the Russian government had been hacking the computer networks of the Democratic National Committee, the Republican National Committee, and some American research institutes for about a year. Days before the 2016 Democratic National Convention, the whistleblower group WikiLeaks uploaded about 20,000 DNC e-mails obtained through the Russian hacks, some of which proved embarrassing to Hillary Clinton.[72]

The Russian government used other means to affect the 2016 elections as well, according to American intelligence agencies. Russian sources planted fake news stories on social media attacking Clinton and sent these stories to voters in key swing states. Efforts to hack the voter registration rolls of at least twenty states were traced to Russian government sources, though there was no solid evidence that the hacks added or removed names from the rolls or changed any votes.[73] The National Security Administration found that Russian military intelligence cyber-attacked at least one American voting software company and tried to access data from more than 100 local American election officials right before Election Day.[74] An American intelligence report in January 2017 concluded, "We assess with high confidence that Russian President Vladimir Putin ordered an influence campaign in 2016 aimed at the US presidential election, the consistent goals of which were to undermine public faith in the US democratic process, denigrate Secretary Clinton, and harm her electability and potential presidency. We further assess Putin and the Russian Government developed a clear preference for President-elect Trump."[75]

The findings were alarming. Elections are the most basic mechanism of a democratic government. They are the means by which elected leaders are motivated to learn citizens' preferences in order to keep their jobs. Allowing foreign involvement in an election destroys this essential domestic check on leaders. If candidates can win elections, especially to the presidency, in part by pleasing foreign interests, then candidates could be induced to act on behalf of those foreign interests, even if those interests might be attempting to undermine the stability of the American economy or the international role of the United States. More fundamentally, foreign interference in domestic elections violates a nation's sovereignty, and with it, the government's claim to public legitimacy and the representation of its citizens.[76]

President Obama moved cautiously during the summer and fall of 2016 in calling out the threat of Russian interference in the presidential election, fearing to undermine citizens' confidence in the election process after candidate Trump charged that the election would be rigged in Clinton's favor. Obama waited until late December to respond with a series of modest economic sanctions against Russia. Some Obama administration officials thought that such a mild response to a threat to the nation's electoral sovereignty was insufficient.[77] But Trump considered the punishment too harsh. He had lobbied the previous summer to remove an anti-Russia plank from the Republican national platform and declared after winning the election that he would relax Obama's sanctions.[78]

In the context of the intensely partisan and polarized atmosphere surrounding the election, the startling information about the Russian hacks offered a meaty opportunity for journalists. The first victim of the controversy was Gen. Michael Flynn, who had been named as President Trump's national security advisor. When Obama announced the sanctions against Russia, the *Washington Post* later revealed, Flynn privately assured the Russian ambassador that the punishments would be reconsidered when Trump took office.[79] Flynn initially denied having done so. But because Flynn had lied to several top Trump administration officials including Vice President Mike Pence about the extent of his contacts with Russian officials, it became apparent that Flynn could be vulnerable to blackmail by Russian leaders who knew the truth. Trump fired Flynn just a month into his presidency while complaining that Flynn had been "treated very, very unfairly by the media."[80]

Extensive media coverage of the Russian hacks made it difficult for Republican congressional leaders to ignore the issue. The House and Senate Intelligence committees were pressured to hold hearings on the Trump–Russia connection. Another independent investigation was launched by the FBI, which added to the controversy. The FBI's director, James Comey, had already been under fire from Democrats for investigating Clinton's use of a private e-mail server while she was secretary of state in the Obama administration. Comey's report, issued in July 2016 at the height of the presidential nomination contest, said that although Clinton would not be charged with any offense, she had been "extremely careless" in using the server.[81] Later, just eleven days before the presidential election in November, Comey announced that new evidence had led to a re-opening of the Clinton investigation. Democrats were outraged. Comey then incurred Republican attacks when he closed the Clinton investigation a second time, only two days before Election Day. Both the FBI and congressional investigations of the Russian election hacks focused intently on Trump's role. Had candidate Trump known about Flynn's ties to Russia? Did President Trump fire Flynn to throw investigators off the trail? The president responded belligerently. Rather than blame Flynn for misleading the administration, Trump castigated journalists for reporting "fake news" and criticized members of the intelligence community for leaking information to the press. The Democrats, he claimed, were peddling the story merely as an excuse for Clinton's loss. He then charged that former President Obama had wiretapped Trump's communications during the campaign.

Trump was not deterred by a lack of evidence. Even the conservative *Wall Street Journal* editorialized about "the damage that Mr. Trump is doing to his Presidency with his seemingly endless stream of exaggerations, evidence-free accusations, implausible denials and other falsehoods." In the face of bipartisan refutation, the *Journal* continued, "the President clings to his assertion like a drunk to an empty gin bottle, rolling out his press spokesman to make more dubious claims."[82] The president's continuing misstatements, it warned, could undermine public trust in even legitimate presidential communications.

After firing Flynn, the president took other steps to contain the damage the story was causing. Comey stated that Trump advised him in February to stop any further investigation of Flynn. When Comey disregarded this "advice," the president fired Comey. The second-in-command at the Department of Justice then appointed former FBI director Robert Mueller as special counsel to continue investigating the Trump–Russian connection. The president responded with a tweetstorm including the following:

7:57 a.m. June 15, 2017: "You are witnessing the single greatest WITCH HUNT in American political history – led by some very bad and conflicted people! #MAGA"

7:53 a.m. June 16, 2017: "After 7 months of investigations & committee hearings about my 'collusion with the Russians,' nobody has been able to show any proof. Sad!"

9:07 a.m. June 16, 2017: "I am being investigated for firing the FBI Director by the man who told me to fire the FBI Director! Witch Hunt"[83]

The president's handling of the media coverage fed the controversy. He stated at various times that there was no evidence of Russian hacking, and that if there were such evidence, then it was the Obama administration's fault for failing to stop the hacking.[84] Reporters' sources conflicted as to whether Trump accepted Putin's denial of the Russian hacking. The president even proposed forming a collaborative U.S.–Russian unit on cybersecurity to guard against future election hacks, to which Republican senator Lindsey Graham responded that it was "not the dumbest idea I've ever heard, but it's pretty close. When it comes to Russia, he's got a blind spot."[85]

Coverage of the Trump–Russia story accelerated as the summer wore on and evidence of collusion became more tangible. It was the focus of the lead story in news aggregators less than a quarter of the time during the president's first 100 days, but 56 percent of the time in July 2017.[86] Journalists pursued the story that Trump's eldest son had agreed to meet Russian envoys to receive what were described as official Russian documents incriminating Clinton[87] and the follow-up that the president had written his son's statement falsely claiming that the meeting had been about Russian adoptions.[88]

A narrative with constant revelations, featuring drama, conflict, and individual protagonists, would have generated immense media coverage under any circumstances. But Trump's cultivation of an intensely hostile relationship with the news media constituted a particular challenge to journalists to ferret out the truth. The president's frequent misstatements, his characterization of the investigation as a media "witch hunt," and his threats to fire the special counsel investigating him[89] elevated a click-worthy story to an epic news event.

CONCLUSION: TRUMP'S TIGHTROPE

Media coverage of President Trump's relationship with Russian leaders demonstrates the high stakes involved in a president's news coverage. National media could not have avoided airing this story extensively because it fits the prevailing definition of news so well. The drama inherent in a president's son meeting with envoys of a traditional enemy power to receive dirt on the opposition candidate, combined with the conflicting stories told by top administration officials, led some writers to describe the events as a "Category 5 hurricane" and a White House "thrust into chaos."[90]

Yet the story led to more than just audiences for advertisers. The front-page coverage of Trump's relationship with Russia, fed by his own hostile interaction with the news media, led journalists to uncover lies by the chief executive and his appointees and information about his financial holdings that Trump had tried to keep private. It also prompted investigations by congressional committees and a special counsel that could potentially lead to the president's impeachment. It is hard to imagine a more consequential line of media coverage. Clearly, presidents' media coverage can enhance their influence by signaling to their supporters which attitudes are appropriate. As Figure 10.2 shows, Putin's approval rating was seriously under water among Republicans in 2014; he had a negative approval rating of 66 points below zero. By Election Day 2016, Republican identifiers' attitudes toward Putin had improved by a remarkable 56 points, to an almost-neutral approval rating of –10. Democrats' attitudes toward Putin became slightly more negative during this time.

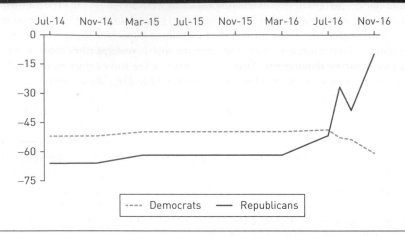

FIGURE 10.2 ■ Vladimir Putin's Net Favorability by Party, 2014–2016

Source: YouGov/Economist polling, 2014–2016; see https://today.yougov.com/publicopinion/archive.

Putin did not change between 2014 and 2016. But when Republican identifiers had learned that Donald Trump thought highly of the Russian leader, their attitudes toward Putin warmed considerably. With the exception of those attending his campaign rallies, Republicans learned of Trump's high regard for Putin through media coverage and Trump's own use of social media. Americans' attitudes toward Putin would not seem to be easy to change, especially because Republican identifiers come disproportionately from the age groups that had experienced the Cold War. Nevertheless, in a relatively short time, Trump's partisans moved from highly negative attitudes toward Putin to near neutrality. People's opinions on this issue closely reflected their partisanship.[91] The polarization of recent American politics has encouraged partisans to take their attitudinal cues from their party's leaders.[92] These cues are transmitted largely through media coverage.

On the other hand, Trump's handling of the Russian issue indicated the problems presidents face when they declare war on the journalists covering them. Although Trump's war with the mainstream media made some strategic sense by appealing to his base and other voters dissatisfied with politics as usual,[93] the president might have as easily advanced other issues—abortion, for instance—on which his most fervent supporters were more enthusiastic than on cooperation with Russia, to maintain ties with his base. Yet at times when it would have been prudent to steer media coverage into areas where the administration was more sure-footed, the president kept tweeting about Russia. Trump's inability to let go of a topic on which he had been criticized had the effect of prolonging media and public attention to his administration's weak points: organizational chaos, efforts to mislead journalists and the public, and a president whose lack of diplomatic experience allowed him to ignore international realities in the face of possible profit.

Perhaps the only saving grace for President Trump was that except for wars, most foreign policy issues do not generate intense public interest. Polls did reflect rising public interest; a Harvard–Harris poll taken at the height of the controversy found that 58 percent of respondents expressed concern about Trump's relationship with Russia, and 73 percent agreed that the investigations of that relationship were interfering with Congress's ability to deal with more important issues, such as the economy.[94] But because economic and domestic social concerns carry more weight with most survey respondents, Trump's handling of the Russia story would probably affect his standing with voters less than would his difficulty in getting health care legislation passed.

The president's use of social media did not always serve his interests either. Trump relied on his most potent media tool, Twitter, almost as often to carry on personal feuds and attacks against individuals and groups he disliked as to promote the policies his administration was trying to sell. Social media are a highly valuable communications tool for political leaders, and Trump's habit of tweeting in the early morning hours, so that journalists began their workday confronted with his latest posts, gave him the opportunity to set the agenda for news coverage for the rest of the day. It was a surprising choice for a president to squander that useful tool on what often were petty aggravations.

Journalists perform a vital role as watchdog on presidential power. A president's followers may cry "sour grapes" when reporters distribute information that could potentially damage his approval rating. Presidents, of course, want journalists to tell the president's side of the story: to persuade readers and viewers that the president's decisions warrant public approval and reelection. And media people are drawn to covering presidents because they are an attractive lure for audiences. Journalists emphasize the drama and controversy of a presidential administration because that is what their viewers and readers seek.

Yet journalists' desire for audiences can lead them to a higher goal. In looking for drama and controversy, journalists have the motivation—their financial survival as media businesses—to bring forward facts that presidents prefer not to emphasize. As one journalist wrote, in expressing concern that President Trump is "excoriat[ing] reporters for committing journalism," "for all our failings, journalism remains an indispensable constraint on power."[95] This inevitable push and pull between presidents and the media may make some citizens uneasy who would prefer to see the nation speak with a single voice. But if journalists' role is to do no more than serve as a mouthpiece for an administration's preferred views, then citizens will lack the information they need to hold their government accountable. The price of a compliant press, as the early Thomas Jefferson realized, would be the loss of a democratic system.

NOTES

1. Thomas Jefferson, letter to Archibald Stuart, 1799.
2. Jefferson, letter to John Norvell, 1807.
3. See, for example, Thomas E. Mann and Norman J. Ornstein, *The Broken Branch* (Oxford: Oxford University Press, 2006), chap. 2.
4. Julia Azari, "Trump Is a 19th-Century President Facing 21st-Century Problems," *Fivethirtyeight.com*, August 28, 2017.

5. See George C. Edwards III, *On Deaf Ears* (New Haven, CT: Yale University Press, 2003); Brandice Canes-Wrone, "The President's Legislative Influence from Public Appeals," *American Journal of Political Science* 45 (April 2001): 313–329; and Andrew W. Barrett, "Press Coverage of Legislative Appeals by the President," *Political Research Quarterly* 60 (December 2007): 655–668.

6. Richard E. Neustadt, *Presidential Power and the Modern Presidents* (New York: Free Press, 1991).

7. Presidents could also exert power through leadership of their party, but presidents differ in the extent to which they serve as party leaders. See Marjorie Randon Hershey, *Party Politics in America*, 17th ed. (New York: Routledge, 2017), chap. 14.

8. For instance, see Elmer E. Cornwell Jr., "The President and the Press," *Annals of the American Academy of Political and Social Science* 427 (September 1976): 53.

9. On mandates, see Julia R. Azari, *Delivering the People's Message* (Ithaca, NY: Cornell University Press, 2014) and Marjorie Randon Hershey, "The Meaning of a Mandate," *Polity* 27 (Winter, 1995): 225–254.

10. Markus Prior, *Post-Broadcast Democracy* (Princeton, NJ: Princeton University Press, 2007).

11. The classic is Herbert J. Gans, *Deciding What's News: 25th Anniversary Edition* (Evanston, IL: Northwestern University Press, 2004).

12. Bill Adair, founder of PolitiFact, quoted by Benjamin Mullin, "What Causes Fake News, and What Are Its Solutions?" May 4, 2017, http://www.poynter.org/2017/what-causes-fake-news-and-what-are-its-solutions-journalists-from-npr-politifact-and-cnn-weigh-in/458582/.

13. Gans, *Deciding What's News*, 9.

14. See Diana C. Mutz, *In-Your-Face Politics* (Princeton, NJ: Princeton University Press, 2015).

15. Theodore H. White's *The Making of the President* series, beginning with his *The Making of the President 1960* (New York: Atheneum House, 1961), demonstrated that well-written reports of candidates' campaign strategies could attract a substantial audience.

16. Timothy E. Cook and Lyn Ragsdale, "The President and the Press," in Michael Nelson, ed., *The Presidency and the Political System*, 5th ed. (Washington, DC: CQ Press, 1998), 332–333.

17. Christopher H. Achen and Larry M. Bartels, *Democracy for Realists* (Princeton, NJ: Princeton University Press, 2016).

18. See Jack Shafer, "Trump Is Making Journalism Great Again," *Politico,* January 16, 2017, http://www.politico.com/magazine/story/2017/01/trump-is-making-journalism-great-again-214638.

19. Lawrence R. Jacobs, "The Presidency and the Press," in Michael Nelson, ed., *The Presidency and the Political System*, 9th ed. (Washington, DC: CQ Press, 2010), 236.

20. David H. Weaver and G. Cleveland Wilhoit, *The American Journalist in the 1990s* (Mahwah, NJ: Lawrence Erlbaum Associates, 1996), chap. 4.

21. Quoted in "New York Times' Executive Editor on the New Terrain of Covering Trump," "Fresh Air," December 8, 2016, http://www.npr.org/2016/12/08/504806512/new-york-times-executive-editor-on-the-new-terrain-of-covering-trump.

22. Glenn Thrush and Michael M. Grynbaum, "Trump Ruled the Tabloid Media," *New York Times*, February 26, 2017, A1.

23. "New York Times' Executive Editor on the New Terrain."
24. Rebecca Riffkin, "Americans' Trust in Media Remains at Historical Low," Gallup Poll, September 28, 2015, http://www.gallup.com/poll/185927/americans-trust-media-remains-historical-low.aspx.
25. See Jonathan McDonald Ladd, "The Role of Media Distrust in Partisan Voting," *Political Behavior* 32 (December, 2010): 567–585.
26. Dylan Byers, "The Media Unload on Trump," CNN Politics, December 10, 2015, http://www.cnn.com/2015/12/10/politics/donald-trump-media-backlash/index.html.
27. Bump, "The White House."
28. Mark Landler and Maggie Haberman, "Trump Again Blames Media in U.S. Divide," *New York Times*, August 23, 2017, A1.
29. Manuel Roig-Franzia and Paul Farhi, "Breitbart," *Boston Globe*, February 19, 2017, https://www.bostonglobe.com/news/nation/2017/02/19/breitbart-new-force-trump-era/3UgdNiS0LzSum1kZWIEX2N/story.html.
30. Pamela Engel, "Donald Trump Vows to Rewrite Libel Laws to Make It Easier to Sue the Media," *Business Insider*, February 26, 2017, http://www.businessinsider.com/donald-trump-libel-laws-sue-media-2016-2.
31. Callum Borchers, "Rachel Maddow's Urgent Warning to the Rest of the Media," *Washington Post*, July 7, 2017, https://www.washingtonpost.com/news/the-fix/wp/2017/07/07/rachel-maddows-urgent-warning-to-the-rest-of-the-media/.
32. Michael M. Grynbaum, Sydney Ember, and Charlie Savage, "Trump's Urging That Comey Jail Reporters Is Denounced as an 'Act of Intimidation,'" *New York Times*, May 18, 2017, A13.
33. Allan Smith, "Trump Goes Off Script During Coast Guard Commencement Speech," *Business Insider*, May 17, 2017, http://www.businessinsider.com/trump-coast-guard-speech-2017-5.
34. Reported in Michael M. Grynbaum, "Latest Bout with Media, Conjures Physical Fight with a Foe," *New York Times*, July 3, 2017, A10.
35. "All Statements from Donald Trump," Politifact.com, http://www.politifact.com/personalities/donald-trump/statements/?list=speaker.
36. See Marjorie Randon Hershey, "The Media," in Michael E. Nelson, ed., *The Elections of 2016* (Washington, DC: CQ Press, 2017): 121–123.
37. Ryan Lizza, quoted in Byers, "The Media Unload on Trump."
38. Chris Agee, "Mass Media in Crisis," *Western Journalism*, January 25, 2017, http://www.westernjournalism.com/mass-media-in-crisis-trumps-war-with-the-press/.
39. See Hershey, ""The Media: Covering Donald Trump," 115–120.
40. "Are Trump and the Media Enemies or Frenemies?" July 5, 2017, https://fivethirtyeight.com/features/are-trump-and-the-media-enemies-or-frenemies/?ex_cid=politicsnewsletter.
41. Survey Monkey poll reported in Mike Allen, "Exclusive: Astonishing Poll about Trump and Media," *Axios,* July 4, 2017, https://www.axios.com/exclusive-astonishing-poll-about-trump-and-media-2453120782.html.
42. Jonathan Lemire, "Trump's Unprecedented Hands-on Messaging Carries Risks," *Las Vegas Sun*, August 6, 2017, https://lasvegassun.com/news/2017/aug/06/trumps-unprecedented-hands-on-messaging-carries-ri/.
43. Heidi N. Moore, "Scaramucci Learned His Press Tactics from Wall Street," *Washington Post*, July 30, 2017, https://www.washingtonpost.com/outlook/scaramucci-learned-his-press-tactics-from-wall-street-theyll-only-get-uglier/.

44. See Timothy E. Cook, *Governing with the News* (Chicago: University of Chicago Press, 1998), chaps. 2 and 3.

45. See, for instance, Jeffrey S. Peake and Matthew Eshbaugh-Soha, "The Agenda-Setting Impact of Major Presidential TV Addresses," *Political Communication* 25, no. 2 (2008): 113–137.

46. D. M. Ryfe, "Franklin Roosevelt and the Fireside Chats," *Journal of Communication* 49, no. 4 (December 1999): 80–103.

47. Susan Milligan, "The President and the Press," *Columbia Journalism Review*, (March/April 2015), https://www.cjr.org/analysis/the_president_and_the_press.php.

48. Mike Isaac and Sydney Ember, "For Election Day Chatter, Twitter Still Dominated Its Social Media Peers," *New York Times*, November 9, 2016, B3.

49. Actually, Twitter reported Trump as having 33 million followers at that time.

50. Amanda Hess, quoted in Melody Kramer, "Here's How to Cover President Trump's Tweets," February 8, 2017, http://www.poynter.org/2017/heres-how-news-organizations-should-cover-president-trumps-tweets/448160/.

51. As reported by Twitter.com.

52. "Did President Trump's Twitter Account Gain Five Million New Bot Followers in Three Days?" Snopes.com, May 31, 2017, http://www.snopes.com/trump-new-bot-followers/.

53. Newspaper subscription data from Pew Research Center in Michael Barthel, "Despite Subscription Surges for Largest U.S. Newspapers, Circulation and Revenue Fall for Industry Overall," June 1, 2017, http://www.pewresearch.org/fact-tank/2017/06/01/circulation-and-revenue-fall-for-newspaper-industry/.

54. I compared President Trump's primary twitter outlet, @realDonaldTrump, with the handle President Obama used most frequently in 2016: @Barackobama. Both presidents also had official "POTUS" handles, but neither of those was as widely used or followed. The time period for both was the period from February 1 until August 31 in 2016, for Obama, and 2017, for Trump.

55. Philip Bump, "The White House Had a Coordinated Message This Month," *Washington Post*, July 3, 2017, https://www.washingtonpost.com/news/politics/wp/2017/06/30/the-white-house-had-a-coordinated-message-this-month-trump-didnt/?utm_term=.4c3a2619cc97.

56. Gregory Korte, "Trump Often Subverts Own Agenda," *USA Today*, August 28, 2017, 3B.

57. Nina Totenberg, "Trump's Criticism of Judges Out of Line with Past Presidents," *Weekend Edition Saturday*, February 11, 2017, http://www.npr.org/2017/02/11/514587731/trumps-criticism-of-judges-out-of-line-with-past-presidents.

58. Alicia Cohn, "Trump Takes Down CNN in WWE Fight Video," *The Hill*, July 2, 2017, http://thehill.com/homenews/administration/340417-trump-takes-down-cnn-in-mock-wrestling-video.

59. Chris Bell, "Trump Gif Maker Apologises for Racist Posts," BBC News, July 6, 2017, http://www.bbc.com/news/blogs-trending-40504203.

60. Brian Bennett, "'This Has to Stop,'" *Los Angeles Times*, June 29, 2017, http://www.latimes.com/politics/la-na-pol-trump-mika-tweets-20170629-story.html.

61. Michael M. Grynbaum, "The Battle of 'Morning Joe,'" *New York Times*, July 1, 2017, A1.

62. Paul Singer, "'Fake News,' by Far, Is at the Top of Trump's Twitter Feed," *USA Today*, July 3, 2017, A1.

63. "Most Americans Disapprove of Trump's Twitter Use," July 12, 2017, https://www
.surveymonkey.com/blog/2017/07/12/americans-disapprove-trumps-twitter-use/.

64. ABC/*Washington Post* poll reported in Philip Bump, "Trump and His Base Live
in a Bubble Where He's Popular and All Is Well," *Washington Post*, July 17, 2017,
https://www.washingtonpost.com/news/politics/wp/2017/07/17/trump-and-his-
base-live-in-a-bubble-where-hes-popular-and-all-is-well/.

65. See, for instance, U.S. Department of State Archive, "United States Relations with
Russia: The Cold War," https://2001-2009.state.gov/r/pa/ho/pubs/fs/85895.htm.

66. James Goldgeier, "Republicans Used to Compare Talking to Moscow to Talking to
Hitler," *Washington Post*, July 17, 2017, https://www.washingtonpost.com/news/
monkey-cage/wp/2017/07/17/republicans-used-to-compare-talking-to-moscow-
to-talking-to-hitler-trumps-startling-new-tweet-shows-thats-changed/.

67. Jeremy Diamond, "Timeline: Donald Trump's Praise for Vladimir Putin," CNN
Politics, July 29, 2016, http://www.cnn.com/2016/07/28/politics/donald-trump-
vladimir-putin-quotes/index.html.

68. *Morning Joe*, December 18, 2015.

69. Josh Rogin, "Trump's Long Romance with Russia," *Bloomberg View*, March 15, 2016,
https://www.bloomberg.com/view/articles/2016-03-15/trump-s-long-romance-
with-russia.

70. Philip Bump, "Trump's Long History of Seeking a Politically Inconvenient Business
Deal in Russia," *Washington Post*, August 29, 2017, https://www.washingtonpost
.com/news/politics/wp/2017/08/28/trumps-long-history-of-seeking-a-politically-
inconvenient-business-deal-in-russia/.

71. Emma Jacobs, "In Europe, Accusations of Russian Meddling in Elections Come as
No Surprise," Public Radio International, April 19, 2017, https://www.pri.org/sto-
ries/2017-04-19/europe-accusations-russian-meddling-elections-come-no-surprise.

72. Greg Miller, Ellen Nakashima, and Adam Entous, "Obama's Secret Struggle to Punish
Russia for Putin's Election Assault," *Washington Post*, June 23, 2017, http://www
.washingtonpost.com/graphics/2017/world/national-security/obama-putin-elec
tion-hacking/.

73. Mike Levine and Pierre Thomas, "Russian Hackers Targeted Nearly Half of
States' Voter Registration Systems," *ABC News*, September 29, 2016, http://abc
news.go.com/US/russian-hackers-targeted-half-states-voter-registration-systems/
story?id=42435822.

74. Philip Bump, "Here's the Public Evidence That Supports the Idea That Russia
Interfered in the 2016 Election," *Washington Post*, July 6, 2017, https://www.wash
ingtonpost.com/news/politics/wp/2017/07/06/heres-the-public-evidence-that-
supports-the-idea-that-russia-interfered-in-the-2016-election/.

75. Office of the Director of National Intelligence and National Intelligence Council,
"Background to 'Assessing Russian Activities in Recent US Elections,'" January 6,
2016, 11.

76. Thanks to Jennifer Nicoll Victor for this point.

77. Miller, Nakashima, and Entous, "Obama's Secret Struggle."

78. Peter Nicholas, Paul Beckett, and Gerald F. Seib, "Trump Open to Shift on Russia
Sanctions, 'One China' Policy," *Wall Street Journal*, January 13, 2017, https://www
.wsj.com/articles/donald-trump-sets-a-bar-for-russia-and-china-1484360380.

79. Greg Miller, Adam Entous, and Ellen Nakashima, "National Security Adviser
Flynn Discussed Sanctions with Russian Ambassador, Despite Denials, Officials

Say," *Washington Post*, February 9, 2017, https://www.washingtonpost.com/world/national-security/national-security-adviser-flynn-discussed-sanctions-with-russian-ambassador-despite-denials-officials-say/2017/02/09/f85b29d6-ee11-11e6-b4ff-ac2cf509efe5_story.html?utm_term=.7981832cd8f3.

80. David Lauter, "What You Need to Know about the Firing of Michael Flynn and Why It Matters for Trump," *Los Angeles Times*, February 15, 2017, http://www.latimes.com/politics/la-na-pol-trump-flynn-questions-20170215-story.html.

81. Michael S. Schmidt and Eric Lichtblau, "Public Scolding of Clinton Fits a Pattern of Taking on Power," *New York Times*, July 6, 2016, A1.

82. "A President's Credibility," *Wall Street Journal*, March 21, 2017, https://www.wsj.com/articles/a-presidents-credibility-1490138920.

83. After Trump's son Donald Jr. admitted meeting with people connected to the Russian government to get negative information about Hillary Clinton (described later in the chapter), Trump raised that to "This is the greatest Witch Hunt in political history. Sad." (on July 11, 2017)

84. Bump, "Here's the Public Evidence."

85. Philip Rucker and David A. Fahrenthold, "Trump Vows to 'Move Forward in Working Constructively with Russia' after Putin Denied Election Hacking," *Washington Post*, July 9, 2017, https://www.washingtonpost.com/news/post-politics/wp/2017/07/09/trump-vows-to-move-forward-in-working-constructively-with-russia-after-putin-denied-election-hacking/?utm_term=.810ae956f20f.

86. Nate Silver, "Trump and Congress Are Probably on a Collision Course over Russia," *Fivethirtyeight.com*, July 26, 2017, https://fivethirtyeight.com/features/trump-and-congress-are-probably-on-a-collision-course-over-russia/?ex_cid=SigDig.

87. Dan Balz, "A Revelation Unlike Any Other in the Russia investigation," *Washington Post*, July 12, 2017, A1.

88. Ashley Parker, Carol D. Leonnig, Philip Rucker, and Tom Hamburger, "Trump Dictated Son's Misleading Statement on Meeting with Russian Lawyer," *Washington Post*, July 31, 2017, A1.

89. Robert A. Graham, "When Will President Trump Fire Robert Mueller?" *The Atlantic*, July 21, 2017, https://www.theatlantic.com/politics/archive/2017/07/when-will-president-trump-fire-robert-mueller/534459/.

90. Philip Rucker and Ashley Parker, "White House under Siege by Trump Jr's Russia Revelations," *The Day*, July 12, 2017, http://www.theday.com/article/20170711/NWS13/170719816/.

91. Scott Clement and Dan Balz, "Poll Finds Trump's Standing Weakened since Springtime," *Washington Post*, July 16, 2017, A1.

92. See, for example, Steven E. Schier and Todd E. Eberly, *Polarized* (Lanham, MD: Rowman & Littlefield, 2016).

93. See, for example, Marc J. Hetherington, "The Election," in Michael Nelson, ed., *The Elections of 2016* (Washington, DC: CQ Press, 2017), chap. 3.

94. Mike Lillis, "Dems Push Leaders to Talk Less about Russia," *The Hill*, June 24, 2017, http://thehill.com/homenews/campaign/339248-dems-push-leaders-to-talk-less-about-russia.

95. Nicholas Kristof, "We're Journalists, Not the Enemy," *New York Times*, August 24, 2017, A23.

11

THE PRESIDENCY AND INTEREST GROUPS

Allies, Adversaries, and Policy Leadership

Daniel J. Tichenor

Images of presidents are prominent in American iconography—think of memorials such as the Washington Monument and Mount Rushmore or of the faces of presidents on coins and currency. Interest groups inhabit a less favored place in American popular culture. Political candidates brand each other, not themselves, as "tools" of the "special interests." Yet because interest groups have political resources that presidents need if they are to govern successfully in the domain of domestic policy, no president can avoid developing relationships with many of these groups. As Daniel J. Tichenor uses historical evidence to show, one key variable affecting president–interest group relations is whether organized interests are affiliated or unaffiliated with the president's political party. A second is whether historical circumstances have granted the president a broad or narrow capacity to exercise policy leadership. The four possible combinations of answers to these two questions range from the highly productive "collaborative breakthrough politics" to the stagnant "adversarial politics-as-usual."

Although Donald Trump broke nearly all the rules in his polarizing and iconoclastic 2016 campaign, he followed a familiar script employed by nearly every
presidential candidate of the modern era when it came to the subject of interest
groups and influential donors. Like previous White House contenders, he vigorously pledged to wage war on powerful interest groups and well-heeled lobbyists
in the nation's capital. To the cheers of rapturous crowds, Trump promised in the
final weeks of the election that he would not let "the Clinton Cartel run this government" and that that he would "drain the swamp in Washington, D.C.," a phrase
that Ronald Reagan made popular decades before.[1] Generations of presidential
candidates across the political spectrum have gotten good political mileage from
telling appreciative voters that the interests of ordinary citizens must be defended
against the welter of Washington lobbying groups that bedevil good government.

Powerful corporations, business lobbies, and Wall Street were a special target of
Trump's ire on the campaign trail as he advocated economic populism. One notable Trump ad run just before the election flashed images of the New York Stock
Exchange and the investment bank Goldman Sachs as the candidate railed against
economic interests "that have robbed our working class, stripped our country of its
wealth, and put that money into the pockets of a handful of large corporations."[2]
Strikingly consistent with lobbying and ethics reforms proposed by Barack Obama
in previous elections, the Trump campaign in October 2016 called for new bans
on lobbying by former government officials and campaign finance restraints on
foreign agents.[3] Trump also reminded voters that his significant wealth set him
apart from all other presidential hopefuls because he could self-finance his campaign and thereby was beholden to no one. As he fittingly tweeted: "Remember, I
am self-funding my campaign, the only one in either party. I'm not controlled by
lobbyists or special interests—only the U.S.A.!"[4] Only a few days after taking the
oath of office, President Trump issued an executive order that he described as an
unprecedented "lobbying ban" that prevented officials from lobbying the agency
they worked in for five years after leaving government service.[5]

What Trump aides failed to acknowledge is that the same order actually removed
key restrictions on lobbyists entering the new administration. In 2009, President
Obama banned people who were registered lobbyists in the preceding year from
taking executive branch jobs. Trump's order revoked this ban. Less than six months
into office, watchdog groups and journalists reported that seventy-four recently
registered lobbyists assumed positions in the new administration, and that forty-
nine of them worked for the very same agencies they used to lobby.[6] After disparaging Wall Street and big corporations for "getting away with murder" during the
election, Trump filled his Cabinet and other administration posts with prominent
business leaders and Wall Street insiders, including many former Goldman Sachs
executives. Instead of breaking up big banks as he promised on the campaign trail,
the early days of the Trump administration emphasized rolling back regulations
on investors and Wall Street, as well as promises of major corporate tax cuts; these
developments led one investment executive to declare in the spring of 2017 that
"the Goldman Sachs faction in the White House has won."[7] The new administration also broke with its predecessor by refusing to disclose logs of those who visit
the 18-acre White House complex; instead visitor logs are to be kept secret until at

least five years after Trump leaves office.[8] Among numerous ethical and transparency concerns, good government groups further warn that President Trump has maintained little separation while in office from hundreds of his own international business holdings that present significant conflicts of interest.[9]

Trump also established an unusually large network of advisory committees comprised mostly of business executives and personal allies to develop policies outside government on issues ranging from infrastructure upgrades to environmental controls. Although other presidents have used advisory groups for various purposes, Trump's groups have drawn lawsuits for ignoring legal requirements to disclose the names of all their members, open their meetings, and release their work-related documents.[10] Moreover, like nearly all modern presidents including Obama, Trump has not hesitated to issue executive orders to shape policy outcomes favored by some of his party's strongest interest group allies and to hold numerous meetings with supportive organized interests. The attention that Trump, again like Obama before him, has devoted to organized interests and lobbying groups underscores a basic fact of contemporary American political life: the national interest group system is as much a fixture in Washington as the modern presidency. Both were born in the protean decades of the early twentieth century, and their relationship to one another has often been uneasy, contentious, and inevitable.

At first blush, modern chief executives appear to have ample incentive to keep their distance from organized interests. Although millions of ordinary citizens either belong to or contribute to various interest groups, most Americans view organized interests in national politics with a level of contempt and suspicion not unlike that of the Constitution's wary architects.[11] As the only officials elected by the entire nation, modern presidents often have cast themselves as guardians of the common good against a host of selfish vested interests. "Fifteen million people in the United States are represented by lobbyists," Harry Truman was fond of saying. "The other 150 million have only one man who is elected at large to represent them—that is, the President of the United States."[12] Likewise, administrations that seem too closely aligned with particular groups risk being charged with serving special interests, as President George W. Bush learned early in his first term when his stands on issues such as Arctic drilling, arsenic levels in drinking water, and global warming provoked criticism that he was cozying up to well-heeled corporate powers.[13] Presidential wariness of organized interests is accentuated by the fact that entrenched Washington lobbies routinely frustrate the president's programmatic goals.

For their part, interest groups would appear to have good reason to concentrate their energies on government institutions other than the presidency. Members of Congress and federal bureaucrats typically enjoy long tenures in office, but a president's hold on power is comparatively brief. The average tenure of postwar presidents has been just over six years. Furthermore, gaining access to the White House can be a tall order for a lobbyist because of the severe constraints on the time and attention of presidents and their advisers. In contrast, the size and specialized work of Congress and the federal agencies make them more accessible to interest groups. As one political insider put it, "There are 535 opportunities in Congress and only one in the White House. Where would you put your effort?"[14] In short, interest group relationships with members of Congress and federal bureaucrats are likely to be longer lasting and more reliable than those with presidents and their top aides.

Despite these significant disincentives to close relations between presidents and interest groups, rarely can either disregard the other. Indeed, they do so at their political peril. Organized interests are crucial elements of presidents' electoral coalitions. In an era of candidate-centered campaigns, interest groups provide money, organizational support, and votes for presidential hopefuls during their primary and general election bids.[15] Once in office, modern presidents largely stake their claims as successful leaders on whether they can build supportive coalitions for their policies with any regularity. Along with political parties, organized interests can offer the White House a potent and efficient means of expanding support for the president's agenda in Congress and other venues. Presidents must also consider, however, that interest groups can just as surely serve as sources of mobilized opposition.

In turn, interest groups cannot ignore the enormous power that modern executives wield in agenda setting, policy formation, budget making, and policy implementation. Presidents can even alter the prevailing interest group system. They can encourage the creation of new organized interests, actively work to demobilize others, and influence how interest groups frame their preferences in the first place.[16] In short, the modern presidency presents interest groups with significant opportunities and constraints. Whether as allies or as rivals, policy-minded presidents and interest groups cannot discount each other in a political system constitutionally designed with the imperative that "ambition must be made to counteract ambition."[17]

One of the most revealing views of the relationship between national interest groups and the White House is provided by their interactions in domestic policymaking. In the next section, I present a theoretical model of president–interest group relations based on the disposition of organized interests toward the president's party (affiliated versus unaffiliated) and on the relative capacities of different presidents to exercise policy leadership in varying historical circumstances (broad versus narrow). From this model, I derive four distinctive forms of president–interest group interaction: collaborative breakthrough politics, adversarial breakthrough politics, collaborative politics-as-usual, and adversarial politics-as-usual. In the rest of the chapter I offer case studies that illuminate each type of interactive politics.

As we shall see, collaboration with the president is frequently less rewarding (and opposition more beneficial) for interest groups than is commonly presumed. Indeed, opposing groups sometimes translate White House antagonism into new sources of organizational vitality. At the same time, modern executives have good reason to frustrate the policy ambitions of even their strongest interest group allies. Presidents often find that the national interest group system can pose major extraconstitutional impediments to their programmatic goals, compounding the challenges of policy leadership in a political system replete with barriers to change. It is little wonder that tensions and resentments abound in president–interest group interactions concerning domestic policymaking, with each side prone to blame the other for lost opportunities.

FRIENDS, FOES, AND POLICY LEADERSHIP: A FRAMEWORK OF PRESIDENT–INTEREST GROUP RELATIONS

The first decades of the twentieth century witnessed an evolution in the presidency that tied executive authority and power to previously scorned forms of rhetorical leadership.[18] During the same period, an unprecedented number and variety of organized interests became actively engaged in Washington lobbying.[19] As Figure 11.1 illustrates, never before had so many organized interests attempted to influence federal policymaking. Conflict and ambivalence characterized modern president–interest group relations from the start. Early activists such as Theodore Roosevelt and Woodrow Wilson frequently warned the public of the sinister influence of organized interests in national politics and spoke eloquently of the president's duty to champion the public good. "The business of government is to organize the common interest against the special interest," Wilson told appreciative voters.[20] Both Roosevelt and Wilson, however, found it difficult to ignore organized interests that could help them govern. During his second term, Roosevelt confided to a close friend that his principled refusal to nurture relationships with corporate interests made leadership challenging. "I am genuinely independent of the big monied men in all matters where I think the interests of the public are concerned," he noted. "But . . . it is out of the question for me to expect them to grant favors to me in return. The sum of this is that I can make no private or special appeals to them, and I am at my wits' end how to proceed."[21] Wilson's administration, by contrast, nurtured close working relationships with business and labor groups during World War I to coordinate industrial production. As the political scientist E. Pendleton Herring observed soon after the war, "In mobilizing the full strength of the country these special interest units gave the government cohesive and responsible organizations with which to deal."[22]

Likewise, more than a few organized interests during the Progressive Era perceived the rise of the modern presidency as a potentially important opportunity to advance their agendas. Consider, for example, the considerable energy and resources that woman suffrage groups such as the National American Woman Suffrage Association and the Congressional Union focused on winning White House support in the 1910s. Inspired by Roosevelt's transformation of the presidency into a "popular steward" of the people, suffragists saw the executive office as a new source of policy dynamism in an often staid American polity. "We knew that [the presidency], and perhaps it alone, would ensure our success," suffragist leader Alice Paul later explained.[23] Wilson was hounded by suffragist groups from his first inauguration in 1913 until the waning days of his second term. Significantly, the tactics that suffragist organizations employed in their pursuit of presidential support included not just conciliatory lobbying, but also highly disruptive anti-administration protests.[24] As modern presidents and interest groups emerged as fixtures in national political life, their ability to recast each other's political calculations and policy fortunes was unmistakable.

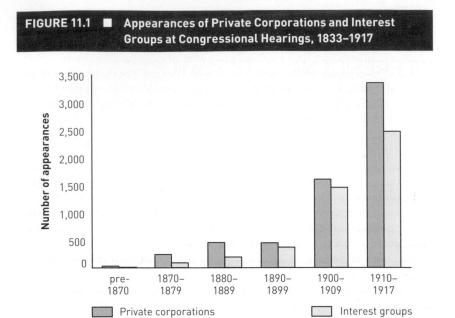

FIGURE 11.1 ■ Appearances of Private Corporations and Interest Groups at Congressional Hearings, 1833–1917

Source: Based on data created by the author from the CIS Index for Congressional Hearings, 23rd–64th Congresses (Washington, DC: U.S. Government Printing Office, 1985).

To capture president–interest group relations in their full richness and complexity would require separate accounts of how each president has dealt with interest groups. But one way to generalize about the interactions between modern presidents and interest groups—that is, to identify patterns and deduce analytical insights about their reciprocal relations—is to focus on two factors that help structure president–interest group politics: (1) the relationship of interest groups to the president's party and (2) the varying opportunities for presidential policy leadership.

It is an old saw of political science that vigorous political parties and interest groups are fundamentally at odds with one other.[25] In truth, both major American parties are linked to interest groups, and each nurtures interest group coalitions that will help its candidates win office and its officeholders govern. "Whether observed in the electoral or lobbying arenas," Mark Peterson notes, "a significant portion of the interest group community reflects ideological positions, takes stands on the issues of the day, or represents constituencies whose orientations are at least compatible with one of the two major parties."[26] While reassuring the general public of their eagerness to stand up to "special interests," modern presidents and their political advisers readily understand the importance of party-affiliated interest groups in constructing successful electoral coalitions and governing majorities. Franklin Roosevelt, for example, established mechanisms by which White House staff members could attend to the groups that made up his loose New Deal coalition, including organized labor, nationality groups, and small farmers.[27] Subsequent presidents have followed suit.[28] Naturally, not every interest group pursues access to, or an alliance with, the White House. For ideological and strategic reasons, groups unaffiliated with the president's party may advance outsider strategies such as campaigns to garner media attention and public support. For the purposes of our analytical model, the relationship of interest groups to the president's party (ranging from closely affiliated to staunchly unaffiliated) is crucial because it takes into account both collaborative and adversarial forms of interaction.

What are the implications of collaborative and adversarial relations when the opportunities for modern executives to advance their domestic policy agendas are broad or narrow? By most accounts, a few presidents have enjoyed a broad opportunity to dominate the policymaking process and to advance their agendas (breakthrough politics). Presidential scholars tend to agree that the political context was exceptionally favorable for Woodrow Wilson, Franklin Roosevelt, Lyndon Johnson, and Ronald Reagan to exercise policy leadership.[29] Most modern presidents have had to struggle with more challenging leadership circumstances in which their opportunities to reshape public policy have been relatively narrow (politics-as-usual).

As Table 11.1 illustrates, four types of interactive politics emerge when we consider together the relationship of interest groups to the president's party (affiliated or unaffiliated) and the relative capacity of a president to exercise policy leadership (broad or narrow).[30] One may predict that collaborative breakthrough politics will involve White House sponsorship and co-optation of interest group allies. When the agendas or behavior of interest groups are at odds with politically dominant presidents, these groups are likely to be marginalized.

Table 11.1 ■ Presidents and Interest Groups: A Model of Interactive Politics

	Relationship of interest groups to the president's party	
President's capacity to exercise policy leadership	Affiliated (Collaborative strategies)	Unaffiliated (Adversarial strategies)
Broad (Breakthrough politics)	Collaborative breakthrough politics *Roosevelt's New Deal for labor, Reagan and the Christian right*	Adversarial breakthrough politics *Roosevelt and the Liberty League, Reagan's assault on liberal citizens' groups*
Narrow (Politics-as-usual)	Collaborative politics-as-usual *George H. W. Bush and the Competitiveness Council, George W. Bush and air quality*	Adversarial politics-as-usual *Carter and energy reform, Clinton and health care reform*

Adversarial breakthrough politics places interest group opponents in the difficult position of challenging presidents who have enormous political capital. If these groups are politically effective, they likely will face intense White House assaults. Even when confronted by powerful White House antagonism, however, oppositional groups may find alternative sources of support in Congress or the bureaucracy because of the fragmented structure of the political system. Indeed, White House antagonism may inspire sympathy for a threatened cause that groups can use to attract new supporters and acquire fresh resources.

The dynamics of collaborative politics-as-usual can produce either weak or strong ties between presidents and the interest groups affiliated with their party. Weak alliances are likely when the president offends affiliated groups by moving toward the political center to secure policy achievements and an independent public image. Presidents who pursue this strategy may presume that, as captives of the president's party, affiliated groups have few alternatives but to maintain at least tacit support for the administration. Nevertheless, strong alliances are possible if the constrained presidents are eager to shore up support from their ideological base by pursuing the policy initiatives endorsed by affiliated interest groups. Collaborative politics-as-usual seems likely to be inhospitable to affiliated groups seeking major policy innovations but more opportune for groups satisfied with incremental policy change.

Finally, adversarial politics-as-usual predictably affords oppositional interest groups numerous chances to frustrate the policy designs of politically constrained presidents by mobilizing grassroots resistance, exploiting alliances with supporters in other branches and levels of government, and pursuing other forms of veto politics. When presidents do not dominate the policymaking process, oppositional groups will play a significant role in helping to set the public agenda and shape new policy initiatives. Under these circumstances the White House may decide to follow the lead of interest groups championing popular causes. To illuminate these distinctive patterns of interactive politics, I next examine several cases of president–interest group relations.

FRANKLIN ROOSEVELT AND INDUSTRIAL UNIONISM: COLLABORATIVE BREAKTHROUGH POLITICS I

Interest groups are attentive to new political openings for their policy goals. During the 1930s organized labor could not resist linking its fortunes to the activist presidency of Franklin Roosevelt and his ambitious New Deal agenda. Labor leaders such as John Lewis of the United Mine Workers (UMW) especially welcomed opportunities to translate New Deal legislative and administrative initiatives into growth for their unions. In particular, these labor leaders hoped to organize unskilled industrial workers who had been largely neglected by the American Federation of Labor (AFL). In 1933 the Roosevelt administration invited a large number of organized interests—including business and labor groups—to participate in drafting the National Industrial Recovery Act (NIRA). Labor activists such as W. Jett Lauck, a Lewis lieutenant, persuaded the White House to include a vague provision in NIRA, Section 7(a), that recognized the right of workers to bargain collectively. Although corporate leaders were reassured by their lawyers that the provision included no administrative mechanism for enforcement, Lauck reported to Lewis that Section 7(a) "will suit our purposes." After NIRA sailed through Congress, Lewis and other union organizers aggressively exploited the popularity of Roosevelt and NIRA to attract more miners to the UMW. "The president wants you to join the union," UMW literature and speakers told workers.[31] Tens of thousands of miners signed union cards and formed lodges with names such as New Deal and Blue Eagle. After only one year of invoking the celebrated names of Roosevelt and the New Deal, the UMW's membership rolls had swollen from 150,000 to more than 500,000.[32]

Lewis and other labor organizers orchestrated a dramatic break with the AFL in 1934, forming the Congress of Industrial Organizations (CIO) to represent millions of unskilled industrial workers.[33] Publicly, CIO leaders professed unwavering support for Roosevelt and the New Deal. In private, they noted the aloof posture that the White House assumed when Sen. Robert Wagner (D-NY) championed legislation to protect unionizing efforts. Roosevelt tepidly endorsed the Wagner Act of 1935, organized labor's Magna Carta, only at the eleventh hour.[34] Although he understood that organized labor was a crucial element of his electoral and governing coalitions, the president took pains to publicly assert his independence from both labor and business interests. During major strikes, for example, Roosevelt was known to tell reporters that labor activists "did silly things." He often sounded centrist tones in urging employers and disgruntled laborers to embrace "common sense and good order."[35]

Lewis and the CIO recognized Roosevelt's lack of enthusiasm for union radicalism but also appreciated that labor reforms such as the Wagner Act and the National Labor Relations Act were powerful catalysts for union organizing and collective bargaining. In 1936 Lewis, David Dubinsky, George Berry, Sidney Hillman, and other labor activists entered into a political marriage of convenience between the CIO and the Democratic Party to reelect Roosevelt. CIO unions contributed significant financial and logistical support to the president's reelection campaign; in fact, Lewis's UMW was the Democratic Party's largest financial benefactor in 1936. In forming the Labor Nonpartisan League, however, Lewis hoped that union votes could be marshaled in future elections to support whichever party or candidate best served the CIO's interests.[36]

After his landslide victory, it became clear that Roosevelt expected organized labor to follow his lead and not the reverse. Like other presidents who have dominated the policy process, Roosevelt intended to dictate the terms of any alliances between the White House and interest groups. Amid labor confrontations with "little steel" in 1937 and 1938, Roosevelt stunned many labor supporters with his comment on the killing of ten steelworkers who were demonstrating in Chicago against Republic Steel Corporation. Denouncing management and unions alike as sponsors of senseless violence, Roosevelt declared "a curse on both your houses." In a Labor Day radio address to millions of listeners, Lewis rebuked the president: "It ill behooves one who has supped at labor's table and who has been sheltered in labor's house to curse with equal fervor and fine impartiality both labor and its adversaries when they become locked in deadly embrace."[37] By the end of the 1930s, Lewis and a few other CIO leaders were convinced that the National Labor Relations Board (NLRB), the courts, and the White House were limiting the labor movement's larger aims. In 1940 Lewis worked in vain to derail FDR's reelection, fearing that it would bring about American entry into war and the concomitant demise of labor's agenda for progressive change. After vain efforts first to launch a third-party challenge and then to back the Republican candidate, Wendell Willkie, in the election, Lewis stepped down as CIO president.[38]

Eager to marginalize and defuse Lewis-style CIO militancy, the Roosevelt White House embraced moderate "labor statesmen" such as Sidney Hillman, president of the Amalgamated Clothing Workers of America and a founder of the CIO. Hillman, in contrast to Lewis, was an unflinching Roosevelt loyalist. He oversaw the creation of the CIO's political action committee, which further cemented the ties between organized labor and the Democratic Party.

After Pearl Harbor, wartime imperatives required extraordinary industrial production and coordination. Labor leaders such as Philip Murray, the new CIO president, and Walter Reuther of the United Auto Workers proposed "industrial councils" that would facilitate efficient wartime production while giving organized labor real influence—along with business and the government—in supervising industries and the workforce. The Roosevelt administration eschewed such ideas. In the end, the AFL, the CIO, and other unions agreed to a no-strike pledge during the war and merely hoped that the war agencies would exercise their robust power over industrial workers benevolently.[39] "Instead of an active participant in the councils of industry," historian Alan Brinkley notes, "the labor movement had become, in effect, a ward of the state."[40] As the war drew to a close, Lewis's vision of an independent labor movement engaged in militant activities was overshadowed by broad CIO and AFL support for a more conciliatory posture. Heartened by the gains and protections that unions had secured during Roosevelt's administration, leaders of organized labor pinned their hopes on a permanent alliance with the Democratic Party.

Presidents with broad opportunities to shape domestic policy are unlikely to leave the interest group system the way they found it. It is hardly surprising that chief executives who have the ability to remake American politics and governance are equally capable of reconstructing the interests that are closest to them. Although Roosevelt did not explicitly favor union expansion or the meteoric rise of the CIO, his influence in those developments was unmistakable. Organized labor benefited a great deal from its ties to a president blessed with the exceptional opportunity to advance major policy changes, but Roosevelt exercised enormous control over the terms of their alliance and the nature of reform. Co-optation was the price of labor's programmatic collaboration, as union militancy and independence gave way to a moderate, bureaucratic style of labor organization.

REAGAN AND THE CHRISTIAN RIGHT: COLLABORATIVE BREAKTHROUGH POLITICS II

During the late 1970s, the Christian right emerged as a new force in conservative politics. For decades after the Scopes trial of 1925 and the repeal of Prohibition in 1933, religious conservatives had retreated from the political sphere into a separate subculture of churches and sectarian educational and social institutions.[41] In the 1960s and 1970s, many social and political changes deeply offended Christian fundamentalists, evangelicals, Pentecostals, and charismatics, who strongly believed that they must resist culturally liberal government policies that favored "secular humanism" over faith-based morality. Organizations formed to advocate what leaders of the new Christian right described as a pro-family agenda, including tax credits for private school tuition, promotion of school prayer, and restrictions on abortion and pornography. The most prominent new group was the Moral Majority, led by televangelist Jerry Falwell. Other new organizations included the Religious Roundtable, which brought together reform-minded fundamentalist and evangelical clergy; the National Christian Action Council; Christian Voice; and Pat Robertson's Freedom Council.[42]

During the presidential campaign of 1980, Ronald Reagan openly courted conservative Christian leaders. Sharing their enthusiasm for restoring traditional values, Reagan pledged his support for their social agenda. He won an early endorsement from Christian Voice, which organized an effective political action committee—Christians for Reagan—on his behalf. The Religious Roundtable invited Reagan to address more than 15,000 ministers at one of its public affairs briefings in summer 1980, another event that helped to coalesce conservative Christians behind his candidacy. The Moral Majority and other groups mobilized voters at the fundamentalist and evangelical grassroots, urging followers to express their religious convictions at the polls.[43] Reagan openly appealed to conservative religious leaders and constituents by supporting the removal of a pro–Equal Rights Amendment plank from the Republican platform and the insertion of an antiabortion plank.[44] His 1980 presidential bid served as an important catalyst for unifying and mobilizing the Christian right, making it a formidable electoral force in American politics.

As president, Reagan appointed a number of Christian right activists to visible administration positions. Morton Blackwell, who served as a liaison between evangelicals and the Reagan campaign organization, was named a special assistant on the White House staff. Robert Billings, the former executive director of the Moral

Majority, received a prominent post in the Department of Education. Gary Bauer, a future director of the Family Research Council, became domestic adviser in Reagan's second term. Reagan also used his "bully pulpit" to advocate Christian right causes, including frequent endorsements of constitutional amendments to prohibit abortion and restore school prayer.[45] Reagan exercised his executive powers to bar the disbursement of public funds to any family-planning organization that discussed abortion as an option with patients. The White House also threw its support behind fundamentalist Bob Jones University in its lawsuit against the Internal Revenue Service, which had revoked the institution's tax-exempt status because of alleged racially discriminatory practices.[46]

If Christian right activists expected the Reagan administration to expend significant political capital on behalf of their social reform agenda, however, they soon discovered that the White House had other priorities. Reagan strategists focused instead on economic issues and a defense buildup. James Baker, the politically moderate White House chief of staff, and Robert Michel, the House Republican leader, set the tone early by serving notice that social issues would not be the administration's top priority. Reagan even reneged on a campaign promise to appear at the 1981 March for Life in Washington, offering instead to meet privately with anti-abortion leaders in the Oval Office. Several of them boycotted the meeting in protest. Paul Weyrich, a central figure in the Christian right movement, organized a conference call among conservative religious leaders in hopes of rallying them to press their social policy goals with the president. Yet few of these leaders were prepared to battle the Reagan White House. Falwell, for instance, argued that to antagonize the administration would be self-defeating.[47] Significantly, at the same time the White House was placing Christian right issues on the back burner, the Moral Majority and other conservative religious organizations dutifully joined a broad coalition of conservative interest groups in rallying behind the president's 1981 Omnibus Budget Reconciliation Act and his Economic Recovery Tax Act.[48] In 1984, although they had few tangible policy gains to show for their alliance with Reagan, prominent Christian right groups threw their full support behind the president's reelection campaign.

The Reagan presidency gave the Christian right and its conservative social agenda enormous symbolic recognition. It also forged an enduring alliance between conservative religious groups and the Republican Party: in every presidential election since 1980, the Christian right has focused its energies on electing the Republican candidate. Ralph Reed, a prominent movement figure, credits Reagan with leading religious conservatives "out of the wilderness" and "giving their concerns a viability in the political system that they had never had before."[49] To be sure, he and many other Christian right activists also lament that they received little more from the Reagan administration than "consolation prizes like speeches by the Gipper to their annual conventions or schmooze sessions in the Roosevelt Room."[50] Yet the Christian right had few alternatives but to remain loyal. Presidents who dominate the political system for a time, such as FDR and Reagan, largely control the terms of their sponsorship of interest group allies. Co-optation is often the price interest groups pay for their engagement in collaborative breakthrough politics. Sometimes the price is high. Unlike organized labor in the 1930s, which benefited from the reform program that Roosevelt framed, however, the Christian right accepted a form of co-optation from Reagan that ensured that its policy goals would be frustrated.

ROOSEVELT AND THE AMERICAN LIBERTY LEAGUE: ADVERSARIAL BREAKTHROUGH POLITICS I

When a president dominates the national policymaking process as thoroughly as Roosevelt did during his first term as president, oppositional groups often have little choice but to shift their political efforts from working with the administration to challenging it with aggressive publicity campaigns and electoral battles. The American Liberty League's crusade against Roosevelt and the New Deal provides an apt illustration of adversarial breakthrough politics.

Early in his presidency, Roosevelt hoped that his administration and its economic recovery experiments would earn the approval of a broad coalition of interests. He was particularly eager to win the support of the business community. But business leaders began to mobilize against Roosevelt when New Deal reformers unveiled a 1934 stock exchange measure that made clear the administration's determination to regulate high finance.[51] In summer 1934 defiant business leaders launched the American Liberty League to serve as an anti–New Deal interest group. The new organization was dominated by prominent executives and corporate lawyers from banking, oil, steel, transportation, automaking, and other industries.[52] The league boasted especially close ties to General Motors and the Du Pont family's financial empire. Claiming to be nonpartisan, the league took pains to include among its officers a handful of conservative Democrats who loathed the New Deal, most notably Al Smith, the 1928 Democratic presidential nominee.[53] All of these officers, including Smith, soon bolted from the Democratic Party, however, which led Arthur Krock of the *New York Times* to conclude that the league's nonpartisanship was a fiction. Instead, he informed readers that the Liberty League was the aegis of Republican patricians determined to guard their business civilization.[54]

League officers initially crowed that their organization would enlist 2 to 4 million in its crusade to defend nineteenth-century economic liberalism against the New Deal. Their efforts fell woefully short: at its peak, the league could claim roughly 75,000 members. Its principal activities focused on reshaping what one leader called "the collective expression of public opinion."[55] The league established offices in the National Press Club building in Washington; issued a profusion of pamphlets, bulletins, and newspaper editorials; and made extensive use of radio to challenge New Deal principles. League spokespersons warned radio listeners that the New Deal threatened "the individual freedom of the worker . . . to sell his own labor on his own terms" and unfairly seized "the accumulation of the thrifty" to distribute it to "the thriftless and unlucky."[56]

Roosevelt handled the league adeptly. He told reporters that he was delighted to learn that its officers were evaluating the New Deal in light of the Ten Commandments. Unfortunately, he noted, they had forgotten the commandment from Jesus to "love thy neighbor as thyself."[57] In his January 1936 message to Congress, Roosevelt declared his pride in having "earned the hatred of entrenched greed," "the unscrupulous money-changers," and the "discredited special interests." In a much-publicized speech to well-heeled members of the Liberty League at Washington's Mayflower Hotel a few weeks later, Al Smith excoriated New Dealers for betraying traditional American ideals in favor of socialist notions of government control and radical collectivism.[58] The choice was clear, Smith declared. Was it to be "Washington or Moscow, the Stars and Stripes or the red flag and the hammer and sickle, the 'Star Spangled Banner' or the 'Internationale?'"

During the 1936 election campaign, as the Republican National Committee and its presidential candidate, Alfred Landon, did their best to strike moderate-to-liberal postures, the Liberty League provided Roosevelt a perfect foil. Landon hoped to distance his party from the Liberty League by running on progressive issues, and he pointedly asked the organization not to publicly endorse his candidacy. Nevertheless, league members contributed lavish sums to defeat Roosevelt and stepped up their anti–New Deal publicity efforts during the campaign. To the chagrin of the Landon team, these high-profile activities only helped New Dealers to brand the Republican Party the tool of wealthy, antigovernment elites. Throughout the 1936 campaign, Roosevelt railed against "economic royalists" who cared little about the plight of most Americans. For his last campaign address outside his home state of New York in 1936, FDR went to Wilmington, the Delaware home of the Du Pont empire, to speak about liberty. He used the occasion to recount a parable of Abraham Lincoln's about a wolf who, after being pulled off the neck of a lamb by the shepherd, denounced the shepherd for destroying liberty. "Plainly, the sheep and the wolf are not agreed upon a definition of the word liberty," Lincoln had quipped.[59]

Not long after Roosevelt won his landslide reelection, the Liberty League chose to shut down rather than retreat into political obscurity. Its failed effort to derail the New Deal illustrates the difficulties oppositional groups can face when squaring off against breakthrough presidents, especially if they lack a large membership base. As we shall see in President Reagan's struggle with liberal citizens' organizations, however, oppositional groups sometimes can prove resilient and even mount effective challenges to breakthrough presidents.

REAGAN'S ASSAULT ON LIBERAL CITIZENS' GROUPS: ADVERSARIAL BREAKTHROUGH POLITICS II

Ronald Reagan, the first modern conservative president with abundant political resources, declared war on liberal advocacy groups concerned with the environment, consumer protection, civil rights, poverty, and other policy issues. Reaganites made no effort to conceal their disdain for these groups, viewing them as "a bunch of ideological ambulance chasers" who profited from bloated government and stood in the way of "regulatory relief."[60] Government retrenchment, the Reagan White House resolved, would require a concerted effort to decrease the groups' resources, size, and influence. The administration set out to demobilize its interest group opponents in 1981 by shrinking government programs they favored, limiting their access to important federal agencies, and eliminating federal grants and contracts that supported their activities.[61]

The Reagan offensive was devastating for some advocacy groups, especially antipoverty organizations. The administration's 1981 social welfare budget cuts spared programs for the elderly, thereby neutralizing senior citizens' lobbies that might have served as powerful allies of advocacy organizations for the poor.[62] Instead, Reagan's effort to "defund the left" by eliminating government grant programs that supported liberal groups took its heaviest toll on a small cluster of poor people's lobbies.[63] When these groups shifted their energies from political advocacy to providing services, however, a number of new groups concerned with the homeless arose and made the Reagan administration's assault on the welfare state the focal point of contentious politics. Organizations associated with the emerging homeless movement of the 1980s engaged in confrontational anti-Reagan protests, building shantytown "Reaganvilles," reminiscent of the Hoovervilles of the Great Depression, and staging attention-getting demonstrations that cast the White House as insensitive to the poor.[64] Ironically, the Reagan administration's constriction of established antipoverty organizations dating back to the Great Society opened the door for new groups to challenge the president's agenda. Presidential antagonism inadvertently encouraged the formation of liberal interest groups.

Beyond its partially effective assault on a handful of antipoverty organizations, the White House plan to enervate liberal groups failed. Reagan's strategists had largely ignored the possibility that resourceful opposition groups might transform open hostility from a powerful, conservative president into a catalyst for liberal organizational growth. National environmental groups, for example, prospered during the 1980s. Denied access to once-friendly federal agencies,[65] environmental organizations launched an effective drive that included aggressive fund-raising, publicity, and coordinated action with congressional allies. As private donations to these groups increased, environmental leaders quipped that James Watt, Reagan's unpopular, anticonservation secretary of the interior, was the "Fort Knox of the environmental movement."[66] The membership rolls of organizations such as the Wilderness Society and the Sierra Club doubled between 1980 and 1985.[67] Finally, environmental groups drove from office two prominent Reagan appointees (Watt and Environmental Protection Agency director Anne Gorsuch) and mounted a successful challenge to the administration's plans for environmental deregulation. Clearly, adversarial breakthrough politics can give oppositional groups the chance to expand and exert influence if they enjoy strong, broad-based constituencies and alternative bases of support within the government.

GEORGE H. W. BUSH, CENTRIST REFORM, AND THE COMPETITIVENESS COUNCIL: COLLABORATIVE POLITICS-AS-USUAL

Presidents with narrow opportunities to exercise domestic policy leadership often have strong political incentives to embrace centrist reforms. By moving toward the political center, these presidents can gain credit among voters for advancing popular, often bipartisan initiatives. In the process, however, they may alienate their party's core interest group allies. George H. W. Bush's endorsements of popular bipartisan measures on the environment and civil rights illustrate this trade-off.

Bush's opportunities for policy leadership were severely limited when he became president in 1989. His party held only 175 seats in the House of Representatives, the fewest of any modern president at the start of a term. Operating within this constrained political environment, the Bush administration hoped to prove its capacity to govern by introducing major environmental reform legislation that would draw considerable congressional, media, and popular support. During his 1988 election campaign, Bush pledged a "kinder, gentler" America and promised to be an "environmental president." As he proclaimed on the campaign trail, "Those who think we are powerless to do anything about the 'greenhouse effect' are forgetting about the 'White House effect.'"[68]

Once in office, Bush stayed on the environmental bandwagon; like Richard Nixon before him, Bush hoped to outmaneuver—or at least keep pace with—congressional Democrats on an issue of enormous popular concern. In July 1989 he sent to Congress an ambitious clean air bill, which was enacted in early 1990 after successful negotiations with Senate Majority Leader George Mitchell (D-ME). The Clean Air Act amendments proved to be Bush's most significant domestic policy achievement.[69] Along the way, however, his administration was required to marginalize traditional Republican interest group allies in business and industry.

At about the same time, the Bush White House endorsed another major centrist reform, the Americans with Disabilities Act (ADA), which had the solid support of the public and liberal political actors but was viewed with dread by many in the business community. The ADA sought to add the disabled to the list of groups protected against discrimination by the 1964 Civil Rights Act. At the urging of a broad coalition of advocates for disability rights, civil rights, and labor, the ADA also required that new or remodeled facilities be made accessible to disabled persons seeking jobs or hoping to make use of public accommodations; existing facilities were to be made accessible whenever "readily achievable." The potential financial costs of complying with ADA requirements were enormous, and Bush administration officials attempted to soften the blow on business by pressuring legislators to eliminate language from the bill permitting aggrieved parties to sue for damages. Congressional Democrats refused, then passed the ADA unaltered. With polls indicating overwhelming public support for civil rights reform on behalf of the disabled, Bush signed the ADA into law.[70]

Conservative critics assailed the Bush administration for approving the Clean Air Act amendments and the ADA.[71] Business groups and other conservative organizations warned administration officials that, in time of recession, new regulatory burdens placed "significant drags on the country's economic recovery."[72] Troubled by those attacks, Bush hoped to appease business groups outside the gaze of the media by limiting the regulatory reach of the Clean Air Act, the ADA, and other initiatives in the implementation process. To this end, Bush created the Council on Competitiveness within the Executive Office of the President. The council, chaired by Vice President Dan Quayle, was to review regulations issued by federal agencies and try to make them less burdensome for the relevant industry. "The president would say that if we keep our hand on the tiller in the implementation phase," recounted a member of the council, "we won't add to the burdens of the economy."[73]

In closed-door meetings, the Competitiveness Council focused on agency regulations that industry representatives complained were excessive. When the Department of Housing and Urban Development proposed ADA-related regulations on how to make apartments more accessible to the disabled, for instance, the council pressured the department to ease the regulations at the behest of construction and real estate interests. As Jeffrey Berry and Kent Portney found, "The new rules were more sympathetic to the industry, and lobbyists for the home builders claimed that hundreds of millions of dollars would be saved each year in aggregate building costs."[74]

The success of some business groups in winning regulatory relief from the Bush administration illustrates perhaps the most promising strategy for interest group allies of politically constrained presidents to achieve incremental policy gains. Avoiding the glare of television lights, interest groups are most likely to benefit from collaborative politics-as-usual by winning favorable regulatory decisions through executive orders or by mobilizing White House pressure on federal agencies for friendly implementation of existing laws. The Competitiveness Council, however, was ultimately unable to operate in secrecy. Liberal public interest groups, media scrutiny, and congressional opponents eventually hamstrung its activities.[75] As the Bush years suggest, the relationship between presidents with limited political power and their party's interest group coalition is often unproductive. And it does not matter which party controls the White House. Liberal interest groups closely aligned with the Democratic Party were frustrated during the Clinton administration when popular centrist reforms were on the agenda. This was particularly true with Clinton's support for the North American Free Trade Agreement (alienating organized labor), the Personal Responsibility and Work Opportunity Reconciliation Act (alienating antipoverty and civil rights groups), and the Defense of Marriage Act (alienating gay and lesbian groups). Clinton's willingness to support these controversial measures highlights that constrained executives have to embrace centrist initiatives even if they estrange interest group allies by doing so.

CLINTON AND HEALTH CARE REFORM: ADVERSARIAL POLITICS-AS-USUAL

Shortly after his unexpected 1948 election, President Truman launched an aggressive campaign to secure national health insurance. Hoping to make the most of his modest political opportunity for programmatic leadership, Truman vigorously nurtured popular support for his ambitious health proposal. The American Medical Association (AMA) and other groups that viewed national health insurance as inimical to their interests launched an intense public relations campaign to depict Truman's plan as socialistic and corrosive of quality medical care. Spending an unprecedented $1.5 million for its publicity counteroffensive, the AMA ran ads claiming that national health insurance would place government bureaucrats between patients and their physicians. Already constrained by the slim Democratic majorities in Congress and by strong resistance from the conservative southern wing of his party, Truman was helpless to save his health plan when public support dwindled.[76]

More than four decades later, Bill Clinton, another Democrat constrained by limited political capacity to remake domestic policy, made universal health care the centerpiece of his administration's reform agenda. He ran effectively on the issue during the 1992 election, receiving a warm reception from voters who agreed that the health care system was in crisis. After a lengthy policy-planning process, in late 1993 Clinton unveiled his much-anticipated Health Security Act, whose name was meant to associate his proposal with one of the federal government's most popular programs, Social Security. In substance, the act called for a new public–private partnership involving "managed competition" and employer mandates.[77] Politically, it made important concessions to large companies and health insurance providers to win their support, while promising universal coverage and limits on soaring medical costs to attract the elderly, consumer groups, unions, religious organizations, and groups representing women, children, and minorities. When the AMA, the U.S. Chamber of Commerce, and several large employers voiced support for principal features of the Health Security Act, it seemed that the Clinton administration had assembled a powerful left–right coalition.

By mid-1994 Clinton's crusade for sweeping health care reform was dead. Critics point to the plan's eye-glazing complexity, resistance from Democrats on the relevant congressional committees, Clinton's failure to streamline his policy agenda, his unwillingness to work with reform-minded Republicans, and high levels of public distrust in government, among other explanations.[78] For our purposes, however, it is useful to concentrate on the significant role that Clinton's interest group adversaries played in derailing health care reform.

Initially, the strongest group opposition to the administration's health care package came from two national organizations with large grassroots constituencies: the Health Insurance Association of America (HIAA) and the National Federation of Independent Business (NFIB). The HIAA represented midsize and small health insurance companies, many of which would go out of business if the Health Security Act became law. Large employers stood to benefit from the Clinton plan, but small businesses represented by the NFIB found intolerable the proposal's mandate that employers pay 80 percent of their employees' health premiums.[79] The Pharmaceutical Research and Manufacturers of America (PhRMA), representing drug companies that stood to lose profits under the Clinton scheme, also joined the opposition. Then, late in 1993 Republican strategists led by William Kristol of the Project for the Republican Future campaigned to persuade a broad set of conservative interest groups to mobilize against even a compromise version of the Health Security Act. Anything but an all-out effort to defeat health care reform, Kristol argued, would jeopardize the political future of the Republican Party and its interest group coalition. Passing the Clinton plan, he insisted, would "relegitimize middle-class dependence for 'security' on government spending and regulation" and thereby revive the Democratic Party's appeal "as the generous protector of middle-class interests."[80] The Christian Coalition, antitax groups, and a variety of other conservative interest groups responded by channeling new resources into the effort to kill health care reform, coordinating their activities with HIAA, NFIB, and PhRMA.

Clinton's interest group adversaries devoted considerable funds to advertising. HIAA spent approximately $14 million on its public relations blitz, which included the "Harry and Louise" television ads, in which a middle-class couple expresses its angst about the Clinton proposal. PhRMA devoted roughly $20 million to its own political advertising campaign. The antireform advertising crusade was designed to minimize public concerns about a health crisis while arousing fears that the president's plan would reduce the quality of medical care, eliminate individual choice of health care providers, encourage bloated government, and dramatically increase taxes to cover the cost of universal coverage. For its part, the 600,000-member NFIB focused on grassroots mobilization, including direct mail and phone bank assaults on the Clinton plan.[81] Against this backdrop, the White House received only modest support for its health care initiative from traditionally Democratic interest groups. The AFL-CIO and other labor groups, for example, had already expended considerable resources fighting one of Clinton's treasured centrist achievements, NAFTA.[82]

Adversarial politics took its toll on public support for Clinton's health care reform, which drifted downward from 67 percent in a September 1993 *Washington Post*/ABC News poll to 44 percent in February 1994.[83] Destined for defeat, the Health Security Act was never put to a vote in either the House or the Senate. The failure of Clinton's major domestic policy initiative presaged the Republican takeover of Congress in November. Many analysts trace the demise of health care reform in 1993 and 1994 to the Clinton administration's strategic missteps, of which there were many. Placed within the context of our theoretical model, however, Clinton's failure to achieve major health care reform reflects the formidable challenges faced by politically constrained presidents who pursue large-scale policy change. It also illustrates the enormous opportunities for interest group adversaries to block the programmatic ambitions of modern presidents in periods of politics-as-usual.

GEORGE W. BUSH: MASTERING COLLABORATIVE POLITICS-AS-USUAL

Like his predecessor, George W. Bush came into office with his party in control of Congress. Yet he received fewer popular votes than his Democratic opponent in the 2000 election, and his Electoral College victory hinged on the controversial intervention of a conservative Supreme Court majority. Moreover, Bush's party lost seats in the congressional elections, leaving Republicans a narrow 221–211 majority in the House and an evenly split Senate that remained Republican thanks only to the vice president's tiebreaking vote. Although Bush was hardly in a position to claim a mandate for bold shifts in public policy, he secured his top priority of a huge tax cut by pursuing a highly partisan strategy.[84] But the Bush administration's opportunities to dramatically reshape domestic policy remained relatively narrow in the first term, even with an ideologically cohesive Republican congressional party and, after September 11, 2001, an unprecedented national security crisis that lent the president new clout. As with his father and Clinton before him, Bush's other successful domestic initiatives—most notably education reform in 2001 and Medicare reform in 2003—were centrist measures that relied on compromise and bipartisan coalitions. The administration's more controversial legislative proposals, such as its initiative to involve faith-based organizations in the delivery of government-funded social services and its efforts to authorize oil drilling in Alaska's Arctic National Wildlife Refuge, were largely frustrated.

Stymied on the legislative front, the Bush White House shifted its attention to regulatory change. As the bastion of politically constrained presidents who hope to alter domestic policies, regulatory action allows an administration to advance its agenda and assist allied organized interests unilaterally, incrementally, and with little public or media attention. In contrast to high-profile lawmaking efforts such as Clinton's ill-fated campaign for sweeping health care reform, an administration can write or revise regulations largely on the president's own authority. Although the Bush White House was certainly not the first to pursue its policy goals through regulation, it proved exceptionally aggressive and successful in its use of this strategy during the first term.

The administration's air quality policies are illustrative. During the 2000 presidential race, Bush pledged to impose controls on power plant emissions of carbon dioxide. In her first days as Bush's director of the Environmental Protection Agency (EPA), Christie Todd Whitman, a former Republican governor of New Jersey, announced plans to carry out this promise. Interest groups representing electric power companies expressed alarm. One of their main lobbyists, Haley Barbour, a former Republican Party chair, threw down the gauntlet in a memorandum to Vice President Dick Cheney: "The question is whether environmental policy still prevails over energy policy with Bush-Cheney, as it did with Clinton-Gore." Barbour urged Cheney, who was heading a task force established by President Bush to conduct a broad review of energy policy, to show that environmental issues did not "trump good energy policy."[85] In March 2001 Bush announced that he would not impose carbon dioxide controls, explaining that "the reality is that our nation has a real problem when it comes to energy."[86]

Industry lobby groups such as the Edison Electric Institute and Electric Reliability Coordinating Council soon pressed the White House for new regulatory changes. One of their targets was a set of rules known as the New Source Review program, which required companies to add new pollution controls when they upgraded or expanded their plants. In a memorandum to Cheney, Whitman warned that any administration effort to undercut New Source Review rules would make it "hard to refute the charge that we are deciding not to enforce the Clean Air Act."[87] In November 2002, however, the administration quietly released a statement from EPA's assistant administrator outlining revisions of the New Source Review program. The rules stipulated that companies would not have to add new pollution control devices if their plant upgrades and construction projects did not cost more than 20 percent of the plant's total value. The rules changes also raised the amount of pollution permitted an entire facility rather than targeting emissions from individual pieces of equipment, and they exempted plants that had installed modern pollution controls from having to make further improvements for ten years, regardless of their emission levels. Twelve states, twenty cities, and numerous environmental groups sued the EPA in response. "Our powerful, bipartisan court challenge says to this administration: 'No, you cannot repeal the federal Clean Air Act by dictatorial edict,'"[88] declared Connecticut attorney general Richard Blumenthal.

Even as opponents of Bush's air quality policies fought these rules changes in the courts, environmental groups noted that lax regulatory enforcement had already paid huge dividends for affected power companies.[89] In addition to loosening air quality controls, Bush's EPA proved far less vigorous than those of previous administrations in cracking down on companies that violated federal environmental laws. The number of lawsuits initiated against companies for environmental violations during Bush's first term declined 75 percent from the number initiated during the last four Clinton years. The $56.8 million in civil penalties that the EPA collected in fiscal 2004 was the lowest amount since 1990.[90]

The Bush White House's approach to environmental policy does not represent an isolated example. New regulations adopted during Bush's first term revised health rules, work safety standards, product safety disclosure requirements, energy regulations, and other measures in a manner that usually favored business and industry allies and drew fire from interest groups representing consumers, labor, the elderly, medical patients, racial minorities, and other constituencies. At the behest of automakers, the National Highway Traffic Safety Administration published a regulation forbidding the public release of some data related to unsafe motor vehicles because the information might cause "substantial competitive harm" to manufacturers. The Mine Safety and Health Administration proposed a new regulation that would dilute rules intended to protect coal miners from black lung disease. Responding to industry complaints, the Department of Labor dropped a rule requiring employers to keep a record of employees' ergonomic injuries. A rule that required hospitals to install facilities to protect workers against tuberculosis was also jettisoned by the administration. In response to lobbying by groups representing lumber and paper companies, Forest Service managers were authorized to approve logging in federal forests without the usual environmental reviews.

These regulatory initiatives inspired little or no public attention. Indeed, it is the unilateral, low-profile character of regulatory change that makes it so attractive to presidents whose efforts to get what they want from Congress are frustrated. During his tenure, George W. Bush honed the skills of collaborative politics-as-usual by regularly winning favorable policy outcomes for his administration and its interest group allies through incremental, regulatory means.

AMBIVALENT ENGAGEMENT: OBAMA, INTEREST GROUPS, AND THE QUEST FOR REFORM

Barack Obama entered the White House in 2009 with transformative political and policy aspirations, hoping to translate his historic 53 percent victory and unified Democratic control of Congress into historic reforms. The major prize he sought, however, was one that had eluded all modern Democratic presidents: universal health care reform. Powerful interest groups were a prominent impediment to such efforts. As Franklin Roosevelt and Harry Truman learned, groups such as the American Medical Association (AMA) were highly effective at both arousing popular anxieties that reform would become "socialized medicine" and mobilizing their stalwart congressional allies. Facing similar resistance in 1965, Lyndon Johnson secured Medicare legislation only after limiting low-cost hospitalization and medical insurance to the elderly. As discussed above, Clinton's health reform efforts in 1993–1994 met their demise at the hands of a welter of powerful interest groups with competing goals. Against this backdrop, Barack Obama entered office well aware that winning over or at least mollifying influential health care lobbyists was critical to achieving reforms that had proven so elusive for his predecessors.

Notwithstanding his spirited denunciation of special interests and influence peddling in Washington, Obama and his aides held quiet meetings with pharmaceutical company lobbyists and executives soon after he entered the Oval Office. A deal was cut in the months that followed: if Big Pharma (the largest drug companies) would support the administration's health care reform plan, the White House would take off the table tough cost controls and other regulatory measures targeting the pharmaceutical industry. In May 2009 drug companies began funding an advertising campaign in support of Obama's health reform blueprints. The Democratic chair of the House Progressive Caucus, Raúl Grijalva, responded to the White House's strategy of courting Big Pharma with disgust. "Are industry groups going to be the ones at the table who get the first big piece of pie," he asked, "and we just fight over the crust?"[91] Despite protests from both liberals and conservatives, the alliance held firm as the administration and drug company leaders and lobbyists advanced the Obama plan.

In the summer of 2009, another bargain was struck on health care reform between the White House and hospitals. In particular, the administration agreed to spare the hospital industry significant limits on its revenues in exchange for its avowed support for health reform and a pledge to contribute a relatively modest

$155 billion in Medicare and Medicaid savings over a decade.[92] At the same time, the once-menacing AMA now desperately looked for stronger guaranteed financing for medical services in the face of fewer paying patients and declining revenues. Likewise, health insurance lobbies such as the American Health Insurance Plans (AHIP) dramatically changed their position on national health reform from the one they maintained during the 1993–1994 struggle. Feeling revenue strains and anxieties similar to those felt by doctors, AHIP welcomed a reform in which the government would require people to have health insurance.[93]

Obama's aggressive strategy of either co-opting or neutralizing the most powerful health care lobbies and interest groups proved crucial to passage of the Patient Protection and Affordable Care Act of 2010. During the two years that Obama advanced health care reform as his top priority, Senate lobbying disclosure forms indicate that roughly 4,500 lobbyists and 1,750 interest groups and corporations sought to influence the reform process. An estimated $1.06 billion was spent on lobbying the issue in 2009–2010.[94] During the long months when Congress remained deadlocked on health care reform, the bargains the Obama White House struck with the pharmaceutical and hospital industries, along with the changing interests of doctors and health insurers, put the administration in position to achieve the landmark reform that had eluded Obama's predecessors.

Even as his administration negotiated with pharmaceutical companies, insurance lobbies, medical professionals, and the hospital industry to secure "Obamacare," the president initiated a series of new rules designed to limit lobbyists' influence in the White House and federal bureaucracy. "If you give up on the idea that your voice can make a difference, then other voices will fill the void: lobbyists and special interests," Obama told Americans during his presidency. He also reminded supporters that the Supreme Court's controversial *Citizens United v. F.E.C.* (2010) ruling enabled conservative special interests and corporate lobbyists to spend lavish sums to defeat him, referencing "the people with $10 million checks who are trying to buy this election and those who are making it harder for you to vote."[95] As noted above, one of the most significant ethics limits imposed by the Obama administration on lobbying was a rule that barred anyone who engaged in official lobbying during the previous two years from getting a job in an executive agency. Another rule prohibited registered lobbyists and the organizations they led from receiving either economic stimulus funds or bank bailout dollars. Registered lobbyists also were blocked from serving on advisory boards to federal agencies that offered recommendations on funding priorities and agency policies.[96] Other new regulations on lobbying included disclosure rules for contacts between executive officials and lobbyists and limits on lobbyists' contacts with certain administration officials.

Many of these new restrictions on executive lobbying, however, proved to be more symbolic than effective. To avoid disclosure rules or to remain eligible for administration appointments, many lobbyists simply chose not to register as an official lobbyist or to report their advising and government advocacy efforts on behalf of private interests as lobbying activities. This loophole was fueled by the ambiguous definition of *lobbying* in the regulations. Although the number of lobbyists registered with Congress fell from about 13,500 in 2007 to 11,000 in 2010, Washington insiders observed that many lobbyists simply chose to ply their trade under the radar. Obama officials contributed directly to undermining their administration's own lobbying and disclosure regulations by meeting with prominent lobbyists hundreds of times away from government property. Executive officials also used private e-mail accounts to communicate with important lobbyists and interest groups in order to avoid having to disclose these contacts.[97] Moreover, like its recent predecessors, the Obama administration provided access to groups and lobbyists that shared its partisan and ideological commitments. An investigation of the White House visitor logs by the *Washington Post* in the Obama years showed a clear partisan divide in access: "Republican lobbyists coming to visit are rare, while Democratic lobbyists are common, whether they are representing corporate clients or liberal causes."[98] Reporters found that Obama officials met with the AFL-CIO's chief lobbyist more than fifty times in Obama's first term and that Obama's reelection team relied on fifteen prominent leaders in the lobbying industry and corporate world to raise millions of dollars for his campaign war chest.[99]

The Obama administration's reform agenda began with exceptionally ambitious goals, reflecting its determination to translate unusually broad political warrants and opportunities into major economic domestic policy breakthroughs, especially in the areas of economic recovery and health care. Yet even though he was the first Democratic president since Franklin Roosevelt to win reelection with over 50 percent of the vote, Obama's second-term reform aspirations entailed bruising confrontations on issues ranging from fiscal balance and gun control to environmental protection and immigration reform. On all of these issues, the White House gained support, absorbed pressure, and endured opposition from the dense network of interest groups in the nation's capital, including diverse citizens' groups, trade associations, corporations, labor unions, professional associations, and intergovernmental lobbies.

Just as most modern presidents facing stiff resistance to their policy agendas in Congress, Obama used executive orders and regulatory discretion to advance policies favored by many of his party's strongest interest group allies, ranging from organized labor to reproductive rights groups.[100] When comprehensive immigration reform languished in Congress, for example, the Obama administration acted unilaterally to provide temporary relief to roughly 800,000 undocumented immigrants who arrived as minors, a program that became known as Deferred Action for Childhood Arrivals (DACA). Modern presidents may gain political points by attacking special interests and lobbyists and they may even, like Obama, make some important inroads on the Washington political culture that has fueled their influence behind closed doors. But successful reform ultimately requires the president to constructively engage diverse interest groups.

CONCLUSION

Political interactions between presidents and national interest groups are an intrinsic feature of contemporary American politics. By studying president–interest group relations as a function of executive leadership opportunities and the partisan and ideological affiliations of interest groups, we can recognize patterns across time, much as Stephen Skowronek's emphasis on regime cycles enables us to forge analytical links between presidents from different historical periods who faced similar political circumstances.[101] The existing scholarly literature underscores the recent development of the institutional resources and political strategies the White House can use to deal with the interest group system.[102] These findings sometimes have led presidential scholars to regard all modern presidents as equally well situated to orchestrate successful relations with organized interests. For example, according to Peterson, "Modern presidents have the institutional means, and have demonstrated the willingness, to influence the interest group system to their own advantage."[103] Our model of interactive politics offers a decidedly different portrait of president–interest group relations, one in which modern executives are frequently confounded in their efforts both to coax allies into supportive coalitions and to thwart opposition groups. Except for rare moments of presidential dominance, interest groups orchestrate effective strategic politics of their own.

Presidents with transformational policy aspirations but ordinary leadership opportunities have routinely found interest group relations trying. Oppositional groups are usually in a good position to frustrate the president's most ambitious programmatic goals, as Clinton's ill-fated crusade for health care reform illustrates. Nurturing and aiding interest group allies can also prove difficult for politically constrained presidents. These executives have strong incentives to endorse centrist measures that are popular but less bold because enactment allows them to point to tangible policy achievements. In the process, however, they routinely alienate affiliated interest groups, as George H. W. Bush learned when he supported the Clean Air Act amendments and the ADA. Indeed, the political allure of such popular centrist initiatives frequently saps the ability of politically constrained presidents to build strong coalitions to support their more partisan measures. During periods of politics-as-usual, they instead may quietly provide succor to their interest group allies through administrative means. But the intense scrutiny that the media and opposition groups devote to White House activities guarantees that such efforts rarely remain secret. When publicized, they may subject the president to charges of catering to special interests and may be contested by interest group adversaries in the federal courts and Congress.

Although most interest groups allied to presidents with constrained leadership opportunities receive fewer tangible benefits than many assume, oppositional groups often find the adversarial politics that prevails during such presidencies hospitable to vibrant and effective activism. As interest groups opposed to Clinton's Health Security program discovered in the 1994 midterm election, countermobilization can have surprising transformational possibilities.

Obviously, interest groups are most rewarded for collaborative relations with the White House during those rare historic moments when breakthrough presidents dominate American governance. But as the Christian right found during the Reagan revolution, such alliances are no guarantee of programmatic achievement. Breakthrough presidents set the terms of collaboration with their allied interest groups, and groups whose goals may jeopardize more important White House objectives may find themselves marginalized in the policy process. Even when the transformational goals of breakthrough presidents and allied interest groups are nearly the same, as was the case with Roosevelt and labor activists in the 1930s, co-optation is typically the price these groups pay to secure dramatic gains for their constituencies.

The sorry history of the American Liberty League illustrates the precarious situation of organized interests that oppose the programmatic ambitions of politically dominant presidents. It is telling, however, that Ronald Reagan, the most recent breakthrough president, dominated domestic policymaking for only a year and that his interest group adversaries prospered during most of his tenure. The scale and variety of the interest group system since the 1970s have been greater than ever before. This important development, as Graham Wilson argues, is part of what forces presidents today to contend with "a thicker structure of constraining institutions (in this case, interest groups)."[104] Thus the likelihood of strained relations between modern presidents and interest groups is greater than ever.

From the beginning, Obama used a repertoire of strategies in dealing with the Washington lobbying community. In a manner akin to other recent presidents, he unflinchingly used executive orders to advance policies that are favorable to some of his party's strongest organized allies, such as new regulations on federal contractors endorsed by labor unions and federations; to reverse Bush administration restrictions on funding for international family planning organizations, which won praise from reproductive rights lobbies; and to restore Endangered Species Act protections supported by environmental groups.[105] He also reached out to traditionally conservative business groups for support on domestic agenda items, such as health care reform, that required an exceptionally broad coalition of support.

Yet Obama also was willing to introduce surprising reforms to national interest group politics, including a series of restrictions on lobbying groups' access to his administration. From the start, he made no effort to conceal his contempt for special interests and highly paid lobbyists for turning the national government "into a game only they can afford to play,"[106] one that was rigged to favor their narrow agendas over the collective good. "In a democracy, the price of access and influence should be nothing more than your voice and your vote," Obama told supporters while endorsing ethics reform, also vowing that special interests "will not run my White House."[107] Despite these reforms, interest groups adapted in predictable fashion. Organized interests aligned with the Democratic Party sought programmatic rewards during the Obama presidency, but they showed limited ability to challenge the White House when it pursues a more centrist or bipartisan policy course. For their part, conservative interest groups routinely pursued adversarial strategies in response to Obama's domestic reform blueprints, and perceived threats from the White House intensified support for them within their base. In the end, Obama's public offensive against special interests and lobbyists was tempered by the need to constructively engage Washington's formidable lobbying community in order to govern.

After waging a grievance-filled campaign in which he lost the popular vote in 2016 (garnering 46.1 percent to Hillary Clinton's 48.2 percent), Trump entered office under leadership circumstances and important constraints on his reform agenda. His greatest opportunities to reshape public policy were initially tied to collaborating with fellow Republicans, who controlled both the House and Senate. This was particularly true given the uncompromisingly conservative legislative agenda advanced by the White House, and unified resistance from Democratic lawmakers whose liberal base insisted on tenacious opposition. After exceptionally unpopular Republican plans to dismantle Obama's signature domestic reform— the Affordable Care Act—failed dramatically in the Senate, Trump issued an executive order designed to undercut "Obamacare" by allowing small businesses to purchase cheaper insurance plans that provide fewer benefits and protections.[108] The action delighted right-wing groups while provoking lawsuits from Blue State attorneys general. Trump also used unilateral executive power to rescind DACA, curtail women's access to free birth control, toughen criminal drug sentencing, and roll back a host of environmental and economic regulations.[109] Consistent with traditional collaborative politics-as-usual, for instance, Trump's Environmental Protection Agency director Scott Pruitt reversed Obama-era protections for Alaska's Bristol Bay, billed by fishermen and scientists as "the most valuable salmon fishery in the world," thirty minutes after a May 2017 meeting with a corporate CEO seeking to build a gold and copper mine at the location.[110] In turn, organized adversaries of the president like Planned Parenthood, the NAACP, the Sierra Club, and the ACLU used White House threats as a catalyst for sharp increases in donations and grassroots activism.[111] Facing chronically low public approval and deprived of major legislative breakthroughs, the Trump White House has declared war on the Washington establishment that has bedeviled his goals. In contrast to Obama's reluctant flexibility toward interest group relations, Trump has zealously assumed the role of an embattled disruptor placing political provocation and retribution above steady governance.

NOTES

1. Eric Garcia, "A History of 'Draining the Swamp,'" *Roll Call*, October 18, 2016.
2. Landon Thomas and Alexandra Stevenson, "Trump's Economic Cabinet Picks Signal Embrace of Wall St. Elite," *New York Times*, November 30, 2016.
3. Russell Berman, "Donald Trump's Last-Ditch Plan to 'Drain the Swamp,'" *The Atlantic*, October 18, 2016.
4. Donald J. Trump, @realDonaldTrump, 2:07pm, January 2, 2016, Twitter; see also Aaron Rupar, "Trump Used to Brag That He Wasn't Controlled by Special Interests," *Think Progress*, June 9, 2016.
5. Isaac Arnsdorf, "Trump Lobbying Ban Weakens Obama Rules," *Politico*, January 28, 2017.
6. Philip Bump, "This Is What Trump's Swamp Looks Like," *Washington Post,* June 1, 2017; Conor Friedersdorf, "Trump Has Filled, Not Drained, the Swamp," *The Atlantic*, September 21, 2017.
7. Heather Long, "Trump Has Done a Big Flip-Flop on Wall Street," CNN Money, April 26, 2017; Thomas and Stevenson, "Trump's Economic Cabinet Picks Signal Embrace of Wall St. Elite."

8. Zeke Miller, "The White House Will Keep Its Visitor Logs Secret," *Time*, April 14, 2017.

9. Kate Brannen, "Trump Family's Endless Conflicts of Interest: Chapter and Verse," *Newsweek,* July 3, 2017; Neil Baron, "Every American Must Be a Watchdog When It Comes to Trump's Conflicts of Interest," *The Hill*, July 11, 2017; Jeremy Venook, "The Trump Administration's Conflicts of Interest," *The Atlantic*, January 18, 2017; Derek Kravitz and Al Shaw, "Trump Lawyer Confirms President Can Pull Money from His Businesses Whenever He Wants," *ProPublica*, April 4, 2017.

10. Anita Kumar, "Trump Hands U.S. Policy Writing to Shadow Groups of Business Execs," *Charlotte Observer,* August 7, 2017.

11. See Jeffrey Berry, *The Interest Group Society* (Glenview, IL: Scott Foresman, 1989), 2–3; and Mark Petracca, "The Rediscovery of Interest Group Politics," in *The Politics of Interests: Interest Groups Transformed,* ed. Mark Petracca (Boulder, CO: Westview Press, 1992), 7–11.

12. Quoted in James Deakin, *The Lobbyists* (Washington, DC: Public Affairs Press, 1966), 7.

13. "Is Bush Poisoning His Well?" *National Journal,* April 14, 2001, 1120–1121.

14. Lyndon Johnson adviser, quoted in Paul Light, *The President's Agenda* (Baltimore: Johns Hopkins University Press, 1999).

15. Stephen Wayne, "Interest Groups on the Road to the White House: Traveling Hard and Soft Routes," in *The Interest Group Connection,* ed. Paul Herrnson, Ronald Shaiko, and Clyde Wilcox (Chatham, NJ: Chatham House, 1998), 65–79.

16. See Benjamin Ginsburg and Martin Shefter, "The Presidency and the Organization of Interests," in *The Presidency and the Political System,* 5th ed., ed. Michael Nelson (Washington, DC: CQ Press, 1988).

17. See Alexander Hamilton, James Madison, and John Jay, *The Federalist Papers,* ed. Clinton Rossiter (New York: New American Library, 1961).

18. Jeffrey Tulis, *The Rhetorical Presidency* (Princeton, NJ: Princeton University Press, 1987).

19. See Elisabeth Clemens, *The People's Lobby: Organizational Innovation and the Rise of Interest Group Politics in the United States, 1890–1925* (Chicago: University of Chicago Press, 1997); and Richard Harris and Daniel Tichenor, "Organized Interests and American Political Development," *Political Science Quarterly* 117, (Winter 2002–2003): 587–612.

20. Quoted in Lewis Eigen and Jonathan Siegel, *The Macmillan Dictionary of Political Quotations* (New York: Macmillan, 1993), 382.

21. Ibid., 381.

22. E. Pendleton Herring, *Group Representation before Congress* (Baltimore: Johns Hopkins University Press, 1929), 51.

23. Quoted in Christine Lunardini and Thomas Knock, "Woodrow Wilson and Woman Suffrage: A New Look," *Political Science Quarterly* 95 (Winter 1981): 671.

24. Daniel Tichenor, "The Presidency, Social Movement, and Contentious Change: Lessons from the Woman's Suffrage and Labor Movements," *Presidential Studies Quarterly* 29 (March 1999): 14–25.

25. Robert Dahl, *Dilemmas of Pluralist Democracy* (New Haven, CT: Yale University Press, 1982), 190.

26. Mark Peterson, "Interest Mobilization and the Presidency," in *The Politics of Interests: Interest Groups Transformed,* ed. Mark Petracca (Boulder, CO: Westview Press, 1992), 239–240.

27. Joseph Pika, "Interest Groups and the White House under Roosevelt and Truman," *Political Science Quarterly* 102 (Fall 1987): 647–668.

28. Bradley Patterson Jr., *The Ring of Power* (New York: Basic Books, 1988), 200–212.

29. William Lammers and Michael Genovese, *The Presidency and Domestic Policy* (Washington, DC: CQ Press, 2000); David Mayhew, *Divided We Govern* (New Haven, CT: Yale University Press, 1991); and Erwin Hargrove and Michael Nelson, *Presidents, Politics, and Policy* (New York: Knopf, 1984).

30. For an excellent typology of interest group liaison (governing party, consensus building, outreach, and legitimation), see Mark Peterson, "The Presidency and Organized Interests: White House Patterns of Interest Group Liaison," *American Political Science Review* 86 (September 1992): 612–625.

31. Robert Zeiger, *John L. Lewis: Labor Leader* (Boston: Twayne, 1988), 64.

32. William Leuchtenburg, *Franklin Roosevelt and the New Deal* (New York: Harper and Row, 1963), 106–107.

33. Ibid., 86.

34. Bruce Miroff, *Icons of Democracy* (New York: Basic Books, 1993), 262.

35. Ibid., 260–262.

36. Leuchtenburg, *Franklin Roosevelt,* 189.

37. Zeiger, *John L. Lewis,* 105–106.

38. Marc Landy, "FDR and John L. Lewis: The Lessons of Rivalry," in *Modern Presidents and the Presidency,* ed. Marc Landy (Lexington, MA: D. C. Heath, 1985), 106–112; and Zeiger, *John L. Lewis,* 109.

39. Alan Brinkley, *The End of Reform: New Deal Liberalism in Recession and War* (New York: Knopf, 1995), 201–226.

40. Ibid., 212.

41. Eric Larson, *Summer for the Gods* (Cambridge, MA: Harvard University Press, 1997), 232–235.

42. John C. Green, "The Spirit Willing: Collective Identity and the Development of the Christian Right," in *Waves of Protest,* ed. Jo Freeman and Victoria Johnson (New York: Rowman and Littlefield, 1999), 156–159.

43. Kenneth Wald, *Religion and Politics in the United States* (Washington, DC: CQ Press, 1992), 234–235.

44. See Ralph Reed, *Active Faith: How Christians Are Changing the Soul of American Politics* (New York: Free Press, 1996), 113–114.

45. James Reichley, *Religion in American Public Life* (Washington, DC: Brookings Institution, 1985), 324–325.

46. Duane Oldfield, *The Right and the Righteous: The Christian Right Confronts the Republican Party* (New York: Rowman and Littlefield, 1996), 118–121.

47. See Reed, *Active Faith,* 114–115.

48. Reichley, *Religion in American Public Life,* 325.

49. Reed, *Active Faith,* 116.

50. Ibid., 115.

51. Leuchtenburg, *Franklin Roosevelt,* 90.

52. See Frederick Rudolph, "The American Liberty League, 1933–1940," *American Historical Review* 56 (October 1950): 19–33.

53. Albert Fried, *FDR and His Enemies* (New York: St. Martin's Press, 1999), 90–91, 120–125.

54. Krock is quoted in Rudolph, "The American Liberty League," 22–23.

55. Ibid., 25.

56. Ibid., 24, 28.

57. Fried, *FDR and His Enemies,* 90.

58. Leuchtenburg, *Franklin Roosevelt,* 178–179.

59. Rudolph, "The American Liberty League," 25.

60. The quote is Reagan's; see Michael S. Greve, "Why 'Defunding the Left' Failed," *Public Interest* 89 (Fall 1987): 91.

61. Peterson, "Interest Mobilization and the Presidency," 226–230.

62. Douglas R. Imig, "American Social Movements and Presidential Administrations," in *Social Movements and American Political Institutions,* ed. Ann Costain and Andrew McFarland (New York: Rowman and Littlefield, 1998), 151–162.

63. Douglas R. Imig, *Poverty and Power* (Lincoln: University of Nebraska Press, 1996), 49–54.

64. Imig, "American Social Movements," 167–169.

65. Mark Peterson and Jack Walker have shown that Reagan ushered in "a virtual revolution" in the access of interest groups to bureaucratic agencies of the federal government. See Peterson and Walker, "Interest Group Responses to Partisan Change," in *Interest Group Politics,* 2nd ed., ed. Allan J. Cigler and Burdett A. Loomis (Washington, DC: CQ Press, 1986), 172.

66. Greve, "Why 'Defunding the Left' Failed," 99.

67. See Christopher Bosso, "The Color of Money: Environmental Groups and the Pathologies of Fund Raising," in *Interest Group Politics,* 4th ed., ed. Allan J. Cigler and Burdett A. Loomis (Washington, DC: CQ Press, 1995), 104; and Richard Waterman, *Presidential Influence and the Administrative State* (Knoxville: University of Tennessee Press, 1989), 134.

68. John Holusha, "Bush Pledges Aid for Environment," *New York Times,* September 1, 1988.

69. Richard Cohen, *Washington at Work: Back Rooms and Clean Air* (New York: Macmillan, 1992); and Norman Vig, "Presidential Leadership and the Environment from Reagan to Clinton," in *Environmental Policy: New Directions for the Twenty-First Century,* 4th ed., ed. Norman Vig and Michael Kraft (Washington, DC: CQ Press, 2000), 104–107.

70. See David Mervin, *George Bush and the Guardianship Presidency* (New York: St. Martin's, 1996), 98–101.

71. See Richard Harris and Sidney Milkis, *The Politics of Regulatory Change: A Tale of Two Agencies* (New York: Oxford University Press, 1996), 292–293.

72. Mervin, *George Bush,* 100.

73. Quoted in Harris and Milkis, *Politics of Regulatory Change,* 289.

74. Jeffrey Berry and Kent Portney, "Centralizing Regulatory Control and Interest Group Access: The Quayle Council on Competitiveness," in Cigler and Loomis, eds., *Interest Group Politics,* 320.

75. Ibid., 336–340.

76. One of the best accounts of this struggle is provided by Paul Starr, *The Social Transformation of American Medicine* (New York: Basic Books, 1982), 350.

77. Jacob Hacker, *Road to Nowhere: The Genesis of President Clinton's Plan for Health Security* (Princeton, NJ: Princeton University Press, 1997).

78. Theda Skocpol, *Boomerang: Health Care Reform and the Turn against Government* (New York: Norton, 1997), 133–188; Allen Schick, "How a Bill Didn't Become a Law," in *Intensive Care: How Congress Shapes Health Policy,* ed. Thomas Mann and Norman Ornstein (Washington, DC: Brookings Institution Press, 1995), 240–251; and Darrell West and Burdett Loomis, *The Sound of Money* (New York: Norton, 1999), 75–108.

79. West and Loomis, *Sound of Money,* 78–82.

80. Skocpol, *Boomerang,* 143–146.

81. West and Loomis, *Sound of Money,* 83–85.

82. Ibid., 79–80.

83. Ibid., 92–93.

84. Douglas Jehl, "Rejoicing Is Muted for the President in Budget Victory," *New York Times,* August 8, 1993, 1, 23; and *Congressional Quarterly Weekly Report,* May 26, 2001, 1251–1254.

85. Christopher Drew and Richard Oppel Jr., "Air War: Remaking Energy Policy," *New York Times,* March 6, 2004, A1.

86. Ibid.

87. Bruce Barcott, "Changing All the Rules," *New York Times,* April 4, 2004, http://www.nytimes.com/2004/04/04/magazine/04BUSH.html?pagewanted=all.

88. Mary H. Cooper, "Air Pollution Conflict," *CQ Researcher,* November 14, 2003, http://photo.pds.org:5012/cqresearcher/document.php?id=cqresrre2003111405.

89. Matthew Wald, "E.P.A. Says It Will Change Rules Governing Industrial Pollution," *New York Times,* November 23, 2002, A1; Drew and Oppel, "Air War," 1; and Don Hopey, "Groups Score Bush on Environment," *Pittsburgh Post-Gazette,* November 10, 2004, 1.

90. Hopey, "Groups Score Bush on Environment," 1.

91. Blumenthal, "The Legacy of Billy Tauzin."

92. "Biden Cheers Deal with Hospitals on Health Care Reform," July 8, 2009, CNN, http://www.cnn.com/2009/POLITICS/07/08/biden.health.care/.

93. Hacker, "The Road to Somewhere," *Perspectives on Politics* 8 (September 2010): 864–865.

94. Aaron Mehta, "Lobbyists Swarm Capitol to Influence Health Reform," Center for Public Integrity, February 24, 2010, http://www.publicintegrity.org/2010/02/24/2725/lobbyists-swarm-capitol-influence-health-reform; and "Health Care Lobbying Boom Continues," CNN Money, March 25, 2011, http://money.cnn.com/2011/03/25/news/economy/health_care_lobbying/index.htm.

95. "Obama's Speech to the Democratic National Convention," *Washington Post,* September 6, 2012; see also Brian Ross, Mathew Mosk, Rhonda Schartz, and Megan Chuchmach, "Democrats Trash Lobbyists in Speeches, but Party with Their Cash," ABC News, September 7, 2012, http://abcnews.go.com/Blotter/demo crats-trash-lobbyists-speeches-party-cash/story?id=17180513.

96. Eliza Newlin Carney, "Lobbyists: Obama's Rules Bring Pain but No Gain," *National Journal,* November 16, 2009; Jeff Zeleny, "Obama Outlines Lobbying Restrictions," *New York Times,* March 20, 2009; Timothy Carney, "A Promising Lobbying Regulation from Obama," *Washington Examiner,* January 31, 2010.

97. Eric Lichtblau, "Across from the White House, Coffee with Lobbyists," *New York Times,* June 29, 2010, http://www.nytimes.com/2010/06/25/us/politics/25caribou .html?pagewanted=all.

98. Ibid; Robert Schlesinger, "Obama Discovers Lobbyists Are Hard to Get Rid Of," *U.S. News and World Report,* May 21, 2012.

99. Eric Lichtblau, "Obama Backers Tied to Lobbies Raise Millions," *New York Times,* October 27, 2012.

100. David Stout, "Obama Moves to Reverse Bush Labor Policies," *New York Times,* January 30, 2009; "Obama Issues Executive Order Reversing GOP Abortion Policy," CNN Political Ticker, January 23, 2009, http://politicalticker.blogs.cnn .com/2009/01/23/obama-issues-executive-order-reversing-gop-abortion-policy/.

101. Stephen Skowronek, *The Politics Presidents Make* (Cambridge, MA: Harvard University Press, 1993).

102. For an excellent review of this literature, see Joseph Pika, "Interest Groups: A Doubly Dynamic Relationship," in *Presidential Policymaking: An End-of-Century Assessment,* ed. Steven Shull (New York: M. E. Sharp, 1999), 59–78.

103. It is telling that Peterson focuses on the political activities of Lyndon Johnson and Ronald Reagan, presidents with exceptional political opportunities to advance policy breakthroughs. See Peterson, "Interest Mobilization and the Presidency," 237.

104. Graham K. Wilson, "The Clinton Administration and Interest Groups," in *The Clinton Presidency: First Appraisals,* ed. Colin Campbell and Bert Rockman (Chatham, NJ: Chatham House, 1996), 231.

105. Stout, "Obama Moves to Reverse Bush Labor Policies."

106. Lynn Sweet, "Obama Acknowledges He Is Not For—Contrary to What He Has Been Saying—a Ban on Lobbyists in the White House," *Chicago Sun-Times,* December 16, 2007.

107. Ibid.; "Obama Vows Ethics Reforms," Associated Press, June 22, 2007; Alexander Bolton, "Senator Obama Finesses His Lobbyist Ties," *The Hill,* April 19, 2007, http://thehill.com/homenews/news/11647-sen-obama-finesses-his-lobbyist-ties. It bears noting that before entering the presidential contest, Obama emerged in 2006 as the Democrats' point person on attacking a Republican "culture of corruption" in the wake of the Jack Abramoff scandal. See "Obama Says It's Time to Clean Up Politics," ABCNews.com, January 18, 2006.

108. Robert Pear, Maggie Haberman, and Reed Abelson, "Trump to Scrap Critical Health Care Subsidies, Hitting Obamacare Again," *New York Times,* October 12, 2017.

109. Chris Cillizza and Sam Petulla, "Trump Has Signed More Executive Orders than Any President in the Last 50 Years," CNN, October 13, 2017; and John Wagner and David Nakamura, "Trump Turns to Executive Powers," *Washington Post,* October 14, 2017.

110. Eric Martinson, "Reversing Obama, Trump ERA Reaches Deal with Pebble Mine Developer," *Alaska Dispatch News,* May 12, 2017.

111. Niraj Choksi, "Nonprofits Opposed to Trump's Ideology See a Surge in Donations," *New York Times,* November 16, 2017; Brian Stelter, "ACLU Racks Up $24.1 Million in Donations Over Weekend," CNN, January 30, 2017; Cale Guthrie Weissman, "All Those Donations Are Giving the ACLU and Planned Parenthood Room," *Fast Company,* February 21, 2017.

12

THE PRESIDENCY AND POLITICAL PARTIES

Sidney M. Milkis

The modern presidency has been anything but supportive of today's Republican and Democratic parties. According to Sidney M. Milkis, most presidents, starting with Franklin Roosevelt, have found the traditional party system too grounded in state and local organizations to be of much help in the effort to forge presidential policies and programs. Indeed, to the extent that the parties have exercised influence through Congress, presidents have sometimes perceived them to be an impediment to national leadership. FDR, Lyndon Johnson, and Richard Nixon each took steps to replace party influence with administration centralized in the bureaucracy and the White House. Ronald Reagan and George H. W. Bush tried to restore some (but not all) of the traditional importance of the political parties, Milkis argues, by "refashioning them into highly untraditional but politically potent national organizations." Their efforts were uneven and met with limited success. Although Bill Clinton did little to sustain the Democratic Party, George W. Bush contributed to, and benefited from, the development of the more national and programmatic Republican Party that emerged with the resurgence and transformation of conservatism during the Reagan presidency. Bush's militant partisanship ultimately became an albatross for his party; nevertheless, party conflict is likely to be an important feature of American politics in the foreseeable future. Indeed, Barack Obama's two terms in office and the first year of Donald Trump's presidency were roiled by partisan divisions that have rattled the resolve of the nation.

The relationship between the presidency and the American party system has always been difficult. The architects of the Constitution established a nonpartisan president who, with the support of the judiciary, was intended to play the leading institutional role in checking and controlling the "violence of faction" that the Framers feared would rend the fabric of representative democracy. Even after the presidency became a more partisan office in the early nineteenth century, its authority continued to depend on an ability to transcend party politics. The president is nominated by a party but, unlike the British prime minister, is not elected by it.

The inherent tension between the presidency and the party system reached a critical point during the 1930s. The institutionalization of the modern presidency, arguably the most significant constitutional legacy of Franklin Roosevelt's New Deal, ruptured the limited but significant bond that linked presidents to their parties. In fact, the modern presidency was crafted with the intention of reducing the influence of the party system on American politics. In this sense Roosevelt's extraordinary party leadership contributed to the decline of the American party system. This decline continued—even accelerated—under the administrations of subsequent presidents, notably Lyndon Johnson and Richard Nixon. Under Ronald Reagan, however, the party system showed signs of transformation and renewal. Reagan and his successor, George H. W. Bush, supported efforts by Republicans in the national committee and the congressional campaign organizations to restore some of the importance of political parties by refashioning them into highly untraditional but politically potent national organizations. George W. Bush further advanced and benefited from the more national and programmatic party that arose with the resurgence and transformation of conservatism during the Reagan presidency.

Yet Bush ultimately became an albatross for the Republican Party in the 2008 election; indeed, his experience suggests that vigorous presidential leadership in the present configuration of executive and party has the defects of its virtues. In the hands of an overweening executive, the party may simply become a means to the president's end, sapping the organization of both its autonomy and its ability to adapt to changing political circumstances. Barack Obama's two terms further advanced developments in the executive-centered party system that Reagan initiated and Bush built upon. Like his Republican predecessors, Obama strengthened his party's capacity to mobilize voters and to advance programmatic initiatives. Like Reagan and Bush, too, his party leadership threatened to subordinate collective responsibility to the White House's political and programmatic ambition. The stunning ascendance of the iconoclastic businessman Donald Trump to the White House and the tumultuous first year of his presidency appeared to confirm that presidency-centered partisanship has denigrated, rather than renewed, the parties' historic function of moderating presidential ambition and mobilizing public support for political values and government policies.

NEW DEAL PARTY POLITICS, PRESIDENTIAL REFORM, AND THE DECLINE OF THE AMERICAN PARTY SYSTEM

The New Deal seriously questioned the adequacy of the traditional natural-rights liberalism of John Locke and the Framers, which emphasized the need to limit constitutionally the scope of government's responsibilities. The modern liberalism that became the public philosophy of the New Deal entailed a fundamental reappraisal of the concept of rights. As Roosevelt first indicated in a 1932 campaign speech at the Commonwealth Club in San Francisco, effective political reform would require, at a minimum, the development of "an economic declaration of rights, an economic constitutional order," grounded in a commitment to guarantee a decent level of economic well-being for the American people. Although equality of opportunity had traditionally been promoted by limited government interference in society, Roosevelt argued, recent economic and social changes, such as the closing of the frontiers and the growth of industrial combinations, demanded that America now recognize "the new terms of the old social contract."[1]

Establishing a new constitutional order would require a reordering of the political process. The traditional patterns of American politics, characterized by constitutional mechanisms that impede collective action, would have to give way to a more centralized and administrative government. As Roosevelt put it, "The day of enlightened administration has come."[2] The concerns Roosevelt expressed at the Commonwealth Club are an important guide to understanding the New Deal and its effects on the party system. The pursuit of an economic constitutional order presupposed a fundamental change in the relationship between the presidency and the party system. In Roosevelt's view, the party system, which was essentially based on state and local organizations and interests and therefore was suited to congressional primacy, would have to be transformed into a national, executive-oriented system organized on the basis of public issues.

In this understanding Roosevelt was no doubt influenced by the thought of Woodrow Wilson. The reform of parties, Wilson believed, depended on extending the influence of the presidency. The limits on partisanship inherent in American constitutional government notwithstanding, the president represented the party's "vital link of connection" with the nation: "He can dominate his party by being spokesman for the real sentiment and purpose of the country, by giving the country at once the information and statements of policy which will enable it to form its judgments alike of parties and men."[3] Wilson's words spoke louder than his actions; like all presidents after 1800, he reconciled himself to the strong fissures within his party.[4] Roosevelt, however, was less willing to work through existing partisan channels, and more important, the New Deal represented a more fundamental departure than did Wilsonian progressivism from traditional Democratic policies of individual autonomy, limited government, and states' rights.

While president-elect, Roosevelt began preparations to modify the partisan practices of previous administrations. For example, convinced that Wilson's adherence to traditional partisan politics in staffing the federal government was unfortunate, Roosevelt expressed to Attorney General Homer Cummings his desire to proceed along somewhat different lines, with a view, according to Cummings's diary, "to building up a national organization rather than allowing patronage to be used merely to build Senatorial and Congressional machines."[5] Roosevelt followed traditional patronage practices during his first term, allowing the chair of the Democratic National Committee (DNC), James Farley, to coordinate appointments in response to local party organizations and Democratic senators. After Roosevelt's reelection in 1936, however, the recommendations of these organizations were not followed as closely. Beginning in 1938 especially, as Edward Flynn, who became the DNC chair in 1940, indicated in his memoirs, "the President turned more and more frequently to the so-called New Dealers," so that "many of the appointments in Washington went to men who were supporters of the President and believed in what he was trying to do, but who were not Democrats in many instances, and in all instances were not organization Democrats."[6] Wilson had taken care to consult with congressional party leaders in the development of his policy program, but Roosevelt relegated his party in Congress to a decidedly subordinate status. He offended legislators by his use of press conferences to announce important decisions and, unlike Wilson, eschewed the use of the party caucus in Congress. Roosevelt rejected as impractical, for example, the Wilsonian suggestion of Rep. Alfred Phillips Jr. "that those sharing the burden of responsibility of party government should regularly and often be called into caucus and that such caucuses should evolve party policies and choice of party leaders."[7] The Roosevelt administration also took action in 1936 to abolish the Democratic National Convention rule that required support from two-thirds of the delegates for the nomination of the president and vice president. This rule had been defended in the past because it guarded the most loyal Democratic region—the South—against the imposition of an unwanted ticket by the less habitually Democratic North, East, and West.[8] To eliminate the rule, therefore, would weaken the influence of southern Democrats (whom Thomas Stokes, a liberal journalist, described as "the ball and chain which hobbled the Party's forward march") and facilitate the adoption of a national reform program.[9] The most dramatic aspect of Roosevelt's attempt to remake the Democratic Party was his twelve-state effort, involving one gubernatorial and several congressional primary campaigns, to unseat conservative Democrats in 1938. Such intervention was not unprecedented; William Taft and Wilson had made limited efforts to remove recalcitrants from their parties. But Roosevelt's campaign took place on a scale that was never before seen and, unlike previous efforts, made no attempt to work through the regular party organization. His action was viewed as such a shocking departure from the norm that the press labeled it "the purge," a term associated with Adolf Hitler's attempt to weed out dissension from Germany's National Socialist Party and Joseph Stalin's elimination of "disloyal" members from the Soviet Communist Party.[10] After the 1938 purge campaign, columnist Raymond Clapper noted that "no President ever has gone as far as Mr. Roosevelt in striving to stamp his policies upon his party."[11]

Roosevelt's massive partisan effort began the process of transforming the parties from local to national and programmatic organizations. At the same time, the New Deal made partisanship less important. Roosevelt's partisan leadership ultimately was based on forging a personal link with the public that would better enable him to make use of his position as leader of the nation, not just of the party that governed the nation.[12] For example, in all but one of the 1938 primary campaigns in which he participated personally, Roosevelt chose to make a direct appeal to public opinion rather than attempt to work through, or reform, the regular party apparatus. This strategy was encouraged by earlier reforms, especially the direct primary, which had begun to weaken the grip of party organizations on the voters. Radio broadcasting also had made direct presidential appeals an enticing strategy, especially for as popular a president with as fine a radio presence as Roosevelt. After his close associate Felix Frankfurter urged him to go to the country in August 1937 to explain the issues that gave rise to the bitter Court-packing controversy, Roosevelt, perhaps anticipating the purge campaign, responded, "You are absolutely right about the radio. I feel like saying to the country—'You will hear from me soon and often. This is not a threat but a promise.'"[13]

In the final analysis, the "benevolent dictatorship" that Roosevelt sought to impose on the Democratic Party was more conducive to corroding the American party system than to reforming it. His prescription for party reform—extraordinary presidential leadership—posed a serious if not intractable dilemma. On the one hand, the decentralized character of politics in the United States could be modified only by strong presidential leadership; on the other, a president determined to alter fundamentally the connection between the executive and the party eventually would shatter party unity.[14] Roosevelt felt that a full revamping of partisan politics was impractical, given the obstacles to party government that are so deeply ingrained in the American political experience. The immense failure of the purge campaign reinforced this view: in the dozen states in which the president acted against entrenched incumbents, he was successful in only two—Oregon and New York.[15] Moreover, Roosevelt and his fellow New Dealers did not view the welfare state as a partisan issue. The reform program of the 1930s was conceived as a "second bill of rights" that they meant to establish as much as possible in permanent programs beyond the vagaries of public opinion and elections. The new rights that Roosevelt pledged the federal government to protect included "the right to a useful and remunerative job" and "the right to adequate protection from the fears of old age, sickness, accident and unemployment."[16] These new rights were never formally ratified as part of the Constitution, but they became the foundation of political dialogue, redefining the role of the national government and requiring major changes in American political institutions.

Thus, the most significant institutional reforms of the New Deal did not promote party government but fostered instead a program that would help the president to govern in the absence of party government—to enable him to become, in Theodore Roosevelt's capacious phrase, "the steward of the public welfare."[17] This program, as embodied in the 1937 executive reorganization bill, would have greatly extended presidential authority over the executive branch, including the independent regulatory commissions. The president and the executive agencies would also be delegated extensive authority to govern, making unnecessary the constant cooperation of party members in Congress. As a presidential committee report put it, with administrative reform the "brief exultant commitment" to progressive government that was expressed in the elections of 1932 and, especially, 1936 would now be more firmly established in "persistent, determined, competent, day by day administration of what the Nation has decided to do."[18] Interestingly, the reorganization bill, which was intended to make partisan politics less necessary, became, at Roosevelt's urging, a party government–style "vote of confidence" for the administration in Congress.[19] Roosevelt initially lost this vote in 1938, when the bill was defeated in the House of Representatives, but he did manage, through the purge campaign and other partisan actions, to keep administrative reform sufficiently prominent in party councils so that a compromise version passed in 1939. Although considerably weaker than Roosevelt's original proposal, the 1939 Executive Reorganization Act was a significant measure. It not only provided authority to create the Executive Office of the President, which included the newly formed White House Office and a strengthened and refurbished Bureau of the Budget, but also enhanced the president's control of the expanding activities of the executive branch. The reorganization act represents the genesis of the institutional presidency, which was equipped to govern independently of the constraints imposed by the regular political process.

The civil service reform that the Roosevelt administration carried out was another important part of the effort to replace partisan politics with executive administration. The original reorganization proposals of 1937 contained provisions to make the administration of the civil service more effective and to expand the merit system. Although the reorganization bill passed in 1939 was shorn of this controversial feature, Roosevelt found it possible to accomplish extensive civil service reform through executive action and other legislation. He extended merit protection to personnel appointed by the administration during its first term, four-fifths of whom had been brought into government outside of merit channels.[20] Patronage appointments had traditionally been used to nourish the party system; the New Deal celebrated an administrative politics that fed instead an executive branch oriented to expanding liberal programs. As the administrative historian Paul Van Riper has noted, the new practices created a new kind of patronage, "a sort of intellectual and ideological patronage rather than the more traditional partisan type."[21] Roosevelt's leadership transformed the Democratic Party into a way station on the road to administrative government. As the presidency developed into an elaborate and ubiquitous institution, it preempted party leaders in many of their limited, but significant, duties: providing a link from government to interest groups, staffing the executive department, contributing to policy development, organizing election campaigns, and communicating with the public.[22] Moreover, New Deal administrative reform was directed not just to creating presidential government, but also to embedding progressive principles in a bureaucratic structure that would insulate reform and reformers from electoral change.

LYNDON JOHNSON'S GREAT SOCIETY AND THE TRANSCENDENCE OF PARTISAN POLITICS

Roosevelt's leadership during the New Deal prepared the executive branch to be a government unto itself and established the presidency rather than the party as the locus of political responsibility. World War II and the Cold War greatly augmented this shift. With the Great Depression giving way to war, another expansion of presidential authority took place, as part of the national security state, further weakening the executive's ties with the party system. As the New Deal prepared for war, Roosevelt spoke not only of the government's obligation to guarantee "freedom from want," but also of its responsibility to provide "freedom from fear"— to protect the American people, and the world, against foreign aggression. The obligation to uphold "human rights" became a new guarantee of security, which presupposed a further expansion of national administrative power.[23] The new requirements of internationalism allowed Harry Truman to persuade Congress to enact an additional administrative reform in 1947, increasing the powers of, and centralizing control over, the national security state. Called the National Security Act, it created the National Security Council, the Central Intelligence Agency, and the Department of Defense.[24]

But the modern presidency was created to chart the course for, and direct the voyage to, a more liberal America. Roosevelt's pronouncement of a "second bill of rights" had begun this task, and it fell to Lyndon Johnson, as one journalist noted, to "codify the New Deal vision of a good society."[25] Johnson's Great Society program entailed expanding the economic constitutional order with policy innovations such as Medicare and, even more significantly, extending those benefits to African Americans.

Johnson's attempt to create the Great Society marked a significant extension of programmatic liberalism and accelerated the effort to transcend partisan politics. Johnson, who came to Congress in 1937 in a special House election as an enthusiastic supporter of the New Deal, well remembered Roosevelt's ill-fated efforts to guide the affairs of his party. He took Roosevelt's experience to be the best example of the generally ephemeral nature of party government in the United States, and he fully expected the cohesive Democratic support he received from Congress after the 1964 election to be temporary.[26] Johnson, like Roosevelt, looked beyond the party system toward the politics of "enlightened administration."

Although Johnson avoided any sort of purge campaign and worked closely with Democratic congressional leaders, he took strong action to de-emphasize the role of the traditional party organization. For example, the Johnson administration undertook a ruthless attack on the DNC beginning in late 1965, slashing its budget to the bone and eliminating several of its important programs, such as the highly successful voter registration division. The president also ignored the pleas of several advisers to replace the amiable but ineffective John Bailey as DNC chair. Instead, he humiliated Bailey, keeping him but turning over control of the scaled-back committee's activities to Marvin Watson, the White House political liaison.[27] Journalists and scholars explain Johnson's lack of support for the regular party organization by invoking his political background and personality. Some observers have suggested that Johnson was afraid the DNC might be built into a power center capable of challenging his authority on behalf of the Kennedy wing of the party.[28] Others have pointed to Johnson's roots in the one-party system of Texas, an experience that inclined him to emphasize a consensus style of politics, based on support from diverse elements of the electorate that spanned traditional party lines.[29] These explanations are not without merit. Yet to view Johnson's failures as a party leader in purely personal terms is to ignore the imperative of policy reform that influenced his administration. Like Roosevelt, Johnson "had always regarded political parties, strongly rooted in states and localities, capable of holding him accountable, as intruders on the business of government."[30] Moreover, from the beginning of his presidency Johnson had envisioned the enactment of an ambitious program that would leave its (and his) mark on history in the areas of government organization, civil rights, conservation, education, and urban affairs. Such efforts to advance the New Deal goal of economic security and also to enhance the "quality of American life" necessarily brought Johnson into sharp conflict with established elements of the Democratic Party, such as the national committee and local machines.[31] As one Johnson aide put it, "Because of the ambitious reforms [LBJ] pushed, it was necessary to move well beyond, to suspend attention to, the party."[32]

Indeed, considerable evidence exists that the Johnson administration lacked confidence in the Democratic Party's ability to act as an intermediary between the White House and the American people. For example, an aide to Vice President Hubert Humphrey wrote to Marvin Watson that "out in the country most Democrats at the State and local level are not intellectually equipped to help on such critical issues as Vietnam and the riots." After a meeting with district party leaders from Queens, New York, White House domestic adviser Joseph Califano reported that "they were . . . totally unfamiliar with the dramatic increases in the poverty, health, education and manpower training areas."[33] The uneasy relationship between the Johnson presidency and the Democratic Party was particularly aggravated by the administration's aggressive commitment to civil rights, which created considerable friction with local party organizations, especially, but not exclusively, in the South. It is little wonder, then, that when riots began to erupt in the cities in the mid-1960s, the president had his special assistants spend time in ghettos around the country instead of relying on the reports of local party leaders.[34]

Lack of trust in the Democratic Party encouraged the Johnson administration to renew the New Deal pattern of institutional reform. In the area of policy development, one of Johnson's most significant innovations was to create several task forces under the supervision of the White House Office and the Bureau of the Budget. These working groups were made up of leading academics throughout the country, who prepared reports in virtually all areas of public policy. The specific proposals that came out of these groups, such as the Education Task Force's elementary education proposal, formed the heart of the Great Society program. The administration took great care to protect the task forces from political pressures, even keeping their existence secret. Moreover, members were told to pay no attention to political considerations; they were not to worry about whether their recommendations would be acceptable to Congress and party leaders.[35] The de-emphasis of partisan politics that marked the creation of the Great Society was also apparent in the personnel policy of the Johnson presidency. As his main talent scout, Johnson chose not a political adviser but John Macy, who was also chair of the Civil Service Commission. Macy worked closely with the White House staff, but especially during the early days of the administration, he was responsible for making recommendations directly to the president. As the White House staff rather grudgingly admitted, Macy's "wheel ground exceedingly slow but exceedingly fine."[36] He uncovered candidates with impressive credentials and experience after careful national searches.

The Johnson administration's strong commitment to merit greatly disturbed certain advisers who were responsible for maintaining the president's political support. James Rowe, who was Johnson's campaign director in 1964 and 1968, constantly hounded Macy, without success, to consider political loyalists more carefully. Rowe believed that Johnson's personnel policy was gratuitously inattentive to political exigencies. At one point he ended a memo to Macy by saying, "Perhaps you can train some of those career men to run the political campaign in 1968. (It ain't as easy as you government people appear to think it is.)" Macy never responded, but the president called the next day to defend his personnel director and to chastise Rowe for seeking to interfere in the appointment process.[37]

The rupture between the presidency and the party made it difficult to sustain political enthusiasm and organizational support for the Great Society. The Democrats' poor showing in the 1966 congressional elections precipitated a firestorm of criticism about the president's inattention to party politics, criticism that continued until Johnson withdrew from the presidential campaign in 1968. Yet Johnson and most of his advisers felt that they had to de-emphasize partisanship if the administration was to achieve programmatic reform and coordinate the increasingly unwieldy activities of government. During the early days of the Johnson presidency, one of his more thoughtful aides, Horace Busby, wrote the president a long memo in which he stressed the importance of establishing an institutional basis for the Great Society. About a year later, Busby expressed great satisfaction that Johnson had confounded his critics by achieving notable institutional changes. In fact, these changes seemed to mark the full triumph of the Democrats as the party to end party politics:

> Most startling is that while all recognize Johnson as a great politician
> his appointments have been the most consistently free of politics of any
> President—in the Cabinet or at lower levels.

> On record, history will remember this as the most important era of
> nonpartisanship since the "Era of Good Feeling" more than a century ago
> at the start of the nineteenth century. Absence of politics and partisanship is
> one reason the GOP is having a hard time mounting any respectable offense
> against either Johnson or his program.[38]

As in the case of the New Deal, however, the institutional innovations of the Great Society did not eliminate "politics" from the activities of the executive branch. Rather, the Great Society extended the merging of politics and administration that had characterized executive reform during the 1930s. For example, to improve his use of the appointment process as a tool of executive administration, Johnson issued an executive order to create a new category of positions in the executive branch, called noncareer executive assignments (NEAs). In recognition of their direct involvement in policymaking, the NEAs were exempted from the usual civil service requirements.

To be sure, the NEAs gave Johnson a stronger foothold in the agencies.[39] But the criteria his administration used to fill these positions emphasized loyalty to Johnson's program rather than a personal commitment to the president. As a consequence, Johnson's active role as manager of the federal service, which John Macy considered unprecedented for a "modern-day Chief Executive," helped to revive the high morale and programmatic commitment that had characterized the bureaucracy during the 1930s.[40] As White House aide Bill Moyers urged in a memo to the president regarding the newly created Department of Housing and Urban Development, the goal of the Great Society was to renew "some of the zeal—coupled with sound, tough executive management of the New Deal days."[41] The legacy of Johnson's assault on party politics was apparent in the 1968 election. By 1966 Democratic leaders no longer felt that they were part of a national coalition. As 1968 approached, the Johnson administration was preparing a campaign task force that would work independently of the regular party apparatus.[42] These actions greatly accelerated the breakdown of the state and local Democratic machinery, placing party organizations in acute distress in nearly every large state.[43] By the time Johnson withdrew from the election in March 1968, the Democratic Party was already in the midst of a lengthy period of decay that was accentuated, but not really caused, by the conflict over the Vietnam War.

Thus the tumultuous 1968 Democratic convention and the reforms of the nominating process, spawned by the McGovern–Fraser Commission, that followed should be viewed as the culmination of long-standing efforts to free the presidency from traditional partisan influences. In many respects, the expansion of presidential primaries and other changes in nomination politics that the commission initiated were a logical extension of the modern presidency. The very quietness of the revolution in party rules that took place during the 1970s is evidence in itself that the party system was forlorn by the end of the Johnson era. Those changes could not have been accomplished over the opposition of alert and vigorous party leaders.[44] Johnson was well aware that the collapse of the regular party apparatus was under way by 1968. From 1966 on, his aides bombarded him with memos warning of the disarray in the Democratic Party organization. Johnson also was informed that reform forces in the states were creating "a new ball game with new rules." These memos indicated that by exploiting the weakened party apparatus, an insurgent with as little national prominence as antiwar senator Eugene McCarthy could mount a head-on challenge to Johnson.[45] The president expressed his own recognition of the decline of party politics in a meeting with Humphrey on April 5, 1968, a few days after he announced his decision not to run for reelection.

Although indicating his intention to remain publicly neutral, Johnson wished the vice president well. But he expressed concern about Humphrey's ability to win the support of the party organization: "This the president cannot assure the vice president because he could not assure it for himself."[46] Like Roosevelt, Johnson had greatly diminished his partisan capital in pursuit of programmatic innovation.

RICHARD NIXON, NONPARTISANSHIP, AND THE DEMISE OF THE MODERN PRESIDENCY

Considering that the New Deal and Great Society were established by replacing traditional party politics with administration, it is not surprising that when a conservative challenge to liberal reform emerged, it entailed the creation of a conservative "administrative presidency."[47]

Until the late 1960s, opponents of the welfare state were generally opposed to the modern presidency, which had served as the fulcrum of liberal reform. Nevertheless, by the end of the Johnson administration it was clear that a strong conservative movement would require an activist program of retrenchment to counteract the enduring effects of the New Deal and Great Society.[48] Opponents of liberal public policy, most of them Republicans, decided that, ideologically, the modern presidency could be a two-edged sword.

The administrative actions of the Nixon presidency were a logical extension of the practices of Roosevelt and Johnson. Nixon's centralization of authority in the White House and reduction of the regular Republican organization to perfunctory status were hardly unprecedented.[49] The complete autonomy of the Committee for the Re-Election of the President (CREEP) from the Republican National Committee (RNC) in Nixon's 1972 campaign was but the final stage of a long process of White House preemption of the national committee's political responsibilities. And the administrative reform program that was pursued after Nixon's reelection, in which he concentrated executive authority in the hands of White House operatives and four cabinet "supersecretaries," was the culmination of a long-standing tendency in the modern presidency to reconstitute the executive branch as a formidable instrument of government.[50] Thus, just as Roosevelt's presidency anticipated the Great Society, Johnson's presidency anticipated the administrative presidency of Richard Nixon. Indeed, the strategy of pursuing policy goals through administrative entities, which had been created for the most part by Democratic presidents, was considered especially suitable by a minority Republican president who faced a Congress and bureaucracy intent on preserving his predecessors' programs. Nixon actually surpassed previous modern presidents in viewing the party system as an obstacle to effective governance.

Yet, mainly because of the Watergate scandal, Nixon's presidency had the effect of strengthening opposition to the unilateral use of presidential power, even as it further attenuated the bonds that linked presidents to the party system. The evolution of the modern presidency now left the office in complete institutional isolation. This isolation continued during the Ford and Carter years, so much so that by the end of the 1970s scholars were lamenting the demise of the presidency as well as of the party system.

THE REAGAN PRESIDENCY AND THE REVITALIZATION OF PARTY POLITICS

Although the emergence of the modern presidency fostered a serious decline in the traditional local and state patronage-based parties, some developments during the Reagan presidency suggested that a phoenix was emerging from the ashes. The erosion of old-style partisan politics and the realignment of partisan allegiance in the South from Democratic to Republican allowed a more national and issue-oriented party system to develop, forging new links between presidents and their parties.

The Republican Party in particular developed a formidable organizational apparatus, which displayed unprecedented strength at the national level.[51] The refurbishing of the Republican organization was due largely to the efforts of William Brock, who, during his tenure as chair of the RNC from 1976 to 1980, set out to rejuvenate and ultimately to revolutionize the national party. After 1976 the RNC and the two other national Republican campaign bodies, the National Republican Senatorial Committee and the National Republican Congressional (House) Committee, greatly expanded their efforts to raise funds and provide services for the party's state and local candidates. Moreover, these efforts carried the national party into activities such as publishing public policy journals and distributing comprehensive briefing books for candidates that demonstrated its interest in generating programmatic proposals that might be politically useful. The Democrats lagged behind in party-building efforts, but the losses they suffered in the 1980 elections encouraged them to modernize the national political machinery, openly imitating some of the devices used by the Republicans. As a result, the traditional apparatus of both parties, which was based on patronage and state and local organizations, gave way to a more programmatic party politics, based on the national organization. Arguably, a party system had finally evolved that was compatible with the national polity forged on the anvil of the New Deal.[52] The revival of the Republican Party as a force to counter government-by-administration reinforced the development of a new American party system. The nomination and election of Ronald Reagan, a far more ideological conservative than Richard Nixon, galvanized the GOP's commitment to programs such as "regulatory relief" and "new federalism" that challenged the institutional legacy of the New Deal. At the same time, Reagan broke with the tradition of the modern presidency and identified closely with his party. The president worked hard to strengthen the Republicans' organizational and popular base, surprising his own political director with his "total readiness" to shoulder partisan responsibilities such as making numerous fund-raising appearances for the party and its candidates.[53] After having spent the first fifty years of his life as a Democrat, Reagan brought the enthusiasm of a convert to Republican activities.

The experience of the Reagan administration suggested how the relationship between the president and the party could be mutually beneficial. A strong Republican Party provided Reagan with the support of a formidable institution, solidifying his personal popularity and facilitating support for his program in Congress. As a result, the Reagan presidency was able to suspend the paralysis that had seemed to afflict the executive office in the 1970s, even though the Republicans still lacked control of the House of Representatives. In turn, Reagan's popularity served the party by strengthening its fund-raising efforts and promoting a shift in voters' party loyalties, placing the Republicans by 1985 in a position of virtual parity with the Democrats for the first time since the 1940s.[54]

Yet the Reagan presidency frequently pursued its program with acts of administrative discretion that short-circuited the legislative process and weakened efforts to carry out broadly based party policies. From the start, in fact, the Reagan White House often pursued programmatic change by using the administrative tactics that characterized the Nixon years. Not only was policy centered in the White House Office and other support agencies in the Executive Office of the President, but much care was taken to plant White House loyalists in the departments and agencies— people who could be trusted to ride herd on civil servants and carry forth the president's program. Most significantly, a wide range of policies to deregulate business were pursued, not through legislative change but by administrative inaction, delay, and repeal. President Reagan's Executive Orders 12291 and 12498 mandated a comprehensive review of proposed agency regulations and centralized the review process in the Office of Management and Budget (OMB).[55] Reagan also appointed the Task Force on Regulatory Relief, headed by Vice President George H. W. Bush, to apply cost-benefit analyses to existing rules. Similarly, the Iran-contra scandal was not simply a matter of the president's being asleep on his watch; rather, it also revealed the Reagan administration's determination to assume a more forceful anti-communist posture in Central America in the face of a recalcitrant Congress and bureaucracy.[56]

Consequently, Reagan did not transform Washington completely. Rather, he strengthened the Republican beachhead in the nation's capital, solidifying his party's recent dominance of the presidency and providing better opportunities for conservatives in the Washington community. Reagan's landslide reelection in 1984 did not prevent the Democrats from maintaining control of the House of Representatives; nor did his plea to the voters during the 1986 congressional campaign to elect Republican majorities prevent the Democrats from recapturing control of the Senate. The 1988 election, in which Vice President Bush defeated the Democratic Massachusetts governor, Michael Dukakis, appeared to confirm the limits of the Reagan revolution, reflecting in its outcome the underlying pattern that had characterized American politics since 1968: Republican dominance of the White House, Democratic ascendancy almost everywhere else. In fact, the 1988 election represented an extreme manifestation of the pattern. Never before had a president been elected while the other party gained ground in the House, the Senate, the state legislatures, and the state governorships. Never before had voters given a newly elected president fewer fellow partisans in Congress than they gave George H. W. Bush.[57]

In the final analysis, Reagan's two terms witnessed a revitalization of the struggle between the president and Congress that marred the Nixon years; indeed, his conservative program became the foundation for more fundamental philosophical and policy differences between the two branches than in the past. The Iran-contra affair and the battles to control regulatory policy were marked not just by differences between Reagan and Congress about policy, but also by the efforts of each to weaken the other. The pursuit of conservative policies through the administrative presidency continued with Bush's elevation to the White House. Facing hostile Democratic majorities in the House and Senate, the Bush administration imposed the burden of curbing environmental, consumer, and civil rights regulations on the Competitiveness Council, chaired by Vice President Dan Quayle. Like its predecessor, the Task Force on Regulatory Relief, the Competitiveness Council required administrative agencies to justify the costs of existing and proposed regulations. The efforts of Republican presidents to compensate for their party's inability to control Congress by seeking to circumvent legislative restrictions on presidential conduct were matched by Democratic initiatives to burden the executive with smothering legislative oversight.[58] Conservatives opposed to liberal reform, then, did not challenge national administrative power but fought a raw and disruptive battle to control its services.

A major, if not the main, forum for partisan conflict during the Reagan and Bush years was a sequence of investigations in which Democrats and Republicans sought to discredit one another. To be sure, ongoing legal scrutiny of public officials was in part a logical response to the Watergate scandal. To prevent another Nixon-style "Saturday Night Massacre," Congress passed the Ethics in Government Act of 1978, which provided for the appointment of independent counsels to investigate allegations of criminal activity by executive officials. Not surprisingly, divided government encouraged the exploitation of the act for partisan purposes. In the 1980s congressional Democrats frequently demanded criminal investigations and possible jail sentences for their political opponents. When Bill Clinton became president in 1993, congressional Republicans turned the tide with a vengeance. As a consequence, political disagreements were readily transformed into criminal prosecutions. Moreover, investigations under the independent counsel statute tended to deflect attention from legitimate constitutional policy differences and to focus the attention of Congress, the press, and citizens alike on scandals. Disgrace and imprisonment thus joined electoral defeat as risks of political combat in the United States.[59]

BILL CLINTON AND THE POLITICS OF DIVIDED DEMOCRACY

The 1992 election contained both optimistic and pessimistic portents for linking the modern presidency and national parties. The Democrats ran an effective campaign; the party not only captured the presidency, but also preserved its majorities in the House and Senate, ending twelve years of divided rule in Washington.

Bill Clinton's victory over George H. W. Bush seemed to represent more than a rejection of the incumbent president; in part, it expressed the voters' hope that the institutional conflict they had witnessed during the era of divided government would now come to an end.[60] This hope was encouraged by Clinton's promise to govern as a "new Democrat," an "agent of change" who would restore consensus to American politics.

Nevertheless, the strong support for independent candidate Ross Perot reflected the continuing erosion of partisan loyalties in the electorate. Perot's campaign, which garnered 19 percent of the popular vote (the most serious electoral challenge to the two-party system since Theodore Roosevelt's 1912 Progressive Party candidacy), suggested just how much presidential politics had become detached from the constraints of party. Perot, a successful businessman, had never held political office of any kind, and his campaign, dominated by thirty-minute infomercials and hour-long appearances on television talk shows, set a new standard for direct, plebiscitary appeals to the voters that threatened to sound the death knell of the party campaign. "Perot hints broadly at an even bolder new order," historian Alan Brinkley wrote in July 1992, "in which the president, checked only by direct expressions of popular desire, will roll up his sleeves and solve the nation's problems."[61]

In the end, however, the American people invested their hope for constructive change more cautiously, in the possibility that Clinton embodied a new form of Democratic politics that could correct and renew the progressive tradition as shaped by the New Deal. During the mid-1980s, Clinton had headed the Democratic Leadership Council (DLC), a group of party moderates who developed many of the ideas that became the central themes of his run for the presidency. As Clinton declared frequently during the campaign, these ideas represented a new philosophy of government, a "new covenant" that in the name of opportunity, responsibility, and community would seek to constrain the demands for economic rights that had been unleashed by the New Deal. The essence of Clinton's message was that the long-standing liberal commitment to guarantee economic welfare through entitlement programs such as Social Security, Medicare, Medicaid, and Aid to Families with Dependent Children had gone too far. The main objective of the new covenant was to correct the tendency of Americans to celebrate individual rights and government entitlements without acknowledging the mutual obligations they had to one another and to their country.[62] Clinton pledged to dedicate his party to the new concept of justice he espoused. But his commitment to control government spending and recast the welfare state was obscured during the early days of his presidency by many traditional liberal actions. No sooner had he been inaugurated than Clinton announced his intention to lift the long-standing ban on homosexuals in the military. The president soon learned, however, the difficulty of resolving such a divisive social issue through "the stroke of a pen." To be sure, the development of the administrative presidency gave chief executives more power to make domestic policy autonomously. Yet when presidents tried to extend national administration to issues that shaped the character of American public life, this power proved inadequate.[63] Most damaging for Clinton was that the issue became a symbol of his inability to revitalize progressive politics as an instrument to redress the economic insecurity and political alienation of the middle class.

The bitter partisan fight over the administration's budget, in summer 1993, reinforced doubts about Clinton's ability to lead the nation in a new, more harmonious direction. Even though his budget plan promised to reduce the deficit, it included new taxes and an array of social programs that Republicans and conservative Democrats perceived as standard "tax and spend" liberalism. In August 1993 Congress enacted a modified version of the plan, albeit by a razor-thin margin and without any support from Republicans, who voted unanimously against it in the House and Senate. Clinton won this narrow, bruising victory only after promising moderate Democrats that he would put together another package of spending cuts in the fall. But this uneasy compromise failed to dispel his political opponents' charge that Clinton was a wolf in sheep's clothing—a conventional liberal whose commitment to reform had expired as soon as he was elected.[64] The deference that Clinton displayed toward traditional liberal causes was, to an extent, understandable; it was a logical response to the modern institutional separation between the presidency and the party. The moderate wing of the party that he represented— including the DLC—was a minority wing. The majority of liberal interest group activists and Democratic members of Congress still preferred "entitlements" to "obligations" and "regulations" to "responsibilities." The media-driven caucuses and primaries, a legacy of the McGovern–Fraser reforms, had given Clinton the opportunity to seize the Democratic nomination as an outsider candidate, but they offered him no means to effect a transformation of his party when he took office.

It is not surprising, therefore, that Clinton's allies in the DLC urged him to renew his "credentials as an outsider" by going over the heads of his party's leaders in Congress and taking his message directly to the people. The new president could "break gridlock," they argued, only by appealing to the large number of independents in the electorate who had voted for Perot—that is, by "forging new and sometimes bipartisan coalitions around an agenda that moves beyond the polarized left-right debate."[65] In fall 1993 Clinton took a page from his former DLC associates by successfully campaigning to secure congressional approval of the North American Free Trade Agreement (NAFTA) with Canada and Mexico. The fight for NAFTA caused Clinton to defend free enterprise ardently and to oppose the protectionism favored by labor unions, one of the most important constituencies in the national Democratic Party. Clinton's victory owed partly to the support of the Republican congressional leadership. No less important was Vice President Al Gore's inspired performance in a debate with Perot, the leading opponent of NAFTA. Gore's optimistic defense of free markets was well received by a large television audience, rousing enough public support for the treaty to persuade a majority of legislators in both houses of Congress to approve it.[66]

It was health care, however, not trade policy that became the defining issue of Clinton's first two years in office. The administration's health care proposal promised to "guarantee all Americans a comprehensive package of benefits over the course of an entire lifetime." The formulation of this program appeared to mark the apotheosis of New Deal administrative politics; it was designed by First Lady Hillary Rodham Clinton and the president's longtime friend Ira Magaziner behind closed doors. Moreover, it would have created a new government entitlement program and an administrative apparatus that signaled the revitalization rather than the reform of the traditional welfare state.[67] Although Clinton made conciliatory overtures to the plan's opponents, hoping to forge bipartisan cooperation on Capitol Hill and a broad consensus among the general public, the possibilities for comprehensive reform hinged on settling differences about the appropriate role of government that had divided the parties and the country for the past two decades. In the end, this proved impossible.[68] By proposing such an ambitious health care reform bill, Clinton angered conservatives. By failing to deliver on his proposal, he dismayed the ardent liberals of his party. Most significantly, the defeat of the health care program created the overwhelming impression that Clinton had not lived up to his campaign promise to transcend the bitter philosophical and partisan battles of the Reagan and Bush years.

Clinton and his party paid dearly for this failure in the 1994 midterm elections. The Republicans gained fifty-two seats in the House and eight in the Senate, taking control of Congress for the first time in forty-two years. The Republicans achieved this victory in a campaign that was unusually ideological and partisan. The charged atmosphere of the election owed much to the efforts of the House minority whip, Rep. Newt Gingrich of Georgia. Gingrich, his party's choice to be the new Speaker of the 104th Congress, persuaded more than 300 House candidates to sign the Republican Contract with America, a "covenant" with the nation that promised to rein in government by eliminating programs, ameliorating regulatory burdens, and cutting taxes. Clinton's attack on the Republican program during the campaign backfired, serving only to abet the Republicans in their efforts to highlight the president's failure to transform the Democratic Party and mute partisan division in Washington.[69] The dramatic Republican triumph in the 1994 midterm elections brought back divided government and with it the institutional confrontation between the president and Congress that Clinton had promised to resolve. The first session of the 104th Congress, in 1995, quickly degenerated into the same sort of administrative politics that had corroded the legitimacy of political institutions in the United States since Nixon's presidency. This time, however, the struggle between the branches assumed a novel form: a Democratic White House versus a Republican Congress.

The battle between Clinton and Congress became especially fierce over legislation to balance the budget. More than any other idea celebrated in the Contract with America, Republicans believed that legislation balancing the budget would give them their best opportunity to control Congress for years to come. The most controversial part of the GOP's program was a proposal to scale back the growth of Medicare, a federal health insurance program for the elderly, by encouraging beneficiaries to enroll in health maintenance organizations and other private managed health care systems. Rallied by their most militantly partisan members in the House, Republicans sought to pressure Clinton to accept their budget priorities by twice shutting down federal government offices and even threatening to force the U.S. Treasury into default. Clinton effectively countered these confrontational tactics. His veto in December 1995 of a sweeping Republican budget bill that not only would have overhauled Medicare but also remade decades of federal social policy roused popular support for the administration. In attacking Medicare and other popular Democratic social policies, such as environmental programs, the

Republicans' assault on programmatic liberalism went beyond what was promised by the Contract with America and gave Clinton the opportunity to take a political stand that most of the country supported.

When Congress returned for the second session of the 104th Congress in January 1996, it was not to Speaker Gingrich's agenda of reducing the role of Washington in the society and economy but to the measured tones of Clinton's third State of the Union message. The president, having outmaneuvered the Republican Congress, now co-opted its most popular theme, declaring that "the era of big government is over."[70] This was not merely a rhetorical flourish. Withstanding furious criticism from liberal Democratic members of Congress and interest group activists, Clinton signed welfare reform legislation in August that replaced the existing entitlement to cash payments for low-income mothers and their dependent children with temporary assistance and a strict work requirement.[71] Clinton conceded that the act was flawed, cutting too deeply into nutritional support for low-income working people and denying support unfairly to legal immigrants. Nevertheless, by requiring welfare recipients to take jobs, it served the fundamental principle Clinton had championed in the 1992 campaign of "re-creating the Nation's social bargain with the poor."[72] Throughout his 1996 reelection campaign, Clinton held firmly to the centrist ground he had staked out after the 1994 elections, campaigning on the same "new" Democratic themes of "opportunity, responsibility, and community" that had served him well during his first run for the White House. He won 49 percent of the popular vote, to Republican nominee Robert Dole's 41 percent and Perot's 8 percent, and 379 electoral votes to Dole's 159.

Yet Clinton's campaign testified to the fragility of the presidency-centered partisanship that arose during the 1980s. Clinton was the first Democratic president since FDR to be elected to a second term, but by focusing on his own campaign he did little to help his party. The Democrats lost two seats in the Senate and gained only a modest nine seats in the House, failing to regain control of either chamber. The president's remarkable political comeback in 1995 was supported by so-called soft money that by law was designated for party-building activities.[73] But these funds were used mostly to mount television advertising campaigns that championed the president's independence from partisan conflicts. Clinton scarcely endorsed the election of a Democratic Congress in 1996; moreover, he raised funds for the party's congressional candidates only late in the campaign. Adding insult to injury, the administration's dubious fund-raising methods led to revelations during the final days of the campaign that reduced Clinton's margin of victory and undermined the Democrats' effort to retake the House.[74]

Clinton's wayward effort to forge a "third way" between the two parties was suggestive of the modern presidency's dominant but uneasy place in the partisan conflict that emerged from the Reagan "revolution." The disjuncture between the bitter partisanship on Capitol Hill and the weakening of partisan affiliation outside it helped to win Clinton a certain following in the country.[75] Yet as the House's impeachment and the Senate's trial of Clinton dramatically revealed, the "extraordinary isolation" of the modern presidency has its limits.[76] Hoping to become a great president in the tradition of Franklin Roosevelt, Clinton instead became the first elected chief executive to be impeached. (Andrew Johnson, the only other president to suffer such an indignity, inherited the office after Lincoln was assassinated.) Just as Reagan and Bush were plagued by independent counsels who investigated alleged abuses in their administrations under the authority of the Ethics in Government Act, so did Clinton have troubles of his own with independent counsels.[77] In early January 1998 Kenneth Starr was authorized to pursue allegations that the president had lied under oath about having an affair with a White House intern, Monica Lewinsky, and that at Clinton's urging his close associate Vernon Jordan had encouraged Lewinsky to perjure herself about the matter.

With Clinton facing an impeachment trial, nearly every political expert predicted that the Republicans would emerge from the 1998 elections with a tighter grip on Congress and, by implication, on the president's political fate.[78] But the Republicans had been preoccupied by the Lewinsky scandal for an entire year and lacked an appealing campaign message. They were unable to increase their 55–45 majority in the Senate and lost five seats in the House, leaving them with a slim 223–211 majority. Clinton, the first Democrat since FDR to be reelected, now became the first president since Roosevelt in 1934 to see his party gain seats in a midterm election. Bitterly disappointed by the results, Republicans fell into soul-searching and recriminations. Ironically, it was the hero of their 1994 ascent to power, Speaker Newt Gingrich, whose political fate was sealed by the elections. Soon after the results were tallied, Gingrich announced that he was resigning not only his leadership position, but also his seat in Congress.

Still, any moral authority Clinton may have had at the beginning of his administration to establish a new covenant of rights and responsibilities between citizens and their government was severely undermined by the public's distaste for his personal conduct.[79] The virulent partisanship that characterized the impeachment process forced Clinton to seek refuge once again among his fellow Democrats in Congress, thereby short-circuiting plans to pursue entitlement reform as the capstone of his presidency.[80] In the wake of the impeachment debacle, Clinton positioned himself as the champion of Social Security and Medicare, urging Congress to invest a significant share of the mounting budget surplus in these unreconstructed liberal programs.[81] Clinton's extraordinary resilience, it seemed, was achieved at the cost of failure to fulfill his promise to forge a Third Way that could reconcile the fundamental differences that sharply divided Democrats and Republicans.

GEORGE W. BUSH, THE WAR ON TERRORISM, AND THE ADVANCE OF EXECUTIVE-CENTERED PARTISANSHIP

The 2000 election testified to the fractious state of American politics. The activist cores of the Democratic and Republican Parties differed starkly on issues such as abortion and the environment, reflecting their fundamental disagreements about the role of government and the relationship between church and state. But the two candidates—Democratic nominee Vice President Gore and the Republican Gov. George W. Bush of Texas—sought to distance themselves from their parties, each of them seeking a strategic center between liberalism and conservatism. The election ended in a virtual tie, a deadlock ultimately resolved by the Supreme Court. The controversial conclusion to the election bitterly divided policy activists but not the American people, many of whom, consistent with the recent pattern of low-turnout elections and public indifference toward politics, had stayed away from the polls.

Like his predecessor, Bill Clinton, candidate Bush sought to forge a "third way," signifying the modern presidency's dominant but uneasy place in contemporary American politics. At its best, Clinton's third way pursued a broad consensus for a limited but energetic national government. All too often, however, his approach degenerated into a politics of expediency that substituted polls and focus groups for leadership. Bush's "compassionate conservatism" seemed to have the same strengths and weaknesses as Clinton's "new covenant." Indeed, Bush's campaign speeches in 2000 bore a striking resemblance to Clinton's during the 1992 and 1996 elections. The Bush administration programs that embodied these values—especially his reform proposals for education, social services, and welfare—invoked many of the ideas incubated in the DLC, the centrist Democratic group that gave rise to several of Clinton's policy initiatives.[82]

Important differences marked Bush's and Clinton's stances toward partisanship, however. Clinton never made clear how his third-way politics would serve the core principles of the Democratic Party; in fact, he and the DLC were highly ambivalent, if not avowedly hostile, toward partisanship. But in compassionate conservatism Bush embraced a doctrine that he and his close advisers hoped would strengthen the appeal of the Republican Party. Bush's rhetoric and policy proposals, his top political strategist, Karl Rove, claimed, were a deliberate attempt to play to conservative values without being reflexively antigovernment.[83] Bush's call for substantial tax cuts appealed to the right's hostility toward government. But the president also acknowledged, columnist E. J. Dionne observed, "that most people do not draw meaning from the marketplace alone, and that the marketplace is not the sole test or most important source of virtue."[84] "The invisible hand works many miracles," Bush said in July 1999. "But it cannot touch the human heart. . . . We are a nation of rugged individuals. But we are also the country of the second chance—tied together by bonds of friendship and community and solidarity."[85]

Bush's ambition to redefine Republican conservatism thus entailed a difficult balancing act between partisanship and bipartisan cooperation. This task was made all the more difficult by the tenuous hold the Republicans had on government. The Senate was evenly split between Democrats and Republicans when Bush took office, with Vice President Dick Cheney breaking the tie. But like Clinton at the beginning of his administration, Bush chose to cooperate with his party's strongly ideological leaders in Congress. Like Clinton, Bush also preferred to solidify his base in the party before reaching out to independent voters. The president's emphasis on traditional conservative issues such as tax cuts, regulatory relief, energy production, and missile defense risked alienating moderate Republicans, a dwindling but pivotal group in the closely divided House and Senate. The president and his party paid dearly for this approach in May 2001, when Sen. James Jeffords of Vermont announced that he was transferring his allegiance from the Republican to the Democratic caucus, giving control of the Senate to the Democrats.[86]

Facing the prospect of partisan obstruction by Senate Democrats, the Bush administration intensified its efforts to consolidate political and policy responsibility within the White House. The first President Bush's top political strategist, Lee Atwater, had worked at the RNC rather than at the White House, helping to sustain for a time the status and independence of the national party organization. In contrast, George W. Bush's principal political consultant, Karl Rove, an Atwater protégé, became a top White House adviser. He staffed a new Office of Strategic Initiatives that oversaw a nearly complete melding of presidential and partisan politics. Rove granted that the national parties that had emerged since the 1980s "were of great importance in the tactical and mechanical aspects of electing a president." But they were "less important in developing a political and policy strategy for the White House." In effect, he said, parties served as a critical "means to the president's end." The emergence of the modern executive office presupposed that "the White House had to determine the administration's objectives" and by implication the party's.[87] By the end of his first summer in the White House, Rove sought to position the president as a nontraditional Republican. Bush stressed education and values, not taxes and defense.[88] Programs such as faith-based initiatives and educational reform were not pursued within Republican councils. Rather, as has been the custom since the development of the modern presidency, the White House advanced these objectives through executive orders and bipartisan cooperation.[89]

However, the president's attention shifted dramatically away from matters such as faith-based initiatives and educational reform when the United States was struck by terrorists of the Al Qaeda network—ensconced in Afghanistan—on September 11, 2001. In the short term, the war on terrorism strengthened the modern presidency and tempered the polarized partisanship that had plagued it during the previous three decades. Hardly a discouraging word was heard when the Bush administration created a White House Office of Homeland Security, imposed tighter restrictions on airports, and embraced deficit spending to help the economy and fight a war in Afghanistan, which harbored the Al Qaeda leaders. Highlighting the need for bipartisanship in a time of national crisis, Bush justified the war on terrorism in words that echoed Franklin Roosevelt. "Freedom and fear are at war," he told a joint meeting of Congress on September 20, 2001. "The advance of human freedom—the great achievement of our time, and great hope of every time—now depends on us. Our nation—this generation—will lift a dark threat of violence from our people and our future. We will rally around the world to this cause by our efforts, by our courage."[90] A strong consensus quickly formed in support of his military response against the Afghan Taliban regime that harbored Al Qaeda and its leader Osama bin Laden: within days of the September 11 attack, Bush's approval rating jumped from 51 to 90 percent.

Jeopardizing the bipartisan support that accrued in the aftermath of 9/11, Bush administration officials, and then the president himself, openly pursued the possibility of another military venture: an invasion of Iraq that, unlike the Persian Gulf War of 1991, would involve a "preemptive" attack and had as its mission the removal of Saddam Hussein from power. Recognizing the country's obsession with homeland security and reluctant to thwart a popular president as the midterm elections approached, Congress passed a resolution in October 2002 authorizing the president to use military force against Iraq "as he determines to be necessary." Although the resolution passed with substantial Democratic support, the Iraq War proved to be a decisive moment that would define Bush as "a divider not a uniter."[91] Running on the war, Bush threw himself into the 2002 midterm election campaign earlier and more energetically than any president in history. Unlike his predecessors, Bush had experienced both united and divided government during his first two years in office. He was convinced that his best strategy for leading Congress was to regain control of the Senate for the Republican Party. The Democrats' inept handling of legislation establishing a Department of Homeland Security, which saw them delay passage until after the election in a dispute over unionized government workers, gave Bush and Republican congressional candidates an issue that they exploited effectively in several close Senate elections. Most controversially, Bush made this issue a cause célèbre in championing Saxby Chambliss's successful Senate challenge to Georgia Democrat Max Cleland, who had lost both legs and an arm in Vietnam. The attack on Cleland for "voting against the president's vital homeland security efforts," which featured a campaign ad that followed footage of Osama bin Laden and Saddam Hussein with an unflattering shot of the Democratic incumbent, infuriated his partisan brethren in Washington and was perhaps the "single largest contributor to the post–September 11 revival of partisan acrimony on the Hill."[92]

In truth, Bush, on Rove's advice, decided well in advance of the elections to become actively involved in the campaign for a Republican majority in Congress.[93] He and Rove recruited strong Republican challengers to incumbent Democratic senators, even to the point of intervening in state party politics to do so. The president's strenuous efforts to raise a campaign war chest and his numerous appearances for GOP candidates strengthened his influence over his party. Several of his appearances were in states where the Republican candidate was trailing and where, if the Democrats had won, Bush risked being blamed for defeat.[94] The results of the election vindicated Bush's decision to take this risk. The Republicans gained two seats in the Senate, transforming them from minority to majority status, and increased their majority in the House of Representatives. An election eve poll indicated that 50 percent of the voters were basing their decision on their opinion of the president, many more than the 34 percent who had done so in 1990 or the 37 percent who had done so in 1998. Of the 50 percent, 31 percent were pro-Bush and only 19 percent opposed him.[95]

Political analysts were quick to describe the historic nature of the Republican victory and to credit Bush as the most successful party-building president since Franklin Roosevelt.[96] Bush could not take all the credit for the Republican gains. Since the late 1970s, the party had been developing into a formidable national organization in which the RNC, rather than state and local organizations, was the principal agent of party-building activities. This top-down approach to party building appeared to many critics to be too centralized and too dependent on television advertising to perform the party's traditional role of mobilizing voters and popular support for government programs. But the Bush White House and the RNC, believing that it had been out-organized "on the ground" by Democrats in the 2000 election, began to put together a massive grassroots mobilizing strategy in

2002. Democrats since the New Deal had relied on auxiliary party organizations such as labor unions to get out the vote. But the GOP created its own national organization to mobilize supporters. Depending on volunteers, albeit closely monitored ones, and face-to-face appeals to voters, the Republicans built on their success in 2002 to mount the most ambitious national grassroots campaign in the party's history for the 2004 elections.[97]

Bush not only benefited from the development of what might be considered the first national party machine in history, he also played a critical role in strengthening it. The White House recruited candidates, raised money to fund their campaigns, and helped to attract volunteers to identify Republican voters and get them out to vote. Just as Ronald Reagan had played a critical part in laying a philosophical and political foundation that enabled the Republican Party to become a solidly conservative and electorally competitive party by 1984, so did Bush make an important contribution in enlarging the core supporters of the party. During his first term, Bush broke Reagan's record for attracting first-time contributors to the Republican Party: under Reagan, 853,595 people donated to the Republican Party for the first time; by the time Bush stood for reelection, he had already attracted more than 1 million new donors to the GOP.[98] More important, although Reagan never converted his personal popularity into Republican control of Congress or the states, Bush approached reelection in 2004 with his party in charge of the House, the Senate, and most governorships. Indeed, the Republican Party had more political control than at any time since the 1920s.

Nevertheless, the centrality of the Bush White House in policymaking, as well as in mobilizing support and framing issues in both the 2002 and 2004 campaigns, suggests that modern presidential politics continued to subordinate partisan to executive responsibility. Reagan made extensive use of executive administration at a time when Congress was usually in the hands of the Democrats. That Bush also made considerable use of administrative mechanisms to achieve his goals, even when his party controlled both houses of Congress, suggested how the administrative presidency impeded the emergence of a more collaborative, party-centered policy process even under the most favorable circumstances. Indeed, subscribing to the "unitary executive" prescribed by Vice President Cheney, Bush became a more zealous defender of presidential prerogatives than his Republican predecessors, and his position only hardened as he fought the war on terrorism.

In domestic policy, the president's staffing practices and aggressive use of the OMB's powers of regulatory review were gauged to maximize presidential control over the civil service. Particularly in areas such as environmental and health and safety regulation, Bush made extensive use of executive orders, signing statements, and regulatory rulemaking to achieve significant departures from past policies. The president also used executive orders to make headway on controversial social issues, such as limiting funding for stem-cell research and denying funds to overseas family-planning organizations that offered abortion counseling. Although these efforts often enjoyed the support of congressional Republicans, they also suggested that the Bush administration preferred to transcend institutions of collective responsibility rather than work through them to achieve compromise or consensus. Even when the administration sought to work with congressional Republicans, it tended to do so in a heavy-handed manner that elicited resentment among GOP legislators. For example, Vice President Cheney, sometimes with Karl Rove in tow, frequently attended the Senate Republicans' weekly strategy sessions, an unusual intrusion that attested to the Bush administration's determination to make the Republican Party on Capitol Hill an arm of the White House.[99]

Bush's partisan administration tied the fortunes of his party to his personal support, which declined after 2004. The administration's ineffectual response to the Hurricane Katrina disaster in 2005 undermined the claim to administrative competence that had previously bolstered the White House and the Republican Party. The negative consequences of Bush's administrative overreaching for the GOP were most evident in the fallout from the White House's imperious management of the war in Iraq and the broader war on terrorism. Determined to wage war on its own terms, the Bush administration, bolstered by solid and largely passive Republican congressional support, made a series of unilateral decisions that departed from historic and legal convention. It chose to deny "enemy combatants" captured in the war on terrorism habeas corpus rights to challenge their detainment in civilian courts, to abrogate the Geneva Conventions and sanction rough treatment (or torture) of detainees during interrogations, and to engage in warrantless surveillance of American citizens suspected of communicating with alleged terrorists abroad. When these controversial decisions were revealed, they provoked widespread condemnation and damaged the GOP's public support. More broadly, the administration's insistence on a free hand to manage the war in Iraq ultimately resulted in the erosion of public confidence in the Republican Party as it became clear that the administration had badly botched postwar reconstruction efforts.

As the 2006 elections revealed, well before the economic crisis that began two years later overwhelmed all other issues, the administration's and the party's prestige was severely (and, in the case of the president, irreparably) wounded by the war. According to a national exit poll taken after the midterm congressional contests, about six in ten voters (59 percent) said they were dissatisfied (30 percent) or angry (29 percent) with President Bush. By a margin of more than two to one, those dissatisfied with Bush supported the Democratic candidate in their district (69 percent to 29 percent), and among those angry with the president, the margin was more than fifteen to one (92 percent to 6 percent).[100] Moreover, several studies appeared to show that general unhappiness with the White House and the war in Iraq contributed not only to the Democrats' taking control of the House and Senate, but also to the substantial gains they made in gubernatorial and state legislative races.[101] Thus, just as previous modern presidents demonstrated insufficient attention to party-building, Bush's experience illustrated the risks posed by overweening presidential partisanship. Ironically, the vigor of the Bush administration's party leadership—and the evident dependence of the GOP on Bush's stewardship—endangered the integrity of the Republican Party. Between 2001 and 2005, the GOP relied heavily for its political sustenance on Bush's personal popularity and prestige as a wartime leader. Both the 2002 and the 2004 elections celebrated executive power, turning on issues of international and domestic security that emphasized the modern presidency's place at the center of government.

The White House also played a dominant role in organizing the massive grassroots efforts that marked Bush's 2004 reelection campaign and in stimulating public participation in these efforts. Campaign officials designed and implemented grassroots programs, concentrated efforts in the battleground states, and deliberately bypassed state and local party leaders to mount a national party offensive.[102] This approach reaped political dividends for GOP candidates in the short run; Bush won 51 percent of the popular vote to Sen. John Kerry's 48 percent, and the Republicans gained three seats in the House and four in the Senate. But it threatened to make the party subservient to presidential authority and to enervate its capacity to hold the president accountable to broader principles. As Stephen Skowronek has warned, the modern GOP appeared to signal a political future in which the party "in effect [becomes] whatever the president needs it to be, and whatever capacity it had to hold its leaders to account would accordingly be lost."[103] The ironic denouement of this development was revealed after the 2008 presidential election, when many Republicans blamed Bush, whom they had previously followed with alacrity, for casting them into the political wilderness.

BARACK OBAMA AND THE RATIFICATION OF EXECUTIVE-CENTERED PARTIES

Democratic senator Barack Obama of Illinois offered the voters "Change We Can Believe In" during the 2008 presidential campaign. Calling on the people to trust in the "audacity of hope," Senator Obama ran an idealistic campaign that sought to reprise the modern presidency's role as "steward of the public welfare." He pledged to bring Americans together and to overcome the raw partisanship that had polarized the Washington community for nearly two decades and that had begun to divide the country during George W. Bush's eight years in office. "In the face of despair, you believe there can be hope," he told the large, enthusiastic audience that gathered in Springfield, Illinois, in February 2007 to hear him announce his candidacy for the presidency: "In the face of politics that's shut you out, that's told you to settle, that's divided us for too long, you believe we can be one people, reaching for what's possible, building that more perfect union."[104] As the child of a white mother from Kansas and a black father from Kenya, a man of color raised in Hawaii and Indonesia, and a reformer schooled in Chicago politics as a member of the post–civil rights generation, Obama seemed to embody the aspirations of the entire nation—to transcend, as no previous modern president could, the racial, ethnic, religious, and economic differences that long had divided the country.

Yet Obama and his leading advisers also saw enormous potential in the national party politics that George W. Bush had practiced. His organizational efforts, in fact, were modeled on the techniques that Republicans had pioneered in 2004. Eschewing the Democrats' traditional reliance on organized labor and other constituency organizations to mobilize the party faithful, Obama promised to strengthen the national party apparatus. He vowed to wage a fifty-state campaign, build grassroots organizations in every state, help elect Democrats down the ballot, and register millions of new voters who would support the party's commitment to depart from the domestic and foreign policies of the previous eight years. Obama's organizational strategy, which combined Internet-based recruiting of volunteers, the use of data files to carefully target potential loyalists, and old-fashioned door-to-door canvassing, elaborated on the tactics that had worked successfully for Bush and the GOP in 2002 and, especially, 2004. The remarkable effectiveness of Obama's fund-raising operation, which drew heavily on Internet-solicited donations, further reflected lessons learned from the Bush campaign. Especially adept at soliciting small donations, Obama became the first major-party candidate to refuse public funds for the general election campaign.[105] Like the formidable Bush–Cheney machine of 2004, the Obama–Biden organization relied in part on the regular party apparatus. DNC chair Howard Dean decided in 2006 to strengthen Democratic organizations throughout the country, an approach that state and local party leaders credited with abetting the party's impressive victories then and in 2008.[106] Just as the Bush–Cheney machine of 2004 resulted in a wide-ranging Republican victory, the Obama–Biden campaign of 2008 yielded not just a decisive triumph at the presidential level but also substantial gains in House and Senate races. This success was in large measure the result of voters' unhappiness with Bush, who had mired the country in an unpopular war and a severe financial crisis. But Obama's sophisticated grassroots campaign linked a vast network of volunteers, elicited enormous enthusiasm among potential supporters, and mobilized the highest voter turnout since 1968. Coming on the heels of the substantial increase in voter participation in the 2004 election, the 2008 campaign appeared to confirm the emergence of a national party system that was ameliorating the chronic voter apathy that had afflicted the presidency-centered administrative state.[107]

Nevertheless, the further development of an executive-centered party system has not eliminated the tension between presidential and party leadership. Hoping to reap the benefits of their party-building efforts during the election, Obama campaign officials announced in January 2009 that the new administration intended to maintain the grassroots campaign in order to press the president's agenda and lay the groundwork for his reelection. Organizing for America (OFA) would be housed in the DNC, now headed by Virginia governor Timothy Kaine, who had endorsed Obama's candidacy early in the primary fight and provided critical support for his general election campaign. Dubbed Barack Obama 2.0 by insiders, the plan called for hiring full-time organizers to mobilize the Internet-based grassroots network forged during the presidential campaign, which had generated a database of 13 million e-mail addresses and tens of thousands of phone bank volunteers and neighborhood coordinators. Although some state-level Democratic officials were enthusiastic about embedding Obama's machine in the DNC because they viewed Organizing for America as an extension of Dean's fifty-state strategy, others expressed concern that it could become a competing political force that revolved around the president's ambitions while diminishing the needs of other Democrats.[108] Just as the 2004 Republican campaign was directed by Bush–Cheney strategists, so was the 2008 Democratic grassroots effort run out of the Obama–Biden headquarters.

The architects of the Obama campaign praised Dean's fifty-state strategy, but they relied almost completely on their own staff, money, and organization, not only to compete in battleground states, but also to make incursions into traditional Republican territory. And just as the Bush–Cheney machine relied on volunteers whose principal loyalty was to the president, so did the Obama–Biden grassroots organization rest in the volunteers' deep admiration for the Democratic standard-bearer.[109] As one liberal blogger fretted toward the end of the 2008 election, "Power and money in the Democratic Party is being centralized around a key iconic figure. [Obama] is consolidating power within the party."[110] Embedding the Obama campaign organization in the DNC only served to reinforce this concern, arousing fears that Obama was building an "Obama party."[111] Obama's aides, including his highly regarded campaign manager, David Plouffe, denied that Obama 2.0 was merely a permanent campaign to advance the president's fortunes. They insisted that the grassroots network's purpose was to deliver on the reform that Obama and his party had promised during the 2008 election. Moreover, the president's political aides assured their partisan brethren that Obama 2.0 would be a force in mobilizing support for Democratic candidates in the 2010 congressional and state races.[112] Congressional Republicans' near-unanimous resistance to the president's main initiatives during his first term—an economic stimulus package, a financial reform program, and Obama's signature accomplishment, a national health care bill—appeared to confirm the need to sustain a strong Democratic organization.

The Patient Protection and Affordable Care Act proved especially polarizing. National health care reform had been the holy grail of progressive politics since the New Deal, and Republicans, spurred by the emergence of the grassroots Tea Party movement, were determined to defeat it. When GOP recalcitrance continued amid the Obama administration's willingness to compromise key features of his plan, most notably a public health care option that would compete with private providers, the president's politics, hitherto "ruthlessly pragmatic," took a decidedly partisan turn.[113] The final push for health care reform featured Obama in a series of campaign-style rallies in Pennsylvania, Missouri, Ohio, and Virginia, where an impassioned president repeatedly taunted Republicans for failing to take on the responsibility of expanding coverage and reducing health care costs. Beyond making public appearances at rallies and town hall meetings to whip up support for reforms among Democrats, Obama deployed Organizing for America to pressure members of Congress into supporting the legislation. In the immediate aftermath of Obama's multistate swing, health care reform was passed into law through the unorthodox—and esoteric—budget reconciliation process, which exploited the Democrats' firm control of both chambers of Congress. Although the Republicans' unwillingness to compromise gave eloquent testimony to their partisan approach to legislating, Obama's leadership throughout the debate—and his acceptance of the use of the reconciliation process, which circumvented the filibuster rules of the Senate, to enact health care reform—revealed a partisan streak of its own. The *New York Times* concluded that "in the course of this debate, Mr. Obama has lost something. . . . Gone is the promise on which he rode to victory less than a year and a half ago—the promise of a 'postpartisan' Washington in which rationality and calm discourse replaced partisan bickering."[114] Shaped by a polarized party system, the signal legislative achievement of the president's first two years became the only major entitlement program ever to become law without a single Republican vote.

The partisan rancor generated by the fight over the health care legislation, which took place amid the stubborn persistence of high unemployment, would haunt the Democrats at the polls. The Republicans gained sixty-three seats in the House to reclaim control of the lower chamber—the worst defeat for a president's party in an off-year election since 1938. In the Senate the GOP added six seats, leaving Obama and the Democrats without the filibuster-proof three-fifths majority needed to enact controversial legislation. And yet, this "shellacking" did not discourage Obama from seeking to build what he termed a New Foundation for American Politics.[115] The White House began to prepare OFA, which was active in both the health care fight and the 2010 campaigns, to mount a strong "ground game" to reelect the president. Moreover, after Obama and congressional Republicans reached an impasse on fiscal policy that almost brought the government into default, the White House launched a "We Can't Wait" initiative, dedicated to advancing policies that the president and his Democratic allies supported through unilateral executive action. During the final two years of his first term, Obama took measures that authorized the Environmental Protection Agency to implement greenhouse gas regulations that were stalled in the Senate; issued waivers that released states from many of the requirements of No Child Left Behind, which Congress had failed to reauthorize, only to bind them to the administration's own education policies; and bypassed the usual confirmation process to make four recess appointments that Senate Republicans had been filibustering.[116] Finally, confirming the adage that policy makes politics, Obama announced in June 2012 an executive initiative that granted relief to an entire category of young immigrants, as many as 1.7 million people, who would otherwise have been subject to deportation. Obama thus elided Republican opposition to the Dream Act, the administration's bill designed to provide a conditional pathway to citizenship for immigrants who were brought to America illegally as children. This measure not only contributed to the president's successful reelection campaign, which saw Hispanics support him by an overwhelming margin, but also, given the importance of the Latino vote to the future of American politics, may have contributed significantly to the development of a new Democratic majority.[117]

In sum, Obama appeared to have bestowed bipartisan legitimacy on an executive-centered party system. Improving on the innovative techniques developed by the Bush–Cheney campaign in 2004, Obama forged a "reciprocal top-down and bottom-up campaign strategy" that mobilized followers to "realize their collective strength."[118] For all the controversy attending it, the health care battle, fueled by lively, sometime vitriolic town meetings throughout the country, confirmed that the recrudescence of partisanship had renewed interest in politics. By pitting Obama's OFA against the new grassroots conservative Tea Party movement, the health care battle showed, as one Democratic congressional staffer observed, that "the age of apathy is over, and that's a good thing."[119] Although the president paid dearly in the coin of public opinion for the partisan nature of the battle over health care reform, his grassroots organization outperformed that of his opponent, former Massachusetts governor Mitt Romney, in the 2012 presidential election, providing the edge in a bitterly contested campaign. Working hand in glove with the Democratic Party and liberal advocacy groups, "Obama's Family" evolved into a "well oiled machine."[120] As one volunteer put it, "There were differences between 2008 and 2012. Everyone was excited in 2008; in 2012 people may have been less passionate, but they worked just as hard. It was more businesslike this time. It wasn't just a bunch of excited people on a major quest to make history. This time it was more about: 'This is important and we're going to do it whatever it takes.'"[121] That sense of mission would continue into Obama's second term: soon after the election, OFA was recast as Organizing for Action, which was established as a non-profit "social welfare" organization that would mobilize grassroots support for the progressive causes championed by Obama and his coalition: implementation of the Patient Protection and Affordable Care Act, immigration reform, climate change legislation, and gun control. President Obama promised his followers that removing his organization from the Democratic National Committee would strengthen its potential as a grassroots advocacy group.[122] Such a move also appeared to advance an *executive-centered* Democratic Party.

CONCLUSION: THE HAZARDS OF EXECUTIVE-CENTERED PARTISANSHIP

Like Republican presidents Ronald Reagan and George W. Bush, Obama's commitment to partisan administration revealed that modern presidents can circumvent partisan gridlock by exploiting executive power for partisan purposes. Taking a longer historical view, however, Obama's special relationship with OFA marked a new stage in the century-long development of presidential partisanship. OFA was a pioneering organization that held the possibility of a new party system that joined executive prerogative, street-level politics, and collective responsibility. At the same time, the very effectiveness of this personal organization, combining a fiercely devoted activist core with the most technically sophisticated campaign organization ever seen in American politics, had sometimes presented the illusion that the president could campaign and govern independently of Congress, the bureaucracy, and the regular party organization.

Even some of OFA's most sympathetic allies feared that its commitment to transformative change had been subordinated if not extinguished by its personal loyalty to the president. As Joe Szakos, the founder and executive director of Virginia Organizing, the leading progressive grassroots group in a key battleground state, explained, Obama's "family," for all its strengths, was not well equipped to orchestrate the building of a reform coalition. OFA could not be a reliable leader, or even partner, of such a coalition, Szakos lamented, because the "the hierarchy of the group and the fact that they are fundamentally about advancing the president's agenda make it very difficult to establish a close, enduring, working relationship with it."[123]

Progressive advocacy groups viewed OFA as an unreliable but potentially powerful ally; Democratic office holders, although they cheered its policy advocacy, tended to be jealous of its familial relationship with the White House. The uneasy relationship between the White House and Democratic legislatures underscored a long-held contention on Capitol Hill that Obama's political operation functioned purely for the president's benefit and not for his party's, an indictment that became especially bitter after the Democrats lost control of the Senate in the 2014 midterm campaign. Obama allies retorted that the president had shared with the Senate campaigns part of his massive lists of volunteer data and supporters' e-mail addresses, considered by his advisers to be sacred documents. But as had been clear throughout the Obama presidency, OFA's personal allegiance to Obama was not portable, and the president's battle cry during the 2014 campaign—that he was not on the midterm ballot but his policies were—did little to extend his personal organization's loyalty to the Democratic Party.[124] Obama thus presided over a greater loss of congressional seats for his party than any two-term president since World War II.[125]

Just as the 2010 elections encouraged Obama to pursue Democratic causes unilaterally, so did the 2014 midterm, which placed the president in opposition to a hostile Republican House and Senate, further encourage him and his grassroots political machine to emphasize the administrative presidency. Indeed, soon after the election, Obama announced an expansion of the deportation relief he provided in the Dreamers initiative, extending protection to an additional 4.3 million unauthorized immigrants.[126] Concurrently, OFA roused its members to support the White House initiative, and, more generally, to shift their focus almost exclusively to administrative politics. As OFA's Executive Director Sara El-Amin wrote in an e-mail of December 12, 2014, "The last month has been a [big deal] for those of us who want to see meaningful action to fix our broken immigration system. But it came towards the end of a frustrating year. House leaders had more than 500 days to hold one simple vote on bipartisan, comprehensive reform, and they failed to act, making it clear that they were just running out the clock on this Congress. That's why President Obama refused to wait any longer." The frustrations Obama and OFA experienced owed in large part to the fiercely divided polity that confronted them. But their response to this bitter factionalism—the celebration of partisan presidential unilateral action—raises the fundamental question of whether the executive of a vast administrative state, even with the tools of instant communication and social media, can truly function as a democratic institution with meaningful links to the public.[127]

This question became a rousing alarm when Donald Trump was elected president. Trump's remarkable and odds-defying ascendance to the presidency in 2016 appeared to complete the fusion of centralized administration and partisanship. Although the substance of Obama's and Trump's messages are radically divergent, their method of communication has nevertheless further ritualized the independent and plebiscitary nature of presidential politicking. Just as Obama relied on OFA and direct mass appeals to mobilize support for his candidacy and programs, so Trump stood apart from most of the GOP "establishment," basing his campaign on cable television, social media (especially his Twitter account), and mass rallies. Indeed, Trump's inaugural address was a rallying cry to his antinomian followers:

You came by the tens of millions to become part of a historic movement, the likes of which the world has never seen before. At the center of this movement is a crucial conviction, that a nation exists to serve its citizens. Americans want great schools for their children, safe neighborhoods for their families, and good jobs for themselves. These are just and reasonable demands of righteous people and a righteous public.[128]

Trump sought to meet these demands during the first year of his presidency with a flurry of administrative actions that changed the trajectory of Obama's program in immigration rights, climate change, criminal justice, civil rights, and foreign trade. Unilateral presidential action became an indispensable feature of executive-centered partisanship during the George W. Bush and Obama years, fueled in no small part by their having to face a Congress when one or both of its chambers was controlled by the other party for substantial periods of their presidencies. One would not think an aggressive administrative strategy would be so pivotal after the GOP won control of the Senate in 2014 and began the Trump administration under unified government in 2017. Nevertheless, Trump's iconoclastic politics made for a very uneasy, indeed often hostile relationship with the GOP's congressional leaders. The White House thus resorted to administrative aggrandizement right from the start, often in the service of highly controversial measures, such as the abandonment of the Trans-Pacific Partnership and the rescission of the deportation relief for Dreamers, that further strained the president's relations with congressional Republicans who remained split in the areas of free trade and immigration.[129]

Beyond the high-stakes battles over domestic and foreign policy that roiled the country during his first year in office, Trump's embrace of unilateral executive power has dramatically exposed the fault lines between the promise of presidential leadership, administrative aggrandizement, and the institutional weakness of political parties. Far from transcending the divisiveness and sectarian interests that form the core of party politics, presidents are now expected to take center stage in the fight over the services for the American state. During the Progressive Era, at the dawn of the modern presidency, Theodore Roosevelt celebrated a new executive office as the "steward of the people" who could temper their infatuation with rights by cultivating the obligations of democratic citizenship. Yet the fracturing of national community forged on the Progressive Era and the New Deal during the past two decades has given rise to a plebiscitary executive that exposes the American people to leaders who scorn the institutional restraints that are a vital ingredient of constitutional government as well as the collaboration that is the sine qua non of organized party politics. Recent developments herald a clarion call, as Hugh Heclo has wisely counseled, for people and their representatives to "think institutionally."[130] But those who would seek to restore the restraints or refinements of institutions must face the imposing obstacle of a government that for years has sacrificed responsible leadership to aggressive and resolute partisan administration. For better or worse, appeals to patience and acts of forbearance have become frail vestiges of a republican form of government that has long been praised—or blamed—for protecting the public from overweening and dangerous ambition.

NOTES

1. Franklin D. Roosevelt, *Public Papers and Addresses,* 13 vols. (New York: Random House, 1938–1950), vol. 1, 751–756.
2. Ibid., 752.
3. Woodrow Wilson, *Constitutional Government in the United States* (New York: Columbia University Press, 1908), 68–69.
4. Arthur S. Link, "Woodrow Wilson and the Democratic Party," *Review of Politics* 18 (April 1956): 146–156. Wilson effectively established himself as the principal voice of the Democratic Party. But he accepted traditional partisan practices concerning legislative deliberations and appointments in order to gain support for his program in Congress, thus failing to strengthen either the Democratic Party's national organization or its fundamental commitment to progressive principles. After 1914 Wilson embraced many elements of progressive democracy, such as direct leadership of public opinion, national administration of commercial activity, and civil service reform. Wilson thus overcame some of the Democratic Party's antipathy toward national administrative power and showed that with the growing prominence of presidential candidates, party leaders in Congress were willing to sacrifice programmatic principles to win the White House. See Scott James, *Presidents, Parties, and the State: A Party System Perspective on Democratic Regulatory Choice, 1884–1936* (New York: Cambridge University Press, 2000). In the end, however, this conversion to advanced progressivism only exposed the yawning gap between, on the one hand, Wilson's pretense to serving as a national progressive leader and, on the other, his allegiance to a decentralized and patronage-based party. See Daniel Stid, *The President as Statesman: Woodrow Wilson and the Constitution* (Lawrence: University Press of Kansas, 1998), esp. chaps. 6 and 8.
5. *Personal and Political Diary of Homer Cummings,* January 5, 1933, box 234, no. 2, 90, Homer Cummings Papers (no. 9973), Manuscripts Department, University of Virginia Library, Charlottesville.
6. Edward J. Flynn, *You're the Boss* (New York: Viking, 1947), 153.
7. Alfred Phillips Jr. to Franklin D. Roosevelt, June 9, 1937; and Roosevelt to Phillips, June 16, 1937, President's Personal File, 2666, Franklin D. Roosevelt Library, Hyde Park, New York.
8. Franklin Clarkin, "Two-Thirds Rule Facing Abolition," *New York Times,* January 5, 1936, IV, 10.
9. Thomas Stokes, *Chip off My Shoulder* (Princeton, NJ: Princeton University Press, 1940), 503. For an assessment of Roosevelt's role in the abolition of the two-thirds rule that also addresses the significance of this party reform, see Harold F. Bass Jr., "Presidential Party Leadership and Party Reform: Franklin D. Roosevelt and the Abrogation of the Two-Thirds Rule" (paper presented at the annual meeting of the Southern Political Science Association, Nashville, Tennessee, November 7–9, 1985).
10. On the purge campaign, see Sidney M. Milkis, *The President and the Parties: The Transformation of the American Party System since the New Deal* (New York: Oxford University Press, 1993), chap. 4; and Susan Dunn, *Roosevelt's Purge: How FDR Fought to Change the Democratic Party* (Cambridge, MA: Harvard University Press, 2010).

11. Raymond Clapper, "Roosevelt Tries the Primaries," *Current History,* October 1938, 16.

12. Morton Frisch, *Franklin D. Roosevelt: The Contribution of the New Deal to American Political Thought and Practice* (Boston: S. T. Wayne, 1975), 79.

13. Frankfurter to Roosevelt, August 9, 1937, box 210, Papers of Thomas G. Corcoran; Roosevelt to Frankfurter, August 12, 1937, reel 60, Felix Frankfurter Papers; both in Manuscript Division, Library of Congress, Washington, D.C.

14. The term "benevolent dictatorship" was coined by Herbert Croly. Croly, a fellow Progressive, criticized Wilson's concept of presidential party leadership along these lines. Although he shared Wilson's view that executive power needed to be strengthened, Croly argued that the "necessity of such leadership [was] itself evidence of the decrepitude of the two-party system." Croly believed that Theodore Roosevelt's 1912 Progressive Party campaign, which scorned the two-party system, championed candidate-centered campaigns, and prescribed that presidents seek political support through direct appeals to public opinion, represented the wave of the future. The emergence of a modern executive and the destruction of the two-party system, he wrote, "was an indispensable condition of the success of progressive democracy." *Progressive Democracy* (New York: Macmillan, 1914), 345, 348. On the Progressive Party and its legacy, see Sidney M. Milkis and Daniel J. Tichenor, "'Direct Democracy' and Social Justice: The Progressive Party Campaign of 1912," *Studies in American Political Development* 8 (Fall 1994): 282–340; and Sidney M. Milkis, *Theodore Roosevelt, the Progressive Party, and the Transformation of American Democracy* (Lawrence: University Press of Kansas, 2009).

15. The purge campaign galvanized opposition to Roosevelt throughout the nation, apparently contributing to the heavy losses the Democrats sustained in the 1938 general elections.

16. The term "second bill of rights" comes from Roosevelt's 1944 State of the Union message, which reaffirmed the New Deal's commitment to an economic constitutional order. Roosevelt, *Public Papers and Addresses,* vol. 13, 40.

17. The term comes from Theodore Roosevelt's New Nationalism speech, a 1910 address, which launched his Progressive Party campaign of 1912—his "Bull Moose" campaign. See Theodore Roosevelt, *The Works of Theodore Roosevelt,* 26 vols. (New York: Scribner's, 1926), vol. 17, 19–20.

18. *Report of the President's Committee on Administrative Management* (Washington, DC: U.S. Government Printing Office, 1937), 53. This committee, headed by Louis Brownlow, played a central role in the planning and politics of executive reorganization from 1936 to 1940. For a full analysis of the commission, see Barry Karl, *Executive Reorganization and Reform in the New Deal* (Cambridge, MA: Harvard University Press, 1963).

19. So strongly did Roosevelt favor this legislation that House Majority Leader Sam Rayburn appealed for party unity before the critical vote on the executive reorganization bill, arguing that its defeat would amount to a "vote of no confidence" in the president. *Congressional Record,* 75th Cong., 3rd sess., April 8, 1938, pt. 5, 5121.

20. Memorandum, "Extending the Competitive Classified Civil Service," Herbert Emmerich to Louis Brownlow, June 29, 1938; and Civil Service Commission statement regarding executive order of June 24, 1938, extending the merit system; both in *Papers of the President's Committee on Administrative Management,* Roosevelt Library; see also Richard Polenberg, *Reorganizing Roosevelt's Government* (Cambridge, MA: Harvard University Press, 1966), 22–23, 184. With the passage

of the Ramspeck Act in 1940, the convulsive movement to reshape the civil service was virtually completed. The Ramspeck Act authorized the president to extend the merit system to nearly 200,000 positions previously exempted by law, many of them occupied by supporters of the New Deal. Roosevelt took early advantage of this authorization in 1941. By executive order he extended the coverage of civil service protection to include about 95 percent of the permanent service. Leonard White, "Franklin Roosevelt and the Public Service," *Public Personnel Review* 6 (July 1945): 142.

21. Paul Van Riper, *History of the United States Civil Service* (Evanston, IL: Row, Peterson, 1958), 327. The merging of politics and administration took an interesting course as a result of the 1939 Hatch Act. Until passage of this bill, which barred most federal employees from participating in campaigns, the Roosevelt administration made use of the growing army of federal workers in state and local political activity, including some of the purge campaigns. Even though the Hatch Act curtailed Roosevelt's ability to continue these activities, the president signed the legislation. He was more interested in orienting the executive branch as an instrument of programmatic reform than he was in developing a national political machine, and the insulation of federal officials from party politics was not incompatible with such a purpose.

22. The task of communicating with the public encouraged FDR and those who staffed the newly created Executive Office of the President to make use of surveys. With the help of the respected pollster Hadley Cantril, the Roosevelt administration learned that the American people viewed the idea of a "second bill of rights" favorably. Oscar Cox to Hadley Cantril, May 3, 1943; Hadley Cantril to Oscar Cox, April 30, 1943; Memorandum, Hadley Cantril to David Niles, James Barnes, and Oscar Ewing, April 30, 1943; "Public Opinion: The NRPB Report and Social Security," Office of Public Opinion Research, April 28, 1943. Roosevelt Library, Oscar Cox Papers, box 100, Lend-Lease Files. On the Roosevelt administration's use of polls, see Robert Eisenger and Jeremy Brown, "Polling as a Means toward Presidential Autonomy: Emil Hurja, Hadley Cantril and the Roosevelt Administration," *International Journal of Public Opinion Research* 10, no. 3 (1998): 239–256; and Theodore Lowi, *The Personal President: Power Invested, Promise Unfulfilled* (Ithaca, NY: Cornell University Press, 1985), 62–66.

23. Roosevelt, *Public Papers and Addresses,* vol. 9, 671–672.

24. Martin Shefter, "War, Trade, and U.S. Party Politics," in *Shaped by War and Trade,* ed. Ira Katznelson and Martin Shefter (Princeton, NJ: Princeton University Press, 2002), 123.

25. Richard A. Rovere, "A Man for This Age Too," *New York Times Magazine,* April 11, 1965, 118. For an account of the influence of Roosevelt and the New Deal on Johnson's presidency, see William E. Leuchtenburg, *In the Shadow of FDR: From Harry Truman to Ronald Reagan,* rev. ed. (Ithaca, NY: Cornell University Press, 1985), chap. 4; and Milkis, *The President and the Parties,* chaps. 7 and 8.

26. Lyndon Baines Johnson, *The Vantage Point: Perspectives of the Presidency, 1963–1969* (New York: Holt, Rinehart and Winston, 1971), 323.

27. Theodore White, *The Making of the President, 1968* (New York: Atheneum, 1969), 107.

28. Rowland Evans and Robert Novak, "Too Late for LBJ," *Boston Globe,* December 21, 1966, 27.

29. David Broder, "Consensus Politics: End of an Experiment," *Atlantic Monthly,* October 1966, 62.

30. Doris Kearns, *Lyndon Johnson and the American Dream* (New York: New American Library, 1976), 256.

31. In a memorandum about one of the early strategy sessions that led to the Great Society, Larry O'Brien, Johnson's chief legislative aide, expressed concern about the acute political problems he anticipated would result from such an ambitious program. Memorandum, Larry O'Brien to Henry Wilson, November 24, 1964, Henry Wilson Papers, box 4, Lyndon Baines Johnson Library, Austin, Texas.

32. Interview with Horace Busby, June 25, 1987.

33. Memorandum, William Connel to Marvin Watson, August 27, 1967, Marvin Watson Files, box 31; Memorandum, Joseph Califano to the president, March 27, 1968, Office Files of the President (Dorothy Territo), box 10; both in Johnson Library.

34. Memorandum, Harry C. McPherson Jr. and Clifford L. Alexander to the president, February 11, 1967, Office Files of Harry McPherson; Memorandum, Sherwin Markman to the president, February 17, 1968, White House Central Files, Subject File, "WE9 (welfare), Exec. February, 1968," box 38; Sherwin J. Markman, Oral History, by Dorothy Pierce McSweeny, tape 1, May 21, 1969, 24–36; all in Johnson Library. Many local Democrats felt threatened by the community action program with its provision for "maximum feasible participation." See Daniel P. Moynihan, *Maximum Feasible Misunderstanding* (New York: Free Press, 1970), 144–145.

35. William E. Leuchtenburg, "The Genesis of the Great Society," *Reporter,* April 21, 1966, 38.

36. Memorandum, Hayes Redmon to Bill Moyers, May 5, 1966, box 12, Office Files of Bill Moyers, Johnson Library. For an excellent book-length treatment of Johnson's personnel policy, see Richard L. Schott and Dagmar S. Hamilton, *People, Positions, and Power: The Political Appointments of Lyndon Johnson* (Chicago: University of Chicago Press, 1983).

37. Memorandum, James Rowe to John W. Macy Jr., April 28, 1965, John Macy Papers, box 504; James H. Rowe, Oral History, by Joe B. Frantz, interview 2, September 16, 1969, 46–47; both in Johnson Library. Rowe's battles with Macy are noteworthy and ironic: as a charter member of the White House Office, he had performed Macy's role for the Roosevelt administration, upholding the principle of merit against the patronage requests of DNC chair James Farley and his successor, Ed Flynn.

38. On the importance of institutional reform, see Draft Memorandum, Horace Busby to Mr. Johnson, n.d., box 52, folder of memos to Mr. Johnson, June 1964; Busby quote is from Memorandum, Horace Busby for the president, September 21, 1965, box 51, Office Files of Horace Busby, Johnson Library.

39. Terry Moe, "The Politicized Presidency," in *The New Direction in American Politics,* ed. John E. Chubb and Paul E. Peterson (Washington, DC: Brookings Institution Press, 1985), 254.

40. Memorandum, Horace Busby to the president, April 21, 1965, and attached letter from John Macy (April 17, 1965), box 51, Office Files of Horace Busby, Johnson Library; Joseph Young, "Johnson Boost to Career People Called Strongest by a President," *Washington Post,* May 16, 1965; Eugene Patterson, "The Johnson Brand," *Atlanta Constitution,* April 30, 1965; and Raymond P. Brandt, "Johnson Inspires

the Civil Service by Appointing His Top Aides from among Career Officials," *St. Louis Dispatch,* May 2, 1965. For a comprehensive treatment of Johnson's management of the bureaucracy, see James A. Anderson, "Presidential Management of the Bureaucracy and the Johnson Presidency: A Preliminary Exploration," *Congress and the President* 1 (Autumn 1984): 137–163.

41.   Memorandum, Bill Moyers to the president, December 11, 1965, box 11, Office Files of Bill Moyers, Johnson Library.

42.   James Rowe became quite concerned on hearing of the task force proposal. He warned the White House staff that this might further weaken the regular party apparatus, which was "already suffering from shellshock both in Washington and around the country because of its impotent status." James Rowe, "A White Paper for the President on the 1968 Presidential Campaign," n.d., Marvin Watson Files, box 20, folder of Rowe, O'Brien, Cooke, Criswell Operation, Johnson Library.

43.   Allan Otten, "The Incumbent's Edge," *Wall Street Journal,* December 28, 1967.

44.   Byron E. Shafer, *Quiet Revolution: The Struggle for the Democratic Party and the Shaping of Post-Reform Politics* (New York: Russell Sage Foundation, 1983). In 1969 the DNC, acting under a mandate from the 1968 Chicago Convention, established the Commission on Party Structure and Delegate Selection. Under the chairmanship first of Sen. George McGovern and, after 1971, of Rep. Donald Fraser, the commission developed guidelines for the state parties' selection of delegates to the national conventions. Their purpose was to weaken the prevailing party structure and to establish a more direct link between presidential candidates and the voters. The DNC accepted all the commission's guidelines and declared in the call for the 1972 convention that they constituted the standards that state Democratic parties, in qualifying and certifying delegates to the 1972 Democratic National Convention, must make "all efforts to comply with." The new rules eventually caused a majority of states to change from selecting delegates in closed councils of party regulars to electing them in direct primaries. Although the Democrats initiated these changes, many were codified in state laws that affected the Republican Party almost as much. For a discussion of the long-term forces underlying the McGovern–Fraser reforms, see David B. Truman, "Party Reform, Party Atrophy, and Constitutional Change," *Political Science Quarterly* 99 (Winter 1984–1985): 637–655.

45.   Memorandum, John P. Roche for the president, December 4, 1967, White House Central Files, PL (Political Affairs) folder; Memorandum, Ben Wattenberg to the president, December 13, 1967, Marvin Watson Files, box 10; Memorandum, Ben Wattenberg to the president, March 13, 1968, Marvin Watson Files, box 11; all in Johnson Library.

46.   Memorandum of conversation, April 5, 1968, White House Famous Names, box 6, Robert F. Kennedy folder, 1968 Campaign, Johnson Library.

47.   Richard Nathan, *The Administrative Presidency* (New York: Wiley, 1983).

48.   Stephen Teles, "Conservative Mobilization against Entrenched Liberalism," in *The Transformation of American Government: Activist Government and the Rise of Conservatism,* ed. Paul Pierson and Theda Skocpol (Princeton, NJ: Princeton University Press, 2007).

49.   On Nixon's party leadership as president, see the Ripon Society and Clifford Brown, *Jaws of Victory* (Boston: Little, Brown, 1973), 226–242.

50.   Nathan, *Administrative Presidency,* 43–56. Toward the end of the Johnson presidency, the administration tried to consolidate further the president's control of

the activities of the executive branch. Johnson's second task force on government organization—the Heineman task force—made many recommendations in 1967 that formed the basis of the Nixon administrative reform program. For example, it called for the reorganization of executive departments and agencies into a smaller number of "superdepartments" that would be "far more useful and much more responsive to, and representative of, Presidential perspectives and objectives than the scores of parochial department and agency heads who now share the line responsibilities of the executive branch." Johnson favored the Heineman task force's central recommendations and planned to implement some of them after his reelection in 1968, but his retirement came sooner than expected. Task Force on Government Organization, "The Organization and Management of the Great Society Programs," June 15, 1967, and "A Recommendation for the Future Organization of the Executive Branch," September 15, 1967, both reports located in Outside Task Forces, box 4, Task Force on Government Organization folder, Johnson Library. See also Peri Arnold, *Making the Managerial Presidency: Comprehensive Reorganization Planning, 1905–1980* (Princeton, NJ: Princeton University Press, 1986), 268.

51. Daniel Galvin, *Presidential Party Building: From Dwight Eisenhower to George W. Bush* (Princeton, NJ: Princeton University Press, 2009).

52. James Reichley, "The Rise of National Parties," in Chubb and Peterson, eds., *New Direction in American Politics,* 191–195. By the end of the 1980s, Reichley was less hopeful that the emergent national parties were well suited to perform the parties' historic function of mobilizing public support for political values and government policies. See his richly detailed study, *The Life of the Parties: A History of American Political Parties* (New York: Free Press, 1992), esp. chaps. 18–21.

53. Rhodes Cook, "Reagan Nurtures His Adopted Party to Strength," *Congressional Quarterly Weekly Report,* September 28, 1985, 1927–1930; David S. Broder, "A Party Leader Who Works at It," *Boston Globe,* October 21, 1985, 14; and interview with Mitchell Daniels, assistant to the president for political and governmental affairs, June 5, 1986.

54. Thomas E. Cavanaugh and James L. Sundquist, "The New Two-Party System," in Chubb and Peterson, eds., *New Direction in American Politics.*

55. Nixon transformed the Bureau of the Budget into the Office of Management and Budget by executive order in 1970, adding a cadre of presidentially appointed assistant directors for policy between the OMB director and the bureau's civil servants. As a consequence, the budget office attained additional policy responsibility and became more responsive to the president. In the Reagan administration, the OMB was given a central role in remaking regulatory policy. See Richard A. Harris and Sidney M. Milkis, *The Politics of Regulatory Change: A Tale of Two Agencies,* 2nd ed. (New York: Oxford University Press, 1996).

56. As the minority report of the congressional committees investigating the Iran-contra affair acknowledged, "President Reagan gave his subordinates strong, clear, and consistent guidance about the basic thrust of the policies he wanted them to pursue toward Nicaragua. There is some question and dispute about *precisely* the level at which he chose to follow the operational details. There is no doubt, however, . . . [that] the President set the U.S. policy toward Nicaragua, with few if any ambiguities, and then left subordinates more or less free to implement it." *Report of the Congressional Committees Investigating the Iran-Contra Affair,* 100th Cong.,

1st sess., House Report 100–433, Senate Report 100–216 (Washington, DC: U.S. Government Printing Office, 1987), 501 (emphasis in original).

57. Michael Nelson, "Constitutional Aspects of the Elections," in *The Elections of 1988,* ed. Michael Nelson (Washington, DC: CQ Press, 1989), 195.

58. Benjamin Ginsberg and Martin Shefter, *Politics by Other Means: The Declining Importance of Elections in America* (New York: Basic Books, 1990).

59. Linda Greenhouse, "Ethics in Government: The Price of Good Intentions," *New York Times,* February 1, 1998, http://www.nytimes.com/1998/02/01/week inreview/blank-check-ethics-in-government-the-price-of-good-intentions .html?pagewanted=all&src=pm; and Cass R. Sunstein, "Unchecked and Unbalanced: Why the Independent Counsel Act Must Go," *The American Prospect* (May–June 1998): 20–27.

60. An exit poll revealed that a plurality of voters now preferred to have the presidency and Congress controlled by the Democratic Party. See William Schneider, "A Loud Vote for Change," *National Journal,* November 7, 1992, 2544.

61. Alan Brinkley, "Roots," *New Republic,* July 27, 1992, 44–45.

62. William Clinton, "The New Covenant: Responsibility and Rebuilding the American Community" (speech delivered at Georgetown University, Washington, D.C., October 23, 1991).

63. On President Clinton's use of executive orders and his attempt to carry out policy "with the stroke of a pen," see Thomas Friedman, "Ready or Not, Clinton Is Rattling the Country," *New York Times,* January 31, 1993, http://www.nytimes .com/1993/01/31/weekinreview/ready-or-not-clinton-is-rattling-the-country .html?pagewanted=all&src=pm. The proposal to lift the ban on gays and lesbians in the military plagued Clinton throughout the critical early months of his presidency. Intense opposition from the respected head of the Joint Chiefs of Staff, Colin Powell, and the influential chair of the Senate Armed Services Committee, Sam Nunn, D-GA, forced Clinton to defer his executive order for six months while he sought a compromise solution. But the delay and the compromise aroused the ire of gay and lesbian activists, who had given strong financial and organizational support to Clinton during the election campaign. In the end, Clinton and the Congress settled on a compromise—the "don't ask, don't tell" policy—that banned gays from serving openly in the military. But the controversy forced the president to betray his campaign promise to focus "like a laser" on the economy. Ann Devroy and Ruth Marcus, "President Clinton's First Hundred Days: Ambitious Agenda and Interruptions Frustrate Efforts to Maintain Focus," *Washington Post,* April 29, 1993, A1.

64. Douglas Jehl, "Rejoicing Is Muted for the President in Budget Victory," *New York Times,* August 8, 1993, 1, 23; and David Shribman, "Budget Battle a Hollow One for President," *Boston Globe,* August 8, 1993, 1, 24.

65. Al From and Will Marshall, "The Road to Realignment: Democrats and the Perot Voters," in *The Road to Realignment: Democrats and the Perot Voters* (Washington, DC: Democratic Leadership Council, 1993).

66. A majority of Republicans in the House and Senate supported the free trade agreement, and a majority of Democrats, including the House majority leader and majority whip, opposed it. David Shribman, "A New Brand of D.C. Politics," *Boston Globe,* November 18, 1993, 15; and Gwen Ifill, "56 Long Days of Coordinated Persuasion," *New York Times,* November 19, 1993, A27.

67. Address to Congress on health care plan, printed in *Congressional Quarterly Weekly Report,* September 25, 1993, 2582–2586; and Robin Toner, "Alliance to Buy Health Care: Bureaucrat or Public Servant?" *New York Times,* December 5, 1993, 1, 38.

68. Adam Clymer, "National Health Program, President's Greatest Goal, Declared Dead in Congress," *New York Times,* September 27, 1994, A1. For a comprehensive treatment of the Clinton health care program, see Cathie Jo Martin, "Mandating Social Change within Corporate America" (paper presented at the annual meeting of the American Political Science Association, New York, 1994). Martin's study shows that health care reform became the victim of "radically different world views about the state and corporation in modern society."

69. Examining exit polls that suggested that a "massive anti-Clinton coalition came together" to produce the "revolution" of 1994. The political analyst William Schneider wrote of the voters' desire for change, "If the Democrats can't make government work, maybe the Republicans can solve problems with less government." Schneider, "Clinton, the Reason Why," *National Journal,* November 12, 1994, 2630–2632.

70. William Clinton, State of the Union address, January 23, 1996, printed in *Congressional Quarterly Weekly Report,* January 27, 1996, 258–262.

71. Many public officials and journalists claimed that the new law put an end to "a sixty-one-year-old entitlement to welfare." In truth, the Aid to Families with Dependent Children (AFDC) program never existed as an entitlement in the sense that Social Security and Medicare did. The program only guaranteed federal matching funds to states that established AFDC programs. See R. Shep Melnick, "The Unexplained Resilience of Means-Tested Programs" (paper delivered at the annual meeting of the American Political Science Association, Boston, September 3–6, 1998).

72. William Jefferson Clinton, "Remarks on Signing the Personal Responsibility and Work Opportunity Reconciliation Act," August 22, 1996, *Weekly Compilation of Presidential Documents,* no. 1484.

73. Anthony Corrado, "Financing the 1996 Elections," in *The Election of 1996,* ed. Gerald Pomper (Chatham, NJ: Chatham House, 1997). In 2002 Congress enacted the Bipartisan Campaign Reform Act, which prohibited the national political parties from raising or spending soft money.

74. Michael Nelson, "The Election: Turbulence and Tranquility in Contemporary American Politics," in *The Elections of 1996,* ed. Michael Nelson (Washington, DC: CQ Press, 1997), 52; Gary Jacobson, "The 105th Congress: Unprecedented and Unsurprising," in Nelson, ed., *Elections of 1996,* 161; and Kathryn Dunn Tenpas, "The Clinton Reelection Machine: Placing the Party Organization in Peril," *Presidential Studies Quarterly* 28 (Fall 1998): 761–768.

75. Clinton's gift for forging compromise was displayed in May 1997 when the White House and the Republican congressional leaders agreed on a plan to balance the budget by 2002. In part, this uneasy deal was made possible by a revenue windfall caused by the robust economy, which enabled the negotiators to avoid the sort of hard choices concerning program cuts and higher taxes that had animated the bitter struggles of the 104th Congress. Richard W. Stevenson, "After Years of Wrangling, Accord Is Reached on Plan to Balance the Budget by 2002," *New York Times,* May 3, 1997, 1. Even so, this rapprochement, which brought about the first balanced budget in three decades, testified to the potential of modern presidents to

advance principles and pursue policies that defy the sharp cleavages that pervade the party system. Indeed, Clinton's third way was emulated abroad as well, with leaders in Britain, Germany, Italy, and Holland attempting to fashion programs that combined market efficiency and social justice. See Jim Hoagland, "Third Way Converts," *Washington Post,* May 20, 1999. In the face of these developments, DLC president Al From, who had often been critical of Clinton's inconsistent commitment to the "third way," credited the president with "modernizing progressive politics for the world." Interview with Al From, June 7, 1999. For a more critical and historical analysis of Clinton's third-way politics, see Stephen Skowronek, *The Politics Presidents Make: Leadership from John Adams to Bill Clinton* (Cambridge, MA: Harvard University Press, 1997), 447–464.

76. The term *extraordinary isolation* is Woodrow Wilson's. See *Constitutional Government in the United States,* 69.

77. Republicans had long opposed reauthorization of the independent counsel statute, considering it an unconstitutional infringement on the executive's prosecutorial authority. But their resistance to Democratic efforts to reauthorize the statute came to an end in 1993 when the Whitewater scandal emerged. Katy J. Harriger, "Independent Justice: The Office of the Independent Counsel," in *Government Lawyers: The Federal Bureaucracy and Presidential Politics* (Lawrence: University Press of Kansas, 1995), 86.

78. Janny Scott, "Talking Heads Post-Mortem: All Wrong, All the Time," *New York Times,* November 8, 1998, A22.

79. Voters distinguished sharply between Clinton, the chief executive, of whom they approved, and Clinton, the man, whom they regarded as immoral and untrustworthy. Just 20 percent of those interviewed in a January 1999 Gallup poll thought Clinton provided good moral leadership, and only 24 percent characterized him as honest and trustworthy, new lows for his presidency. "Good Times for Clinton the President, but Personal Reputation Hits New Low," Gallup News Service, January 23, 1999, http://www.gallup.com/poll/4096/good-times-clinton-president.aspx.

80. Interview with Will Marshall, president, Progressive Policy Institute, June 14, 1999.

81. David E. Rosenbaum, "Surplus a Salve for Clinton and Congress, *New York Times,* June 29, 1999, http://www.nytimes.com/1999/06/29/us/planning-for-a-surplus-the-politics-surplus-a-salve-for-clinton-and-congress.html.

82. New Democrats accused Bush of trying to steal their politics. As DLC president Al From wrote in spring 1999, Bush's effort to call himself a "compassionate conservative" appeared to be an effort by Republicans "to do for their party what New Democrats did for ours in 1992—to redefine and capture the political center." Al From, "Political Memo," *The New Democrat* 11 (May/June 1999): 35. Many Republicans agreed. One skeptical conservative revealed that if he wanted to know the Bush campaign's position on a particular issue, he would consult the DLC magazine, *The New Democratic Blueprint.* Interview with Bush campaign adviser, not for attribution, November 13, 2001.

83. Interview with Karl Rove, November 15, 2001.

84. E. J. Dionne Jr., "Conservatism Recast," *Washington Post,* January 27, 2002.

85. George W. Bush, "Duty of Hope," speech, Indianapolis, Indiana, July 22, 1999, http://www.georgewbush.com.

86. Tish Durkin, "The Scene: The Jeffords Defection and the Risk of Snap Judgments," *National Journal,* May 26, 2001.

87. Rove interview. Rove believed that Atwater, a friend of his for twenty years, had made a mistake by going to the RNC. Political power fell into the hands of White House Chief of Staff John Sununu. A leading conservative in Washington who worked in the Bush administration indicated that he strongly urged Rove to work at the White House, not the RNC, "where organizational frustrations were rampant." Interview with conservative journalist, not for attribution, November 13, 2001.

88. Fred Barnes, "The Impresario: Karl Rove, Orchestrator of the Bush White House," *Weekly Standard,* August 20, 2001, http://www.weeklystandard.com/Content/ Protected/Articles/000/000/000/129ddfbx.asp.

89. On January 29, 2001, Bush created a White House office to, among other things, "eliminate unnecessary legislative, regulatory, and other bureaucratic barriers that impede faith-based and other community efforts to solve social problems." Executive Order 13199, "Establishment of Faith-Based and Community Initiatives." He also ordered the Departments of Labor, Education, Health and Human Services, and Housing and Urban Development, as well as the attorney general's office, to establish Centers for Faith-Based and Community Initiatives within their departments. These centers would perform internal audits, identifying barriers to the participation of faith-based organizations in providing social services and forming plans to remove those barriers. Executive Order 13198, "Agency Responsibilities with Respect to Faith-Based and Community Initiatives," January 29, 2001. As for education, from the start Bush and his advisers viewed it as the central issue distinguishing Bush as a different kind of Republican. George W. Bush, State of the Union address, *Washington Post,* January 29, 2002, http://www.washingtonpost .com/wp-srv/onpolitics/transcripts/sou012902.htm; and Rove interview. But the No Child Left Behind law, enacted in 2002, seemed less a use of government to serve conservative principles than an uneasy compromise between liberal demands for more spending and conservative insistence on standards. Bush trumpeted his alliance with the liberal Democratic icon Sen. Edward M. Kennedy in passing education reform legislation in 2001.

90. George W. Bush, address to the joint session of Congress and the nation, January 20, 2002, http://www.whitehouse.gov.

91. Gary C. Jacobson, *A Divider, Not a Uniter: George W. Bush and the American People,* 2nd ed. (Boston: Longman, 2010).

92. Ibid., 71.

93. In seeking a Republican Senate, Bush faced a daunting challenge: the average loss for the president's party in post–World War II midterm elections was four Senate seats. Even worse from the Republicans' standpoint, their party was more exposed in 2012 than were the Democrats: twenty Republican seats were at stake in the election, compared to fourteen Democratic seats. No president's party had taken control of the Senate away from the other party in a midterm election since 1882.

94. Bush was the featured attraction at sixty-seven fund-raising events that raised a record $141 million in campaign contributions for the Republican Party and its candidates. Moreover, throughout the fall, Bush campaigned ardently for Republican nominees. For example, in the five days leading up to the election, he traveled 10,000 miles to speak at Republican rallies in seventeen cities in fifteen states.

95. Adam Nagourney and Jane Elder, "In Poll, Americans Say Both Parties Lack Vision," *New York Times,* November 3, 2002, http://www.nytimes.com/2002/11/03/ us/2002-campaign-voters-poll-americans-say-both-parties-lack-clear-vision .html?page wanted=all&src=pm. An election eve Gallup Poll reported that 53 percent would be using their vote "in order to send a message that you support [or oppose] George W. Bush." Of these, 35 percent said they would vote to support him and 18 percent said they would vote to express their opposition. David W. Moore and Jeffrey M. Jones, "Late Shift toward Republicans in Congressional Vote," November 4, 2002, http://www.gallup.com/poll/7123/late-shift-toward-republicans-congressional-vote.aspx.

96. Rhodes Cook, "Bush, the Democrats, and 'Red' and 'Blue' America," *Rhodes Cook Newsletter,* October, 2003, http://www.rhodescook.com.

97. Interview with Matthew Dowd, political strategist for the Bush–Cheney Campaign, July 8, 2004; see also Matt Bai, "The Multilevel Marketing of the President," *New York Times Magazine,* April 25, 2004, 45–46. Dowd insisted that a centralized grassroots campaign was not an oxymoron. The "ground war" was built with community volunteers, but "once they volunteered, we ask them to do certain things. A national organization has to have a consistent message and mechanics. If the message is not consistent, if tasks are not systematically assigned, the campaign will implode. This was the message of the [failed Howard] Dean campaign: letting people loose can get the candidate in trouble. The message and organization must be relatively disciplined." The centralized grassroots campaign was not without spontaneity, however. "The campaign headquarters gave people tasks, but volunteers on the ground had some flexibility in determining how to carry out those tasks. It was local volunteers, for example, who learned that model homes in subdivisions were a good place to register new voters."

98. The average contribution of the new donors was less than $30. RNC press release, October 1, 2003. Personal interview with Christine Iverson, RNC press secretary, July 7, 2004.

99. Jonathan Mahler, "After the Imperial Presidency," *New York Times Magazine,* November 9, 2008, 44.

100. Bush was much more of a drag on his party's candidates than was former president Clinton in 1994. More than a third (36 percent) of the electorate said they voted to oppose Bush; compare that with the 27 percent who voted to oppose Clinton in 1994 and the 21 percent who voted likewise in 1998, the year Congress impeached the president. "Centrists Deliver for Democrats," Pew Research Center, November 8, 2006, http://www.pewresearch.org/2006/11/08/centrists-deliver-for-democrats/.

101. Ralph Thomas and Andrew Garber, "Even in State Races, Anti-Bush Mood Played Major Role," *Seattle Times,* November 9, 2006, 1.

102. Sidney M. Milkis and Jesse Rhodes, "George W. Bush, the Republican Party, and the 'New' American Party System," *Perspectives on Politics* 5 (September 2007): 461–488.

103. Stephen Skowronek, "Leadership by Definition: First Term Reflections on George W. Bush's Leadership Stance," *Perspectives on Politics* 3 (December 2005): 829.

104. Barack Obama, Announcement for President, February 10, 2007, http://www .barackobama.com.

105. Alec MacGillis, "Obama Camp Relying Heavily on Ground Effort," *Washington Post,* October 12, 2008, http://articles.washingtonpost.com/2008–10–12/politics/ 36876 255_1_obama-effort-obama-organization-marshall-ganz.

106. Ari Berman, "The Dean Legacy," *The Nation,* February 28, 2008, http://www.the-nation.com/article/dean-legacy. Former aide to Vice President Gore and Harvard professor Elaine Kamarck offers preliminary evidence that Dean's contributions did make a difference in the 2006 campaigns. See Kamarck, "Assessing Dean's Fifty-State Strategy in the 2006 Midterm Elections," *Forum* 4, no. 3 (2006), http:/www.bepress.com/forum/v014/iss3/art5.

107. "Voting Turnout," http://elections.gmu.edu/voter_turnout.htm.

108. Peter Wallsten, "Retooling Obama's Campaign Machine for the Long Haul," *Los Angeles Times,* January 14, 2008, http://articles.latimes.com/2009/jan/14/nation/na-obama-army14.

109. Adam Nagourney, "Dean Argues His 50-State Strategy Helped Obama Win," *International Herald Tribune,* November 12, 2008.

110. Dana Goldstein and Ezra Klein, "It's His Party," *The American Prospect,* August 18, 2008, http://prospect.org/article/its-his-party.

111. Ibid.

112. Lisa Taddeo, "The Man Who Made Obama," *Esquire,* November 3, 2009, http://www.esquire.com/features/david-plouffe-0309.

113. Alec MacGillis, "Sounds Great but What Does He Really Mean?," *Washington Post,* May 10, 2009, http://articles.washingtonpost.com/2009–05–10/opinions/36845928_1_ pragmatism-obama-supporters-president-obama.

114. David Sanger, "Big Win for Obama, but at What Cost?," *New York Times,* March 21, 2010, A1.

115. Remarks by the President on the Economy, Georgetown University, April 14, 2009, Office of the White House Press Secretary, http://www.whitehouse.gov/the-press-office/remarks-president-economy-georgetown-university.

116. In a decision that called into question the president's recess appointments, a federal appeals court ruled that Obama violated the Constitution when he installed three officials on the National Labor Relations Board. Charlie Savage and Steven Greenhouse, "Court Rejects Obama Move to Fill Posts," *New York Times,* January 25, 2013, http://www.nytimes.com/2013/01/26/business/court-rejects-recess-appointments-to-labor-board.html?pagewanted=2&_r=1. For a detailed account of the "We Can't Wait Initiative," see Kenneth Lowande and Sidney M. Milkis, "'We Can't Wait': Barack Obama, Partisan Polarization, and the Administrative Presidency," *The Forum* 12 (1), 2014: 3–27.

117. David Klaidman and Andrew Romano, "President Obama's Executive Power Grab," *Daily Beast,* October 22, 2012, http://www.thedailybeast.com/newsweek/2012/10/21/president-obama-s-executive-power-grab.html; and Ryan Lizza, "The Party Next Time: The GOP's Demographic Dilemma," *New Yorker,* September 2012, http://www.newyorker.com/reporting/2012/11/19/121119fa_fact_lizza. According to exit polls, Obama won about 70 percent of the Hispanic vote. For example, see Mark Hugo Lopez and Paul Taylor, "Latino Voters in the 2012 Election," Pew Research Hispanic Center, November 7, 2012, http://www.pewhispanic.org/2012/11/07/latino-voters-in-the-2012-election/.

118. Hugh Heclo, "The Once and Future Chief Executive: Prophesy versus Prediction," remarks delivered at the fourth annual symposium in Honor of Ronald Reagan, "The Future of the American Presidency," Regent University, Virginia Beach, Virginia, February 6, 2009.

119. Interview with Democratic congressional staff member, July 19, 2009.

120. Interview with OFA volunteer, December 4, 2012. For a detailed account of how the OFA combined sophisticated targeting and old fashioned canvassing, see Sasha Issenberg, "Obama Does It Better," *Slate*, October 29, 2012, http://www.slate.com/ articles/news_and_politics/victory_lab/2012/10/obama_s_secret_weapon_demo crats_have_a_massive_advantage_in_targeting_and.single.html.

121. Interview with OFA volunteer, December 3, 2012.

122. E-mail message from OFA volunteer, January 8, 2013; and http://www.barack obama.com/about/about-ofa/.

123. Joe Szakos (president, Virginia Organizing), interview with Sidney M. Milkis and John W. York, July 21, 2014.

124. Phillip Rucker and Robert Costa, "Battle for the Senate: How the GOP Did It," *Washington Post*, November 5, 2014. The Republicans picked up 9 seats in the Senate and 13 in the House. The GOP majority in the Senate became 54–46; its 247–188 edge in the House gave the Republicans the largest majority it has enjoyed since 1948.

125. Between 2008 and 2015, Democrats have lost 13 Senate seats, 69 House seats, 913 state legislative seats, 11 governorships, and 32 state legislative chambers. The only president in the past seventy-five years who came close was Dwight Eisenhower, who witnessed a similar decline for the GOP during his presidency. Juliet Eilperin, "Obama, Who Once Stood as Party Outsider, Now Works to Strengthen Democrats," *Washington Post*, April 25, 2016, https://www.washingtonpost.com/ politics/obama-who-once-stood-as-party-outsider-now-works-to-strengthen-democrats/2016/04/25/340b3b0a-0589-11e6-bdcb-0133da18418d_story.html.

126. Immigrants would be eligible to apply for three years of relief from deportation, and work permits, if they arrived in the United States before 2010, and arrived in the United States under the age of 16; or arrived in the United States before 2010, and have at least one child who is a U.S. citizen or legal resident.

127. Obama's ambitious immigration initiative was tied up in the federal courts until the Trump administration rescinded it on taking office. Adam Litak and Michael D. Shear, "Supreme Court Tie Blocks Obama Immigration Plan, *New York Times*, June 23, 1916, http://www.nytimes.com/2016/06/24/us/supreme-court-immi gration-obama-dapa.html?_r=0. For a detailed case study of OFA and its advance of executive-centered partisanship, see Sidney M. Milkis and John W. York, "Barack Obama, Organizing for Action and Executive-Centered Partisanship," *Studies in American Political Development*, vol. 31, issue 1, April 2017: 1–23.

128. "The Inaugural Address." January 20, 2016. The White House: Office of the Press Secretary.

129. For a detailed account of the Trump's partisan administration, see Sidney M. Milkis and Nicholas Jacobs, "'I Alone Can Fix It': Donald Trump, The Administrative Presidency, and the Hazards of Executive-Centered Partisanship," *Forum*, vol. 15, issue 3 (November 2017), https://www.degruyter.com/view/j/for.2017.15. issue-3/for-2017-0037/for-2017-0037.xml.

130. Hugh Heclo, *On Thinking Institutionally* (New York: Oxford University Press, 2008).

13

THE INSTITUTIONAL PRESIDENCY

John P. Burke

Not until 1857 did Congress appropriate funds for a White House staff—just enough to hire one clerk. More than a half-century later, President Woodrow Wilson had only seven full-time aides. Growth in the size of the White House staff began in earnest during the presidency of Franklin Roosevelt, and, with occasional lapses, the growth has yet to abate. The major challenge for presidents—not just for Roosevelt and his Democratic successors, such as Bill Clinton and Barack Obama, but also for conservative Republicans such as George W. Bush and Donald Trump—has been to keep pace with an ever-expanding bureaucracy. Ironically, John P. Burke argues, the size and complexity of the modern presidential staff have caused the White House itself to take on "the character of a bureaucratic organization." Burke chronicles a number of the strategies presidents have adopted—with varying success—to make good use of their staffs.

Analysis of the workings of the White House staff, both by people who have served on it and by scholars, has a peculiar if not schizophrenic quality. For some, the staff is simply a reflection of the personality, style, and managerial skills of the incumbent president. Others emphasize characteristics of the presidency that seem to endure from administration to administration. Both of these perspectives have some merit. Presidents do seem to leave their imprint—for better or for worse—on the office. The formal and hierarchical arrangements of the Dwight Eisenhower, Richard Nixon, Ronald Reagan, George H. W. Bush, and George W. Bush presidencies and the more collegial, informal, ad hoc patterns in the John Kennedy, Lyndon Johnson, and Bill Clinton White Houses can be linked to the organizational preferences and "work ways" of each of these chief executives. Yet the White House staff, now made up of some 2,000 employees in significant policymaking positions, also serves as an organizational context that can—just as in any bureaucracy—set limits on what a president can do and sometimes thwart even the best of presidential intentions. For the skillful president, the White House staff is like very hard clay that can be molded only with great effort, patience, and understanding; for the less skilled it can become a hard rock, if not a brick wall, that resists presidential management and control.

A full analysis of how presidents have succeeded or failed at this "organizational artistry" would require a detailed account of the presidential staff system that has evolved since the late 1930s and a close examination of the efforts of each of the presidents from Franklin Roosevelt through Donald Trump to organize and manage the institutional presidency. What follows is only part of that larger project: an outline of some of the institutional characteristics of the modern presidency and the managerial challenges they present to incumbent presidents.[1]

One point that deserves mention is how odd the need for organizational leadership would have seemed to presidents in the nineteenth and early twentieth centuries. Thomas Jefferson managed his office with one secretary and a messenger. Sixty years later, in the administration of Ulysses Grant, the size of the staff had grown to three. By 1900 the staff consisted of a private secretary (formally titled "secretary to the president"), two assistant secretaries, two executive clerks, a stenographer, three lower-level clerks, and four other office personnel. Under Warren Harding the size of the staff grew to thirty-one, but most staff members were clerical. Herbert Hoover managed to persuade Congress to approve two more secretaries to the president, one of whom he assigned the job of press aide.

It was common practice for early presidents to hire immediate family and other relatives as their secretaries, an indication that their few staff members functioned as personal aides rather than as substantive policy advisers. John Quincy Adams, Andrew Jackson, John Tyler, Abraham Lincoln, and Ulysses Grant all engaged their sons as private secretaries. George Washington, James Polk, and James Buchanan employed their nephews. James Monroe employed his younger brother and two sons-in-law. Zachary Taylor hired his brother-in-law.

Early presidents also paid the salaries of their small staffs out of their own pockets. Not until 1857 did Congress appropriate money ($2,500) for a single presidential clerk. As recently as the Coolidge presidency, the entire budget for the White House staff, including office expenses, was less than $80,000.[2] By 1963 it had climbed to $12 million. In 2009 the corresponding figure for the Executive Office of the President was estimated conservatively at $375 million. Other estimates, taking into account items that are paid for by departments and agencies, put the total at over $1 billion.[3]

As demands on the presidency mounted, more help was needed. Grappling with the Great Depression of the 1930s, President Roosevelt's solution was to "muddle through." Early in his administration he experimented with a form of cabinet government but quickly became dissatisfied with its members' parochial perspectives, infighting, and tendencies to leak information to the press—problems encountered by many of Roosevelt's successors who also took office thinking that the cabinet would play a central role in their policymaking. Roosevelt then moved to a series of coordinating bodies that included relevant cabinet officers and the heads of the new agencies that were created as part of the New Deal. Another of FDR's managerial strategies was to borrow staff from existing departments and agencies; these employees remained on their home agencies' personnel budgets while they were "detailed" to the White House. In fact, the legislative whirlwind of Roosevelt's first 100 days was the product of a loosely organized group of assistants, many of whom did not have formal positions on the White House staff.

Roosevelt's patchwork arrangement worked, but just barely. In an interview with a group of reporters shortly after his reelection in 1936, Roosevelt publicly attributed his victory to the failure of his Republican opponent, Gov. Alfred Landon of Kansas, to seize on the president's chief weakness. "What is your weakness?" one of the reporters asked. "Administration," replied the president.[4] Clearly something needed to be done.

Roosevelt had already taken steps to rectify his administrative problems by forming the Committee on Administrative Management, headed by Louis Brownlow. Roosevelt's creation of the Brownlow Committee was not the first presidential effort to seek administrative advice on how to make the presidency work more effectively. But it was the Brownlow Committee that most clearly and directly focused on the need for a larger, reorganized White House staff.[5] Concluding that "the President needs help," Brownlow and his associates proposed that "to deal with the greatly increased duties of executive management falling upon the president, the White House staff should be expanded."[6] After initially rejecting the then-controversial proposal, Congress passed the revised recommendations of the Brownlow Committee in the Reorganization Act of 1939.[7] Significant increases in the staff resources available to the president also followed passage of the Employment Act of 1946, which created the Council of Economic Advisers; the National Security Act of 1947, which led to the development of the National Security Council and its staff; and the recommendations of the 1947 Hoover Commission on the Reorganization of the Executive Branch.[8] During Eisenhower's presidency, existing units within the White House Office (itself the core unit of the White House staff) were more clearly defined, and new offices were created. Eisenhower also designated Sherman Adams as the first White House chief of staff and assigned him significant authority to oversee and coordinate the domestic policy component of the staff system.[9]

From the handful of aides that Roosevelt and his predecessors could appoint, the numbers have increased steadily in each succeeding administration. By 1953 the size of the White House Office was about 250. Twenty years later, it had grown to almost 500. In 1977, criticizing the size of the staff as a symptom of the "imperial presidency," Jimmy Carter reduced it by 100 employees, mostly by moving them to other parts of the executive bureaucracy. By 1980, Carter's last year in office, the size of the staff had inched back up to 500, and it has remained at about that size ever since. When other administrative units under direct presidential control (the larger Executive Office of the President) are included—such as the Office of Management and Budget (OMB), the National Security Council, and the Council of Economic Advisers—the number of staff swells to about 2,000. Physically, the Executive Office of the President has spilled out from the East and West wings of the White House to occupy first the Old Executive Office Building next door, which was once large enough to house the Departments of State, War, and Navy, and then the New Executive Office Building on the north side of Pennsylvania Avenue, as well as other, smaller buildings in the vicinity.

A marked change in the character of the presidency has thus occurred. By recognizing that the American executive is an institution—a presidency, not merely a president—we can better understand the office, how it operates, the challenges it faces, and how it affects our politics.

THE INSTITUTIONAL PRESIDENCY

If the presidency is best understood as an institution, then clearly it should embody some of the characteristics of an institution. But what do terms such as *institution, institutional,* and *institutionalization* mean? Our concern is the organizational character of the presidency—its growth in size, the complexity of its work ways, and the general way in which it resembles a large, well-organized bureaucracy. More specifically, an institution is complex in what it does (its functions) and how it operates (its structure), and it is well bounded—that is, differentiated from its environment.[10]

Complex Organization

Institutions are complex: they are relatively large in size, each part performs a specialized function, and some form of central authority coordinates the parts' various contributions to the work of the whole. The first aspect of complexity—the increase in size of the institutional presidency—can easily be seen by comparing the White House staff available to President Roosevelt in 1939, before the adoption of the Brownlow Committee's recommendations, with the staff at work in the Bush, Obama, or Trump White House. The eight-person list of members of the White House staff in the 1939 *United States Government Manual* (see Table 13.1) is dwarfed by the long list of staff members currently serving under President Trump. A comparison of the Roosevelt and Trump staffs also illustrates the second aspect of organizational complexity: increasing specialization of function. Roosevelt's aides were, by and large, generalists; they were simply called secretary to the president or administrative assistant. The staff list for the Trump White House includes titles such as strategic communication director, special assistant to the president for legislative affairs, special assistant to the president and director of media affairs, deputy chief of staff for policy, and many others.

Table 13.1 ■ The White House Office, 1939	
Secretary to the president	Stephen Early
Secretary to the president	Brig. Gen. Edwin M. Watson
Secretary to the president	Marvin H. McIntyre
Administrative assistant	William H. McReynolds
Administrative assistant	James H. Rowe Jr.
Administrative assistant	Lauchlin Currie
Personal secretary	Marguerite A. LeHand
Executive clerk	Rudolph Forster

Source: United States Government Manual, 1939 (Washington, DC: U.S. Government Printing Office, 1939).

Other units of the White House staff operate within functionally defined, specialized areas, such as national security or environmental quality. In fact, one of the primary causes of the growth of the White House staff has been the addition of these units: the Bureau of the Budget (created in 1921, transferred from the Treasury Department in 1939, and reorganized as the OMB in 1970); the Council of Economic Advisers (1946); the National Security Council (1947); the Office of the United States Trade Representative (1963); the Office of Policy Development (1970); the Council on Environmental Quality (1970); the Office of Science and Technology Policy (1976); the Office of Administration (1977); and the Office of National Drug Control Policy (1989). All told, the once relatively simple tasks of the president's staff—writing speeches, handling correspondence, and orchestrating the daily schedule—have evolved into substantive duties that affect the policies presidents propose and the ways they deal with the steadily increasing demands placed on the office.

The staff assigned to the vice president is another institutional resource. Although vice presidents in the nineteenth through the mid-twentieth centuries had little in the way of staff and were headquartered on Capitol Hill, recent vice presidents have become key presidential advisers and powerful players within the White House. Starting with Walter Mondale under Carter, vice presidents have had an office in the West Wing. They are also now served by a large staff, including vice presidential economic and domestic policy aides, staff for communication strategy and speechwriting, assistants for public engagement and intergovernmental affairs, a legislative affairs unit, a national security adviser and staff, plus a chief of staff to keep it all on track. As Joel Goldstein observes, "The vice presidency is no longer a sinecure. It matters now. A lot. An office that was 'nothing' has become a robust political institution."[11] This has held true under Trump's vice president,

Mike Pence, who not only has inherited the staff resources available to his recent predecessors, but also has emerged as a close presidential adviser and liaison to Capitol Hill.

The final characteristic of institutional complexity is the presence of a central authority that coordinates the contributions of the institution's functional parts. For the presidency, such authority resides nominally in the president. Since the 1950s, however, coordinating authority has gradually been taken over by the White House chief of staff, who performs substantive roles in policymaking and, in most cases, wields day-to-day authority over the workings of the White House staff. A recent book on the history of the office has as its main title *The Gatekeepers,* and a very telling subtitle: *How the White House Chiefs of Staff Define Every Presidency.*[12] Still, when presidents encounter difficulties, the chief of staff is often the first head to roll. The rocky start of the Trump presidency, for example, led to Reince Priebus's resignation after a mere six months on the job.

Differentiation from Environment

The complexity of the presidency and its reliance on expert advice have given the institution a unique place in the policy process, differentiating it from its political environment. One way this has occurred is through increased White House control of new policy initiatives. Presidents now routinely try to shape the nation's political agenda, and the staff resources they have at their disposal make it possible for them to do so. John Kennedy, Lyndon Johnson, and especially Richard Nixon, with his creation of the Domestic Council, emphasized White House control of policy formulation, de-emphasizing the involvement of the cabinet and the bureaucracy. Carter and Reagan began their terms of office by promising to rely more on the cabinet. They quickly found that goal unworkable in practice and turned inward to the White House staff for policy advice. Clinton, George W. Bush, and Obama followed this pattern, and their domestic and economic initiatives were largely the work of their White House staffs.

For Trump, the problem was compounded by a poor transition to the presidency marked by a failure to move swiftly in filling subcabinet and other executive branch positions. He lagged well behind George W. Bush and Obama. Of 591 key federal positions tracked by the *Washington Post,* by September 1 of the first year, Obama had 310 confirmed, Bush had 294, while Trump had only 117. Trump had not even nominated anyone for 366 positions.[13] As well, tensions developed between Trump and some of his main cabinet officers, notably Attorney General Jeff Sessions and Secretary of State Rex Tillerson.

Those outside the White House—Congress, the bureaucracy, the news media, and the public—have responded to presidential direction of the national agenda by expecting more of it. Political lobbying and influence seeking, especially by those directly involved in Washington politics, focus on the president. Although American politics remains highly decentralized, incremental, and open to multiple points of access, those seeking to influence national politics try to cultivate the people who have the most to do with policy proposals: the White House staff.

A second aspect of the presidency that differentiates it from the surrounding political environment is the way parts of the staff are organized explicitly to manage external relations with the media, Congress, and various constituencies. The press secretary and staff coordinate, and in many cases control, the presidential news passed on to the media.[14] Since 1953 specific staff assistants also have been assigned to lobby Congress on the president's behalf. Today White House lobbying efforts are formally organized within the large, well-staffed Office of Legislative Affairs. The establishment of special channels of influence for important constituent groups is another way presidents manage their relations with the political environment. This practice began in the administration of Harry Truman, when David Niles became the first staff aide explicitly assigned to serve as a liaison to Jewish groups. Eisenhower hired the first black presidential assistant, E. Frederic Morrow, and added a special representative from the scientific community as well. In 1970 Nixon created the Office of Public Liaison as the organizational home within the White House staff for the aides serving as conduits to particular groups. By the time Jimmy Carter left office in 1981, special staff members were assigned to consumers, women, the elderly, Jews, Hispanics, white ethnic Catholics, Vietnam veterans, and gay men and lesbians, as well as to such traditional constituencies as African Americans, labor, and business.[15] Under George W. Bush, senior adviser Karl Rove was placed in charge of constituency groups. The pattern continued under Obama with the appointment of Valerie Jarrett, a longtime member of his inner circle, as senior adviser in charge of both the public liaison and intergovernmental affairs offices. As Rove was to Bush, Jarrett was to Obama, serving as one of his closest and most influential advisers.

The increasing differentiation of the presidency as a discrete entity thus complements its increasing complexity and reliance on expertise as evidence of its status as an institution.

EFFECTS OF AN INSTITUTIONAL PRESIDENCY

Even if the presidency bears the marks of an institution, do its distinctly institutional characteristics—as opposed to the individual styles, practices, and idiosyncrasies of each president—matter? Despite the tremendous growth in the size of the president's staff, perhaps it remains mainly a cluster of aides and supporting personnel, with their tasks, organization, and tenure varying greatly from administration to administration or even changing within the tenure of each president. After all, observers of the presidency, both scholarly and journalistic, have noted enormous differences between the Kennedy and Eisenhower White Houses, between Johnson and Nixon, Carter and Reagan, Reagan and George H. W. Bush, George W. Bush and Obama, and even Bush father and Bush son. It is the personality, character, and distinctive behavior of each of these presidents that have generally attracted the attention of press and public. This has certainly been the case for Trump, whose persona looms especially large in his presidency.

Some of these observations are accurate, but to the extent that the institutionalized daily workings of the presidency transcend the personal ideologies, character, and idiosyncrasies of those who work within it (especially the president), it also makes sense to analyze the presidency from an institutional perspective. Not only do many of the presidency's institutional characteristics affect the office, but the effects are negative as well as positive. The institutional presidency can help determine the success or failure of a particular president.

External Centralization: Presidential Control of Policymaking

The creation of a large presidential staff has centralized much policymaking power within the presidency. This development has both positive and negative aspects. On the positive side, an institutional presidency that centralizes control of policy can protect the programs that the president wishes to foster. The Washington political climate is usually not receptive to new political initiatives, which must compete for programmatic authority and budget allocations against older programs that are generally well established in agencies and departments, have strong allies on Capitol Hill, and enjoy a supportive clientele of special interest groups.

In creating the Office of Economic Opportunity (OEO), Lyndon Johnson, a president whose legislative skills were unsurpassed, recognized precisely this problem. The OEO was designed to be a central component of Johnson's War on Poverty. As Congress was considering the legislation to create the OEO, three departments—Commerce; Labor; and Health, Education, and Welfare—lobbied to have it administratively housed within their respective bailiwicks. Johnson, recognizing that this would subordinate the OEO to whatever other goals a department might pursue, lobbied Congress to set up the OEO so that it would report directly to the president. Johnson was especially swayed by the views of Harvard economist John Kenneth Galbraith, who warned, "Do not bury the program in the departments. Put it in the Executive offices, where people will know what you are doing, where it can have a new staff and a fresh man as director."[16]

The centralization of power in presidents' staffs has not always redounded to their advantage. One of the worst effects of increasing White House control of the policy process, especially in foreign policy, has been to diminish or even exclude other sources of advice. Since the creation of the National Security Council (NSC) in 1947, presidents have tended to rely for advice on the council's staff, especially the president's assistant for national security (also known as the NSC advisor). Ironically, Congress's intent in creating the NSC was to check the foreign policy power of the president by creating a deliberative body whose members would provide an alternative source of timely advice to the president.

Except during Eisenhower's presidency, the NSC has not generally functioned as an effective deliberative body. What has developed instead is a large, White House–centered NSC staff, headed by a highly visible national security assistant, that often dominates the foreign policymaking process.[17] The reasons why the NSC staff and the national security assistant have come to dominate are plain: proximity to the Oval Office, readily available staff resources, and a series of presidents whose views about decision-making processes differed from Eisenhower's. Beginning with McGeorge Bundy under Kennedy and continuing with Walt Rostow under Johnson, Henry Kissinger under Nixon, and Zbigniew Brzezinski under Carter, most national security assistants not only have advocated their own policy views, but also have eclipsed other sources of foreign policy advice, especially the secretary of state and the State Department.

Perhaps the best testimony to the problems created by centralizing control of foreign policy in the NSC staff can be found in the memoirs of three recent secretaries of state. Cyrus Vance, who served under Carter, repeatedly battled Brzezinski. Vance's resignation as secretary of state in 1980, in fact, was precipitated by the administration's ill-fated decision—from which Vance and the State Department were effectively excluded—to try to rescue the American hostages in Iran.[18]

Alexander Haig, Reagan's first secretary of state, encountered similar problems with the NSC. In his memoirs, Haig claims he had only secondhand knowledge of many of the president's decisions. In a chapter tellingly titled, "Mr. President, I Want You to Know What's Going on Around You," Haig reported,

> William Clark, in his capacity as National Security Adviser to the President, seemed to be conducting a second foreign policy, using separate channels of communications . . . bypassing the State Department altogether. Such a system was bound to produce confusion, and it soon did. There were conflicts over votes in the United Nations, differences over communications to heads of state, mixed signals to the combatants in Lebanon. Some of these, in my judgment, represented a danger to the nation.[19]

George Shultz, Haig's successor as secretary of state, also found himself cut out of a number of important decisions by the NSC staff. The most notable was the Reagan administration's secret negotiations with Iran to exchange arms for the release of American hostages in Lebanon and its covert, illegal use of the profits generated by the arms sales to fund the contra rebels in Nicaragua. The arms deal violated standing administration policy against negotiating for hostages, and the disclosure of the secret contra funds undermined congressional support for Reagan's policies in Central America. The affair not only bespoke Shultz's conflicts with the NSC, but also was politically damaging to the president.

Some exceptions have been noted to the general pattern of NSC dominance in foreign policymaking: one occurred during the Ford administration, another in the elder Bush's presidency. In both cases a reasonable balance was struck in the advisory roles of the State Department and the NSC. But the two cases are revealing about the conditions under which excessive centralization can be avoided. In both presidencies the same individual, Brent Scowcroft, served as the NSC advisor, and he deliberately crafted his job to be a "neutral" or "honest" broker of the foreign policymaking process.[20] Furthermore, in both administrations the secretaries of state had extensive White House staff experience. Kissinger had served under Nixon as NSC advisor, and for part of his tenure in the Nixon and Ford administrations he was simultaneously NSC advisor and secretary of state. Bush's secretary of state, James Baker, had served as White House chief of staff and as secretary of the Treasury under Reagan.

The making of foreign and national security policy in George W. Bush's presidency offers another variant. During the first term, NSC advisor Condoleezza Rice, a longtime Bush confidant, was generally considered both a policy coordinator and a policy adviser, much like her mentor Brent Scowcroft in the George H. W. Bush presidency. George W. Bush, however, had other powerful voices in his inner circle during his first term: Secretary of State Colin Powell, Secretary of Defense Donald Rumsfeld, and Vice President Dick Cheney, all of whom had served in previous administrations. Rumsfeld and Cheney were chiefs of staff under Ford, and Powell was Reagan's NSC advisor. Rumsfeld and Cheney also had served as defense secretary, and Powell had been chair of the Joint Chiefs of Staff.

The events of September 11, 2001, radically transformed many of the internal dynamics of the Bush presidency. Although a foreign policymaking process with substantial participation by the cabinet developed after September 11, the White House staff remained a powerful force. According to one account, the "outline of the war plan often emerge[d] from the private conversations" of Bush and Rice.[21] The NSC added two new offices to deal with counterterrorism and computer security, and other White House units were created as well. Most notably, Bush signed an executive order creating the Office of Homeland Security, with a mandate to coordinate federal efforts to prevent and respond to domestic terrorism. The White House unit predated the establishment of a cabinet-level Department of Homeland Security in December 2002 (which Chief of Staff Andrew Card and members of his staff played the major role in creating). However, the White House's Office of Homeland Security remained in place after the department came into being.[22]

In domestic and economic policy, Bush too centralized policymaking in the White House.[23] The White House staff was the dominant force in such areas as tax reform, education, the patients' bill of rights, and the faith-based initiatives proposal. In fact, in at least one of these issue areas, education policy, reports surfaced that the secretary of education was not pleased with the dominant role taken by the White House.[24] In Bush's second term, the White House played a major role in his ill-fated response to Hurricane Katrina and his failure to secure reforms in Social Security policy. Here centralization proved problematic. Despite his sharp policy differences with Bush, President Obama also centralized policymaking in the White House. Four longtime associates, David Axelrod, Peter Rouse, Valerie Jarrett, and David Plouffe, played important roles as "senior advisors" at various points in his presidency. Each left an indelible imprint on the administration's policy development. As one early account noted, although Obama built "a cabinet of prominent and strong willed players . . . he is putting together a governing structure that will concentrate more decision making over his top domestic priorities in the White House" than in the departments.[25] These observations proved prophetic. Not only were Obama's senior advisors influential, but new White House offices were also created to coordinate energy, health care, urban policy, and other initiatives. Indeed, the media took note of the proliferation of White House policy "czars" (the media's label, not the White House's).[26]

In the early Trump presidency, the pattern continued. Although his staff was riven by internal conflict and often performed poorly, it still held sway over departments and agencies. Cabinet members were caught short by and ill informed about a number of Trump's initiatives, including executive orders dealing with travel bans on immigrants and other visitors from several predominantly Muslim nations, the presence of transgender personnel in the military, the pardon of Sheriff Joe Arpaio, and Trump's controversial response to white supremacist demonstrations in Charlottesville, Virginia. They indicate the negative consequences of too much White House intervention, even when not directly by the president.

Internal Centralization: Hierarchy, Gatekeeping, and Presidential Isolation

The centralization of policymaking power by the White House staff has been accompanied by a centralization of power within the staff by one or two chief aides. This internal centralization is further evidence of the institutional character of the presidency, and it too affects the way the institutional presidency operates, providing both opportunities and risks for the president.

On the positive side, centralization of authority within a well-organized staff system can ensure clear lines of responsibility, well-demarcated duties, and orderly work ways. When presidents lack a centralized, organized staff system, the policymaking process suffers.

The travails of Franklin Roosevelt's staff illustrate the problems that can arise from lack of effective organization. Roosevelt favored a relatively unorganized, competitive staff system, one in which the president acted as his own chief of staff. But rather than establishing regular patterns of duties and assignments and an orderly system of reporting and control, Roosevelt often gave several of his staff assistants the same assignment, pitting them against each other.

Some analysts have argued that redundancy—two or more staff members doing the same thing—can benefit an organization.[27] But in Roosevelt's day, staff resources were minimal. Worse, his staff arrangements generated jealousy and insecurity among his aides, neither of which is conducive to sound policy advice or effective administration. As Patrick Anderson observes, "Roosevelt used men, squeezed them dry, and ruthlessly discarded them. . . . The requirement [for success] was that they accept criticism without complaint, toil without credit, and accept unquestioningly Roosevelt's moods and machinations."[28]

In addition to making the staff more effective, a system in which one staff member serves as chief of staff or is at least *primus inter pares* (first among equals) is advantageous to a president for other reasons. It can protect the president's political standing, for example. A highly visible staff member with a significant amount of authority within the White House can act as a kind of lightning rod, handling politically tough assignments and deflecting political controversy from the president to himself or herself.

Perhaps the best example of this useful division of labor comes from the Eisenhower presidency. Part of Eisenhower's success as president derived from a leadership style in which he projected himself as a chief of state who was above the political fray, while allowing his assistants, especially Sherman Adams, the flinty former governor of New Hampshire who was Eisenhower's chief of staff, to seem like prime ministers concerned with day-to-day politics. A 1956 *Time* magazine feature on Eisenhower's staff reported that Adams's scrawled "O.K., S.A." was tantamount to presidential approval. Although it was really Eisenhower who made the decisions, Adams's reputation as the "abominable 'No!' man" helped to "preserve Eisenhower's image as a benevolent national and international leader" and protect his standing in the polls.[29]

A well-organized, centralized staff can also work against a president. Corruption and the abuse of power are among the dangers of elevating one assistant to prominence and investing that person with a large amount of power. Sherman Adams proved politically embarrassing to Eisenhower when he was accused of accepting gifts from a New England textile manufacturer. Eisenhower found it personally difficult to ask his trusted aide to resign and delegated the job to Vice President Nixon. The political and personal problems Eisenhower experienced from relying on, and then having to fire, Adams seem to be part of a pattern: Truman and Harry Vaughan, Johnson and Walter Jenkins, Nixon and Bob Haldeman, Reagan and Donald Regan, and George H. W. Bush and John Sununu.

Another two-edged consequence of a centralized staff system is that a highly visible assistant with a large amount of authority can act as a gatekeeper, controlling and filtering the flow of information to and from the president. Both Hamilton Jordan under Carter and Regan under Reagan were criticized for limiting access to the president and selectively screening the information and advice the president received. Joseph Califano Jr., Carter's secretary of health, education, and welfare, had repeated run-ins with Jordan. While lobbying Dan Rostenkowski, the Democratic representative from Illinois and influential chair of the Health Subcommittee of the House Ways and Means Committee, on a hospital cost containment bill, Califano found that Rostenkowski also resented the treatment he was receiving from Jordan. "He never returns a phone call, Joe," Rostenkowski complained. "Don't feel slighted," Califano replied. "He treats you exactly as he treats most of the Cabinet."[30] In July 1979 Carter fired Califano and finally designated Jordan his first chief of staff.

Donald Regan, who succeeded James Baker as Reagan's chief of staff in 1985, acquired tremendous power in domestic policymaking, played a major role in important presidential appointments, and was even touted in the media as Reagan's prime minister. Immediately on taking office, Regan flexed his political muscles by revamping the cabinet council system, substituting instead two streamlined bodies: the Economic Policy Council and the Domestic Policy Council. Regan retained control of the two councils' agendas. Subsequent council reports to President Reagan also flowed through Regan: "The simplified system strengthened Regan's direct control over policy, establishing him as a choke point for issues going to the President."[31]

Regan certainly was effective at centralizing power in his hands, but his attempts to exercise strong control over the policymaking process did not always serve the president's interests. In the realm of domestic policy, the tactics of Regan and his staff frequently upset House Republicans.[32] In the realm of foreign affairs, Regan was the first chief of staff to play a major role in both making and implementing policy. His attempts to influence foreign policy precipitated the resignation of Robert McFarlane, the national security advisor, and led to the selection of Adm. John Poindexter, a Regan ally, as McFarlane's replacement. The Regan-dominated, Poindexter-led NSC soon embroiled the Reagan administration in the politically embarrassing Iran-contra affair.[33] Centralized authority of the kind that Regan practiced is preferable to organizational anarchy. But as hierarchy and centralization develop within the White House staff, presidents can find themselves isolated, relying on a small core group of advisers. If that occurs, the information the president gets will already have been selectively filtered and interpreted. Discussions and deliberations will be confined to an inner circle of like-minded advisers. Neither development is beneficial to the quality of presidential decision making or to the formulation of effective policy proposals.

George W. Bush also centralized domestic policymaking. During his first term, chief of staff Andrew Card and Karl Rove played central roles. Their importance, especially Rove's, did not go unnoticed in the press. Questions were raised about the White House's overemphasis on loyalty and discipline, its ideological insularity, and the need for Bush to have other channels of information and advice.[34] Concerns about an insular "Bush bubble" persisted into his second term.

For Barack Obama, his selection of Rahm Emanuel as chief of staff brought on board someone with impressive credentials who was likely to hew to the strong chief of staff model. Emanuel had been Clinton's chief White House political advisor (akin to Rove), he had strong political credentials as the fourth-ranking Democrat in the House of Representatives, and he had a reputation as a tough and demanding manager and fierce partisan infighter. Emanuel's reputation became a reality during his tenure as chief of staff. Unlike some of his problematic predecessors, he moved on and soon was elected the mayor of Chicago. Emanuel was succeeded by William M. Daley, a former secretary of commerce under Bill Clinton and the son and brother of two famed mayors of Chicago. Daley, however, was a weaker chief of staff than Emanuel, outflanked by aides closer to the president. A similar fate befell Gen. James A. Jones, Obama's first national security advisor.

During the tenure of both Daley and Jones, influence and power remained firmly lodged in the White House, albeit in the hands of other chief aides. Obama's senior advisors—Axelrod, Jarrett, Rouse, and later Plouffe—formed an important and influential source of advice on domestic issues, just as they had been during the 2008 campaign and earlier in Obama's career. With respect to national security and foreign policy, Jones was succeeded by his deputy, Thomas Donilon. Donilon and his deputy NSC advisor, Denis McDonough, exercised significant influence over the administration's policies. Like the senior advisors on domestic and political affairs, both had strong ties to Obama before he became president. Overall, this pattern was reinforced when McDonough was appointed White House chief of staff at the start of Obama's second term and when Susan Rice, another longtime Obama associate who had been serving as ambassador to the UN, replaced Donilon as NSC advisor in July 2013. For this president, longtime association, trust, and personal familiarity mattered, and those who filled the bill ended up in key White House positions. As with George W. Bush, however, critics noted a degree of insularity and isolation in policy deliberation, which may have not served either president well on important occasions.

For President Trump, the White House has remained the center of action. But from the beginning of his administration, it was riven with warring factions, marked with an unusual degree of turnover at its highest levels, and vexed by Trump's own problematic decision-making proclivities and management style. His initial national security advisor, Lt. Gen. Michael Flynn, was forced to resign after less than a month on the job following revelations of questionable telephone contacts with the Russian ambassador during the transition period. Although Flynn initially denied that anything of substance had been discussed, the conversations had been taped by intelligence officials and Flynn had misled Vice President Pence and chief of staff Reince Priebus, who had initially defended him. Lt. Gen. H. R. McMaster was appointed to replace Flynn. His first order of business was to restore the morale of the NSC staff, remove several controversial appointees, and improve the deliberative processes of the national security system.

As for Priebus, he initially seemed a good and complementary fit for the politically inexperienced, quintessential "outsider" president. An "establishment Republican," Priebus had been chairman of the Republican National Committee for six years, with a wide array of party and "inside-the-Beltway" contacts and experience. From the start of the Trump presidency until his resignation six months later, however, Priebus was unable to instill order in the free-wheeling Trump White House or to mobilize resources to advance the president's agenda, especially the failed effort to replace Obamacare. Most notably, he failed to contain the infighting among other senior aides such as strategist Stephen K. Bannon (who was himself forced out a few weeks later), Trump's daughter Ivanka and son-in-law Jared Kushner, media spokesperson Kellyanne Conway, policy advisor Stephen Miller, and others. As James Pfiffner observes, "Priebus could not impose order or create a regular policy process because the factions could not agree on the administration's main directions."[35] Those disagreements, moreover, were played out in the press, often fueled by leaks criticizing other staff members. Priebus was replaced by Gen. John Kelly, who had been serving as secretary of homeland security. Like McMaster, Kelly faced the daunting task of restoring discipline and order to a haphazard and chaotic staff system. He especially sought to control access to Trump and the materials that crossed the president's desk, much like his stronger predecessors. Both Kelly and McMaster also faced the continuing challenges of dealing with Trump's impulsive decision making and communication style. No modern presidency, going all the way back to FDR's, experienced so much and so early change in personnel.[36]

Bureaucratization

As the top levels of the White House staff have gained authority and political visibility, the rest of the staff has taken on the character of a bureaucratic organization. Among its bureaucratic characteristics are complex work routines, which often stifle originality and reduce differences on policy to their lowest common denominator. Drawing on his experience in the Carter White House, Greg Schneiders complained that if one feeds "advice through the system . . . what may have begun as a bold initiative comes out the other end as unrecognizable mush. The system frustrates and alienates the staff and cheats the President and the country."[37] Schneiders also noted that the frustrations of staffers do not end with the paper flow:

> There are also the meetings. The incredible, interminable, boring, ever-multiplying meetings. There are staff meetings and task force meetings, trip meetings and general schedule meetings, meetings to make decisions and unmake them and to plan future meetings, where even more decisions will be made.[38]

"All of this might be more tolerable," Schneiders suggested, "if the staff could derive satisfaction vicariously from personal association with the President." But few aides have any direct contact with the president: "Even many of those at the highest levels—assistants, deputy assistants, special assistants—don't see the President once a week or speak to him in any substantive way once a month."[39] Similarly, Karen Hult observes that "so much of it is symbolic." In her view, staff members "want to get close to the president because it signals . . . the person really has the president's ear. Now, of course, the more people you have like that, the less likely they really are to have the president's ear."[40]

What develops as a substitute for work satisfaction or personal proximity to the president are typical patterns of organizational behavior: "bureaucratic" and "court" politics. With regard to court politics, for example, White House staff members often compete for assignments and authority that serve as a measure of their standing and prestige on the staff and ultimately with the president. Sometimes these turf battles are physical in character, with staff members competing for larger office space and closer proximity to central figures in the administration, especially to the president and the Oval Office in the West Wing. At the beginning of each presidential term, journalists take an intense interest in the size of staff offices and their location in relation to the president; these are taken as signs of relative power and influence by the Washington political community.

Not only are staff members concerned about their standing within the White House, but they also care about how they are perceived by outsiders. Patterns of behavior—bureaucratic politics—can develop that relate to a staff member's place in the organization: "Where one stands depends on where one sits." Staff members often develop allies on the outside—members of the press, members of Congress, lobbyists, and other political influentials—who can aid the programs and political causes of particular parts of the institutional presidency or the personal careers of staffers. Conversely, they can also create hostility and enmity among those outside the staff who compete with them for the president's attention. One classic example of this is the "us versus them" attitude that develops between White House staff members (inside) and the regular departments (outside) in domestic and economic policy and between the NSC staff (inside) and the State Department (outside) in foreign policy. In part, such attitudes may stem from different views and perspectives of a personal nature. But these attitudes may also inhere in the endemic bureaucratic competition and politics that any complex, bureaucratic institution generates. The internal rivalries within the "Trump court" were especially prevalent in his early presidency, as was tension and suspicion between staff in the White House and his cabinet officers.

Politicization

As a response to the bureaucratization of the White House staff, presidents are increasingly politicizing the institutional presidency. That is, they are attempting to make sure that staff members heed their policy directives and serve the president's political needs, rather than their own.

In most cases, the president's reasons for politicizing the staff are understandable. The Constitution's system of shared powers deals presidents a weak hand in Washington. To advance their goals, presidents need broad agreement among their aides and assistants with regard to their political programs and policy goals. President Nixon, for example, created the Domestic Council as a discrete unit within the White House staff to serve as his principal source of policy advice on domestic affairs because he feared that the agencies and departments were staffed with unsympathetic liberal Democrats.

The difficulty for presidents comes in determining to what extent they should politicize their staffs. Excessive politicization can limit the range of opinions among (and thus the quality of advice from) the staff. Taken to extremes, politicization may result in a phalanx of like-minded sycophants.

Excessive politicization can also weaken the objectivity of the policy analysis at the president's disposal, especially if the newly politicized staff unit has a tradition of neutral competence and professionalism. As Terry Moe summarized the argument, "Politicization is deplored for its destructive effects on institutional memory, expertise, professionalism, objectivity, communications, continuity, and other bases of organizational competence."[41]

The part of the president's staff in which politicization has been most noticeable—and the debate over politicization most charged—is the OMB. When Nixon created the Domestic Council he also reorganized the old Bureau of the Budget into the present OMB. Although the Bureau of the Budget was an arm of the presidential staff and certainly not wholly above politics, it was regarded as a place where neutral competence was paramount—that is, "a place where you were both a representative for the President's particular view and the top objective resource for the continuous institution of the Presidency."[42]

Nixon increased the number of political appointees in the OMB. Moreover, some functions once assigned to professionals were given to political appointees; for example, presidentially appointed program associate directors were placed in the OMB's examining divisions.[43] The effects of these changes have been noticeable: greater staff loyalty to political appointees, less cooperation with other parts of the White House staff and with Congress, and reduced impartiality and competence in favor of ideology and partisanship. The role of the OMB in the policy process has also changed: it now gives substantive policy advice—not just objective budget estimates—and takes an active and visible role in lobbying Congress.

The experience of the Reagan administration is particularly revealing of the risks of excessive politicization in budget making, an area where expertise and objective analysis must complement the policy goals expressed in the president's budget proposal. Reagan relied heavily on the OMB, especially during the directorship of David Stockman, both in formulating an economic policy and in trying to get its legislative provisions passed by Congress. Stockman himself concluded— and announced that conclusion in the title of his memoirs—that the so-called Reagan revolution failed.[44] Part of Stockman's thesis was that Reagan was done in by normal Washington politics, which is particularly averse to a budget-conscious president. But Stockman's own words reveal a politicized, deprofessionalized OMB, which may not have been able to give the president the kind of objective advice that he needed, at times, to win over his critics and political opponents:

> The thing was put together so fast that it probably should have been put together differently. . . . We were doing the whole budget-cutting exercise so frenetically . . . juggling details, pushing people, and going from one session to another. . . . The defense program was just a bunch of numbers written on a piece of paper. And it didn't mesh.[45]

The politicization of the OMB cannot explain all of Stockman's difficulties. But as Stockman's account attests, Reagan and his advisers needed hard questioning, objective analysis, and criticism of the sort that the old Bureau of the Budget, but not the new OMB, could provide a president. For Trump, politicization seems problematic among officials dealing with climate change and global warming, which Trump has questioned.

PUTTING THE PRESIDENT BACK IN

Since its inception under Franklin Roosevelt, the institutional presidency has undoubtedly offered presidents some of the important resources they need to meet the complex policy tasks and expectations of the office. But as we have seen, the by-products of an institutional presidency—centralization of policymaking in the president's staff, hierarchy, bureaucratization, and politicization—have detracted from as well as served presidents' policy goals.

Presidents are not, however, simply at the mercy of the institution. Having emphasized the institutional character of the presidency, we should not neglect the presidential character of the institution. Although the presidency is an institution, it is an intensely personal one, which can take on a different character from administration to administration, from one set of staff advisers to another. Presidents and their staffs are by no means hostages to the institution. They have often been able to benefit from the positive resources it provides while deflecting or overcoming the institutional forces that detract from their goals. This is part of presidential leadership.

The most obvious management task a president faces is to recognize on first being elected that organizing and staffing the White House are matters of highest priority. All of Washington and the media wait in eager anticipation for the president-elect to announce the names of the new cabinet. But it is how presidents-elect organize the White House staff and select the people who work for them that will make or break their presidencies.[46]

Clinton's difficulties during his first years as president can be attributed in great measure to his failure, during the transition period before he took office, to understand what it takes to create an effective staff system. According to one report, "Though it had studied the operations of every other major government agency, [Clinton's transition team] assigned no one to study the workings of the White House."[47] This failure was "an insane decision," according to one senior Clinton aide. "We knew more about FEMA [Federal Emergency Management Agency] and the Tuna Commission than we did about the White House. We arrived not knowing what was there, had never worked together, had never worked in these positions."[48]

Clinton's early appointments of top aides exhibit another pattern of which presidents need to be wary: the tendency to offer staff positions to longtime political loyalists and campaign workers. As one Clinton aide noted, "Unable to shift from a campaign mode, it [Clinton's transition team] made staffing decisions with an eye to rewarding loyal campaign workers instead of considering the broader task of governing."[49] Presidents surely need assistants who are personally loyal to them and share their deeply held political views. But presidents also need aides who are adept in Washington politics or have expertise in a particular policy area. Too many friends from Little Rock, Sacramento, or rural Georgia can doom a presidency very quickly.

In contrast, George W. Bush had a more successful transition to office, despite the unusual circumstances of determining who won the 2000 election. Much preliminary planning had been undertaken before the election, including the selection of a chief of staff. Furthermore, even as the uncertainty over how Florida voted dragged on (not to be settled until December 12), transition planning was well under way in the Bush camp. Bush made a particularly wise choice in placing Cheney in charge of the transition. Cheney was not only a veteran of past administrations, he was also a participant in the outgoing Ford and senior Bush transitions. Bush's early selection of Card as chief of staff enabled White House planning and organization to proceed on course. By the end of the first week of January, Bush was only a week behind where Clinton had been in picking his cabinet, he was well ahead in announcing White House appointments, and he had made significant progress in planning his policy agenda.[50]

Like Bush, Barack Obama used his transition period wisely in preparing to take office. During summer 2008, John Podesta, a former Clinton chief of staff, was assigned to head Obama's pre-election transition. Podesta ambitiously began by developing lists of potential nominees, formulating a legislative agenda, reviewing President Bush's executive orders, planning for Obama's first 100 days in office, and organizing the postelection transition. On November 6, two days after the election, Obama tapped Rahm Emanuel as chief of staff, and in the ensuing weeks key White House staff appointments were announced. Cabinet appointments also were swiftly made public, often in teams that stressed Obama's agenda and priorities.

Obama was somewhat less surefooted in his choice of department heads. On the one hand, by December 19 his roster of cabinet nominees was complete. No transition since Nixon's in 1968 had made swifter progress. But this progress came at a price. Ethical questions arose with regard to several of the nominees, and it took until April 28, when Kansas governor Kathleen Sebelius was confirmed to head the Department of Health and Human Services, for the cabinet to be fully in place.

Donald Trump's experience will likely provide the textbook case on what not to do in managing a transition—or perhaps even a presidency—effectively. He was positioned to benefit from new federal legislation providing candidates with assistance in transition planning before Election Day. Governor Chris Christie of New Jersey was assigned the task and assembled a team. Reports indicated that transition planning was well underway, but Trump fired Christie shortly after Election Day, concerned about his loyalty and political viability. Much of the pre-election work was discarded and a new team was put in place; valuable time was lost. In assembling a White House staff, Trump, who lacked prior governmental experience and thus a talent pool to draw upon, essentially turned to campaign loyalists and family members Jared Kushner and Ivanka Trump. As noted earlier, this approach proved a recipe for chaos and internal tension. More generally, day-to-day management was challenging for this president. As Pfiffner notes, Trump "has haphazardly managed the White House, publicly undercutting his top officials and refusing to coordinate his policy decisions with them."[51]

Beyond striking a good balance between loyalty on the one hand and Washington experience and policy expertise on the other, presidents must also be aware of the strengths, and especially the weaknesses, of the various ways of organizing the staff members they have selected. For example, to reduce some of the negative effects of relying on a large White House staff, Eisenhower complemented his use of the formal machinery of the NSC and Adams's office with informal channels of advice. In foreign affairs, he turned not just to his trusted secretary of state, John Foster Dulles, but also to a network of friends and associates with political knowledge and substantive experience, such as his brother Milton Eisenhower and Gen. Alfred Gruenther, the supreme allied commander in Europe. Eisenhower also held regular meetings with his cabinet and with congressional leaders to inform them of his actions, to garner their support, and to hear their views and opinions.[52]

When dealing with his staff, Eisenhower encouraged his aides to air their disagreements and doubts in a candid and straightforward manner. He especially emphasized the need to avoid expressing views that simply reflected departmental or other bureaucratic interests. Herbert Brownell, his attorney general from 1953 until 1957, recalls that "time after time" Eisenhower would tell his cabinet members, "You are not supposed to represent your department, your home state, or anything else. You are my advisers. I want you to speak freely and, more than that, I would like to have you reflect and comment on what other members of the cabinet say."[53] Minutes of Eisenhower's NSC meetings reveal a president who was exposed to the policy divisions within his staff and who engaged in lively discussions with Dulles, Nixon, Harold Stassen, Henry Cabot Lodge, and others. But

Eisenhower was also careful to reserve for himself the ultimate power of decision. Although they had a voice in the process, neither the NSC nor Adams decided for the president.

Kennedy dismantled most of the national security staff that had existed under Eisenhower, preferring instead to use smaller, more informal and collegial decision-making forums. Kennedy's abandonment of more formal procedures may have been unwise, but his experience with the "Ex-Com" (his executive committee of top foreign policy advisors) offers lessons about how presidents can make good use of informal patterns of seeking and giving advice. In April 1961 Kennedy's advisors performed poorly, steering him into an ill-conceived, poorly planned, hastily decided, and badly executed invasion of Cuba—the Bay of Pigs disaster. In the aftermath of that fiasco, Kennedy commissioned a study to find out what had gone wrong. On the basis of its findings, he reorganized his decision-making procedures—including major changes in the Central Intelligence Agency—and explored the faults in his own leadership style. By the time of the Cuban missile crisis in October 1962, Kennedy and his advisors had become an effective decision-making group. Information was readily at hand, the assumptions and implications of policy options were probed, pressures that could lead to a false group consensus were avoided, and Kennedy deliberately concealed his own policy preferences—sometimes absenting himself from meetings—to facilitate candid discussions and to head off a premature decision.

In addition to developing a suitable leadership style, presidents can also take steps to deal with the bureaucratic tendencies that crop up in their staffs. Kennedy's New Frontier agenda, for example, included a number of programs, such as the Peace Corps, that did not resemble traditional bureaucracies, and his personal style generated loyalty and trust. Eisenhower lacked the youthful vigor of his successor, but his broad organizational experience made him a good judge of character with a sure instinct for what and how much he could delegate to subordinates and how best to organize and use their various talents. As with members of his cabinet, Eisenhower emphasized to his staff aides that they worked for him, not for the NSC, Adams, or anyone else.

Finally, although the tendencies toward centralization of policymaking within the White House and politicization of the advisory process have been powerful, all presidents have the capacity to choose how they will act and react within a complex political context populated by other powerful political institutions, processes, and participants. Too much politicization weakens any special claims of expertise, experience, and institutional primacy that the president might make in a particular policy area. Too much centralization eclipses the role of other political actors in a system that is geared to share, rather than exclude, domains of power; it may also set in motion a powerful reaction against the president.

Presidents would be well advised not to neglect the observation about presidential success that Richard Neustadt made nearly sixty years ago: "Presidential power is the power to persuade."[54] But what presidents also need to know is that the character and intended audience of that persuasion must be tailored not just to the requirements of legislative bargaining and enhancing popular support, but also to the institutional character of the presidency itself.

NOTES

1. For a fuller account, see John P. Burke, *The Institutional Presidency: Organizing and Managing the White House from FDR to Clinton* (Baltimore: Johns Hopkins University Press, 2000).

2. Stephen J. Wayne, *The Legislative Presidency* (New York: Harper and Row, 1978), 30.

3. Bradley H. Patterson, *To Serve the President: Continuity and Innovation in the White House Staff* (Washington, DC: Brookings Institution, 2008), 31–32.

4. Quoted in Louis Brownlow, *A Passion for Anonymity: The Autobiography of Louis Brownlow,* vol. 2 (Chicago: University of Chicago Press, 1958), 392.

5. I use the term *larger* to refer to the Brownlow Committee's recognition that the president needed greater staff resources and its recommendations that the Bureau of the Budget be brought over from the Treasury Department and that the Executive Office of the President be created. In its advice on increasing the size of the president's immediate staff, the committee's recommendations were rather modest: the addition of six administrative aides who would avoid the political spotlight and have a "passion for anonymity." These new positions added a more formal structure to the Roosevelt White House and set out new responsibilities for the once–ad hoc staffing arrangement. It is also interesting to note that Roosevelt rejected Brownlow's recommendations that the position of a chief of staff be created and that a more hierarchical, formally organized White House be established; their implementation would await FDR's successors. For further analysis of FDR and the institutional presidency, see Matthew J. Dickinson, *Bitter Harvest: FDR, Presidential Power, and the Growth of the Presidential Branch* (Cambridge: Cambridge University Press, 1997). For fuller discussion of earlier reorganization efforts, see Peri Arnold, *Making the Managerial Presidency: Comprehensive Reorganization Planning, 1905–1980* (Princeton, NJ: Princeton University Press, 1986).

6. President's Committee on Administrative Management, *Administrative Management in the Government of the United States* (Washington, DC: U.S. Government Printing Office, 1937), 4.

7. The initial Brownlow Committee recommendation for reorganizing the executive branch also included proposals to redefine the jurisdiction of cabinet departments, regroup autonomous and independent agencies and bureaus, and give the president virtually unchecked authority to determine and carry out the reorganization and any needed in the future. The more controversial proposals were either dropped or made more palatable in the reorganization act passed by Congress in 1939.

8. For further discussion of the Brownlow and Hoover Commissions, as well as other efforts at reorganizing the presidency, see Arnold, *Making the Managerial Presidency.*

9. On the growth of the White House staff during the Eisenhower presidency, see John Hart, "Eisenhower and the Swelling of the Presidency," *Polity* 24, no. 4 (1992): 673–691.

10. The characteristics of institutionalization are adapted, in part, from Nelson Polsby, "The Institutionalization of the U.S. House of Representatives," *American Political Science Review* 62, no. 1 (1968): 144–168. On the notion of the presidency as an institution, also see Lester Seligman, "Presidential Leadership: The Inner Circle and Institutionalization," *Journal of Politics* 18, no. 3 (1956): 410–426; Norman

Thomas and Hans Baade, eds., *The Institutionalized Presidency* (Dobbs Ferry, NY: Oceana Press, 1972); Robert S. Gilmour, "The Institutionalized Presidency: A Conceptual Clarification," in *The Presidency in Contemporary Context,* ed. Norman Thomas (New York: Dodd, Mead, 1975), 147–159; John Kessel, *The Domestic Presidency: Decision-Making in the White House* (North Scituate, MA: Duxbury Press, 1975); Lester Seligman, "The Presidency and Political Change," *Annals* 466 (March 1983): 179–192; John Kessel, "The Structures of the Carter White House," *American Journal of Political Science* 27, no. 3 (1983): 431–463; John Kessel, "The Structures of the Reagan White House," *American Journal of Political Science* 28, no. 2 (1984): 231–258; Colin Campbell, *Managing the Presidency* (Pittsburgh, PA: University of Pittsburgh Press, 1986); and Peri Arnold, "The Institutionalized Presidency and the American Regime," in *The Presidency Reconsidered,* ed. Richard Waterman (Itasca, IL: F. E. Peacock, 1993), 215–245.

11. Joel K. Goldstein, *The White House Vice Presidency: The Path to Significance, Mondale to Biden* (Lawrence: University Press of Kansas, 2016), 2.

12. Chris Whipple, *The Gatekeepers: How the White House Chiefs of Staff Define Every Presidency* (New York: Crown, 2017); also see Terry Sullivan, ed., *The Nerve Center: Lessons in Governing from the White House Chiefs of Staff* (College Station: Texas A&M University Press, 2004).

13. The full data was 117 confirmed, 107 nominated but awaiting confirmation, 2 awaiting nomination, and 366 with no nominee (total of 591). "Tracking How Many Key Positions Trump Has Filled So Far," *Washington Post,* September 1, 2017, https://www.washingtonpost.com/graphics/politics/trump-administration-appointee-tracker/database/.

14. On White House relations with the media, see Martha J. Kumar, *Managing the President's Message: The White House Communications Operation* (Baltimore: Johns Hopkins University Press, 2007).

15. For further discussion, see Joseph Pika, "Interest Groups and the Executive: Federal Intervention," in *Interest Group Politics,* ed. Allan J. Cigler and Burdett A. Loomis (Washington, DC: CQ Press, 1983), 298–323.

16. Galbraith quoted in Lyndon Johnson, *Vantage Point: Perspectives of the Presidency, 1963–69* (New York: Holt, Rinehart and Winston, 1971), 76. For a more extensive analysis of White House centralization, see Andrew Rudalevige, *Managing the President's Program: Presidential Leadership and Legislative Policy Formulation* (Princeton, NJ: Princeton University Press, 2002).

17. On the development of the role of NSC adviser, see John P. Burke, *Honest Broker? The National Security Advisor and Presidential Decision Making* (College Station: Texas A&M University Press, 2009).

18. Cyrus Vance, *Hard Choices: Critical Years in America's Foreign Policy* (New York: Simon and Schuster, 1983), 409–410.

19. Alexander Haig, *Caveat: Realism, Reagan, and Foreign Policy* (New York: Macmillan, 1984), 306–307.

20. On Scowcroft's role as honest broker, see Burke, *Honest Broker?,* 151–197.

21. Jane Perlez, David Sanger, and Thom Shanker, "From Many Voices, One Battle Strategy," *New York Times,* September 23, 2001.

22. For further discussion on centralization post–September 11, see John P. Burke, *Becoming President: The Bush Transition, 2000–2003* (Boulder, CO: Lynne Rienner, 2004), 175–180, 186–188.

23. There were, however, some exceptions. Early in the new administration, Vice President Cheney was asked to develop a comprehensive energy program. Bush also chose a special task force to flesh out his campaign proposals for Social Security reform.

24. See, for example, Noam Scheiber, "Rod Paige Learns the Hard Way," *New Republic,* July 2, 2001; and Diana Schemo, "Education Chief Seeks More Visible Role," *New York Times,* August 5, 2001.

25. Peter Baker, "Reshaping White House with a Domestic Focus," *New York Times,* December 20, 2008.

26. On presidential "czars," see Mitchel A. Sollenberger and Mark J. Rozell, *The President's Czars: Undermining Congress and the Constitution* (Lawrence: University Press of Kansas, 2012).

27. Martin Landau, "Redundancy, Rationality, and the Problem of Duplication and Overlap," *Public Administration Review* 29 (1969): 346–358.

28. Patrick Anderson, *The President's Men* (Garden City, NY: Anchor Books, 1969), 10.

29. Fred I. Greenstein, *The Hidden-Hand Presidency* (New York: Basic Books, 1982), 147. Adams's counterpart in foreign affairs was Secretary of State John Foster Dulles.

30. Joseph A. Califano Jr., *Governing America: An Insider's Report from the White House and the Cabinet* (New York: Simon and Schuster, 1981), 148.

31. Ronald Brownstein and Dick Kirschsten, "Cabinet Power," *National Journal,* June 28, 1986, 1589.

32. Bernard Weinraub, "How Donald Regan Runs the White House," *New York Times Magazine,* January 5, 1986, 14.

33. On the involvement of the chief of staff in foreign policy, see David A. Cohen, Chris J. Dolan, and Jerel A. Rosati, "A Place at the Table: The Emerging Foreign Policy Roles of the White House Chief of Staff," *Congress and the Presidency* 29 (Autumn 2002): 119–149.

34. See, for example, Ron Suskind, *The Price of Loyalty: George W. Bush, the White House, and the Education of Paul O'Neill* (New York: Simon and Schuster, 2004).

35. James Pfiffner, "Why John Kelly Can't Tame the White House Chaos," *Washington Post,* August 18, 2017.

36. In addition to Flynn, Priebus, and Bannon, other top officials fell by the wayside during Trump's first six months in office: press secretary Sean Spicer, deputy NSC advisor K. T. McFarland, deputy chief of staff Katie Walsh, communications director Mike Dubke, and his replacement, Anthony Scaramucci, who lasted just eleven days on the job, plus FBI director James Comey. For a more extensive comparative analysis, see Kathryn Dunn Tenpas, "Why Is Trump's Staff Turnover Higher than the 5 Most Recent Presidents?" *Bookings Institute Report,* January 19, 2018.

37. Greg Schneiders, "My Turn: Goodbye to All That," *Newsweek,* September 24, 1979, 23.

38. Ibid.

39. Ibid.

40. Quoted in Baker, "Reshaping White House with a Domestic Focus."

41. Terry M. Moe, "The Politicized Presidency," in *The New Direction in American Politics,* ed. John Chubb and Paul Peterson (Washington, DC: Brookings Institution Press, 1985), 235.

42. Hugh Heclo, "OMB and the Presidency: The Problem of 'Neutral Competence,'" *Public Interest* 38 (Fall 1975): 81.

43. Ibid., 85.

44. David A. Stockman, *The Triumph of Politics: Why the Reagan Revolution Failed* (New York: Harper and Row, 1986).

45. Quoted in William Greider, *The Education of David Stockman and Other Americans* (New York: Dutton, 1982), 33, 37.

46. For an analysis of the Carter through Clinton transitions, see John P. Burke, *Presidential Transitions: From Politics to Practice* (Boulder, CO: Lynne Rienner, 2000). For an early analysis of the Obama transition, see John P. Burke, "The Obama Presidential Transition: An Early Assessment," *Presidential Studies Quarterly* 39, no. 3 (September 2009): 572–602; a fuller account can be found in Martha Joynt Kumar, *Before the Oath: How George W. Bush and Barack Obama Managed a Transition of Power* (Baltimore: Johns Hopkins University Press, 2015).

47. Jack Nelson and Robert Donovan, "The Education of a President," *Los Angeles Times Sunday Magazine,* August 1, 1993, 14.

48. Quoted in ibid.

49. Ibid.

50. For further analysis of the George W. Bush transition, see Burke, *Becoming President.*

51. Pfiffner, "Why John Kelly Can't Tame the White House Chaos."

52. On Eisenhower's "binocular" use of informal and formal patterns of advice, see Greenstein, *Hidden-Hand Presidency,* 100–151. On his decision-making processes, see John P. Burke and Fred I. Greenstein, with Larry Berman and Richard Immerman, *How Presidents Test Reality: Decisions on Vietnam, 1954 and 1965* (New York: Russell Sage Foundation, 1989).

53. Herbert Brownell with John P. Burke, *Advising Ike: The Memoirs of Attorney General Herbert Brownell* (Lawrence: University Press of Kansas, 1993), 294.

54. Richard E. Neustadt, *Presidential Power: The Politics of Leadership* (New York: Wiley, 1960).

THE PRESIDENCY AND THE BUREAUCRACY

The Levers of Presidential Control

David E. Lewis and Terry M. Moe

"Chief executive" is not a presidential title that appears in the Constitution. Indeed, the constitutional separation of powers grants considerable authority over the executive branch, or bureaucracy, to Congress as well as to the president. Nonetheless, modern presidents work hard to maximize their control of the bureaucracy and to shift the balance of political power in their own favor. David E. Lewis and Terry M. Moe explain why presidents seek to make themselves "chief executives," and, after reviewing the constitutional and historical aspects of the relationship between the presidency and the bureaucracy, they offer case studies in the areas of personnel, budgets, and regulatory review to illuminate how presidents do it—and why they usually succeed.

On January 3, 2013, President Barack Obama signed into law the 2013 National Defense Authorization Act—which, among other things, purported to limit the president's ability to transfer detainees out of military prisons in Guantánamo Bay and Afghanistan. Accompanying the president's signature was a ten-paragraph "signing statement" expressing dissatisfaction with many provisions of the new law.[1] With regard to the limits on his ability to transfer detainees, the signing statement read, "In the event that these statutory restrictions operate in a manner that violates constitutional separation of powers principles, my Administration will implement them in a manner that avoids the constitutional conflict." In other words, the president would comply with these provisions only if he felt doing so would not interfere with his constitutional authority.

When Obama was a candidate for the presidency in 2007 and 2008, he actually spoke out against such use of presidential signing statements,[2] telling the *Boston Globe,* for example, that it was a "problem" that President Bush "has attached signing statements to legislation in an effort to change the meaning of the legislation, to avoid enforcing certain provisions of the legislation that the President does not like, and to raise implausible or dubious constitutional objections to the legislation."[3] Yet once he became president himself, Obama attached signing statements to at least twenty different pieces of legislation during his first term alone, challenging multiple provisions in each law.

What was President Obama trying to do? The answer: just what President Bush was trying to do. By telling government agencies what he considered the law to mean, and thus how he expected the law to be carried out, Obama was attempting to exercise control over the bureaucracy—and in so doing, to shape public policy. Writ large, this is what all modern presidents do. Sometimes they use signing statements, but far more often they rely on other, better known levers of presidential power, such as appointments, budgets, and regulatory review. Whatever the mechanisms, all presidents routinely and systematically take actions throughout their terms of office that are designed to bring the bureaucracy more fully under their control. Indeed, they have little choice. Almost all important policies are carried out by public agencies of one kind or another, and any president who hopes to be a strong leader and put his stamp on the nation's public policy must therefore control the bureaucracy. Or at least gain as much control as possible.

Throughout our nation's history, presidents have made a good deal of progress on this front. During the nineteenth century, there was very little bureaucracy because the departments and agencies of the executive branch were few in number and small in size and scope. Presidents tended to be weak and Congress strong. But as the federal government began addressing the burgeoning problems of industrial society during the early decades of the twentieth century, particularly during the New Deal of the 1930s, American bureaucracy grew enormously. And as the bureaucracy grew, so did the presidency, which evolved into a complex institution whose specialized components—the Office of Management and Budget (OMB), the National Security Council, the White House domestic policy staff, the White House appointments unit, and many others—are devoted largely to providing the president with the capacity to impose centralized control on the bureaucracy.[4] These developments are among the defining features of modern American government: a government that is bureaucratic and presidentially led.

Yet presidential control is far from complete. Precisely because bureaucracy is so central to public policy, Congress cares about the bureaucracy too. Indeed, this is putting it mildly. Congress knows that, unless it can shape the substance of bureaucratic action, the laws its legislators write and the benefits they attempt to bring home to constituents and powerful interest groups are worth little more than the paper on which they are written. Congress has formidable weapons to employ, moreover, in bringing its preferences to bear: it authorizes the agencies' programs, supplies the agencies' money, and oversees the agencies' behavior.

The stage is set, then, for an ongoing struggle between the president and Congress over which branch controls the bureaucracy—a struggle that is guaranteed, even encouraged, by a Constitution that puts no single branch in charge, and indeed barely deals with the bureaucracy at all. Any effort to understand presidential leadership must understand the nature of this perpetual battle over the bureaucracy, how presidents have responded to it, and how well they have done—and can be expected to do—in gaining the upper hand.

The challenge facing presidents is a daunting one. But despite the obstacles that the American system of checks and balances puts in their way, and despite the awesome powers of a turf-conscious Congress, presidents have inherent advantages in the struggle to control the federal bureaucracy—advantages that have allowed them, slowly but surely, to outmuscle Congress (much of the time) and play the predominant role in harnessing the bureaucracy toward their own ends. We are not saying that presidents reign supreme. We are saying that, although separation of powers is naturally brutal to presidents, they have made it less so through strategic and aggressive action.

In the first part of the chapter, we show that a distinctive logic governs this struggle for control. Along the way, we explain how decisions about the bureaucracy are made in the political process, the relative roles that the president and Congress play, and the forces that give rise to key presidential advantages. In the second part, we detail how presidents have used their inherent advantages through various levers of power. Specifically, they have increased their strategic use of presidential appointees across the government, they have extended their control over the federal budget, and they have centralized the review of agency rulemaking in their own hands. Through these actions they have gained more control over the nation's bureaucracy, and over its policies and governance, than the constitutional fragmentation of power would otherwise provide.

THE PRESIDENT, THE CONGRESS, AND THE DYNAMICS OF CONTROL

To understand the dynamics of control, we need to start at the beginning with how the bureaucracy is organized. Although this topic may seem sterile and far removed from politics, it is anything but. Organization matters. Everyone in the political process knows that the specifics of agency organization—mandates, structures, personnel systems, locations in the hierarchy of government, and more—have profound consequences for how policies are interpreted and carried out, as well as for which politicians and groups are in a position to exercise control. Because decisions about organization are matters of strategy and struggle, they are intensely political.[5]

Within Congress, the legislative designers of public agencies tend to view the bureaucracy in parochial terms. As individual actors in a fragmented system, legislators and interest groups are not held responsible for the performance of the bureaucracy as a whole, as presidents are. They have little concern for broad issues of management, efficiency, and coordination, as presidents do. Interest groups have their eyes on their own interests and not much else. Legislators have their eyes on their own electoral fortunes, and thus on the special (often local) interests that can bring them security and popularity in office. For both interest groups and legislators, politics is not about the system. It is about the pieces of the system, and about ensuring the flow of benefits to constituents and special interests. As we see in the following sections, political parties modify these tendencies somewhat. But the tendencies remain fundamental.

What are the implications for how the bureaucracy gets organized? In any particular case, of course, a winning legislative coalition wants an agency that will carry out its favored policies effectively. But this is not simply a matter of designing organizations to be effective. For what an agency actually does will depend on who controls it and what they want it to do. If control of the agency falls into the "wrong" hands, the most effective organization in the world will not help. The key challenge a legislative coalition faces is to ensure its own control and to insulate against the control of others.

The way to accomplish such control most directly is to specify the agency's organization in great detail by establishing decision procedures, standards, timetables, personnel rules, and other structural features. A strategically designed compendium of such rules serves to tell the agency precisely what to do and how to do it. In this way, the legislative coalition that passes the law is able to exercise control *ex ante,* embedding its interests in formal restrictions that, by giving the "right" direction to agency behavior, also insulate it from future influence by opponents. The benefits of insulation do not come cheap because restrictive rules can easily undermine the agency's effectiveness by denying it the discretion it needs to do a "good" job. But in a world of political uncertainty, where enemies abound, this is a price worth paying if the agency is to be protected.

Presidents are prime targets of this strategy, even when legislative coalitions regard the current incumbent as friendly. The reason is that all presidents, for institutional reasons, use their power in ways that are threatening to legislators and groups. As national leaders with a broad, heterogeneous constituency, presidents think in grander terms than members of Congress about social problems and the public interest, and they tend to resist specialized appeals. Moreover, because presidents are held uniquely responsible by the public for virtually every aspect of national performance, and because their leadership turns on effective governance, they have strong incentives to seek centralized control of the bureaucracy, both for themselves and for their policy agendas.

Legislative coalitions often have reason, then, to try to insulate agencies from presidential influence. All the formal restrictions mentioned here help to do that: by specifying the features of agencies' organization—and thus the rules that ultimately guide their behavior—in excruciating detail, they help to insulate agencies from external control, including presidential control. Other restrictions are aimed directly at presidents themselves. The independent commission, for example, is a popular structural form that restricts presidents' appointment and removal powers, as well as their budgetary and managerial reach. Similarly, legislation is sometimes crafted to limit the number of presidential appointees in an agency and to use civil service hiring procedures and professional credential requirements as protections against presidential control.

So although presidents are nominally in charge of the entire executive branch, the American political system makes it very difficult for them to exercise genuine control. This is a built-in problem, ultimately traceable to the constitutional separation of powers and its far-reaching consequences for politics. The bureaucracy is a product of this politics. It is heavily influenced by the fragmented, decentralized forces that animate congressional decision making, and it is slowly pieced together over time—agency by agency, program by program, unit by unit, procedure by procedure—with little overarching concern for the whole and with conscious, strategic effort to insulate its components from possible opponents. The bureaucracy is not designed to be centrally controlled by presidents, or by anyone else. Yet controlling it is essential to presidential leadership.

What can presidents do?

Presidential Discretion and Unilateral Power

There is actually quite a lot that presidents can do to control the bureaucracy. In the fractious, often chaotic politics that separation of powers tends to generate, presidents enjoy important advantages over Congress in the ongoing struggle for control. Over time, these advantages have allowed presidents to move the structure of the bureaucratic system, however haltingly and episodically, along a presidential trajectory—shifting the balance of power in their favor, and giving them greater (if still very imperfect) control.

Presidents are greatly advantaged by their position as chief executive, which gives them many opportunities to make unilateral decisions about structure and policy. If they want to develop their own institutional capacity (by beefing up the apparatus of the institutional presidency), review or revise agency decisions, coordinate agency actions, make changes in agency leadership, or otherwise impose their views on the bureaucracy, they can simply act—claiming the legal right to do so—and leave it to Congress and the courts to react. For reasons discussed later, Congress often finds this difficult or impossible to do, and the president wins by default. The ability to win by default is a cornerstone of the presidential advantage.

Why do presidents have powers of unilateral action?[6] Part of the answer is constitutional. The Constitution, rather than spelling out their authority as chief executive in detail through specific enumerated powers—a strategy favored by those among the Framers who were most concerned with limiting the executive—is largely silent on the nature and extent of presidential authority, especially in domestic affairs. It broadly endows presidents with the "executive power" and charges them to "faithfully execute the laws" but says little else. This very ambiguity, as Richard Pious notes, "provided the opportunity for the exercise of a residuum of unenumerated power."[7] The proponents of a strong executive at the Constitutional Convention were well aware of that.

The question of what the president's formal powers really are, or ought to be, will always be controversial among legal scholars. But two things seem reasonably clear. One is that if presidents are to perform their duties effectively, they must be (and in practice are) regarded as having certain legal prerogatives that allow them to do what executives do: manage, coordinate, staff, collect information, plan, reconcile conflicting values, and so on. This is what it means, in practice, to have the executive power.[8] The other is that, although the content of these prerogative powers is often unclear, presidents have been aggressive in pushing an expansive interpretation: rushing to claim the gray areas of the law, asserting their rights of control, and exercising them—whether or not other actors, particularly in Congress, happen to agree.[9] Many of the same arguments can be made for the president's role as commander in chief, but the presidential advantages are stronger and more obvious when it comes to war and foreign policy, so we continue to highlight the grounds for unilateral presidential action in the domestic realm, and in governance generally.[10]

The courts, which have the authority to resolve ambiguities about the president's proper constitutional role, generally have not chosen to do so. Certain contours of presidential power have been clarified by major court decisions—on the removal power, for instance, and executive privilege—and justices have sometimes offered their views on the president's implied or inherent powers as chief executive. But the political and historical reality is that presidents have largely defined their own constitutional role by pushing out the boundaries of their prerogatives.[11]

Congress can do nothing to eliminate presidents' executive power. Presidents are not Congress's agents. They have their own constitutional role to play and their own constitutional powers to exercise, powers that are not delegated to them by Congress and thus cannot be taken away. Any notion that Congress makes the laws and that the president's job is simply to execute them—to follow orders, in effect—overlooks what separation of powers is all about: presidents have authority in their own right, coequal to Congress and not subordinate to it.

Precisely because presidents are chief executives, however, what they can and cannot do is also shaped by the goals and requirements of the laws they are charged to execute. And Congress has the right to be as specific as it wants in writing these laws, as well as in designing the agencies that administer them. If Congress likes, it can specify policy and structure in enough detail to narrow agency discretion considerably, and with it the scope of presidential control. It can also impose requirements that explicitly qualify and limit how presidents may use their prerogative powers—as it has done, for example, in protecting members of independent commissions from removal and in mandating civil service protections.[12]

Yet these sorts of restrictions ultimately cannot contain presidential power. To begin with, presidents are powerful players in the legislative process, and because discretion is the foundation of their power and ultimate success in controlling the bureaucracy, they will fight for statutes that give them as much discretion as possible, and they can veto those that don't. All legislation, as a result, is inevitably shaped to some degree by the presidential drive to increase administrative discretion.[13] In addition, legislators have their own incentive to craft bills that delegate considerable discretion to agencies and presidents in order to pursue their own goals. Legislators' main concern, politics aside, is for the effective provision of benefits to their constituents. For problems of even moderate complexity, especially in an ever-changing and increasingly interdependent and complicated world, this requires putting most aspects of policy and organization in the hands of agency professionals and allowing them to use their expert judgment to flesh out the details. It requires, in other words, the delegation of discretion. And once this is done—as it regularly is, year in and year out—presidents and agencies do the actual governing, not Congress.

Thus, although legislators and groups may try to protect their agencies by burying them in rules and regulations, a good deal of agency discretion will remain, and presidents cannot readily be prevented from turning it to their own advantage. They are centrally and supremely positioned in the executive, they have great flexibility to act, they have a vast array of powers and mechanisms at their disposal, they have informal means of persuasion and influence, and they, not Congress, are the ones who are ultimately responsible for day-to-day governance. Even when Congress directly limits a presidential prerogative, such as the removal power, presidents have the flexibility simply to shift to other avenues of discretionary action.

In part, Congress's problem is analogous to the classic problem a board of directors faces in trying to control management in a private firm.[14] The board, representing owners, tries to impose rules and procedures to ensure that management will behave in the owners' best interests. But managers have their own interests at heart, and their expertise and day-to-day control of operations allow them to strike out on their own. Congress faces the same problem with presidents. However much it tries to structure things, presidents can use their own institution's—and through it, the bureaucracy's—informational and operational advantages to promote the presidential agenda.

Yet Congress's situation is even worse than the corporate analogy would suggest. In business settings, the owners may well have control problems, but they also have supreme authority over their managers, whom they have the right to hire and fire, and thus they have major levers for gaining the upper hand. In American politics, Congress has no such authority. Its executive officers—presidents—have all the resources for noncompliance that corporate managers do, and in addition they are not Congress's agents. Presidents have formal authority in their own right. Congress does not hire them, it cannot fire them short of impeachment, and it cannot structure their powers and incentives in any way it might like. Yet Congress is forced to entrust them with the execution of the laws. From a control standpoint, this is your basic nightmare.

It is also important to recognize that, although Congress can try to limit presidential prerogatives by enacting statutes, presidents are greatly empowered through statutory law whether Congress intends it or not. Some legislative grants of power to the presidency are explicit, such as the negotiation of tariffs and the oversight of mergers in the foreign trade field. But the most far-reaching additions to presidential power are implicit. When new statutes are passed, almost regardless of what they are, they increase presidents' total responsibilities and give them a formal basis for extending their authoritative reach into new realms. At the same time, the new statutes add to the total discretion available for presidential control, as well as to the resources contained within the executive.

It may seem that the proliferation of statutes would tie presidents in knots as they pursue the execution of each one. But the opposite is true: the aggregate effect of all these statutes on presidents is liberating and empowering. Presidents, as chief executives, are responsible for *all* the laws—and, inevitably, those laws turn out to be interdependent and conflicting in ways that the individual statutes themselves do not recognize. As would be true of any executive, the president's proper role is to rise above a myopic focus on each statute in isolation, to coordinate policies by taking account of their interdependence, and to resolve statutory conflicts by balancing their competing requirements. All of this affords presidents substantial discretion, which they can use to impose their own priorities on government.[15]

Congress's Collective Action Problems

Another major source of presidential advantage deserves equal emphasis. Presidents are unitary actors who sit alone atop their own institution, the Executive Office of the President. Within that institution, what they say goes. In contrast, Congress is a collective body that can make decisions only through the laborious aggregation of member preferences. As such, it suffers from serious collective action problems that presidents not only avoid, but can exploit.

This crucial fact of political life is too often overlooked. Scholars and journalists tend to reify Congress, treating it as an institutional actor like the president and analyzing their interbranch conflicts accordingly. The president and Congress are portrayed as fighting it out, head to head, over matters of institutional power and prerogative. Each is seen as defending and promoting its own institutional interests. The president wants power, Congress wants power, and they struggle for advantage.

This portrayal misconstrues things. Congress is made up of hundreds of members, each a political entrepreneur, each dedicated to reelection, each serving a district or state. Although they have a common stake in upholding the institutional power of Congress, this is a collective good, not an individual one, and can only weakly motivate their behavior.[16] Members of Congress are trapped in a classic prisoner's dilemma: all of them might benefit if they could cooperate in defending or advancing Congress's power, but each has a strong incentive to free ride if supporting the collective good is politically costly to them as individuals. Just as most citizens, absent taxation, would not voluntarily pay their share of the national defense, so most legislators will not flout their constituents or key interest groups in order to protect congressional power. If a legislator is offered a veterans' hospital or a new highway in exchange for supporting a bill that, among other things, happens to reduce Congress's power relative to the president's, there is little mystery as to where the stronger incentives would lie.

The internal organization of Congress, especially its party leadership, imposes a modicum of order and gives it a certain capacity to guard its power.[17] Indeed, in recent decades, with the parties ever more polarized and party-line votes increasingly common, it may appear that party leaders have been strong enough to stifle the fractious inclinations of their members, coordinate behavior, and get Congress to defend itself by acting coherently as an institution. But there is less institutional strength here than meets the eye.

What has happened in recent decades, more fundamentally, is that the constituencies within each party have become more homogeneous, mainly because the conservative South has become more Republican and the liberal Northeast has become more Democratic. Party leaders—who are elected by their members and highly sensitive to their needs—have been better able to mobilize the members to vote together because there are many more issues on which they already agree. Not so, however, when they don't agree. Constituency is still in the driver's seat, and much of what looks like leader power is really a reflection of shared constituency concerns and ideology. Leaders have no license to force members to do what they don't want to do or don't really care about—such as taking costly action to protect Congress's institutional power relative to the president's—in the face of competing inducements to behave otherwise.[18]

The party that doesn't occupy the presidency, of course, does have an electoral reason—although it is not directly related to protecting Congress as an institution—for challenging the president. If its members can make him look bad, and if they can tarnish his party's label, then they are more likely to win the next election. In addition to the forces of constituency, then—which can easily be centrifugal and thus can be played upon by presidents—legislators have a "shared electoral fate" that shapes their political calculus and may induce them to take on the president when he tries to enhance his power. There is a flip side to this phenomenon, however, that works in the opposite direction and undercuts its efficacy: legislators in the president's own party have a shared electoral fate in seeing that he wins, and they have an incentive to undermine any effort by Congress to strike back at him or foil his plans. This is just another example of how complex the congressional decision process is, and how many collective action problems stand in the way of strong, coherent legislative action.

Presidents are not hobbled by collective action problems. Supreme within their own institution, they can simply make authoritative decisions about what to do and then do it. On occasion, their interests as individuals may conflict with those of the presidency as an institution. The short-term pressures on them to enhance the loyalty of an agency like the OMB, for example, could cause them to overly politicize it, and this could undercut the institutional presidency's long-term capacity for expertise and competence.[19] But most of the time, presidents' personal drive for leadership motivates them to do things that actively promote and nurture the power of their institution—because it is through their institutional power that they are able to get things done, and to succeed. Thus not only is the presidency a unitary institution, but there is also substantial congruence between the president's individual interests and the interests of the institution.

In sum, presidents have both the will and the capacity to promote the power of their own institution, but individual legislators have neither and cannot be expected to promote the power of Congress in a coherent and forceful way. This basic imbalance means that presidents will behave imperialistically and opportunistically, but that Congress will not do the same by formulating an offensive of its own, and indeed will not even be able to mount a consistently effective defense of its authority against presidential encroachment.

Congress's situation is all the worse because its collective action problems do more than weaken its will and disable its capacity for action. They also allow presidents to manipulate legislative behavior to their own advantage by getting members to support or at least acquiesce in the growth of presidential power. One reason for this has already been established by political scientists: in any majority-rule institution with a diverse membership, so many different majority coalitions are possible that, with the right manipulation of the agenda, outcomes can be engineered to allow virtually any alternative to win against any other.[20] Put more simply, agenda setters can take advantage of the collective action problems inherent in majority-rule institutions to get their own way.

Presidents have at least two important kinds of agenda-setting power. First, because Congress is so fragmented, presidentially initiated legislation is the most coherent force in setting the legislative agenda. The issues Congress deals with each year are fundamentally shaped by the issues presidents decide are salient.[21] Second, presidents set Congress's agenda when they or their appointees in the bureaucracy act unilaterally to alter the status quo—by making the Environmental Protection Agency less aggressive in enforcing the Clean Air Act, for example, or by having the Occupational Safety and Health Administration conduct fewer on-site inspections of worker safety. This sort of thing happens all the time, and Congress is forced to react or acquiesce. In either case, presidents can choose their positions strategically, with an eye to the various majorities in Congress, and engineer outcomes more beneficial to the presidency than they could if dealing with a unified opponent.[22]

Presidential leverage is greatly enhanced by the maze of obstacles that stand in the way of each congressional decision. A bill must pass through subcommittees, committees, and floor votes in both the House of Representatives and the Senate; it eventually must be passed in identical form by both houses; and it is threatened along the way by rules committees, filibusters, holds, and other procedural roadblocks. Every one of these veto points must be overcome if Congress is to act. Presidents, in contrast, need to succeed with only one to ensure that their newly determined status quo will prevail.

More generally, the transaction costs of congressional action are enormous. Not only must coalitions somehow be formed among hundreds of legislators across two houses and a variety of committees—a challenge that requires intricate coordination, persuasion, trades, promises, and all the rest—but owing to scarce time and resources, members must also be convinced that the issue at hand is more deserving than the hundreds of other issues competing for their attention. Party leaders and committee chairs can help, but the obstacle-strewn process of generating legislation remains incredibly difficult and costly. And because it is, the best prediction for most issues most of the time is that Congress will take no positive action at all. Whatever members' positions on an issue, the great likelihood is that *nothing will happen.*

When presidents use unilateral powers and discretion to shift the status quo, what they want most from Congress is no formal response at all—which is exactly what they are likely to get. This would be so in any event, given the multiple veto points and high transaction costs that plague congressional choice. But it is especially likely when presidents and their agents enter the legislative process on their own behalf, dangling rewards, threatening sanctions, offering side payments, and, perhaps most importantly, mobilizing the legislators in their own party to come to their support.[23] Presidents are especially well situated and endowed with political resources to do this. And again, blocking congressional action is fairly easy, especially given that, should all else fail, presidents can use their veto.

Whether presidents are trying to block or to push for legislation, the motivational asymmetry between them and Congress adds mightily to their cause. Presidents are strongly motivated to develop an institutional capacity for controlling the bureaucracy as a whole, and, when structural issues are in question, they take the larger view. How do these structures contribute to or detract from the creation of a presidential system of control? Legislators are driven by localism and special interests, and they are little motivated by these sorts of systemic concerns. This basic motivational asymmetry has a great deal to do with what presidents are able to accomplish when they attempt to block or steer congressional outcomes.

On issues affecting the institutional balance of power, then, presidents care intensely about securing changes that promote their institutional power, whereas legislators typically do not. Members of Congress are unlikely to oppose incremental increases in the relative power of presidents unless the issue in question directly harms the special interests of their constituents, which, if presidents play their cards right, can often be avoided. On the other hand, legislators are generally unwilling to do what is necessary to develop Congress's own capacity for strong institutional action. Not only would doing so often require that they put constituency concerns aside for the sake of the common good, which they have strong incentives not to do, but it also would tend to call for more centralized control by party leaders and less individual member autonomy, which they find distinctly unattractive.

When institutional issues are at stake in legislative voting, then, presidents have a motivational advantage: they care more about their institution than legislators do about theirs. This asymmetry means that presidents will invest more of their political clout in getting what they want. It also means that the situation is ripe for trading. Legislators may fill the airwaves with rhetoric about the dangers of presidential power, but their weak individual stakes in overcoming these dangers allow them to be bought off with the kinds of particularistic benefits (and sanctions) that they really do care about. This does not mean that presidents can perform magic. If what they want requires affirmative congressional action, the obstacles are many and the probability of success is low. But their chances are still much better than they otherwise would be, absent the motivational asymmetry between them and legislators. And if all presidents want to do is block congressional action, which often is all they need to preserve their control over the bureaucracy, then the asymmetry can work wonders in cementing presidential faits accomplis.

THE LEVERS OF PRESIDENTIAL CONTROL: THREE CASES

Presidents have used their institutional advantages to enhance their control over the bureaucracy. In this section, we describe three important examples of how they have done this in the areas of personnel, budgets, and regulatory review. In each case, Congress has been either unwilling or unable to protect its own power, and the net result has been a shift in the balance of power toward presidents.

Personnel

During the middle and late 1800s, members of Congress were actively involved in the spoils system, which, in doling out government jobs to the party faithful, was the foundation of the American party system. Control of spoils gave them control over appointments to the bureaucracy, and thus substantial control over the bureaucracy itself. American society, however, was undergoing disruptive changes—industrialization, immigration, urbanization—and these changes gave rise to massive social problems, as well as to new political groups demanding governmental action to solve them. A government that traditionally had done very little, and could get away with being staffed by appointees who lacked expertise and experience, was now expected to perform at a much higher level.

As a result, Congress was under pressure to adopt a merit system for government personnel. The first step came with the Pendleton Act in 1883, which created the Civil Service Commission and brought 10.5 percent of federal jobs under the umbrella of merit appointment. The proportion of merit-protected civil servants then grew, decade by decade, as did the protections afforded federal employees under the system. Presidents had the authority to add jobs to the merit system and, at the end of their terms, often "blanketed in" their political appointees, ensuring that the latter couldn't be fired en masse by the next president. Meanwhile, business and civic groups continued the drumbeat for civil service expansion, as did the emerging federal employee unions, and Congress responded by adding new classes of employees to the system. By the 1930s more than 80 percent of federal jobs had become part of civil service.[24]

During the Great Depression, Franklin Roosevelt led the federal government into new areas of economic and regulatory activity. Scores of new agencies were created to counter the depression and, later, to mobilize for World War II. The bureaucracy grew by leaps and bounds. Federal employment soared.[25] Most of the new jobs were originally filled with appointees recommended by Democratic Party officials, but these positions were then blanketed in as the New Deal drew to a close, thus protecting them from future dismissal.[26]

The expansion of bureaucracy presented all subsequent presidents with a fundamental challenge. If they wanted to be strong leaders, they needed to control the tangle of departments, agencies, boards, and commissions that populated the government and carried out policy. This was especially true for Dwight Eisenhower, the first Republican to become president in twenty years, because upon assuming office in 1953, he faced a bureaucracy filled with Democrats.

Supported by a Republican Congress hungry for jobs, President Eisenhower acted through executive order to create 800–1,000 new appointed positions, hoping to rein in the sprawling New Deal bureaucracy.[27] Subsequent presidents have continued to add appointees to the federal personnel system. And, more fundamentally, they have worked to develop the president's institutional capacity to find, recruit, and select loyal appointees. The number of political appointees has nearly doubled from 1,778 at the end of the Eisenhower administration to about 2,846 in 2012, a number that will surely increase as President Obama fills out his second term team. These increases have come under both Democratic and Republican presidents, with the largest increase occurring during the presidency of Jimmy Carter—for reasons we soon discuss.

Why wouldn't Congress simply forbid modern presidents to expand the numbers of appointees? One reason is evident in the Eisenhower experience. He entered office with Republican majorities in Congress. They wanted him to be successful and, with Republicans in high-level executive positions, to move policy in a more conservative direction. They also knew that, as members of the president's party, they could recommend candidates for appointment and, when successful, win the appreciation of the appointees and their group supporters, along with their endorsements and campaign support.

More generally, the data show that during periods of unified government—when the presidency and Congress are controlled by the same party—significantly larger increases in the number of political appointees occur than during periods of divided government.[28] Yet even when Congress is controlled by the opposition party, serious efforts to reduce the number of appointees have gained little traction. This is true despite repeated claims by think tanks, academics, and former government officials that there are too many political appointees in the bureaucracy, threatening its expertise and "neutral competence."[29] Congress's problem is that, because the president can veto any legislation he doesn't want, a fair portion of his own party would have to go along if the number of appointees were to be cut—and they are unlikely to do that. In addition, the majority party's willingness to cut the number of appointees is inhibited by the hope that its own candidate will win the presidency in the next election.

The dynamic at work here, therefore, favors the president. Congress is not a unified institution intent on maximizing its power relative to the president's. It is a factionalized institution rife with collective action problems, and it is vulnerable to presidential imperialism. Historically, Congress has occasionally resisted presidential efforts to increase the number of political appointees, and it has occasionally succeeded in pressuring presidents to reduce the numbers in specific agencies. But overall, presidents have increased the penetration of appointees in the bureaucracy quite dramatically.

Targeting Management Agencies. The career civil service, whose members are neither hired nor fired by presidents, is obviously a major impediment to presidential leadership of the bureaucracy. Presidents took strategic action *within* the existing federal personnel system to affect the numbers and placement of political appointees. But until Jimmy Carter, no modern president had seriously tried to change the system itself. Civil service reform had been contemplated in broad reorganization packages, notably under Roosevelt (via the Brownlow Committee) and Eisenhower (via the second Hoover Commission), but such reform had never been a high priority on its own.[30] This isn't so surprising: genuine reform requires controversial new legislation, which is extraordinarily difficult and politically costly to achieve. With so many other ways to enhance their power over the bureaucracy through unilateral action, presidents have had little incentive to pursue it.

Carter's situation was different from that of his predecessors. With the massive growth of government in the 1960s under Lyndon Johnson's Great Society, followed in the early 1970s by the dramatic expansion of federal regulation—with the creation of the Environmental Protection Agency and the Occupational Safety and Health Administration, for example—Carter oversaw a bureaucracy much bigger, more complex, and more expensive than they had. And by the mid-1970s, in a worsening atmosphere of stagflation and energy shortages, Americans were fed up. Strong antigovernment, antitax sentiments swelled within the electorate, and politicians—including Carter—responded with pledges of reform.[31]

It was easy to portray civil service reform as part of this broad movement for better, more effective government. But for Carter it was much more than that: it was a way to make the civil service system more responsive to the presidency, and thus to enhance the president's capacity to control the bureaucracy. The kind of reform he had in mind amounted to nothing less than a clear shift in the balance of institutional power.

In the early spring of 1978, barely a year after assuming office, Carter placed a comprehensive proposal for civil service reform before Congress.[32] Among other things, he aimed to divide the Civil Service Commission into two parts. One, the Office of Personnel Management (OPM), would be headed by a single presidential appointee and given substantial discretion in crafting personnel policies for federal employees. The other, the Merit Systems Protection Board, would be an adjudicatory agency for handling employee appeals and grievances. In addition, Carter pushed for the creation of the Senior Executive Service (SES), a flexible corps of about 8,000 high-level administrators who could be moved from job to job at the discretion of the president and his subordinates and whose ranks would include some 800 political appointees.[33]

Nothing about this proposal could have fooled legislators into seeing civil service reform as a simple attempt to achieve "good government." It was also—and obviously—a bold attempt to expand presidential power over personnel and thus over the entire bureaucracy. Congress responded just as we would expect. Legislators simply did not care much about the balance-of-power issue and, with a few exceptions, did not oppose this clear shift in authority and discretion to the president. Virtually all the political controversy was stimulated by other aspects of the bill that were tangential to the power issue but affected veterans' organizations and public sector unions—constituency interests that, unlike the collective good of institutional power, motivate members of Congress to take action.[34]

The dynamics of control favored the president. Carter had a Democratic majority in Congress and so was in a strong position to begin with. Plus, most of the political conflicts between the president and Congress, and within Congress itself, centered on special-interest concerns—which excited negative votes even among many Democrats at points along the way—but not on whether Congress was yielding too much authority to the president in an institutional power struggle. In the end, Carter compromised on the veterans' and labor issues and won on what he really cared about. The Civil Service Reform Act transferred governance of the federal personnel system from an independent commission to a presidential agency (OPM) headed by a political appointee and endowed with greater discretion; it increased the number of appointees in the OPM from six to twelve; it embedded them more deeply into the structure of the agency; and it created the SES—a hugely important innovation that allowed presidents to move thousands of high-level careerists from job to job and gave them hundreds of additional appointees to work with as well. All in all, the act resulted in a tremendous boost for presidential power.

Strengthening the White House Personnel Operation. Along with the increase in the number of political appointees, the White House personnel operation has grown more sophisticated in how it fills these positions.[35] Truman was the first president to have a White House aide designated specifically to handle personnel issues. And up through the Eisenhower administration, it was common for the national party to have an office close to the White House to handle appointments. With the advent of John Kennedy's administration, however, a dedicated White House staff emerged both to recruit appointees and to manage the patronage pressures on the new administration.

Since that time, presidents have increasingly professionalized and institutionalized the personnel process.[36] President Kennedy employed three personnel officials. President Nixon employed twenty-five to thirty. Today the number is higher still, and can exceed 100 when new presidents are transitioning into office. Starting with Nixon, presidents began employing professional recruiters to help identify qualified persons for top executive posts. Recent presidents have also regularized a process for handling patronage requests from campaign staff, the party, interest groups, and influential members of Congress through an ever more formal division between policy and patronage efforts.

The growing sophistication of the personnel operation has allowed presidents to take more and more control of the appointments process—leaving less to their party and their department and agency heads. Throughout much of the twentieth century, presidents were involved directly in filling only the top executive positions. In recent decades, they have increasingly sought to assert their influence over all appointed positions.

Congress hasn't done anything to slow the development of the White House personnel operation. In part, legislators recognize that presidents need to make appointments and thus need to get organized for that purpose. But of course, bigger issues are at stake. The president's institutional capacity is related directly to his ability to shift the balance of power with Congress in his favor. Congress could have tried to keep the president's institutional capacity to a minimum—for example, by restricting the amount of money appropriated for presidential operations, or by restricting his discretion (much of it grounded in the OPM and the SES) in allocating appointees across the bureaucracy. But it hasn't done these things. In the final analysis, presidents hold most of the cards: they can veto anything Congress enacts, members of their own party support them anyway, and power issues don't mobilize legislators to rise up and defend their institution.

Congressional Response through Inaction? One area where recent Congresses have attempted to limit presidents is by refusing to use their power to confirm presidential nominees to executive and judicial posts, done with the goal of gaining leverage in negotiations with the president. Congressional efforts have met with mixed success, subject to the same limitations that influence their ability to check the president in other areas. According to data from the *Washington Post,* for example, President Obama had filled only 75 percent of the key executive-branch policymaking positions by the eighteen-month mark in his first term.[37] His record with regard to judges was even worse.

Some of the reluctance to confirm Obama nominees was partisan, due to a determined Republican minority in the Senate inclined to oppose administration appointees, particularly if it gave them an election issue to trumpet. Both Republicans and Democrats in the Senate also placed "holds" on nominations in the hope of stopping the president's agenda or securing concessions on matters of individual concern. Holds are requests by senators to keep nominations from coming to the floor with an implied threat to hold up Senate business with dilatory actions such as filibusters. For example, Senator Richard Shelby (R-AL) held up dozens of Obama's nominees because he was concerned about a tanker contract and funding for a proposed counterterrorism center in his home state.[38] Democratic senator Robert Menendez (D-NJ) placed holds on Obama's nominees to head the White House Office of Science and Technology Policy and the National Oceanic and Atmospheric Administration over a policy disagreement about U.S. foreign policy in Cuba.[39]

Recent presidents have increasingly resorted to recess appointments in order to avoid these sorts of problems. The Constitution allows the president to fill administrative positions during a recess of the Senate, and presidents have simply waited for the Senate to go into recess and then filled key posts unilaterally. President Obama used this authority to make thirty-two recess appointments during his first term in office. President George W. Bush made 171 of them during his two terms.[40]

The continued use of this power ultimately led to a significant constitutional confrontation between the president and Congress. In late 2011 Congress sought to prevent President Obama from filling certain administration posts by using an artifice to avoid going into formal recess. Although all members had gone home, a senator showed up every three days to gavel the Senate into and out of order, thus keeping it "in session." Obama claimed that the Senate was actually in recess, and in early January 2012 he made recess appointments of people vehemently opposed by Republicans to the National Labor Relations Board and the Consumer Financial Protection Bureau. Congressional Republicans were outraged, arguing that Obama had acted beyond his constitutional authority.

Budgets

In the late 1800s and early 1900s, as government became bigger, more bureaucratic, and more complex in the course of responding to the nation's growing social problems, Congress began to have serious difficulties dealing with the national budget.[41] Its own fragmented organization was part of the problem. Congress was divided into policy-based committees, and bureaucratic agencies each submitted their budgetary requests to these committees directly, without coordination. This diffusion of control made it difficult for Congress to establish priorities in its spending, or even to reconcile expenditures with revenues—leading to frequent deficits.

These problems came into sharp relief in the aftermath of World War I, precipitating a fiscal crisis that pushed the nation's debt from $1 billion to $25 billion. Congress responded by enacting the Budget and Accounting Act of 1921, which created the Bureau of the Budget (BOB) within the Treasury Department, authorized it to pull together the budget estimates of every agency into a single federal budget, and made presidents responsible for improving the economy and efficiency of administration. The intention was to compensate for Congress's collective action problems by creating a more coherent, coordinated structure for the budget.[42]

The BOB, however, soon became a foundation for the expansion of presidential power. With authority not only to collect agency budget estimates but also to revise them—and thus to bring them into line with his own priorities and policy goals— the president now had a far stronger institutional capacity for directing national policy. Presidents gradually began to use the budget as a policy tool by adjusting budget estimates to promote their own legislative goals. The budget evolved into a document that described presidential aspirations for what government should do and how it should do it. By the end of the New Deal and World War II, after two decades of Democratic presidents and Democratic congressional majorities, a general expectation had emerged that presidents would take the lead on the budget and that Congress would use the president's budget as a starting point for its own deliberations. This deference to the president was bolstered by the fact that the BOB had far-reaching expertise and detailed inside knowledge about what the bureaucracy was (and was not) doing and how much its programs actually cost, which gave the president's team an information advantage over Congress.

Presidential control of the budgetary process—and through it, public policy— had received a significant boost in 1939. Franklin Roosevelt, worried that the inability to manage the fast-growing New Deal bureaucracy might threaten his reelection, as well as the New Deal itself, asked Congress to help him create an institutional apparatus for housing agencies that would be truly presidential and not really part of the larger bureaucracy, where the agencies would be vulnerable to more congressional intervention. Large Democratic majorities agreed to empower their president by authorizing the creation of the Executive Office of the President and placing the BOB under its rubric. The Budget Bureau was now, in every sense, an arm of the presidency.

When Republicans finally regained control of both branches in 1953, they could have acted to roll back the BOB and the power of the presidency. But they didn't, because the power was now theirs. Over time, the BOB grew in size, and its career staff gained greater and greater influence in matters ranging from the details of administration and spending to the broader contours of public policy. The bureau also became an important source of institutional memory for the president, as well as for Congress. It provided vital transition advice to new presidents, monitored the management performance of different bureaucratic agencies, and helped presidents use the budget to accomplish their larger political goals. The BOB viewed its mission as serving the presidency as an institution, rather than any one individual president.

But presidents, characteristically, wanted more. In particular, they wanted the BOB to be responsive to their individual needs and political agendas; they also wanted it to be a more powerful control mechanism overall. The vehicle for change was Richard Nixon's Reorganization Plan no. 2, which, under "reorganization authority" granted to the president by Congress, would become law unless disapproved by either the House or the Senate. Nixon proposed that political appointees replace career civil servants as heads of the bureau's operating divisions; that its functions in program management, coordination, and information be expanded; and that all functions vested by law in the BOB—now to be renamed the Office of Management and Budget—be transferred to the president. The point of this plan, clearly, was to give the OMB greater control of the bureaucracy, to make OMB more responsive to the president, and to expand presidential power.[43] Legislators saw Nixon's proposal for what it was. But the institutional issues, even with Congress in the hands of the Democratic Party, were not sufficient to galvanize opposition, especially because Congress actually had to act in order to block the plan. The Senate never even voted on a resolution of disapproval. The House did, but the Nixon forces put together a coalition of Republicans and southern Democrats that prevailed.[44]

If Congress had a budgetary moment in the sun, it came in the midst of the Watergate crisis—an episode of presidential excess that, needless to say, raised the specter of the imperial presidency and gave presidential power a very bad name, at least for a while. In the budgetary realm, the symbol of Nixon's imperial misbehavior was that he had impounded (refused to spend) certain funds appropriated by Congress, arguing that legislators' spending was profligate and a cause of inflation.[45] Congress responded by passing the Congressional Budget and Impoundment Control Act of 1974, which made it more difficult for presidents to impound money, and, more generally, created a new and more centralized congressional budgetary process for countering presidential power.

In passing the 1974 budget act, Congress was not only recognizing that excessive presidential power was a problem, it was also recognizing its own collective action problems, and the new law was fully intended as a remedy. The act included three main provisions. First, it created new budget committees in each chamber that would set an overall annual budget ceiling, as well as ceilings for each policy area, in order to limit what the appropriations committees could spend. Second, it established a series of deadlines and procedures to usher each year's budget legislation through Congress. Finally, it created the Congressional Budget Office to provide Congress with its own source of fiscal expertise as a counterbalance to the power of the OMB.[46]

This reform has been a colossal failure. Members of Congress still wanted to bring home the bacon to their constituents, and the act provided no mechanism to force them or their committees to stick to the targets set by the budget committees. The budget committees themselves, moreover, could and did change (meaning increase) the targets throughout the legislative year. Nor did Congress abide by the procedures and deadlines designed to promote speedy, coherent decision making.

These problems became sorely apparent in the 1980s. President Reagan pushed for lower taxes and higher defense spending; Congress sought to protect entitlements and social programs. Deficits ballooned. With its reforms not working, Congress added still other mechanisms to get control over the budget.[47] One device involved automatic spending cuts: if deficits hit certain prespecified levels, cuts would go into effect on all programs not specifically exempted from the process. Another device involved hard spending caps, augmented by "pay as you go" requirements stipulating that all new spending proposals must identify a new source of revenue (or cuts in other programs) to compensate for the new spending. Ultimately, both devices failed. Members of Congress used accounting tricks, program exemptions, and clever scoring to maneuver around their own rules. Having designed these reforms because they knew they couldn't trust themselves, they proved they were right. Even during periods of fiscal surplus, such as the late 1990s, the budget caps were exceeded by close to $60 billion per year.

Congress's most overt capitulation came in 1996. Controlled by Republicans for the first time in forty years, and thus by conservatives who had long railed against the Democrats' "irresponsibility" in overspending, it passed the Line Item Veto Act. This was, to be sure, at least partly an act of ideology. But it was also rooted in a simple recognition that Congress's collective action problems made it inherently incapable of controlling the budget. What the act did was to give presidents—in this case, a Democratic president, Bill Clinton—the power to single out specific spending or revenue items within a larger bill and to veto only those items. These vetoes would then prevail unless Congress passed another bill to reinstate the spending. In June 1998, however, the Supreme Court struck down the act as unconstitutional.

In recent years, economic adversity and partisan polarization have combined to bring the budget—and the deficit—to center stage, accompanied by political fireworks that illuminate once again just how debilitating Congress's collective action problems can be. Republicans opposed to taxes and spending took control of the House in 2011 and refused to increase the nation's debt ceiling—which Congress needed to do by August 3, 2011, if the nation were to avoid defaulting on its obligations—unless Democrats agreed to drastic cuts in spending without any increases in taxes. The Democrats, in control of the Senate and led by President Obama, insisted on softer spending cuts and higher taxes on the wealthy. As August 3 loomed, every attempt at compromise failed, bringing the national economy, and indeed the world economy, to the brink of crisis.

Finally, at the last hour, Congress kicked the can down the road by passing the Budget Control Act of 2011, which itself did little to reduce the long-term deficit. Instead, it temporarily raised the debt ceiling and set up a bipartisan "super committee" of representatives and senators to come up with a legislative solution by the end of the year. If the committee failed, massive spending cuts onerous to Republicans and Democrats alike would go into effect automatically on January 2, 2013. On about that same date, the Bush tax cuts were already set to expire, raising everyone's taxes if nothing were done. The result: a "fiscal cliff" so dangerous to the national economy that, optimists hoped, members of all political stripes would have incentives to agree on a solution—and act.

But this was expecting too much. The super committee failed miserably, and most of 2012 was then wasted as legislators looked toward the November elections and refused to bite the bullet on the deficit issue. After the election, a victorious Obama demanded a comprehensive legislative fix, but Congress remained dead-locked. Just hours before the nation was set to fall off the fiscal cliff, Congress managed to produce legislation that increased taxes on the wealthy, but it avoided dealing with spending issues and delayed the "automatic" spending cuts, thus, once again, kicking the can down the road to the edge of yet another fiscal cliff. The nation's recent budgetary wars are an especially vivid demonstration of Congress's incapacities as an institution and of the reasons why, over more than a century of modern history, budgetary power has been shifted incrementally but relentlessly toward the president. In his second term, President Obama's leader-ship was frustrated by House and Senate Republicans. But the larger lesson is that, just as presidents before him did, President Obama was the one forcing the budgetary action, setting the budgetary agenda, controlling most of the pivotal expertise, and operating the levers of power. He couldn't have everything he wanted. But his budgetary levers did allow him to exercise leadership in a system that is heavily stacked against it.

Regulation

Appointments and budgets have long been fundamental levers of presidential power. Another is regulatory review, which in recent decades has become a main-stay of the modern presidency and a telling barometer of how much the institu-tional balance of power has shifted in the president's favor.[48]

The first traces of regulatory review emerged in the early 1970s, when President Nixon, acting unilaterally, instituted the Quality of Life Review program under the OMB. His real target was the Environmental Protection Agency (EPA), newly created in 1970, which had been devising antipollution rules that stood to cost industry billions of dollars a year at a time when the national economy—Nixon's main concern—was headed for trouble. The administration required the EPA to submit its rules to the OMB for prepublication review so that other agencies could comment, economic costs could be analyzed, and pressure could be applied to bring the EPA's rules more in line with the president's program. The EPA wasn't Nixon's only target. In the early 1970s, six other regulatory agencies had been cre-ated, and twenty-nine new regulatory statutes had been enacted.[49] Nixon wanted to gain control of all this because it affected his entire economic agenda.

Environmental, labor, and other liberal interest groups were not pleased with the president's moves, nor was Congress. The new agencies had been created to engage in aggressive regulation, and Nixon, without any clear statutory authority, was trying to replace their priorities with his. Still, it wasn't clear at this point whether regulatory review was simply a Nixon power grab, which would soon be over, or something bigger.

It turned out to be something bigger, although its ultimate proportions could hardly have been anticipated at the outset. When Gerald Ford became president in 1974, he too faced serious economic problems and expanded Nixon's early system of regulatory review as a means of attacking them. Jimmy Carter's election in 1976 gave Congress and Democratic constituencies hope that the EPA and other regulatory agencies would be unleashed, but this was not to be. Carter took even more aggressive action on regulatory review than his Republican predecessors had. In his Executive Order 12044, agencies were told to prepare—for all rules having major economic consequences—regulatory analyses that rigorously evaluated their cost-effectiveness. Carter also created a new organizational arrangement, led by the OMB and other presidential agencies, for carrying out the reviews. With these developments, it became clear that regulatory review was not merely a Nixon or a Republican device to frustrate liberal ideals. It was a *presidential* device—one that would serve presidential interests regardless of party.

When Ronald Reagan took office in 1981, he pushed regulatory review to unprecedented heights. He began quickly, appointing a Task Force on Regulatory Relief that promptly suspended some 200 pending regulations and prepared a hit list of existing regulations for review. He followed up with the groundbreaking Executive Order 12291, which brought regulatory agencies under presidential control as never before.[50] The executive order required agencies to submit all proposed rules to the OMB's Office of Information and Regulatory Affairs (OIRA) for prepublication review, accompanied by rigorous cost-benefit analyses and evaluations of alternative approaches. In a departure from past practice, the OMB now allowed agencies to issue rules only when the benefits exceeded the costs; it also required them to choose among possible rules so as to maximize the net benefits to society as a whole. Moreover, the OMB now asserted the right to delay proposed rules indefinitely while review was pending.[51]

Environmental groups, especially, were furious and launched all-out attempts to persuade Congress to break the president's hold on regulatory review. Pressure to do so had been building for more than ten years, as frustration with past presidents escalated demands for a congressional counterattack. But now, with the Reagan agenda so aggressive, these groups were pulling out the stops.

How did Congress respond? It did not take on the president directly—say, through major legislation declaring that Executive Order 12291 was null and void. Instead, its approach was piecemeal, fragmented, and altogether predictable from a constituency-dominated institution: special interest legislation—such as the 1982 amendments to the Endangered Species Act, the 1984 amendments to the Hazardous and Solid Waste Act, and the 1986 Superfund amendments—that, through countless new restrictions, narrowed the EPA's discretion, hobbled it with cumbersome administrative burdens, and, on very specific items, directed the president and the OMB not to interfere. For the most part, legislators and groups attacked the president by burying the EPA in more bureaucracy and trying to insulate its decisions from presidential interference.[52]

At the same time, another drama was unfolding over the OIRA. This agency was created during the Carter years for other purposes, and only later did Reagan, acting unilaterally, vest it with authority for regulatory review.[53] The problem was that it had to weather the congressional budgetary process every year to get funding and, to make matters worse, its authorization was set to expire in 1983. In principle, then, the OIRA was very vulnerable to congressional attack.

What happened? The OIRA's opponents were able to block its reauthorization for a few years. But Congress continued to fund the OIRA, which continued to carry out its regulatory review activities. Eventually, a compromise was struck. The OIRA was reauthorized, but Reagan agreed that its head would henceforth be subject to Senate confirmation and its processes made more public.[54] These were not serious concessions, considering that Congress could have put the OIRA out of business. The president held the upper hand. And regulatory review churned on, shaping and delaying regulations and infuriating its opponents.

The Bush years witnessed more of the same. Although the more moderate George H. W. Bush was not as zealous about regulatory review as Reagan, he left the basic structure of Executive Order 12291 in place, and the OIRA continued to do its presidential job. Interest groups, meanwhile, continued to nibble away at the OIRA through piecemeal congressional action. Environmental groups scored an indirect success (with Bush's assistance) when Congress passed and Bush signed the Clean Air Act of 1990, which buried the EPA in more bureaucratic constraints and timetables intended to guide its future behavior.[55] Environmentalists also took direct shots at the OIRA, whose authorization was set to run out again. In 1990 legislative opponents agreed to reauthorize the OIRA if Bush would accept certain restrictions on its activities, but wrangling within Congress caused the effort to collapse. By default, the OIRA wasn't reauthorized.[56] Nonetheless, Bush (and later Bill Clinton) succeeded in getting it funded.

Legislative opponents did score a big (but temporary) victory: the Senate never confirmed a nominee to head the OIRA during George H. W. Bush's administration. But the president simply acted unilaterally, shifting regulatory review from the OIRA to the Competitiveness Council, a purely presidential unit headed by Vice President Dan Quayle.[57] The Competitiveness Council, which earlier had been assigned issues ranging from legal reform to job training, dove quickly into regulatory review, with staff assistance from the OIRA. For the remainder of the Bush presidency, opponents trained their ire on the council, going after it in the usual ways.[58] But they were never able to deny it funding, they had no influence over its personnel or appointments, and they never passed legislation to challenge its activities.[59]

Bill Clinton retook the White House for the Democrats in 1993 and immediately got rid of the Competitiveness Council, evoking a joyous response from many legislators and interest groups. But Clinton's action was largely symbolic, because he surely did not get rid of regulatory review. Indeed, he fully embraced it as essential to his leadership. During his first year in office, Clinton issued Executive Order 12866, which, in the course of repealing Reagan's Executive Order 12291, imposed a review structure that was very similar to Reagan's, even retaining cost-benefit requirements. The difference was that the new structure was better suited to Clinton's agenda, which was more proregulation than Reagan's. Accordingly, regulatory review was returned to the OIRA; environmental, labor, and other such groups were granted greater access to the process; and only the most costly rules were targeted for review.[60]

What made the Clinton years unusual is that, after Congress shifted from Democratic to Republican control in 1995, the president came under pressure from Congress to use his powers of regulatory review more forcefully than he wanted to. With Clinton insisting on using regulatory review as he saw fit, Republicans pushed ahead with bills to impose heavy new restrictions on the regulatory agencies.[61] These failed to become law because Congress, as usual, was unable to take bold action, and the president ultimately prevailed—another reflection of the presidential advantage.

Republicans in Congress did succeed in enacting the Congressional Review Act of 1996, which, by streamlining its own procedures, made it easier for Congress to overturn proposed regulations and thus to participate in regulatory review. Yet the review act hasn't worked. The streamlined procedures have been used successfully just once, in 2001, to overturn controversial ergonomics regulations promulgated by the Clinton Labor Department. Even in this case, legislative action was successful only because the newly elected president, George W. Bush, supported the repeal. Congress's problems are always the same: the obstacles to collective action are huge, and the president can veto.

By the election of 2000, the device of presidential review of regulation was firmly in place. Both President Bush and President Obama made minor changes to the process, attempting to lengthen its reach. President Bush strengthened his regulatory powers in 2007 by issuing Executive Order 13422.[62] The new order required that every regulatory agency have a regulatory policy review office headed by a presidential appointee. These offices were directed to supervise the development of new rules, as well as to impose new criteria (such as proof of market failure) that increased the threshold for issuing any new rules. Their most significant role, however, was to oversee how agencies use "guidance" documents—that is, informal statements that instruct businesses as to how agency rules will be interpreted and enforced. White House officials and business groups were concerned that agency careerists were using these guidance documents to work around the presidential restrictions they didn't like, and the new regulatory offices were designed to extend presidential control to these informal practices. Congressional critics hit the roof, and in the summer of 2007 the Democratic House voted to prohibit the OIRA from using any federal money to enforce Bush's executive order. No action was forthcoming from the Senate, however, and the order remained in effect, as did the new regulatory offices and the extension of presidential power.[63]

By the time Obama became president in January 2009, Democrats had no illusions that he would relegate this tool of presidential power to the dustbin. He would keep it and, like his predecessors, Republican and Democrat alike, use it aggressively toward his own policy ends. One of his first steps was to issue an executive order reversing Bush's Executive Order 13422 and its intrusion into agency decision making. But his biggest early move was his high-profile choice to head the OIRA: Cass Sunstein, a legal scholar from the University of Chicago (and more recently, Harvard), who was widely admired for his creativity, his brilliance, and his innovative approaches to public policy rooted in the new behavioral economics. Sunstein went on to become "one of the Obama administration's most provocative figures," as the *New York Times* put it. He enraged liberals with his aggressive use of cost-benefit analysis and his alleged weakening of agency rules. He enraged conservatives by endorsing significant rules on, for example, Obama's new health care law that the conservatives claimed would hamper business and economic growth and by seeking to rationalize the nation's entire regulatory system through a "retrospective review" of all past agency rules. Sunstein wasn't acting alone. He was Obama's choice, Obama's agent. And the OIRA, once again, was serving as a major means of leverage in forwarding the president's agenda.[64]

Regulatory review has been an arena of ongoing struggle between the presidency and Congress—a struggle sparked continually by the imperialistic initiatives of presidents and one that presidents have dominated time and again. Regulatory review is now a routine part of government. Presidents began it, built it up, and have used it regularly to pursue their agendas in the face of interest group and legislative hostility. Congress did not rise up and pass major legislation to stop them, although it had the power to do so. It did not refuse to fund the review agencies, although it had the power to do that, too. Instead, it succeeded only in imposing minor restrictions, while presidents expanded their power relentlessly.

CONCLUSION

The story of the president, Congress, and the bureaucracy is not entirely a story of presidential triumph. Separation of powers creates a system of government that is distinctly unfriendly to presidents. It fragments authority, multiplies sources of opposition, creates a bureaucracy resistant to central control, and produces a political setting hostile to any kind of forceful, coherent leadership in a host of other ways.

But presidents are strongly motivated to lead and are reluctant to accept a system that is stacked against them. Their strategy has been to modify the architecture of the system to make it more presidential, and it is through this effort that the story becomes brighter for them. For whatever separation of powers does to frustrate their leadership, it also gives them critical advantages over Congress in the politics of institution building and bureaucratic control.

Presidents derive important advantages from their capacity for unilateral action. These involve powers that Congress cannot readily stop them from exercising and that allow them to shift the status quo on their own, winning by default when Congress fails to react effectively. They also benefit because they are unitary decision makers motivated to protect and promote their own institution, whereas Congress is vulnerable to serious collective action problems and unable to take coherent, forceful action on its own behalf. The combination produces a built-in asymmetry in the president's favor when the two branches struggle for power.

The three case studies in this chapter illustrate how these presidential advantages play out in American politics. In matters of personnel, the budget, and regulatory review, presidents have clearly been aggressive in building their own institutions for controlling the vast government bureaucracy. In contrast, Congress has typically been disorganized, ineffective, and even passive in response. Presidents did not always get their way in these cases, and Congress did not always fail to act. But changes in the institutional balance of power came about because presidents were pushing and shoving to occupy new institutional terrain, and Congress did not have what it took to stop them.

The future promises more of the same. The dynamic is built in, an unavoidable outgrowth of the institutional system and the way it structures incentives. All future presidents, whether Republican or Democrat, liberal or conservative, will find that their presidencies are defined and their legacies ultimately determined by how successfully they deal with the formidable economic and social challenges that face our nation, and they will have no choice but to push for as much discretion and institutional capacity as they can get. They will need these things if they are to exercise forceful, coherent leadership, and they need them if they are to overcome the impediments that the separation of powers system places in their way. There will be no backing down, no going back. They need power. And they will pursue it.

NOTES

1. Barack Obama, "Statement by the President on H.R. 4310," Office of the White House Press Secretary, January 3, 2013, http://www.whitehouse.gov/the-press-office/2013/01/03/statement-president-hr-4310.

2. Laura Meckler, "Obama Shifts View of Executive Power," *Wall Street Journal*, March 30, 2012, http://online.wsj.com/article/SB10001424052702303812904577292273665694712.html.

3. Devin Dwyer, "President Obama Issues 'Signing Statement' Indicating He Won't Abide by Provision in the Budget Bill," ABC News, April 15, 2011, http://abcnews.go.com/blogs/politics/2011/04/president-obama-issues-signing-statement-indicating- he-wont-abide-by-provision-in-budget-bill/.

4. Terry M. Moe, "The Politicized Presidency," in *The New Direction in American Politics*, ed. John E. Chubb and Paul E. Peterson (Washington, DC: Brookings Institution, 1985); and John P. Burke, *The Institutional Presidency* (Baltimore: Johns Hopkins University Press, 1992).

5. For a more fully developed discussion of these issues, see Terry M. Moe, "The Politics of Bureaucratic Structure," in *Can the Government Govern?*, ed. John E. Chubb and Paul E. Peterson (Washington, DC: Brookings Institution, 1989); and David E. Lewis, *Presidents and the Politics of Agency Design* (Stanford, CA: Stanford University Press, 2003).

6. For a detailed review, see Terry M. Moe and William G. Howell, "A Theory of Unilateral Action," *Presidential Studies Quarterly* 29 (December 1999): 850–871; and William G. Howell, *Power without Persuasion: The Politics of Direct Presidential Action* (Princeton, NJ: Princeton University Press, 2003).

7. Richard Pious, *The American Presidency* (New York: Basic Books, 1979), 38.

8. Harold H. Bruff, "Presidential Power and Administrative Rulemaking," *Yale Law Journal* 88 (1979): 451–508; Harold H. Bruff, "Presidential Management of

Agency Rulemaking," *George Washington Law Review* 57 (1989): 533–595; Lloyd N. Cutler, "The Case for Presidential Intervention in Regulatory Rulemaking by the Executive Branch," *Tulane Law Review* 56 (April 1982): 830–848; and Peter Strauss, "The Place of Agencies in Government: Separation of Powers and the Fourth Branch," *Columbia Law Review* 84 (April 1984): 573–669.

9. Pious, *American Presidency.*

10. See, for example, Andrew Rudalevige, *The New Imperial Presidency* (Ann Arbor: University of Michigan Press, 2006); and Gordon Silverstein, *Imbalance of Powers: Constitutional Interpretation and the Making of American Foreign Policy* (New York: Oxford University Press, 1997).

11. On how the courts have approached presidential power, and particularly presidential powers of unilateral action, see, for example, Joel L. Fleishman and Arthur H. Aufses, "Law and Orders: The Problem of Presidential Legislation," *Law and Contemporary Problems* 40 (Summer 1976): 1–45; Thomas Cronin and Michael Genovese, *The Paradoxes of the American Presidency* (New York: Oxford University Press, 1998); and Silverstein, *Imbalance of Powers.*

12. Louis Fisher, *The Politics of Shared Power* (Washington, DC: CQ Press, 1993); and Strauss, "The Place of Agencies in Government."

13. Craig Volden, "A Formal Model of the Politics of Delegation in a Separation of Powers System," *American Journal of Political Science* 46 (January 2002): 111–133.

14. Eugene Fama and Michael Jensen, "Separation of Ownership and Control," *Journal of Law and Economics* 26 (June 1983): 301–325.

15. Pious, *American Presidency;* Bruff, "Presidential Power and Administrative Rulemaking"; Bruff, "Presidential Management of Agency Rulemaking"; Strauss, "The Place of Agencies in Government"; and Cutler, "The Case for Presidential Intervention in Regulatory Rulemaking by the Executive Branch."

16. Mancur Olson, *The Logic of Collective Action,* 2nd ed. (Cambridge, MA: Harvard University Press, 1971).

17. Gary Cox and Mathew McCubbins, *Legislative Leviathan* (Berkeley: University of California Press, 1993). See also Gary Cox and Mathew McCubbins, *Setting the Agenda* (New York: Cambridge University Press, 2005).

18. On the relative roles of constituency and party, see, for example, David W. Rohde, *Parties and Leaders in the Postreform House* (Chicago: University of Chicago Press, 1991); J. H. Aldrich, "Political Parties in and out of Legislatures," in *The Oxford Handbook of Political Institutions,* ed. R. A. W. Rhodes, Sarah A. Binder, and Bert A. Rockman (New York: Oxford University Press, 2006); and Keith Krehbiel, "Where's the Party?" *British Journal of Political Science* 23 (April 1993): 235–266.

19. Hugh Heclo, "The OMB and the Presidency: The Problem of Neutral Competence," *Public Interest* 38 (Winter 1975): 80–98.

20. Richard D. McKelvey, "Intransitivities in Multidimensional Voting: Models and Some Implications for Agenda Control," *Journal of Economic Theory* 12 (June 1976): 472–482.

21. See John Kingdon, *Agendas, Alternatives, and Public Policies* (Boston: Little, Brown, 1984); Paul Light, *The President's Agenda* (Baltimore: Johns Hopkins University Press, 1982).

22. Thomas H. Hammond, Jeffrey S. Hill, and Gary J. Miller, "Presidents, Congress, and the 'Congressional Control of Administration' Hypothesis" (paper presented

at the annual meeting of the American Political Science Association, Washington, D.C., 1986).

23. George C. Edwards III, *Presidential Influence in Congress* (San Francisco: W. H. Freeman, 1980); and Stephen J. Wayne, *The Legislative Presidency* (New York: Harper and Row, 1978).

24. Sean M. Theriault, "Patronage, the Pendleton Act, and the Power of the People," *Journal of Politics* 65 (February 2003): 50–68; Ronald N. Johnson and Gary D. Libecap, *The Federal Civil Service System and the Problem of Bureaucracy* (Chicago: University of Chicago Press, 1994); and Martin West, "Bargaining with Authority: The Political Origins of Public-Sector Collective Bargaining," manuscript, Brown University, 2006.

25. It increased from 603,587 employees to 3,332,356 between 1933 and 1944. Susan B. Carter, Scott Sigmund Gartner, Michael R. Haines, Alan L. Olmstead, Richard Sutch, and Gavin Wright, eds., *Historical Statistics of the United States: Earliest Times to Present, Millennial Edition*, vol. 5 (New York: Cambridge University Press, 2006), 5–127.

26. By the end of the Truman administration, close to 90 percent of all federal civilian employees were governed by the civil service system. David E. Lewis, *The Politics of Presidential Appointments* (Princeton, NJ: Princeton University Press, 2008), 20.

27. Lewis, *Politics of Presidential Appointments*, 70.

28. Ibid., chaps. 4–5.

29. National Commission on the Public Service, *Leadership for America: Rebuilding the Public Service* (New York: Free Press, 1989); and National Commission on the Public Service, *Urgent Business for America: Revitalizing the Federal Government for the 21st Century* (Washington, DC: Brookings Institution Press, 2003).

30. Richard Polenberg, *Reorganizing Roosevelt's Government 1936–1939* (Cambridge, MA: Harvard University Press, 1966); and Peri E. Arnold, *Making the Managerial Presidency* (Princeton, NJ: Princeton University Press, 1986).

31. Felix A. Nigro, "The Politics of Civil Service Reform," *Southern Review of Public Administration* 20 (September 1979): 196–239.

32. Patricia W. Ingraham, "The Civil Service Reform Act of 1978: The Design and Legislative History," in *Legislating Bureaucratic Change: The Civil Service Reform Act of 1978*, ed. Patricia W. Ingraham and Carolyn Ban (Albany: State University of New York Press, 1984); and Harlan Lebo, "The Administration's All-Out Effort on Civil Service Reform," *National Journal*, May 27, 1978, 837–838.

33. Nigro, "The Politics of Civil Service Reform." The original design allowed for a little over 9,000 SES employees, but the number has varied somewhat over time and has generally been in the neighborhood of 8,000. Also, of the 800 political appointees, 350 were in newly created positions and 450 were moved into the SES from the old system.

34. Arnold, *Making the Managerial Presidency*; and Ann Cooper, "Carter Plan to Streamline Civil Service Moves Slowly toward Senate, House Votes," *Congressional Quarterly Weekly Report*, July 15, 1978, 1777–1784.

35. For a good review, see Bradley H. Patterson Jr. and James P. Pfiffner, "The Office of Presidential Personnel," in *The White House World*, ed. Martha Joynt Kumar and Terry Sullivan (College Station: Texas A&M University Press, 2003); and Thomas J. Weko, *The Politicizing Presidency: The White House Personnel Office, 1948–1994* (Lawrence: University Press of Kansas, 1995).

36. Lewis, *Politics of Presidential Appointments,* 27–30.

37. David E. Lewis, "Presidential Appointments in the Obama Administration: An Early Evaluation," in *The Obama Presidency: Change and Continuity,* ed. Andrew Dowdle, Dirk van Raemdonck, and Robert Maranto (New York: Routledge, 2011).

38. Shailagh Murray, "Sen. Shelby Releases Hold on Nominees," *Washington Post,* February 9, 2010, http://www.washingtonpost.com/wp-dyn/content/article/2010/02/08/AR2010020804199.html.

39. Juliet Eilperin, "Nominations on Hold for Two Top Science Posts," *Washington Post,* March 3, 2009, http://www.washingtonpost.com/wp-dyn/content/article/2009/03/02/AR2009030202425.html.

40. "The Noel Canning Decision and Recess Appointments Made from 1981–2013," Memorandum, Congressional Research Service, February 4, 2013, Washington, D.C.

41. Presidents had much earlier earned a reputation as guardians of the Treasury against extensive spending by Congress. As early as 1909, Congress asked the secretary of the Treasury to estimate revenue for the coming year, determine whether there was likely to be a deficit, and make recommendations for cuts or other sources of revenue to cover the deficits. Fisher, *Politics of Shared Power,* 220–221.

42. Ibid., 222–223.

43. Hugh Heclo, "The OMB and the Presidency"; Moe, "The Politicized Presidency"; and Arnold, *Making the Managerial Presidency.*

44. "Congress Accepts Four Executive Reorganization Plans," *Congressional Quarterly Almanac, 1970* (Washington, DC: Congressional Quarterly, 1971), 462–467.

45. Whether Nixon was correct is contestable. See Fisher, *Politics of Shared Power,* 226–227.

46. Ibid., 129–130.

47. Ibid., 141–152.

48. The basic history of regulatory review is well known. The following account relies largely on William F. West and Joseph Cooper, "The Rise of Administrative Clearance," in *The Presidency and Public Policy Making,* ed. George C. Edwards III, Steven A. Shull, and Norman C. Thomas (Pittsburgh, PA: University of Pittsburgh Press, 1985); Elizabeth Sanders, "The Presidency and the Bureaucratic State," in *The Presidency and the Political System,* 3rd ed., ed. Michael Nelson (Washington, DC: CQ Press, 1990), 409–442; Thomas O. McGarity, *Reinventing Rationality: The Role of Regulatory Analysis in the Federal Bureaucracy* (Cambridge: Cambridge University Press, 1991); and Robert V. Percival, "Checks without Balance: Executive Office Oversight of the Environmental Protection Agency," *Law and Contemporary Problems* 54 (Autumn 1991): 127–204.

49. Percival, "Checks without Balance," 139.

50. To this already stringent set of procedures, Reagan later added Executive Order 12498, which required agencies to submit annually a program outlining all significant regulatory actions planned for the coming year so that the OMB would have plenty of time to review them without the pressure of statutory deadlines.

51. Peter M. Benda and Charles H. Levine, "Reagan and the Bureaucracy: The Bequest, the Promise, and the Legacy," in *The Reagan Legacy: Promise and Performance,* ed. Charles O. Jones (Chatham, NJ: Chatham House, 1988).

52. Percival, "Checks without Balance," 175.

53. Benda and Levine, "Reagan and the Bureaucracy."

54. Ann Cooper, "OMB Regulatory Review," *Congressional Quarterly Almanac, 1986* (Washington, DC: Congressional Quarterly, 1987), 325.

55. Jonathan Rauch, "The Regulatory President," *National Journal,* November 30, 1991, 2902–2906.

56. Kitty Dumas, "Administration Deal Pushes Paperwork Reduction Act," *Congressional Quarterly Weekly Report,* October 27, 1990, 3602; and Janet Hook, "101st Congress Leaves behind Plenty of Laws, Criticism," *Congressional Quarterly Weekly Report,* November 3, 1990, 3699.

57. Rauch, "The Regulatory President."

58. Kirk Victor, "Quayle's Quiet Coup," *National Journal,* July 6, 1991, 1676–1680.

59. On the failed attempt to deny the council funding, see Susan Kellam, "Social Security Riders Thrown from Senate Treasury Bill," *Congressional Quarterly Weekly Report,* September 12, 1992, 2712–2713; and Susan Kellam, "Conferees Cut $200 Million, Pave Way to Approval," *Congressional Quarterly Weekly Report,* September 26, 1992, 2936.

60. Executive Order 12866, 58 *Federal Register* 51735 (1993). This order also repealed Reagan's Executive Order 12498.

61. See, for example, John H. Cushman Jr., "Republicans Plan Sweeping Barriers to New U.S. Rules," *New York Times,* December 25, 1994, A1.

62. Robert Pear, "Bush Directive Increases Sway on Regulation," *New York Times,* January 30, 2007.

63. Jim Abrams, "House Balks at Bush Order for New Powers," *Washington Post,* July 3, 2007.

64. Sunstein returned to Harvard in August 2012. For perspectives on his years at the OIRA, see, for example, John M. Broder, "Powerful Shaper of U.S. Rules Quits, with Critics in Wake," *New York Times,* August 3, 2012 (from which the quote in the text is taken); James L. Gattuso and Diane Katz, "Red Tape Rising: Obama-Era Regulation at the Three-Year Mark," Heritage Foundation, March 13, 2012, http://www.heritage.org/research/reports/2012/03/red-tape-rising-obama-era-regulation-at-the-three-year-mark.

15

THE PRESIDENT
AND CONGRESS

Matthew J. Dickinson

The renowned presidential scholar Richard Neustadt described the American system of constitutional government as one of "separated institutions sharing powers." One implication of this description is that it is difficult for the president to accomplish much without the support or the acquiescence of Congress. Political parties developed as a bridge between the constitutionally separated branches early in American history. A president could count on the support of most of his fellow partisans in Congress, as well as that of some legislators who belonged to the opposition party but who shared the president's views. In recent decades, however, the two parties have become ideologically polarized, which, as Matthew J. Dickinson shows, makes it hard for the president to find allies across the partisan divide. Barack Obama promised in his first campaign for the presidency in 2008 to transcend partisan divisions, but, like all recent presidents, found from experience that he had little choice but to govern through his congressional party. Donald Trump's failed effort to repeal and replace Obama's Affordable Care Act illustrates the problems that a president who tries to rely on his own party can have, even when that party controls both houses of Congress.

Shortly after 1 a.m. on July 28, 2017, in one of the more dramatic moments in recent Senate history, Arizona Republican Senator John McCain approached the center of the Senate floor, extended his right arm with thumb pointing down, and softly declared "No." With that vote, McCain apparently ended the Republicans' seven-year effort to repeal the Patient Protection and Affordable Care Act, better known as Obamacare, at least for the immediate future.[1] Senators Susan Collins (R-ME) and Lisa Murkowski (R-AK) joined McCain, all forty-six Senate Democrats, and two independents in rejecting the Republican effort to undo President Barack Obama's signature domestic legislative achievement.

The defeat was a bitter blow to President Donald Trump and the Republican leadership in Congress, both of whom had made replacing Obamacare a litmus test of their ability to fulfill their campaign promises and implement the Republican agenda. Not surprisingly, Trump's immediate response was to take to Twitter, his preferred communication medium, to castigate McCain and the other Senators who voted no, tweeting: "3 Republicans and 48 Democrats let the American people down. As I said from the beginning, let ObamaCare implode, then deal. Watch!"[2] Trump also reportedly called Senate Majority Leader Mitch McConnell to berate him for "bungling" the health care vote.[3] In the days after the Senate vote Trump continued to issue public condemnations, using a press conference, rally speeches, and Twitter to place much of the blame for the failure to repeal Obamacare squarely on McConnell and Republicans in Congress.

Republican legislators fired back, albeit in a less direct manner. According to media reports, McConnell privately questioned Trump's understanding of the legislative process and speculated that Trump's presidency might be fatally compromised by the series of controversies it had endured during his first six months in office.[4] McConnell's criticisms resonated with many congressional Republicans who faulted Trump for what they saw as his inconsistent and ill-informed public statements regarding their replacement health care bill, the American Health Care Act (AHCA). Some party members argued that Trump's "strong-arm" tactics made it more difficult for them to craft a winning coalition for repeal and replace.[5] And more than one pundit interpreted McCain's crucial "no" vote as payback for disparaging comments made by then-candidate Trump about McCain's war record.[6]

The finger-pointing and recriminations among Republicans were understandable. After watching Democrats repeatedly rebuff repeal attempts during the previous seven years, the 2016 elections had finally given Republicans control of the Presidency along with majorities in the Senate and House. As a result, Party leaders were cautiously optimistic that they were on the cusp of finally achieving their long-promised goal of a Republican health care bill. For his part, Trump had made replacing Obamacare a centerpiece of his successful 2016 presidential campaign. In an era of nationalized elections, in which Congress members' electoral prospects are increasingly yoked to the president's, Trump and Republican legislators had a common interest in working together to repeal and replace Obamacare.

Why, then, did they fail in their attempt to achieve their goal, and what, if anything, does this failure indicate regarding their legislative prospects more generally? In the immediate aftermath of the vote against AHCA, many media stories blamed Trump for his failure to use his "bully pulpit" to close the deal.[7] Others speculated about McCain's motives, and whether his "no" vote was rooted in personal animosity toward Trump, disgust with the lack of Senate deliberation, his maverick tendencies, or perhaps was even related to his brain cancer.

However, there were more fundamental forces conspiring to undercut the Republican repeal-and-replace effort. To begin, the Senate repeal bill McCain voted against served only as a legislative placeholder designed to allow congressional debate regarding repealing and replacing Obamacare to continue. Had he supported it, the odds still remained against Republicans achieving that objective. Despite party majorities in both chambers of Congress that were united on the need to repeal Obamacare, Republicans never achieved any consensus on what should replace it. Conservative Republicans sought a total repeal of Obamacare and a return to a primarily market-driven system of health care. Moderates wanted to retain some features of Obamacare, including Medicaid expansion and the requirement that insurers provide at least a minimum amount of health coverage.[8] No matter how McCain voted on the bill in question, it's not clear how McConnell and House Speaker Paul Ryan were going to bridge these fundamental ideological divides in order to pass repeal and replace.

Similarly, although critics may be right that Trump misplayed his political cards in dealing with Congress, the reality is that the 2016 elections dealt him a far weaker hand than is often acknowledged. Not only did he win just 46.1 percent of the popular vote, with almost 3 million fewer votes than his opponent Hillary Clinton, he also ran behind the vast majority of Republican congressional candidates in their districts.[9] Moreover, he entered office lacking the traditional presidential "honeymoon" with the public, as evidenced by his historically low approval ratings. If Richard Neustadt was correct in characterizing the presidency as a "weak" office, Trump's was particularly so right from the start.[10]

Although it is common for the media to describe the Trump presidency as not "normal," there's no evidence to date that his atypical behavior, such as his prolific use of social media and general flouting of traditional norms of behavior, has done anything to change the dynamics governing presidential–congressional relations.[11] Instead, when it comes to dealing with Congress, Trump's experiences to date seem quite typical; he spent his first seven months grappling with the same forces that bedeviled his predecessors Bill Clinton, George W. Bush, and Obama. Those forces are the culmination of trends dating back at least three decades, to a series of electoral and constituency-related developments whose cumulative effect has been to winnow out ideologically moderate members from both the House and the Senate. That process has produced two ideologically cohesive and opposed congressional parties: liberal Democrats and conservative Republicans. It has also reduced presidents' incentive to reach across the political aisle for support in enacting their legislative agenda.

Under the constitutional system of "separated institutions sharing powers," to use Neustadt's apt description, the president and members of Congress are compelled to share the responsibilities of governing. But the Constitution also ensures that they will do so from fundamentally separate vantage points because they have different constituencies, terms of office, and responsibilities. In theory, during an era of nationalized elections, a shared party affiliation between the president and members of Congress can help to bridge these otherwise distinct institutional perspectives. With control of enough seats in Congress, presidents should find it easier to legislate primarily through their party majority, exercising a form of "responsible party government" in which the voters hold both president and party responsible for policy outcomes.

But there are significant risks to legislating exclusively through one's own party. To begin, it means a president's legislative fortunes depend heavily on avoiding the party defections that divided Republicans during the Senate health care debate. Moreover, as Trump has discovered—and as presidents Clinton, Bush, and Obama did before him—the same conditions that promote party government also encourage the minority party to unite in opposition to majority rule. This reduces the incentive for bipartisan action, and instead motivates presidents and their majority party to pursue policies that many moderate voters perceive as too extreme. If enough voters act on this perception, the resulting electoral backlash can cost the president and his (someday her) party their congressional majority.

The Democrats' successful effort to pass Obamacare in 2010 perfectly illustrates this dynamic. Despite promising to govern in a bipartisan fashion, Obama was forced to push health care legislation through both congressional chambers by relying only on his party's support; not a single Republican voted in favor of Obamacare. In midterm elections that fall, Democratic legislators who voted for Obamacare along with the $800 billion stimulus bill were punished by voters, and Democrats lost sixty-three seats and their House majority.[12] Nor does this wave election appear to be an isolated event. The president's party also lost significant seats in the 1994, 2006, and 2014 midterms—losses attributed in part to the public's opposition to key portions of the president's legislative agenda.

The recent midterm losses provide a cautionary lesson for Trump and Republicans in Congress as they pursue their legislative agenda while looking ahead to the 2018 congressional elections. In an era of polarized parties and nationalized elections, presidents may see no alternative to legislating exclusively through their party caucus. But doing so can exact a heavy electoral price.

The remainder of this chapter develops these initial observations in more detail. I begin by sketching the limits on Trump's first-term efforts to enact a Republican agenda, focusing in particular on the failed attempt to repeal and replace Obamacare. I then explain those limits in the context of the fundamental forces shaping presidential–congressional relations, starting with the constitutional design of the government and the creation and evolution of political parties. Although parties helped to ameliorate some of the centrifugal political tendencies inherent in the American political system during the nation's first century, they never completely bridged the Constitution-based separation of the president and Congress. This was partly because congressional and presidential elections did not always move to the same rhythms. Nor did party labels always accurately reflect the ideological leanings of representatives and senators, which meant that a Democratic or Republican president could not always rely on full party support in Congress.

The recent strengthening of ideological differences between the two parties reflects in part a process of partisan sorting, particularly in the South, where during the past two decades most conservative Democrats in Congress either became or, more commonly, were replaced by Republicans. As a consequence, party labels today more accurately reflect members' ideology. Recent elections have done nothing to halt this trend toward party purification; indeed, both parties' gains in the last several House and Senate elections typically came at the expense of their more moderate members. The result is that by some measures, Congress today is more polarized than it has been since at least the post–Civil War Reconstruction era. This creates incentives for the president's party to come together in support of their president's legislative agenda. However, it also motivates the opposing party in Congress to unify in opposition. That dynamic, in the context of the nationalization of congressional elections in which a party's electoral fortunes are increasingly linked to the president's, may be contributing to a level of electoral volatility in congressional elections not seen since the late nineteenth century.

Under these political conditions, presidents' legislative prospects can be impaled on the horns of a dilemma. Presidents may take office promising to work with Congress on a bipartisan basis, but they will find it difficult to act on these inclinations due to a dwindling number of moderates. By abandoning their professed desire to legislate in bipartisan fashion in favor of a more partisan strategy aimed at mobilizing their party majority in Congress, however, they risk inciting a backlash among more moderate voters. What, then, is a president's best legislative strategy under current conditions? I conclude the chapter by exploring the possibilities for presidential influence in Congress during the contemporary era of polarized parties and nationalized elections.

THE 2016 ELECTIONS: THE DAWN OF A NEW ERA—OR A CONTINUATION OF THE OLD ONE?

In the aftermath of the 2016 elections, in which they recaptured the presidency while holding on to their majorities in both the House and the Senate, Republicans had reason for optimism. Assuming the party held together, they had the votes to enact the most sweeping partisan agenda in decades, including repealing Obamacare, slashing corporate tax rates as part of tax reform, passing a comprehensive immigration bill, investing in infrastructure spending, and undoing Obama-era environmental regulations. In the House, after losing only six seats, Republicans retained a healthy forty-seven-seat cushion, 241–194. In the Senate Republicans lost two seats, but still possessed a 52–48 seat majority.[13] "Welcome to the dawn of a new unified Republican government," House Speaker Ryan declared after the election, adding that, "If we are going to put our country back on the right track, we have got to be bold, and we have to go big."[14]

Closer inspection revealed dark clouds in that new dawn. Ideological fissures within the Republican congressional caucus threatened to fracture their working majority and their ability to pass their agenda. In the House, Republicans were divided between the Freedom Caucus, which included approximately thirty-six of the most conservative House Republicans, and the Tuesday Group, consisting of forty to fifty of the most moderate Republicans. The two caucuses had very different views on how to achieve the party's goals, including replacing Obamacare.[15] In the Senate, the Republicans' slim four-seat margin was not nearly enough to overcome a Democratic filibuster under current Senate rules—a fact that would force Republicans to attempt to pass their major legislative initiatives, starting with repeal and replace, using reconciliation procedures as part of the budget process. The use of reconciliation prevented a Democratic filibuster, but it also meant only budget-related items could be included in the Republican health care bill. This limited McConnell's ability to build a working coalition through legislative side payments. And, because only one bill could be taken up under reconciliation at a time, it prevented simultaneous action on the rest of Trump's legislative agenda. That put added pressure on the Senate Republican leadership to bypass the usual committee deliberations in order to pass health care legislation quickly.

For his part, Trump took office in January 2017 with little leverage to bridge his party's internal differences in pursuit of his legislative agenda. He won the election despite the opposition of most Republican Party leaders to his candidacy, and on the promise that he would "drain the swamp" in Washington, D.C.—a pledge that reportedly did not endear him to his fellow Republicans in Congress.[16] Moreover, despite generating huge crowds at his campaign rallies, he lost the popular vote, which weakened his claim to a popular mandate. And a significant portion of those who voted for him did so primarily as a vote against Clinton, rather than in support of his agenda.[17] This partly reflected the fact that although Trump campaigned on lofty promises to restore America's economic prosperity, to bring back jobs, and to "make America great again," those promises were not backed by a detailed policy agenda or clearly articulated political principles, making it hard to know what he stood for. Moreover, his divisive campaign rhetoric and penchant for blunt, personal attacks on his political rivals had not endeared him to voters, as indicated by his historically low favorability ratings at the start of his presidency.

Table 15.1 ■ Pre-Inauguration Favorability Ratings of Presidents-Elect Since 1993			
	Favorable %	Unfavorable %	No opinion %
Donald Trump (Jan. 4–8, 2017)	40	55	5
Barack Obama (Jan. 9–11, 2009)	78	18	5
George W. Bush (Jan. 15–16, 2001)	62	36	2
Bill Clinton (Jan. 18–19, 1993)	66	26	8

Source: Data from Gallup, http://news.gallup.com/poll/201977/trump-pre-inauguration-favorables-remain-historically-low.aspx.

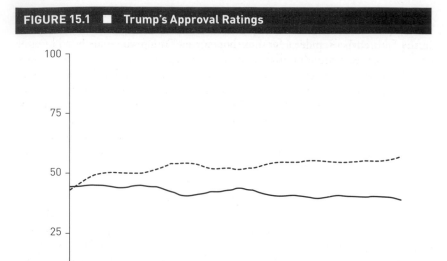

FIGURE 15.1 ■ Trump's Approval Ratings

Source: Data from HuffPost Pollster, http://elections.huffingtonpost.com/pollster/trump-job-approval.

Similarly, Trump's public approval rating, as measured by the *Huffington Post* aggregate poll, stood at an anemic 44 percent when he took office, about 2 percent below his popular vote percentage, and also historically low for an incoming president. It remained there, more or less, through the first weeks of his presidency; once Congress began debating health care in March, Trump's approval began slipping. By the time McCain cast his dramatic vote against the Republican repeal plan in late July, Trump's approval was only 39 percent—another historic low this early in a presidency.

Trump's tepid popular support underscored his lack of pull with the Republican congressional caucus. He ran ahead of the Republican House candidate in only 34 of 212 contested House districts won by Republicans—hardly a sign of potent presidential coattails.[18] Although Trump received more votes in the states of six of sixteen fellow Republicans who won Senate races in 2016, only one of those senators faced a competitive race, and none would face voters for another six years—two years after Trump's term was scheduled to end.

Nor was it clear, after running a campaign characterized by polarizing rhetoric and personal attacks on opponents and erstwhile allies alike, that Trump could adopt a more unifying persona once in office.[19] The early signs on this score were not reassuring; as president, Trump continued his pattern of using Twitter both to ridicule his political opponents and to express his opinions with apparently little if any vetting from advisors. Indeed, for those hoping that Trump would surround himself with experienced aides who might restrain his tendencies to tweet first and think later, his initial White House staff selections sent a mixed signal at best. Trump appointed Steve Bannon, the outspoken editor of the right-wing *Breitbart News,* as his chief political strategist. Stephen Miller, who shared Bannon's economic nationalist views and his penchant for controversy, was hired as a policy adviser.

Reince Priebus, the former chair of the Republican National Committee, was selected as chief of staff, ostensibly to strengthen Trump's ties to the Republican Party and to serve as a counterpoint to Bannon's antiestablishment views. However, Priebus was not close to Trump, and it soon became obvious that he lacked the clout to counter Bannon's influence. Nor could he stem the White House infighting that developed early in Trump's presidency (to say nothing of reining in the president's use of Twitter). The primary combatants were Bannon and White House Senior Adviser Jared Kushner, who as Trump's son-in-law was well situated to influence the president's decisions, and who early on staked out his own portfolio handling Mideast issues and reorganizing government.[20] Within a matter of weeks, Trump's White House had splintered into three factions, headed by individuals—Bannon, Priebus, and Kushner—whose only shared characteristic was a complete lack of governing experience.

Trump's inexperience, combined with a factionalized White House staff whose senior members were also learning on the job, led to a series of early policy missteps, beginning with a proposed ban on immigration from six predominantly Muslim nations that was immediately blocked in court. Trump also found his presidency embroiled in controversy due to allegations that members of his campaign staff may have colluded in Russian attempts to influence the 2016 presidential election. These allegations claimed an early victim when, less than a month into Trump's presidency, his national security advisor, Mike Flynn, was forced to resign when it was revealed he had hidden the extent of his contact with Russian officials during the post-election presidential transition. Less than two months later Trump fired FBI director James Comey, who had been spearheading the Russian collusion investigation. Trump's critics charged him with obstructing justice—a potentially impeachable offense. In response, Deputy Attorney General Rod J. Rosenstein appointed former FBI director Robert Mueller as special prosecutor, charged with investigating Trump's Russian ties and all related issues, including his motivations for firing Comey. Mueller's appointment practically guaranteed that the Russian problem would continue to fester under the glare of the media spotlight, further weakening Trump's ability to exert political influence on behalf of his legislative agenda.

Under these less than auspicious political conditions, Trump decided, evidently on the advice of Speaker Ryan, to make repealing Obamacare his first legislative priority—a decision he would later regret.[21] The effort began in earnest in the House in early March, when Republicans introduced the American Health Care Act (AHCA). Ryan touted the legislation as the first step in a three-stage plan to rework the nation's health care system. If passed, AHCA would partially repeal Obamacare by eliminating tax penalties for people who opted to forgo health insurance, roll back state-by-state expansions of Medicaid, and replace government-subsidized insurance policies offered exclusively in the Affordable Care Act's market-places with tax credits. Assuming Republicans were able to pass AHCA, step two would entail using regulatory powers to stabilize insurance markets, and step three would be to pressure Democrats to support additional provisions to complete the remainder of the replacement process.[22]

Ryan scored early victories when two key House committees—Energy and Commerce, and Ways and Means—approved AHCA on straight party-line votes. But in an indication of problems to come, when AHCA went to the Budget Committee, three members of the House Freedom Caucus broke with the leadership to oppose the bill, and it was voted out by a narrow 19–17 margin. The Freedom Caucus members objected to provisions in AHCA extending Obamacare's Medicaid expansion for another four years, its failure to immediately repeal all of Obamacare's tax increases, and the inclusion of refundable tax credits to help people buy insurance, which they saw as another entitlement. For many conservative Republicans, these provisions were evidence that AHCA was merely "Obamacare 2.0."

House Republicans on the other end of the ideological spectrum, including members of the Tuesday Group caucus, opposed AHCA's cuts to the Medicaid expansion under Obamacare, particularly after the Congressional Budget Office (CBO) estimated that if passed, AHCA would cause an additional 24 million individuals to drop health insurance within a decade. Ryan proved unable to bridge the divide between his party's wings. The Tuesday Group persistently opposed proposals that its members perceived to be too conservative, while the Freedom Caucus blocked versions of AHCA that they felt did not go far enough in repealing Obamacare. The acrimony between the two groups became so pronounced that New Jersey Representative Tom MacArthur resigned as the Tuesday Group's co-chair after criticism from fellow members for attempting to broker a health care deal with the Freedom Caucus.[23]

As Ryan and his leadership team struggled to fashion a bill that both party moderates and conservatives could accept, Trump acted mostly as cheerleader-in-chief, rather than a hands-on negotiator. He publicly praised AHCA as a "great bill," while making full use of the perquisites at his command, including hosting private lunches and dinners for lawmakers at the White House, sharing rides on *Air Force One,* and even scheduling a bowling event. However, beyond statements from aides suggesting that Trump's two health care priorities were removing health care taxes and eliminating the mandate, and Trump's own admission that there were some things in AHCA he didn't like, he seemed content to let party leaders fashion the details of the legislation. At the same time, he warned of an "electoral bloodbath" in 2018 if Republicans failed to repeal Obamacare.

After two weeks of intense negotiations following the Budget Committee vote, House Republicans appeared to be at an impasse, with Ryan still ten to fifteen votes short of the majority needed to pass AHCA. Freedom Caucus members were determined to repeal the requirement that health plans provide at least a minimum set of benefits. They argued that the only way to reduce premiums was to give insurers the option of providing low-cost, bare-bones coverage. But moderates, including members of the Tuesday Group, sought to preserve what they saw as one of the most popular parts of Obamacare. Ultimately, in a bid to keep conservatives on board, the House Rules committee inserted a waiver into AHCA allowing the low-cost coverage option. Despite this concession, Republicans remained divided. Frustrated, Trump pushed for a vote of the full House, hoping the prospect of legislative defeat would change the minds of enough of the roughly thirty Republicans who indicated they were leaning toward a "no" vote on AHCA.

On the day of the scheduled vote, Ryan—after consulting Trump—pulled the legislation from the floor, citing a lack of support. News reports described the decision as a stinging defeat for Trump. He responded by initially blaming Democrats, predicting they would come to the bargaining table when Obamacare collapsed, and expressing his readiness to move on to tax reform. But in what would prove to be a recurring pattern throughout the health care debate, Trump subsequently seemed to change positions by shifting the blame for the failure to repeal onto Republicans. He tweeted that his followers should watch a Fox news segment in which the host demanded Ryan's resignation as Speaker.

Even as media reports suggested health care repeal was dead, negotiations between rank-and-file House legislators continued behind the scenes. A month after Trump professed his readiness to move on to tax reform, ongoing negotiations between members of the Freedom Caucus and Tuesday Group produced a plan to allow some states to opt out of selected provisions of the revised health care act. When the leadership agreed to add $8 billion over five years to cover people with serious preexisting conditions, the framework for an agreement was in place. On May 4, 2017, as one of its first legislative acts of the new session, the House voted 217–213 in favor of the revised AHCA bill. Twenty Republicans, more than half of whom were members of the Tuesday Group, joined all House Democrats in voting against the bill.

A pleased Trump summoned members of the victorious coalition for a photo opportunity in the White House Rose Garden, where he praised the legislation as "a great plan," adding, "I actually think it will get even better. . . . This has brought the Republican party together."[24] Despite Trump's optimism, however, the House process revealed ominous warning signs for Republicans as the debate moved to the Senate. Despite a forty-seven-vote buffer, House Republicans had barely managed to pass AHCA, and only did so after revising the bill in a way that made it less likely to get support from the more moderate members of the Republican Senate caucus, in which Republicans could afford to lose only two votes. Moreover, in the unlikely event that Ryan's counterpart McConnell could modify the House bill in a way that attracted enough Senate support to pass, there was no guarantee the amended bill could then win a majority of votes in the more conservative House Republican caucus again.

Operating under the constraints imposed by reconciliation, McConnell and Republican senators took up the House health care bill. In order to expedite the process by minimizing early opposition, McConnell decided to eschew open committee hearings—a decision that some Republicans, including McCain, would later cite as a reason why they could not support the bill. Instead, most of the early negotiations took place behind closed doors among only Republicans. After some false starts, McConnell finally revealed draft legislation to the full Senate on

June 22, posting the text online. Despite his plea for Republicans to refrain from publicly criticizing the draft legislation, it was immediately clear that deep divisions within the party remained.[25] Conservatives, including Rand Paul (R-KY), Mike Lee (R-UT), Ron Johnson (R-WI), and Ted Cruz (R-TX), sought amendments to allow insurance companies to weaken Obamacare's minimum coverage provisions.[26] Moderates like Collins opposed efforts to defund Planned Parenthood. But it was the inclusion of a provision that slowed Medicaid spending from the current baseline that most clearly divided Republicans along ideological lines, with moderates strongly opposed to the benefit reduction.

Even more than during the House negotiations, Trump avoided engaging in bargaining with senators as they debated how to amend the AHCA bill.[27] Instead, he again used social media and other platforms to alternatively promote Republican efforts and to warn about the dire consequences of failure. But his public pronouncements often proved counterproductive, as when he turned on the very House bill that he had enthusiastically celebrated with Ryan and his team only weeks prior, calling it a "mean" piece of legislation. Nor did he provide much guidance to Republicans regarding his preferred outcome. Instead, on even the most basic question, such as whether Congress should repeal Obamacare, repeal and immediately replace it, or wait for it to falter, Trump adopted shifting positions.[28] His overriding objective seemed to be getting a legislative victory. How to do so appeared of less concern.

When it became clear that McConnell could not bridge the divide separating conservatives and moderates, and the Republican effort again seemed poised to fail, the Senate majority leader floated the possibility of substituting a pared-down version of comprehensive repeal legislation, dubbed the "skinny" bill, which did not include the controversial House Medicaid provision. McConnell hoped to attract enough Senate support to send a partial repeal bill to a conference with the House, where Republicans from both chambers could then try to negotiate more comprehensive repeal legislation.

On July 25, in a crucial procedural vote on a motion to proceed to a final vote, two moderate Senate Republicans, Collins and Murkowski, voted "no," signaling their likely opposition to passing a Senate version of AHCA. However, McCain—making a dramatic return to the Senate after revealing less than a week earlier that he had been diagnosed with brain cancer—voted with his Republican colleagues to proceed to a vote. His support allowed Vice President Pence to break the tie, and the motion passed by the slimmest of margins, 51–50.

Pence's vote set the stage for twenty hours of debate, evenly divided between the two parties, and voting on a sequence of amended versions of the House bill. The next day, in what was another ominous sign for Republicans, a vote to pass a comprehensive counterpart to the House AHCA legislation was defeated, with nine Republicans joining all forty-six Democrats and two independents in opposition.[29] That left the skinny bill as the Republicans' last, best option for keeping the repeal process alive.

At 10 p.m. on July 27, the text of the skinny bill, titled the Health Care Freedom Act (HCFA), was finally released.[30] Meanwhile, four senators, including McCain, warned that they would only support the skinny bill if they received assurances that should it pass the Senate, the bill would then go to a joint House–Senate conference for further amending, rather than directly back to the House floor for a vote. Ryan assured them that this would be the case, but evidently McCain remain unconvinced.[31]

An hour after the HCFA text was published, the CBO scoring of the bill, required under reconciliation, was released. It indicated that HCFA would increase premiums over the next decade, leave 16 million more Americans without health insurance (7 million of whom would be previously covered by Medicaid), and would cut $235 billion from Medicaid spending. None of these findings were likely to reassure wavering Republican moderates, despite McConnell's plea that the skinny bill was only meant to move debate along.

As the clock ticked toward the final vote, suspense built on the Senate floor. McCain's earlier vote to proceed had significantly heightened the drama, and the audience, for his vote on the skinny bill. As the roll call votes were announced, he could be seen engaging Pence, who was poised to cast the tie-breaking vote if necessary, in an animated conversation. And then, shortly after 1 a.m., McCain cast his dramatic vote against his party's bill—an action that elicited gasps and applause from some of the gathered senators.

In explaining his decision, McCain reiterated his desire to repeal Obamacare but argued that the skinny bill was an inadequate vehicle for doing so. In a press release issued after the vote, McCain stated, "We must now return to the correct way of legislating and send the bill back to committee, hold hearings, receive input from both sides of the aisle, heed the recommendations of [the] nation's governors, and produce a bill that finally delivers affordable health care for the American people." However, McCain's call for a return to "regular" legislative procedures with bipartisan input seemed unrealistic, given Congress's recent history of relying on unorthodox lawmaking procedures in order to overcome the minority party's use of obstructionist tactics.[32]

Seeking to take advantage of Republicans' divisions, Senate Minority Leader Chuck Schumer offered to work with them to "fix" Obamacare. His words also rang hollow given the recent history of partisan polarization in Congress. Obamacare had originally passed Congress with nary a Republican vote in favor, and not one Democrat had supported any of the Republican repeal-and-replace efforts to date. The fixes suggested by Schumer for Obamacare, such as retaining subsidies to lower premiums for high-cost enrollees, were not likely to attract much Republican support.

The failure to repeal Obamacare serves as a reminder that however atypical Trump's presidency seemed to be, the 2016 elections did little to change the legislative dynamics characterizing presidential–congressional relations dating back at least three decades. During the presidential campaign, Trump presented himself as the master of the art of the deal—the title of his best-selling book. His outsider status, business experience, and lack of party ties, he told his supporters, would allow him to break the partisan polarization and gridlock characterizing recent Congresses. Nearly twelve months into his presidency, however, none of these attributes appeared to have helped Trump change the partisan dynamics that had dominated his predecessors' legislative efforts.

This should surprise no one. The tension between Trump's desire to overcome the polarization dividing the parties in Congress and his need to rely on his partisan majority to enact his legislative agenda is not new.[33] It is a tension that inheres in the presidency as legislative leader and that dates back to the creation of the constitutional system and the formation of political parties. When Thomas Jefferson took office as president in 1800, it marked the first change in party control of that office in history. In Jefferson's inaugural address, he reminded his audience, "We have called by different names brethren of the same principle. We are all Republicans, we are all Federalists." Jefferson's election, however, owed much to voters' rejection of some of his predecessor John Adams's Federalist policies, such as the Alien and Sedition Acts.

But if the tension between presidents' desire to govern in bipartisan fashion while also implementing their own partisan agenda has deep historical roots, it has indisputably become more pronounced in recent decades. This is because of the increasing polarization of parties in Congress and the nationalization of congressional elections—developments that the Framers of the Constitution likely never anticipated but with which modern presidents, including Trump, must grapple on a daily basis.

CONGRESS, THE PRESIDENT, AND POLITICAL PARTIES, 1789–1960

The Constitution sets the basic parameters that govern the president's relationship with Congress. For the two branches to fulfill their constitutional obligations, from legislating to conducting foreign policy to managing the bureaucracy, they must actively collaborate. Consider what is arguably their most significant function: to make laws. Article I, Section 1, specifies that "all legislative Powers herein granted shall be vested in a Congress of the United States" consisting of "a Senate and House of Representatives." Article I, Section 7, establishes much of the president's legislative role: before bills passed by Congress can become law they must be signed by the president or, if vetoed, be passed again by at least two-thirds of the members in each house. Article II, Section 3, adds that the president shall recommend to Congress "such Measures as he shall judge necessary and expedient." Modern presidents have interpreted this phrase as an invitation to submit a legislative program, and legislators have come to expect them to do so. To be sure, proposing legislation is no guarantee that it will be enacted, but doing so provides the president with significant power to set the congressional agenda.[34]

So it goes across the range of the national government's functions. In foreign affairs, Congress declares war, but the president is commander in chief of the armed forces. Presidents appoint ambassadors and negotiate treaties, but only with the Senate's advice and consent. Congress establishes the executive departments and a system of federal trial and appeals courts, but presidents appoint their members, including Supreme Court justices—again with Senate approval. Moreover, Congress establishes and funds all government departments and agencies, and determines who controls appointments to them.

Clearly, the Constitution requires Congress and the president to work together if the shared powers of the national government are to be exercised. The Constitution also ensures that the two branches will do so from decidedly different perspectives because the president, the House, and the Senate represent distinct constituencies and serve different terms of office.

To become president, one must win a majority of Electoral College votes, and these are apportioned according to the number of each state's representatives and senators in Congress. Because of the evolution of a winner-take-all voting system, in which the candidate with the most popular votes in a state receives all of its electoral votes, presidential candidates typically hew to the ideological center of the political spectrum.[35] For would-be presidents there is no electoral payoff from attracting a significant minority of a state's popular vote.[36]

Representatives are selected through a single-member, simple-plurality voting system from electoral districts where constituencies are much smaller and often more homogeneous than the nation as a whole.[37] Depending on a district's makeup, a candidate for the House might succeed by staking out a relatively extreme ideological position. Moreover, because the entire House is up for election every two years, it tends to be more responsive than the president to prevailing political passions.[38]

Senators act on yet a third set of political imperatives. Although they also are chosen by a simple plurality of the popular vote, their states vary widely in size and diversity of population.[39] Generally speaking, senators represent constituencies that are more populous and heterogeneous than House districts, which reduces the likelihood that senators will be beholden to ideologically extreme viewpoints.[40] In addition, because senators serve for six years, with only one-third of the chamber up for election at a time, the Senate as a whole is unlikely to be as responsive to the political forces that influence presidential or House elections.

In sum, presidents, senators, and representatives come to their shared constitutional tasks with different political needs and goals. This was the Framers' original intent: as Madison explained in *The Federalist* No. 51, with power apportioned among the branches in this way, it will be difficult for any branch to abuse its authority.[41] But the Framers also hoped to establish an effective government, and in this respect the original constitutional scheme had several defects.

First, the presidential selection system did not provide the presidency with a strong enough electoral base to resist congressional encroachment. By 1800 presidential nominations were determined by congressional caucuses, each controlled by a single political faction. Moreover, as James Sterling Young documents, the Framers' emphasis on limited government, together with the tendency for each branch to jealously protect its institutional prerogatives, prevented the president and Congress from addressing many national problems during the nation's early years. Citizens, in turn, did not develop a strong attachment to a national government that seemed largely ineffectual.[42]

To address these problems in the decade after the Constitution's ratification, the nation's leading politicians gravitated toward a single solution: political parties. The Constitution makes no mention of parties, but their precursors were already evident during George Washington's administration, when debates broke out among his advisers on issues such as the constitutionality of the Neutrality Proclamation and the creation of a central bank. These disputes highlighted the growing ideological divide between those, led by Secretary of the Treasury Alexander Hamilton, who favored a strong presidency and a more powerful national government and those, led by Secretary of State Thomas Jefferson and Rep. James Madison, who sought to limit national authority, particularly presidential authority.

By the Third Congress (1793–1795), voting within both chambers was occurring along clearly discernible party lines, as the two major political factions mobilized support among legislators on important issues. Their efforts spilled into the electoral arena as well. When Washington published his farewell address in 1796, he warned of "the baneful effects of the spirit of party generally."[43] Washington's warning notwithstanding, in 1796 the presidential election to determine his successor showed early evidence of party cleavages among the political elite, and by 1800 the race between Jefferson and Adams for president had become overtly partisan.

Despite the Framers' deep antipathy toward parties, they developed because they performed a number of useful functions. First, by providing the presidency with a popular base of support, parties rescued the office from its dependence on Congress. The process by which the presidency gained an independent electoral base involved several steps. To begin with, the Electoral College was transformed from an independent body that both nominated and elected the president to an instrument of the parties. By 1800 competing slates of presidential electors in each state were pledging before the election to vote as a bloc on behalf of a particular candidate.[44] This change provided the means for parties to aggregate electoral support across state lines behind a single candidate, increasing the possibility that their candidate would win a majority in the Electoral College.

The use of the party ballot fostered the election of a national figure as president; without it, electoral votes would usually have been scattered among a host of local favorites. But to provide the president with a truly independent electoral base, an additional link to the voters was required. This connection was established by the development of mass-based political parties that nominated presidential candidates and mobilized the electorate to support them. The advent of the national convention, first used by a major party in 1832, moved the presidential nominating process out of the hands of the congressional caucus and into the hands of local and state political leaders.

Meanwhile, the growth of mass-based campaigns organized by parties helped create within the citizenry an attachment to the national government. By the 1820s, spurred by the sharper competition for the presidency, popular participation in elections began to rise.[45] In the 1824 presidential election, less than 30 percent of the eligible electorate voted. In 1840, sixteen years and four elections later, turnout jumped to almost 80 percent. The presidency and the national government had become visible and durable parts of the political landscape.

Parties served an additional function: they provided a means to bridge the constitutional gap between president and Congress. If voters' choices in presidential and congressional elections were driven by party allegiances, a single party would likely control both branches after each election. And if candidates elected on the same party ticket shared a similar ideological outlook, presidents could capitalize on these shared preferences to convince Congress to pass their legislative program. Voters could then reasonably hold the party accountable for the policies the government produced. In this way political parties might compensate in part for the centrifugal tendencies inherent in the Constitution.[46]

In truth, throughout the nineteenth century, the promise of "responsible party" government proved greater than the reality. For one thing, parties were loosely knit federations of factions led by state and local chieftains, not unified national bodies organized around a coherent party program. Second, presidents possessed few tools for enforcing party discipline in Congress. They had to share their most potent weapon, political patronage, with members of the legislative branch. And with the rise of the nonpartisan civil service and the decline of patronage-based parties beginning in the late nineteenth century, this tool became less effective as a source of presidential leadership. Third, unified party government could not be taken for granted: even when political parties reached their apex of influence during the sixty-eight years from 1832 to 1900, divided government existed in some form for thirty-two of those years—nearly half the time. Nor did unified party control always translate into congressional support for a president's policies. As noted earlier, presidents, senators, and representatives from the same party respond to different political incentives because of their varying constituencies and terms of office. In short, what the Constitution set apart, the parties only partially put together.

Except for dramatic periods of electoral realignment, when presidential and congressional elections were subject to the same intense political pressures, legislators seldom felt a shared sense of political fate with presidents. Moreover, the ties that bound the two branches began to fray during the first half of the twentieth century, as the services that the parties traditionally provided were undermined gradually by progressive reforms. The advent of the direct primary further weakened party leaders' control over the nomination of political candidates.[47] Ballots that were provided to voters by the parties and cast publicly gave way to the Australian, or secret, ballot, making it harder for party officials to enforce discipline in elections. Civil service reforms, beginning in 1883 with the Pendleton Act, reduced the value of patronage as a source of presidential influence in Congress. Collectively, these developments sent the parties into a slow but inexorable decline that extended throughout the twentieth century. The result was a further unraveling of the weak bonds linking the presidency and Congress.

THE ERA OF INCUMBENCY AND INSULATION, 1960–1984

In the 1960s political parties sank to their nadir of influence. Congress entered what Morris Fiorina describes as the "era of incumbency and insulation," in which the outcomes of presidential and congressional elections seemed increasingly independent.[48] As Figure 15.2 depicts, voting studies revealed a growing tendency for voters to split their ticket between a presidential candidate of one party and a

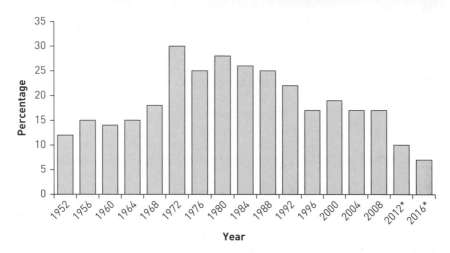

FIGURE 15.2   ■   Split-Ticket Voting in Presidential Election Years (1952–2016)

	'52	'56	'60	'64	'68	'72	'76	'80	'84	'88	'92	'96	'00	'04	'08	'12*	'16*
Dem Pres/ Dem Cong	39	39	45	59	40	31	42	35	36	40	48	44	43	43	46	47	47
Dem Pres/ Rep Cong	2	2	4	9	7	5	9	8	6	7	10	13	10	7	9	4	3
Rep Pres/ Dem Cong	10	13	10	6	11	25	16	20	20	18	12	4	9	10	8	4	4
Rep Pres/ Rep Cong	49	45	41	26	42	40	34	38	39	34	30	38	39	40	38	44	46
N	1009	1151	1187	947	776	1293	1280	762	1144	1030	1124	855	814	674	1294	26565	24558

Source: American National Election Studies data and CNN national exit polls.

* 2012 and 2016 data are from CNN national exit polls.

House candidate of the other. At the same time, as Figure 15.3 shows, the number of self-identified independent voters was on the rise. Although scholars dispute how to interpret this development, it suggests at the very least that the party affiliation of officeholders was becoming less important to voters.[49]

Electoral reforms and other developments after the 1968 elections further diminished the importance of parties in the presidential nominating process. In 1972, for the first time, a majority of delegates to the presidential nominating conventions were selected in primaries. The primaries weakened the party leaders' traditional role as gatekeepers to nomination.[50] Meanwhile, campaign finance reforms designed to minimize the influence of private money in elections helped

FIGURE 15.3 ■ Self-Identified Independent Voters (1952–2016)

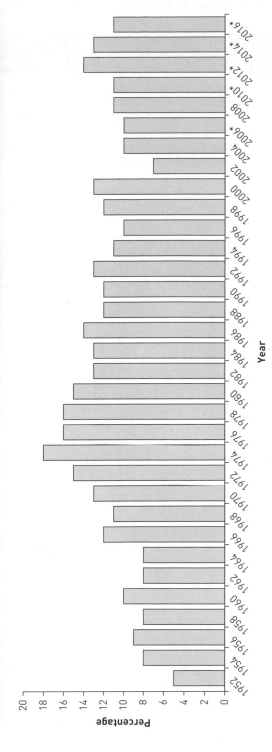

Party Identification 3-Point Scale

	'52	'54	'56	'58	'60	'62	'64	'66	'68	'70	'72	'74	'76	'78	'80	'82	'84	'86	'88	'90	'92	'94	'96	'98	'00	'02	'04	'06*	'08	'10*	'12*	'14*	'16*
Democrat (incl. leaners)	59	58	52	58	53	56	62	55	56	54	51	52	51	54	52	55	48	50	47	52	50	47	52	51	50	49	50	49	51	45	47	45	47
Independent	5	8	9	8	10	8	8	12	11	13	15	18	16	16	15	13	13	14	12	12	13	11	10	12	13	7	10	9	11	11	14	13	11
Republican (incl. leaners)	36	34	39	34	37	36	31	32	33	33	34	31	33	30	33	32	40	36	41	36	37	41	38	37	37	43	41	39	37	44	39	42	42
N	1689	1088	1690	1737	1864	1237	1536	1263	1531	1490	2695	2492	2833	2269	1612	1403	2228	2157	2026	1965	2473	1780	1706	1267	1790	1466	1194	1516	2293	25396	5894	16479	17375

Source: American National Election Studies data and Gallup polls.

*2006, 2010, 2012, 2014, and 2016 data are calculated from the average of Gallup party affiliation polls for that year.

to elevate the importance of single-issue and more ideologically extreme interest groups as sources of candidate funding. The public's growing use of radio and television encouraged congressional candidates to take their campaigns directly to the people, with minimal reliance on party organizations. The result was that the candidate-centered campaign replaced the party-mediated campaign.

No longer needing to cater as strongly to party leaders' interests, members of Congress proved particularly adept at putting together their own coalitions to win reelection. The benefits of incumbency for senators and representatives began to rise. The percentage of the popular vote that incumbents gained between their first and second elections to Congress—the "sophomore surge" attributable to incumbency— rose from about two percentage points in the 1950s to seven percentage points in the 1970s. In the same period, the number of marginal congressional races, those in which the winning candidate won with 55 percent or less of the popular vote, declined, signifying a decrease in party competition.[51] The congressional swing ratio, formally defined as the number of seats a party gains in the House for every 1 percent increase in its national popular vote, also declined—another indication that congressional races were less responsive to shifting national political forces than in the past.

According to Fiorina, at least part of this heightened incumbency effect reflected legislators' effective use of casework to bolster their support among their constituents. Because helping people solve their problems with government is a nonpartisan and nonideological service, it also contributed to the voters' sense that parties mattered less than ever.[52] Finally, incumbents proved more adept than challengers at using the new campaign finance regulations to raise money, even though studies showed that money was more crucial to the challenger's chances of electoral success. This further padded the incumbent advantage.

Whatever the explanation for the rise in incumbent reelection rates, Democrats, as the majority party in Congress at the time these changes were occurring, benefited disproportionately, especially in the House. In the forty years from 1954 to 1994, the Democrats never lost control of the House, even though Republicans won six of ten presidential elections and increased their share of the national popular vote in congressional races.[53] The Republicans had slightly better luck in the Senate, winning control of that chamber from 1981 to 1987, but the outcomes of senatorial elections also diverged from the national trends influencing presidential races.

By the mid-1980s, Congress and the presidency appeared more separated from each other than ever. Presidential coattails, never very long in American elections, were diminishing. The proportion of congressional districts carried by a congressional candidate of one party and the presidential candidate of the other jumped from less than 5 percent in 1900 to more than 40 percent in 1984. As a result, presidential landslides no longer guaranteed large gains for the president's party in Congress. Although Richard Nixon was reelected overwhelmingly in 1972, winning 520 electoral votes and 62 percent of the popular vote, the Republicans gained only twelve House seats and lost two in the Senate; the Democrats retained control of both chambers. Similarly, in 1984 Reagan won a landslide reelection with 525 electoral votes and 59 percent of the popular vote, but his party gained only sixteen House seats—not nearly enough to capture control—and lost two in the Senate. Two years later Reagan's party lost its Senate majority as well.

The result of all these changes was an increased occurrence of divided government. From 1947 to 1991, the parties divided control of Congress and the presidency for twenty-four of forty-four years.[54] Without a sense of shared political fate, members of Congress saw little virtue in working closely with the president to address national issues. Critics decried what they saw as a decline in collective responsibility in Washington and the concomitant failure of the political system to address major national concerns, such as the burgeoning budget deficit and the growth in spending on entitlement programs.[55]

For many scholars, the solution to divided government and legislative gridlock was to return to strong political parties. But not everyone agreed that divided government meant gridlock. A study by David Mayhew showed that from 1946 to 1990 the legislative process was no more prone to deadlock under divided government than under unified control.[56] One reason was that neither the Democrats nor the Republicans were an ideologically homogeneous party in the post–World War II era. Conservative Democrats rarely faced serious opposition in elections in the one-party South, which enabled them to accrue enough seniority in Congress to become a potent conservative force within their otherwise liberal party. The Republicans, too, although a mostly conservative party, included a liberal wing of legislators centered in the Northeast.

Party labels, therefore, did not clearly distinguish legislators' ideological preferences. Democratic conservatives and Republican liberals frequently crossed party lines to vote with the opposition, and presidents could cultivate bipartisan coalitions of support. The especially heterogeneous nature of the Democratic Party allowed both Democratic and Republican presidents to mobilize bipartisan coalitions on many issues, which explains Mayhew's finding that Dwight Eisenhower, Richard Nixon, and Ronald Reagan were able to persuade a Congress controlled by Democrats to pass significant legislation. They did so by mobilizing coalitions consisting of a majority of Republicans and the minority conservative wing of the Democratic Party. Alternatively, Lyndon Johnson relied on Republicans to overcome opposition from conservative Democrats to his civil rights legislation.

Even as the scholarly community debated Mayhew's findings, changes were under way that threatened to undercut the implications of his research.[57] First, the two parties started shedding their more moderate members as early as 1964. As each became more ideologically cohesive during the next three decades, they also grew more distinct from one another. In the 1970s, congressional races became more attuned to national political trends. Although district-level factors were still critical in determining the outcomes of House races, by the 1990s it was no longer true that, in the words of former House Speaker Thomas "Tip" O'Neill Jr., "all politics is local." Congress had entered a new, more partisan era of increasingly nationalized politics—one with significant ramifications for the president's legislative role.

CONGRESS AND THE PRESIDENT IN THE POST–REFORM ERA: TOWARD MORE RESPONSIBLE PARTY GOVERNMENT?

Scholars were slow to recognize the changing nature of congressional elections and political parties. With hindsight it is clear that by the mid-1970s the decline of parties, however steep, had been arrested. Split-ticket voting peaked in 1972, when 30 percent of voters supported a congressional candidate of one party and the presidential candidate of the other. From then on it declined, falling to 7 percent according to 2016 exit polls—the lowest total in more than sixty-five years. Similarly, the percentage of voters labeling themselves "pure" independents—that is, those who do not even lean toward a party—plateaued at 18 percent in 1974. It then declined slowly, bottoming out at 7 percent in 2002, the lowest percentage since 1952, before increasing again, but not to the peak post–World War II levels seen in the 1970s. In 2016, 11 percent of surveyed adults self-identified as independent.[58] Meanwhile, the number of self-identified strong Democrats increased from a low of 15 percent in 1972 to 20 percent in 2012, while those identifying themselves as strong Republicans nearly doubled, from a low of 8 percent in 1978 to 15 percent in 2012.[59]

At the same time, congressional races became even more responsive to national forces. One can construct a rough measure of the relative importance of national and local forces in House elections by regressing the House district vote on the previous election's House district and presidential vote and using the coefficients for the presidential vote as a proxy for national political trends.[60] As Figure 15.4 shows, by 1976 the relative influence of national forces in House races in presidential election years had begun to rebound, after declining through the 1960s. Beginning in 2000, national forces proved more important than local influences on House races. The same trend is visible in House midterm elections (see Figure 15.5), with national influences growing stronger during the period 1986–1994 and finally transcending local influences in the 2006 midterm election. The trend toward nationalized elections shows no evidence of abating; the 2014 and 2016 House elections are the most nationalized elections dating back at least to 1952.

What explains this turnabout in party influence? Scholars cite several causes that collectively transformed and revitalized the parties and made members of Congress more responsive to national forces. First, the Republicans began making inroads among voters in the once solidly Democratic South, which changed both parties' geographical base. A precipitating event was the Democratic Party's embrace of civil rights under John Kennedy and Lyndon Johnson, fueled by the surge of liberal Democrats into Congress in the 1958 and 1964 elections. Some conservative southern voters reacted to the 1964 Civil Rights Act and 1965 Voting Rights Act by switching parties, and young voters just entering the electorate were more likely than in the past to become Republicans. In 1964 only 17 percent of southern voters called themselves Republicans. Twenty years later the number had

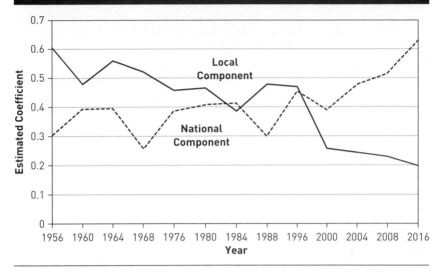

FIGURE 15.4 ■ Decomposition of Presidential-Year House Elections, Contested Seats Only (1956–2016)

Sources: For 2000, 2004, 2008, and 2016, author's calculations using data from swingstateproject .com, polidata.us, and the DailyKos elections site. For previous years, data provided by Arjun Wilkins, Stanford University.

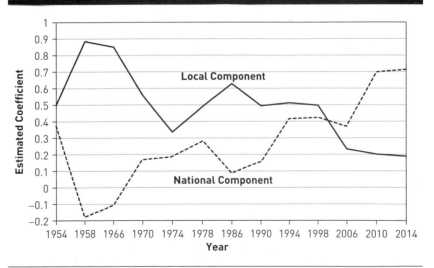

FIGURE 15.5 ■ Decomposition of Midterm House Elections, Contested Seats Only (1954–2014)

Source: For 1998, 2006, 2010, and 2014, author's calculations using data from swingstateproject .com, polidata.org, yahoo.com, and DailyKos elections site.

increased to 31 percent, and in 2000 it was 37 percent—the same proportion as outside the South. This trend was encouraged by the Republicans' "southern strategy," which was designed to split the Democratic Party by emphasizing the parties' differences on social issues such as school busing, abortion, school prayer, affirmative action, and crime. At the same time, thanks in large part to the Voting Rights Act, African Americans' electoral participation in the South rose, and they voted overwhelmingly Democratic.

But differences on social issues tell only part of the story. Partisan sorting within the electorate was also helped by the Republican Party's adoption of a more libertarian economic platform against the backdrop of an increasingly affluent society. As Americans became wealthier on average, their support for economic redistribution and government-run social programs declined. Upper-income citizens in particular were more likely to identify with the Republican Party and its advocacy of an "ownership" society.[61] The result was a consistent economic bias in presidential voting, at least through 2012, with higher-income voters more likely to vote Republican.

Population shifts from the East and Midwest to the West and South (that is, from the Rust Belt to the Sun Belt) accentuated these trends.[62] Moderate Republicans in the East found themselves marginalized in a national party whose center was moving to the more conservative southern and Rocky Mountain states. The decennial redistricting process, in which House seats are reapportioned to take account of changes in population, contributed to the partisan restructuring. In particular, the creation of "majority–minority" congressional districts, in which a majority of the eligible voters belong to a racial or an ethnic minority, helped accentuate the party divisions. First established by the Justice Department after Congress amended the Voting Rights Act in 1982, these districts increased minority representation in Congress, nearly all of it Democratic.[63] But they also helped to increase the Republican vote in neighboring districts. The result was further ideological polarization between the two parties: representatives elected in majority–minority districts, particularly African Americans, were typically on the extreme left of the Democratic Party. At the same time, because the surrounding areas were "bleached" of minority voters, adjacent districts became more likely to elect conservative Republicans.

The changing nature of campaign finance also contributed to the parties' transformations. In the early 1970s Congress passed the first of a series of reforms designed to mitigate the influence of big money in politics by providing public funding for presidential races, capping individual contributions to all federal campaigns, and requiring public disclosure of campaign expenses. Decisions by the Supreme Court equating some types of campaign spending with free speech, however, allowed single-issue interest groups, whose views frequently were well outside the ideological center of the electorate, to become an important source of campaign funding.[64] The influx of special interest money and the increased participation of issue activists, particularly in congressional nominating contests, tended to reward more ideologically extreme candidates. Much of this money flowed from groups outside a candidate's state or district. No longer were congressional races local affairs; national political actors now also influenced them.

At the same time, the parties took advantage of campaign regulations that, until Congress passed the 2002 Bipartisan Campaign Reform Act (commonly known as the McCain–Feingold Act), allowed them to raise unlimited amounts of money for "party-building" exercises. These "soft money" contributions became an important source of campaign funds and helped transform political parties. Instead of the loose federations of locally controlled, vote-mobilizing organizations of the past, parties became synonymous with their national committees, which focused on fund-raising and on candidate recruitment and training. These committees became adept at using their resources in ways that maximized their party's seats in Congress, further contributing to the nationalization of congressional elections.

Although the McCain–Feingold Act outlawed soft money contributions to parties in national elections, presidential candidates benefited from spending by independent organizations that could legally accept such unregulated contributions. In 2004 and 2008, 527 and 501(c) groups—named after the relevant election law subsections in the tax code—acted much like "shadow" parties by spending money on "issue advocacy" campaigns closely linked to particular candidates. In 2008 spending by 527 groups, although down from the amount spent in 2004, totaled almost $258 million. By 2012, however, spurred on by controversial court rulings that loosened restrictions on campaigns donations, money began flowing toward independent expenditure-only committees, better known as super PACs.[65] The courts ruled that under the First Amendment free speech rights these groups may raise unlimited sums of money from corporations, unions, associations, and individuals, and they can spend that money to overtly advocate for or against political candidates, as long as spending is not coordinated with those candidates. In response, more than 1,200 super PACs participated in the 2012 election, collectively spending more than $600 million in independent expenditures. During the 2016 elections, the number of active super PACS climbed to 2,394, and they spent more than $1 billion across all congressional and presidential races. As was the case with the 527 groups, most of that money was raised and spent by issue activists with distinctly partisan leanings.

The two major political parties, meanwhile, continued to raise and spend "hard money" (money raised under federal contributions limits and contributed directly to candidates) on behalf of their congressional and presidential candidates. In the 2016 election, the Democratic and Republican Parties in combination funneled more than $3.5 billion to their candidates through their parties' national, congressional, and senatorial campaign committees.[66]

Evidence on voter turnout suggests that the transformation of the parties affected electoral participation in two somewhat contradictory ways. On the negative side, faced with candidates espousing widely divergent political views, voters were left to choose between extremes or not participate at all. For a growing number of voters, the second option seemed for a time to be more palatable. Political scientists began attributing some of the decline in voter turnout in presidential and congressional elections that began after 1964 to public dissatisfaction with the partisan and ideological tone of public debate.[67]

On the positive side, both parties became increasingly effective at spending the money they raised to get out the vote. Although turnout among eligible voters in presidential elections declined steadily to a post-1964 low of 51.7 percent in 1996, it increased in successive elections, peaking at 61.7 percent in 2008, the highest turnout rate in forty years, before declining slightly across the next two presidential elections. In 2016, the turnout among eligible voters stood at 60.2 percent. Turnout also went up in the 2010 midterm elections, reaching 41 percent, the highest since the 1994 midterm elections and the second highest since 1982 before also declining to 36.7 percent in the 2014 midterms.[68]

Even with the increase in turnout, voters still often faced a choice in the general election between two ideologically extreme candidates. This is because the role of money and the influence of partisan issue activists can be stronger in primaries and caucuses, when turnout among moderate voters tends to be lower. The result is that moderate candidates are often weeded out in the nominating phase. The consequence, as Figures 15.6 and 15.7 show, is an increasingly polarized House and Senate; as moderates are replaced by more partisan legislators, the ideological middle in Congress shrinks, leaving no overlap between congressional Republicans and congressional Democrats on which to construct a bipartisan coalition.[69]

The reduction in the two parties' moderate wings creates the conditions for what David Rohde and John Aldrich call "conditional party government." When political parties in a legislative body are evenly matched and internally unified, Rohde and Aldrich argue, rank-and-file legislators may find it in their electoral interest to strengthen their party's leaders and to act in ways that bolster the party's "brand name" nationally. In the House, institutional reforms pushed primarily

FIGURE 15.6 ■ Polarization in the House

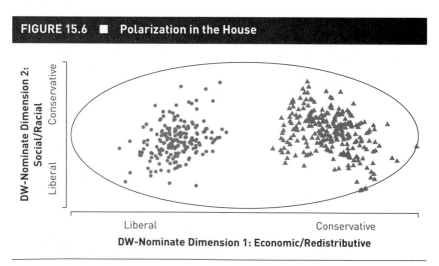

Source: Based on 115th House rankings at https://voteview.com/congress/house.

FIGURE 15.7 ■ **Polarization in the Senate**

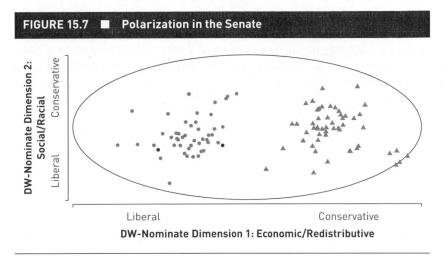

DW-Nominate Dimension 2:
Social/Racial
Conservative — Liberal

Liberal   Conservative
DW-Nominate Dimension 1: Economic/Redistributive

Source: Based on 115th Senate rankings at https://voteview.com/congress/senate.

by liberal Democrats from 1970 to 1977 helped facilitate strong party leadership. These included a "subcommittee bill of rights" that weakened the power of committee chairs, rule changes that enhanced the Speaker's powers, and a revitalization of the majority-party caucus as a decision-making forum.[70] These reforms granted more power to Democratic Speakers Tip O'Neill, Jim Wright, and Tom Foley in the 1970s, 1980s, and early 1990s. Their Republican successors, Newt Gingrich and Dennis Hastert, exercised similarly strong leadership after the 1994 Republican congressional takeover.[71]

The GOP's 1994 takeover provided compelling evidence that congressional races were more susceptible to national forces than they had been in the 1960s. Through a combination of population shifts, effective candidate recruitment, a focused agenda, and extensive fund-raising, the Republicans, led by Gingrich, had positioned themselves to capitalize on voter dissatisfaction with the Bill Clinton administration and the Democratic Congress in the 1994 midterm election. In dramatic fashion, they picked up fifty-three House seats and eight Senate seats to take control of both chambers for the first time in forty years. Subsequent events revealed just how partisan Congress had become. Legislators in the Republican-controlled House could not persuade their Senate counterparts to sign on fully to their conservative Contract with America, and in the winter of 1995–1996 partisan wrangling over the federal budget led to several government shutdowns. Congressional Republicans followed this fight with the bitterly partisan impeachment and trial of President Clinton in 1998–1999.

Although George W. Bush's election in 2000—in conjunction with Republican control of the House and Senate—muted these overt signs of partisan conflict for a time, conflict reemerged after the Democrats retook both houses of Congress in 2006, most notably in Democratic efforts to link further spending on the Iraq War to a fixed timetable for withdrawing U.S. troops. Bush, using his veto, rebuffed those efforts and actually increased troop levels— the so-called surge. In turn, congressional Democrats quashed Bush's efforts to reform Social Security.

Despite Obama's promise to govern in bipartisan fashion, his eight years in office saw no reduction in partisan polarization, particularly after the rise of the Tea Party movement that fueled Republicans' regaining their House majority in 2010. Efforts by the Tea Party–backed Republican legislators to link the passage of appropriation bills and raising the debt limit to a repeal of Obamacare led to yet another government shutdown for two weeks in October 2013. Although Republicans would not achieve their objective, they would vote to repeal parts or all of Obamacare more than fifty times during Obama's last six years in office.

Other data support these highly visible indicators of growing partisan conflict. The difference between Republican and Democratic mean party ideology scores in Congress reached a low from 1968 to 1972 and then climbed steadily thereafter.[72] Party unity scores, a measure of roll call votes in Congress in which a majority of the legislators of one party vote against a majority of the other, reached record levels in the House in 2011 at 75.8 percent, up from about 30 percent in 1970, and remained at near-record high levels through 2016, which saw a 73.4 percent unity score.[73] The number of individual party votes, defined as the percentage of times the average Democrat or Republican votes with his or her party in roll calls that split the two parties, also increased steadily in this period, from below 60 percent for both parties in 1970 to about 90 percent in 2011.[74] Since 1968 the importance of party affiliation in explaining roll call voting by legislators has also grown stronger.[75] Voting analysis indicates that the 114th Congress (2015–2017) was the most polarized since the post–Civil War Reconstruction era, and there is no evidence as yet that the 2016 elections reversed this trend.[76]

Perhaps the most significant development affecting congressional voting has been the collapse of social issues as a cross-cutting influence on party alignments. For most of the twentieth century, many Democrats were more conservative than Republicans on social issues like racial integration or abortion. This meant that on many important votes, presidents could construct bipartisan coalitions of support. However, although social issues still exercise an important influence on legislators' votes, since the 1990s these issues have increasingly operated to reinforce party differences regarding the proper role of government in economic redistribution—the issue that historically most clearly differentiates Republicans and Democrats. As a result, on nearly every issue, voting in Congress today breaks down along liberal Democratic and conservative Republican lines.[77]

Clearly, partisan politics now dominates the way Congress conducts business. This development has had profound consequences for a president's legislative prospects.

POLITICS, PARTISANSHIP, AND PRESIDENTIAL INFLUENCE IN CONGRESS

Under unified government, the development of ideologically distinct, internally cohesive parties and the nationalization of congressional elections can, in theory, strengthen the president's hand on Capitol Hill. Indeed, this is precisely the rationale behind the notion of responsible party government, a theory of governing most famously espoused in a 1950 report by a committee of political scientists who were seeking to reform the American two-party system.[78] The report was a response to the concern that it was often difficult to differentiate Republicans' views in Congress from Democrats'. Critics argued that partisan blurring on issues like civil rights left voters without any real choice in elections. Moreover, the lack of distinct party alternatives weakened political accountability and undercut presidential leadership by making it difficult to hold either party responsible for enacting—or failing to enact—the president's legislative programs. The cure, according to responsible party advocates, was to develop more clearly differentiated, internally cohesive parties characterized by strong party loyalty and distinct party platforms, preferably within the context of unified government.

By the 1990s the two parties had evolved along the lines long sought by responsible party advocates. Democratic and Republican legislators were no longer "tweedle-dee and tweedle-dum," as critics had dubbed them four decades earlier. But the extreme partisan polarization that characterized the new party system revealed a dark side to the practice of responsible party government. Debate in Congress became increasingly contentious, as each party closed rank on behalf of its policy objectives and in opposition to the other party's preferences. The more transparent congressional proceedings—a product of sunshine laws that opened committee hearings to the public; the increased use of recorded teller votes, which made public how legislators voted; the introduction of live televised coverage of Congress by C-SPAN; and the increasingly hothouse media environment in which these policy debates played out, particularly with the rise of Internet-based political blogs—exacerbated partisan differences and made political compromise more difficult to achieve. Congress appeared increasingly unable or unwilling to address significant national problems such as deficit reduction or entitlement reform. Legislative productivity, even under unified government, decreased compared to what it had been in less polarized Congresses.[79] In response, the public grew increasingly dissatisfied with both Congress and the president. When Obama left office in January 2017, his approval stood at 56.1 percent in the *Huffington Post* aggregate poll—his highest approval since midway through his first year in office. In contrast, Congress's approval stood at 15 percent, and it had dropped as low as 10 percent during Obama's presidency—the lowest level ever recorded during the thirty-two years in which pollsters have asked the public to evaluate Congress.[80]

In his victory speech on Election Night in 2016, President-elect Trump sought to reach across party lines to unify the nation, saying, "To all Republicans and

Democrats and independents across this nation, I say it is time for us to come together as one united people. . . . I pledge to every citizen of our land that I will be president for all Americans."[81] It is a familiar refrain. Each of the previous three presidents—Clinton, Bush, and Obama—entered office preaching the virtues of bipartisanship. But, in this increasingly partisan congressional era, they found it difficult to follow their own sermons. Whipsawed between two ideologically extreme parties, all three presidents fell back on their own party's majority in Congress to enact their most important legislation. In Clinton's first year as president, the Democratic-controlled Congress passed his 1993 omnibus deficit reduction bill, which made a significant down payment on reducing the deficit by raising tax rates for high-income earners, increasing the gasoline tax, and raising the tax on corporate incomes above $1 million. The bill barely passed the House by 218–216, without a single Republican vote in favor, and squeaked by in the Senate by a 51–50 vote, again without the support of a single Republican.[82]

The signature domestic initiative of George W. Bush's first year was a ten-year, $1.35 trillion tax cut. In a strategy necessitated by the bicameral nature of the legislative process, Bush initially supported the larger, $1.65 trillion tax reduction bill that was passed by the Republican-controlled House. Then, to win approval from the Senate, where the Republicans held a one-vote majority, he agreed to reduce the size of the tax cut. The final version of the tax bill passed with unanimous Republican support in both chambers, but with only twelve of fifty Senate Democrats and twenty-eight of 181 House Democrats voting in favor—a coalition only slightly more bipartisan than the one that enacted Clinton's deficit reduction legislation.[83]

Similarly, both of Obama's major domestic initiatives in his first year in office were enacted with almost no Republican support. His $800 billion economic stimulus bill passed the House without a single Republican vote in support, and with only three moderate Republicans backing it in the Senate. And, as noted above, not a single Republican voted in favor of his health care legislation.

Nor is it surprising that all three presidents adopted similar strategies for passing their major legislation. Their choice of tactics was dictated by structural factors that influence how presidents bargain with Congress in this highly partisan era. First, under the Constitution, tax bills must originate in the House, a practice that historically has been extended to spending bills as well. Second, the correlation between House members' roll call votes and the level of support for the president by the voters in their districts has been increasing steadily since 1978.[84] Finally, the House has evolved institutionally in ways that empower the majority party. Thus, under unified government the president's initial policy preference is likely to receive a favorable response in the House. For this reason, both Bush and Obama chose to stake out their economic policy position in that chamber first and then moderate that stance as needed for passage through the Senate, as Trump tried to do in his bid to repeal and replace Obamacare.

It is equally noteworthy, however, that all three of Trump's predecessors appeared to suffer a midterm backlash from voters disillusioned with policies produced by relying almost exclusively on majority-party support. Clinton and Democrats lost control of both the House and Senate in 1994, two years into his presidency, and he faced unified Republican majorities in Congress thereafter. Bush's Republicans lost their majority status in both congressional chambers after six years of his presidency—an outcome partly explained by the backlash to his effort to reform Social Security. And Democrat's House majority disappeared in 2010 when voters punished them for supporting Obama's economic stimulus and health care bills. They would lose their Senate majority four years later in an election in which Republicans sought to make the vote a referendum on Obama's presidency.

Given this historical record, what can Trump do to pass his legislative agenda without jeopardizing his party's congressional majority? One answer is to focus on issues that have the potential to bridge the partisan divide by attracting some support from the other party. Thus, despite facing a Democratic-controlled Senate early in his first term after Senator Jim Jeffords defected from the Republican Party, Bush was able to attract enough Democratic support to pass the No Child Left Behind law. Republicans supported No Child Left Behind because it instituted mandatory student testing. Democrats favored it because it increased education spending. This suggests Trump would do well to focus his legislative agenda during the next two years on policies such as immigration and tax reform that have at least some potential to attract bipartisan support.

Indeed, after the failure to repeal and replace Obamacare, there were signs that Trump had grown disillusioned with a strategy—which so far had proved ineffective—of relying solely on Republicans to pass his legislative agenda. In early September 2017, Trump unexpectedly bypassed the Republican leadership to strike a deal with Senate and House minority leaders Chuck Schumer and Nancy Pelosi to increase the government's debt limit and borrowing authority, and to finance the government for another three months, thus avoiding a potential fiscal crisis. The legislation included more than $15 billion in aid to areas devastated by Hurricane Harvey. That deal had initially been rejected by Republican leaders who had hoped to pass relief aid in a separate bill and to use the impending deadline for raising the debt ceiling and extending borrowing authority as leverage to enact spending concessions from Democrats. With Trump's decision, however, Republicans reluctantly signed on to the appropriations bill without extracting any corresponding spending cuts.

A week later media accounts indicated that Trump had reached an agreement in principle with Schumer and Pelosi that would ensure protections for "dreamers"—children of undocumented immigrants for which Obama, through his 2012 Deferred Action for Childhood Arrivals (DACA) program, had granted legal protection.[85] On September 5, 2017, Trump announced he was ending the DACA program, arguing that it had been established by an unconstitutional exercise of unilateral executive authority, and he challenged Congress to come up with a comprehensive immigration policy within a six-month period that would address the status of the dreamers. Before the Republicans in Congress could act, however, Pelosi and Schumer announced that they had reached an immigration deal with Trump that would provide legal status for dreamers in return for funding stronger border security. Significantly, in what appeared to contradict perhaps Trump's most memorable campaign promise, the deal would exclude money to build a wall along the U.S.–Mexico border. In a series of tweets following their announcement, Trump cautioned that the deal was still under negotiation, and that the wall was already under construction using existing funding, but he did express support for providing dreamers with some form of legal status that would allow them to remain in the United States.

It is far too early to know whether these two examples reflect a longer-term shift in bargaining strategy by Trump and, if so, whether it will be successful. In such a highly polarized environment, immigration remains one of the few issues, along perhaps with tax reform, in which it appears possible for the Republican president to work with Democrats in Congress. Even on these issues, however, it is important for Trump to avoid framing the discussion in ways that activate deep-seated party differences. This is often easier said than done, particularly when the opposing party is determined to gain a debating advantage through framing tactics. When Obama pressed Congress to pass a bank bailout bill during his first year in office, conservative Republicans labeled the Obama administration's plan for the federal government to buy bank assets "socialism." The Republican strategy made sense in light of public opinion surveys indicating that, although 54 percent of Americans supported the government's "temporarily taking over major U.S. banks" in order to stabilize them, only 37 percent supported "temporarily nationalizing" banks for the same purpose.[86] When the debate was framed in terms of "nationalizing" banks—which many people view as a code word for socialism—public support for Obama's policy dropped.

In addition to using his agenda-setting power wisely, Trump has a second powerful tool with which to influence the legislative process: the presidential veto. Although Bush did not veto a single bill during his first term, he issued twelve vetoes during his second term, all but one of them when Congress was controlled by the Democratic Party. Similarly, ten of Obama's twelve vetoes occurred after Republicans took control of both chambers of Congress in the 2014 midterm elections. Of course, the veto is a negative weapon, better at preventing action than at ensuring a positive outcome and thus not always an appropriate bargaining tool. However, the threat of a veto can move congressional deliberations closer to a president's preferred outcome. To date, Trump has issued no vetoes, but that will surely change if Republicans lose their congressional majority.

The limited number of issues that have bipartisan appeal, and the difficulty in framing those issues to attract both Republican and Democratic support, is a reminder that a president's influence in Congress is predicated primarily on institutional and political forces that are not easily amenable to presidential influence.[87] However, given the large, enthusiastic crowds Trump attracted to his campaign rallies, and his effort to position himself as an outsider beholden to neither major party, he might be tempted to respond to legislative opposition by "going public" to promote his agenda.[88] Indeed, during his first year in office Trump held a number of well-attended campaign-style rallies designed to mobilize his base and pressure legislators to support his program.

However, it will be surprising if Trump's rallies boost his popularity. Nor are they likely to yield concessions by congressional Democrats—or even by Republicans threatening to break with the president. Much research by political scientists finds only limited success for presidents who try to augment their legislative influence by mobilizing public support.[89] For that strategy to be effective, four conditions must be met. First, the president must already be in good standing with the public. Second, the public must pay attention to and understand the arguments the president is making. Third, the president's general popularity must be fungible—that is, it must translate into support for the president's stance on specific issues. Finally, opposition members of Congress must not be equally able or willing to mobilize countervailing support among their own constituencies.[90] In this regard, it is telling that political scientists who try to demonstrate the effectiveness of going public usually cite the same example: Ronald Reagan's first-term success in getting Congress to pass his tax and spending bills.[91] Even in that case, there is reason to question whether Reagan's rhetorical appeals carried the day.[92] Whether or not they did, it is unlikely that Trump can replicate Reagan's tactics. Almost twelve months into his presidency, his approval ratings are the lowest ever recorded this early in a president's first term. Moreover, history suggests that in the absence of a mobilizing event, his approval ratings are not likely to significantly improve during the remainder of his term.

Even if Trump regains some popularity, it is not clear how fungible it will be in terms of influencing lawmakers. Already there is a deep partisan divide in how Americans evaluate his job performance. Previous presidents saw strong partisan divides, but not to the extent Trump is currently experiencing. As Figure 15.8 shows, the partisan division in Trump's support after his three months in office is greater even than that experienced by presidents George W. Bush and Obama, who had previously exhibited the greatest partisan polarization in approval ratings as measured by Gallup polls. Given the likelihood that Trump's already low approval ratings will not appreciably rise, and that his support is already deeply divided by party, it appears highly unlikely that he can leverage his public support as a tool for moving Democratic legislators. Instead, efforts to go public will, as George Edwards persuasively argues, mostly fall on "deaf ears."[93]

Considering this rather pessimistic prognosis regarding the limits on presidential influence in Congress, Trump may be tempted to avoid legislative bargaining altogether by relying instead on so-called unilateral actions—executive orders and directives, administrative rulemaking, and signing statements—to accomplish his policy objectives. This can be an effective means for achieving incremental, short-term policy change, as illustrated by Obama's DACA directive. However, as Trump's reversal of Obama's directive illustrates, policies made through unilateral actions are susceptible to being countermanded by presidents using the same unilateral methods.[94]

Moreover, as Trump discovered with his initial executive order placing a temporary ban on immigration from six Muslim-majority nations, because these unilateral directives are typically based on the advice of specialized presidential advisers who often do not fully understand the president's broader vantage point, such orders may work in the long term to lessen a president's influence rather than extend it.[95] Trump's initial travel ban order was blocked by a district court, as was a revised order designed to meet the legal objections raised during the first court challenge. Trump appealed these decisions, and in December the Supreme Court allowed a modified ban to go into effect while Trump's legal challenge works its

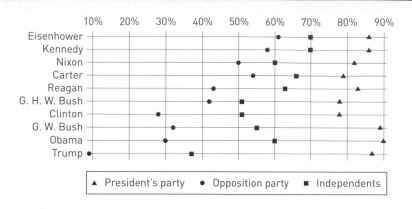

FIGURE 15.8 ■ Partisan Divide in Presidential Approval

▲ President's party ● Opposition party ■ Independents

Source: http://www.huffingtonpost.com/entry/presidential-approval-ratings-are-more-partisan-than-ever_us_58f9647ce4b00fa7de12dbcc.

way through the court system. Whatever the final court ruling, however, the backlash to Trump's efforts to institute a travel ban likely contributed to his historically low approval ratings. As Richard Neustadt warned, when it comes to making significant and enduring policy change and protecting the president's sources of power, reliance on executive orders and other acts of "command" are a poor substitute for bargaining with Congress.[96]

Where does this leave Trump nearly a year into his presidency? In his study of the policy process during the post–World War II era, Charles O. Jones shows that patterns of lawmaking vary considerably under conditions of both unified and divided government.[97] Nonetheless, Trump's success in Congress will be influenced by some fundamental features of the current political landscape. First, with even fewer liberal Republicans and conservative Democrats than in the recent past, the 115th Congress (2017–2019) is likely to be as polarized as its immediate predecessors. Despite their forty-seven-seat House majority, on many issues the Republican caucus remains divided. In the Republican-controlled Senate, Democrats still retain enough seats to use procedural rules to block most action. This makes legislating solely through the Republican caucus a risky proposition. However, the limited number of issues that can conceivably receive bipartisan support in Congress may leave Trump little choice on how to proceed.

Second, history indicates that Trump's window of opportunity to be an agent of change may close rapidly. During the post–World War II era, only George W. Bush saw his party gain seats in Congress during the first midterm election, and that was in the aftermath of the 9/11 terrorist attacks. The average first-term midterm losses for the president's party dating back to Harry Truman in 1946 has been just under twenty-five seats in the House and slightly less than two seats in the Senate.[98]

This means Trump has little time to move his legislative agenda before lawmakers focus more on the upcoming elections than on working with the president. After the midterm elections, if history holds, Trump's congressional support is likely to be even weaker.

As an additional reminder of the ephemeral nature of his political capital, Trump would do well to remember Obama's response early in his presidency to Republicans' request for him to consider their draft of an economic stimulus bill. When presented the draft by Republican representative Eric Cantor, Obama rejected it, reportedly saying, "Elections have consequences, and at the end of the day, I won. So I think on that one I trump you."[99] Because Obama's statement seemed to ignore the fact that the Republicans with whom he was negotiating had also won their elections to Congress, it likely did little to further his goal of creating a bipartisan atmosphere. Two years later Obama's party had lost their House majority, in part due to public opposition to Obama's stimulus bill.

Similarly, in the aftermath of his reelection in 2004, Bush proclaimed, "I earned capital in the campaign, political capital, and now I intend to spend it." When Bush tried to expend that capital by reforming Social Security, the effort failed soundly. In his memoirs Bush conceded that if he had to "do it all over again, I would have pushed immigration reform . . . as the first major initiative" of his second term because it "had bipartisan support." Instead, as he acknowledged, the effort to push social security "widened the partisan divide."[100] It also contributed to Republicans losing their congressional majority in 2006.

A decade later Donald Trump won the presidential election by promising to use his outsider status and deal-making prowess to end legislative gridlock and restore American greatness. When it came to repealing Obamacare, however, Trump's first foray into the legislative realm followed the familiar path trod by his immediate predecessors—one that relied solely on the president's party to achieve a legislative objective. But after failing to repeal Obamacare, and to enact any other major legislation in his first seven months in office, Trump showed signs of recalibrating his bargaining strategy by adopting a more bipartisan approach to dealing with Congress. It is too early to know whether this represents a fundamental shift and, if so, whether it will produce the legislative breakthroughs he promised on the campaign trail—and at what cost to his core support. However, he may judge that it is a risk worth taking. The alternative is to govern in a purely partisan manner—a strategy that recent history indicates may gain Trump a few legislative victories, but which may also risk his Republican majority in Congress, and his dream to be a transformational president.

NOTES

*The chapter benefited from the research assistance of Avery White, Danny Zhang, Martina Berger, Martin Naunov, Day Robins, Kate Reinmuth, and Maggie Joseph.

1. As of mid-September 2017, Senate Republicans were still scrambling to craft a replacement bill before reconciliation provisions expired at the end of the month.

2. https://twitter.com/realDonaldTrump/status/890820505330212864?ref_src= twsrc%5Etfw&ref_url=https%3A%2F%2Fwww.vox.com%2F2017%2F7%2F28 %2F16054746%2Ftrump-senate-vote-skinny-repeal-defeat-tweets (accessed August 28, 2017).

3. Matt Flegenheimer and Maggie Haberman, "Mitch McConnell's 'Excessive Expectations' Comment Draws Trump's Ire," *New York Times,* August 9, 2017, https://www.nytimes.com/2017/08/09/us/politics/mitch-mcconnell-trump-health-care.html?mcubz=3&_r=0 (accessed September 10, 2017).

4. These included allegations that members of Trump's campaign team—perhaps with Trump's tacit encouragement—had colluded with Russian efforts to influence the 2016 presidential election, and then had engaged in a coverup to hide their tracks. "McConnell, in Private, Doubts if Trump Can Save His Presidency," *New York Times,* August 22, 2017, https://www.nytimes.com/2017/08/22/us/politics/mitch-mcconnell-trump.html?_r=1 (accessed August 28, 2017).

5. https://www.theatlantic.com/politics/archive/2017/08/trumps-mitch-session/536505/ (accessed August 28, 2017).

6. Shortly after announcing his candidacy, in discussing McCain's war record, Trump noted, "He was a war hero because he was captured. . . . I like people who weren't captured."

7. As evidence, critics cited Trump's clumsy public effort to pressure Murkowski, via tweets and through Interior Secretary Ryan Zinke, after she voted no on both the repeal and repeal-and-replace legislation. See, more generally, W. James Antle, "Trump's Closing Pitch Leaves Republicans Wanting More," *Washington Examiner,* July 25, 2017, http://www.washingtonexaminer.com/trumps-closing-healthcare-pitch-leaves-republicans-wanting-more/article/2629575.

8. Matthew Dickinson, "Why the Republican Effort Failed: There Was No There, There," http://sites.middlebury.edu/presidentialpower/2017/07/28/why-the-repeal-effort-failed-there-was-no-there-there/.

9. In contrast, House Republican candidates outpolled their Democrat opponents in 2016 in the aggregate by a bit more than 1.3 million votes. See http://history .house.gov/Institution/Election-Statistics/Election-Statistics/ (accessed September 14, 2017).

10. Richard Neustadt, *Presidential Power and the Modern Presidents* (New York: Free Press, 1990), p. ix.

11. See, for example, Jennifer Rubin, "This Is Not a Normal President," *Washington Post,* May 1, 2017, https://www.washingtonpost.com/blogs/right-turn/wp/2017/05/01/ this-is-not-a-normal-president/?utm_term=.bd3f696a94d3 (accessed September 16, 2017).

12. Brendan Nyhan et al., "One Vote Out of Step? The Effect of Salient Roll Call Votes in the 2010 Election," American Politics Research (2012), http://themonkeycage.org/ wp-content/uploads/2012/03/nyhanetal_published.pdf (accessed August 30, 2017).

13. Democrats held forty-six seats, but the two Senate independents, Bernie Sanders (I-VT) and Angus King (I-ME), caucused with them.

14. http://www.npr.org/2016/12/22/505618360/-dawn-of-a-new-unified-republican-government-coming-in-2017 (accessed September 14, 2017).

15. Drew DeSilver, "What Is the House Freedom Caucus, and Who's in It?" Pew Research Center (October 20, 2015).

16. On this point, see Steve Bannon's comments in his *60 Minutes* interview, https://www.cbsnews.com/news/60-minutes-breitbart-steve-bannon-declares-war-on-the-gop/ (accessed September 14, 2017).

17. George Edwards, "No Deal: Donald Trump's Leadership of Congress" (Paper presented at the 2017 meeting of the American Political Science Association, San Francisco, CA), https://www.researchgate.net/publication/319184368_NO_DEAL_DONALD_TRUMP%27S_LEADERSHIP_OF_CONGRESS (accessed August 30, 2017).

18. This only includes victorious Republicans who faced a Democratic challenger.

19. On this score, Trump had no doubts; he boasted that he could be "more presidential" than any president but Lincoln. https://www.washingtonpost.com/video/politics/trump-i-can-be-more-presidential-than-all-us-presidents-except-lincoln/2017/07/25/d416d2ea-7193-11e7-8c17-533c52b2f014_video.html?utm_term=.a04cd62152c1.

20. See, for example, Sarah Ellison, "The Inside Story of the Kushner-Bannon Civil War," *Vanity Fair,* April 14, 2017, https://www.vanityfair.com/news/2017/04/jared-kushner-steve-bannon-white-house-civil-war (accessed August 30, 2017).

21. Glenn Thrush and Maggie Haberman, "Trump the Dealmaker Projects Bravado," *New York Times,* March 23, 2017, https://www.nytimes.com/2017/03/23/us/politics/trump-health-care-bill-regrets.html?mcubz=3&_r=0 (accessed September 15, 2017).

22. Robert Pear and Thomas Kaplan, "The G.O.P.'s High-Risk Strategy for Health Law Repeal," *New York Times*, March 11, 2017.

23. Deirdre Walsh, "Tom MacArthur Resigns as Co-chair of Moderate Tuesday Group," CNN, May 23 2017.

24. Shane Goldmacher, "Trump Savors Health Care Win: Hey, I'm President," *Politico*, May 4, 2017, http://www.politico.com/story/2017/05/04/trump-health-care-win-238005.

25. Burgess Everett, "Inside McConnell's Plan to Repeal Obamacare," *Politico,* June 22, 2017.

26. Ibid.

27. Glenn Thrush and Jonathan Martin, "On Senate Health Bill, Trump Falters in the Closer's Role," *New York Times*, June 27, 2017.

28. David Graham, "As I Have Always Said: Trump's Changing Positions on Health Care," *Atlantic,* July 28, 2017, https://www.theatlantic.com/politics/archive/2017/07/as-i-have-always-said-trumps-ever-changing-position-on-health-care/535293/ (accessed August 31, 2017).

29. Under Senate rules, because the bill had not been "scored" by the CBO, it needed sixty votes to pass.

30. See https://www.budget.senate.gov/imo/media/doc/HealthCareFreedomAct.pdf.

31. http://thehill.com/policy/healthcare/344244-ryan-assures-gop-senators-house-will-go-to-conference.

32. On this point, see Barbara Sinclair, *Unorthodox Lawmaking,* 5th ed. (Washington, DC: CQ Press, 2017).

33. See, for example, James A. Morone, "One Side to Every Story," *New York Times,* February 17, 2009, http://www.nytimes.com/2009/02/17/opinion/17morone.html? pagewanted=.

34. See George C. Edwards III and Andrew Barrett, "Presidential Agenda Setting in Congress," in *Polarized Politics,* ed. Jon R. Bond and Richard Fleisher (Washington, DC: CQ Press, 2000), 109–133; and Andrew Rudalevige, *Managing the President's Program: Presidential Leadership and Legislative Policy Formulation* (Princeton, NJ: Princeton University Press, 2002).

35. The exceptions are Maine and Nebraska; in both states it is possible to split electoral votes between candidates, as was the case with Nebraska in 2008, when one of its five electoral votes went to Obama, and Maine in 2016, when Trump won one of the state's four electoral votes.

36. The classic case is Ross Perot, who received 19 percent of the popular vote in 1992 but did not win a single Electoral College vote.

37. This is not mandated in the Constitution, but it gradually became the norm in the United States and is now based in statute.

38. Since the Twenty-second Amendment was ratified in 1951, presidents can be reelected only once.

39. Senators were not popularly elected until 1914, after ratification of the Seventeenth Amendment.

40. See Gerald C. Wright and Michael Berkman, "Candidates and Policy in U.S. Senatorial Elections," *American Political Science Review* 80 (June 1986): 576–590.

41. James Madison, *Federalist Papers,* no. 51 (Norwalk, CT: Easton Press, 1979), 347.

42. James Sterling Young, *The Washington Community, 1800–1828* (New York: Columbia University Press, 1966).

43. George Washington, Farewell Address, 1796, http://avalon.law.yale.edu/18th_century/washing.asp.

44. See Richard McCormick, *The Presidential Game: The Origin of American Presidential Politics* (New York: Oxford University Press, 1984).

45. Ibid.

46. E. E. Schattschneider, *Party Government* (New York: Farrar and Rinehart, 1940).

47. In 1901 Florida became the first state to use a presidential primary.

48. Morris Fiorina, "Epilogue: The Era of Incumbency and Insulation," in *Continuity and Change in House Elections,* ed. David Brady, John Cogan, and Morris Fiorina (Stanford, CA: Stanford University Press, 2000).

49. Some researchers believe scholars misinterpreted survey results and overestimated the actual increase in the number of "true" independent voters. See Bruce E. Keith, David B. Magleby, and Candice J. Nelson, *The Myth of the Independent Voter* (Berkeley: University of California Press, 1992); and Jody Baumgartner and Peter L. Francia, *Conventional Wisdom and American Elections* (Lanham, MD: Rowman and Littlefield, 2007).

50. How much that gatekeeping role weakened is a matter of some dispute. Some scholars argue that party activists continued to exert a discernible influence on the nominating process. See, for instance, Marty Cohen, David Karol, Hans Noel, and John Zaller, *The Party Decides: Presidential Nominations before and after Reform* (Chicago: Chicago University Press, 2008). But Noel concedes that was not the case in the 2016 Republican presidential nominating process: "Why Can't the Party Stop Trump?" *New York Times,* March 1, 2016, https://www.nytimes.com/2016/03/01/opinion/campaign-stops/why-cant-the-gop-stop-trump.html?mcubz=3(accessed September 21, 2017).

51. On the incumbency advantage, see Andrew Gelman and Gary King, "Measuring the Incumbency Advantage without Bias," *American Journal of Political Science* 34 (November 1990): 1142–1164. On the declining marginals, see David Mayhew, "Congressional Elections: The Case of the Vanishing Marginals," *Polity* 6 (Spring 1973): 295–318.

52. The classic statement of this thesis is Morris Fiorina, *Congress: Keystone of the Washington Establishment,* 2nd ed. (New Haven, CT: Yale University Press, 1989).

53. Republican popular support in congressional elections peaked at 48 percent in 1968 and reached 46 percent in 1980.

54. For a readable overview of the issues, see Morris Fiorina, *Divided Government* (New York: Macmillan, 1992).

55. For example, see Gary Jacobsen, *Politics of Congressional Elections,* 5th ed. (New York: Longman, 2001), 237–270; and Morris Fiorina, "The Presidency and Congress: An Electoral Connection?" in *The Presidency and the Political System,* 5th ed., ed. Michael Nelson (Washington, DC: CQ Press, 1988), 431.

56. David Mayhew, *Divided We Govern: Party Control, Lawmaking, and Investigations, 1946–1990* (New Haven, CT: Yale University Press, 1991).

57. Looking at new data through 1997, for instance, Sarah Binder finds that policy gridlock is higher under conditions of divided government. Sarah H. Binder, "Congress, the Executive, and the Production of Public Policy," in *Congress Reconsidered,* 7th ed., ed. Lawrence C. Dodd and Bruce I. Oppenheimer (Washington, DC: CQ Press, 2001), 293–314.

58. The 2016 figure, however, comes from a Gallup poll, while the previous ones are based on ANES studies, so comparisons should be read with caution. Clearly, however, the number of self-proclaimed independents has declined since its earlier peak.

59. ANES figures on strong partisanship are not yet available for 2016.

60. The figures control for whether an incumbent representative is running. Note that figures are unavailable for the elections immediately after the decennial census, including the 2012 election, because the congressional districts have been redrawn to reflect population shifts. Figures through 1996 are based on data provided by Arjun Samuel Wilkins from Stanford University.

61. See Nolan McCarty, Keith Poole, and Howard Rosenthal, *Polarized America* (Cambridge, MA: MIT Press, 2006).

62. See Bruce Oppenheimer, "Deep Red and Blue Congressional Districts: The Causes and Consequences of Declining Party Competitiveness," in *Congress Reconsidered,* 8th ed., ed. Lawrence C. Dodd and Bruce I. Oppenheimer (Washington, DC: CQ Press, 2005), 135–158.

63. Fifteen new black-majority districts and nine new Latino-majority districts were established in 1992.

64. In 1976 the Supreme Court ruled in *Buckley v. Valeo* that campaign finance regulations prohibiting individuals from making campaign expenditures independent from a candidate's campaign violated constitutionally protected free speech.

65. In *Citizens United v. the Federal Election Commission,* the Supreme Court struck down the ban on electioneering by unions and corporations contained in the McCain–Feingold Act. In *SpeechNow.org v. Federal Election Commission,* the D.C. Circuit Court of Appeals ruled that the provisions of the Federal Election Campaign Act limiting the source and size of contributions to independent expenditure-only PACs violate the First Amendment.

66. Data based on Federal Election Commission records as reported on the Open Secrets website. See www.opensecrets.org/parties/.

67. Regarding declining turnout, see Stephen Ansolabehere and Shanto Iyengar, *Going Negative: How Political Advertising Alienates and Polarizes the American Electorate* (New York: Free Press, 1996); and Morris Fiorina and Theda Skocpol, eds., *Civic Engagement in American Democracy* (Washington, DC: Brookings Institution Press, 1999).

68. All turnout data are from Michael McDonald's website, http://www.electproject .org.

69. Based on DW-Nominate scores reported at http://voteview.com/polarized_america .htm. These scores are derived from an analysis of congressional voting records dating back to 1789 that finds the primary issue differentiating liberal, moderate, and conservative members of Congress is their views regarding the role of the government in the economy.

70. See David W. Rohde, *Parties and Leaders in the Post-Reform House* (Chicago: University of Chicago Press, 1991); and John H. Aldrich and David W. Rohde, "Congressional Committees in a Partisan Era," in Dodd and Oppenheimer, eds., *Congress Reconsidered,* 8th ed., 251.

71. Steven S. Smith and Gerald Gamm, "The Dynamics of Party Government in Congress," in Dodd and Oppenheimer, eds., *Congress Reconsidered,* 8th ed., 196.

72. Gary Jacobson, "Party Polarization in National Politics: The Electoral Connection," in Bond and Fleisher, eds. *Polarized Politics,* 13.

73. *Vital Statistics in Congress* (Washington, DC: Brookings Institution, 2016), https:// www.brookings.edu/multi-chapter-report/vital-statistics-on-congress/(accessed Sept. 17, 2017).

74. Ibid.

75. Jacobson, "Party Polarization in National Politics," 27.

76. "The End of the 114th Congress," https://voteviewblog.com/2016/12/18/the-end-of-the-114th-congress/ (accessed September 17, 2017).

77. "The Collapse of the Voting Structure—Possible Big Trouble Ahead," Voteview Blog (January 12, 2017), https://voteviewblog.com/2017/01/12/the-collapse-of-the-voting-structure-possible-big-trouble-ahead/ (accessed September 17, 2017).

78. See "Toward a More Responsible Two-Party System: A Report of the Committee on Political Parties," *American Political Science Review* 44, no. 3 (1950), part 2, supplement.

79. For evidence that high levels of party polarization decrease legislative productivity, see Lawrence C. Dodd and Scot Schraufnagel, "Reconsidering Party Polarization and Policy Productivity: A Curvilinear Perspective," in *Congress Reconsidered,* 9th ed., ed. Lawrence C. Dodd and Bruce I. Oppenheimer (Washington, DC: CQ Press, 2008), 393–418.

80. All data from http://elections.huffingtonpost.com/pollster/. For comparable measures from Gallup, which shows a longer time trend, see also http://news.gallup .com/poll/1600/congress-public.aspx.

81. Transcript, Election Night Speech, http://www.latimes.com/politics/la-na-pol-trump-election-night-speech-20161108-story.html (accessed September 17, 2017).

82. See "Final Vote Results for Roll Call 406," http://clerk.house.gov/evs/1993/r011406. xml; and "U.S. Senate Roll Call Votes 103rd Congress—1st Session," United States Senate, http://www.senate.gov/legislative/LIS/roll_call_lists/vote_menu_103_1.htm.

83. Ten House Republicans and twenty-nine Democrats did not vote. See "Final Vote Results for Roll Call 149," http://clerk.house.gov/evs/2001/r011149.xml; and "A Bill to Provide for Reconciliation Pursuant to Section 104 of the Concurrent Resolution on the Budget for Fiscal Year 2002," http://www.senate.gov/legislative/LIS/roll_call_lists/roll_call_vote_cfm.cfm?congress=107&session=1&vote=00170.

84. Jacobsen, *The Politics of Congressional Elections,* 253.

85. Under DACA, Obama directed the Department of Homeland Security to stop deporting undocumented immigrants who came to this country before age sixteen, had resided in the United States for five years or more, and were in college or were high school graduates or serving in the military. They must also not have had criminal records. Julia Preston and John H. Cushman Jr., "Obama to Permit Young Migrants to Remain in U.S.," *New York Times,* June 15, 2012, http://www.nytimes.com/2012/06/16/us/us-to-stop-deporting-some-illegal-immigrants.html?pagewanted=all&_r=0.

86. Frank Newport, "Americans' Views on Bank Takeovers Appears Fluid," Gallup, February 24, 2009, http://www.gallup.com/poll/116065/americans-views-bank-takeovers-appear-fluid.aspx.

87. Charles O. Jones, *The Presidency in a Separated System,* 2nd ed. (Washington, DC: Brookings Institution, 2005), 355.

88. For a cogent summary of the reasons behind, and the effectiveness of, this strategy, see Samuel Kernell, *Going Public: New Strategies of Presidential Leadership,* 4th ed. (Washington, DC: CQ Press, 2007).

89. See, for instance, Jon R. Bond and Richard Fleisher, *The President in the Legislative Arena* (Chicago: University of Chicago Press, 1990); and Brandice Canes-Wrone, *Who Leads Whom? Presidents, Policy and the Public* (Chicago: University of Chicago Press, 2005).

90. For further evidence of the limited fungibility of popularity, Trump need only consult his predecessors' experiences. After the September 11, 2001, terrorist attacks, George W. Bush capitalized on his high approval ratings to push a number of war-related initiatives through Congress. But on most of his other legislative proposals that became law, Bush's success came not from public appeals, but from bargaining and compromise. And the strategy became increasingly moot as Bush's approval ratings dipped into historically low territory, culminating with the loss of Republican control of both houses in the 2006 midterm elections. Bush's father, George H. W. Bush, also enjoyed stratospheric popularity ratings when he led a successful international coalition against Iraq, which had invaded neighboring Kuwait, in the Persian Gulf War. But that support dissipated quickly in the economic downturn that followed, and Bush was voted out of office in 1992. His successor, Bill Clinton, enjoyed his highest popularity ratings while being impeached by the Republican-controlled House and acquitted in the Senate.

91. See, for example, Kernell, *Going Public,* 140–167; Theodore Lowi, *The Personal Presidency: Power Invested, Promise Unfulfilled* (Ithaca, NY: Cornell University Press, 1985).

92. Marc Bodnick, "Going Public Reconsidered: Reagan's 1981 Tax and Budget Cuts," *Congress and the Presidency* 17 (Spring 1990): 13–28

93. George C. Edwards III, *On Deaf Ears: The Limits of the Bully Pulpit* (New Haven, CT: Yale University Press, 2007).

94. Matthew J. Dickinson and Jesse Gubb, "The Limits to Power without Persuasion," *Presidential Studies Quarterly* 46 (February 2016): 48–72.

95. See https://www.whitehouse.gov/the-press-office/2017/01/27/executive-order-protecting-nation-foreign-terrorist-entry-united-states.

96. See Neustadt, *Presidential Power and the Modern Presidents,* esp. 33–35.

97. Jones identifies five distinct patterns of lawmaking: straight partisanship, competitive partisanship, bipartisanship, competitive bipartisanship, and cross-partisanship. Charles O. Jones, *The Presidency in a Separated System,* 2nd ed. (Washington, DC: Brookings Institution, 2005), 341–354.

98. This average includes Democratic losses in 1966 and Republican losses in 1974.

99. Eric Cantor, "What the Obama Presidency Looked Like to the Opposition," *New York Times,* January 14, 2017, https://www.nytimes.com/2017/01/14/opinion/sunday/eric-cantor-what-the-obama-presidency-looked-like-to-the-opposition.html?mcubz=3 (accessed September 21, 2017).

100. George W. Bush, *Decision Points* (New York: Crown, 2010), 306.

16

THE PRESIDENCY AND THE JUDICIARY

David A. Yalof

During the past half century, Democratic and Republican presidents have benefited from an informal alliance they've forged with the judicial branch of government. When successful, such an alliance can produce judicial support for many of the administration's policies, as well as judicial deference to the executive's interpretation of many aspects of those policies. Although President Donald Trump suffered through a mostly rocky first six months in office, his successful appointment of a Supreme Court justice and numerous highly conservative federal judges may stand as his administration's most lasting legacy. David A. Yalof calls attention to mounting evidence that unlike President Obama, who deemphasized the judiciary as a means of waging his administration's most significant political battles, President Trump has proven himself a reliable conservative in the judicial arena. Indeed, he has borrowed from the playbook of Presidents Reagan and George W. Bush, among others, in making judicial appointments that appeal to conservative interest groups and many of the social conservatives who make up perhaps the most loyal part of his political base. This effort should pay dividends in the near future, as the Trump administration's most controversial policies (such as the proposed travel ban) are likely to end up before the courts (including the Supreme Court), where extremely conservative judges such as his own appointee, Justice Neil Gorsuch, will be waiting. In that sense, a strategic alliance forged between this unorthodox chief executive and like-minded courts may once again prevail.

On January 20, 2017, the day that Donald Trump took the oath of office as forty-fifth president of the United States, Republican Party control of the levers of federal government was nearly absolute. In addition to controlling the executive branch, Republicans also controlled both houses of Congress—along with a four-seat majority in the Senate, the GOP enjoyed an astounding forty-seven-seat margin in the House of Representatives. No Republican president since Herbert Hoover had enjoyed such a large working margin in the lower chamber. Yet despite these clear advantages, it would be a rocky first six months for Trump and the GOP. Long-promised legislation to repeal the Patient Protection and Affordable Care Act (also known as "Obamacare") had met with considerable intra-party divisions, frustrating the president and his supporters at every turn. Thus as the summer of 2017 turned to fall, President Trump was still looking for his party's first high-profile legislative victory [1] and the chance to celebrate a new era for "getting things done" in Washington.

Fortunately for Trump and his allies, they could point to at least one clear marker of success during the first half of 2017: the appointment of Judge Neil Gorsuch to the U.S. Supreme Court. Even with Republicans holding a relatively narrow working majority in the Senate, the Gorsuch nomination moved through that chamber without delay. In a period spanning less than ten weeks, Senate Republicans shepherded the Gorsuch nomination through countless meetings with Senators, four days of confirmation hearings, a Senate rule change that outlawed filibusters of high court nominees, and then finally, through a Senate floor debate culminating in a 54–45 vote for the nominee. Once the Senate jettisoned the filibuster rule, the final outcome was never in doubt, as all fifty-two Republicans (joined by just two Senate Democrats) supported Gorsuch throughout the process. In that respect, the process of appointing Gorsuch appeared not all that different from the process at work in so many other high court appointments in the post-Bork era: fierce rhetoric was heard on both sides, followed usually by a Senate vote in favor of confirmation.[2]

Certainly the Gorsuch appointment was not free of controversy. Because the vacancy first arose upon the death of Justice Antonin Scalia on February 13, 2016, Democrats proclaimed that with nearly a year left in his presidency, the power to name a new justice rightfully belonged to President Barack Obama. True to form, the Democratic president named Judge Merrick Garland of the D.C. Circuit as his nominee exactly a month following the death of Scalia. Senate consideration of the nomination was another matter, however, as Senate Majority Leader Mitch McConnell (R-KY) and his fellow Republicans united behind the position that only President Obama's successor was entitled to fill the vacant seat. With Senate Republicans in control of the process, Garland's nomination was doomed from the outset; and once the November election was over, his nomination expired without any formal action taken. Democratic senators complained that the chamber had ignored its constitutional duty to consider Garland; *The New York Times* called out the Republicans for their "abuse of power" that had resulted in a "stolen seat."[3] All such arguments fell on deaf ears, however, as the GOP exulted in Trump's nomination of Gorsuch.

Just as controversial was the Senate majority's decision on April 6, 2017, to eliminate the filibuster for Supreme Court nominees. The procedural change (in this instance accomplished by a party line vote) marked a new low point in inter-party relations within an upper legislative chamber whose members had traditionally prided themselves on their capacity to maintain collegial relations across the aisle. The Democrats got the ball rolling in this regard in November 2013, when they eliminated the filibuster for most other nominations, including those to the lower courts. Yet the Gorsuch nomination marked a historical moment in Supreme Court confirmation politics. Going forward, future presidents whose party also controls the Senate will no longer need bipartisan approval for their nominees.

More telling, although the Republicans enjoyed a near record margin of control in the House, it was the U.S. Senate and its narrow 52–48 split that produced the most important achievement of Donald Trump's first six months in office. It was a meaningful victory as well, as the Gorsuch appointment may have direct implications for the president in forging a lasting legacy. Why? Because the judiciary can so often make or break a president's policy agenda. For that reason above all, many modern presidents have sought to shape the courts in their own image and then forge alliances with the judiciary once it is in friendly hands. If successful, these strategic alliances can offer extraordinary benefits; by contrast, a president who ignores the judiciary (or in extreme cases, one who goes to war with the courts) can find his administration hampered from making his long-term policy initiatives stick—if they can get those policies passed in the first place. Numerous Democratic presidents benefitted as the judiciary helped advance progressive causes during the middle and late twentieth century; Republican presidents for their own part emphasized the role of the courts to achieve important political gains and to energize a party base that has grown increasingly concerned about social issues.

As president, Franklin Roosevelt depended on the courts in general (and the Supreme Court in particular) to validate his progressive New Deal policy agenda; he quickly grew frustrated with Court resistance during his first term. Progressive animus toward a hardline conservative Court actually began with his cousin Theodore's open attacks on the judiciary, continued with calls by Sen. Robert M. LaFollette and others for reforms that would allow Congress to override Supreme Court decisions, and then culminated in fierce contests over the confirmation of Herbert Hoover's Supreme Court nominees during the early 1930s.[4] When the Court's majority refused to defer to the political branches, Roosevelt struck against the Court with the most provocative move of all: an (unsuccessful) attempt to "pack the court" by adding justices (one per year for every current justice who had already reached the age of seventy, up to a maximum of fifteen justices sitting at one time). FDR knew the Court would prove a thorn in his party's progressive agenda if he did not engage in such battles forcefully and on his own terms.

FDR lost the court-packing battle, but ultimately won the war over constitutional interpretation. Subsequent Democratic chief executives quickly came to view the courts as allies in progressive policymaking, especially during Earl Warren's reign as chief justice from 1953 until 1969. Presidents John F. Kennedy and Lyndon B. Johnson, for example, welcomed court intervention against southern resistance to civil rights policies. Meanwhile, Democratic presidents who tried to avoid the judiciary for particular purposes enjoyed only occasional success in doing so. When President Jimmy Carter sought to unilaterally annul a mutual defense treaty with China in 1979, the Court rejected attempts by Republican members of Congress to stop him.[5] President Clinton did not prove so fortunate in 1997 when the high court ordered him to defend himself against a sexual harassment lawsuit alleging actions that occurred prior to his term as president.[6] Once again, a chief executive who sought to duck the courts proved unable to do so, and witnesses' testimony in *Jones v. Clinton* gave rise to events that led to his eventual impeachment by the House of Representatives.

Among the modern Republican presidents, Richard Nixon looked to the judiciary for gains that could not be achieved by a Congress controlled by the Democratic opposition. In fact, Nixon's interest in rolling back the rights of the accused and curtailing controversial court-imposed desegregation strategies informed his Supreme Court selections and his administration's litigation strategies in the high court as well.[7] Politically speaking, these strategies also proved effective at dividing the Democrats and opening the way for the emergence of a new conservative coalition. President Ronald Reagan took this approach a step further, focusing on lower court appointments as the key to transforming the constitutional landscape in a more conservative direction. More recently, President George W. Bush put his own stamp on the process, placing extremely conservative judicial nominees on the courts through the use of recess appointments and other controversial tactics. With some success, the Bush administration pressured the courts (including the Supreme Court) to back its agenda for fighting the war on terrorism after the attacks of September 11, 2011. These Republican presidents viewed the courts as crucial allies in the policy battles they wished to wage against or around a resistant Congress.

President Obama offered a markedly different perspective on the role of courts in the political system. Specifically, he hoped to create a broader and more diverse Democratic coalition that could pursue political ends without the help of (or interference from) the courts. He soon learned the folly of this approach, however. President Obama's victory in *National Federation of Independent Business v. Sebelius*[8]—which upheld the bulk of his administration's signature legislative achievement in health care policy—was achieved only narrowly, and with a key vote cast by a Republican appointee, Chief Justice John Roberts. Beyond litigation over the Affordable Care Act, the Obama administration was dragged into court repeatedly to defend its policy achievements against constitutional attack. President Obama's final record before the Supreme Court featured significant highs and lows. Although he won significant victories in the health care case and in a lawsuit brought by Arizona to curb federal immigration policies, the landmark campaign finance case of *Citizens United v. F.E.C.*[9] haunted the Democrats for years; at a minimum, it gave rise to a storm of super PAC money flowing into Republican coffers during the 2012 election campaign.

With Congress seemingly unwilling to pass comprehensive immigration reform, President Donald Trump attempted to enact immigration policy on his own through controversial executive orders that faced judicial scrutiny as well. The Trump administration's initial immigration ban—by which the federal authorities limited travel from six mostly Muslim countries for 90 days and suspended the nation's refugee program for 120 days—expired before reaching the Supreme Court. Yet another version of the administration's travel ban, issued on September 24, 2017, would have placed varying levels of restrictions on foreign nationals from eight different countries including Venezuela and North Korea. This latest form of the ban was still making its way through the lower courts at the time this book went to press. Few doubt that one or more of the administration's travel bans will eventually end up before the Supreme Court. Once there, Justice Neil Gorsuch will be in a position to exert considerable influence over their fate.

From the moment a president first exercises the substantial powers vested in him by the Constitution, the third branch of government provides a wellspring of opportunity, as well as dangers, to his policy agenda. Through rulings that defer to the executive, the judiciary can validate the president's most controversial actions, and in some cases bestow upon them a measure of credibility. On the other hand, litigation may present significant pitfalls, as the courts may undermine the president's political hopes through negative rulings. In that respect, the circumstances facing President Trump in his first few months as president were not so different from that faced by all the modern presidents who preceded him: win over the courts or risk imperiling your agenda at the outset. Of course the forty-fifth president did enjoy at least one advantage unavailable to most of his predecessors: upon his arrival in Washington, D.C., a Supreme Court vacancy was already waiting for him. President Trump's quick move to fill that vacancy was to be expected; that such action would mark the signature achievement of his young presidency was the real surprise.

PRESIDENTIAL CAMPAIGNS AND THE JUDICIARY

Even before presidents take office, they must address critical questions concerning their views on controversial legal precedents and the ways they hope to shape the judiciary. Occasionally during the nineteenth and twentieth centuries, the Supreme Court and related issues figured prominently in campaigns for the presidency.[10] In the 1800 race between President John Adams and Vice President Thomas Jefferson, the latter owed his victory largely to his party's steadfast denunciation of the controversial Alien and Sedition Acts of 1798, which criminalized the act of criticizing government officials. The Federalist Party had supported the legislation, and Adams signed it. The law provided a forum for Federalist judges to rail against Republican editors and publishers at sedition trials. The voters put the judiciary on trial in the election of 1800, and the judiciary lost.

A half-century later, the recently formed Republican Party used the Supreme Court's decision in *Dred Scott v. Sandford* as an effective target of Northerners' frustrations during the election campaign of 1860.[11] The *Dred Scott* decision invalidated the Missouri Compromise of 1820, which had divided U.S. territories into free and slave states. In the process, the Court aggressively articulated the theory that slaves were the personal property of their owners. Running on the Republican ticket, Abraham Lincoln alleged that the timing and substance of *Dred Scott* pointed to a conspiracy by the Democrats to nationalize slavery. According to political scientist Donald Grier Stevenson, the 1860s were the nadir of Supreme Court influence, largely because Lincoln's 1860 victory placed the mostly Democratic Court on the losing side of the presidential election.[12]

During the twentieth and early twenty-first centuries, the Supreme Court has only rarely been a factor in presidential elections. The Court's low profile in election campaigns stands in marked contrast to the high profile it has assumed as a national policymaker. The Court was on Franklin D. Roosevelt's mind during the 1936 election only because the justices had recently stymied the president's New Deal initiatives by invalidating the National Industrial Recovery Act and the Agricultural Adjustment Act, among other pieces of legislation.[13] Still, to the surprise of many, Roosevelt maintained a "studied silence" about the Court during his first reelection campaign. This silence was strategic, as Roosevelt enjoyed only a five-point lead in the Gallup poll that summer, and, with some other surveys predicting his defeat, "deliberately raising the Court question seemed foolhardy."[14] Later it would appear that Roosevelt fumbled away the opportunity to create a mandate for the Court-packing plan he unveiled after the election, a bold initiative to expand the number of justices that went down to an embarrassing defeat in 1937. Thus, at one of those rare moments in history when voters were focused on Court-related issues, they were denied a rich debate among the presidential candidates over how they would address the constitutional crisis that was brewing.

The same pattern prevailed in subsequent decades, as the Court and constitutional matters provided mostly side stories in presidential elections. Harry Truman, John Kennedy, and Lyndon Johnson barely discussed the Court during their respective campaigns. Dwight Eisenhower sought to distinguish his preferred method of judicial selection from that of the Democrats, who he believed awarded judgeships on the basis of patronage and partisanship. Yet Eisenhower rarely highlighted this point in his most important campaign speeches. And when he nominated California governor Earl Warren (to pay back a campaign debt) and circuit court judge John Marshall Harlan (promoted by Ike's close friend and former legal partner Attorney General Herbert Brownell) to the Court, critics barely stirred.

Richard Nixon's campaign for the presidency in 1968 marked the first concerted attempt by a major-party candidate in the twentieth century to place the Supreme Court and its recent rulings squarely before the voters. Blaming the Warren Court and its "pro-felon" decisions such as *Miranda v. Arizona* for the civil unrest sweeping the country, Nixon promised that he would appoint only conservative "law and order" judges who would "strictly interpret" the Constitution and not "make law."[15] Nixon's campaign strategy made political sense, especially in the South, where resentment against civil rights and other liberal initiatives had spilled over into resentment against the Warren Court. By securing a Republican plurality in the South for the first time in history, Nixon showed that when legal issues were carefully couched in the right electoral rhetoric, they could make a difference.

Although Nixon's 1968 campaign changed the rhetoric of future campaigns, subsequent elections were not affected by Court-related issues to nearly the same degree. Running for reelection in 1972, President Nixon could point to his nomi-nation of four moderate-to-conservative justices as proof of his sincerity. But it was the relative prosperity of the country (and its fear of an increasingly liberal Democratic Party) that propelled Nixon into office for a second term. Eight years later, Ronald Reagan went a step further during his own White House campaign by targeting Supreme Court decisions that were politically divisive, even among Republican voters. Reagan directed his fiercest criticism at *Roe v. Wade,* which cre-ated a constitutional right to abortion, observing that the decision was "an abuse of power worse than Watergate."[16] Reagan also decried other controversial rulings banning Bible readings and prayer in the public schools, protecting non-obscene pornography as free expression, approving busing as a means of facilitating racial integration in the schools, and upholding certain affirmative action programs. Reagan even borrowed from Nixon's playbook by denouncing Supreme Court deci-sions that protected the rights of the accused.

Reagan's anti-Court rhetoric may have shored up the support of the most socially conservative Republicans, but those voters were certain to vote Republican in any case. Reagan's 1980 and 1984 election victories owed to the state of the country's economy more than anything else. Still, it was telling that Reagan was never punished for such rhetoric by more moderate Republican voters. Democratic presidential nominee Walter Mondale's repeated harping on the conservative lean-ings of the Supreme Court proved little match for the peace and prosperity the country enjoyed in 1984. And when Massachusetts governor Michael Dukakis hammered Vice President George H. W. Bush on social issues and the future com-position of the Court in 1988, his attacks barely registered with the crucial swing voters who had elected Reagan twice and then elected Bush despite his controver-sial social agenda.

Arkansas governor Bill Clinton's successful effort to bring many of these same swing voters back to the Democratic fold in 1992 was notable for its lack of emphasis on Court-related issues. During President George H. W. Bush's term, the Supreme Court had curtailed abortion rights, first in *Webster v. Reproductive Health Services* (1989) and then in *Planned Parenthood v. Casey* (1992).[17] In these two decisions the Court narrowly saved *Roe v. Wade,* while opening the door to more government restrictions going forward. Clinton and the Democrats could have made the Court an issue in the 1992 election; perhaps the young president's advisors learned some-thing from the Dukakis and Mondale failures. Although Court-related rhetoric is now considered an essential aspect of every presidential campaign, it apparently sways relatively few voters.

Still, voters continue to inquire as to candidates' positions on those issues related to the judiciary. Since 1968, all presidential candidates have provided their views on the right to abortion (all Republican candidates have opposed the right; Democrats have supported it), affirmative action (Republicans oppose; Democrats support with qualifications), and the "philosophy of judging" that the candidate favors (Republicans tend to support "strict interpretation"; Democrats support the notion of a "living Constitution").

Regardless of its effect on the actual vote, Court-related political campaigning has implications for judicial selections after the election takes place. Stated simply, winning presidential candidates tend to keep their promises in this context. The socially conservative Republican presidents (Nixon, Reagan, Bush I, and Bush II) routinely appointed conservative jurists to the Court. (President George H. W. Bush's appointment of the more moderate David Souter in 1990 was a notable exception.) George W. Bush's bold proclamations during both the 2000 and 2004 presidential campaigns that he hoped to appoint more Supreme Court justices in the conservative mold of Scalia and Clarence Thomas heightened expectations among his most conservative supporters that Bush would shift the high court further to the right. His appointments of Chief Justice Roberts and Justice Samuel Alito clearly satisfied these Republican constituencies.

By contrast, Presidents Clinton and Obama appointed moderate-to-liberal jurists to the Court. As a presidential candidate in 2008, Barack Obama said he hoped to appoint judges who would be "sympathetic enough to those who are on the outside, those who are vulnerable, those who are powerless." Three years earlier, that had been the basis of Senator Barack Obama's vote against John Roberts's nomination as chief justice. Now as president, it provided some indication of his commitment to nominate more liberal justices to the high court. Obama's selections of Judge Sonia Sotomayor and Solicitor General Elena Kagan to the Court in 2009 and 2010, respectively, offered proof that his commitment to reverse conservative gains on the court matched his rhetoric in at least this one respect.

During the 2016 Republican primaries, businessman Donald Trump offered his own novel approach to campaigning on the issue of judicial selections. Seeking to reassure conservative constituencies of his allegiance to their cause, Trump released two separate lists of judges in advance of Election Day: one during May and a second in September. Trump promised that he would draw on the pool of twenty-one names on the two lists combined to nominate a successor to Justice Scalia. True to his word, just a few days after his inauguration he narrowed the original pool down to three names, including that of his eventual nominee, Judge Neil Gorsuch.[18] Future presidential candidates (Democrat or Republican) may well employ the same device in hopes of locking down constituencies they need in a tough general election contest.

LIKE A "BOLT OF LIGHTNING"? PRESIDENTIAL APPOINTMENTS TO THE U.S. SUPREME COURT

An individual's appointment to any federal court—but especially to the United States Supreme Court—has been likened to the spin of a roulette wheel or a bolt of lightning that can strike anywhere without warning. Harvard law professor Thomas Reed Powell summed it up this way: "The selection of Supreme Court Justices is pretty much a matter of chance."[19]

In truth, the process of identifying and selecting candidates for the Supreme Court has undergone a dramatic transformation in the modern era. The identification of Supreme Court nominees by presidents originated as a private affair, handled entirely by the president and perhaps a small coterie of his closest advisers. George Washington worked alone after his first inauguration in 1789 to sort through the multitude of written suggestions he received concerning whom he should place on the new Court.[20] Thomas Jefferson consulted with legislators from his party, and Ulysses S. Grant and Woodrow Wilson sought the advice of cabinet members. Sitting Supreme Court justices have managed to break into this inner circle of advisers on occasion. Most notably, Chief Justice William Howard Taft exerted considerable influence over the Court appointments made by Presidents Warren Harding and Calvin Coolidge during the 1920s. To the extent that the attorney general played a role, it was simply as an adviser, with no special resources to draw on other than his own expertise on Court-related issues. Presidents huddled with the attorney general and any other trusted advisers to toss around the names of potential nominees. Once a short list was identified, little research was conducted other than perhaps to invite comment informally from congressional leaders or officials in the organized bar.

Since the mid-twentieth century, however, a confluence of factors has transformed the political environment that shapes the recruitment of candidates for the Supreme Court. These factors include the following:[21]

1. *Growth and bureaucratization of the Justice Department.* From a modest-sized agency in the late nineteenth century, the Justice Department has grown into a mammoth enterprise, assuming many litigation functions on behalf of the federal government that previously were performed by the individual agencies. Especially significant was the creation of the Office of Legal Counsel (OLC) in the 1930s. The OLC was conceived of as a bureaucratic resource for the attorney general, serving him in his role as legal adviser to the president. In recent years, the heavily politicized OLC has been headed by an assistant attorney general with a staff of about twenty lawyers. Since the 1980s, Republican presidents in particular have relied heavily on the OLC and other Justice Department lawyers to generate lists of candidates for the federal judiciary, including the Supreme Court.

2. *Growth and bureaucratization of the White House staff.* The White House staff underwent a growth spurt of its own, expanding from just thirty-seven in the early 1930s to more than 900 by the late 1980s.[22] Beginning with President Kennedy, who consulted regularly with White House counsel Theodore Sorenson, presidents have increasingly relied on staff lawyers to assist in vetting prospective judicial candidates and, more recently, as a source of independent legal research. When President Obama sought to fill the Supreme Court seat vacated by John Paul Stevens, he turned to the vice president's chief of staff, Ron Klain, a former chief counsel to the Senate Judiciary Committee, to head that process.

3. *Growth in the size and influence of the federal judiciary.* Congress's creation of many new federal judgeships during the twentieth century shaped the process of judicial recruitment in significant ways. Although accused of moving slowly in submitting candidates for federal judgeships, Barack Obama still managed to

appoint 329 judges during his two terms as president. Moreover, some of these federal judgeships—including all of those on the Court of Appeals for the D.C. Circuit—are unencumbered by typical considerations of senatorial courtesy, the legislative norm that allows senators of the president's party to all but dictate local appointments. Such judgeships are thus available as a testing ground for future Supreme Court justices. Federal appellate judges who prove to be ideologically compatible with the president's agenda may find themselves on short lists for elevation to the Supreme Court, either by the president who appointed them or by a later president of the same party. President Reagan followed this practice, nominating to the high court two judges, Robert Bork and Antonin Scalia, whom he had earlier appointed to the D.C. Circuit. President Clinton nominated two jurists to the Court, Ruth Bader Ginsburg and Stephen Breyer, who were appointed to circuit court judgeships by President Carter more than a decade earlier. When Donald Trump identified a pool of twenty-one potential Supreme Court nominees during his 2016 presidential campaign, more than half were sitting federal judges. President Trump's first Supreme Court pick was a federal judge straight out of central casting: Judge Neil Gorsuch of the U.S. Court of Appeals for the Tenth Circuit. Because these prospective justices have already issued multiple rulings from the federal bench, they have fashioned a judicial portfolio that makes their behavior on the Supreme Court that much more predictable.

4. *Increased participation by interest groups, including the organized bar, in the selection process.* Although organized interests occasionally mobilized to defeat Supreme Court nominees in the nineteenth and early twentieth centuries, the level and intensity of interest group participation in the modern process is unprecedented. Since World War II, interest groups have extended their influence into the early stages of judicial selection. The American Bar Association has been rating nominees to all federal courts since the early 1950s; outright negative (or even unenthusiastically positive) recommendations can damage a nominee substantially, if not derail the nomination altogether. Other groups, such as the Alliance for Justice, People for the American Way, and the Leadership Conference on Civil Rights, have made Supreme Court appointments a high priority for their organizations. During the George W. Bush administration, the Federalist Society, an organization of conservatives seeking reform of the American legal system, enjoyed unprecedented influence in the judicial selection process. By some accounts, the withdrawal of Harriet Miers's Supreme Court nomination (and the subsequent selection of Samuel Alito in her place) was shaped largely by the actions and commentary of Federalist Society luminaries such as Robert Bork, Randy Barnett, and John Yoo.[23] In 2016, the executive vice president of the Federalist Society, Leonard Leo, helped Donald Trump generate his own list of names for high court consideration.

5. *Increased media attention before and during Supreme Court confirmation hearings.* In the not-so-distant past, the media's spotlight would fall on a prospective Supreme Court justice only after being nominated, and even then the process of confirming the nominee was mostly an inside-the-beltway diversion. Today the

entire process—extending from rumors of a pending vacancy to the final confirmation vote—is a thoroughly public matter. National reporters assigned to cover the Supreme Court provide their readers with updated short lists of the candidates the president is considering. In a nod to this reality, Bill Clinton strategically floated the names of candidates to a hungry media contingent even before he decided on his final selections. This practice of "politics by trial balloon" provided Clinton with advance warning of the opposition he was inviting; it may also have provided the administration's enemies too much influence over the selection process. For example, in 1993 Senator Orrin Hatch and Senate Minority Leader Robert Dole of Kansas torpedoed the prospective Supreme Court nomination of Interior Secretary Bruce Babbitt with their not-so-subtle public hints about Babbitt's lack of judicial experience.[24] President Clinton's failure to commit to Babbitt before he underwent Hatch and Dole's rhetorical assault may have rescued the administration from considerable embarrassment. Yet it also invited public attacks from critics who might otherwise have feared the wrath of a White House already significantly invested in that candidate. More recently, President Obama's short list of prospective candidates underwent intense scrutiny in the media and elsewhere during the spring of 2009 and 2010.

6. *Advances in legal research technology.* In 1956, Attorney General Herbert Brownell sought to investigate the record of a prospective nominee for the Court, New Jersey Supreme Court justice William Brennan. To perform the task, Brownell did what any first-year law student would have done at that time: he read the printed New Jersey court reports, skimming Brennan's written opinions for clues to his philosophy. By the end of the twentieth century this quaint method of legal research had given way to computer searches conducted using the databases of LEXIS/NEXIS and WESTLAW, which in turn allowed officials to gather all of a prospective candidate's past judicial opinions, scholarship, and public commentary at the click of a mouse. Justice Department officials can even construct elaborate word searches to pinpoint the candidate's most controversial statements.

These advances in research technology are a double-edged sword: media outlets and opposition interest groups are just as likely to discover negative information about prospective candidates. Eleventh-hour revelations, such as the news that Supreme Court nominee G. Harrold Carswell had given a speech at a Ku Klux Klan rally (which helped to undermine his nomination in 1970), seem far less likely in the computer age. The ease of information gathering may also contribute to a streamlining of the selection process that favors lackluster candidates whose bland inoffensiveness renders them capable of surviving intense scrutiny of their backgrounds and opinions. For all the conservative critics' frustrations at some of Justice Souter's rulings, many have forgotten that it was Souter's complete lack of a controversial, substantive record on important legal issues—and thus the difficulty of attacking him—that made his candidacy so appealing to the George H. W. Bush administration.

These changes in the political landscape have profoundly influenced the process by which prospective Supreme Court nominees are identified and selected. In recent administrations, high-level political operatives who did not want to expend all of the president's political capital on a confirmation fight have bat-tled ardent ideologues hell-bent on transforming the constitutional landscape through the selection of right-thinking Supreme Court justices. The factors that have shaped the political environment for Supreme Court recruitment have tilted the Court toward professional judges and lawyers whose records and experiences tended to occur outside of the political arena. Whereas governors, U.S. senators, and even some high-profile presidential candidates once garnered serious consideration for the Supreme Court, candidates with relatively uncon-troversial public profiles now dominate short and long lists for the high Court. (See Table 16.1.)

Table 16.1 ■ Positions Held by Supreme Court Nominees at the Time of Their Nominations, 1937–2017			
Nominee	Year	Appointing president	Position previously held
Hugo Black	1937	Roosevelt	U.S. senator
Stanley Reed	1938	Roosevelt	U.S. solicitor general
Felix Frankfurter	1939	Roosevelt	Law professor
William O. Douglas	1939	Roosevelt	SEC chairman
Frank Murphy	1940	Roosevelt	U.S. attorney general
James Byrnes	1941	Roosevelt	U.S. senator
Harlan Stone (CJ)	1941	Roosevelt	U.S. Supreme Court associate justice
Robert Jackson	1941	Roosevelt	U.S. attorney general
Wiley Rutledge	1943	Roosevelt	Federal appellate judge
Harold Burton	1945	Truman	U.S. senator
Fred Vinson (CJ)	1946	Truman	U.S. secretary of the treasury
Tom C. Clark	1949	Truman	U.S. attorney general
Sherman Minton	1949	Truman	Federal appellate judge
Earl Warren (CJ)	1953	Eisenhower	Governor of California
John M. Harlan	1954	Eisenhower	Federal appellate judge
William Brennan	1956	Eisenhower	New Jersey Supreme Court judge
Charles Whittaker	1957	Eisenhower	Federal appellate judge

Nominee	Year	Appointing president	Position previously held
Potter Stewart	1958	Eisenhower	Federal appellate judge
Byron White	**1962**	**Kennedy**	**Deputy attorney general**
Arthur Goldberg	**1962**	**Kennedy**	**U.S. secretary of labor**
Abe Fortas	1965	Johnson	Private practice, presidential adviser
Thurgood Marshall	**1967**	**Johnson**	**U.S. solicitor general**
Abe Fortas (CJ, withdrew)	1968	Johnson	U.S. Supreme Court associate justice
Homer Thornberry (withdrew)	1968	Johnson	Federal appellate judge
Warren Burger (CJ)	1969	Nixon	Federal appellate judge
Clement Haynsworth (rejected)	1969	Nixon	Federal appellate judge
G. Harrold Carswell (rejected)	1970	Nixon	Federal appellate judge
Harry Blackmun	1970	Nixon	Federal appellate judge
Lewis Powell	1971	Nixon	Private practice
William Rehnquist	**1971**	**Nixon**	**Asst. attorney general**
John Paul Stevens	1975	Ford	Federal appellate judge
Sandra Day O'Connor	1981	Reagan	Arizona appellate judge
William Rehnquist (CJ)	1986	Reagan	U.S. Supreme Court associate justice
Antonin Scalia	1986	Reagan	Federal appellate judge
Robert Bork (rejected)	1987	Reagan	Federal appellate judge
Douglas Ginsburg (withdrew)	1987	Reagan	Federal appellate judge
Anthony Kennedy	1987	Reagan	Federal appellate judge
David Souter	1990	Bush I	Federal appellate judge

(Continued)

		Appointing	
Nominee	**Year**	**president**	**Position previously held**
Clarence Thomas	1991	Bush I	Federal appellate judge
Ruth Bader Ginsburg	1993	Clinton	Federal appellate judge
Stephen Breyer	1994	Clinton	Federal appellate judge
John Roberts (CJ)	2005	Bush II	Federal appellate judge
Harriet Miers (rejected)	**2005**	**Bush II**	**White House counsel**
Samuel Alito	2005	Bush II	Federal appellate judge
Sonya Sotomayor	2009	Obama	Federal appellate judge
Elena Kagan	**2010**	**Obama**	**U.S. solicitor general**
Merrick Garland (nomination expired at end of the Obama presidency)	2016	Obama	Federal appellate judge
Neil Gorsuch	2017	Trump	Federal appellate judge

Source: Compiled by the author.

Note: Nominees who came directly from executive or legislative branches are highlighted in bold.

President Barack Obama's ascension to the White House offered the prospect of a more daring approach to Supreme Court selections. First, the forty-fourth president enjoyed numerous political advantages over his most recent predecessors: by capturing 53 percent of the popular vote in 2008, Obama could rightfully claim a greater electoral mandate than Bill Clinton or George W. Bush, neither of whom ever broke the 51-percent mark in an election. Counting independents who caucused with the Democrats, Obama's party enjoyed a minimum eighteen-seat advantage in the Senate for much of his first two years in office, putting him tantalizingly close to a filibuster-proof majority in that chamber. Second, emboldened by his own experience as an instructor of constitutional law at the University of Chicago, President Obama took a more hands-on role in the selection process. Accordingly, he was in a strong position to champion a bolder nominee over the objections of more cautious advisors. Finally, during his first term as president Obama was tasked with replacing two reliable members of the moderate-to-liberal wing of the Court (Justices David Souter and John Paul Stevens), thus affording him a bit more latitude than if he was charged with replacing a key swing vote or a conservative.

With these advantages, Barack Obama could have nominated a big-name "pol" to the high court in the tradition of John Marshall, Hugo Black, and Earl Warren. Instead, he veered from modern selection patterns only modestly, and in a manner calculated more to defuse the political opposition than to excite his Democratic supporters. Neither of the two candidates he named—Judge Sonya Sotomayor and Solicitor General Elena Kagan—was a seasoned politician experienced in the rough-and-tumble world of legislating or governing. Judge Sotomayor identified as a career jurist, having served for seventeen years as a federal judge (she previously served on both a federal district court and a U.S. Court of Appeals). A year later, Obama's successful nomination of Solicitor General Elena Kagan gave the court its first justice with no previous judging experience in nearly forty years.[25] Still, Kagan's primary credentials—she had served as Harvard Law School dean before becoming solicitor general—distinguished her as a high-profile participant in the politics of the ivory tower, but not in the partisan politics of Washington, D.C. Both nominees were confirmed easily by modern standards: the Senate approved Sotomayor by a 68–31 vote, while Kagan garnered a 63–37 show of support.

As a candidate for president in 2016, Donald Trump flouted political norms on a regular basis. One might have predicted that he would go on to flout traditional norms in choosing a successor to Justice Scalia's seat as well. Perhaps Trump's first Supreme Court nominee would come from the ranks of Republican governors; at a minimum, Trump could have named the first state judge to the high court since Sandra Day O'Connor's appointment in 1981. Instead, President Trump played his first Supreme Court nomination by the book, deferring to strong political forces within the Republican Party that demanded a tried and true conservative. During the campaign he had asked Leonard Leo of the Federalist Society, a nationwide organization of conservative lawyers, to generate a list of names that he would in turn release to the public. According to Jeffrey Toobin, Leo "knew how to play the game—how to find a nominee who met Trump's ideological requirements as well as his own, while observing the proprieties expected of judicial nominees."[26] The lists of nominees Trump released in May and September of 2016 were dominated by reliably conservative judges including Gorsuch, a jurist with especially close ties to Leo's Federalist Society Network. President Trump then gave his most conservative supporters the judge they hoped for, naming Gorsuch as the latest in a string of highly qualified conservative Supreme Court nominees hailing from the U.S. Courts of Appeals.

TOO MUCH COURTESY? PRESIDENTIAL APPOINTMENTS TO THE LOWER FEDERAL COURTS

With 866 full-time federal judgeships now in existence, modern presidents have at their disposal a bulk of opportunities to place their overall stamp on judicial policymaking. Even under the most difficult of circumstances, a president can expect to fill as many as forty to fifty vacancies on the federal bench each year.

Still, the vast majority of lower federal court appointments remain the product of well-honed connections between judicial candidates and their sponsoring

U.S. senators. Jimmy Carter's short-lived attempt to displace this patronage system with merit-based "nominating commissions" ran into political obstacles and was disbanded quickly by his successor, Ronald Reagan. Subsequent presidents have tried to balance the demands of individual senators with the chief executive's goal of shaping the ideological makeup of the federal judiciary.[27] To that end, considerations of merit and ideology have played a significant role in the elevation of candidates to the courts of appeals, at least since the 1980s. President George W. Bush's aggressive campaign for extremely conservative judicial nominees rankled Senate Democrats so much that they filibustered ten of his most objectionable nominees during his first term as president. President Bush responded by offering two of those filibustered nominees (Charles Pickering and William Pryor) recess appointments to the U.S. Courts of Appeals, effective until the end of the following congressional session.[28] Even amid all this conflict, between 2001 and 2008, President Bush appointed sixty-two judges to the courts of appeals and 261 judges to the district courts, amassing an appointments record similar to that of other two-term presidents in the modern era.

Left-wing critics of President Obama complained that he was reluctant to appoint more committed liberal ideologues to the federal bench as a counterbalance to the ardent conservatives chosen by George W. Bush. The liberal Alliance for Justice, normally a loyal supporter of Democratic presidents, feared that Obama often ignored nominees from beyond the ideological safety zone—individuals who could be "counters to the Posners, the Easterbrooks."[29] By contrast, the most extreme of Obama's liberal nominees, California State Justice Goodwin Liu, saw his nomination to the Ninth Circuit filibustered in 2010, and then withdrawn the following year.

On the other hand, Obama's final total of 329 Article III judicial appointments in eight years matched his two predecessors, at least in quantity. Additionally, the Obama administration made great strides in diversifying the bench. For example, Obama appointed more women and Hispanics to federal judgeships than any president in history, and he appointed more Asian Americans (19) to the bench than all of his predecessors combined. In raw percentages, 42 percent of Obama's judges were female, while 37 percent were racial or ethnic minorities. By the time Obama left office in January 2017, white male judges constituted a minority of U.S. Courts of Appeals judges for the first time ever. The so-called "Obama judges" stand as the most diverse group in U.S. history in terms of terms of gender, ethnicity, and nationality.

Obama's more cautious approach to appointing ideologically extreme judges may have been his own reasoned reaction to the political environment in which he found himself. As was noted above, Senate opposition to lower court nominations has steadily increased in recent times. Between 1939 and 1977, the Senate Judiciary Committee approved nearly all lower court nominees for a full Senate vote on the merits; just one court of appeals nominee and six district court nominees received negative committee votes during that entire thirty-eight-year period.[30] By comparison, since the early 1980s, more than twice as many nominees have been reported out of committee unfavorably. According to the Congressional Research Service, all the objections raised against these nominees concerned their ideological orientation.[31] Many other candidates were left to wither in committee, with no action at all taken on their nominations. The Senate's decision to outlaw the filibustering of lower court nominees in November 2013 unclogged the process for President Obama's lower court nominees in the short term, but it did little to soothe the harsh partisanship that has infected the appointment process.

President Trump faced similar challenges in his early efforts to restock the courts. Although the Trump administration moved slowly in filling executive posts, it moved rapidly to nominate federal judges: Indeed, by nominating forty-four individuals to the bench during his first seven months as president, Donald Trump outpaced Presidents Obama and George W. Bush on this score. That said, Trump was not able to overcome the legacy of partisanship that has caused so many lower court confirmation battles in recent decades. In particular, Senate Democrats in 2017 showed an increased willingness to block Trump's nominees to the courts of appeals through the use of "blue slips," a Senate tradition that accords to senators of either party virtual veto power over nominees from their home state. Several key Senate Republicans (including Majority Leader Mitch McConnell and Judiciary Committee Chairman Chuck Grassley [R-IA]) suggested that the blue slip policy should either be limited to district court nominations or be eliminated entirely. If that happens, President Trump and his successors will enjoy far more discretion over the lower court selection process than did Presidents Bush and Obama—so long as the Senate remains in friendly partisan hands.

"MAY IT PLEASE THE COURT": PRESIDENTIAL INFLUENCE ON THE JUDICIAL PROCESS

The growth and bureaucratization of the Justice Department have facilitated more than just a thorough vetting of prospective Supreme Court nominees. They have also made possible greater White House involvement in the cases that flow to the Supreme Court, the lower federal courts, and the various state courts. The federal government has long been the busiest litigant in the federal courts and the Supreme Court; each day countless new lawsuits are filed against federal agencies such as the Department of Health and Human Services and the Department of Defense. Executive branch lawyers settle many such lawsuits, but others go to trial either before an administrative law judge or in a federal court.

Drawing on social scientist Marc Galanter's landmark framework for understanding the systematic features of a legal system, the executive branch is a "repeat player"—that is, a litigating actor engaged in many similar cases over time.[32] Accordingly, the federal government enjoys a number of advantages in the litigation process, including expertise, informal relationships with the other actors, a prior "bargaining reputation," and the ability to "play the odds" for advantages that may accrue only in later cases. All of these factors weigh heavily in the government's favor in most forms of litigation.

Recent presidents have sought to use these advantages to gain through the courts what they could not attain elsewhere, whether because of congressional inertia, concerted interest group opposition, or White House fears that legislative solutions would redound to the detriment of fellow party members in Congress. Unable to enact conservative modifications to the Voting Rights Act in the early 1990s, for example, the George H. W. Bush administration supported private legal efforts to overturn congressional districts that were drawn to protect certain racial groups. The Clinton administration switched sides and, beginning in 1993, supported many of those same districts. The Justice Department under Clinton also aggressively prosecuted Microsoft Corporation for antitrust violations in the late 1990s; by contrast, George W. Bush encouraged his own Justice Department to adopt a less aggressive approach in the Microsoft litigation. Following complaints that the United States had not adequately responded to unfair trade practices by China, the Obama administration in 2012 filed a lawsuit against that nation, charging that it had provided auto and auto parts companies with at least $1 billion in illegal export subsidies. Executive branch agencies with litigation expertise may also lend behind-the-scenes assistance in legal cases in which the government is not a direct party. Thus the Clinton administration lent support to private plaintiffs suing tobacco companies and gun manufacturers in the mid-to-late 1990s.

The federal government's repeat-player advantage also pays dividends for the White House when it takes an interest in cases before the Supreme Court. The solicitor general, who represents the United States in most such cases, enjoys an especially close relationship with the justices, no matter which party controls the White House. Not surprisingly, the solicitor general's office has enjoyed an extraordinary level of success before the Court, as reflected both in the Court's rulings on cases and, even more dramatically, in the Court's selection of which cases to hear.[33] Although frequently a petitioner or respondent before the Supreme Court, the solicitor general influences matters more subtly by submitting amicus curiae ("friend of the court") briefs in cases in which the U.S. government is not directly involved but in which it nonetheless takes an interest in the outcomes. In the 1960s Archibald Cox became the first solicitor general to aggressively involve his office in the filing of amicus briefs. From 1961 to 1965, Cox's office filed an average of seventeen amicus briefs per year, including twenty-eight in 1963 alone.[34] During the 1970s and 1980s, the federal government routinely filed amicus briefs in 20 percent to 30 percent of all cases decided by the Court, and sometimes in as many as half.

This high level of amicus filings by the U.S. government, which has held steady in recent years, is driven largely by perceptions that the Supreme Court serves as an important venue for deciding a range of politically significant legal issues. The Reagan administration in particular sought to use the amicus brief as a tool of constitutional change, and it achieved considerable success in this regard under its first solicitor general, Charles Fried.

The solicitor general and the president at times may differ on legal strategy. During the Nixon administration, Solicitor General Erwin Griswold declined to argue for the government before the Supreme Court in two cases involving national security and the military draft. The Carter administration's attorney general, Griffin Bell, engaged in a well-reported feud on the president's behalf with

Solicitor General Wade McCree concerning how to handle the controversial affirmative action case *Regents of the University of California v. Bakke* (1978).[35] Still, most solicitors general are chosen in the first place for their compatibility with the president's agenda, and they act accordingly to defend the president's interests. President Obama was so pleased with Elena Kagan's performance as his first solicitor general that he promoted her to the U.S. Supreme Court.

In the so-called "Obamacare litigation" that followed passage of the Affordable Care Act in 2010, the White House was on the defensive throughout. By refusing to take potential constitutional objections to the act more seriously when it was drafted, the Obama administration forfeited the chance to insert more favorable judicial review provisions into the text of the legislation. When the law was narrowly upheld in 2012, President Obama barely escaped a deathblow to his signature legislative achievement, and perhaps his reelection chances as well.

The fate of immigration lawsuits during the Obama presidency are also instructive. Throughout President Obama's first term in office, administration officials urged the Immigration and Naturalization Service (INS) and other agencies to strike a careful balance between enforcement and accommodation. Obama himself sought alternatives to deportation for those who would have qualified under legislative initiatives such as the Dream Act that failed to pass Congress. Into this political thicket arrived Arizona S.B. 1070 (the Support Our Law Enforcement and Safe Neighborhoods Act), which authorized local police to check the immigration status of every person stopped for other reasons. Whether or not the federal government was already authorized to make such stops, Arizona was assuming federal regulatory powers that might undermine consistent enforcement of the law and which threatened already delicate U.S. relations with Mexico and other Latin American states. Still, the Obama administration was hesitant to file a lawsuit, both because polls showed majority support for the law and because a court challenge would require administration lawyers to seek the overturning of a democratically passed law absent an explicit federal law in conflict with it.

The Justice Department finally filed suit against the State of Arizona fully two-and-a-half months after the Arizona law had technically been in place.[36] The primary considerations for filing were more political than legal. With five lawsuits already filed by civil rights groups and others, a failure to participate might be viewed as a sign of governmental apathy by groups at the core of the Democratic Party's constituency. Additionally, laws such as Arizona's S.B. 1070 were starting to pop up all around the country, as federal inaction on S.B. 1070 had encouraged frustrated state lawmakers to take matters into their own hands. In sum, the Department of Justice's lawsuit was a matter of defense—Arizona (and other states) had forced the administration's hand, compelling the Department of Justice to enter an arena that might offer limited prospects for success. Once again, the Obama administration narrowly escaped catastrophe in the courts: on June 25, 2012, the Court by a 5–3 vote nullified most of the more controversial provisions of the Arizona law.[37] Yet just four years later the same Court refused to countenance President Obama's attempts to exempt a class of individuals from the threat of deportation. Thus in *United States v. Texas* (2016)[38] the high court upheld a lower court injunction blocking President Obama's efforts to delay deportation of less than half of the 11 million undocumented aliens then living in the United States. Not to be outdone, President Trump's continued efforts to enact more restrictive immigration policies through executive decree should eventually end up before the high court as well.

PRESIDENTS AND THE JUDICIARY: AN UNEASY COURTSHIP

On April 2, 2012, President Barack Obama declared at a Rose Garden press conference that he was confident the Supreme Court would not overturn his signature health care law. Obama argued that it would be "unprecedented" for the Court to make such a dramatic power play over Congress; he warned against such an "extraordinary step of overturning a law that was passed by a strong majority of a democratically elected Congress."[39] Less than three months later, the Obama administration barely averted disaster, as the Supreme Court fell just one vote short of short-circuiting Obamacare. Though hailing from the very opposite end of the political spectrum, President Trump was equally critical of aggressive judicial rulings, especially those that upended his administration's controversial travel ban. Shortly after he took office in January 2017, Trump lashed out on several occasions at U.S District Judge James Robart, who had placed a nationwide hold on Trump's first travel ban. Then in March 2017 the president blasted yet another judicial ruling that blocked a revised version of the travel ban, suggesting it was a politically motivated decision that made the United States look "weak."[40]

Presidents Obama and Trump are not the first chief executives to take issue with the judicial branch's intrusion into national politics. The greater surprise is that President Obama felt he could achieve some measure of lasting success without judicial validation of his administration's signature achievements. Certainly President Obama should have known better—as a former constitutional law instructor, he was aware that there was nothing so "extraordinary" about the Supreme Court invalidating a law passed by a coordinate branch of government. Even without such legal training, President Trump instinctively knew that courts could be a valuable partner in the political wars he planned to wage, and thus his administration moved with lightning speed to fill Justice Scalia's high court seat as well as many of the most critical vacancies on the federal appellate courts.

Regardless of party, presidents who seek to cajole or threaten courts in hopes of steering them away from political battles do so at their own peril, and with little real hope of success. The far better strategy—and one with a track record of success—is to seek an alliance with the courts, integrating a carefully conceived litigation strategy as well as the strategic use of judicial appointments as part of an overall comprehensive approach to national policymaking. In this respect, time is very much on the chief executive's side. The president may suffer some setbacks in the short term, but over the long run presidents will be able to stock the lower courts (and in most cases, the Supreme Court as well) with likeminded jurists who are increasingly receptive to the president's initiatives. The scholar Robert Dahl

noted more than half a century ago that rather than holding firm to minority positions, the Court's policies over time normally fall into line with the views that are
dominant among the elected lawmaking majorities.[41] That should be good news
indeed for the president's supporters, so long as they can exhibit the patience necessary for such lasting change to occur.

NOTES

1. That first major victory would not come until December 22, 2017, when President Trump signed into law the Tax Cuts and Jobs Act of 2017.
2. Between 1993 and 2017, the only Supreme Court nominee to be denied a seat on the Court was Harriet Miers, President George W. Bush's nominee in 2005. After conservatives complained that she lacked the proper credentials for the high court, Miers formally withdrew her nomination on October 27, 2005.
3. Editorial, "Neil Gorsuch, the Nominee for a Stolen Seat," *New York Times*, January 31, 2017.
4. William Leuchtenburg, *The Supreme Court Reborn* (New York: Oxford University Press, 1995), 83.
5. See *Goldwater v. Carter*, 444 U.S. 996 (1979).
6. See *Clinton v. Jones*, 520 U.S. 681 (1997).
7. See generally, Kevin McMahon, *Nixon's Court* (Chicago: University of Chicago Press, 2011).
8. 567 U.S. 519 (2012).
9. 558 U.S. 310 (2010).
10. For a full discussion of the preconditions for such Court-related campaigns, see Donald Grier Stevenson Jr., *Campaigns and the Court: The U.S. Supreme Court in Presidential Elections* (New York: Columbia University Press, 1999).
11. *Dred Scott v. Sandford*, 60 U.S. 393 (1857).
12. Stevenson, *Campaigns and the Court*, 103.
13. See *United States v. Butler*, 297 U.S. 1 (1936); and *Schechter Poultry Corp. v. United States*, 295 U.S. 495 (1935).
14. Leuchtenburg, *The Supreme Court Reborn*, 107.
15. *Miranda v. Arizona*, 384 U.S. 436 (1966).
16. *Roe v. Wade*, 410 U.S. 113 (1973); Reagan is quoted in Stevenson, *Campaigns and the Court*, 204.
17. *Webster v. Reproductive Health Services*, 492 U.S. 490 (1989); and *Planned Parenthood v. Casey*, 505 U.S. 833 (1992).
18. "President Trump Narrows Supreme Court Nomination Down to Three Judges," *Christian Science Monitor*, January 24, 2017.
19. Quoted in David M. O'Brien, *Storm Center: The Supreme Court in American Politics*, 8th ed. (New York: W. W. Norton, 2008), 35.
20. John Anthony Maltese, *The Selling of Supreme Court Nominees* (Baltimore: Johns Hopkins University Press, 1995), 24.
21. The discussion of these factors is borrowed from David A. Yalof, *Pursuit of Justices* (Chicago: University of Chicago Press, 1999).
22. Stephen Hess, *Organizing the Presidency* (Washington, DC: Brookings Institution Press, 1988), 5.

23. The leading work on this topic is Steven M. Teles, *The Rise of the Conservative Legal Movement* (Princeton, NJ: Princeton University Press, 2008).

24. Richard Berke, "Hatch Assails Idea of Justice Babbitt," *New York Times,* June 9, 1993, A17.

25. Prior to Kagan, the last non-judge to receive a U.S. Supreme Court appointment was Assistant Attorney General William Rehnquist, who took his seat on the Court in January 1972. President George W. Bush's nomination of White House counsel Harriet Miers in 2005 would have enjoyed this distinction as well, but the subsequent withdrawal of her nomination left the string of judges nominated to the high court intact.

26. Jeffrey Toobin, "The Conservative Pipeline to the Supreme Court," *The New Yorker,* April 17, 2017.

27. For a fuller discussion of Carter's nominating commissions, as well as the politics of lower court appointments in general, see Sheldon Goldman, *Picking Federal Judges: Lower Court Selection from Roosevelt through Reagan* (New Haven, CT: Yale University Press, 1997).

28. Although the lower court appointment process was marked by considerable strife during both the 107th and 108th Congresses, by the end of his first term President George W. Bush had still managed to see 204 of his 260 nominees confirmed, with another twenty-four nominees still pending. After securing his reelection in November 2004, the emboldened president promised to renominate twenty of the unconfirmed candidates, including seven of the nominees filibustered by Senate Democrats during his first term. The conflict between President Bush and the Democratic minority in the Senate began to heat up even more during spring 2005, as Senate Majority Leader Bill Frist (R-TN) threatened to use his party's majority to permanently change Senate rules to prevent future filibusters on judicial nominees (this maneuver was nicknamed the "nuclear option"). Eventually a compromise was brokered by the so-called Gang of 14—a group of seven Senate Republicans and seven Senate Democrats who were determined to head off the looming crisis. Under the May 2005 agreement, the seven Senate Democrats agreed to allow five of the seven controversial nominees a vote by the entire Senate (all five were confirmed eventually); they further agreed to support future Democratic filibusters on nominees only in "extraordinary circumstances." In return, the seven Senate Republicans agreed to reject the "nuclear option" favored by party leaders.

29. Sheldon Goldman, Elliot Slotnick, and Sara Schiavoni, "Obama's Judiciary at Midterm," *Judicature* 94, no. 6 (2011): 272.

30. Denis Rutkus and Susan Smelser, "U.S. Circuit and District Court Nominations: Senate Rejections and Committee Votes Other than to Report Favorably," Congressional Research Service Report, March 24, 2009.

31. Ibid.

32. See Marc Galanter, "Why the 'Haves' Come Out Ahead: Speculations on the Limits of Legal Change," *Law and Society Review* 9 (Fall 1974): 95–151.

33. Rebecca Mae Salokar, *The Solicitor General: The Politics of Law* (Philadelphia: Temple University Press, 1992), 106–150.

34. Lincoln Caplan, *Tenth Justice* (New York: Vintage Books, 1987), 197.

35. *Regents of the University of California v. Bakke,* 438 U.S. 265 (1978).

36. See Jerry Markon and Michael Shear, "Justice Department Sues Arizona over Immigration Law," *Washington Post,* July 7, 2010, A1.

37. *Arizona v. United States*, 567 U.S. 387 (2012).

38. 579 U.S. ___ (2016).

39. Carolyn Kaster, "Obama: Supreme Court Overturning Health Care Would Be 'Unprecedented,'" CBS News, April 2, 2012, http://www.cbsnews.com/8301– 503544_162–57408181–503544/obama-supreme-court-overturning-health-care- would-be-unprecedented/.

40. Eugene Scott, "Trump Criticizes Latest Court Ruling against Travel Ban," CNN Politics, June 13, 2017, http://www.cnn.com/2017/06/13/politics/trump-tweet- ban-ninth-court/index.html.

41. Robert A. Dahl, "Decision-Making in a Democracy: The Supreme Court as a National Policymaker," *Journal of Public Law* 6 (Fall 1957): 279–295.

17

THE PRESIDENCY AND UNILATERAL POWER

A Taxonomy

Andrew Rudalevige

Hemmed in by the Constitution, presidents are continually tempted to act unilaterally. Doing so promises quick and decisive action and the opportunity to transform their preferences directly into public policy. Thus, throughout American history, but especially since the mid-twentieth century, presidents have interpreted the "executive power" granted them in Article II very broadly, as evidenced by George W. Bush's expansive claims regarding presidential conduct of the Global War on Terror, Barack Obama's generous exegesis of environmental and immigration law, and Donald Trump's early flurry of deregulatory initiatives. Presidents have been aided in this effort by their status as a unitary actor, by the growth of a massive administrative establishment, and, not least, by the willingness of the other branches to delegate power to them. In this chapter, Andrew Rudalevige provides a history and taxonomy of the president's unilateral powers in war and peace, and explores the real limits, both substantive and normative, of their going it alone.

In early 2016, campaigning to become president, Donald J. Trump argued that the incumbent in the White House was a weak leader. His evidence? Barack Obama's frequent use of unilateral administrative tools to advance policy goals. "We have a president that can't get anything done," Trump told an interviewer, "so he just keeps signing executive orders all over the place."[1]

A little more than a year later, as President Trump marked his first hundred days in office, the White House issued a press release headlined in breathless capital letters: "TAKING EXECUTIVE ACTION." It went on to claim that "President Trump has accomplished more in his first 100 days than any other President since Franklin Roosevelt."[2] The evidence? That Trump had signed more executive orders in that period than anyone from Truman through Obama.[3]

Trump had clearly discovered what so many of his predecessors had: the temptations and rewards of unilateral action. Like Obama, Trump had found advancing a legislative agenda to be difficult (though unlike Obama, his own party was in charge of both chambers of Congress). Like Obama, who argued in 2011 that "we can't wait for an increasingly dysfunctional Congress to do its job"—and George W. Bush, who bragged in 2004 that when "Congress wouldn't act . . . I signed an executive order. That means I did it on my own"[4]—Trump found that executive actions proved a more tractable way of claiming his administration was making progress on promised policy changes. As the president tweeted in mid-October, "Since Congress can't get its act together on HealthCare, I will be using the power of the pen to give great HealthCare to many people – FAST."[5]

Indeed, in the American constitutional system of intertwined institutions, doing things "on my own" is hugely tempting. Acting unilaterally promises quick and decisive action, the chance to short-circuit the tedious parliamentary procedures in which legislators delight, and to directly transform presidential preferences into public policy. As Bill Clinton aide Paul Begala put it, "Stroke of the pen, law of the land. Kind of cool."[6] Cool enough, anyway, for President Clinton to issue 364 executive orders in his eight years as president; during their subsequent terms, George W. Bush offered 288 orders, and Obama another 276 of his own.[7] Nor, as discussed later in this chapter, do executive orders constitute anything close to the whole of potential unilateral actions by the president—many other such actions are less visible but can reach even farther.

How much can the president do on his own? Certainly the president's roles as head of an expansive executive branch, as commander in chief, and, not least, as beneficiary of the constitutional grant of an amorphous "executive power" combine to empower presidential unilateralism, especially in times of national emergency. The fact that Congress is a divided body run by collective choices affords presidents inherent advantages: even if they don't get the last say, presidents often get to make the first move. That shapes the landscape over which subsequent options range. "The executive, in the exercise of its constitutional powers," Alexander Hamilton observed, "may establish an antecedent state of things, which ought to weigh in the legislative decision."[8] Yet presidents—who, after all, bear the name of "presider" rather than "decider"—form only one part of a system grounded in checks and balances. Congress is the first branch of government described in the Constitution. As James Madison argued, the executive's powers "must pre-suppose the existence of the laws to be executed," since "to see the laws faithfully executed constitutes the essence of the executive authority."[9] During the ratification debate, defenders of the Constitution did not dispute opponents' contention that "to live by one man's will [becomes] the cause of all men's misery." Instead, they sought to show that the president's will would be hemmed in by institutional checks, backstopped by Congress's power to impeach and remove him from office.[10] This early debate highlights a recurring dispute in American history: Can presidents act only when the Constitution, or Congress, gives them permission to act? Or can presidents act whenever they have not been forbidden to do so? Indeed, can presidents go even further and disregard "the legislative decision" if they think it is inconsistent with their own constitutional duties and the national interest? The answer to these questions has been forged not by scholarship but by history, worked out in practice through interbranch contestation.

The remainder of this chapter traces that practice, cataloging the tools of executive discretion and the scope of their use. The last four decades have witnessed both broad claims of unilateral presidential power and occasions of congressional backlash against those claims. President Obama's executive actions were an "existential threat to this nation," warned one member of Congress; a senator likewise cautioned President Trump that he "can sign whatever executive orders he likes, but the law is the law."[11] But on the whole, the presidential power to do things "on my own" has expanded. This raises the age-old question of efficiency versus accountability. In a system as large and fragmented as ours, there is real value in clear leadership. On the other hand, presidential leadership is not by definition virtuous, especially if it does violence to constitutional tenets. In 1952 Supreme Court Justice Robert Jackson put it this way:

> The claim of inherent and unrestricted presidential powers has long been a persuasive dialectical weapon in political controversy. . . . [But] with all its defects, delays and inconveniences, men have discovered no technique for long preserving free government except that the Executive be under the law, and that the law be made by parliamentary deliberations.[12]

THE EXECUTIVE POWER

In 1926 the journalist H. L. Mencken made a typically mordant observation: "No man would want to be President of the United States in strict accordance with the Constitution."[13]

A quick scan of Article II suggests why. The president is given the ability to grant reprieves and pardons, unchecked. But most of the office's other enumerated powers come with an asterisk of sorts. The president's treaties must be ratified, and appointments confirmed, by the Senate. The president may propose laws, but Congress must pass them; he may veto bills, but Congress can override him. He may conduct wars, but Congress declares them. The president may "require, in writing," the advice of his department heads, but Congress creates and funds the departments. Very little, it would seem, can be done by the president alone.

On the other hand, the first sentence of Article II declares that "the executive power shall be vested in a President of the United States of America." That "executive power" is nowhere defined. James Wilson, the most persuasive advocate of a strong executive at the Constitutional Convention, assured his colleagues that the only strictly executive powers under the Constitution were to carry out the laws and appoint personnel.[14] Nonetheless, the wording of the vesting clause has suggested to many—and certainly to many presidents—a broader reading.

For one thing, the parallel language pertaining to Congress in Article I includes a qualifier: "All legislative powers *herein granted* shall be vested in a Congress of the United States, which shall consist of a Senate and House of Representatives." Proponents of presidential authority as early as the George Washington administration argued that this discrepancy means the executive power goes beyond the brief list of powers noted above. Others link the vesting clause to other clear or implied authorities. Grover Cleveland, for example, argued that the president possesses "a grant of all the power necessary to the performance of his duty in the faithful execution of the laws." Others, including the Supreme Court, have suggested that inherent powers are implied by the president's oath of office to "preserve, protect, and defend the Constitution," or by the title of commander in chief, even in peacetime, especially now that large standing armies have become a permanent part of American governance.[15] Most presidents have believed that as long as an initiative was not specifically forbidden by the Constitution, then it was (as Theodore Roosevelt put it) "not only [the President's] right but his duty to do anything that the needs of the Nation required,"[16] This logic had special force in times of national emergency, which activated what the seventeenth-century English philosopher John Locke called "prerogative"—the power of the executive "to act according to discretion, for the publick good, without the prescription of the Law, and sometimes even against it." Abraham Lincoln argued, in the context of the Civil War, that "measures, otherwise unconstitutional, might become lawful, by becoming indispensable to the preservation of the constitution, through the preservation of the nation." After the September 11, 2001, terrorist attacks, George W. Bush's Justice Department advised him that no statute could "place any limits on the President's determinations as to any terrorist threat, the amount of military force to be used in response, or the method, timing, and nature of the response. These decisions, under our Constitution, are for the President alone to make."[17]

These claims have hardly gone unchallenged. After the Civil War, the Supreme Court upbraided Lincoln, arguing that any notion that the Constitution could be suspended by some "theory of necessity" was "pernicious" and "false." In 2004 the Court likewise reminded Bush that "a state of war is not a blank check for the President." William Howard Taft, rebutting his one-time mentor, Roosevelt, stated that "the President can exercise no power which cannot be fairly and reasonably traced to some specific grant of power. . . . There is no undefined residuum of power which he can exercise because it seems to him to be in the public interest."[18] The range of presidential discretion has also ebbed and flowed with political tides. In the 1970s, reacting to the steady expansion of the office (and the more recent growth spurt spurred by the Vietnam War and the Watergate scandal) into what Arthur Schlesinger Jr. enduringly called the "imperial presidency," legislators pushed back.[19] In a series of enactments, they sought to create a much greater role for Congress in interbranch relations. Even a partial list of laws enacted during that decade gives a sense of the scope of Congress's ambition: the War Powers

Resolution, the Intelligence Oversight Act, the Foreign Intelligence Surveillance Act, the Congressional Budget and Impoundment Control Act, the Freedom of Information Act, the Independent Counsel Act. In 1980 former president Gerald Ford complained that congressional efforts had been so successful that "we have not an imperial presidency but an imperiled presidency."[20]

Yet the next thirty-plus years would see presidents regain much of the ground they had lost, either by their own initiative or because Congress was unwilling to commit the time and political capital necessary to enforce the rules it had imposed. Presidents retained a solid base of authority grounded in their ability to grab the spotlight and set the public agenda, as well as in the commander-in-chief power and in executive authority over policy implementation through appointments and centralized management. Especially after Ronald Reagan's election in 1980, they refined these tools to enhance their influence over bureaucratic agencies and avoid legislative dictation. Further, Congress let the consultation procedures laid out in law—especially in the War Powers Resolution and Intelligence Oversight Act—be enforced on presidential terms, which is to say, rarely.[21] Even Congress's ultimate weapon, the process of impeaching the president, was exercised in late 1998 in the face of such hostile public opinion that it failed, bringing the independent counsel statute down with it as collateral damage. After the September 11 attacks, an array of broad new discretionary powers were granted to the president, and older ones were reasserted. Thus, when Donald Trump arrived in the Oval Office he found it already equipped with a full toolkit of unilateral powers.

THE GROWTH OF EXECUTIVE UNILATERALISM: THE TOOLS AT HAND

How has historical practice equipped presidents for unilateral action? The answer is wide ranging, but in general presidents have engaged in strategies to control bureaucratic behavior and thus influence policy implementation, or they have exercised powers that flow from specific emergency situations.

Controlling Bureaucratic Behavior

The president's power as chief executive expanded in concert with the growth of the executive establishment. More than 4 million people now work for the executive branch, spread across fifteen cabinet departments and nearly sixty independent agencies.[22] They report to the president but often have conflicting loyalties. Legislative power over their agencies' statutory missions and budgets; the contrast between the long tenure granted to civil servants and the relatively short presidential term; the conflicting demands of relevant interest groups and the national interest—all these mean that the president's preferences are far from automatically enforced upon the permanent government. This requires presidents to bargain with the bureaucracy, much as they must with members of Congress: many directives that we think of as "unilateral" had their origins outside the Executive Office of the

President. Even those that spring from the White House itself normally go through a long process of "clearance" that allows the departments and agencies to weigh in and sometimes even to exercise an informal veto over an order's issuance.[23]

But coordinating bureaucratic behavior is worth the effort, for it means controlling policy. Thus presidents have reacted to that challenge in various ways. One tactic has been to centralize functions in a large White House organization that can serve either to ride herd on or simply to evade the wider executive branch. The personal staff available to presidents has grown from a handful of aides under Franklin Roosevelt to as many as 2,000 assistants with substantive duties under Barack Obama. New staff units can be created by each president to reflect personal priorities or societal concerns, such as health care reform (Barack Obama) or trade policy (Donald Trump). These aides do not require Senate confirmation and do not suffer from divided loyalties; they give the president the resources to coordinate, or sometimes compete with, the advice given by bureaucratic actors. Critics worry that centralization leads to the appointment of White House "czars" who are not accountable to Congress even as they oversee Senate-confirmed agency heads.[24] Occasionally the temptation to use loyal staffs to carry out policy has overtaken presidents' better judgment, as in the 1980s Iran-contra scandal that saw National Security Council aides engaged in covert military operations and financial chicanery.[25]

From its position astride the annual budget process, the Office of Management and Budget (OMB) in particular gives the president powerful leverage over bureaucratic behavior. Since 1921 federal law has required a unified executive budget, affording presidents a useful mechanism for managing their agenda. In 1939 Franklin Roosevelt moved the OMB's predecessor, the Bureau of the Budget, from the Treasury department to the Executive Office of the President. Over time, the OMB has picked up various management functions, as reflected in its current name, including the central clearance of draft presidential directives noted above. Its ability to link funding recommendations to agency behavior and performance, even tacitly, gives it real clout.

Another method for controlling bureaucratic behavior is controlling the people who run the bureaucracy.[26] As the Reagan administration credo had it, "Personnel Is Policy."[27] Presidents pay close attention to those personnel, starting with the 5,200 executive branch political appointments each president gets to make, ranging from the cabinet secretaries all the way to posts deep within the bureaucracy. By appointing personal loyalists throughout the executive branch—even, sometimes, to ostensibly nonpartisan positions such as inspector general and U.S. attorney—presidents have sought, in the words of one aide to George W. Bush, to "implant their DNA throughout the government." To clone that DNA more widely, they have developed aggressive personnel recruitment and vetting operations. Reportedly, the search for those personally loyal to the new president slowed the Trump administration's efforts to fill subcabinet posts across the wider executive branch.[28] These efforts can be counterproductive. Loyalty that overshadows competence can lead to performance in office that reflects badly on the president.

Although high-level appointees must receive Senate confirmation, the sheer size of the federal government means that many appointments have been vested directly in the president—a population expanded by more than 200 positions by congressional action in 2012.[29] The "recess appointment," which derives from a provision in Article II that allows presidents to fill vacancies while the Senate is in recess, is another useful unilateral tool for circumventing the confirmation process. President Reagan made nearly 250 recess appointments in eight years, Clinton nearly 140, and George W. Bush more than 170.[30] But starting in 2007 the Senate held pro forma sessions even during breaks in the legislative year, a practice that continued through the Obama and Trump administrations. The idea was that the Senate would never formally be in recess, thus preventing recess appointments. Nonetheless, in January 2012 President Obama installed Richard Cordray as head of the new Consumer Financial Protection Bureau. Obama declared that the pro forma sessions did not conduct Senate business (this was mostly true) and therefore should not count as sessions at all (this was entirely dubious). The Supreme Court ultimately ruled against Obama, though upholding presidents' general power to make such appointments during recesses of ten days or more.[31]

Controlling Process

One of the president's most important duties is to "faithfully" execute the law. But the vagueness of many congressional enactments means that the specifics of that fidelity are subject to interpretation. In other cases, presidents may believe that part of a statute is unconstitutional and should not be executed. Presidents have therefore sought unilateral influence over the specifics of policy implementation. They use devices ranging from the subtle manipulation of the agency rulemaking process to the issuance of direct administrative commands.

Rulemaking and Regulatory Review. For many reasons, including the complexity of contemporary issues and legislative lassitude, Congress often writes statutes that delegate authority to the executive branch to write the rules that transform the law's general intent into specific governmental action.

The importance of the rulemaking process rose as the federal government grew. By the 1970s federal regulation reached into most corners of American life. Because the rulemaking process is so complex, the regulations issued by executive agencies serve as a low-profile instrument for effecting tangible policy change, sometimes in ways not anticipated by a statute's sponsors.[32] For example, in early 2002 Congress passed the No Child Left Behind (NCLB) education reform act. But how its testing and accountability requirements would affect schools and students was not clear until the Department of Education issued rules governing what kind of tests were required and how state standards for measuring pupil performance would be defined. The department continued to issue revised regulations throughout both terms of the Bush administration, even as the act's reauthorization languished. When Barack Obama took over, the law was still not reauthorized, so he effectively rewrote parts of it through his "Race to the Top" funding initiative and by offering states waivers from key NCLB requirements in exchange for their adopting his preferred policy direction. Congress finally replaced NCLB in late 2015, reining in these tools, only to see the Obama administration issue new regulations to which many legislators objected—in early 2017 they invoked the little-used Congressional Review Act to rescind Obama's rules.[33] Yet the Trump administration, in its turn, also interpreted the new law in ways not foreseen by state-level educators and their congressional allies.[34]

Part of the appeal of the personnel strategy is that it helps ensure that even lower-level appointees are in tune with administration policy preferences when it comes to writing regulations. It is no accident that the Department of Education is one of the most politicized agencies in the federal government.[35] Environmental, workplace safety, and health care policies have also attracted a good deal of recent attention from presidents seeking to shape regulatory outcomes. Rules written by the Environmental Protection Agency (EPA) were particularly controversial under Obama. As his legislative initiatives against climate change stalled in Congress, Obama's EPA issued a series of new rules known as the Clean Power Plan (CPP), which opponents charged went well beyond the authority granted the agency by the Clean Air Act. The Trump administration reacted by halting some of the CPP rules not yet fully in effect, declining to defend others in court, and announcing it would rewrite still others. Trump also sought to reverse—or simply not enforce— Obama-era regulations reining in the financial sector and those extending broader rights to the employees of federal contractors.

One key mechanism helping presidents shape these regulatory outcomes more systematically is the OMB's process of "central clearance." In February 1981, after fits and starts in this direction by earlier presidents, Ronald Reagan issued Executive Order 12291, which declared that "regulatory action shall not be undertaken unless the potential benefits to society for the regulation outweigh the potential costs to society." The OMB's Office of Information and Regulatory Affairs (OIRA) was granted authority to recommend that regulations be withdrawn if they did not meet that test. In 2011 the Obama White House added a requirement that old or redundant rules be regularly reviewed and reconsidered—and in 2017, President Trump directed that for every new regulation proposed, federal agencies had to come up with two that should be removed from the books.[36] Despite intermittent congressional grumbling about the elevation of White House ideology over agency expertise, and worries that presidents are usurping the rulemaking power formally vested directly in those agencies, it has remained in place across presidencies of both parties for more than thirty-five years.

Signing Statements and Item Vetoes. Another means that presidents use to direct policy implementation is the issuance of signing statements when they sign bills into law. These statements give the president a chance to comment on various aspects of the new statute: to congratulate its sponsors or complain about media coverage, but also, more crucially, to influence its judicial interpretation, guide agency rulemaking, and announce how the executive branch will enforce any disputed provisions. Although examples of signing statements can be found as far back as the Monroe administration, Reagan and his successors pioneered a more systematic usage. George W. Bush's use of signing statements to declare certain items within bills unconstitutional attracted considerable attention because of the scale and scope of their issuance. By one count, he issued more statements than all other presidents combined, recording nearly 1,200 objections to parts of more than 170 laws—including 116 separate objections to the Consolidated Appropriations Act of 2005 alone.[37] A 1986 memo by Reagan aide Samuel Alito (who now sits on the Supreme Court) noted that "our primary objective is to ensure that Presidential signing statements assume their rightful place in the interpretation of legislation." Alito acknowledged the "potential increase of presidential power" these statements entailed and the likely resentment they would stir in Congress. He also asked a key question: "What happens when there is a clear conflict between the congressional and presidential understanding? Whose intent controls?"[38] Alito offered no answer to this question. But presidents have answered clearly: "mine!"

Most commonly, signing statements serve as a means for the president to object to congressional incursions across the border between Articles I and II. Barack Obama claimed that "no one doubts that it is appropriate to use signing statements to protect a president's constitutional prerogatives," and he issued about thirty-five such statements during his administration.[39] Provisions requiring certain types of appointments, or that presidents submit legislation, are common targets; presidents usually say they will interpret such statutes as suggestions rather than dictates. Presidents have routinely included language in signing statements that rejects what Donald Trump called "clearly unconstitutional provisions" in foreign policy-making: those "that purport to displace the President's exclusive constitutional authority."[40] In early 2013 an Obama signing statement regarding language constraining the president's discretion over the detention of foreign fighters in the war on terror decried "unwarranted interference by Members of Congress. [This section of the law] . . . could interfere with my ability as Commander in Chief to make time-sensitive determinations about the appropriate disposition of detainees in an active area of hostilities. . . . My Administration will implement it to avoid the constitutional conflict."[41]

Such avoidance effectively means ignoring a statute's intent. After Reagan issued a national security directive with strict enforcement provisions governing leaks of sensitive information, Congress passed a bill forbidding the enforcement of those provisions. Reagan signed the bill but stated in doing so that he would enforce his directive, not the ban. Since that language "impermissibly interfered with my ability to prevent unauthorized disclosures of our most sensitive diplomatic, military, and intelligence activities," Reagan said, "in accordance with my sworn obligation to preserve, protect, and defend the Constitution, [it] will be considered of no force or effect."[42] This tactic aroused particular controversy in late 2005 when George W. Bush asserted that he would construe the Detainee Treatment Act's ban against "cruel, inhuman, or degrading treatment or punishment" of prisoners captured in the War on Terror "in a manner consistent with the constitutional authority of the President to supervise the unitary executive branch and as Commander in Chief and consistent with the constitutional limitations on the judicial power."[43] Bush's argument was that congressional regulation of detainee treatment was itself unconstitutional because it overrode the president's authority as commander in chief to conduct the war as he saw fit. Yet whether that power was exclusively executive was far from clear. Others pointed to Congress's Article I power to "make rules for . . . the regulation of the land and naval forces" and "rules concerning capture on land or water."

In any case, signing statements provide a clear example of how presidents claim the right to determine how—even if—laws will be implemented. The language presidents use to assert that claim may be formulaic, but the claim itself is a broad affirmation of the executive power. Still, the practical effect of signing statements on policy implementation is hard to determine. A 2008 report by a congressional auditor found that executive agencies had implemented twenty of twenty-nine selected statutory provisions in accordance with the president's directions, but that courts had placed little reliance on them in parsing the meaning of statutes.[44] Signing statements are a variant of the line-item veto most state governors have. Unlike those governors, presidents may not veto specific provisions of legislation. But this has not stopped them from long claiming the right to refuse to spend appropriated funds when, as in Ulysses Grant's declaration, these funds are "of purely private or local interest." At times Congress has given presidents discretionary impoundment power in order to limit expenditures. President Nixon upped the ante by arguing that this was not necessary—that although Congress had the power to appropriate funds, the executive power covered their actual expenditure. "The Constitutional right of the President of the United States to impound funds," he claimed, "is absolutely clear." Nixon's impoundments eventually encompassed about a fifth of the federal government's discretionary spending, aimed largely at programs whose passage he had opposed.[45] That practice was made illegal by the 1974 Impoundment Control Act and declared unconstitutional in the 1975 case *Train v. City of New York*.[46] Still, the issue of presidential control of spending has never gone away. Times of budget deficit tend to revive pressure for some form of line-item veto, peaking in 1996 when Congress provided the president with "enhanced rescission" power. This allowed the president's vetoes of specific spending or revenue items to go into effect unless Congress passed a bill to reinstate them (a bill that could itself be vetoed). President Clinton used briefly what one senator called "the most significant delegation of authority by the Congress to the President since the Constitution was ratified," but the law was declared unconstitutional by the Supreme Court in 1998. With budget deficits pushing $1.5 trillion annually when Barack Obama took office, a bipartisan group of senators made similar proposals in the spring of 2009.[47] Interestingly, as battles over spending continued into Obama's second term, threats to default on the $16 trillion national debt by failing to raise the statutory debt limit prompted another call for unilateralism: Obama could ignore the debt limit law, it was argued, because an obscure clause in the Fourteenth Amendment to the Constitution held that "the public debt of the United States . . . shall not be questioned." Obama, however, declined to read the Constitution this way.

Executive Orders, Memoranda, and other Directives. A crucial instrument for executing the law is the presidential directive. These take various forms and names, including executive orders, proclamations, national security decision documents, and presidential memoranda.[48] By whatever name, they are presidential actions intended to shape the manner in which the president's powers are carried out by the executive branch. Such directives can serve not just as complements to statute—that is, seeking to shape its implementation—but as substitutes for legislation presidents failed to convince Congress to adopt.

The best-known unilateral presidential directive is the executive order, a formal document aimed at, and governing the actions of, government officials and agencies. Recent presidents have issued an average of three per month during their terms—and at least 30,000 overall since 1789.[49]

Executive orders typically make for uninspiring reading. They lay out careful definitions; they set agency priorities and procedures, prodding the development of future action; they structure institutions by organizing task forces, reorganizing agencies, and shaping decision-making processes. Sometimes they are largely symbolic—an early Trump order, for instance, declared that "it shall be the policy of the executive branch to reduce crime in America."[50] But the dull prose disguises their real power to control national security strategy or to effect new and important policies. Presidents have used executive orders to create everything from Indian reservations to marine sanctuaries and to mold policies ranging from federal procurement (a multibillion-dollar tool to influence private-sector behavior) to the treatment of suspected terrorists detained at Guantánamo Bay. Orders can determine how, and how aggressively, a statute is implemented—note in this regard the sharp contrast between Obama's and Trump's priorities in enforcing immigration law, or Trump's efforts to temporarily bar refugees from entering the United States. Nor are other directives less potentially potent. The Louisiana Purchase was consummated by an executive order in the form of a proclamation, as was the emancipation of the slaves during the Civil War. One study found that of a "top ten" list of high-salience executive actions taken by Obama—including the Clean Power Plan, gun control efforts, the DACA program protecting immigrants who had entered the United States illegally as children, the swap of Taliban detainees for a captured American serviceman, and delays in implementing portions of the Affordable Care Act—none were achieved via formal executive order. Instead, Obama used tools like memoranda to department heads, national security directives, and implementation guidance issued by executive agencies in order to move these policies forward.[51]

A recent trend has been for new presidents to kick off their terms by issuing multiple directives designed to set the symbolic tone for their administration. One of Bill Clinton's first actions in January 1993 was to end a "gag rule" that had, in the Reagan and George H. W. Bush administrations, prohibited abortion counseling and referrals by family planning clinics that received federal funds. George W. Bush reversed Clinton's order in January 2001. Eight years later, Barack Obama restored it. Eight years after that, Donald Trump put the gag rule back in place. He also issued a flurry of other directives reversing Obama administration policies concerning everything from limits on cross-country energy pipelines to the federal approach toward "sanctuary cities" reluctant to enforce immigration law.

As this "ping pong of presidential power" suggests, executive orders are both powerful and constrained.[52] Although they have the force of law, they can be overturned not only by subsequent administrations, but also by congressional action or court ruling. Obama's 2014 effort to forestall the deportation of perhaps 4 million parents of American citizens, for instance, never took effect.[53] Trump's orders regarding the "travel ban" and sanctuary cities were also delayed or pared down in court. Obama aide David Plouffe admitted that "you can't just sit there and kind of fantasize about what would be great to do. In a lot of these areas, there are limits."[54]

Still, outright negation of a presidential directive is relatively rare. And in the interim, such orders can give the president power to mold or remold the policy landscape, thereby shaping Hamilton's "antecedent state of things." Like regulations, executive orders often move under the political radar screen. Unlike regulations, their formulation may legally evade public comment. Although the number of executive orders issued annually by presidents has dropped since the early 1940s, the number of significant orders has risen dramatically—one survey found that the proportion of substantively significant orders tripled from the 1950s to the 1990s.[55] And, as noted, other types of directives can substitute for executive orders: in 2013, for instance, Obama issued just twenty executive orders all year—but forty-one presidential memorandums.

The ability to utilize any of these directives increases with the size of the U.S. Code, since they often embody the unintended consequences of vague statutory language or past congressional delegation. Clinton's 1996 set-aside of millions of acres of Utah land as a national monument, for example, rested on a 1906 statute long forgotten by Congress, but not by presidents. Franklin Roosevelt closed the banks in 1933 under authority granted to Woodrow Wilson in World War I. Even congressional efforts to constrain executive authority sometimes legitimate it. In 1977 Congress passed the International Emergency Economic Powers Act (IEEPA) to limit the use of certain emergency powers. But by providing a statutory process for declaring emergencies as a means of preventing economic transactions with disfavored regimes, Congress legitimized a previously shadowy claim to power—and presidents invoked the act to issue executive orders declaring thirty "national emergencies" between 1979 and 2000, when the law was reauthorized. In September 2017 President Trump even threatened to invoke the IEEPA to block American trade with any country doing business with North Korea, in the wake of that nation's provocative series of nuclear tests.[56]

Presidential directives are less contentious when clearly grounded in a statute, or when they move in areas unaddressed by congressional enactment. Greater controversy occurs when orders seek to elide those enactments. As Clinton aide Rahm Emanuel put it in 1998, "Sometimes we use [an executive order] in reaction to legislative delay or setbacks. Obviously, you'd rather pass legislation that can do X, but you're willing to make whatever progress you can on an agenda item."[57] For example, in mid-2012 President Obama directed the Department of Homeland Security to defer all deportations of young illegal immigrants who met certain other conditions. This happened to be the population that would have been protected by the so-called Dream Act the administration favored—but that act had failed to win congressional approval in 2010.[58] In 2017, President Trump announced that he would rescind Obama's directive, though he challenged Congress to grant the "Dreamers" legal status through legislation.

Orders can also stir up opposition when they rely not on clearly delegated authority, but on a broadly conceived sense of the executive power. Consider, for instance, the brief and vague justification offered by Harry Truman when he nationalized America's steel mills: it was done "by virtue of the authority vested in me by the Constitution and laws of the United States, and as President of the United States."[59] Federal courts tend to move case by case when considering executive orders, but they usually give presidents the benefit of the doubt when Congress has failed to decide an issue over a prolonged period. Practice trumps theory: a case in the early twentieth century suggested that since "government is a practical affair, intended for practical men," courts should presume that "unauthorized acts [by the president] would not have been allowed [by Congress] to be so often repeated as to crystallize into a regular practice."[60] Presidents, then, may proceed confidently in the absence of congressional disapproval. Even when faced with it, they often choose to act on the assumption that Congress will acquiesce eventually; often, they are right.

Emergency Powers in Peace and War

Crises empower the executive branch. A menacing world enhances the value of centralized leadership's swift decision-making capacity. By the middle of the twentieth century, which was marked by wars cold and hot, the United States had settled into a seemingly perpetual period of crisis. What would have been "emergencies in policy" in the world before World War II, Richard E. Neustadt wrote in 1960, quickly became business as usual—"a way of life."[61] With the threat of nuclear Armageddon, and then international terrorism, as the backdrop, national security became the primary justification for unilateral executive action in the post–World War II era. Such action was often encouraged and empowered by legislative delegation.

Domestic Crisis. Because threats to security do not always come from abroad, presidents may wield emergency powers during periods of economic instability, domestic unrest, or natural disaster. "In the event Congress shall fail to act, and act adequately, I shall accept the responsibility, and I will act," Franklin Roosevelt declared in 1942. "The President has the powers, under the Constitution, and under Congressional acts, to take measures necessary to avert a disaster." Roosevelt was seeking a law authorizing wage and price controls, and he got one. Indeed, although FDR relied heavily on executive initiatives to attack the Great Depression and rally the nation (he issued 654 executive orders in 1933 alone), in most cases he received quick and sometimes retroactive congressional approval.

Subsequent presidents have also received blanket authority from Congress to deal with economic crises. Richard Nixon was able to impose wage and price controls and take the dollar off the gold standard in August 1971. The Emergency Economic Stabilization Act of 2008 gave George W. Bush's Treasury department wide discretion to disburse $700 billion in funds to prop up the collapsing banking sector. Presidential authority over efforts to help the economy was augmented yet again by the $787 billion stimulus act passed in 2009.[62]

Domestic Unrest and Natural Disaster. Presidential emergency powers include stand-by authority to call out federal troops or take control of state national guards in order to quell domestic unrest or deter violence. Such authority has been used in the United States to put down strikes, protect mail delivery, and impose order during natural disasters and urban riots.

During the nineteenth century, the most common use of presidential police power involved labor unrest. Hoping to prevent violence between strikers and company security forces, presidents often used troops to break strikes. In the 1950s and 1960s, presidents deployed federal troops or state national guards to keep the peace during efforts to enforce racial desegregation. In 1957 Dwight Eisenhower sent troops to Little Rock, Arkansas, to protect children enrolling in integrated schools from angry mobs. During the late 1960s, when lawless disorder was instead in inner cities or linked to U.S. involvement in Vietnam, soldiers again were used frequently to maintain the peace. As recently as 1992, George H. W. Bush sent Marines to help quell the looting triggered by the acquittal of white Los Angeles police officers accused in the severe beating of Rodney King, an African American suspect.

Presidential emergency powers are also invoked frequently during natural disasters. By declaring a local state of emergency, the president sets in motion government machinery that can provide immediate food, shelter, and police protection, as well as longer-term federal aid. Barack Obama declared multiple states of emergency after "Superstorm" Sandy devastated the mid-Atlantic coast—just before the 2012 election. One of Donald Trump's first external tests was reacting to the one-two punch of Hurricanes Harvey and Irma in Texas and Florida, respectively, in the early fall of 2017. But such powers can be a double-edged sword. In August 1992 Florida residents complained bitterly about the government's tardy response to Hurricane Andrew, hurting then-president George H. W. Bush in November. Far worse, after Hurricane Katrina hammered the Gulf Coast in 2005, federal officials' slow reaction to, and even apparent denial of, the chaos in New Orleans prompted widespread anger at the perceived incompetence of George W. Bush's administration.[63] Trump's seeming indifference to hurricane-stricken Puerto Rico, by comparison to Texas and Florida, elicited bitter criticism too.[64] Expectations for presidential action in response to domestic unrest and natural disasters may be inflated (not least by presidential promises), but they are no less real for that.

War Powers. In foreign relations, and most of all in times of war, presidential powers reach their greatest expanse. Since 1789 the United States has entered into myriad hostilities of all shapes and sizes, from declared wars to brief "police actions." In each instance, presidents have asserted claims to inherent powers to deal with the threat at hand.[65]

These claims often are based on a broad reading of the executive power. The 1936 Supreme Court decision *U.S. v. Curtiss-Wright*—a text cherished by presidents, though by few scholars of constitutional law—spoke of the "very delicate, plenary, and exclusive power of the President as the sole organ of the federal government in the field of international relations—a power which does not require as a basis for its exercise an act of Congress."[66] When Franklin Roosevelt sought to aid

Adolph Hitler's enemies, despite legislative efforts to maintain American neutrality, he declared first a "limited" and then (after the fall of France) an "unlimited" state of emergency. Roosevelt also concluded a series of executive agreements making important commitments to foreign governments. Most famously the United States transferred fifty destroyers to Britain in return for eight Caribbean naval bases. The attorney general's opinion justifying the agreement was grounded partly in the "plenary powers of the President as Commander-in-Chief of the Army and Navy and as head of state in its relations with foreign countries."[67]

This formulation stuck. When President Reagan sent Marines to Lebanon in 1982, for instance, he said the troops had been deployed under his "constitutional authority with respect to the conduct of foreign relations and as Commander-in-Chief." Truman never sought congressional approval for the Korean War; and although George H. W. Bush did for the first Gulf War, he said he did not need to: "I didn't have to get permission from some old goat in the United States Congress to kick Saddam Hussein out of Kuwait." An interesting twist in such cases was the erroneous claim that decisions by international organizations such as the United Nations and the North Atlantic Treaty Organization (NATO) could substitute for congressional action in activating presidential war powers—or that congressional approval was not required because the events in question (like the 2011 NATO operation against the Qaddafi regime in Libya) were not actually "hostilities."[68]

On the whole, presidents have resisted admitting to an absolute need for external authorization of any sort in such circumstances; instead they may assert, as George W. Bush's Justice Department wrote in 2002, that "the Constitution grants the President unilateral power to take military action to protect the national security interests of the United States. . . . This independent authority is *supplemented* by congressional authorization."[69] Even so, wartime also tends to lead to broad congressional grants of executive authority to prosecute war, on both the military and economic fronts. Woodrow Wilson and Franklin Roosevelt, during World Wars I and II, respectively, received such grants. Congress also authorized the first Gulf War in 1991 and the second in 2003, voting in the latter case to grant largely unfettered autonomy to George W. Bush to renew the fight with Saddam Hussein. In 1964 and 2001, even more expansive discretionary powers were delegated to the president to allow him to respond to outside aggression: the disputed Gulf of Tonkin attacks in Vietnam and the terrorist attacks on New York and Washington. In September 2001 Congress resolved that "the president has authority under the Constitution to take action to deter and prevent acts of international terrorism against the United States" and authorized "all necessary and appropriate force against those nations, organizations, or persons he determines planned, authorized, committed, or aided the terrorist attacks that occurred on September 11, 2001, or harbored such organizations or persons, in order to prevent any future acts of international terrorism against the United States." This wide authority was used almost immediately to overthrow the Taliban regime in Afghanistan and was critical to justifying far-flung executive action across three administrations and counting. It was used to support President Obama's decisions to utilize remote drone strikes to kill suspected militants (including several American citizens) in a number of nations far from Afghanistan, despite worries about due process and presidential accountability; to justify expanding the use of American force against the so-called Islamic State terrorist group in Iraq and Syria, starting in 2014; and even to take the fight to similar groups in Sudan and Congo. Donald Trump did the same, and extended its umbrella even to military clashes with the Syrian government itself.[70]

Presidents do not always inform Congress about their actions abroad. The use of executive agreements to cut binding deals with foreign leaders is one way presidents can institute policy change without going through the arduous process of seeking Senate ratification of a treaty. The Congressional Research Service found that more than 18,500 executive agreements have been entered into since 1789—more than 17,000 of them from 1939 on.[71] The Case–Zablocki Act of 1972 was supposed to make sure that such agreements were reported to Congress, but enforcement of this requirement has been spotty. George W. Bush chose an executive agreement rather than a treaty to formalize a long-term arrangement with Iraq about the continued presence of U.S. troops in that country, while Obama did the same in concluding a multilateral deal seeking to stall Iran's nuclear program in exchange for lifting sanctions on that nation.[72]

Covert action is also largely an executive operation. The CIA and other intelligence organizations have long constituted a "secret arm of the executive, with a secret budget."[73] "Black ops" helped guide the overthrow of governments in Iran, Guatemala, and Laos in the 1950s but failed to do so in Cuba in the 1960s and Nicaragua in the 1980s. Covert operations remain an important weapon in the foreign affairs arsenal. CIA officers were among the first to arrive in Afghanistan in 2001 and Iraq in 2003, and "human intelligence" has been demonstrated to have particular value in the battle against terrorism. In the aftermath of the September 11 attacks, actions such as the operation of "black sites" in various places around the world and the practice of "extraordinary rendition" were justified by the same claims about executive power that underlay the dispute about interrogation techniques noted earlier.[74] Although Congress has sought to require consultation before, and notification after, intelligence operations, presidents have been reluctant to comply. In part, they suspect correctly that Congress has trouble keeping secrets. Sometimes, however, secrecy is simply a useful means to fend off legislative interference. Confidentiality and accountability coexist uneasily at best, as suggested by the struggle over whether to publish a 2014 Senate Intelligence Committee report detailing the use of torture in the war on terror.[75] And covert action can occur at home as well as abroad. During World War II, Franklin Roosevelt directed his attorney general to surveil "persons suspected of subversive activities against the Government of the United States." This policy extended most infamously to FDR's executive order authorizing the detention of more than 100,000 Japanese Americans in internment camps for the duration of the war. During the Vietnam War, Lyndon Johnson and Richard Nixon used the intelligence agencies to investigate Americans and determine whether they posed threats to national security, a program that included interception of mail and phone calls, break-ins, and the use of informers to infiltrate antiwar groups.[76] And a month after the 9/11 attacks, George W. Bush issued a secret executive order authorizing the National Security Agency (NSA) to track communications between suspected terrorists abroad and

Americans within the United States. Though this order violated the 1978 Foreign Intelligence Surveillance Act, which generally required a warrant by a special court in order to conduct such surveillance, the administration argued that the president had a "well-recognized inherent constitutional authority as Commander in Chief and sole organ for the Nation in foreign affairs to conduct warrantless surveillance of enemy forces for intelligence purposes to detect and disrupt armed attacks on the United States." By this reasoning, any statute that sought to limit the president's "core exercise of Commander in Chief control" was unconstitutional and did not need to be enforced.[77]

Later Congress changed the law to allow the wiretapping program, and it extended that approval in 2012 and again in 2018, with minor changes.[78] But the Bush administration never said it needed a new statute, and its reasoning in its defense of the wiretapping program extended to a variety of unilateral claims stemming from the commander-in-chief power. Similar language was used to justify the president's power to designate individuals—even U.S. citizens—as "enemy combatants" who could be held indefinitely without charge, removed from normal judicial processes, and tried by military commissions established by presidential decree.[79] The methods used to interrogate those detainees were likewise deemed to be within the commander in chief's sole purview, as made clear by the signing statement to the Detainee Treatment Act. President Obama backed away from some of these broader claims, seeking to ground his actions in statutes such as the 2001 authorization—but he nonetheless sought to hold fast to his autonomy in the national security sphere. Documents leaked from a disaffected NSA employee in the summer of 2013 made it clear that a variety of expansive post-9/11 surveillance programs remained in place under the Obama administration, taking advantage of generously vague statutory language and aggressive executive-branch readings of that language.[80]

SECRECY AND EXECUTIVE PRIVILEGE

A final issue deserves mention: the power to impose a cloak of secrecy over executive branch actions. Checking presidential power requires that others know what the president is doing; the penchants for executive secrecy and for excluding Congress from decision making are linked. Federal law mandates that executive orders and proclamations be published, but it allows for secret orders to protect the public interest in dealing with military or intelligence matters. Presidents also issue classified executive directives drafted through the National Security Council staffing process. In the mid-1980s secret directives underlay the policies that devolved into the Iran-contra scandal. In the 1990s such directives dealt with emerging issues of counterintelligence and cyber-warfare. In the 2000s they shaped national strategies toward ballistic missile defense and the War on Terror.[81] More generally, presidents control classification procedures and intelligence gathering, and the amount of "secret" information has grown enormously. Manipulation of the classification process can shape the information legislators have—or do not have—when making decisions about presidential initiatives.

A related issue is the exercise of "executive privilege," which, when claimed as an offshoot of Article II's "executive power," prevents congressional oversight of—or, as presidents would say, meddling with—administration behavior. Although the phrase dates only to the 1950s, the practice of executive privilege extends back to the Washington administration. From the start, most presidents have claimed the right to determine what, in James Polk's phrase, is "compatible with the public interest to communicate."[82] Later, as the Executive Office of the President grew, claims of privilege expanded to include other links in the advisory chain, based on the model of lawyer–client privilege. Nixon's attorney general, Richard Kleindienst, told a Senate hearing that "your power to get what the President knows, is in the President's hands."[83] That argument ran aground on the shoals of Watergate, when a unanimous Supreme Court ruled in the 1974 case of *U.S. v. Nixon* that the president had to release the incriminating tape recordings that subsequently forced his resignation from office. But although Nixon lost that battle, presidents won the war, since the Court also held that some sort of communications "privilege is . . . inextricably rooted in the separation of powers under the Constitution." When "military, diplomatic, or sensitive national security secrets" were at stake, the Court owed the president "great deference." In 1994 a circuit court endorsed a "presidential communications privilege" that, when invoked, made documents "presumptively privileged."[84] The idea was to protect the confidentiality of the advice presidents receive to ensure it would be given freely.

In itself this doctrine is a reasonable offshoot of the separation of powers. But it can be taken too far. The Clinton administration, for example, refused a congressional request for documents dealing with its policy toward Haiti on the grounds that Congress had no power to conduct oversight of foreign affairs.[85] Barack Obama began his presidency by sending memoranda telling executive agencies that he was "committed to creating an unprecedented level of openness in Government" and that "in the face of doubt, openness prevails" in questions involving Freedom of Information Act requests.[86] In at least some cases, however, the temptations of secrecy overrode these good intentions. Obama invoked executive privilege in 2012 over a failed gun-tracking operation run by the Department of Justice and aggressively utilized the "state secrets" doctrine in court filings that threatened (the administration claimed) to reveal details of its counterterrorism tactics.[87] In the spring of 2013, the administration was revealed to have examined the e-mail and phone records of a number of news organizations in the pursuit of prosecuting those leaking classified information to the media, sparking fresh controversy over privacy and accountability.[88] Donald Trump's administration took an even stronger stand against leaks, as the FBI created a new counterintelligence unit to investigate such cases. The press "cannot place lives at risk with impunity," Attorney General Jeff Sessions declared in August 2017.[89] In his own testimony before a Senate committee that June, Sessions had set out a novel claim of prospective privilege, refusing to answer questions about conversations with the president on the grounds that Trump might in future decide executive privilege applied to those conversations.[90]

"PERFECTLY COORDINATE"

An aide to President John Kennedy once observed, "Everybody believes in democracy—until they get to the White House."[91] Congress is the first branch of government, and it remains the institution with the greatest potential power over the workings of government. Yet from the other end of Pennsylvania Avenue, Congress's version of democracy seems frustratingly slow and polarized, the challenges of presidential leadership loom as immense, and the enumerated powers of the office appear limited. Successful leadership, it has long seemed to presidents, depends on arguing that "we can't wait"—on evading congressional constraint by expanding the bounds of executive power.

The result is that presidents have pushed to do things on their own: to define the vague terms of their charter expansively. Sometimes Congress has pushed back, but often it has not. Sometimes it has even helped presidents to get the powers they want. As the federal government grew enormously in size and scope, presidents' administrative authority grew with it. The broad outcome has been an accretion of precedents for unilateral presidential power, despite latent congressional authority and occasional periods of congressional resurgence.

Few would argue that presidents should not enjoy at least some discretionary authority when administering laws and carrying out executive functions. Looking ahead, the key questions concern the scope of that authority and who gets to define it. The theory of the "unitary executive"—that the executive power is indivisible—is unobjectionable to the extent that it holds that all of the executive powers under the Constitution are exercised by the president. But problems arise when, as in recent iterations of the theory, it holds further that only the president can determine what those powers actually are.[92] As Madison wrote in *The Federalist* No. 49, "The several departments being perfectly co-ordinate, . . . none of them . . . can pretend to an exclusive or superior right of settling the boundaries between their respective powers." Much as the president might prefer it, he is not alone in his responsibilities. Nor is the president always right.

One of the president's mandates, then, is to exercise leadership through coalition, not command; by persuasion, not dictate. As heavy reliance on unilateral action becomes the norm, it reinforces itself, potentially undermining democratic accountability. Hence the concern that arose when President Trump argued he had "complete" pardon power as a hedge against an ongoing investigation into his administration arising from Russian interference in the 2016 election.[93]

Although the presidency still has potent tools readily at hand, presidents may want to rethink their automatic resort to these tools. When the contributions of other political actors are neither desired nor valued, both the quality and legitimacy of the president's decisions are lessened. More pragmatically, as setbacks mount the president may be left out on a lonely limb, without support from others who have a stake in the choices he has made. George W. Bush aide Jack Goldsmith has written eloquently of the irony that results when "the hard power of prerogative" is undermined by the president's failure to "take the softer aspects of power seriously."[94] As Obama himself noted in early 2013, initiatives that involve legislative outreach are more likely to be "thoroughly embraced, whereas had I just moved ahead with an executive order, there would have been a huge blowback that might have set back the cause for a long time."[95] There are risks not just to the polity, then, but also to the president, in acting alone.

NOTES

1. Christopher Ingraham, "Six Times Trump Said Executive Orders Were Bad before He Decided They Were Actually Good," Wonkblog, *Washington Post*, April 25, 2017, https://www.washingtonpost.com/news/wonk/wp/2017/04/25/six-times-trump-said-executive-orders-were-bad-before-he-decided-they-were-actually-good/?utm_term=.838fd16708d1.

2. The April 25, 2017, White House release is at https://www.whitehouse.gov/the-press-office/2017/04/25/president-trumps-100-days-historic-accomplishments.

3. This was accurate if counting from 1949, after Truman was elected in his own right, but not from 1945, when Truman first took office. See Andrew Rudalevige, "Trump May Have the 'Most Executive Orders' since Truman—But What Did They Accomplish?" Monkey Cage, *Washington Post*, April 28, 2017, https://www.washingtonpost.com/news/monkey-cage/wp/2017/04/28/trump-may-have-the-most-executive-orders-since-truman-but-what-did-they-accomplish/?utm_term=.46262b23a87d.

4. "Remarks by the President on the Economy and Housing," Office of the White House Press Secretary, October 24, 2011, http://www.whitehouse.gov/the-press-office/2011/10/24/remarks-president-economy-and-housing; "President's Remarks at Faith-Based and Community Initiatives Conference," The White House, March 3, 2004, http://georgewbush-whitehouse.archives.gov/news/releases/2004/03/20040303–13.html (and see Executive Orders 13199 and 13279).

5. Tweet of October 10, 2017, https://twitter.com/realDonaldTrump/status/917698839846576130. More generally see Andrew Rudalevige, "Candidate Trump Attacked Obama's Executive Orders; President Trump Loves Executive Orders," Monkey Cage, *Washington Post*, October 17, 2017, https://www.washingtonpost.com/news/monkey-cage/wp/2017/10/17/candidate-trump-attacked-obamas-executive-orders-president-trump-loves-executive-orders/?utm_term=.ec41211430b8.

6. Quoted in James Bennet, "True to Form, Clinton Shifts Energies Back to U.S. Focus," *New York Times,* July 5, 1998.

7. See http://www.archives.gov/federal-register/executive-orders/disposition.html for a list of orders from 1933 on.

8. Alexander Hamilton, "Pacificus," no. 1, 1793, The Founders' Constitution, http://press-pubs.uchicago.edu/founders/print_documents/a2_2_2–3s14.html. A more formal analysis of the "first mover" advantage may be found in William G. Howell, "Unilateral Powers: A Brief Overview," *Presidential Studies Quarterly* 35 (September 2005): 417–439.

9. James Madison, "Letters of Helvidius," nos. 1–4, 1793, The Founders' Constitution, http://press-pubs.uchicago.edu/founders/documents/a2_2_2–3s15.html.

10. "Cato," Letter V, 1787, http://www.constitution.org/afp/cato_05.htm; in response, see especially Alexander Hamilton, *The Federalist*, no. 69.

11. Ginger Gibson, "Rep. Stockman Threatens Obama Impeachment over Guns," *Politico,* January 14, 2013, http://www.politico.com/blogs/on-congress/2013/01/rep-stockman-threatens-obama-impeachment-over-guns-154141.html; Sen. John McCain (R-Ariz.) tweet of January 25, 2017, https://twitter.com/SenJohnMcCain/status/824265645911117825.

12. Jackson, concurring opinion to *Youngstown Sheet & Tube v. Sawyer,* 343 U.S. 579 (1952).

13. H. L. Mencken, *Notes on Democracy* (New York: Dissident Books, [1926] 2009), 139.

14. Indeed, later scholars argued, if the president was vested with vast executive authority, why bother to authorize him to (for instance) seek written opinions from his department heads? See David Gray Adler and Michael A. Genovese, "Introduction," in *The Presidency and the Law: The Clinton Legacy,* ed. Adler and Genovese (Lawrence: University Press of Kansas, 2002).

15. Grover Cleveland, *The Independence of the Executive* (Princeton, NJ: Princeton University Press, 1913), 14–15; in *In re Neagle* (135 U.S. 1 [1890]), the Court agreed that the oath must, "by necessary implication," be read to "invest the President with self-executing powers; that is, powers independent of statute."

16. Theodore Roosevelt, *An Autobiography* (New York: Da Capo Press, 1985), 372.

17. John Locke, *"Second Treatise of Government,"* ed. C. B. Macpherson (Indianapolis, IN: Hackett, [1690] 1980), 84; "Abraham Lincoln to Albert Hodges," April 4, 1864, reprinted in *The President, Congress, and the Constitution,* ed. Christopher H. Pyle and Richard M. Pious (New York: Free Press, 1984), 65; George W. Bush, Office of Legal Counsel opinion of September 25, 2001, http://www.usdoj.gov/olc/warpowers925.htm. See also Thomas Jefferson's earlier formulation, in which he argued that "to lose our country by a scrupulous adherence to written law, would be to lose the law itself, with life, liberty, property and all those who are enjoying them with us; thus absurdly sacrificing the end to the means." "Jefferson to Colvin, September 10, 1810," reprinted in Pyle and Pious, eds., *President, Congress, and the Constitution,* 62.

18. *Ex parte Milligan,* 71 U.S. (4 Wall.) 2 (1866); *Hamdi v. Rumsfeld,* 542 U.S. 507 (2004); William Howard Taft, "Our Chief Magistrate and His Powers (1916)," in Pyle and Pious, eds., *President, Congress, and the Constitution,* 70–71.

19. Arthur M. Schlesinger Jr., *The Imperial Presidency* (Boston: Houghton Mifflin, 1973); for updated detail and a bibliography, see Andrew Rudalevige, *The New Imperial Presidency: Renewing Presidential Power after Watergate* (Ann Arbor: University of Michigan Press, 2006).

20. Gerald Ford interview in *Time,* November 10, 1980, 30. See also G. Calvin Mackenzie, *The Imperiled Presidency* (Lanham, MD: Rowman & Littlefield, 2017).

21. Louis Fisher and David Gray Adler, "The War Powers Resolution: Time to Say Goodbye," *Political Science Quarterly* 113 (Spring 1998): 1–20.

22. This figure includes approximately 700,000 postal employees and 1.5 million uniformed military personnel.

23. The value of this process was made clear in early 2017, when President Trump issued a number of directives—notably his first "travel ban" order—absent any such consultation, leading to substantive flaws, political blowback, and unfavorable judicial rulings. For a broader discussion see Andrew Rudalevige, "Executive Orders and Presidential Unilateralism," *Presidential Studies Quarterly* 42 (March 2012): 138–160; Rudalevige, "Executive Branch Management and

Presidential Unilateralism: Centralization and the Formulation of Executive Orders," *Congress and the Presidency* 42 (Winter 2015): 342–365.

24. See, e.g., Mitchel A. Sollenberger and Mark Rozell, *The President's Czars: Undermining Congress and the Constitution* (Lawrence: University Press of Kansas, 2012); Justin S. Vaughn and José D. Villalobos, *Czars in the White House* (Ann Arbor: University of Michigan Press, 2015).

25. See John P. Burke, "The Institutional Presidency," chap. 13, this volume; David E. Lewis, "Staffing Alone: Unilateral Action and the Politicization of the Executive Office of the President," *Presidential Studies Quarterly* 35 (September 2005): 496–514. New staffs can be created by executive order but must receive congressional appropriations to become permanent.

26. David E. Lewis, *The Politics of Presidential Appointments* (Princeton, NJ: Princeton University Press, 2008).

27. Quoted in Thomas J. Weko, *The Politicizing Presidency: The White House Personnel Office, 1948–1994* (Lawrence: University Press of Kansas, 1994), 89.

28. Bush aide quoted in Mike Allen, "Bush to Change Economic Team," *Washington Post,* November 29, 2004, A1. On Trump see, inter alia, Peter Baker and Julie Hirschfeld Davis, "Trump, an Outsider Demanding Loyalty, Struggles to Fill Top Posts," *New York Times,* February 18, 2017, https://www.nytimes.com/2017/02/18/us/ politics/trump-candidates-top-posts.html?_r=0; Michael Scherer and Alex Altman, "Trump's Loyalty Test," *Time,* May 18, 2017, http://time.com/4783929/presi dent-trump-loyalty-test/. More generally, see Richard Nathan, *The Administrative Presidency* (New York: Macmillan, 1983); Lewis, *Politics of Presidential Appointments.*

29. Via the 2011 Presidential Appointment Efficiency and Streamlining Act (Pub. L. No. 112–166), which removed the requirement for Senate confirmation from agency, advisory board, and EOP positions, including the various assistant secretaries for management in the cabinet departments.

30. Simendinger, "Help Wanted," 29; Henry Hogue, *Recess Appointments: Frequently Asked Questions,* Report RS21308 (Washington, DC: Congressional Research Service, January 9, 2012).

31. See *National Labor Relations Board v. Noel Canning, Inc.,* 573 US _ (2014).

32. Cornelius Kerwin and Scott Furlong, *Rulemaking: How Government Agencies Write Law and Make Policy,* 4th ed. (Washington, DC: CQ Press, 2010).

33. Dana Goldstein, "Obama Education Rules Are Swept aside by Congress," *New York Times,* March 9, 2017, https://www.nytimes.com/2017/03/09/us/every-student-succeeds-act-essa-congress.html?_r=0.

34. Alyson Klein, "Trump Education Department Releases New ESSA Guidelines," *Education Week,* March 13, 2017, http://blogs.edweek.org/edweek/campaign-k-12/2017/03/trump_education_dept_releases_new_essa_guidelines.html; Michael J. Petrilli, "Betsy DeVos's Team Stumbles on ESSA," *The Flypaper* (blog), Thomas B. Fordham Institute, June 15, 2017, https://edexcellence.net/articles/betsy-devoss-team-stumbles-on-essa.

35. Lewis, *Politics of Presidential Appointees,* chap. 3.

36. Executive Order 13563, "Improving Regulation and Regulatory Review," January 18, 2011; Executive Order 13771, "Reducing Regulation and Controlling Regulatory Costs," January 30, 2017.

37. Thanks to Christopher Kelley for this count of signing statement objections as of October 15, 2008, available at http://www.users.muohio.edu/kelleycs; "Statement

on Signing the Consolidated Appropriations Act, 2005," *Public Papers of the Presidents,* December 8, 2004, http://www.presidency.ucsb.edu/ws/index.php?pid= 64673&st=&st1=.

38. Samuel A. Alito Jr., to Litigation Strategy Working Group, "Using Presidential Signing Statement to Make Fuller Use of the President's Constitutionally Assigned Role in the Process of Enacting Law," National Archives, RG 60, Files of Stephen Galebach, Accession 060–89–269, box 6.

39. Michael Abramowitz, "On Signing Statements, McCain Says 'Never,' Obama and Clinton 'Sometimes,'" *Washington Post,* February 25, 2008, A13; "Statement by the President," Office of the White House Press Secretary, March 11, 2009, http://www .whitehouse.gov/the_press_office/Statement-from-the-President-on-the-signing- of-HR-1105; Phillip J. Cooper, *By Order of the President: The Use and Abuse of Executive Direct Action,* 2nd rev. ed. (Lawrence: University Press of Kansas, 2014), chap. 8. For a list of Obama's signing statements see http://www.coherentbabble .com/listBHOall.htm.

40. "Statement by President Donald J. Trump on the Signing of H.R. 3364," Office of the White House Press Secretary, August 2, 2017, https://www.whitehouse.gov/the- press-office/2017/08/02/statement-president-donald-j-trump-signing-hr-3364. More generally see Cooper, *By Order of the President;* Christopher S. Kelley, ed., *Executing the Presidency* (Albany: State University of New York Press, 2006), chap. 4.

41. "Statement by the President on H.R. 4310," Office of the White House Press Secretary, January 3, 2013, http://www.whitehouse.gov/the-press-office/2013/01/ 03/statement-president-hr-4310.

42. "Statement on Signing the Treasury, Postal Service and General Government Appropriations Act," September 22, 1988, http://www.presidency.ucsb.edu/ws/ index.php?pid=34878.

43. "President's Statement on Signing of H.R. 2863," Office of the White House Press Secretary, December 30, 2005, http://georgewbush-whitehouse.archives.gov/news/ releases/2005/12/20051230–8.html.

44. *Presidential Signing Statements: Agency Implementation of Selected Provisions of Law,* GAO-08–553T, U.S. Government Accountability Office, March 11, 2008; it is not clear whether GAO's analysis covered a representative sample of such statements. A circuit court once scolded the Reagan administration's effort to avoid parts of a con- tracting act by saying "this claim of right for the President to declare statutes uncon- stitutional and to declare his refusal to execute them . . . is dubious at best." See *Ameron v. U.S. Army Corps of Engineers,* 787 F.2d 875 (3d Cir. 1986). But see also 18 *Opinions of the Office of Legal Counsel* 199 (1994), available at http://www.justice .gov/olc/nonexcut.htm, listing Supreme Court decisions that purportedly con- doned signing statements.

45. James Sundquist, *The Decline and Resurgence of Congress* (Washington, DC: Brookings Institution, 1981), 202ff; Schlesinger, *Imperial Presidency,* 239.

46. *Train v. City of New York,* 420 U.S. 35 (1975).

47. Rudalevige, *New Imperial Presidency,* 141–149 (the quote from Sen. Ted Stevens is on p. 148); "Unlikely Team Pushes Line-Item Veto Bill," CBS News, March 4, 2009, http://www.cbsnews.com/stories/2009/03/04/politics/100days/main4842 840.shtml.

48. The Supreme Court ruled in 1879 that there is no material difference between proclamations and executive orders, nor is there much practical difference between

executive orders and the other forms of presidential orders described most comprehensively in Cooper, *By Order of the President*. See also Graham Dodds, *Take Up Your Pen: Unilateral Presidential Directives in American Politics* (Philadelphia: University of Pennsylvania Press, 2013); Gregory Korte, "Obama Issues 'Executive Orders by Another Name,'" *USA Today*, December 16, 2014, https://www.usatoday .com/story/news/politics/2014/12/16/obama-presidential-memoranda-executive-orders/20191805/.

49. President Trump's order on Restoring State, Tribal, and Local Law Enforcement's Access to Life-Saving Equipment and Resources of August 28, 2017, was Executive Order 13809. However, haphazard record-keeping before 1946 likely means that between 15,000 and 50,000 directives were never recorded. In 1946 Congress mandated that the text of all nonclassified executive orders, executive branch announcements, proposals, and regulations be published in the *Federal Register*. See Mayer, *Stroke of a Pen*.

50. Executive Order 13776, issued February 2, 2017.

51. Andrew Rudalevige, "The Obama Administrative Presidency: Some Late-Term Patterns," *Presidential Studies Quarterly* 46 (December 2016): 868–890.

52. Daniel P. Gitterman, *Calling the Shots: The President, Executive Orders, and Public Policy* (Washington, DC: Brookings Institution Press, 2017), 41.

53. Andrew Rudalevige, "The Supreme Court Didn't Answer Its Own Questions on Immigration," Monkey Cage, *Washington Post*, June 24, 2016, https://www.washing tonpost.com/news/monkey-cage/wp/2016/06/24/the-supreme-court-didnt-answer-its-own-questions-on-immigration-heres-what-comes-next/?utm_term= .e7023511ad30.

54. Quoted in Jeff Zeleny, "Four More Years, Yes, but It's the First One That Really Counts," *New York Times,* January 23, 2012, A12.

55. Mayer, *With the Stroke of a Pen*, 79–87; for a different time series but similar findings, see William Howell, *Power without Persuasion* (Princeton, NJ: Princeton University Press, 2003), 83–85.

56. Alexander Smith, "North Korea Crisis: Trump Threatens to Stop U.S. Trade with China," NBC News, September 4, 2017, https://www.nbcnews.com/news/world/ north-korea-crisis-could-trump-stop-u-s-trade-china-n798561.

57. Quoted in Alexis Simendinger, "The Paper Wars," *National Journal,* July 25, 1998, 1737.

58. Kevin Loria, "DREAM Act Stalled, Obama Halts Deportations for Young Illegal Immigrants," *Christian Science Monitor,* June 15, 2012. The acronym stands for Development, Relief, and Education for Alien Minors.

59. Executive Order 10340.

60. *U.S. v. Midwest Oil*, 236 U.S. 459 (1915).

61. Richard E. Neustadt, *Presidential Power and the Modern Presidents* (New York: Free Press, 1990), 3.

62. Nigel Bowles, *Nixon's Business* (College Station: Texas A&M Press, 2005); Pub. L. No. 110–343; Pub. L. No. 111–5.

63. U.S. House, "A Failure of Initiative: Final Report of the Select Bipartisan Committee to Investigate the Preparation for and Response to Hurricane Katrina" (Washington, DC: U.S. Government Printing Office, 2006), http://katrina.house.gov.

64. See, e.g., Gregory Krieg, "Trump's Puerto Rico Response is Confirming His Critics' Worst Fears," CNN, September 28, 2017, http://www.cnn.com/2017/09/28/poli tics/donald-trump-puerto-rico-response-mess/index.html.

65. For a useful review—but also a useful reminder of the conditions under which congressional power might be exercised in such instances—see William G. Howell and Jon C. Pevehouse, *While Dangers Gather: Congressional Checks on Presidential War Powers* (Princeton, NJ: Princeton University Press, 2007).

66. See *U.S. v. Curtiss-Wright Export Corp. et al.,* 299 U.S. 304 (1936); for a skeptical take of presidents' reading of this case, see Louis Fisher, "The Sole Organ Doctrine," *Presidential Studies Quarterly* 37 (March 2007): 139–152.

67. Barton J. Bernstein, "The Road to Watergate and Beyond: The Growth and Abuse of Executive Authority since 1940," *Law and Contemporary Problems* 40 (Spring 1976): 58–86.

68. Charlie Savage and Mark Landler, "White House Defends Continuing Role in Libya Operation," *New York Times,* June 16, 2011, A16; Louis Fisher, "War Power," in *The American Congress: The Building of Democracy,* ed. Julian E. Zelizer (Boston: Houghton Mifflin, 2004), 696. Note that the War Powers Resolution specifically prohibits the use of treaty obligations as an approval mechanism.

69. Office of Legal Counsel, "Authority of the President under Domestic and International Law to Use Military Force against Iraq" (emphasis added), October 23, 2002, http://www.justice.gov/olc/2002/iraq-opinion-final.pdf, 1, 7. But see Howell and Pevehouse, *While Dangers Gather,* for an analysis of how presidents anticipate congressional reaction to their own choices.

70. See Charlie Savage, *Power Wars,* rev. ed. (New York: Back Bay Books, 2017), chap. 8; Rudalevige, "Obama Administrative Presidency"; Gene Healy, "9/14 Changed Everything," Cato Institute, September 14, 2017, https://www.cato.org/blog/914-changed-everything; Rita Siemion, "Trump Administration Says Its Broad Powers under the 2001 AUMF Are Plenty," *JustSecurity,* August 2, 2017, https://www.justsecurity.org/43831/trump-administration-broad-powers-2001-aumf-plenty/.

71. Michael John Garcia, "International Law and Agreements: Their Effect upon U.S. Law," Congressional Research Service, Report RL 32528, February 18, 2015, https://fas.org/sgp/crs/misc/RL32528.pdf.

72. Kiki Caruson and Victoria Farrar-Meyers, "Promoting the President's Foreign Policy Agenda: Presidential Use of Executive Agreements as Policy Vehicles," *Political Research Quarterly* 60 (2007): 631-644; Glen S. Krutz and Jeffrey S. Peake, *Treaty Politics and the Rise of Executive Agreements* (Ann Arbor: University of Michigan Press, 2011); Andrew Rudalevige, "Executive Agreements and Senate Disagreements," Monkey Cage, *Washington Post,* March 10, 2015, https://www.washingtonpost.com/news/monkey-cage/wp/2015/03/10/executive-agreements-and-senate-disagreements/?utm_term=.c8e61e5fed14.

73. Bernstein, "The Road to Watergate," 81; more generally, see John Prados, *Safe for Democracy: The CIA's Secret Wars* (Chicago: Ivan Dee, 2006).

74. Rudalevige, *New Imperial Presidency,* chap. 7; Jane Mayer, *The Dark Side* (New York: Doubleday, 2008).

75. Deb Reichmann, "Democrats Say GOP Is Trying to Bury Torture Report," PBS, June 2, 2017, http://www.pbs.org/newshour/rundown/democrats-say-gop-trying-bury-torture-report/.

76. Bernstein, "Road to Watergate," 64; Robert H. Jackson, *That Man: An Insider's Portrait of Franklin D. Roosevelt* (New York: Oxford University Press, 2003), 68–73.

77. U.S. Department of Justice, *Legal Authorities Supporting the Activities of the National Security Agency Described by the President,* January 19, 2006, http://www.justice .gov/opa/whitepaperonnsalegalauthorities.pdf, 1–2, 10–11, 17, 30–31.

78. See the FISA Amendments Act of 2012, Pub. L. No. 112–238; Charlie Savage, "With Clock Ticking, House Intelligence Committee Releases its Version of a 702 Surveillance Bill," Power Wars Blog, November 30, 2017, https://www.charliesav age.com/?p=1783.

79. Office of Legal Counsel (OLC), memorandum re: Applicability of 18 U.S.C. §4001(a) to Military Detention of United States Citizens, June 27, 2002; president's military order of November 13, 2001; and see OLC memorandum re: Authority for Use of Military Force to Combat Terrorist Activities within the United States, October 23, 2001, which was criticized in but not quite rescinded by a subsequent OLC decision of January 15, 2009. These memoranda and opinions are collected at the Justice Department site, http://www.usdoj.gov/opa/documents/olc-memos.htm.

80. See Savage, *Power Wars.*

81. George H. W. Bush called these national security directives, Clinton called them presidential decision directives, George W. Bush called them national security presidential directives, and Obama calls them presidential policy directives. See Cooper, *By Order of the President.*

82. Mark J. Rozell, *Executive Privilege,* 2nd rev. ed. (Lawrence: University Press of Kansas, 2002); Louis Fisher, *The Politics of Executive Privilege* (Durham, NC: Carolina Academic Press, 2004).

83. Richard Kleindienst, Hearings before the Senate Subcommittee on Intergovernmental Relations, "Executive Privilege, Secrecy in Government, Freedom of Information," 93rd Cong., 1st sess., April 10, 1973.

84. *U.S. v. Nixon,* 418 U.S. 683 (1974); *In re Sealed Case,* 121 F. 3d 729 (D.C. Circuit 1998).

85. Rozell, *Executive Privilege,* 106–107.

86. See the memoranda of January 21, 2009, and Executive Order 13489 relating to the Presidential Records Act, http://www.whitehouse.gov/briefing_room/executive_orders.

87. Richard Serrano, "Obama Invokes Executive Privilege over Fast and Furious Documents," *Los Angeles Times,* June 20, 2012; Savage, *Power Wars*, chap. 9.

88. Sari Horwitz, "Attorney General Holder Says He'll Protect Journalists' Rights," *Washington Post,* May 30, 2013; Aamer Madhani, "Holder Tries to Reassure Media on Leak Investigations," *USA Today,* May 31, 2013.

89. Charlie Savage and Eileen Sullivan, "Leak Investigations Triple Under Trump, Sessions Says," *New York Times*, August 4, 2017, https://www.nytimes.com/ 2017/08/04/us/politics/jeff-sessions-trump-leaks-attorney-general.html.

90. Charlie Savage, "Explaining Executive Privilege and Sessions's Refusal to Answer Questions," *New York Times,* June 15, 2017, https://www.nytimes.com/2017/06/15/ us/politics/executive-privilege-sessions-trump.html.

91. Quoted in Thomas E. Cronin, "'Everybody Believes in Democracy until He Gets to the White House,'" *Law and Contemporary Problems* 35 (1970): 573–625.

92. Steven G. Calabresi and Christopher S. Yoo, *The Unitary Executive: Presidential Power from Washington to Bush* (New Haven, CT: Yale University Press, 2008). For a more expansive variant, see John Yoo, *War by Other Means* (New York: Atlantic, 2005);

Jess Bravin, "Judge Alito's View of the Presidency: Expansive Powers," *Wall Street Journal,* January 5, 2006, A1.

93. Peter Baker, "Trump Says He Has 'Complete' Power to Pardon," *New York Times,* July 22, 2017, https://www.nytimes.com/2017/07/22/us/politics/donald-trump-jeff-sessions.html.

94. Jack L. Goldsmith, *The Terror Presidency* (New York: Norton, 2007), 215.

95. Franklin Foer and Chris Hughes, "Barack Obama Is Not Pleased," *The New Republic,* January 27, 2013, http://www.newrepublic.com/article/112190/obama-interview-2013-sit-down-president#.

18

PRESIDENTIAL POWER AND PUBLIC POLICY

Roger B. Porter

A president's interactions with most of the institutions and actors chronicled in this book, including private actors such as political parties, interest groups, voters, and the media, and public institutions such as Congress, the Supreme Court, and the bureaucracy, affect presidential leadership of public policy. Roger B. Porter, a scholar and a veteran of several administrations, first notes the ways in which some of these institutions and actors have been changing during the past half century, notably Congress, the media, the executive branch, organized interests and think tanks, and, as made manifest in the normalization of divided government, the voters and parties. These changes have required corresponding changes in the ways presidents pursue their public policy goals. In particular, the presidency has been transformed into three presidencies, according to Porter: the legislative presidency, the administrative presidency, and the rhetorical presidency.

In November 2016, America's voters took an unprecedented step, electing as president a candidate who had never before run for or held public office—federal, state, or local, nor served in the nation's military forces. Donald Trump's candidacy was built on a powerful premise that voters wanted two types of change that he promised.

The first was a change in policy, a promise to "Make America Great Again," an appeal to those who felt left behind, forgotten, and ignored. He promised to stand up for them, protect the jobs that remained, and bring back the jobs that had left.

The second promised change was to "drain the swamp," to overcome the inertia, topple the vested interests, and break free from the gridlock that afflicted federal policymaking in Washington, D.C. Doing so, he argued, required a leader who was neither part of the system nor beholden to it. The president and the presidency would be at the center of this new effort to transform the American government and the nation.

A first task for a newly elected president is assembling his team, staffing his administration. Donald Trump made good on his promise to represent change by appointing, with a few notable exceptions, individuals to his White House staff and cabinet who had little or limited experience in the executive branch of the federal government.

Several of his senior appointees heading departments or agencies were serving in the Congress (Justice, Interior, Health and Human Services, Office of Management and Budget, Central Intelligence Agency) or as state governors (Agriculture, Energy, the United Nations) or had military experience (Defense, Homeland Security, National Security Adviser). Only three cabinet members had significant previous experience in the executive branch (Transportation, Veterans Affairs, U.S. Trade Representative). A larger than normal number of the initially appointed or nominated senior officials had no previous governmental experience (State, Treasury, Commerce, Labor, Housing and Urban Development, Education, Small Business Administration, White House Chief of Staff, White House Chief Strategist, National Economic Council, Council of Economic Advisers, along with his oldest daughter and a son-in-law who were appointed to senior positions in the White House).

Not only did Trump bring with him fresh faces, but he had a favorable situation vis-à-vis the Congress. Like his three immediate predecessors (Bill Clinton, George W. Bush, and Barack Obama), Donald Trump entered the White House with majorities of his political party in both the U.S. Senate and House of Representatives.[1] These circumstances provide a fresh and new opportunity to re-examine a central question. How much power does the president have, and how does he exercise that power in shaping the nation's public policies?

THE ORIGINAL DESIGN

When those whom George Washington later referred to as "the Framers"[2] gathered in Philadelphia in the summer of 1787, they were filled with a multitude of concerns and impulses. Two ideas dominated their discussions. First, virtually all the delegates recognized and accepted the need for a stronger central government. The loose arrangements adopted in the wake of the successful revolution had proven inadequate. At the same time the delegates were acutely aware of the potential for abuse associated with concentrated power.[3]

Under the Articles of Confederation and Perpetual Union—note the optimism embodied in that phrase—there was no chief executive, no president of the United States. The arrangement reflected the skepticism toward executive power found in the thirteen states. Governors were effectively subservient to legislatures.[4] In eight of the states, the governor was elected by the legislature. In ten of the states, the governor was elected for a one-year term.

At the Constitutional Convention some delegates seriously advanced the idea of a plural executive—a three-member body with one member coming from the Northern states, one from the Southern states, and one from the Middle States. The commanding presence of George Washington presiding over the Convention served to allay the fears of many delegates. Over the summer they finally settled on a single executive, who could succeed himself, and who was elected in the first instance independently from the legislature. The president, however, was to be given few formal powers. The office of the presidency that emerged was a unique entity born in the soil of skepticism regarding the ability to exercise power wisely, and of the potential for abuse associated with concentrated power. At the same time, as James Wilson of Pennsylvania declared in arguing successfully for a single executive, what was needed was someone who could provide "energy, dispatch, and responsibility" to the new government.[5] They and succeeding generations have looked to the president to provide leadership and vision.

Perhaps the most clearly articulated exposition of presidential power is that advanced by Richard Neustadt in his book by that title.[6] First published in 1960, Neustadt's argument rests on three central claims. First, the president is the focus of enormous expectations and is constantly pressed to respond to a wide variety of pressures and appeals. In this sense, he is like a clerk. Whether the president can become a leader is for Neustadt an open question, but that he is a clerk is beyond dispute. Second, the president seeks to respond to these pressures in a system of separate institutions sharing power. The president's capacity to act on his own, to command, is limited. He requires the agreement and acquiescence of others; thus, the essence of presidential power is the power to persuade.

Neustadt's third claim is that in seeking to persuade others the president has two assets in addition to his limited formal powers: his *professional reputation*, how he is viewed by those with whom he must deal in the Congress, in organized interest groups, and the media; and his *public prestige*, how he is viewed by those in the country at large. As his public prestige rises, it positively influences his professional reputation. As his professional reputation is strengthened, his ability to persuade is enhanced.

To what extent does this formulation of presidential power remain valid today? What has changed since 1960? Have these changes reinforced or altered the argument that presidential power is the power to persuade?

FIVE MAJOR INSTITUTIONAL DEVELOPMENTS

The Congress

One set of institutional developments involves the Congress. In 1960, power in Congress resided in a small number of hands. Lyndon Johnson was, in Robert

Caro's memorable phrase, the Master of the Senate.[7] Sam Rayburn, the Speaker, played a similar role in the House of Representatives. An entrenched seniority system accentuated the role of committee chairmen. Dwight Eisenhower could negotiate with Lyndon Johnson and Sam Rayburn confident that once agreement was reached, they could deliver the votes.

Much has changed. In the mid-1970s, the leadership was challenged by a large class of newly elected members eager for a larger role without the lengthy wait for seniority to confer its benefits. This led, among other things, to an expansion in the number of subcommittees and the importance of their role. A greater sharing of power was accentuated when several committee chairs were successfully challenged and replaced.

Eventually, this produced a reaction and a sea change led by a Republican majority in both the House and Senate following the 1994 mid-term elections. The new Speaker, Newt Gingrich, successfully instituted a series of measures that both strengthened the power of the Speaker and the leadership while at the same time providing term limits for committee chairs.[8]

Greater democratization is also reflected in the growth of congressional caucus organizations, with which Congressional leaders must deal. The first modern caucus organization was formed in 1959. Today there are nearly 300 caucus organizations in the House, the Senate, or both chambers.

Congress has also greatly enhanced its own capabilities and reduced its dependence on the executive branch. Personal and committee staffs have grown nearly threefold since 1960. The Congressional Budget Office, created in 1974, is a highly professional bipartisan resource that Congress now relies on for estimates of the costs of programs and proposals. The Congressional Research Service has grown fourfold since 1960.[9]

As Congress has become less dependent on the executive for information and analysis, the ties between individual members of Congress and their constituents have strengthened as party organizations have receded. Congressional candidates largely raise their own campaign funds and build their own organizations. The amount of time members of Congress spend in their home districts and states has risen steadily. Before 1970, House and Senate members averaged two or three days each month at home. By 1980, House members were spending an average of about ten days each month at home. The House and Senate now rarely hold votes on Mondays or Fridays, permitting members to utilize a Tuesday to Thursday schedule in Washington when Congress is in session.

The transportation and communication revolutions, computers, and the Internet have changed the work style of members of Congress, their staffs, and the House and Senate as institutions. Since the 1960s the percentage of House members' personal staff located in a representative's home district has more than doubled. Today it approaches 50 percent. One consequence of these trends is that members of Congress spend less time with their colleagues, on either side of the aisle, outside of formal sessions and meetings.

Another major development is the increased use of procedural devices designed to delay and block action. The time taken to complete the confirmation process for presidential nominees has lengthened as senators increasingly seek to extract concessions as the price of permitting nominees a confirmation vote. The number of times senators use procedural devices, most prominently the filibuster, to block or delay consideration of legislation or nominations has increased dramatically over the past forty years. It is now considered routine that sixty votes in the Senate are needed to pass major legislation. A relatively new device, used by a determined minority party, is to stall, delay, and even fail to appoint conferees to conference committees.

Congress has also experienced a higher level of polarization than at any time in the past century.[10] Sean Theriault found voting patterns that reveal that the Senate has become 29 percent more polarized and House polarization has increased 47 percent during the period from 1973 to 2005.[11] Such polarization, understandably, makes reaching bipartisan agreements more difficult.[12]

Party leaders in Congress often feel like they are walking a tightrope with the need to satisfy the members of their caucus, reducing their flexibility in negotiations with their counterparts and with the president. Moreover, the dwindling number of competitive congressional districts has caused many members of Congress to be more wary of primary challengers and therefore more tied to what they perceive as the inclinations of primary voters.

The frustration associated with these tactics has led to a series of adaptations. The number of bills enacted by the Congress has declined while the length of bills has increased. Legislative leaders increasingly resort to omnibus pieces of legislation, as well as the use of budget reconciliation and continuing resolutions. The combination of these developments has significantly transformed the Congress, producing a legislative body that is more polarized and responsive to its constituents, whose enhanced internal capacity makes it less dependent on the executive, and whose embrace of obstructionist procedural devices has made producing outcomes more difficult and challenging.

The Executive Branch

The executive branch of the government over this period has also undergone significant change. The number of presidentially appointed officials has risen sharply. This reflects the creation of new departments and an increase in the number of political appointees in traditional departments. Since the early 1960s Congress has created six cabinet-level departments bringing the total to fifteen. By January 20, 2001, Senate-confirmed positions had grown to roughly 500 cabinet and subcabinet posts, and the president also had the opportunity to appoint 2,000 or so non-Senate-confirmed political aides. In short, presidents have far greater latitude in filling their administration with political appointees whom they select and whom they can replace. In August 2012, President Obama signed the Presidential Appointment Efficiency and Streamlining Act, which reduced by one-third the number of executive branch positions that require Senate confirmation.[13]

At the same time, the president's immediate resources have expanded in their reach and scope, including the Office of Management and Budget.[14] New entities dealing with trade, economic and domestic policy, the environment, drug control, science and technology, and homeland security have joined the Executive Office of the President. In short, the president has substantially more capacity to oversee and direct the activities of his branch of the government.

Organized Interests and Think Tanks

The milieu in which presidents operate and policy is made, however, has become more congested, complicated, and robust with the growth of organized interests and think tanks. The trade and professional groups that dominated the interest group landscape decades ago have been supplemented by a host of nonprofit and public interest organizations active in lobbying government. Gathering accurate data on this phenomenon is not easy, and a variety of researchers have produced varying estimates, but the direction and magnitude are unmistakable. The most careful studies suggest that the number of such organizations has grown between four- and fivefold since 1960.[15] It is not merely the growth in organized interests that has reshaped the policy landscape, but also the establishment of a host of research institutions, "think tanks," filled with highly educated, industrious, and creative individuals advancing ideas, producing analysis, and generating estimates. Moreover, many of these think tanks devote much of their attention and effort more to shaping current governmental deliberations than influencing scholarly debate. The arena in which public policies are contested is now more thickly settled and is arguably richer with a host of ideas and analyses competing for the attention of policy makers.

The Media

A fourth development concerns the transformation of the media in recent decades. In 1960 the three television networks each presented a nightly fifteen-minute national news broadcast. Those days have given way to a time of intense competition between and within the media. Print, electronic, and digital news organizations now vie with one another for readers and viewers. The twenty-four-hour news cycle is filled with scores of active and often aggressive news organizations. To this milieu is an expanding social media, including Twitter accounts with millions of avid followers, a form of communication used often many times a day by the president, as well as by those who support and oppose him.

These technological developments have contributed to a traditional emphasis on openness and transparency, with the adoption and greater use of means to illuminate what is occurring inside government. Media organizations, interest groups, and individuals actively utilize the Freedom of Information Act, the Government in the Sunshine Act, the Federal Register Act, the Administrative Procedure Act, the Federal Advisory Committee Act, the Negotiated Rulemaking Act, the Regulatory Flexibility Act, the Small Business Regulatory Enforcement Fairness Act, and the Congressional Review Act, not simply to find out what is happening inside government but to actively advance their interests.

As late as 1972, 40 percent of congressional committee meetings were closed to the public. By the start of the 104th Congress in 1995, House Republicans passed a rule that all committee and subcommittee meetings must be open unless it would pose a threat to national security. Both Houses of Congress now televise their proceedings and the twenty-four-hour news cycle has become a way of life.

In short, the media is more intense and intrusive. There is greater transparency and scrutiny of decision making within the executive branch as well as negotiations between branches. Debates are now shaped by the democratization of public discussion through the use of social media.

The Phenomenon of Divided Government

Not least, the phenomenon of divided government has become a dominant feature in the past four and a half decades. During the seven decades from 1899 to 1969 unified government was the norm, with the president and a majority in both houses of Congress from the same political party for fifty-six of those seventy years. During the forty-eight years from 1969 to 2017 the norm of unified government has given way to one of divided government, with unified government the case for twelve and a half years and divided government for thirty-five and a half years.[16]

What are the consequences of these five developments for the exercise of presidential power? How have they altered the ways in which presidents provide leadership and pursue policy goals? Significantly, the president's formal powers have changed little in the past half century. What has changed, in part in response to these developments, is what one might call the three presidencies—the legislative presidency, the administrative presidency, and the rhetorical presidency.

THE LEGISLATIVE PRESIDENCY

The legislative presidency involves at least three distinct roles for the president. His success, particularly in economic and domestic policy, is closely tied to (1) his skill in initiating, (2) his capacity to shape legislation and build coalitions, and (3) his willingness to block, if he feels it necessary. How ambitious or targeted an agenda should he propose? How early and how extensively should he engage? How much time and political capital should he expend? How skillful is he in negotiating?

The Budget and Accounting Act of 1921 first required the president to submit a unified federal budget to the Congress. This annual rite has the potential to serve as a starting point for the appropriations process. The Budget and Impoundment Control Act of 1974 required the president to present a budget with five-year spending projections related to his annual budget proposal.

Likewise, since Franklin D. Roosevelt's administration, the president has advanced a legislative program, often ambitious and frequently detailed, that has helped to focus the attention of Congress and to establish a set of priorities for public policy. These proposals, many outlined in his State of the Union Address, have served to fill a desire for ideas and policies that deserve attention and to clarify national priorities.

The president has the opportunity of a first mover, to take the initiative while recognizing that his initial proposals are merely the starting point for what is frequently a lengthy process of give and take between various interests, parties, constituencies, and ideas. In responding to this opportunity, presidents weigh a host of factors. Dwight Eisenhower and Jimmy Carter, who entered office in 1953 and 1977, respectively, each came into office at a time of unified government yet took quite different initial approaches. President Eisenhower, cautious and eager to avoid mistakes, embraced a careful deliberate approach.[17] President Carter, deeply committed to fulfilling his campaign promises, sent a host of initiatives to the Congress only to conclude later that he had initially overloaded his legislative agenda.[18]

Two developments have served to transform federal budgeting in recent years. First, more and more budgeting comprises intergenerational transfers that are not subject to the appropriations process. Second, with the increased complexity of the tax code, multiple budget baselines, competing estimates, and the expanded use of refundable tax expenditures, budgeting has become much more complicated. This has led to reliance on omnibus budget reconciliation acts, and more recently of continuing resolutions, as a means of bringing some order and a measure of finality to the annual budget process. No longer is the president's budget proposal with its assumptions and estimates the only game in town.

Over the past three decades, bipartisan majorities enacted the major budget and tax legislation during times of divided government. Over the same period, highly partisan majorities enacted major budget and tax legislation during times of unified government. Table 18.1 also includes four additional major pieces of legislation dealing with welfare, financial services, education, and health care. Each of these confirms this pattern. The measures enacted during times of divided government were the product of a conscious effort by the president to orchestrate and participate in negotiating a bipartisan agreement.

An instructive example of the legislative presidency is to compare the ways presidential leadership and contextual factors influence outcomes. Since the late 1960s and early 1970s the federal government has assumed a major role in environmental policy. During the 1988 general election, both presidential candidates articulated strong support for achieving reductions in air pollution. Within days of assuming office, in his first major address to a joint session of Congress, President George H. W. Bush called for "a new attitude about the environment." He announced that he would soon send legislation for a "new, more effective Clean Air Act" and reiterated that "the time for study alone has passed, and the time for action is now."[19]

In crafting his legislative proposal, administration officials held extensive consultations with members of the House and Senate, both Republican and Democrat, seeking their input and exploring options. By June his administration had drafted and transmitted a detailed bill which was the subject of Senate Environment and Public Works Committee hearings and later lengthy negotiations involving administration officials and Senators producing an Administration-Leadership Agreement that, among other things, established the SO_2 allowance trading system. The legislation embodying the agreement passed the Senate 89–11 with the support

Table 18.1   ■   Bipartisan and Partisan Majorities under Unified and Divided Government

The Economic Recovery Tax Act of 1981

(H.R. 4242, 97th Congress)

	Aye		Nay		Not voting	
	Democrats	Republicans	Democrats	Republicans	Democrats	Republicans
House	113	169	93	1	21	12
Senate	25	41	7	1	12	11

The Omnibus Budget Reconciliation Act of 1981

(H.R. 3982, 97th Congress)

	Aye		Nay		Not voting	
	Democrats	Republicans	Democrats	Republicans	Democrats	Republicans
House	47	185	186	6	6	–
Senate	30	49	13	1	3	3

The Tax Equity and Fiscal Responsibility Act of 1982

(H.R. 4961, 97th Congress)

	Aye		Nay		Not voting	
	Democrats	Republicans	Democrats	Republicans	Democrats	Republicans
House	122	103	118	89	1	–
Senate	9	43	35	11	1	–

The Omnibus Budget Reconciliation Act of 1982

(H.R. 6955, 97th Congress)

	Aye		Nay		Not voting	
	Democrats	Republicans	Democrats	Republicans	Democrats	Republicans
House	91	152	141	34	6	3
Senate	18	48	26	6	1	–

(Continued)

Table 18.1 ■ (Continued)

The Deficit Reduction Act of 1984

(H.R. 4170, Amendment to H.R. 2163, 98th Congress)

	Aye		Nay		Not voting	
	Democrats	Republicans	Democrats	Republicans	Democrats	Republicans
House	223	95	31	66	9	3
Senate	22	52	22	1	1	2

The Tax Reform Act of 1986

(H.R. 3838, 99th Congress)

	Aye		Nay		Not voting	
	Democrats	Republicans	Democrats	Republicans	Democrats	Republicans
House	176	116	74	62	2	2
Senate	33	41	12	11	2	1

The Balanced Budget and Emergency Deficit Control Reaffirmation Act of 1987

(H.J. Res. 324, 100th Congress)

	Aye		Nay		Not voting	
	Democrats	Republicans	Democrats	Republicans	Democrats	Republicans
House	125	105	111	65	19	5
Senate	31	33	21	13	2	–

The Omnibus Budget Reconciliation Act of 1990

(H.R. 5835, 101st Congress)

	Aye		Nay		Not voting	
	Democrats	Republicans	Democrats	Republicans	Democrats	Republicans
House	181	47	74	126	3	2
Senate	35	19	20	25	–	1

The Omnibus Budget Reconciliation Act of 1993

(H.R. 2264, 103rd Congress)

	Aye		Nay		Not voting	
	Democrats	Republicans	Democrats	Republicans	Democrats	Republicans
House	217	0	38	175	0	1
Senate	48	1	5	44	1	1

The Personal Responsibility and Work Opportunity Reconciliation Act of 1996

(H.R. 3734, 104th Congress)

	Aye		Nay		Not voting	
	Democrats	Republicans	Democrats	Republicans	Democrats	Republicans
House	98	230	99	2	2	3
Senate	25	53	21	0	1	0

The Balanced Budget Act of 1997

(H.R. 2015, S. 947, 105th Congress)

	Aye		Nay		Not voting	
	Democrats	Republicans	Democrats	Republicans	Democrats	Republicans
House	50	219	152	8	1	2
Senate	21	52	24	3	–	–

The No Child Left Behind Act of 2001

(H.R. 1, 107th Congress)

	Aye		Nay		Not voting	
	Democrats	Republicans	Democrats	Republicans	Democrats	Republicans
House	198	186	10	35	3	1
Senate	48	43	2	6	1	0

(Continued)

Table 18.1 ■ (Continued)

The Economic Growth and Tax Relief Reconciliation Act of 2001

(H.R. 1836, 107th Congress)

	Aye		Nay		Not voting	
	Democrats	Republicans	Democrats	Republicans	Democrats	Republicans
House	14	216	197	0	4	1
Senate	13	49	38	0	0	0

The Emergency Economic Stabilization Act of 2008

(H.R. 1424, 110th Congress)

	Aye		Nay		Not voting	
	Democrats	Republicans	Democrats	Republicans	Democrats	Republicans
House	221	47	3	145	7	6
Senate	41	33	10	15	1	–

The American Recovery and Reinvestment Act of 2009

(H.R. 1, 111th Congress)

	Aye		Nay		Not voting	
	Democrats	Republicans	Democrats	Republicans	Democrats	Republicans
House	244	0	10	178	–	1
Senate	59	2	0	37	–	1

The Dodd–Frank Wall Street Reform and Consumer Protection Act of 2009

(H.R. 4173, 111th Congress)

	Aye		Nay		Not voting	
	Democrats	Republicans	Democrats	Republicans	Democrats	Republicans
House	234	3	19	173	2	2
Senate	57	3	1	38	–	–

The Patient Protection and Affordable Care Act of 2010

(H.R. 3590, 111th Congress)

	Aye		Nay		Not voting	
	Democrats	Republicans	Democrats	Republicans	Democrats	Republicans
House	219	0	34	178	–	–
Senate	60	0	0	39	–	1

The Budget Control Act of 2011

(S.365, 112th Congress)

	Aye		Nay		Not voting	
	Democrats	Republicans	Democrats	Republicans	Democrats	Republicans
House	95	174	95	66	3	–
Senate	46	28	7	19	–	–

The American Taxpayer Relief Act of 2012

(H.R. 8, 112th Congress)

	Aye		Nay		Not voting	
	Democrats	Republicans	Democrats	Republicans	Democrats	Republicans
House	172	85	15	151	3	5
Senate	49	40	3	5	1	2

of 87 percent of Republican senators and 91 percent of Democratic senators. The legislation passed the House of Representatives 401–21 with the support of 87 percent of Republican members and 96 percent of Democratic members.[20]

Twenty years later, another new president took office with an ambitious agenda. Foremost on his environmental legislative agenda was climate change. The American Clean Energy and Security Act of 2009, popularly known as the Waxman–Markey bill, included an economy-wide cap-and-trade system to reduce carbon dioxide (CO_2) emissions. It passed the House of Representatives by a slender margin, 219–212, with support from 83 percent of the Democratic members but only 4 percent of Republican members. In the summer of 2010 the U.S. Senate abandoned its efforts to pass similar legislation.

What distinguished these two efforts, and how does one explain the two outcomes? Weighing the many factors that contributed is neither easy nor precise, but the exercise is instructive. During those two decades there was a substantial increase in polarization in the Congress understandably making reaching bipartisan agreements more difficult.

There are, of course, other factors. In 1989, the president took the initiative in crafting a bill. Gridlock in the Congress had blocked legislation for more than a decade and success was unlikely without presidential commitment and leadership. In doing so, his administration engaged in extensive consultations with members of Congress and affected interest groups before advancing a detailed draft legislative proposal. These consultations not only influenced the shape of the proposal but facilitated the negotiation of an agreement.

The priority in the president's hierarchy of objectives also played a role. President Obama focused much of his legislative attention and political capital during his first two years on an economic stimulus bill, health care, and financial services regulation. Climate change legislation received less emphasis and attention from the White House.

The composition of Congress also played a role. President Bush, facing larger opposition majorities in the Congress than any elected president in U.S. history, had little choice but to pursue a bipartisan solution. Moreover, if he wanted legislation that embodied the market-oriented approach to environmental regulation that he favored, it was imperative that he take the initiative and demonstrate his commitment to his preferred approach. In the negotiations and subsequent consideration of floor amendments, he judiciously used the threat of his veto to ensure that the final legislation reflected his approach. Personal factors also played a role. President Bush cared deeply about the issue and advanced a proposal that was more ambitious than that of his predecessors or than preferred by some in his administration. At the same time, he had developed and maintained a set of relationships with members of the House from his service in that body as well as during the eight years he presided over the Senate—relationships that proved crucial at certain points when particular killer amendments threatened to derail the legislation. Not least, the bipartisan process of inclusion in the more than 130 hours of negotiations on the bill was crucial in building and sustaining a majority.

President Obama, with large Democratic majorities in both the House (256–178 with one vacancy) and the Senate (59–41 including two Senators in the Democratic caucus who identified themselves as independents), left much of the initiative to his party's congressional leadership. His administration officials worked closely with these leaders to shape particular provisions but deferred on key points regarding how best to produce the desired majorities. The attention during his first two years focused on three major pieces of legislation dealing with economic stimulus, health care, and financial institution regulation. While climate change legislation passed the House by a slender margin in 2009, it had neither the momentum nor the bipartisan base on which to secure passage in the Senate.

The November 2010 midterm elections produced a return to divided government. Republicans picked up a net change of sixty-three seats and a 242–193 majority in the House. Republicans also added a net of six Senate seats, shrinking the Democratic majority to 53–47. During divided government, the norm for the past four and a half decades, the president's legislative role, in certain respects, becomes more important. His single most powerful tool, the veto, always makes him a player.[21]

In the past half century, Democratic and Republican presidents have rarely chosen to threaten and even more rarely to use their veto when dealing with Congressional majorities of their own party.[22] Instead, they have relied heavily on the judgment of congressional leaders regarding how best to construct a legislative majority. Unsurprisingly, those majorities have overwhelmingly proven partisan in their composition.

Divided government is at once both challenging and liberating for the legislative presidency. Congressional leaders of both parties publicly acknowledge the president's pivotal role and repeatedly call for his leadership, particularly on large national issues. Rarely do they challenge his efforts to lead or initiate. At the same time, given that the successful legislative outcomes under divided government are invariably a product of negotiation, the relationships that the president and his lieutenants develop are crucial. Given that sustaining a veto only requires one-third plus one in a single house of the Congress, the president's ability to prevail when he chooses to use it, particularly when he has prepared the ground for such an action, is overwhelming.[23]

At the beginning of his second term, Barack Obama pushed hard for gun control and immigration legislation. In the first case, his agenda appeared to be driven by the tragic shooting of twenty children and six adults at the Sandy Hook Elementary School in Newtown, Connecticut. Within weeks, an interagency task force under Vice President Biden had produced a set of proposals that the president advanced. The most consequential measures required legislation, and he sought to rally public support for their enactment.

The November 2012 election and its results elevated immigration, a longstanding maturing issue that had proven legislatively intractable for a decade. In this instance, the legislative initiative seemed to come from a bipartisan group of eight senators—four Democrats and four Republicans—who announced progress toward a bipartisan approach.[24] While expressing support for comprehensive immigration reform, the president's strategy seemed to be a version of leading from behind when he declared: "And if Congress is unable to move forward in a timely fashion, I will send up a bill based on my proposal and insist that they vote on it right away."[25]

In the wake of his 2016 election, Donald Trump entered office with high expectations. All new beginnings are hopeful, and the outset of his administration was no exception. Among the legislative challenges for the new administration was that the 2016 campaign was more a movement than an exercise in securing support for a comprehensive set of policies. His small campaign staff, a fraction of the size of his opponent's staff, had a limited policy operation and the new administration entered office with little in the way of detailed policies. Moreover, his personal relationships with members of Congress were few and not particularly deep.

Like his three immediate predecessors, Trump entered office with majorities from his party in both the houses of the Congress. These majorities represented both an opportunity and a challenge. The opportunity is to secure early victories and build momentum. A challenge is the pressure to begin with large, often controversial issues, such as repealing and replacing the Affordable Care Act or undertaking fundamental tax reform. Even if one merely needs a simple majority in the Senate for proposals that are folded into the reconciliation process, securing a majority in both chambers is difficult, especially if those majorities are thin, as in the case of the 52–48 Republican Senate majority. Success often rests on building relationships and trust. Doing so requires much patience, focus, and persistence.

Nine months into the first year of his presidency, Trump had signed fifty-eight pieces of legislation, fifteen of which employed the Congressional Review Act to repeal regulations issued in the waning weeks of the Obama administration.[26] None of these bills, however, were widely viewed as a significant legislative victory. The repeated efforts to repeal and replace the Affordable Care Act, the administration's signature legislative priority, failed to achieve a majority in the Senate. The president fashioned a bipartisan agreement for disaster relief in the wake of hurricanes and flooding in Texas, Florida, and Puerto Rico and for a temporary extension to the debt limit. But, whether the issue was health care, taxes, immigration, or infrastructure, reaching agreement between the administration and the Congress on other legislation had thus far proved elusive.

The most significant development in recent decades with respect to the legislative presidency has been the increased polarization in Congress. It has made the path to enacting legislation more difficult. Congress has sought to micromanage the executive branch more and more. As frustration with the process has grown, the executive branch has sought to do more itself. What evidence is there that policymaking is now more dominated by the president and the executive branch?

THE ADMINISTRATIVE PRESIDENCY

Some terms have many meanings and mean different things in different contexts. The administrative presidency is used in this chapter to refer to what presidents do in exercising the executive power they are granted under the Constitution.[27] It embraces a host of activities—nominating and appointing officials and judges; overseeing the flow of regulations that implement statutory provisions; exercising discretion in the efficient enforcement of laws; filing suits or seeking injunctions; providing guidance to examiners; deploying and commanding military forces; issuing directives, executive orders, and presidential memoranda; and negotiating treaties and executive agreements. Such activities are at the heart of what executives do.

The executive branch over which the president presides is, in Stephen Bailey's felicitous phrase, "a many splintered thing."[28] A central presidential task is to produce comprehensive and coherent policies amid the competing priorities and mandates conferred by Congress in legislation and to accommodate the wide range of interests within executive departments and agencies. In issuing regulations, directives, executive orders, and the like, carefully established procedures help ensure informed decision making. Successive administrations have maintained and strengthened many of these processes, as well as entities such as the Office of Information and Regulatory Affairs in the Office of Management and Budget, which help exercise oversight and quality control.

Presidents take their administrative tasks seriously, devoting much time and attention to selecting those whom they appoint and considering the internal processes they use in shaping policy. Like their principal lieutenants, presidents are eager to expand the discretion they have been given and to make wise use of it. They want flexibility to adapt to new circumstances and developments. They desire to leave an impact and are often frustrated by the lack of action on their legislative proposals.

As the challenges grow associated with enacting the budgets and legislation they desire, it is natural that presidents turn to administrative means to achieve their ends. There is nothing new about this phenomenon. Scholars have devoted considerable attention in recent years to developing theories and examining data exploring the president's ability to act independently or, as it is sometimes put, unilaterally.[29]

Some scholars attach much significance to the president's ability as a first mover—that by acting first those with a different view are put in the position of having to organize and respond. The president can pick the time and means when he acts. Others may grumble but their capacity to overturn, whether through the Congress or the courts, is limited. Presidents are thus tempted, the theory goes, to do administratively all that they feel they can "get away with."[30]

The administrative actions taken by the president and his appointees are often described as independent or unilateral. Such actions are unilateral in the sense that they do not require the agreement or concurrence of Congress or the courts. The world of the administrative presidency, however, is filled with much nuance and subtlety. Crafting regulations, orders, and directives is time-consuming and the subject of much debate and deliberation. The procedures used involve multiple steps and many parties. These processes encourage the representation of the wide variety of interests and perspectives found throughout the executive branch. In the administrative presidency, policy is always the product of many hands.

Executive orders, for example, are only issued by the president. Many are routine; some are symbolic; others are more substantive. Andrew Rudalevige examined nearly 300 executive orders over the period 1947–1987 and discovered, unsurprisingly, that the written record reveals an executive branch full of contending views and interests, and that "the issuance of executive orders often involves persuasion rather than simply command: it incorporates wide consultation across the executive branch and, frequently, White House ratification of what agencies wanted to do in the first place."[31] His examination of the available written record revealed only a part of the interplay and adjustments involved in crafting and implementing the executive orders of greatest consequence. His understated conclusion: "the issuance of executive orders seems to involve as much about consultation as command."[32]

A large part of the administrative presidency involves matters and organizational issues about which members of Congress have limited interest. Moreover, such orders disproportionately involve how the executive branch will carry out its functions and guide its employees.[33] They reflect choices about how best to implement or execute the laws.

Many of the most aggressive executive actions taken by the president involve national security considerations or are taken during times of crisis or international conflict—where the Congress and the courts have proven more deferential—partially because these actions deal with classified matters, partially because of the clarity of the president's role as commander in chief, and partially because the president is seen as having a greater claim to superior and more comprehensive information.

When one reviews the most consequential examples of presidents initiating unilateral action, the recent examples—Nixon's imposition of wage and price controls, Carter's implementation of the agreement to release American diplomats held by Iran, Reagan's cost-benefit analysis for federal regulations, and Clinton's creation of national monuments—reveal a pattern that is more complicated than appears at first glance.[34]

For example, Richard Nixon's action on wage and price controls was the product of a fierce internal struggle within his administration and taken in accordance with provisions in the Economic Stabilization Act of 1970, which gave the president stand-by powers to "issue such orders as he may deem appropriate to stabilize prices, rents, wages and salaries."[35] Ironically, Nixon had opposed the legislation when it was debated in Congress and vowed he would not use the authority the Congress had provided.[36] Ultimately, Nixon chose to act counter to the advice tendered by a majority of his senior advisers, but his actions were consistent with what Congress had explicitly authorized and many in Congress had urged him to do.

In instances where they are at the edge of their discretion, presidents and their advisers consciously anticipate the potential reaction—judicially and legislatively. Will it produce a challenge in the courts?[37] Will it encourage members of the Senate to hold up nominees?[38] Will it prompt oversight hearings or affect appropriation requests? In the conduct of the administrative presidency there is a good deal of give and take, assessments and calculations, and the interplay of short-term advantages and potential longer-term difficulties.

The use of his administrative powers was on full display as President Obama began his second term. Empowered by a fresh electoral mandate, freed from the prospect of facing voters again, and with his public approval ratings rising, he outlined an ambitious agenda in his State of the Union address. His proposals included tax reform and investments in infrastructure, early childhood education, and manufacturing. He called for legislation to address climate change, immigration, and to increase the minimum wage. He devoted much of his address to the issue of gun violence. Weeks before, at the prayer vigil honoring the victims of the tragic shootings at Sandy Hook Elementary School in Newtown, Connecticut, the president vowed to "use whatever power this office holds to engage my fellow citizens—from law enforcement to mental health professionals to parents and educators—in an effort aimed at preventing more tragedies like this."[39]

Despite strong public support, the president discovered that his administrative authority was limited. Of the thirty-seven initiatives proposed by the task force chaired by Vice President Biden, only eighteen could be accomplished administratively.[40] The president ordered federal law enforcement officers to conduct background checks on gun owners before returning weapons seized during investigations,[41] and the Centers for Disease Control and Prevention to study the causes of gun violence.[42] He mandated that executive branch agencies make relevant records available to the National Instant Criminal Background Check System.[43] Other proposals involved encouraging private sellers to use a licensed gun dealer with the capacity to run a background check on potential buyers.

The most substantial reforms the Biden-led task force identified, however, needed congressional action—requiring background checks for all gun sales; banning military-style assault weapons, high-capacity magazines, and the possession of armor-piercing ammunition; and imposing stronger penalties for gun trafficking. Existing gun control laws limit executive discretion. A 1986 law prohibits the Bureau of Alcohol, Tobacco, Firearms and Explosives from conducting more than one unannounced inspection per year on a gun dealer. The federal government is required to destroy background check records within twenty-four hours of approval.[44] Designed to protect privacy, the law makes it challenging to identify falsified sales records and to prosecute gun traffickers. Changing those restrictions requires legislation as do those proposals that involve new funding for training new police officers or hiring school counselors able to identify and connect troubled children with appropriate mental health services.[45]

During his first presidential campaign, Barack Obama promised Latino voters that he would prioritize immigration reform and establish a pathway to citizenship for illegal immigrants.[46] Choosing to elevate health care reform, President Obama delayed the debate on immigration until late in his first term. When Congress proved unwilling to pass the Dream Act, he determined to act administratively. While acknowledging the need for Congress to enact comprehensive immigration reform, he instructed his secretary of homeland security, Janet Napolitano, to direct her department not to initiate deportment proceedings against a precise and narrowly defined set of young immigrants.[47] The directive was symbolically powerful but, in practice, changed little. The memorandum reassured young illegal immigrants that they would not be deported, but most immigration enforcement targets workplaces rather than schools. Limited law enforcement resources understandably focus on deporting those with criminal records. Moreover, the memorandum did not grant new rights that formed an important part of the Dream Act, such as eligibility for in-state tuition at state colleges and universities. President Obama acknowledged that his measure "falls short of where we need to be—a path to citizenship. It's not a permanent fix. This is a temporary measure that lets us focus our resources wisely while offering some justice to these young people."[48] Executive actions are important tools available to the president as he seeks to advance his policies and priorities. But, as presidents discover, the scope of what they can accomplish through such actions is often limited.[49]

Eager for action, and intent on showing his supporters concrete results, Donald Trump issued more executive orders during his first 100 days than any other president since Franklin D. Roosevelt.[50] By October 25, 2017, he had issued fifty-two executive orders, ninety presidential proclamations, and eighty-five presidential memoranda.[51]

Most of these administrative actions concerned the routine business of government or, in the case of most presidential proclamations, acknowledged holidays such as Columbus Day and Father's Day, or encouraged particular activities such as National School Lunch Week or Fire Prevention Week. The overwhelming majority of presidential memoranda and executive orders established councils, clarified responsibility, or set in motion initiatives by federal departments and agencies, such as expanding apprenticeships or reviving the National Space Council.

Other executive orders were more consequential, such as establishing regulatory reform task forces throughout the executive branch or imposing sanctions with respect to the situation in Venezuela and imposing additional sanctions with respect to North Korea.[52] The ability to make policy through such administrative actions, however, is limited. They can be challenged in the courts, as in the case of changes in immigration policy, or forced by the actions of others such as the deadline for suits filed by state attorneys general.[53]

THE RHETORICAL PRESIDENCY

The rhetorical presidency is something of a residual category. For purposes of this chapter, it involves those actions and measures that a president undertakes with the intent of exercising influence that do not revolve around legislation and do not involve taking an executive or administrative action.[54]

This conception of the rhetorical presidency is broader than moving people through the eloquence of a speech or fireside chat. It is more than providing reassurance during a time of crisis or stiffening the resolve of citizens in the face of challenge as did Winston Churchill and Franklin Roosevelt during the Second World War. It is not using presidential speeches or public appeals to try to move or advance a particular piece of legislation by encouraging citizens to contact and pressure their members of Congress to approve the policy preferences advocated by the president.

An important aspect of this expanded concept of the rhetorical presidency involves getting individuals, organizations, and governments to either make different decisions than they would otherwise make, support causes they might otherwise neglect, or embrace goals they might otherwise not elevate. It has three principal elements.

One element of the rhetorical presidency involves *motivating* individuals and organizations to think and act differently. A crucial element of Ronald Reagan's efforts to reduce drug abuse was his rhetorical campaign urging youth to "Just Say No." His successor, through hundreds of appearances and by his example, encouraged all Americans to render voluntary service. The "Thousand Points of Light" he selected and honored daily inspired tens of thousands of similar efforts.

Bill Clinton, long a champion of better race relations, did not propose or sign new civil rights legislation, nor did he initiate an array of administrative actions to advance civil rights. He did launch "The President's Initiative on Race" in which he "asked Americans to join in open and honest discussions about race."[55] This initiative sought to promote better relations through public discussions in town halls across the country and provided a manual for use in conducting community discussions. Likewise, in his 1996 State of the Union Address, he issued challenges to teachers, schools, and parents regarding a host of education issues, from requiring students to wear school uniforms to teaching character education.[56]

The initiatives of the Obama administration to secure voluntary commitments from corporations to hire veterans and a campaign against childhood obesity illustrate the range of causes the president can champion. Likewise, Trump and his administration have sought to draw favorable attention to businesses that invest in new plants and equipment in the United States, thereby creating jobs for American workers, and to criticize companies that are considering moving manufacturing operations from domestic to international locations.

A second element of the rhetorical presidency involves *mobilizing* individuals, organizations, and governments to behave in particular ways. Sometimes presidents do this by calling on others, including their predecessors, to undertake a task, such as the public appeal for funds to assist those whose homes and lives were shattered by the Southeast Asian tsunami and Hurricane Katrina.

This element of the rhetorical presidency is particularly salient in the realm of foreign policy, where presidents can only partially pursue their objectives through legislative and administrative actions. Whether carefully constructing coalitions to respond to international aggression or seeking support for imposing economic sanctions against Iran designed to deflect it from its pursuit of nuclear weapons, presidents act other than through legislative and administrative means.

The rhetorical presidency involves a president's relationships with foreign leaders as well as with opinion makers. The relationships established by Roosevelt and Churchill, Reagan and Thatcher, George H. W. Bush and Gorbachev, Bill Clinton and Tony Blair, and George W. Bush and Tony Blair influenced the effectiveness of numerous foreign policy initiatives.

A third element of the rhetorical presidency involves *educating* citizens regarding the choices the country faces and persuading them and their elected officials to deal with reality. In many respects this is the most difficult and most important element of the rhetorical presidency, because often it involves elevating longer-term considerations rather than attending to shorter-term needs. It involves attending to general rather than particular interests. It is the kind of rhetorical leadership demonstrated by George Washington and Abraham Lincoln among others. Doing so is neither easy—it requires patience and tenacity—nor sometimes welcome. But it is the president who is better positioned than any other political leader to undertake this challenging and necessary task. The rhetorical presidency rests on trust, credibility, charisma, perseverance, timing, and personal relationships.

A CASE STUDY: EDUCATION POLICY

Presidents have engaged and elevated education as an important national public policy for more than fifty years, discussing it repeatedly during presidential campaigns, leading the fight to create a cabinet-level Department of Education, and urging greatly expanded federal funding. Like most areas of public policy, education is complicated, engaging government at the federal, state, and local levels.

Presidents in seeking to advance an agenda on education employ all three tools—legislative, administrative, and rhetorical. Despite facing larger opposition majorities in the House and Senate than any elected president in U.S. history, George H. W. Bush recognized the need for legislation to accomplish much of what he wanted to achieve with respect to education policy. His opening series of legislative proposals, outlined within three weeks of his inauguration, included an Excellence in Education Act as well as subsequent legislative initiatives. He secured overwhelming votes in both the House and the Senate but was only able to achieve a modest amount of what he wanted legislatively, frustrated by a rolling Senate filibuster.

Rhetorically, he sought to *motivate* (through a national literacy campaign and visits to schools, etc.), to *mobilize* (through a Summit Conference on Education with Governors that led to national education goals and a commitment from the nation's governors to undertake education reform within their states and to embrace the idea of national standards), and to *educate* by shifting the debate from one dominated by funding levels to one of ideas—championing choice, site-based management, merit pay, establishing standards for what students should know and be able to do, and testing to see whether they had achieved those standards. He secured a carefully negotiated agreement with all fifty governors to embrace six national education goals announced in his 1990 State of the Union Address and implemented and monitored over the next ten years through the National Education Goals Panel. He established the President's Education Policy Advisory Board (PEPAB) consisting of business, labor, governors, local officials, and educators to advise him and met with them frequently.

Administratively, when the nation's governors complained that excessive federal regulations were stifling innovation and the most efficient use of federal funds, he worked with the National Governors Association to canvass all governors for a list of specific federal rules and regulations and then reported back to them on what the federal government would do to address their concerns. The capacity to change some of those regulations with the stroke of a pen was strictly limited by specific provisions in legislation which necessitated that the regulations be written in a particular way. Those regulations that could be changed administratively were changed or eliminated; for those regulations that could only be changed with new legislation the administration offered, and many of the governors accepted the invitation, to jointly petition the Congress with a request for changes in current legislation. Some of that occurred; much did not.

This brief case study illuminates how presidents simultaneously employ legislative, administrative, and rhetorical tools. The leadership they provide, and that in many respects only they are in a position to provide, requires great patience, persistence, and the powers of persuasion.

CONCLUSIONS

Presidential leadership is becoming more rather than less challenging. The constitutionally ordained division of power with its accompanying set of checks and balances confirms that the president still must share or compete with other political institutions for power and influence. The president's limited formal powers have not been substantially enhanced. The Framers' vision in this respect remains intact.

In exercising power and shaping policy, the president has three sets of tools at his disposal. He must use them wisely. The first constitutes the legislative presidency. Many of his goals and aspirations require legislation and appropriations. The land is thick with laws and those laws, however challenging to enact, have great force.

The president retains the capacity to initiate, through both his annual federal budget and his legislative program. His ability to draw attention to an issue and to press for action is greater than any other single actor. Moreover, through the use of his veto power and the credibility of his threat to exercise it, he has a powerful bargaining tool in using his legislative power. But while he has the capacity to initiate, he must bring others along.

Congress has become less dependent on the executive branch for information and analysis. The world of policy has become more congested with competing voices and ideas. Greater polarization in the Congress has made the legislative presidency increasingly challenging. Yet it is possible. The wheels of government continue to turn. Much is done in the context of crises. Procedural challenges have not stopped the growth of government programs and the articulation of policy.

The sheer magnitude of the enterprise of government has enhanced the role of the chief executive. He presides over the branch of government with extensive power to regulate, administer, and enforce. The president's control over the executive branch has strengthened to some extent, but so has the capacity of those with whom he must compete with and share power. The increased length and detailed provisions in legislation still leave considerable discretion to executive branch officials. But there are more watchful eyes—in the Congress, among highly organized interest groups, in a vigilant media operating in an ever more expansive, transparent, and competitive environment.

In directing the executive branch, presidents have increased difficulty in putting those officials requiring Senate confirmation in place. In crafting regulations, the number of comments has risen as the policy world has gone electronic. Now there are many more comments to consider in the process of issuing regulations and a greater threat of challenges when they exceed their bounds. Presidents discover, or are reminded once in office, that their capacity to act "unilaterally" is limited, although less so in the realm of foreign affairs. Whether the issue is guns or immigration, what can be accomplished with the stroke of a pen is modest and may well produce battles within their own branch of government as well. As legislation has become longer and more detailed, the discretion afforded those who implement those laws remains substantial, even if more limited.

The president also has the opportunity, if he seizes it, to motivate, mobilize, and educate—three pillars of the rhetorical presidency. His success rests in large part on the trust and credibility he has earned among those with whom he works in government and in the nation at large. Successfully orchestrating his legislative, administrative, and rhetorical powers is his challenge and his opportunity.

NOTES

1. Interestingly, during the period of the modern presidency since Franklin Roosevelt, all seven Democratic presidents entered office with Democratic majorities in both houses of Congress. Of the seven Republican presidents, only three (Dwight Eisenhower, George W. Bush, and Donald Trump) had Republican majorities in both houses of Congress.

2. Richard Beeman, *Plain, Honest Men—The Making of the American Constitution* (New York: Random House, 2009), ix.

3. Carol Berkin, *A Brilliant Solution: Inventing the American Constitution* (New York: Harcourt, 2002); Ray Raphael, *Mr. President: How and Why the Founders Created a Chief Executive* (New York: Vintage Books, 2012).

4. Akhil Reed Amar, *America's Constitution: A Biography* (New York: Random House, 2005), 59.

5. Beeman, *Plain, Honest Men,* 127.

6. Richard E. Neustadt, *Presidential Power* (New York: John Wiley & Sons, 1960).

7. Robert A. Caro, *Master of the Senate* (New York: Alfred A. Knopf, 2002).

8. The Republican Party in both the House and the Senate continues to maintain a system of term limits for committee chairs.

9. See U.S. Office of Personnel Management, *Federal Employment Statistics Report,* December 2011, http://www.opm.gov/policy-data-oversight/data-analysis-documentation/federal-employment-reports/employment-trends-data/2011/december.

10. An excellent essay discussing this phenomenon and the scholarship associated with it is David W. Rohde and Meredith Barthelemy, "The President and Congressional Parties in an Era of Polarization," *The Oxford Handbook of the American Presidency,* ed. George C. Edwards III and William G. Howell (Oxford: Oxford University Press, 2009), 289–310.

11. Sean M. Theriault, "Party Polarization in the U.S. Congress: Member Replacement and Member Adaptation," *Party Politics* 12, no. 4 (2006): 483–503. This study concluded "that member adaptation accounts for one-third of the total party polarization in both the House and Senate. Member replacement accounts for the other two-thirds, the lion's share of which has been the replacement of moderate southern Democrats by conservative Republicans. Republicans in both chambers are polarizing more quickly than Democrats. If the Democratic senators have taken one step toward their ideological home, House Democrats have taken two steps, Senate Republicans three steps and House Republicans four steps."

12. Nate Silver, "So Few Swing Districts, So Little Compromise," *New York Times,* December 28, 2012, A16.

13. Presidential Appointments Efficiency and Streamlining Act of 2011, S.769, 112th Congress (2012), http://www.gpo.gov/fdsys/pkg/BILLS-112s679enr/pdf/BILLS-112s679enr.pdf.

14. Shelley Lynne Tomkin, *Inside OMB: Politics and Process in the President's Budget Office* (New York: M. E. Sharpe, 1998).

15. Frank R. Baumgartner and Beth L. Leech, *Basic Interests: The Importance of Groups in Politics and in Political Science* (Princeton, NJ: Princeton University Press, 1998), 109.

16. When George W. Bush entered office the Senate was evenly split 50–50 between those Senators caucusing with the Republican and Democratic Parties. The Republican

Party had control procedurally with Vice President Cheney casting the tie-breaking vote for such matters as majority leader, committee chairs, and others. Five months later, on May 24, 2001, Vermont's Republican senator, Jim Jeffords, announced he was changing his party affiliation to Independent and would caucus with the Democratic members of the Senate, giving that party majority control.

17. *The Eisenhower Diaries*, ed. Robert H. Ferrell (New York: W. W. Norton, 1981), 226.

18. Jimmy Carter, *Keeping Faith* (New York: Bantam Books, 1982), 87.

19. "Address before a Joint Session of Congress" (February 9, 1989) in *Public Papers of the Presidents of the United States: George H. W. Bush, 1989* (Washington, DC: Government Printing Office, 1990).

20. Kathy McCauley, Bruce Barron, and Morton Coleman, *Crossing the Aisle to Cleaner Air* (Pittsburgh, PA: University of Pittsburgh Institute of Politics, 2008).

21. Charles M. Cameron, *Veto Bargaining: Presidents and the Politics of Negative Power* (Cambridge: Cambridge University Press, 2000).

22. During times of unified government, Jimmy Carter vetoed thirty-one bills; Bill Clinton, none; George W. Bush, one; and Barack Obama, two. See U.S. Senate, *Summary of Bills Vetoed, 1789–present*, http://www.senate.gov/reference/Legislation/Vetoes/vetoCounts.htm.

23. Two of Jimmy Carter's thirty-one vetoes were overridden. Nine of Ronald Reagan's seventy-eight vetoes were overridden. One of George H. W. Bush's forty-four vetoes was overridden. Two of Bill Clinton's thirty-seven vetoes were overridden. Four of George W. Bush's twelve vetoes were overridden. Neither of Barack Obama's two vetoes were overridden. See U.S. Senate, *Summary of Bills Vetoed, 1789–present*, http://www.senate.gov/reference/Legislation/Vetoes/vetoCounts.htm.

24. Alan Gomez, "Senators Announce Deal to Overhaul Immigration System," *USA Today*, January 28, 2013, http://www.usatoday.com/story/news/politics/2013/01/28/senators-immigration-changes/1869763/.

25. Remarks by the president on Comprehensive Immigration Reform, White House Office of the Press Secretary, January 29, 2013, http://www.whitehouse.gov/the-press-office/2013/01/29/remarks-president-comprehensive-immigration-reform.

26. White House website, http://www.whitehouse.gov (accessed October 25, 2017).

27. The term *administrative presidency* has most closely been associated with Richard Nathan and his book by that title published in 1983, foreshadowed by his book *The Plot That Failed: Nixon and the Administrative Presidency* (New York: John Wiley, 1975). In this sense it refers to the efforts of presidents to gain control of the executive branch through expanding the number of political appointees and using various measures to ensure their loyalty to him and his policies. An excellent symposium on "The Administrative Presidency," organized by Bert A. Rockman, appeared in *Presidential Studies Quarterly* 39 (March 2009).

28. Stephen Bailey, "The President and His Political Executives," *Annals of the American Academy of Political and Social Science* 307 (September 1956), 24.

29. Kenneth R. Mayer, *With the Stroke of a Pen: Executive Orders and Presidential Power* (Princeton, NJ: Princeton University Press, 2001). Steven A. Shull, *Policy by Other Means: Alternative Adoption by Presidents* (College Station: Texas A&M University Press, 2006). Kenneth R. Mayer, "Going Alone: The Presidential Power of Unilateral Action," and Richard W. Waterman, "Assessing the Unilateral Presidency," in *The Oxford Handbook of the American Presidency* provide useful assessments of much of the recent scholarship on the subject.

30. William G. Howell, *Power without Persuasion: The Politics of Direct Presidential Action* (Princeton, NJ: Princeton University Press, 2003).

31. Andrew Rudalevige, "The Contemporary Presidency: Executive Orders and Presidential Unilateralism," *Presidency Studies Quarterly* 42 (2012), 138.

32. Ibid., 145.

33. Eager to promote gun safety, President Clinton issued a Memorandum on Child Safety Lock Devices for Handguns to Executive Departments and Agencies in part so that "the Federal Government can serve as an example of gun safety for the Nation" as well as to apply pressure on Congress to act. *Public Papers of the Presidents of the United States: William J. Clinton, 1997, Book I* (Washington, DC: Government Printing Office, 1998), 239.

34. Kenneth R. Mayer, "Going Alone: The Presidential Power of Unilateral Action," 427.

35. Richard Nixon, Executive Order 11615, 36 FR 15727, August 17, 1971.

36. "The Economy: The Law Nixon Used," *Time*, August 30, 1971.

37. The crafting of a response to a state request for a Medicaid waiver, for example, might well involve officials from the Department of Health and Human Services, the Department of Justice, the Office of Management and Budget, and the White House Counsel's Office and the White House Office of Economic and Domestic Policy. In most instances, the legal counsels from these executive departments and agencies would be reluctant to approve a request that would likely be challenged in the courts.

38. Mary Landrieu (D-LA) only lifted her several-month hold on the nomination of Jack Lew for director of the Office of Management and Budget after she received adequate assurances from the secretary of interior regarding permits for deep and shallow water drilling in the Gulf of Mexico. Scott Wong and Abby Philip, "OMB's Jack Lew Confirmed after Hold Lifted by Mary Landrieu," *Politico,* November 18, 2010; and Eric Pianin, "Lew Confirmed as OMB Chief after Landrieu Gets Her Way," *Fiscal Times*, November 19, 2010. Similarly, Senator Jesse Helms (R-NC) only lifted his several-month hold on eight senior Treasury Department nominees after receiving a letter promising that the administration would not issue regulations on a Caribbean trade agreement until Congress had devised a "legislative solution" to address his concerns. "Helms Abandons His Hold on Nominees," *Washington Times*, August 7, 2001.

39. Remarks by the president at Sandy Hook Interfaith Prayer Vigil, Newtown, Connecticut, December 16, 2012, http://www.whitehouse.gov/the-press-office/2012/12/16/remarks-president-sandy-hook-interfaith-prayer-vigil.

40. "Now Is the Time: The President's Plan to Protect Our Children and Our Communities by Reducing Gun Violence," January 16, 2013, http://www.whitehouse.gov/sites/default/files/docs/wh_now_is_the_time_full.pdf.

41. "Presidential Memorandum—Tracing of Firearms in Connection with Criminal Investigations," January 16, 2013, http://www.whitehouse.gov/the-press-office/2013/01/16/presidential-memorandum-tracing-firearms-connection-criminal-investigati.

42. "Presidential Memorandum—Engaging in Public Health Research on the Causes and Prevention of Gun Violence," January 16, 2013, http://www.whitehouse.gov/the-press-office/2013/01/16/presidential-memorandum-engaging-public-health-research-causes-and-pre-0.

43. "Presidential Memorandum—Improving Availability of Relevant Executive Branch Records to the National Instant Criminal Background Check System,"

January 16, 2013, http://www.whitehouse.gov/the-press-office/2013/01/16/presidential-memorandum-improving-availability-relevant-executive-branch.

44. "A Broken System for Tracking Guns," *New York Times*, December 31, 2012, A18.

45. "Now Is the Time: The President's Plan to Protect Our Children and Our Communities by Reducing Gun Violence," January 16, 2013.

46. Barack Obama speech to the League of United Latin American Citizens, July 8, 2008, http://realclearpolitics.com/articles/2008/07/obamas_speech_to_lulac.html.

47. Memorandum from Secretary Janet Napolitano to David V. Aguilar, Alejandro Mayorkas, and John Morton, "Exercising Prosecutorial Discretion with Respect to Individuals Who Came to the United States as Children," June 15, 2012, http://www.dhs.gov/xlibrary/assets/s1-exercising-prosecutorial-discretion-individuals-who-came-to-us-as-children.pdf.

48. Barack Obama speech to the National Association of Latino Elected and Appointed Officials Annual Conference, June 22, 2012, http://www.whitehouse.gov/the-press-office/2012/06/22/remarks-president-naleo-annual-conference.

49. On the day he delivered his 2013 State of the Union Address, President Obama issued an executive order, "Improving Critical Infrastructure Cybersecurity." Its objective was to establish voluntary standards to help facilitate the rapid dissemination of information regarding cyberthreats to utility companies. It was issued, in part, because of frustration stemming from an inability to secure legislation acceptable to the president. As Andy Ozment, the White House senior director for cybersecurity, acknowledged to a conference of regulatory utility commissioners, "An executive order is not magical; it does not create new power or authority for any government agencies." See Hannah Northey and Annie Snider, "Obama Poised to Issue Executive Order," *E&E News PM*, February 12, 2013.

50. Andrew Rudalevige, "Candidate Trump Attacked Obama's Executive Orders. President Trump Loves Executive Orders," *Washington Post,* October 17, 2017.

51. White House website, http://www.whitehouse.gov (accessed October 25, 2017).

52. For a useful early assessment of the regulatory reform efforts by the new admin istration, see Ted Gayer, Robert Litan, and Philip Wallach, *Evaluating the Trump Administration's Regulatory Reform Program*, Brookings Institution, October 20, 2017, https://www.brookings.edu/research/evaluating-the-trump-administrations-regulatory-reform-program/.

53. An early assessment is found in Andrew Rudalevige, "Trump May Have the 'Most Executive Orders' since Truman. But What Did They Accomplish?" *Washington Post*, April 28, 2017.

54. This use of the term *rhetorical presidency* is different from that used by Jeffrey Tulis in his excellent studies describing active presidential leadership of popular opinion. See Jeffrey R. Tulis, "The Two Constitutional Presidencies," in *The Presidency and the Political System*, ed. Michael Nelson.

55. "One America in the 21st Century—the President's Initiative on Race," March 1998, https://www.ncjrs.gov/pdffiles/173431.pdf.

56. *Public Papers of the Presidents of the United States: William J. Clinton, 1996, Book I* (Washington, DC: Government Printing Office, 1998), 81.

19

THE PRESIDENCY AT WAR

The Limits of Agency in Wartime Presidential Leadership

Andrew J. Polsky

The Constitutional Convention was on the verge of voting to grant Congress the power "to make war" when Pierce Butler, a delegate from South Carolina, voiced his concern that Congress might not even be in session when the need arose to respond to foreign invasion. Persuaded, James Madison of Virginia and Elbridge Gerry of Massachusetts moved to substitute "declare war" for "make war," thereby "leaving to the Executive the power to repel sudden attacks." That exception to the general rule of congressional initiative in decisions to go to war has been broadened almost beyond recognition throughout American history, and especially since World War II. Andrew J. Polsky observes that the president's constitutional authority as commander in chief has always allowed him to order U.S. troops to go anywhere, including places where their presence was all but certain to provoke a war. During most of American history, the armed forces were too small for presidents to make much use of this authority, except when Congress voted to increase the nation's military apparatus in preparation for a war that Congress intended to declare. The massive standing army, navy, and air force that have existed since the mid-1940s, however, have given presidents from Harry Truman to Donald Trump the means to exercise the commander in chief's power to deploy forces on a scale that has rendered Congress's war-declaring authority almost meaningless. Even, Polsky writes, "the possibility of war invites presidential initiative, yielding an opportunity structure that offers expansive possibilities for the chief executive."

In June 2017, President Donald Trump made his first significant commitment in a military conflict, authorizing the Pentagon to send as many as several thousand additional American troops to Afghanistan to prop up the faltering government of President Ashraf Ghani.[1] As a candidate, Trump at times condemned ongoing U.S. military interventions in Syria/Iraq and Afghanistan. As president, however, he found it more difficult to watch the demise of a friendly government in an unsettled part of the world. In recent years, a resurgent Taliban movement had destabilized much of Afghanistan, putting the survival of the Kabul government at risk. With his decision, Trump extended what was already the longest war in American history.

Skeptical observers might be forgiven for thinking that they had seen this movie before.[2] In February 2009, less than a month after he assumed office, President Barack Obama approved the deployment of 17,000 more troops to Afghanistan. In that instance, the Taliban, having revived after the 2001 American-led invasion, threatened to derail scheduled elections and undermine the regime of then-President Hamid Karzai. The president decided he needed to act immediately to buy time to formulate a long-term strategy.[3]

If the script seemed familiar, the two presidents chose different approaches for how best to direct the filming. Obama determined from the outset to keep close tabs on the use of force during his watch. He insisted that he would define the limits of American intervention—both its goals and its duration. By contrast, Trump delegated the responsibility for managing the conflict to Secretary of Defense James Mattis. The president maintained that wars ought to be directed by proven military professionals. Critics accused him of "outsourcing" the war to avoid the political fallout if things went badly.[4] It remained to be seen whether Trump's hands-off exercise of wartime leadership would yield more lasting results.

War presents a president with a dynamic opportunity structure, which permits varying degrees of agency. By *agency* I mean two things: first, that the actors involved might have made other choices (or that other actors in the same positions might have chosen differently), and, second, that different choices might have had significantly different consequences. In the lead-up to a conflict and in its opening stages, a president demonstrates broad agency. Several factors—the constitutional powers of the office, the military resources at the disposal of any modern commander in chief, and the rallying effect of a national security crisis—combine to give him sweeping freedom of action. A wartime president can capitalize on these circumstances to frame national war goals and define military strategy on his own terms. But the window in which a president exercises unchecked agency closes swiftly. His initial choices foreclose possibilities; the actions of other players, ranging from the troops under his command to allies and adversaries, eliminate others. Especially if the conflict drags on, other political actors, deferential at the start, will begin to reassert themselves, while public support becomes problematic.

We also should understand the exhaustion of agency to be "lumpy" rather than linear. Along the way, the window can be reopened by military developments and/ or the electoral clock, though not as widely as at the outset of the conflict and not for long. In the later stages of a war, a president becomes a captive of circumstances, so much so that, in terms of the outcome, it may make no difference who occupies the White House. An open question at the beginning of the Trump presidency, with a public weary of ongoing wars in Iraq/Syria and Afghanistan, is whether he retains meaningful space to assert agency in those conflicts.

THE PRESIDENTIAL PATH TO WAR

A national security crisis increases the scope of presidential discretion. As the crisis erupts, a president may choose among multiple possible responses, including non-intervention. The constitutional division of powers bestows broad authority on the chief executive as the commander in chief of the armed forces and as the nation's diplomatic leader, and presidents have exploited both roles to make war more likely. They still face potential resistance from the public and Congress. By adroitly managing the circumstances, however, presidents have been able to influence public opinion in ways that their words alone cannot. Congress, too, can find itself with little choice but to approve a presidential request to authorize military operations.

A threat to the United States, even a direct attack, can be met in various ways, and over the years presidents have demonstrated considerable latitude in their responses. In each of the world wars of the twentieth century, the United States avoided becoming a belligerent for more than two years. Woodrow Wilson at the outset of World War I urged Americans to remain neutral in thought as well as deed. He maintained that neutral status until 1917, deflecting pressures from the warring nations to take sides and even efforts from within his own administration to propel the United States into the conflict.[5] A generation later, when Germany invaded Poland in 1939 to begin World War II, Franklin Roosevelt hoped that by providing support for Great Britain and France he could keep the conflict at a distance. After France surrendered in June 1940, he sought to assist the British with "all aid short of war," aware that the American people still opposed intervention.[6] To say that presidents exercise agency amid dangerous international circumstances, however, is not to claim they control the situation. When Wilson declared that if Germany initiated unrestricted submarine warfare he would opt for war, he ceded to Berlin the power to decide whether and when the United States would be drawn into the conflict.[7]

George W. Bush demonstrated again the scope of presidential discretion in the aftermath of the 9/11 terrorist attacks. His administration quickly orchestrated a military operation to topple the Taliban regime in Afghanistan, which had harbored Osama bin Laden and Al Qaeda during the planning of the attacks. Faced with the question of what to do next, the president found himself operating under the most permissive circumstances, abetted by American primacy on the international stage and the relaxation of domestic inhibitions about using American power in the wake of 9/11. As political scientist Gideon Rose puts it, "The administration's leading figures found themselves with extraordinary freedom of action, greater in some ways than any of their predecessors had ever had, and the only question was how they would use it."[8] Exploiting this freedom, the administration planned and launched an invasion of Iraq, even though its government had played no role in the 9/11 attacks.

Sometimes a president may decide against intervention in an international conflict. This alternative becomes more appealing in the wake of military interventions that have gone awry. When confronted with a widening civil war in Syria in 2013, Barack Obama wavered before eventually deciding against committing American ground forces. His decision reflected the chastening experiences of the protracted wars in Iraq and Afghanistan that had yielded continuing instability and violence, all at great cost to the United States in lives and treasure. It became clear over the next three years, however, that inaction may also impose a high price. In Syria, civil war continued; the erosion of central government authority created an opening for a new extremist group, the Islamic State (popularly called ISIS); the violence aggravated a refugee crisis that spilled over far beyond the borders of Syria; and Russia stepped in to give direct military backing to the regime of President Bashar al-Assad. The Syrian civil war underscores a sobering truth: when considering whether to embark on a military conflict, a president may have to choose from a set of only bad options.

Much of the president's flexibility when faced with a situation that may lead to war derives from the constitutional powers vested in the office. The Framers understood the importance of a unified military chain of command, so they established the president as the commander in chief of the armed forces and of the militia (now the National Guard) when called into national service. Significantly, in a constitutional system otherwise filled with elaborate institutional checks, the president acts as commander in chief without securing approval from any other branch of the government. Even in peacetime the president exercises military command, which permits him to issue orders that make a conflict more likely. On multiple occasions presidents have positioned American forces in a way that could easily provoke a violent response from a potential foe or increase the pressure on Congress to approve the use of force. As early as 1845, President James Polk ordered General Zachary Taylor to take a small American army into disputed territory along the Texas–Mexico border. With congressional Whigs and northern Democrats hostile to Polk's expansionist designs, his action courted trouble at home and with America's neighbor to the south.[9] Similarly, George W. Bush dispatched American forces to Kuwait in 2002 before asking Congress to approve a resolution authorizing the use of force in the event that Saddam Hussein failed to comply with American demands for full inspection of his regime's alleged weapons of mass destruction (WMD). Bush also steered the United Nations to support the American position, capitalizing on the prestige of his secretary of state, General Colin Powell, to win over skeptical delegates.[10] In their role as commander in chief, several presidents have exercised military command with the clear intent of provoking a potential adversary to fire the first shot. Polk hoped to induce an armed Mexican response and create a cause for war. When the Mexicans obliged by attacking an American cavalry detachment, Polk asked Congress to recognize that a state of war existed, brought on by Mexico's "aggression." Legislative opposition to Polk's expansionist agenda collapsed.[11] Abraham Lincoln thought along the same lines when he sent a ship to resupply Fort Sumter in Charleston Harbor, which was under siege by secessionist forces, in April 1861. The Confederates bombarded the fort into surrender, an attack that helped unify the North to defend the Union.[12]

Presidents have resorted to manipulating circumstances during national security crises in part because they encounter stubborn resistance to military intervention from key political actors. The American people are not easily persuaded to embrace war.[13] Franklin Roosevelt may have seen American entry into the Second World War as inevitable by mid-1941, but he failed to sell his view to the public. For all his supposed rhetorical gifts, a poll taken at the beginning of December 1941, just a week before the Japanese bombed Pearl Harbor, found that only one in three Americans favored joining the war—a figure unchanged since the French collapse eighteen months earlier.[14] Strikingly, despite the imminent threat of conflict with Germany, Japan, or both, the House of Representatives in August 1941 approved the extension of peacetime conscription by a single vote. As this narrow margin suggests, the legislature may express popular doubts about the need for military action. Lawmakers, particularly from the opposition party, will press a president to exhaust all alternatives to war—especially diplomacy and economic sanctions—before resorting to arms. For example, in the run-up to the 1991 Gulf War, Democrats in Congress urged President George H. W. Bush to postpone a military campaign and give sanctions more time to force Saddam Hussein to withdraw from Kuwait, which his army had occupied the previous summer.[15]

In a test of will between Congress and the executive over whether to go to war, however, the latter holds the stronger hand. This is partly a residue of the constitutional design. The Framers did give Congress the power to declare war, a choice consistent with their preference for careful deliberation in matters of consequence. Early presidents doubted their constitutional authority to engage in military action without congressional approval (though their reservations did not deter them from sending troops to wage war against Indians standing in the path of westward expansion).[16] On the other hand, as Joseph Avella points out, the Framers rejected language that would have left the power to "make war" in legislative hands. From this distinction, the advocates of presidential discretion have inferred that the Framers contemplated situations in which the use of force would fall short of war and thus not require legislative approval.[17] Presidential control over lesser military actions also comports with Alexander Hamilton's vision of the executive as the branch capable of acting with energy to meet a crisis. Initiative, then, rests with the president. For Congress to respond it must overcome the problems of a cumbersome, collective body. More than that, if a president chooses to exercise his authority to order American forces into combat, Congress has few options.

One tool the Framers placed in legislative hands, control over the appropriations needed to create and sustain a military establishment, has ceased to be a meaningful curb on presidents as they contemplate war. Under Article I, it falls on Congress to establish and finance the nation's armed forces, to call state militia into national service, and to impose standards upon the state militia. The article prohibits the use of any army appropriation for longer than two years, a legacy of colonial mistrust of standing armies. For the better part of the next 150 years, the United States maintained only a modest peacetime military, which helped contain any impulse toward executive bellicosity. Only when war loomed did Congress expand the armed forces, as in the War of 1812, the Spanish–American War, World War I, and World War II. In some cases (the Mexican War and the Civil War), legislative approval came after the war began. But with the rise of the United States as a world power at the end of the nineteenth century, this ad hoc approach began to give way to a new national security structure. Since the end of World War II, presidents have had at their disposal a massive permanent military apparatus to plan and execute large-scale troop deployments. Indeed, the United States has maintained a standing military establishment in peacetime that dwarfs any of the nation's pre-twentieth-century wartime forces. With its endorsement of this military transformation, Congress effectively surrendered its constitutional power to deny presidents the means to wage war. Although in theory Congress might deny funding for the military on the eve of a conflict, in reality such an action is politically inconceivable.

Presidents also use their military and diplomatic powers to help win congressional approval for military action. The formal constitutional power to declare war has become an anachronism, last invoked in December 1941. Just the same, most presidents have deemed it prudent to secure legislative endorsement before they embark on a major military operation. Harry Truman dismissed the need for congressional approval when he decided in June 1950 to intervene to help South Korea when it faced a North Korean invasion. But when the war took an abrupt turn for the worse several months later, following the entry of communist Chinese troops, Truman discovered that going it alone leaves a president isolated and vulnerable to sharp congressional criticism.[18] Subsequent presidents usually have taken pains to obtain some form of congressional backing for military action. Because the president determines the timing of such requests, any vote on Capitol Hill occurs under circumstances that maximize the likelihood that lawmakers will go along and thus share responsibility for the conflict. Lyndon Johnson sought and received congressional endorsement of American escalation in Vietnam following putative attacks by North Vietnamese torpedo boats on U.S. Navy vessels in the Tonkin Gulf in August 1964. George W. Bush similarly asked Congress to authorize military operations against Iraq and Saddam Hussein in October 2002. With midterm elections pending, he and his advisers realized that in the post-9/11 political climate, Democrats would fear being tagged with the label "soft on terrorism." They responded by giving strong support to the resolution, especially leaders such as Senators John Kerry, Hillary Clinton, and Joseph Biden, all of whom harbored future presidential aspirations.[19]

In sum, the possibility of war invites presidential initiative, yielding an opportunity structure that offers expansive possibilities for the chief executive. It may be risky for a president to settle the question of war without regard for the preferences of the public or Congress. But he can certainly shape circumstances to make conflict more likely and perhaps unavoidable. In so doing, he can put Congress on the defensive, with neither the means nor the political will to derail him. A recent example confirms the presidential advantage. When Barack Obama decided in 2011 to give direct U.S. military support to Libyan rebels, he declined to seek congressional authorization. In response, apart from some ritual harrumphing from the Republican opposition and the left wing of the Democratic Party, Congress did nothing.[20]

A FREE HAND

In the opening stage of a military conflict, a president enjoys wide latitude as he seeks to accomplish the multiple tasks he faces as a wartime leader. At home he can count on a degree of congressional support that he rarely enjoys on most policy matters. The public rallies behind the war effort as well, a process encouraged by strong media support. With the political foundation for waging war in place, a president can turn to his other immediate leadership challenges: defining the nation's political objectives in going to war, finalizing decisions about military means and strategy, making sure that the military approach is consistent with the political goals he has specified, and putting in place the framework for the postwar order he envisions.[21] Presidential discretion in these matters is striking. Of particular importance, the commander in chief establishes war goals and chooses the path to achieve them without any check on his power, a degree of executive agency beyond that permitted by the political system in other areas.

Congress readily gives a president the tools he requests at the beginning of a conflict. In the era before the United States maintained a large standing military, lawmakers moved quickly to create an army suited for war virtually from scratch, expanding the regular force and summoning the militia into national service. (When Abraham Lincoln took these measures on his own authority at the beginning of the Civil War, Congress ratified his actions as soon as it returned to session.) Even controversial measures, ranging from conscription to sweeping federal controls over the economy, have been approved promptly when the United States entered a major conflict. Amid early mobilization difficulties for World War I, Woodrow Wilson received unprecedented emergency economic powers under the Overman Act and authority to place railroads under federal direction through the Federal Control Act of 1918.[22] Congressional deference extends beyond measures directly related to war mobilization to include significant restrictions on civil liberties. The Wilson administration secured congressional backing for a series of measures targeted at critics of American intervention: the 1917 Espionage Act allowed fines and prison for interfering with recruitment and authorized the postmaster general to block the mailing of literature he found seditious; the October 1917 Trading with the Enemy Act required that all foreign language publications clear certain pieces with the post office before publication; the Alien Act of 1918 let the government deport or incarcerate foreign residents suspected of disloyalty or merely accused of belonging to organizations that advocated violent overthrow of the government; and the May 1918 Sedition Act permitted jailing anyone who said anything disloyal or abusive about the government or the army.[23] Similarly, George W. Bush asked for and received sweeping domestic police powers soon after 9/11 under the USA PATRIOT Act. Only when presidents seek higher taxes for war-related increases in expenditures has Congress "pushed back," granting some of the requests but preferring to finance the war in part either by borrowing or by delaying votes until after congressional elections.

As with Congress, the public falls in line behind the president once he makes a decision for war. This is not surprising, given the tendency for public opinion to follow elite signals. With most political leaders lined up in favor of military intervention, the media typically communicate information supportive of the president's war policy.[24] Dissenting voices at first tend to be marginal political figures; other criticism comes from the leaders of the enemy nation, whose perspective will be dismissed by most Americans. Only in the case of the Vietnam War did press skepticism bedevil a president from the outset: by the time Lyndon Johnson chose escalation in 1965, American reporters in Saigon already dismissed official military accounts as the "Five O'Clock Follies."[25] In subsequent conflicts the Pentagon has taken great care to promote a positive image of American war capabilities and of U.S. troops on the front lines. The Iraq invasion in 2003, for example, saw the use of embedded reporters accompanying American troops on the successful drive to Baghdad to allow the public back home to experience vicariously the danger and the triumph.

With Congress and the public behind the war, a president turns his attention to the things he needs to do to ensure a successful outcome. He must first define the purpose of military action. Although war requires achieving some degree of military success over an adversary, presidents always seek broader political goals, ranging from unconditional surrender (in total wars) to preserving a friendly regime faced with invasion or insurgency. Presidents enjoy a free hand in their initial formulation of war goals. Sometimes a president envisions war as a vehicle for far-reaching, even transformative, political objectives, as when Woodrow Wilson hoped to bring about a new global order in which differences between nations would be resolved not by recourse to violence, but through an international organization.[26] In this vein, too, George W. Bush saw the invasion of Iraq as a means not only to uncover and eliminate Saddam Hussein's WMDs and to depose the dictator, but also to establish a functioning liberal society in the heart of the Middle East that would set in motion similar constructive upheavals throughout the region. Few within a president's inner circle or elsewhere in the American political system have asked hard questions about whether the goals that a president frames are realistic.

Unfettered presidential agency extends to the choice of military means, the selection of commanders, and the definition of military strategy. By making the president the commander in chief of the armed forces, the Framers vested national political and military leadership during a military conflict in the same hands. This arrangement reduces the possibility of friction between political objectives and military means. But because a president must still delegate the conduct of the war to civilian and military subordinates, he cannot take for granted that the planning and conduct of military operations will conform to his aims. Here, again, presidents have latitude in how they set out to execute their wars. Some presidents have chosen to be very hands-on in their role as commander in chief, not trusting the military to fight the war as they intend. Lincoln, who decided at the beginning of the Civil War to seek to restore the Union rather than destroy slavery, disavowed a proclamation by General John C. Frémont, his commander in Missouri, confiscating rebel sympathizers' property and freeing their slaves. Other presidents have preferred to exercise minimal supervision over military planning and strategy. Woodrow Wilson dispatched General John J. Pershing to France in 1917 to command the American Expeditionary Force without ever sitting down with him to discuss how he proposed to use the troops who would follow.[27]

The lead-up to the invasion of Iraq in 2003 demonstrated a new variation on presidential discretion. Bush left the planning of the invasion and postwar arrangements to subordinates, effectively transferring his agency to their hands. Presidential scholars have identified management style as a key individual variable across administrations.[28] Bush's preferred approach stands apart. With his training in business management and background in business, he declared himself to be the first chief executive officer (CEO) president. As he understood this model, the leader establishes the broad goals of the organization, then leaves subordinates with considerable latitude to achieve the objectives while holding them accountable for their performance.[29] For the invasion of Iraq, responsibility rested with civilian leaders in the Pentagon. The result was an unusual fusion of hands-on direction and modern corporate management: the president's express political agents, notably Secretary of Defense Donald Rumsfeld, exercised close supervision over the planning process. Rumsfeld clashed in turn with the military over the size of the invasion force. The uniformed leadership wanted to send 350,000 troops, but he insisted on a smaller, more agile contingent. Further, after bureaucratic battles with the State Department, Rumsfeld secured Pentagon responsibility for planning the postwar restoration of Iraq, a task to which he then devoted minimal attention. The president offered no guidance, despite the very ambitious vision he articulated for the future of Iraq. An opponent of American military efforts at "nation-building," Rumsfeld made clear that he wanted a quick exit following the anticipated regime change in Baghdad. His decisions about troop levels and his casual approach to postwar stability operations (as they are known in military parlance) later drew sharp criticisms when the occupation of Iraq went poorly. In view of the outcome, then, it's worth emphasizing that Bush *chose* to empower his defense secretary in the planning process.[30]

THE WINDOW CLOSES

Wartime presidential freedom of action swiftly diminishes. Often before a president appreciates it, he goes from muscular to muscle-bound. Several factors combine to reshape the opportunity structure in a way that sharply limits his capacity to shape events. The president's first choices foreclose alternatives that might have contributed to success, both in military terms and in realizing his broader political goals. Actions by his key agents on the ground—the military commanders and the troops fighting the war—also may undermine his policy. If no progress is visible as the conflict continues and casualties mount, cracks develop at home in the facade of national unity. The media, the public, and Congress all turn against a war they once supported. But a president who begins a war and believes in its necessity finds it impossible, psychologically and politically, to embrace withdrawal without victory. Further, as he looks for a diplomatic solution to the fighting, he also discovers that he lacks leverage over key foreign actors, including allies, client regimes that the United States has backed, and adversaries.

A president's initial military decisions shape the entire conflict, narrowing his later options. If he uses too few troops, imposes too many or too few restrictions on the troops' use, or ends the fighting too soon, he cannot start over or reverse course. In the 1991 Persian Gulf War, George H. W. Bush accepted a military assessment that only remnants of Saddam Hussein's army had escaped Kuwait, too few to defend the regime against an internal uprising. The president and his advisers expected Saddam to be ousted quickly by his own people, thereby satisfying an unstated administration goal. It soon became clear that much of Saddam's politically reliable Republican Guard had survived. It proved more than enough to suppress the rebellion. By that point Bush had declared victory, and American troops could not intervene.[31] A dozen years later, George W. Bush, determined to be rid of Saddam for good, accepted an invasion plan that sent just over 100,000 American and coalition troops into Iraq. This was enough to accomplish the mission of regime change but far too few to ensure order in Iraq afterwards. In the power vacuum that followed Saddam's defeat, many discontented Iraqis took up arms, and the United States found itself facing a burgeoning insurgency for which the American military had neither the "boots on the ground" nor the counterinsurgency techniques to cope.[32] Nor were there adequate reinforcements at home, because the military was still pursuing Al Qaeda in Afghanistan and the Bush administration had decided against a major expansion of the military in the wake of 9/11.[33]

Wartime presidents also may find their control over events compromised and constrained by the actions of the troops in the field. As commander in chief, the president sits atop a chain of command extending all the way down to the most junior officers and enlisted personnel. As with all principal–agent relations in large organizations, however, effective control may be difficult to exercise, no matter how hands-on a president chooses to be. When the United States intervenes to topple a regime or thwart an insurgency, one key political goal will be winning the hearts and minds of the local population. But whether a president can achieve this objective rests on his military subordinates on scene, and the prospects for success can be compromised, possibly even derailed, by what those subordinates do under the stress of combat. Excessive civilian casualties caused by American military operations damaged the local standing of the United States in Vietnam and Afghanistan; in Iraq, photographs of American military police abusing detainees at the Abu Ghraib prison severely tarnished the American image not just there, but across the Arab world.[34] Nor do the difficulties arise only with those at the bottom of the military hierarchy: even senior commanders may stumble in achieving a president's goals. General William Westmoreland in Vietnam proved to be a poor choice for the kind of unconventional warfare American forces faced, while successive American commanders in Iraq after the end of the invasion campaign in 2003 could not stem the rising insurgency and spreading violence that swept across that nation over the next three years. Presidents can change commanders, of course, but such a move comes with a political price. Replacing a commander represents an admission that a war has not gone according to plan, which reflects badly on the leadership at the top.[35]

Difficulties with getting subordinates to pursue the policy the president has established may extend to key political appointees. At times Woodrow Wilson found himself working at cross purposes with his most important aides. He sent Colonel Edward M. House to Europe in 1918 to act as a go-between with the British and French governments. To the president's chagrin, House agreed to let the Allied military commanders set the military terms for any armistice, failing to appreciate that these would have lasting political ramifications and affect any peace conference.[36] George W. Bush appointed Donald Rumsfeld to be secretary of defense in part because both men agreed that the United States military should not be used for postwar "nation-building." Rumsfeld remained wedded to this view even as Iraq spiraled downward into chaos after 2003, while the president was determined to do whatever was necessary to create the kind of postwar Iraq he had envisioned—even if that required the use of American troops indefinitely. Yet despite their different perspectives, Bush retained his defense secretary for three more years, again reluctant to take a step that would be seen as an acknowledgment of policy failure.[37]

As the fighting continues and casualties mount, domestic backing for wars erodes. Wartime unity has always been short-lived, much to presidents' chagrin. The media take increasing note of (and, indeed, may magnify, due to their professional biases and commercial incentives) setbacks and difficulties. Accordingly, the American people will be exposed to many stories about the lack of measurable military progress, the failings of client regimes being propped up by American support, and the ongoing losses among American troops. Add to this the disenchantment of political elites. In particular, defections among a president's partisan allies will have a significant effect on public views of the war.[38] Domestic dissent then begins to mount, too. During the Vietnam War, Lyndon Johnson faced massive antiwar demonstrations by 1967, less than two years after his decision to escalate American involvement. Polls demonstrated widespread public doubts about the war.[39] A similar pattern appeared after the 2003 invasion of Iraq. By late 2005 public backing for the war had declined, and prominent members of Congress, led by Representative John Murtha, a Vietnam veteran, began to urge American withdrawal.[40] Lawmakers' endorsement of an antiwar position represents a pivotal moment, for it signals that the opposition has entered the political mainstream.

Antiwar protest has always unsettled wartime presidents. The right to oppose a war enjoys constitutional protection. Moreover, when dissent moves from the political margins into the mainstream, it is a strong indication that something has gone amiss on the battlefield. But most presidents do not view antiwar opposition as a warning sign of policy failure and take the opportunity to reconsider their strategy and their war goals. Instead, presidents regard protests as unpatriotic, giving aid and comfort to the enemy and undermining the morale of the troops fighting to protect the nation. This reaction is understandable and has some foundation. At times America's adversaries have encouraged domestic opponents of a president's war policies. During the Civil War, Democratic "Copperheads" were encouraged by the Confederacy to believe that only Lincoln's obstinacy stood in the way of peace. During the Vietnam War, the communist leadership in Hanoi closely monitored the size of antiwar demonstrations in the United States and invited leaders of the peace movement to visit the North Vietnamese capital to witness the destruction of civilian targets by American bombers. Influencing American hearts and minds, in short, has always been part of enemy war strategy.

Faced with a rising tide of dissent yet convinced their choice of war was correct, presidents find themselves squeezed into a narrow policy space. Mounting domestic opposition removes from the table one possible response to military stalemate: a major escalation of the American military commitment. Congress will not pull the plug on funding a war so long as American troops remain in combat, but legislative agreement to sustain a larger force is another matter. Opposition to a war may be strong enough to cost a president's party control of Congress, as in the case of the Republicans in the 2006 midterm elections. At the same time, presidents who begin wars that degenerate into stalemate do not disengage from the conflict. Persuaded that they made the right call in choosing military action, they remain too invested in it to reverse their initial decision.[41] And their core supporters continue to stand behind that decision.[42] Sometimes, indeed, a president's backers become more convinced of the rationale for war. Even after no WMDs were found in Iraq, polls in the following years showed that the percentage of Republicans who believed Saddam possessed such a capability had increased.[43] Rather than withdraw, then, a president doubles down on his commitment, escalating the rhetoric about the dangers of defeat. As the public became more discouraged by the Iraq War, Bush issued increasingly dire warnings about terrorists following departing American troops back to the American homeland.[44]

The loss of presidential agency extends to the diplomatic arena, too. Presidents must deal with allies and coalition partners, client regimes, and adversaries and the governments that support them. Each of these relationships poses challenges that become more difficult over the course of a conflict. Just because nations fight on the same side does not mean they share many common interests. Indeed, in the case of the United States and the Soviet Union in World War II, the two countries shared almost nothing in common besides a determination to bring about the total defeat of Nazi Germany. Presidents may find themselves with scant leverage over allies and coalition partners, and the little they have declines over time. The Bush administration struggled to put together a significant coalition to join in the Iraq invasion, and coalition partners regarded the postwar chaos and episodes of terror directed at their own citizens as reason to scale back or terminate their commitments.

Client regimes have been a source of frustration to every president who has backed a government trying to suppress an insurgency, whether in Vietnam, Iraq, or Afghanistan. These regimes struggle to establish their legitimacy in the eyes of their own people. To give in to American demands for reform would validate the insurgents' charge that the regime is a mere puppet of the United States. Making matters worse, the United States intervenes without making reform a condition for aid, even as the president declares the client regime's survival to be a vital matter of American national security.[45] The president is therefore without leverage when the regime leader—for example, Hamid Karzai in Afghanistan—balks at American demands to clean up corruption or broaden the political base of his government.

Most frustrating are the efforts to negotiate with the enemy. Limited wars, in which the United States does not seek the complete destruction of the adversary, usually require diplomatic engagement with the opposing side. Presidential actions may influence the timing of negotiations. For example, Lyndon Johnson's decision to halt bombing of North Vietnam above the 20th parallel in March 1968 finally drew Hanoi to the bargaining table. But the Vietnam War also shows that an adversary may see political advantage in refusing to talk. Although Johnson tried for three years following the American escalation in South Vietnam in 1965 to persuade Hanoi to join peace talks, he succeeded only after the war had destroyed his reelection prospects.[46] The other side may prefer to let the swelling current of discontent in the United States weaken the president's hand or conclude that the next election will bring about a peaceful "regime change" in Washington, with a new president who is not committed to staying the course. And Vietnam does not represent the worst diplomatic scenario, because Johnson at least knew who spoke for the enemy. More recent conflicts in Iraq and Afghanistan have seen factionalized insurgencies with shadowy backers in neighboring countries, a situation that leaves a president without a clear negotiating counterpart.

THE ENDGAME

The decline of presidential agency during a war may not trace a straight line, but it is irreversible. Wars are inherently volatile, and circumstances may restore a measure of latitude for a political leader. Developments on the battlefield sometimes create new military or political possibilities. Further, when a new president takes office amid an ongoing war, he can take steps effectively denied his predecessor. In either case, however, the partial reopening of the window of agency does not last. Absent victory, which in limited wars becomes less likely over time, a president will need to define an exit strategy.[47] Once he does, he finds himself in an opportunity structure bereft of options that would let him exercise any meaningful influence on the course of events. If he has not managed to put in place the elements of a postwar settlement by the time American troops stop fighting, he will surely lack the means to do so afterward.

Through war-driven circumstances, presidents sometimes receive new opportunities to shape events. Probably the most significant expansion in a president's agency came during the Civil War. At the outset of the conflict in April 1861, Abraham Lincoln decided to limit the nation's war goals to restoring the Union, fearing that an antislavery focus would alienate important political constituencies in the North. During the next fifteen months, however, pressure for emancipation mounted, a consequence of slaves fleeing into Union lines, rising casualties that led the northern public to demand a greater return for the sacrifices being made, and the realization that slave labor was an important cornerstone of the Confederate war effort. Lincoln seized the moment in September 1862 to publish the preliminary Emancipation Proclamation and formally transform the conflict into a total war to destroy the foundation of the South's social order.[48] War may also place in the president's hands new tools for pursuing his objectives. At the start of the Iraq invasion in 2003, the American military could call on no recent experience in counterinsurgency (COIN) warfare, a critical deficiency as violence spread during the next several years. Through experience earned at a terrible cost, the troops developed new methods for improving population security—or, more accurately, relearned techniques not used since the Vietnam War. These in turn were codified in a new COIN doctrine, which became the basis for the operational approach that animated the troop surge ordered by George W. Bush at the beginning of 2007. In combination with other factors, notably the rejection of extremist violence by a significant part of the Iraqi Sunni minority (the Anbar Awakening), COIN methods helped lessen the level of violence in Iraq and yielded a measure of stability by early 2008.[49] Absent the COIN approach, Bush would have had no good alternatives—as noted earlier, neither escalation nor withdrawal was politically possible.

American politics also can restore a degree of presidential freedom of action during a war. A newly elected president who inherits an ongoing military stalemate benefits from "second-chance" agency, giving him room to take some steps not possible under his predecessor. Public discontent with the conflict, which likely contributed to the incoming president's election, means he has to find a path out of the war. Still, the American people will grant him both more time and greater flexibility. Public support for the war in Afghanistan was already low by the time Barack Obama took office in 2009, and his fellow Democrats were especially eager to see an end to the American combat role. But all seemed prepared to give Obama a grace period to find a way out, and Democrats in Congress were much less willing to demand withdrawal than they had been when Bush persisted in Iraq after 2006.[50] Obama demonstrated agency not only in his decision to send additional forces to Afghanistan, but also in redefining war aims—the United States and its allies would seek merely to degrade the Taliban insurgency rather than defeat it—and in limiting the duration of the surge so the troops would begin to return home in 2011.[51]

Yet the increased agency that a president claims soon disappears, marking a return to the larger dynamic of a decline in his ability to control events. Once Lincoln redefined his war goals to include emancipation, he could never turn back; after his surge decision, Bush became little more than a cheerleader for his new commander in Iraq, General David Petraeus. Obama found himself in a similar position in Afghanistan. Having committed additional American troops for eighteen months, he could do little to shape the fighting, stem the corruption of the Karzai regime in Kabul, or persuade Pakistan to cease giving support and safe havens to insurgent leaders.[52] Troop withdrawals in particular compromise a president's agency. When Richard Nixon began to pull American troops out of Vietnam in 1969, his national security adviser, Henry Kissinger, cautioned that the process could never be reversed. For the American people, Kissinger said, troop withdrawals are like salted peanuts—give them a taste, and they'll only want more, and no president will be able to resist the pressure.[53] Further, when troop withdrawals begin, the American people cease to care about the outcome of the conflict, causing presidential warnings about the dire consequences of defeat to fall on deaf ears. The disengagement process also reduces a president's diplomatic leverage. Client regimes, insurgents, and any neighboring countries supporting the insurgents recognize that the United States is leaving and begin to position themselves for the new state of affairs after the Americans are gone.

By the end of a conflict, a president's ability to shape a postwar settlement has disappeared. Back home, the public turns its attention to peacetime concerns. Although isolationism represents an extreme reaction to the high price of war, a lack of interest in the aftermath—in peace building—is common. Congressional deference to presidential leadership, so evident at the outset, will diminish over the course of a conflict, then vanish completely as soon as peace returns. Abroad, peace spells the weakening or dissolution of wartime alliances and coalitions, no longer held together by the glue of necessity. Woodrow Wilson discovered how powerless a president can be at the moment of his triumph. After negotiating the armistice that ended World War I in November 1918, he failed to secure the kind of peace agreement that he had used to justify American intervention and saw the Senate reject his plan for a League of Nations.[54] Other presidents have experienced similar frustrations at the end of their wars. For example, when the last American troops left Iraq, the Obama administration failed to negotiate a "status of forces" agreement that would have kept a residual American military presence in that country to help ensure stability and preserve U.S. influence. The emergence of ISIS stemmed in no small degree from that failure.[55]

When Donald Trump took office in 2017, he inherited two long and unpopular wars with no attractive policy options. As a candidate he had captured popular frustration with the lack of meaningful success at nation-building, while not committing to any specific course of action. But even though he did not tie his own hands, Trump found himself with minimal freedom of action. In Afghanistan, the deployment of additional troops might buy the local regime more time, but it isn't evident how that time could be used to achieve better results than previous troop surges. Delegating responsibility to his defense secretary and the military may serve to keep the spotlight off the White House, but the move doesn't address the plain fact that the United States has never been able to create a basis for a political solution in Afghanistan. In Syria/Iraq, the recapture of territory from ISIS in 2017 seemed likely to drive the insurgents underground while empowering regional powers such as Iran that are deeply hostile to American interests. The American people years ago turned their collective back on Iraq. Neither they nor their elected representatives in Congress would support any significant American escalation. It may be, then, that the best Trump can do is to manage these conflicts until he can turn them over to his successor.

CONCLUSION

War presents the president with a dynamic opportunity structure that invites popular misunderstanding. The broad possibilities for the president to exercise agency at the outset and in the early stages of a conflict have led many to conclude that war magnifies presidential power. Much has been written about whether presidents have overstepped their constitutional role by leading the nation into frequent military conflicts and how this proclivity might be curbed. Yet the quick and ultimately irreversible decline in wartime presidential agency points in another direction: presidents find themselves with too little power to achieve the political objectives they establish in going to war.

Presidents themselves have not recognized this pattern. War first throws open a window of agency. For a president, it may be a heady moment, tantalizing with possibilities for escaping the ordinary restraints imposed by the American political system, reshaping the behavior of other nations, and even establishing a new global order. But the moment passes quickly, and unless a president seizes it he will fall far short of his goals. Some, including Lyndon Johnson in Vietnam and George W. Bush in Iraq, failed to assert firm direction over military policy early on when their choices had the greatest impact. Most waited too long to set in place the elements of their postwar vision and found themselves thwarted by the indifference of the American public, revived congressional assertiveness, media skepticism, and the loss of diplomatic leverage. Once the window closes, a wartime president is very much the captive of circumstances, not their master.

NOTES

1. Mark Landler and Michael R. Gordon, "As U.S. Adds Troops in Afghanistan, Trump's Strategy Remains Undefined," *New York Times*, June 18, 2017, https://www.nytimes.com/2017/06/18/world/asia/us-troops-afghanistan-trump.html.
2. "The Groundhog Day War in Afghanistan," *New York Times*, May 29, 2017, https://www.nytimes.com/2017/05/29/opinion/afghanistan-troops-trump-taliban.html?_r=0.
3. Bob Woodward, *Obama's Wars* (New York: Simon and Schuster, 2010), 96 97.
4. Michael R. Gordon, "Trump Gives Mattis Authority to Send More Troops to Afghanistan," *New York Times*, June 13, 2017, https://www.nytimes.com/2017/06/13/world/asia/mattis-afghanistan-military.html.
5. For a fuller discussion of Wilson's efforts to navigate the perilous shoals of neutrality, see Andrew J. Polsky, *Elusive Victories: The American Presidency at War* (New York: Oxford University Press, 2012), 86–95.
6. Ibid., 142–143.
7. After warning a potential adversary that certain actions would provoke an American military response, a president can still decide not to make good on the threat. Doing so, however, has negative reputational consequences, making the United States look feckless. Barack Obama found himself in this position when he warned the Syrian government not to cross a "red line" by using poison gas against rebels in the civil war there. His subsequent failure to act emboldened the Syrian regime.
8. Gideon Rose, *How Wars End: Why We Always Fight the Last Battle* (New York: Simon and Schuster, 2010), 270.
9. John H. Schroeder, *Mr. Polk's War: American Opposition and Dissent, 1846–1848* (Madison: University of Wisconsin Press, 1973), chap. 1.
10. Gary R. Hess, *Presidential Decisions for War,* 2nd ed. (Baltimore: Johns Hopkins University Press, 2009), 235–246; Michael R. Gordon and General Bernard E.

Trainor, *Cobra II: The Inside Story of the Invasion and Occupation of Iraq* (New York: Pantheon, 2006), 130.

11. Schroeder, *Mr. Polk's War,* chap. 1.

12. Polsky, *Elusive Victories,* 35–36.

13. On ambivalent popular attitudes toward war, see Dominic Tierney, *How We Fight: Crusades, Quagmires, and the American Way of War* (New York: Little, Brown, 2011).

14. Polsky, *Elusive Victories,* 154.

15. Hess, *Presidential Decisions for War,* 189.

16. David P. Currie, "Rumors of War: Presidential and Congressional War Powers, 1809–1829," *University of Chicago Law Review* 67 (Winter 2000): 1–40; William D. Adler, "'Generalissimo of the Nation': Warmaking and the Presidency in the Early Republic," *Presidential Studies Quarterly* 43 (June 2013): 412–426.

17. Joseph R. Avella, "The President, Congress, and Decisions to Employ Military Force," in *The Presidency Then and Now,* ed. Phillip G. Henderson (Lanham, MD: Rowman and Littlefield, 2000), 51–52.

18. Hess, *Presidential Decisions for War,* chap. 1.

19. Polsky, *Elusive Victories,* 283.

20. By contrast, Obama decided that he would seek congressional authorization to intervene in Syria before ultimately rejecting the military option. Michael R. Gordon and Jackie Calmes, "President Seeks to Rally Support for Syria Strike," *New York Times,* September 1, 2013, http://www.nytimes.com/2013/09/02/world/middleeast/syria.html.

21. These tasks are discussed in greater detail in Polsky, *Elusive Victories,* Introduction.

22. Arthur Link and John W. Chambers, "Woodrow Wilson as Commander-in-Chief," in *The United States Military under the Constitution of the United States, 1789–1989,* ed. Richard Kohn (New York: NYU Press, 1991), 326–330.

23. Kendrick A. Clements, *The Presidency of Woodrow Wilson* (Lawrence: University Press of Kansas, 1992), 153.

24. John R. Zaller, *The Nature and Origins of Mass Opinion* (New York: Cambridge University Press, [1992] 1995), chap. 6.

25. Kathleen J. Turner, *Lyndon Johnson's Dual War: Vietnam and the Press* (Chicago: University of Chicago Press, 1985), 140–141.

26. Polsky, *Elusive Victories,* 96–98.

27. Ibid., 37, 103–104. Wilson chose his "hands-off" approach in part because he believed Lincoln had been too meddlesome in military matters.

28. For an overview, see Joseph A. Pika, John Anthony Maltese, and Norman C. Thomas, *The Politics of the Presidency,* 5th ed. (Washington, DC: CQ Press, 2002), 144ff.

29. For a discussion of the Bush approach, see James P. Pfiffner, "The First MBA President: George W. Bush as a Public Administrator," *Public Administration Review* 67 (January–February 2007): 6–20.

30. Polsky, *Elusive Victories,* 284–288.

31. Hess, *Presidential Decisions for War,* chap. 6; Thomas E. Ricks, *Fiasco: The American Military Adventure in Iraq* (New York: Penguin Books, 2006), 4–6.

32. Analysts debate whether the insurgency might have been averted had more troops been available. One school holds that Iraqi society was so badly fragmented that conflict among Sunnis, Shiites, and Kurds was inevitable. That said, there seems little doubt that the scale of the insurgency would have been much more limited had the invading forces imposed order quickly. See Rose, *How Wars End,* 273–276.

33. Polsky, *Elusive Victories,* chap. 6.

34. Ricks, *Fiasco,* 378–380; Hess, *Presidential Decisions for War,* 267–268.

35. For a discussion of Johnson's decision to retain Westmoreland, see Lewis Sorley, *A Better War: The Unexamined Victories and Final Tragedy of America's Last Years in Vietnam* (Orlando, FL: Harvest/Harcourt, 1999), 15–16.

36. Clements, *Presidency of Woodrow Wilson,* 165–167. I do not mean to suggest that compliance problems only arise once the United States is at war. While the nation was still neutral, Wilson and Roosevelt alike encountered difficulties with willful subordinates determined to thwart presidential preferences. See Polsky, *Elusive Victories,* 92, 141–142.

37. Polsky, *Elusive Victories,* 304–307.

38. Matthew A. Baum and Tim J. Groeling, *War Stories: The Causes and Consequences of Public Views of War* (Princeton, NJ: Princeton University Press, 2009).

39. Larry Berman, *Lyndon Johnson's War: The Road to Stalemate in Vietnam* (New York: W. W. Norton, 1989), 85–86.

40. Stephen Benedict Dyson, "George W. Bush, the Surge, and Presidential Leadership," *Political Science Quarterly* 125, no. 4 (2010–2011): 565.

41. Andrew J. Polsky, "Staying the Course: Presidential Leadership, Military Stalemate, and Strategic Inertia," *Perspectives on Politics* 8 (March 2010): 127–139.

42. Brandon Rottinghaus, "Following the 'Mail Hawks': Alternative Measures of Public Opinion on Vietnam in the Johnson White House," *Public Opinion Quarterly* 71, no. 3 (2007): 1–25.

43. Jack Snyder, Robert Shapiro, and Yaeli Bloch-Elkon, "Free Hand Abroad, Divide and Rule at Home" (paper presented at the 2007 Annual Meeting of the American Political Science Association, August 30–September 2, 2007), 21–22.

44. Polsky, *Elusive Victories,* 310–311.

45. Douglas Macdonald, *Adventures in Chaos: American Intervention for Reform in the Third World* (Cambridge, MA: Harvard University Press, 1992).

46. Polsky, *Elusive Victories,* 247–250.

47. The need to identify a way out of a conflict has become more urgent in the modern period as the United States has found itself in a series of unwinnable conflicts. For a careful analysis of this challenge, see Dominic Tierney, *The Right Way to Lose a War: America in an Age of Unwinnable Conflicts* (New York: Little, Brown, 2015).

48. James M. McPherson, *Abraham Lincoln and the Second American Revolution* (New York: Oxford University Press, 1991), chap. 4.

49. See Dyson, "George W. Bush, the Surge, and Presidential Leadership," 572–573; Polsky, *Elusive Victories,* 313–314.

50. Woodward, *Obama's Wars,* 101–102.

51. Polsky, *Elusive Victories,* 335–336.

52. Ibid., 337–339.

53. Henry Kissinger, *Ending the Vietnam War* (New York: Simon and Schuster, 2003), 586–88, as quoted in Rose, *How Wars End,* 347n.

54. For a compelling and thorough account, see Margaret MacMillan, *Paris 1919: Six Months That Changed the World* (New York: Random House, [2001] 2003).

55. This is not to suggest that negotiating such an agreement was necessarily feasible, given the fierce resistance of the Iraqi government at the time.

"THE FIRING, RETIRING, AND EXPIRING OF PRESIDENTS"

Impeachment, Disability, Resignation, and Death— From the Constitutional Convention to Donald Trump

Michael Nelson

When granting the president a fixed, four-year term, the Framers of the Constitution added emergency exits: an impeachment process to remove presidents judged by Congress to be guilty of "Treason, Bribery, or other high Crimes and Misdemeanors," and a much vaguer provision for removing presidents on grounds of "Inability to discharge the Powers and Duties" of the office, which was later clarified by the addition of the Twenty-fifth Amendment in 1967. The Framers also acknowledged in the Constitution that a president's term might be ended prematurely by death or resignation. Historically, Michael Nelson shows, all four of these eventualities have arisen. Donald Trump's presidency raises the possibility that any one of them might arise in his case.

Creating the presidency was one of the boldest acts of the Constitutional Convention of 1787.[1] The Articles of Confederation included no executive branch. The governors of most states were weak, often elected by their legislatures to a one-year term and entrusted with few powers. Convinced by experience that "energy in the executive is a leading character in the definition of good government," the delegates created a unitary executive chosen independently of Congress for a four-year term with substantial powers.[2] They also acknowledged in the document that a president might die or choose to resign from office before the term expires. In addition, anticipating that opponents of ratifying the Constitution would attack the presidency as a thinly disguised monarchy reminiscent of the one Americans had overthrown in the revolutionary war, the delegates added two "emergency exits" to bring the tenure of a seriously flawed president to a close prior to the end of the four-year term.[3]

One way of removing such a president from office is impeachment. Both the process and the grounds for impeachment and removal were spelled out in the Constitution in language that has never been altered. By a majority vote of the House of Representatives and a two-thirds vote of the Senate, a president can be impeached and removed for committing "Treason, Bribery, or other high Crimes and Misdemeanors." The second way of removing a president involves disability. In case of a presidential "Inability to discharge the Powers and Duties of the said Office," the president would be temporarily (or permanently—the wording was not clear) removed. Neither the meaning of "Inability" nor any process for determining if it existed were specified, however. The Twenty-fifth Amendment, which became part of the Constitution in 1967, did not define inability but it did create a process for deciding whether a president is disabled.

Historically, deaths in office—four by natural causes, four by assassination—have been by far the most common cause of presidents not completing their terms. Two presidents have been impeached but not removed, although the one president ever to resign did so in the face of certain impeachment and removal. As for disability, one recent president has invoked the Twenty-fifth Amendment but none has been displaced from office for more than a couple hours or against his will. Even so, fairly serious discussions of impeaching President Donald Trump or declaring him disabled occurred as early as his first few months in office. In all cases—death, impeachment and removal, resignation, and disability—the Constitution designates that the powers and duties of the presidency are transferred to the vice president.

This chapter addresses each of these forms of presidential removal, its origins in the Constitution, its history during the more than two centuries that have followed, and the recent controversies concerning Trump. It begins by describing what the Constitution provides, as well as the laws and practices that have clarified and sometimes obscured the document's meaning.

THE CONSTITUTION AND THE LAW

While granting the president a fixed four-year term, the Constitution of 1787 addressed four ways that the term might be brought to a premature end. Provisions relating to impeachment were included in both Article I, the legislative article, and Article II, which deals with the presidency. Article I specifies that "the House of Representatives . . . shall have sole Power of Impeachment" and "the Senate shall have the sole Power to try all Impeachments." The House, in other words, is to function roughly like a grand jury, deciding whether there is enough evidence to indict the president, and the Senate is to act like a trial jury, deciding whether the evidence is sufficient to convict. During the trial of a president, "senators shall be on oath or affirmation" and "the Chief Justice shall preside." For the president to be removed from office at the conclusion of the trial, "the concurrence of two-thirds of the Members [of the Senate] present" is required. Although the penalty for a negative vote is limited to "removal from Office and disqualification to hold and enjoy any Office" in the future, a president who is "convicted shall nevertheless be liable and subject to Indictment, Trial, Judgment and Punishment according to Law." The constitutional grounds for impeachment were stated in Article II: "Treason, Bribery, or other high Crimes and Misdemeanors."

Impeachment and each of the other three ways that a president's term might end prematurely were also addressed in another provision of Article II:

> In Case of the Removal of the President from Office, or of his Death,
> Resignation, or Inability to discharge the Powers and Duties of the said
> Office, the Same shall devolve on the Vice President, and the Congress
> may by Law provide for the Case of Removal, Death, Resignation
> or Inability, both of the President and Vice President, declaring
> what Officer shall then act as President, and such Officer shall act
> accordingly, until the Disability be removed, or a President shall be
> elected.

Multiple ambiguities attend these constitutional provisions. Concerning impeachment, for example, what is a "high Crime and Misdemeanor"? No clear answer can be found in the records of the Constitutional Convention. Concerning "inability," what defines a president as disabled and who has the authority to make that judgment? Again the record is unhelpful. At one point in the convention, John Dickinson of Delaware rose to ask, "What is the extent of the term 'disability' & who is to be the judge of it?"[4] The delegates adjourned for the week and never revisited the matter.

Concerning all four methods, what actually happens when a president vacates the office? Does the vice president become president for the remainder of the four-year term or merely acting president until a special election can be called? Much hinges on the antecedent of "the Same" in the clause "the Same shall devolve on the

Vice President." Does it refer back to "the said Office," in which case the vice president becomes president, or to the office's "Powers and Duties," which suggests that the vice president merely fills in temporarily? The latter is what the delegates seem to have intended, but they did not make this clear.[5] Further, by placing "Inability" in the same clause as "Removal," "death," and "resignation"—all three of the latter final rather than possibly temporary states—did the Constitution mean that a president who was removed for illness or injury could not return to office upon recovery? And, finally, would Congress actually "by Law provide" an answer to the question of "what Officer shall then act as President" in the event that both the presidency and the vice presidency become vacant—and if so, what line of succession would that law create?

As the sections of this chapter that follow make clear, some of these questions have been addressed through practice and precedent. Others have been answered by the enactment of laws or constitutional amendments. In 1792, 1886, and 1947 Congress passed bills that created, then changed, and then changed again the line of presidential succession that follows the vice president, as well as initially providing for and then rejecting a special election for a new president. In 1965 Congress proposed and by 1967 enough states ratified a new Twenty-fifth Amendment to the Constitution. Section 1 of the amendment explicitly stated that if the president dies, resigns, or is impeached and removed, "the Vice President shall become President" in every sense of the word. Without defining inability, the amendment also created procedures both for a president to transfer the "powers and duties of his office" to the vice president and for others in the government, including the vice president, to effect that transfer—in all cases temporarily, "until no inability exists." In order to ensure that a vice president always would be available to perform his or her responsibilities under the amendment, Section 2 provides that if the vice presidency becomes vacant a new vice president must be appointed.

In 1933, the Twentieth Amendment already had addressed two other possible situations. It stipulates that if a president-elect were to die before the start of the term, the vice president–elect would be inaugurated as president. The amendment also states that, if by inauguration day, no presidential candidate has received either a majority of electoral votes or the support of a majority of state delegations in the House, the vice president–elect, chosen by a simple majority vote of the Senate, would act as president until a president was chosen. Other provisions of the amendment deal with equally remote but real possibilities: for example, that a vice president–elect might not be chosen or that either a winning presidential or vice presidential candidate might die before receiving "elect" status when Congress counts the electoral votes in early January.

DEATH

It isn't clear which of four ways the presidency could become vacant before the end of the four-year term the framers of the Constitution thought would be the most common. As it happens, all of the delegates to the Constitutional Convention were dead before any of these contingencies arose.[6] Starting with George Washington, the first eight presidents all completed the one or two terms to which they were elected. As a result, during the country's first fifty-two years under the Constitution, its provisions regarding death, impeachment, resignation, and disability never had to be invoked.

This changed in 1841, when William Henry Harrison, at sixty-eight the oldest president ever elected until Ronald Reagan in 1980, fell ill after giving a two-hour inaugural address on a cold and wet day and died just one month later. During the 122 years that followed, seven additional presidents died. Indeed, a useful if grim mnemonic for remembering most of these deaths is that from 1840 to 1960 every president elected in a year ending in zero died in office. Four died of natural causes: Harrison, Zachary Taylor in 1850, Warren G. Harding in 1923, and Franklin D. Roosevelt in 1945. Four others were assassinated: Abraham Lincoln in 1865, James A. Garfield in 1881, William McKinley in 1901, and John F. Kennedy in 1963. Since the Kennedy assassination, no president has died in office, although serious attempts were made on the lives of Gerald R. Ford in 1975 and Reagan in 1981.

Harrison's death on April 4, 1841, aroused several of the ambiguities in the original Constitution. Specifically, did Vice President John Tyler remain vice president, merely acting as president until a special election could be held, or did he succeed fully to the office and title of president for the remaining three years and eleven months of Harrison's four-year term? Former president John Quincy Adams, who after leaving office had been elected to the House of Representatives, was among those who thought that Tyler only assumed temporarily the powers and duties of the presidency. Tyler, who was at his home in Williamsburg, Virginia, when he received word of Harrison's death, disagreed. He immediately set out for Washington by coach and, soon after he arrived on April 6, took the oath of office and gave a kind of inaugural address to an audience gathered in the Capitol. Adams and most members of Congress acquiesced to Tyler's claim but some actively disagreed. When a motion was offered in the House to appoint a committee to "wait on the President of the United States," an amendment was offered to strike "President of the United States" and substitute "Vice President, on whom, by the death of the late President, the Powers and Duties of the office of President have devolved."[7] The motion failed. The majority of members seemed to realize that not much was to be gained by alienating the person who, whether as president or acting president, would be wielding the powers of the office for some time.

By acting boldly and decisively in a constitutionally ambiguous situation, the "Tyler Precedent" was established, so much so that when President Taylor died in office nine years later, also of natural causes, no doubts were raised about what was to happen next. Without controversy, Vice President Millard Fillmore became president and remained so for the twenty months left in Taylor's four-year term. But Tyler's and Taylor's deaths, as well as those of the other six presidents and the nine vice presidents who have died in office, left the vice presidency vacant. An accidental explosion on a naval warship in February 1844 that killed the secretary of state, the secretary of war, and five others spared President Tyler his life and the country a double vacancy only because he happened to be below deck.

If Tyler or any other president of that era who was in office without a vice president had died, resigned, become disabled, or been impeached and removed, a succession act passed by Congress in 1792 pursuant to Article II of the Constitution would have applied. The act provided that in the absence of both a president and vice president, the president pro tempore of the Senate or, if that office was vacant, the Speaker of the House would become acting president.[8] If the double vacancy occurred with more than six months left in the four-year term, Congress would call a special election for a new president and vice president.

Although Lincoln's death on April 14, 1865, six weeks after he was inaugurated for his second term, was the first to come at the hands of an assassin, there once again was no uncertainty about Vice President Andrew Johnson's right to succeed him as president. Neither the Lincoln assassination nor those of the other three presidents who have been murdered—or the five upon whom serious assassination attempts were made (Andrew Jackson, Harry S. Truman, Ford, Reagan, and President-Elect Franklin D. Roosevelt)—was part of a serious, organized effort to launch a revolution or coup d'état. This is not to say that none of them were politically motivated—John Wilkes Booth and his small band of fellow conspirators hoped that killing Lincoln would save the Confederacy, for example—but rather that they originated on the fringes of political ferment.[9]

Garfield's assassination four months after taking office in 1881 was of this kind. His killer, Charles Guiteau, had deluded himself into thinking that he would have a better chance of being appointed to a prominent position in the administration if Vice President Chester A. Arthur became president. "I am a Stalwart," Guiteau declared when his bullet struck Garfield, "and Arthur will be President!"[10] The slaying triggered a reevaluation, prompted by President Arthur, of the 1792 succession act. When Arthur took office, not just the vice presidency both also the presidency pro tempore of the Senate and the Speakership of the House—the only two offices in the existing line of succession—were vacant. Once Arthur raised the issue, others noted that the 1792 act had been passed before political parties were clearly established and did not take account of the subsequent reality that a Senate president or House Speaker who succeeded to the presidency might be a member of the opposite party from the late president. A new succession act was passed in 1886. It established a cabinet-centered line of succession, with the heads of each department listed according to the order in which their departments were created: the secretary of state first, then the secretary of the treasury, and so on. The new act also granted Congress discretion about whether to call a special election rather than requiring it to do so.

Sixty years later, the line of succession again was revised, this time at the instigation of Truman, whose ascent to the presidency when Franklin Roosevelt died left the vice presidency vacant. Truman believed strongly that "the office of the President should be filled by an elective officer."[11] He failed to persuade Congress that "a special election [should be] called for the purpose of electing a new President and Vice President"; indeed, Congress decided that anyone who succeeded to the presidency should serve whatever remained of the four-year term, foreclosing the special election option that the 1792 act required and the 1886 act allowed. Truman did succeed in persuading Congress to restore elected officials to the front of the line, just behind the vice president. In contrast to the 1792 act, the Speaker of the House was ranked first and the president pro tempore of the Senate, which over time had become an honorary rather than a leadership position, second. Conferred on the longest-serving member of the majority party, it usually has been held by senators in their eighties or nineties. Cabinet members followed the Speaker and the president pro tempore in the order in which their departments were created.

Lincoln and Arthur were essentially unguarded when gunmen assassinated them. The same was true in 1901, when President McKinley was murdered. Three assassinations in thirty-six years spurred Congress to assign the Secret Service, whose main job had been pursuing counterfeiters, to guard the president. Over time, the guarding has grown steadily more intense, rendering personal contact with the president by ordinary citizens much less frequent and much more restricted. One consequence has been that presidents are more insulated against assassins than ever. As of 2018, no president had been assassinated in nearly fifty-five years. Another, less fortunate effect has been to wall off presidents from spontaneous encounters with ordinary citizens and everyday life. What recent president has ever run into a neighbor while walking the dog, hunted for a parking space, sat in the middle seat on an airplane, or waited in line at an ATM?

IMPEACHMENT AND RESIGNATION

Andrew Johnson, the first president to take office after a presidential assassination, was also the first president to be impeached. But his was not the first instance of the impeachment power being employed. In 1805 Supreme Court Justice Samuel P. Chase was impeached. Urged on by President Thomas Jefferson, whose newly triumphant Democratic-Republican Party resented the defeated Federalist Party's continued hold on the judiciary, the House of Representative voted to impeach the highly partisan but indisputably competent Chase on grounds that seemed overtly political. Chase survived his Senate trial, Jefferson abandoned impeachment as a strategy for attacking the courts, and impeachment itself became regarded with suspicion.

Although their effort failed, Jefferson and his allies in the House were not entirely baseless in thinking of impeachment as an intrinsically political act. The Constitution itself is vague on this point. To be sure, during the course of the Constitutional Convention, the grounds for impeachment became steadily less political. Initially, the delegates voted that the president and other officials would be impeachable for "malpractice or neglect of duty." That came to be seen as too vague and, therefore, too readily devolvable into impeachment for simple unpopularity in Congress or the country—exactly what the Framers hoped to avoid by granting the president a fixed four-year term. Subsequent suggestions, including impeachment for "corruption" or "maladministration," came to be seen as similarly overbroad.[12] Eventually, the convention joined "Treason" and "Bribery" as impeachable offenses with "high Crimes and Misdemeanors," a term borrowed from fourteenth-century English common law that was as apolitical sounding as it was hard to define.

But even as the appropriate grounds for impeachment were becoming less political during the course of the convention, the process for deciding whether a president should be impeached and removed became more political. Initially, the delegates assigned the impeachment process to the Supreme Court alone, then to the Court and the House of Representatives, and only near the end of their deliberations to the House and Senate. In other words, the process, initially in the hands of unelected legal officials, eventually was entrusted to elected political officials. And the punishments Congress was able to impose were limited to removal from office and disqualification from holding office in the future—both of them political penalties—not imprisonment or civil damages of the kind a court could exact.

Jefferson's failed attempt to remove Justice Chase made clear that the impeachment power would not be employed lightly. As unpopular as President Tyler became after vetoing a series of bills passed by the Whig-controlled Congress, for example, an attempt by Rep. John Botts to persuade the House to impeach him went nowhere. One important reason is the vagueness of the phrase "high Crimes and Misdemeanors." Treason is defined in Article III of the Constitution as "levying war against [the United States], or in adhering to their enemies, giving them aid and comfort." Bribery is defined in statutory laws that bar the offering, giving, or accepting of rewards in exchange for official favors. But does "high Crimes and Misdemeanors" include only serious crimes in the usual sense of the word—that is, violations of the criminal law? Or does it extend, as Alexander Hamilton argued in *Federalist* no. 65, to any "abuse or violation of some public trust"—that is, "to injuries done immediately to the society itself," which may, Hamilton wrote, "with peculiar propriety be denominated as POLITICAL," whether or not a criminal statute has been violated?[13]

The three serious attempts to impeach and remove a president—Johnson in 1868, Nixon in 1974, and Clinton in 1998–1999—all hinged on some variation of these complexities. In each instance, either the law, the facts, or both were unclear.

Andrew Johnson: Clear Facts, Unclear Law

As president, Johnson became embroiled in a series of bitter controversies about the post–Civil War Reconstruction of the South with the Radical Republicans, the wing of the party that took control of Congress in the 1866 midterm election, nineteen months after he succeeded to the presidency.[14] Johnson, a Democrat from Tennessee, was a pro-Union senator when the war broke out, the only southern member of Congress not to leave when his state seceded. Lincoln put him on the ticket when he ran for reelection in 1864 as a way of broadening his appeal to Democratic voters. When Johnson became president after Lincoln died, however, he commanded none of the loyalty from congressional Republicans that the twice-elected, victorious commander in chief had enjoyed. After Secretary of War Edwin

M. Stanton, a Lincoln appointee, sided more with Congress on Reconstruction-related issues than with the president, Johnson decided to fire him. Congress protected Stanton by passing the Tenure of Office Act and then overriding Johnson's veto of the bill on March 2, 1867. The new law forbade the president from removing any Senate-confirmed appointee from office until the Senate approved the nomination of a successor, reversing the First Congress's decision in 1789 to uphold the president's unilateral authority to remove executive officials.[15]

After Congress went into recess in 1867, Johnson took advantage of a loophole in the new law that allowed him to act in Congress's absence. He suspended Stanton as secretary of war and replaced him with Gen. Ulysses S. Grant. Reconvening in 1868, however, the Senate disapproved Johnson's action, and Grant turned the office back to Stanton. Johnson thought he had Grant's promise to ignore the Senate vote and thereby force a confrontation with Congress and, ultimately, a decision by the Supreme Court about the constitutionality of the Tenure of Office Act. But Grant decided not to jeopardize his own presidential ambitions by siding with the president and alienating congressional Republicans. In February 1868, acting in explicit defiance of the law, Johnson fired Stanton and appointed Gen. Lorenzo Thomas to replace him. After Thomas tried, unsuccessfully, to persuade Stanton to vacate the building, the House voted on February 21 to open an impeachment inquiry against the president.

The House took little time to act. The ardently radical Committee on Reconstruction quickly prepared an eleven-article impeachment resolution, which the House approved by a 126–47 vote on March 2 and 3, 1868, after only two days of debate. The first eight articles dealt with various aspects of Johnson's violation of the Tenure of Office Act. Article IX accused him of violating another recently enacted law when he bypassed the nation's highest-ranking military officer, the general of the army, to give an order to a general in the field. (Johnson considered this law unconstitutional too.) Articles X and XI charged that Johnson's inflammatory speeches in the 1866 midterm election campaign had sought to bring Congress into "disgrace, ridicule, hatred, contempt, and reproach." With most of the strongly Democratic southern states still not restored to Congress, both chambers were overwhelmingly Republican.

Seven members of the House were appointed to present the case for removal in the Senate trial. The facts were not in dispute. Johnson had taken the actions and spoken the words of which he was accused. The controversy instead was over the law. The president's lawyers argued that he was entitled to violate any statute he regarded as unconstitutional in order to bring the issue before the Supreme Court. The lawyers also argued, more narrowly, that the Tenure of Office Act did not bar Johnson from firing Stanton because Stanton had been appointed by a different president. They dismissed Article IX and, especially, Articles X and XI as frivolous. Even rude criticism of Congress did not rise to the level of a high crime and misdemeanor.

Thirty-six votes in favor of even a single article in the fifty-four-member Senate would have been enough to remove Johnson. By most reckonings, twelve senators (nine of them Democrats) were Johnson supporters and thirty were Johnson opponents. That left the decision in the hands of twelve undecided Republicans, some of whom dreaded the prospect that under the law prevailing at the time, Senate president pro tempore and Radical hard-liner Benjamin Wade of Ohio would succeed to the presidency if Johnson were removed. In votes taken on May 16 and May 26, 1868, seven of the twelve voted not to convict the president. As a result, the margin in favor of removal was 35–19, one vote shy of the required two-thirds. Johnson completed his term as president on March 4, 1869.

Richard Nixon: Clear Law, Unclear Facts

On June 17, 1972, more than a century after Johnson's razor-thin acquittal, five burglars secretly employed by the Committee to Re-elect the President (better known by its acronym, CREEP) were caught breaking into the offices of the Democratic National Committee in the Watergate hotel and office complex in Washington.[16] The chain of command that had authorized the break-in, along with a host of other illegal and unethical campaign activities, reached high into the administration of President Richard Nixon. In an effort to avoid embarrassing revelations, Nixon and some of his closest aides in the White House responded to news of the burglary by trying to obstruct official investigations into what happened. It took the next two years for a combination of actions to bring to light persuasive factual evidence of Nixon's involvement in the Watergate cover-up. These actions included diligent investigations by reporters Bob Woodward and Carl Bernstein of the *Washington Post* in 1972 and 1973; hearings by a special Senate committee chaired by Democratic senator Sam Ervin of North Carolina during the summer of 1973; testimony before the Ervin committee by White House counsel John Dean and other participants in the Watergate affair regarding their own, each other's, and (in Dean's case) the president's culpability; and the release of secret White House tape recordings that Nixon had made.

In February 1974 the House Judiciary Committee began to consider impeaching the president for "high Crimes and Misdemeanors" in the second of only three serious presidential impeachment inquiries in American history. In contrast to Johnson's impeachment, this time the law was clear: if Nixon had obstructed justice by ordering a cover-up of the burglars' crimes, then he had committed an impeachable offense by any definition of the term. After the tapes were released—some by Nixon in response to political pressure, and the rest after the Supreme Court ruled against him unanimously on July 24 in the case of *United States v. Nixon*—the facts became clear as well. As the recording of a June 23, 1972, conversation between the president and his chief of staff, H. R. Haldeman, revealed, Nixon had ordered Haldeman to tell the Central Intelligence Agency (CIA) to ask the Federal Bureau of Investigation (FBI) to back off its criminal investigation of the Watergate break-in on bogus national security grounds. "They," said Nixon, referring to CIA officials, "should call the FBI in and say that we wish, for the country, don't go any further into this case."[17]

Between July 27 and 29, even before the "smoking gun" tape was released, the Judiciary Committee decided to recommend three articles of impeachment to the full House of Representatives on the basis of evidence that already was available. Article I, which the committee approved by a bipartisan 27–11 vote, charged that

Nixon had violated his oath to "preserve, protect, and defend the Constitution" as well as his constitutional responsibility to "take Care that the Laws be faithfully executed" with actions that obstructed the administration of justice in the Watergate case. These actions included withholding evidence, condoning perjury, approving the payment of "hush money" to the five men who were caught breaking into the Watergate, interfering with lawful investigations, and making false and misleading statements.

Article II, approved by 28–10, contended that the president had misused and abused both his executive authority and the resources of various executive agencies, including the FBI, the CIA, the Internal Revenue Service, and the Justice Department's Criminal Division and Office of Watergate Special Prosecution Force. This article included the Watergate cover-up and other misdeeds, such as a covert break-in, sponsored by White House operatives, into the office of Dr. Lewis Fielding, who was psychiatrist to former Defense Department employee Daniel Ellsberg. As was the case with Article I, all twenty-seven committee Democrats voted for the article and a narrow majority of the seventeen Republicans voted against it. Article III, approved along party lines by 21–17, charged Nixon with contempt of Congress for not cooperating with the Judiciary Committee's impeachment investigation.

Because the committee's working standard for an impeachable offense was that it be an indictable crime "to the manifest injury of the people of the United States," it voted down two other proposed articles of impeachment.[18] The first, which faulted the president for secretly bombing Cambodia during the Vietnam War, was judged not to be criminal. The second, Nixon's alleged evasion of income taxes, was found to be a personal rather than a political crime.

The release of the smoking gun tape on August 5 led even Nixon's staunchest Republican supporters in Congress to abandon him. With impeachment by the House and conviction by the Senate all but certain, Nixon resigned as president on August 9. But as Article I of the Constitution stipulated, Nixon's resignation left him "liable and subject to Indictment, Trial, Judgment and Punishment" for the criminal laws he violated in the course of obstructing justice in the Watergate investigation. On Sunday morning, September 8, 1974, Nixon's successor as president, Gerald Ford, announced that he was exercising his constitutional power to grant Nixon a "full, free and absolute pardon . . . for all offenses against the United States which he . . . has committed or may have committed."[19] Ford's exercise of the pardon power—the only constitutional power of the presidency that cannot be checked by Congress or the Supreme Court—freed Nixon from prosecution for any federal crime.

In announcing the pardon, Ford noted several reasons for his decision, including the former president's deteriorating health and the difficulty of securing a fair trial. More than anything else, Ford said, "someone must write 'The End'" to the Watergate affair, lest "ugly passions . . . again be aroused."[20] Nixon received the pardon with a statement conceding only "mistakes and misjudgments" in his handling of the crisis. Responding to critics who complained that Ford should have insisted on a stronger apology, administration officials maintained that, legally, the act of accepting the pardon was a confession of guilt by the former president.

Although Ford paid a severe political price for the unpopular Nixon pardon, it was his presence in the vice presidency that facilitated the impeachment inquiry and Nixon's subsequent resignation. Ford became vice president on December 6, 1973, through an unprecedented process made possible by the Twenty-fifth Amendment, which at the time had only been in the Constitution for six years. Section 2 of the amendment states: "Whenever there is a vacancy in the office of the Vice President, the President shall nominate a Vice President, who shall take office upon a majority vote of both Houses of Congress." A vacancy occurred when Nixon's previous vice president, Spiro T. Agnew, resigned on October 10, 1973, as part of a plea bargain that spared him from imprisonment for cash bribes he had taken ever since his days in local office in Maryland. If the new amendment had not been in place, Agnew's resignation would have left the vice presidency vacant. Under the terms of the Succession Act of 1946, any effort to remove the Republican Nixon from the presidency would have elevated Speaker of the House Carl Albert, a Democrat, to the office. Albert also had a serious drinking problem, another complication. Politically, this would have severely challenged Congress's ability to evaluate Nixon's case on its merits, free of starkly partisan considerations. But because the amendment triggered the nomination of Ford, who was the House Republican leader and widely admired for his integrity, Congress did not have to worry about overturning the results of the 1972 election by replacing a Republican president with a Democrat.

Bill Clinton: Unclear Law, Unclear Facts

A century separated the impeachments of Johnson and Nixon. Only a quarter-century passed between the impeachments of Nixon and Bill Clinton.[21]

The roots of Clinton's impeachment lay in the Ethics in Government Act of 1978, a Watergate-era measure that had been renewed at Clinton's urging in 1993. As modified by the courts, the act required a panel of federal judges to appoint an independent counsel whenever the attorney general concluded that a high-level executive official may have committed a crime. In 1994 the panel appointed former Reagan administration solicitor general Kenneth Starr to investigate Clinton's possible involvement during the late 1970s in an Arkansas real estate scheme known as Whitewater. In subsequent years, Starr's investigation broadened, eventually centering on the president's testimony in a sexual harassment lawsuit brought against him by Paula Jones, a former Arkansas state employee. The suit ultimately was thrown out of federal court, but by then Clinton had testified in a sworn deposition that he never had "sexual relations" or "an affair" with former White House intern Monica Lewinsky, who was one of several women about whom Jones's attorneys asked him. In January 1998, when Starr obtained evidence from a Lewinsky confidante that Clinton had a sexual affair with Lewinsky that lasted from late 1995 to early 1997, he decided that Clinton's deposition was perjurious. He also suspected the president of obstructing justice by trying to persuade Lewinsky to lie about their affair when giving her own deposition in the Jones case in return for his help in getting her a lucrative job in New York.

Clinton's relationship with Lewinsky became public on January 21, 1998, and dominated the news for more than a year. For months Clinton maintained that he was innocent. "I did not have sexual relations with that woman, Miss Lewinsky," he angrily declared on January 26. "I never told anyone to lie. Not a single time. Never." But on August 6, in exchange for a promise of immunity from prosecution for perjury, Lewinsky testified to Starr's Whitewater grand jury that she and the president had a number of sexual encounters in the White House while denying that he had urged her to lie under oath. DNA evidence that the president had ejaculated onto a blue dress that Lewinsky had saved and not cleaned confirmed her testimony, although Clinton maintained that Lewinsky's repeated performance of oral sex on him did not constitute sexual relations because they did not have intercourse.

When the federal courts ruled that Starr had the authority to subpoena Clinton to testify before the grand jury, the president agreed to appear on August 17. Although Clinton admitted in a televised address that evening that his relationship with Lewinsky "was not appropriate. In fact, it was wrong," Starr believed that the president had lied to the grand jury about the full extent of his wrongdoing. Zealously fulfilling one of the independent counsel's responsibilities under the Ethics in Government Act, Starr shared with the House Judiciary Committee his opinion that the president had committed impeachable offenses.

In Clinton's case, neither the facts nor the law was clear. By itself, his affair with Lewinsky was neither a crime nor an impeachable offense. But had he lied under oath, tampered with a witness by urging Lewinsky to lie, or obstructed justice by trying to trade her silence for a job? Starr said yes, Clinton said no. Even if he had, would these attempts to protect himself from public embarrassment and marital discord rise to the level of a high crime and misdemeanor? Clinton again said no. The Republican Congress delivered a mixed verdict.

In December 1998, Democrats on the Judiciary Committee urged that the House vote to censure rather than impeach Clinton for "making false statements" as well as for having "violated the trust of the people, lessened their esteem for the office of the President, and dishonored the presidency."[22] The Republican majority on the committee voted down the censure resolution. Republican members argued that the Constitution provided only for impeachment, with no mention of censure. More to the point, they were determined to settle for nothing less than driving Clinton from office.

On December 19, the House adopted two articles of impeachment recommended by the Judiciary Committee and rejected two others. By a vote of 228–206, with only five Republicans and five Democrats crossing party lines, the House approved an article that accused Clinton of giving the grand jury "perjurious, false and misleading testimony" on August 17 concerning his relationship with Lewinsky. After voting down another of the committee's proposed articles, which involved perjury in Clinton's deposition in the Paula Jones lawsuit, by 205–229, the House adopted a second article by 221–212, charging the president with obstruction of justice for a series of actions to "delay, impede, cover up, and conceal the existence of evidence," including trying to buy Lewinsky's silence with a job in New York. Five Democrats voted for this article, and twelve Republicans voted against it. The

House then rejected the final proposed article, which loosely accused the president of abuse of power and "a pattern of deceit and obstruction," by a vote of 148–285. Republican unity accounted for the two articles' passage; their disunity allowed House Democrats to defeat the other two.

The Senate formally convened on January 7, 1999, to deal with the articles of impeachment approved by the House. After a five-week trial, on February 12 senators voted 45–55 against conviction on Article I—twenty-two votes short of the two-thirds majority necessary to remove the president. Ten Republicans joined all forty-five Democrats in voting "not guilty." The Senate divided 50–50 on Article II, with five Republicans joining all the Democrats in voting not to convict.

The Politics of Impeachment

What accounts for the varying ways Congress dealt with the Johnson, Nixon, and Clinton impeachment controversies? As might be expected from a constitutional process that entrusts impeachment and removal to elected officials, partisan politics is one important element. An overwhelmingly Republican Congress (191–46 in the House and 42–11 in the Senate) impeached and came within one vote of removing the Democrat Johnson. A solidly Democratic Congress (242–191 in the House and 56–42 in the Senate) forced the Republican Nixon to resign in the face of certain impeachment and removal. And a strongly Republican House (226–207) impeached Clinton, a Democrat.

A Congress controlled by the opposition party may be a necessary condition for impeaching a president, but clearly it is not a sufficient one. Most recent presidents have faced such a Congress for at least part of their time in office without being impeached. A second part of the explanation is the president's standing with the voters. Even without polls to measure how unpopular Johnson was, the results of the 1866 midterm election made clear to all that he had little public support. Nixon's job approval rating in the Gallup Poll sank below 30 percent in late 1973 and stayed there. Clinton's case is more complicated. His party actually gained five House seats in the 1998 midterm election, the first time this happened during a president's second term since 1822. His job approval rating remained above 60 percent during the entire controversy, soaring to 73 percent in December 1998 when the House was voting to impeach him. House Republicans, however, were motivated by fear of their chamber's party leaders, who were determined to force out the president, as well as by the knowledge that the greatest possible threat to their reelection would come from the equally anti-Clinton Republican primary voters in their districts. Representing more politically competitive states and enjoying longer terms of office, a significant number of Republican senators broke ranks and supported Clinton on the final votes.

A third element in explaining impeachment politics is the immediate practical consequence of removal. To remove one president is to install another. Enough moderate Republicans dreaded the prospect of the radical Senate president pro tempore Wade becoming president that they held their noses and stood by Johnson. In Nixon's case, Democratic Speaker Albert may not have been an acceptable successor but Republican Vice President Ford was. Clinton's case is again less clear.

Congressional Democrats would have been happy and Republican legislators unhappy to see Vice President Al Gore succeed to the presidency—and for the same reason: it would give him the advantages of incumbency in the 2000 presidential election. But the fervency of both parties' primary electorates prevented them from acting on this basis.

Finally, public attitudes toward impeachment in general color the likelihood that a president may be impeached. During the 184-year period from 1789 to 1973, only one president, Johnson, underwent the process, and that failed effort seemed to discredit impeachment as a "vengefully political act," such that in the judgment of the political scientist Clinton Rossiter: "I do not think we are likely ever again to see such a trial."[23] Rossiter, who published these words in 1960, was proven wrong just fourteen years later. From 1974 to 1999 two presidents were in effect impeached; more to the point, every president since Clinton has been the object of a grassroots campaign to impeach him by opposition party activists. In the contemporary climate of bitter partisan polarization, impeachment strikes many as just another method of "politics by other means."[24]

DISABILITY

One knows when a president has died or been impeached and removed from office. But, as Dickinson asked at the Constitutional Convention, "What is the extent of the term disability?" The Constitution's only answer, both in its original form and as altered by the Twenty-fifth Amendment, is that it is an "Inability to discharge the Powers and Duties of the said Office." The delegates to the Constitutional Convention did not discuss the question. Nearly two centuries later, the authors of the amendment discussed but explicitly chose not to answer it. It is clear from Congress's deliberations what disability is not—namely, incompetence, laziness, unpopularity, or impeachable conduct. As to what disability is, they thought that any definition they might write into the Constitution in the mid-1960s would be rendered obsolete by changes in medical science and terminology. Broadly speaking, however, disability clearly includes severe mental illness and physical incapacity, as well as more far-fetched situations such as a president being kidnapped by an enemy power.

What the amendment's authors did provide was a constitutional answer to Dickinson's second question: "who is to be the judge of it?" Historically, the lack of an answer in the original Constitution had immobilized the government when situations of obvious presidential disability occurred. In 1881 Garfield lay dying for eighty days after he was shot by an assassin. At one point his cabinet unanimously recommended that Vice President Arthur become acting president. Arthur refused. To assume power while Garfield was alive and without his blessing, the vice president believed, would be politically reckless and constitutionally uncertain. In 1919 Woodrow Wilson was felled by a stroke from which he never fully recovered during the remaining nineteen months of his term. Urged by some cabinet members to assume Wilson's powers and duties, Vice President Thomas R. Marshall said, "I am not going to seize the place and then have Wilson—recovered—come around and say, 'Get off, you usurper!'"[25]

In contrast to Garfield, Wilson, and other presidents who were disabled for briefer periods of time (notably Grover Cleveland, who pretended to be on vacation for five weeks while actually boarding a ship to have cancerous growths removed from his mouth and jaw), President Dwight D. Eisenhower worked out an arrangement with Vice President Nixon in response to his own heart attack in 1955, ileitis attack in 1956, and mild stroke in 1957. Eisenhower asked Nixon to preside over cabinet meetings and perform the public functions of the presidency while he recovered and eventually sent the vice president a letter authorizing him to become acting president either at the president's request or, if the president were too incapacitated to make the request, on his own initiative. As soon as Eisenhower recovered, he would resume his powers and duties. Eisenhower wrote his letter out of concern that in an age of nuclear weaponry and Cold War confrontation with the Soviet Union, the nation could not afford even a brief period without a functioning president. But it was a letter, lacking constitutional status.

It took the Twenty-fifth Amendment to remedy this deficiency.[26] The amendment, which the states ratified eighteen months after Congress proposed it in 1965, covers three possible situations in Sections 3 and 4. In the first, the president is "unable to discharge the powers and duties of his office" and recognizes this condition—say, before or after undergoing surgery. A simple letter from the president to the Speaker of the House and the president pro tempore of the Senate is all it takes to make the vice president the acting president. A subsequent presidential letter declaring that the disability is ended restores the president's powers and duties.

In the second situation, the president is disabled but, perhaps having sunk into a coma, is unable to say so. Should this happen, either the vice president or the head of any of the fifteen executive departments may call a meeting of the vice president and cabinet to discuss the situation. If both the vice president and a majority of the heads of the departments declare the president disabled, the vice president would become acting president—again, until the president writes to the leaders of Congress to announce an end to the disability.

The third situation is the most troubling. It involves instances, such as questionable mental health or severe physical impairment, in which the president's ability to fulfill the office is in doubt because the president claims to be able but the vice president and the cabinet disagree. The amendment provides that, if this were to happen, the vice president becomes acting president until Congress can resolve the matter. Congress would have a maximum of three weeks to decide whether the president is disabled, with a two-thirds vote of both the House and the Senate needed to overturn the president's judgment. But because the Twenty-fifth Amendment only transfers power to the vice president for as long as the presidential disability lasts, a subsequent claim of restored health by the president would set the whole process in motion again—and, possibly, again and again.

Some critics of the amendment argued that it vests too much power in the executive branch to make disability determinations. An alternative proposal was to create a disability commission that included members of all three branches, perhaps joined by some physicians. Senator Birch Bayh, the amendment's chief author, defended his version by saying that any move to strip power from the president by officials outside the administration risked violating the constitutional separation of powers. In the end, both to satisfy the critics and to preclude the possibility that a president might fire some or all department heads in order to forestall a disability declaration, the amendment authorized Congress, at its discretion, to substitute another body for the cabinet.

By most accounts, Sections 3 and 4 of the Twenty-fifth Amendment failed their first serious test. In 1981 Reagan was seriously wounded by an assassin's bullet. While he was at the hospital undergoing major surgery, cabinet and staff members gathered at the White House in the absence of Vice President George Bush, who was returning from a trip to Houston. When White House counsel Fred Fielding mentioned that there was a constitutional way to "pass the baton temporarily" to the vice president, he was ignored, and when fellow staff member Richard Darman noticed that Fielding had prepared a document for the transfer of power, he took it away and locked it in a safe.[27] Even as Soviet forces assembled at the Polish border, the main concern of those around the president was to maintain the pretense that he was strong and able. Four years later, somewhat bizarrely, Reagan did transfer power to Bush in anticipation of being unconscious during a minor surgical procedure, but only after claiming that he was not doing so under the terms of the Twenty-fifth Amendment. Still, a precedent was established, raising expectations that the amendment would work as intended in future administrations, at least for the easy cases when the transfer of power was brief and initiated by the president. This precedent was followed in 2002 and 2007 when George W. Bush cited the amendment in transferring authority to Vice President Richard Cheney just before being anesthetized for minor procedures.

Still less clear is whether a president realistically could be relieved of the office's powers and duties against his or her will. All of those involved in making such a decision owe their positions to the president. Even if Congress replaced the cabinet with, say, a committee of physicians, the vice president's agreement would still be essential. Could a vice president be expected to overcome the fear expressed in pre-Twenty-fifth Amendment times by Arthur and Marshall that they would be branded a "usurper" by the president's supporters or by the president himself?[28]

PRESIDENTIAL REMOVAL AND DONALD TRUMP

Challenges to Donald Trump's constitutional legitimacy were an ongoing part of his presidency, starting the day after the election when protesters in several cities chanted "Not my president!" On the eve of Trump's inauguration, the respected civil rights leader and sixteen-term Democratic congressman John Lewis of Georgia said that he did not regard Trump as a "legitimate president."[29] Efforts to find a way to remove Trump from office began almost immediately after he took the oath.

Impeachment talk moved from left-wing social media to mainstream telecasts and publications and the halls of Congress less than four months into the term, after Trump fired FBI director James Comey on May 9, 2017, for continuing to investigate possible criminal links between Russia and the Trump election campaign. As the president publicly explained the firing two days later, "I said to myself, I said, 'You know, this Russia thing with Trump and Russia is a made-up story. It's an excuse by the Democrats for having lost an election that they should have won.'"[30] According to Comey, in a private meeting on February 14, the day after Michael Flynn resigned as national security advisor after lying to Vice President Mike Pence about conversations he had during the postelection transition with the Russian ambassador, Trump told him, "I hope you can see your way clear to letting this go, to letting Flynn go. He is a good guy." Comey said he took the request "as a direction" but continued the investigation.[31] On May 13 a prominent Democratic constitutional scholar, Laurence Tribe, argued in the *Washington Post* that Trump's expression of "hope" that Comey would drop the Flynn investigation and his subsequent firing of the director constituted obstruction of justice. This, Tribe argued, was an even worse "high Crime and Misdemeanor" than the ones that drove Nixon from office because it "involv[ed] national security matters vastly more serious than the 'third-rate' burglary that Nixon tried to cover up in Watergate."[32]

As Trump's first year in office unfolded, various Democratic members of the House of Representatives introduced impeachment resolutions.[33] Most Republicans either defended Trump or remained silent, but Senator John McCain said that the controversy was of "Watergate size and scale" and Representative Justin Amash of Michigan declared that Comey's allegations, if true, were grounds for impeachment.[34]

On May 17, eight days after Comey was fired, Deputy Attorney General Rod Rosenstein appointed former FBI director Robert S. Mueller III as special counsel to investigate the allegations about Russia and the Trump campaign. Rosenstein made the decision because Attorney General Jeff Sessions had recused himself from the matter on March 2 after it was revealed that during his Senate confirmation hearing he had failed to mention two meetings with the Russian ambassador. Then and later Trump was furious at Sessions for ceding control of the investigation. On July 19 he told the *New York Times* that if Sessions "was going to recuse himself he should have told me before he took the job and I would have picked somebody else."[35] For weeks afterward, Trump belittled Sessions in a series of tweets and interviews.

Mueller made clear that he would turn over any evidence that Trump had obstructed justice to Congress as part of a possible impeachment proceeding. Depending on the results of Mueller's investigation, as well as on continuing congressional and media revelations of other troubling presidential conduct, public opinion may turn so strongly against Trump as to persuade enough Republican members that it is politically safe to abandon him. Strong though Republican voters' early support for Trump was, a measurable number of them began leaving the party because they disapproved of him so strongly.[36] Trump's insistent unwillingness to admit that Russia had worked on his behalf gave the July 2017 revelation that Donald Jr. and Trump's son-in-law Jared Kushner had met with a Russian lawyer the previous June the appearance of a cover-up, even though the meeting produced nothing and did not include the candidate himself. Trump and Kushner took the meeting because they had been promised "official documents" that would "incriminate Hillary" as part of "Russia and its government's support for Mr. Trump."[37]

Any decision to remove a president is also, by implication, a decision to place someone else in the office, and many Republican members of Congress would be much happier with President Pence than President Trump. Pence remained unwaveringly loyal to Trump's policies but consistently distanced himself from controversial "stories about the time before he joined the ticket."[38] He even created a political action committee—the Great America Committee—to fund his political travel, something no previous vice president had done. Personal loyalty to Trump among Republican legislators, never great to begin with, was shredded by his disrespectful treatment of Sessions, as well as by threats to senators such as Dean Heller and Lisa Murkowski.[39] The Democrats may well take control of the House in the 2018 midterm election and, depending on the extent of Trump's unpopularity, conceivably could buck the odds and win the Senate even though they will be defending twenty-six seats and the Republicans only eight. Such an outcome would make impeachment by a majority of the Democrat-controlled House considerably more likely and perhaps alarm enough Republican senators so that a two-thirds majority for removal could be forged in that chamber. As argued above, the likelihood that a president will be impeached rises when the president is unpopular, the opposition party controls Congress, the vice president is an acceptable alternative, and impeachment is regarded as an acceptable form of opposition.

Finding the impeachment process still too difficult to navigate, some critics who wanted Trump forced from office offered the Twenty-fifth Amendment as an alternative. By the time Democratic representative Jamie Raskin of Maryland introduced a bill in June 2017 to remove the Trump-appointed cabinet from disability determinations and replace it with a "Commission on Presidential Capacity" consisting mostly of physicians and psychiatrists, a few conservative columnists, including Ross Douthat and George F. Will, and former Republican officials such as Eliot Cohen had already argued that Trump was unfit by reason of temperament, character, and mental health to be president. By July nearly sixty thousand self-identified "mental health professionals" had signed a petition declaring that "Trump manifests a serious mental illness" and "should be removed from office" under the terms of the amendment.[40]

To the extent that the disability approach to removing Trump was based on ease of accomplishment, it probably is misguided. Even if the cabinet was replaced by a medical board, the amendment cannot be used against an unwilling president without the vice president's agreement. And if the president were to appeal an adverse decision to Congress, as Trump certainly would, a two-thirds majority of both chambers, not just of the Senate, would have to vote against him. Even if they did, he could start the process all over again by claiming that his disability was ended. The premise of the amendment is that in cases of disability—unlike those of death, resignation, or impeachment—the president retains the office even when shorn of its powers and duties, and that these should be restored to him as soon as he is well.

NOTES

1. With apologies to Clinton Rossiter, from whom I borrowed this title. Rossiter, *The American Presidency* (Baltimore: Johns Hopkins University Press, 1987). Originally published in 1960.

2. "The Federalist Papers, Nos. 69–73," in *The Evolving Presidency: Landmark Documents, 1787–2015*, ed. Michael Nelson (Washington, DC: CQ Press, 2016), 24. Alexander Hamilton wrote the quoted statement, which appears in *The Federalist* no. 70.

3. For a detailed overview of the creation of the presidency, see Sidney M. Milkis and Michael Nelson, *The American Presidency: Origins and Development, 1776–2014* (Washington, DC: CQ Press, 2016), chaps. 1–2.

4. Ibid., 40.

5. Ibid., 58–60.

6. James Madison was the last surviving delegate until his death in 1836.

7. Milkis and Nelson, *American Presidency*, 151.

8. Some, including James Madison, have argued that the constitutional reference to "Officer" applies only to executive branch officials, not members of Congress. See Akhil Reed Amar and Vikram David Amar, "Is the Presidential Succession Law Constitutional? *Stanford Law Review* (1995–1996): 118–123.

9. Some attempts, such as John Hinckley's shooting of President Reagan in 1981, had entirely nonpolitical motives. Hinckley wanted to impress actress Jodie Foster.

10. Candace Millard, *Destiny of the Republic: A Tale of Madness, Medicine, and the Murder of a President* (New York: Doubleday, 2011), 168.

11. Harry Truman, "Special Message to the Congress on the Succession to the Presidency," The American Presidency Project, http://www.presidency.ucsb.edu/ws/?pid=12201.

12. Erwin C. Hargrove and Michael Nelson, *Presidents, Politics, and Policy* (Baltimore: Johns Hopkins University Press, 1984), 33–35.

13. "The Federalist Papers: No. 65," Avalon Project, http://avalon.law.yale.edu/18th_century/fed65.asp.

14. For a fuller understanding of the Johnson impeachment, see David O. Stewart, *Impeached: The Trial of President Andrew Johnson and the Fight for Lincoln's Legacy* (New York: Simon and Schuster, 2009); and Michael Les Benedict, *The Impeachment and Trial of Andrew Johnson* (New York: W. W. Norton, 1973).

15. "James Madison's Defense of the President's Removal Power," in Nelson, *The Evolving Presidency*, 43–47.

16. For a fuller understanding of the Nixon impeachment effort and resignation, see Stanley I. Kutler, *The Wars of Watergate: The Last Crisis of Richard Nixon* (New York: Alfred A, Knopf, 1990); and Theodore H. White, *Breach of Faith: The Fall of Richard Nixon* (New York: Scribner, 1975).

17. "Transcript of a Recording of a Meeting Between the President and H. R. Haldeman, The Oval Office, June 23, 1972," Nixon Library, https://www.nixonlibrary.gov/forresearchers/find/tapes/watergate/trial/exhibit_02.pdf.

18. "Proposed Articles of Impeachment against Richard Nixon," in Nelson, *The Evolving Presidency*, 210–214.

19. "Gerald R. Ford's Pardon of Richard Nixon," in Nelson, *The Evolving Presidency*, 214–217.

20. Ibid.

21. For a fuller understanding of the Clinton impeachment, see Peter Baker, *The Breach: Inside the Impeachment and Trial of William Jefferson Clinton* (New York: Scribner, 2000); and Ken Gormley, *The Death of American Virtue: Clinton vs. Starr* (New York: Crown, 2010).

22. Michael Nelson, "Removal of the President and the Vice President," in *Guide to the Presidency and the Executive Branch* (Washington, DC: CQ Press, 2013), 520.

23. Rossiter, *The American Presidency*, 38, 194.

24. Benjamin Ginsberg and Martin Shefter, *Politics by Other Means: The Declining Importance of Elections in America* (New York: Basic Books, 1990).

25. Gene Smith, *When the Cheering Stopped: The Last Years of Woodrow Wilson* (New York: Time-Life Books, 1964), 123.

26. For an account of the enactment of the amendment, see John D. Feerick, *The Twenty-fifth Amendment* (New York: Fordham University Press, 1976).

27. Garrett M. Graff, *Raven Rock: The Story of the U.S. Government's Secret Plan to Save Itself While the Rest of Us Die* (New York: Simon and Schuster, 2017), 279; and Richard Reeves, *President Reagan: The Triumph of Imagination* (New York: Simon and Schuster, 2005), 39.

28. An additional concern with the amendment is that it does not provide for the possibility of a disabled vice president. Congress can substitute a different body for the cabinet in presidential disability determinations but not for the vice president.

29. Madeline Conway, "John Lewis: 'I Don't See This President-Elect as a Legitimate President,'" *Politico,* January 13, 2017, http://www.politico.com/story/2017/01/john-lewis-donald-trump-not-legitimate-president-233607.

30. Mark Hensch, "Trump Says 'Made Up' Russia Story Part of Decision to Fire Comey," *The Hill,* May 11, 2017, http://thehill.com/policy/national-security/fbi/333056-trump-made-up-russia-story-part-of-comey-firing.

31. Martin Finucane, "Comey Testimony Includes Good News, Bad News for Trump," *Boston Globe,* June 7, 2017, https://www.bostonglobe.com/news/nation/2017/06/07/comey-testimony-includes-good-news-bad-news-for-trump/YAxfv8So1HnJoHo4fIrGbO/story.html.

32. Laurence H. Tribe, "Trump Must Be Impeached. Here's Why," *Washington Post*, May 13, 2017, https://www.washingtonpost.com/newssearch/?datefilter=All%20Since%202005&query=Trump%20Must%20Be%20Impeached.%20Here%E2%80%99s%20Why&sort=Relevance&utm_term=.5f561a73dae0.

33. See Michael Nelson, *Trump's First Year* (Charlottesville: University of Virginia Press, 2018), chap. 9.

34. Anna Giaritelli, "McCain: Trump Scandals Have Reached 'Watergate Size and Scale,'" *Washington Examiner,* June 15, 2017, http://www.washingtonexaminer.com/mccain-trump-scandals-have-reached-watergate-size-and-scale/article/2623309; and Cristina Marcos, "First Republicans Talk Possibility of Impeachment for Trump," *The Hill,* May 17, 2017, http://thehill.com/homenews/house/333803-first-republicans-talk-impeachment-for-trump.

35. Peter Baker, Michael S. Schmidt, and Maggie Haberman, "Citing Recusal, Trump Says He Wouldn't Have Hired Sessions," *New York Times,* July 19, 2017, https://www.nytimes.com/2017/07/19/us/politics/trump-interview-sessions-russia.html.

36. Brendan Nyhan, "Why Trump's Base of Support May Be Smaller Than It Seems," *New York Times*, July 19, 2017, https://www.nytimes.com/2017/07/19/upshot/why-trumps-base-of-support-may-be-smaller-than-it-seems.html.

37. Dan Balz, "A Revelation Unlike Any Other in the Russia Investigation," *Washington Post*, July 11, 2017, https://www.washingtonpost.com/politics/a-revelation-unlike-any-other-in-the-russia-investigation/2017/07/11/7985fa14-666b-11e7-8eb5-cbccc2e7bfbf_story.html?utm_term=.a2cae984778c.

38. Rebecca Savransky, "Pence Responds to Trump Jr., Emails: He's 'Not Focused on Stories about the Campaign,'" *The Hill*, July 11, 2017, http://thehill.com/homenews/administration/341473-pence-not-focused-on-stories-about-the-campaign.

39. Megan Trimble, "Trump Warns GOP Senator over Obamacare Repeal," *U.S. News*, July 19, 2017, https://www.usnews.com/news/national-news/articles/2017-07-19/donald-trump-warns-dean-heller-over-health-care-vote; and Erica Martinson, "Trump Administration Threatens Retribution against Alaska over Murkowski Health Votes," *Alaska Dispatch News*, July 26, 2017, https://www.adn.com/politics/2017/07/26/trump-administration-signals-that-murkowskis-health-care-vote-could-have-energy-repercussions-for-alaska/.

40. John Gartner, "Mental Health Professionals Declare Trump Is Mentally Ill and Must Be Removed," Change.org, n.d., https://www.change.org/p/trump-is-mentally-ill-and-must-be-removed.

INDEX